D1567664

# Outdoor Program Administration

## Principles and Practices

**Association of Outdoor Recreation
and Education**

**Editors**

Geoff Harrison, MS
Boise State University

Mat Erpelding, MA
College of Western Idaho

**Human Kinetics**

Library of Congress Cataloging-in-Publication Data

Outdoor program administration : principles and practices / Geoff Harrison, Mat Erpelding, [editors].
   p. cm.
  Includes bibliographical references and index.
  ISBN-13: 978-0-7360-7537-4 (hardcover)
  ISBN-10: 0-7360-7537-2 (hardcover)
  1.  Outdoor recreation--Planning. 2.  Outdoor recreation--Management.  I. Harrison, Geoff, 1970- II. Erpelding, Mat, 1975-
  GV191.66.O88 2012
  790.06'9--dc23

2011037869

ISBN-10: 0-7360-7537-2 (print)

ISBN-13: 978-0-7360-7537-4 (print)

The web addresses cited in this text were current as of September 2011, unless otherwise noted.

**Acquisitions Editor:** Gayle Kassing, PhD

**Developmental Editor:** Melissa Feld

**Assistant Editor:** Rachel Brito

**Copyeditor:** John Wentworth

**Indexer:** Dan Connolly

**Permissions Manager:** Martha Gullo

**Graphic Designer:** Joe Buck

**Graphic Artist:** Keri Evans

**Cover Designer:** Keith Blomberg

**Photographer (cover):** Juan Carlos Muñoz / age fotostock

**Visual Production Assistant:** Jason Allen

**Art Manager:** Kelly Hendren

**Associate Art Manager:** Alan L. Wilborn

**Illustrations:** © Human Kinetics, unless otherwise noted

**Printer:** Sheridan Books

Printed in the United States of America

10 9 8 7 6 5 4 3 2 1

The paper in this book is certified under a sustainable forestry program.

**Human Kinetics**
Website: www.HumanKinetics.com

*United States:* Human Kinetics
P.O. Box 5076
Champaign, IL 61825-5076
800-747-4457
e-mail: humank@hkusa.com

*Canada:* Human Kinetics
475 Devonshire Road Unit 100
Windsor, ON N8Y 2L5
800-465-7301 (in Canada only)
e-mail: info@hkcanada.com

*Europe:* Human Kinetics
107 Bradford Road
Stanningley
Leeds LS28 6AT, United Kingdom
+44 (0) 113 255 5665
e-mail: hk@hkeurope.com

*Australia:* Human Kinetics
57A Price Avenue
Lower Mitcham, South Australia 5062
08 8372 0999
e-mail: info@hkaustralia.com

*New Zealand:* Human Kinetics
P.O. Box 80
Torrens Park, South Australia 5062
0800 222 062
e-mail: info@hknewzealand.com

E4531

# Contents

Preface   ix

## Part I   Outdoor Program Foundations   1

### Chapter 1   The Outdoor Program Administrator   3
*Geoff Harrison, MS, and Mat Erpelding, MA*

Outdoor Program Administration Defined . . . . . . . . . . . . . . . . . . . . . . . . . . . .4
Outdoor Program Administrator Defined . . . . . . . . . . . . . . . . . . . . . . . . . . . .4
Skill Sets for Outdoor Program Administrators . . . . . . . . . . . . . . . . . . . . . . . .4
Administrative Competence . . . . . . . . . . . . . . . . . . . . . . . . . . . . . . . . . . . .8
Acquiring Skills. . . . . . . . . . . . . . . . . . . . . . . . . . . . . . . . . . . . . . . . . . . .8
Professional Maintenance . . . . . . . . . . . . . . . . . . . . . . . . . . . . . . . . . . . . .10
Administrative Challenges. . . . . . . . . . . . . . . . . . . . . . . . . . . . . . . . . . . . .12
Summary. . . . . . . . . . . . . . . . . . . . . . . . . . . . . . . . . . . . . . . . . . . . . . . .13

### Chapter 2   History of Outdoor Recreation in the United States: An Outdoor Program Administrator's Perspective   15
*Steven P. Guthrie, PhD, Bryan J. Cavins, EdD, and Jerome Gabriel, MEd*

The Beginnings of Environmentalism and Outdoor Recreation: 1825 to 1880 . . . . . . . . . . . . . . .16
The Beginnings of a Profession: 1880 to 1920 . . . . . . . . . . . . . . . . . . . . . . . . .16
National Environmental Consciousness and Outdoor Recreation Evolves: 1920s to 1960s . . . . . . .20
Adventure Programming Emerges: 1960s to 1990. . . . . . . . . . . . . . . . . . . . . . . .22
Outdoor Adventure Programming Today (1990 to Present). . . . . . . . . . . . . . . . . . .24
Summary. . . . . . . . . . . . . . . . . . . . . . . . . . . . . . . . . . . . . . . . . . . . . . . .29

### Chapter 3   Dimensions of Outdoor Recreation Programs   31
*Todd Bauch, MEd, and Steve Hutton, MA*

Three Service Sectors of Outdoor Recreation Programs. . . . . . . . . . . . . . . . . . . . . . . . . .31
Common Programmatic Types . . . . . . . . . . . . . . . . . . . . . . . . . . . . . . . . . . . .33
Common Facilities or Resources of Outdoor Programs . . . . . . . . . . . . . . . . . . . . . .34
Outdoor Program Administrative Structures and Models . . . . . . . . . . . . . . . . . . . . .35
Summary. . . . . . . . . . . . . . . . . . . . . . . . . . . . . . . . . . . . . . . . . . . . . . . .38

### Chapter 4   The Future of Outdoor Program Administration   39
*Laurlyn K. Harmon, PhD, and Susan L. Johnson, MS*

Evolving Participant Characteristics . . . . . . . . . . . . . . . . . . . . . . . . . . . . . . . . .40
Staffing . . . . . . . . . . . . . . . . . . . . . . . . . . . . . . . . . . . . . . . . . . . . . . . . .44
Professionalization of the Field: Standards, Certifications, Accreditation. . . . . . . . . . . . . . .44
Youth and the Outdoors . . . . . . . . . . . . . . . . . . . . . . . . . . . . . . . . . . . . . . .45
Technology and the Outdoors . . . . . . . . . . . . . . . . . . . . . . . . . . . . . . . . . . . .46
Sustainability. . . . . . . . . . . . . . . . . . . . . . . . . . . . . . . . . . . . . . . . . . . . . .47
Collaborations and Partnerships . . . . . . . . . . . . . . . . . . . . . . . . . . . . . . . . . . .50
Outcome Assessment. . . . . . . . . . . . . . . . . . . . . . . . . . . . . . . . . . . . . . . . .50
Summary. . . . . . . . . . . . . . . . . . . . . . . . . . . . . . . . . . . . . . . . . . . . . . . .51

## Part II    Program Design and Implementation    53

**Chapter 5**  Administrative Risk Management . . . . . . . . . . . . . . . . . . . 55
*Mat Erpelding, MA, and Geoff Harrison, MS*

Terms and Definitions of Risk Management . . . . . . . . . . . . . . . . . . . . . . . . .55
Creating a Comprehensive Risk-Management Plan . . . . . . . . . . . . . . . . . . . .56
Summary. . . . . . . . . . . . . . . . . . . . . . . . . . . . . . . . . . . . . . . . . . . . . . . . .65

**Chapter 6**  Designing and Developing Outdoor Recreation
and Education Programs. . . . . . . . . . . . . . . . . . . . . . 67
*Todd Miner, EdD, and Heidi Erpelding-Welch, MS*

Vision . . . . . . . . . . . . . . . . . . . . . . . . . . . . . . . . . . . . . . . . . . . . . . . . . . .67
Mission Statement . . . . . . . . . . . . . . . . . . . . . . . . . . . . . . . . . . . . . . . . . .68
Strategic Plan. . . . . . . . . . . . . . . . . . . . . . . . . . . . . . . . . . . . . . . . . . . . .71
Sustainability. . . . . . . . . . . . . . . . . . . . . . . . . . . . . . . . . . . . . . . . . . . . .75
Dealing With Change: Evolve to Survive and Thrive. . . . . . . . . . . . . . . . . . .82
Summary. . . . . . . . . . . . . . . . . . . . . . . . . . . . . . . . . . . . . . . . . . . . . . . . .82

**Chapter 7**  Legal Considerations in Outdoor Recreation . . . . . . . . . . . 83
*Brent Wilson, JD, and Tracey Knutson, JD*

Negligence. . . . . . . . . . . . . . . . . . . . . . . . . . . . . . . . . . . . . . . . . . . . . . . .85
Legal Definition (Elements) of Negligence . . . . . . . . . . . . . . . . . . . . . . . . . .85
Negligence and Related Theories of Liability . . . . . . . . . . . . . . . . . . . . . . . . .88
Defenses Against Negligence . . . . . . . . . . . . . . . . . . . . . . . . . . . . . . . . . . .94
Role of Insurance in Legal Liability Matters. . . . . . . . . . . . . . . . . . . . . . . . .104
Summary. . . . . . . . . . . . . . . . . . . . . . . . . . . . . . . . . . . . . . . . . . . . . . . .107

**Chapter 8**  Budgeting and Financial Operations
of Outdoor Programs . . . . . . . . . . . . . . . . . . . . . . . 109
*Tim J. Moore, MS, and Geoff Harrison, MS*

Budget Components . . . . . . . . . . . . . . . . . . . . . . . . . . . . . . . . . . . . . . . . .110
Budget-Development Strategies . . . . . . . . . . . . . . . . . . . . . . . . . . . . . . . . .114
Forecasting Expenses and Revenue . . . . . . . . . . . . . . . . . . . . . . . . . . . . . .120
Summary. . . . . . . . . . . . . . . . . . . . . . . . . . . . . . . . . . . . . . . . . . . . . . . .126

**Chapter 9**  Marketing Outdoor Programs. . . . . . . . . . . . . . . . . . . . . 129
*Geoff Harrison, MS, and John McIntosh, PhD*

Marketing Basics . . . . . . . . . . . . . . . . . . . . . . . . . . . . . . . . . . . . . . . . . .129
Identifying the Market. . . . . . . . . . . . . . . . . . . . . . . . . . . . . . . . . . . . . . .130
Marketing Mix. . . . . . . . . . . . . . . . . . . . . . . . . . . . . . . . . . . . . . . . . . . .132
Developing a Marketing Plan. . . . . . . . . . . . . . . . . . . . . . . . . . . . . . . . . .138
Branding . . . . . . . . . . . . . . . . . . . . . . . . . . . . . . . . . . . . . . . . . . . . . . . .140
Marketing Methods . . . . . . . . . . . . . . . . . . . . . . . . . . . . . . . . . . . . . . . .141
Summary. . . . . . . . . . . . . . . . . . . . . . . . . . . . . . . . . . . . . . . . . . . . . . . .144

**Chapter 10** Access and Permitting for Use
of Public Lands. . . . . . . . . . . . . . . . . . . . . . . 145

*Rachel M. Peters, MA*

Outdoor Programs on Public Lands. . . . . . . . . . . . . . . . . . . . . . . . . . . . . . . . .145
Permitting Defined . . . . . . . . . . . . . . . . . . . . . . . . . . . . . . . . . . . . . . . . . .147
Management Agencies and Regulations. . . . . . . . . . . . . . . . . . . . . . . . . . . . . .148
Permitting Tips . . . . . . . . . . . . . . . . . . . . . . . . . . . . . . . . . . . . . . . . . . . .159
Summary. . . . . . . . . . . . . . . . . . . . . . . . . . . . . . . . . . . . . . . . . . . . . . . .162

**Chapter 11** Environmental Stewardship. . . . . . . . . . . . . . . . . . 163

*Whitney Ward, PhD, and Will Hobbs, PhD*

History of Environmental Stewardship in the United States . . . . . . . . . . . . . . . . . .163
Major Impacts of Recreation Today . . . . . . . . . . . . . . . . . . . . . . . . . . . . . . . .166
Applied Environmental Stewardship . . . . . . . . . . . . . . . . . . . . . . . . . . . . . . . .168
Integration of Environmental Stewardship and Recreation . . . . . . . . . . . . . . . . . .172
Summary. . . . . . . . . . . . . . . . . . . . . . . . . . . . . . . . . . . . . . . . . . . . . . . .174

**Chapter 12** Developing Policies, Procedures, and Guidelines
for Outdoor Programs . . . . . . . . . . . . . . . . . . . . . . . 175

*Mat Erpelding, MA, Curt Howell, MA, and Brien Sheedy, MA*

Characteristics of Quality Policy, Procedure, and Guideline Documents. . . . . . . . . . .176
Considerations Specific to Developing Policies and Procedures. . . . . . . . . . . . . . . .178
Developing Administrative Policies and Procedures . . . . . . . . . . . . . . . . . . . . . . .187
Developing Field Policies and Procedures . . . . . . . . . . . . . . . . . . . . . . . . . . . . .187
Summary. . . . . . . . . . . . . . . . . . . . . . . . . . . . . . . . . . . . . . . . . . . . . . . .196

**Part III** Staffing Considerations                                197

**Chapter 13** Staff Recruitment and Supervision . . . . . . . . . . . . . . . . 199

*Jeff Turner, PhD, and Leigh Jackson-Magennis, MEd*

Human Resource Planning . . . . . . . . . . . . . . . . . . . . . . . . . . . . . . . . . . . . . .199
Staff Selection . . . . . . . . . . . . . . . . . . . . . . . . . . . . . . . . . . . . . . . . . . . . .206
Staff Supervision . . . . . . . . . . . . . . . . . . . . . . . . . . . . . . . . . . . . . . . . . . .211
Summary. . . . . . . . . . . . . . . . . . . . . . . . . . . . . . . . . . . . . . . . . . . . . . . .217

**Chapter 14** Staff Training . . . . . . . . . . . . . . . . . . . . . . . . . . . . 219

*Bruce Saxman, MA, and Tom Stuessy, PhD*

Needs Assessment . . . . . . . . . . . . . . . . . . . . . . . . . . . . . . . . . . . . . . . . . . .219
Staff-Training Progression . . . . . . . . . . . . . . . . . . . . . . . . . . . . . . . . . . . . . .220
Mentoring . . . . . . . . . . . . . . . . . . . . . . . . . . . . . . . . . . . . . . . . . . . . . . . .222
Staff-Training Assessment . . . . . . . . . . . . . . . . . . . . . . . . . . . . . . . . . . . . . .223
Mechanisms for Training Assessment and Evaluation of Staff. . . . . . . . . . . . . . . . .224
Staff-Training Designs: Integrated Training Model. . . . . . . . . . . . . . . . . . . . . . . .226
Activity-Specific Training . . . . . . . . . . . . . . . . . . . . . . . . . . . . . . . . . . . . . . .228
Staff Appraisal . . . . . . . . . . . . . . . . . . . . . . . . . . . . . . . . . . . . . . . . . . . . .233
Summary. . . . . . . . . . . . . . . . . . . . . . . . . . . . . . . . . . . . . . . . . . . . . . . .233

**Chapter 15** Staff Assessment . . . . . . . . . . . . . . . . . . . . . 235

*Jenny Kafsky, PhD, and Mark Wagstaff, EdD*

The Basics and Purpose of Staff Assessment . . . . . . . . . . . . . . . . . . . . . . . . . .235
An Effective Environment for Assessment . . . . . . . . . . . . . . . . . . . . . . . . . . . . .236
Assessment Criteria. . . . . . . . . . . . . . . . . . . . . . . . . . . . . . . . . . . . . . . . . . . . .240
Assessment Tools. . . . . . . . . . . . . . . . . . . . . . . . . . . . . . . . . . . . . . . . . . . . . . .241
An Effective Assessment System . . . . . . . . . . . . . . . . . . . . . . . . . . . . . . . . . . .250
Summary. . . . . . . . . . . . . . . . . . . . . . . . . . . . . . . . . . . . . . . . . . . . . . . . . . . . .256

## Part IV   Facilities and Programs                       259

**Chapter 16** Rental Operations. . . . . . . . . . . . . . . . . . . . . . 261

*Rob Jones, MS*

Planning . . . . . . . . . . . . . . . . . . . . . . . . . . . . . . . . . . . . . . . . . . . . . . . . . . . . .261
Purchasing. . . . . . . . . . . . . . . . . . . . . . . . . . . . . . . . . . . . . . . . . . . . . . . . . . . .265
Rental Center Operations . . . . . . . . . . . . . . . . . . . . . . . . . . . . . . . . . . . . . . . .268
Summary. . . . . . . . . . . . . . . . . . . . . . . . . . . . . . . . . . . . . . . . . . . . . . . . . . . . .278

**Chapter 17** Indoor Climbing Walls. . . . . . . . . . . . . . . . . . . 279

*John Bicknell, MA, and Guy deBrun, MS*

History of Artificial Climbing Walls . . . . . . . . . . . . . . . . . . . . . . . . . . . . . . . .279
Climbing Wall Facilities and Construction . . . . . . . . . . . . . . . . . . . . . . . . . . .280
Climbing Wall Activities . . . . . . . . . . . . . . . . . . . . . . . . . . . . . . . . . . . . . . . . .284
Climbing Wall Management . . . . . . . . . . . . . . . . . . . . . . . . . . . . . . . . . . . . . .287
Summary. . . . . . . . . . . . . . . . . . . . . . . . . . . . . . . . . . . . . . . . . . . . . . . . . . . . .292

**Chapter 18** Challenge Course Management. . . . . . . . . . . . . 293

*Christina Carter Thompson, MS, and Adam Bondeson, BA*

Challenge Terms . . . . . . . . . . . . . . . . . . . . . . . . . . . . . . . . . . . . . . . . . . . . . . .293
History . . . . . . . . . . . . . . . . . . . . . . . . . . . . . . . . . . . . . . . . . . . . . . . . . . . . . .294
Challenge Course Program Design and Outcomes . . . . . . . . . . . . . . . . . . . . .294
Primary Influences on Challenge Programming . . . . . . . . . . . . . . . . . . . . . . .295
Challenge Course Facilities . . . . . . . . . . . . . . . . . . . . . . . . . . . . . . . . . . . . . . .296
Designing and Choosing a Course. . . . . . . . . . . . . . . . . . . . . . . . . . . . . . . . . .301
Bidding Process . . . . . . . . . . . . . . . . . . . . . . . . . . . . . . . . . . . . . . . . . . . . . . .304
Building Process . . . . . . . . . . . . . . . . . . . . . . . . . . . . . . . . . . . . . . . . . . . . . . .304
The Challenge Course Administrator . . . . . . . . . . . . . . . . . . . . . . . . . . . . . . .304
Organizational Support and Resources . . . . . . . . . . . . . . . . . . . . . . . . . . . . . .311
Summary. . . . . . . . . . . . . . . . . . . . . . . . . . . . . . . . . . . . . . . . . . . . . . . . . . . . .311

**Chapter 19** Land-Based Programming . . . . . . . . . . . . . . . . . . . . . . . . . 313

*Curt Howell, MA*

Incident Prevention and Incident Response. . . . . . . . . . . . . . . . . . . . . . . . . . . . . . . . . . . . 314
Cost Analyses . . . . . . . . . . . . . . . . . . . . . . . . . . . . . . . . . . . . . . . . . . . . . . . . . . . . . 315
Determining Learning Outcomes . . . . . . . . . . . . . . . . . . . . . . . . . . . . . . . . . . . . . . . . 317
Risk Management . . . . . . . . . . . . . . . . . . . . . . . . . . . . . . . . . . . . . . . . . . . . . . . . . . . 318
Backpacking . . . . . . . . . . . . . . . . . . . . . . . . . . . . . . . . . . . . . . . . . . . . . . . . . . . . . . . 318
Climbing . . . . . . . . . . . . . . . . . . . . . . . . . . . . . . . . . . . . . . . . . . . . . . . . . . . . . . . . . . 320
Caving Programs. . . . . . . . . . . . . . . . . . . . . . . . . . . . . . . . . . . . . . . . . . . . . . . . . . . . 323
Mountaineering. . . . . . . . . . . . . . . . . . . . . . . . . . . . . . . . . . . . . . . . . . . . . . . . . . . . . 325
Ski Programs . . . . . . . . . . . . . . . . . . . . . . . . . . . . . . . . . . . . . . . . . . . . . . . . . . . . . . . 326
Cycling . . . . . . . . . . . . . . . . . . . . . . . . . . . . . . . . . . . . . . . . . . . . . . . . . . . . . . . . . . . . 328
Summary. . . . . . . . . . . . . . . . . . . . . . . . . . . . . . . . . . . . . . . . . . . . . . . . . . . . . . . . . . 330

**Chapter 20** Water-Based Programming. . . . . . . . . . . . . . . . . . . . . . . . 333

*Chris Stec, BS, and Geoff Harrison, MS*

Incident Prevention and Incident Response: Needs Assessment . . . . . . . . . . . . . . . . . . 333
Water-Based Programming: Flat Water . . . . . . . . . . . . . . . . . . . . . . . . . . . . . . . . . . . . 343
Water-Based Programming: Moving-Water and Whitewater Venues . . . . . . . . . . . . . . . 346
Water-Based Programming: Open Water. . . . . . . . . . . . . . . . . . . . . . . . . . . . . . . . . . . 351
Summary. . . . . . . . . . . . . . . . . . . . . . . . . . . . . . . . . . . . . . . . . . . . . . . . . . . . . . . . . . 355

**Chapter 21** Special Events Programming. . . . . . . . . . . . . . . . . . . . . . . 357

*Brent Anslinger, BS, and Amy Anslinger, BS*

Special Event Options . . . . . . . . . . . . . . . . . . . . . . . . . . . . . . . . . . . . . . . . . . . . . . . . . 358
Risk Management for Special Events and Competitions. . . . . . . . . . . . . . . . . . . . . . . . 367
Assessing and Planning for Your Event . . . . . . . . . . . . . . . . . . . . . . . . . . . . . . . . . . . . 367
Staffing . . . . . . . . . . . . . . . . . . . . . . . . . . . . . . . . . . . . . . . . . . . . . . . . . . . . . . . . . . . 373
Managing the Event. . . . . . . . . . . . . . . . . . . . . . . . . . . . . . . . . . . . . . . . . . . . . . . . . . 374
Developing Timelines for Successful Events . . . . . . . . . . . . . . . . . . . . . . . . . . . . . . . . 375
Putting the Planning Into Motion . . . . . . . . . . . . . . . . . . . . . . . . . . . . . . . . . . . . . . . . 375
Summary. . . . . . . . . . . . . . . . . . . . . . . . . . . . . . . . . . . . . . . . . . . . . . . . . . . . . . . . . . 376

References and Resources   377

Index   389

About the Editors   399

About the Contributors   401

# Preface

As the outdoor recreation and education professions continue to become an essential part of an economically successful society, the need for effective and experienced administrators increases. Outdoor program administrators lead programs in universities, municipalities, nonprofit organizations, military, social services, and parks and recreation. The diversity of programming associated with outdoor recreation requires professionals to be adept at working in complex environments. The Association of Outdoor Recreation and Education (AORE) has become the definitive source for current and emerging recreation professionals in the various sectors. *Outdoor Program Administration: Principles and Practices* provides professionals with the information needed for improving administrative practices.

## ORGANIZATION OF THE BOOK

*Outdoor Program Administration: Principles and Practices* has four parts:

**>> Part I: Outdoor Program Foundations.** Chapter 1 discusses what is necessary for becoming an effective outdoor program administrator. Chapter 2 presents a history of programming as it relates to outdoor recreation. This chapter is valuable for administrators working on proposals and presentations to supervisors. Chapter 3 explores the types of programs and the sectors where outdoor recreation is commonly offered. While some programs are considered historical models, determining the type of program an organization will operate affects future planning. Chapter 4 discusses the future of outdoor recreation administration as increased demand and improved technology begin to influence the decisions administrators have to make.

**>> Part II: Program Design and Implementation.** Chapter 5 covers the importance of viewing risk management as a gestalt process not limited to field programming. Chapter 6 details the basic techniques for establishing a vision statement and a mission statement when developing programs. Chapter 7 looks at the legal considerations for an outdoor recreation administrator. Chapters 8 and 9 provide detailed information about financial operations and marketing techniques to increase program success. Chapter 10 provides extensive information about the process of gaining access and securing permits to public and private lands. Chapter 11 discusses current and future trends regarding environmental stewardship. Chapter 12 discusses considerations in writing effective field policies and procedures for those who supervise participants.

**>> Part III: Staffing Considerations.** Chapter 13 discusses staff recruitment and supervision from the perspective of human resources. Chapter 14 is dedicated to the development and ongoing staff training necessary for maintaining a safe and successful outdoor program. Accurate evaluation of staff through the development of rubrics and measures is the focus of chapter 15.

**>> Part IV: Facilities and Programs.** This part addresses issues specific to a host of outdoor recreation facilities and technical leadership programs:

- Challenge programs
- Special events
- Water-based programs
- Land-based programs
- Rental centers
- Climbing walls

Chapters 16 through 21 discuss specific programming and management aspects of each topic. Outdoor recreation administrators should understand the general management principles discussed in previous chapters and discipline-specific components detailed in these chapters.

## AUTHORSHIP OF THE BOOK

The AORE worked hard to find professionals in administrative roles of the various sectors of outdoor recreation and education. Most of the chapters are coauthored. As a result of the extensive number of authors involved in this project, chapter presentations may vary. Proceeds from the book will benefit the Association of Outdoor Recreation and

Education, and most of the authors donated their authoring stipend back to the association.

## CONSIDERATIONS

*Administrators* are concerned with the overall vision and direction of outdoor recreation programs. They are responsible for setting the course of the organization. *Managers* have discipline-specific skills in implementing policies, procedures, and directives to meet organizational objectives. Unfortunately, many outdoor recreation administrators need to function in both roles consistently as the result of an organization's staffing hierarchy. As a consequence, the term *administrator* is used to designate a professional in charge of an outdoor recreation program in any sector (nonprofit, commercial, government). *Management* is referenced as a set of skills essential for effective administration. This book addresses a range of programs, and it is recognized that some programs will have both administrative responsibilities for setting the course for success and specific management responsibilities for ensuring various aspects of the daily operations are completed.

The four categories of skills—human, outdoor, educational, and management—are introduced in this text as a means of organizing the broad base of knowledge and abilities required of outdoor recreation administrators. Each of these skill areas is addressed throughout the text; however, management skills serve as the focal point for the content of the text.

**»» Audience.** This book serves as a desk reference for outdoor recreation administrators and as an upper-level textbook for students in outdoor recreation administration courses. This book is a reference to both field instructors and administrators alike.

**»» General reference, not prescriptive.** While the content presented in this text is extensive, by no means is it an exhaustive compilation of all possible challenges faced by administrators. The perspective is generalized to a broad base of business sectors and outdoor program designs. This is not a prescriptive text that all outdoor program administrators must follow, because missions and delivery structures will vary from organization to organization.

**»» Overlap.** While each chapter addresses specific topics, the amount of overlap across subjects is immense. A chapter might reference other areas in the book that cover a specific topic, and keep in mind that the index is the place to find common terms and their locations throughout the book.

# Outdoor Program Foundations

# Chapter 1

# The Outdoor Program Administrator

*Geoff Harrison, MS, and Mat Erpelding, MA*

Since the 1960s outdoor recreation programming has become increasingly more structured and professionalized. Outdoor activity participation has increased by 4.4 percent from an estimated 208 million to 217 million since 2000 (Cordell, 2008). This growth has fueled the still-emerging professional field of outdoor program administration. Whether the outdoor program administrator is serving at a university, a government municipal parks and recreation program, a nonprofit agency, or a military welfare and recreation (MWR) program, duties are multifaceted and require the ability to apply educational theories, human psychology, management practices, and outdoor skills. Outdoor program administrators work in environments that range from meeting with an advisory board at a retreat center to leading a group of participants up the summit ridge of a snow-capped peak. This book emphasizes the discipline-specific knowledge related to the operations and management of an outdoor program. This first chapter includes a brief introduction to the profession. Key sections in the chapter include the following:

- Outdoor program administration defined
- Outdoor program administrator defined
- Management skills
- Outdoor program administrator minimum skill competencies
- Skill acquisition for the emerging professional
- Professional maintenance

Although an outdoor program administrator should have extensive experience outdoors, outdoor skills are not the emphasis of this book. The mixed nature of workplace responsibilities requires outdoor recreation professionals to demonstrate effectiveness in the following dimensions: human skills, outdoor skills, management skills, and educational skills. The contents of this book, though targeted at administrative professionals working in the field of outdoor recreation, include common principles and practices transferable to many other administrative positions in the fields of recreation, tourism, and sport management. In this chapter we first discuss the skills one needs to be an effective outdoor program administrator; this is followed by a discussion of the work experience, training, and educational experience necessary for success in the field. This chapter also covers many of the unique responsibilities and issues that distinguish outdoor program administrators from other recreation professionals.

# OUTDOOR PROGRAM ADMINISTRATION DEFINED

*Outdoor program administration* is the creation and implementation of programs that use outdoor environments for a deliberate recreational or educational experience. Outdoor program administrators are commonly responsible for the following types of programs:

- Adventure education
- Environmental education
- Outdoor education
- Guiding
- Military morale and welfare
- Municipal parks and recreation
- Wilderness therapy
- Summer camps

Outdoor program administration is a specialized profession because it might require both effective outdoor skills for working outside the office and effective management skills for working within an administration. Although the previous list of possible programs is not exhaustive, all of these programs have a common thread: Outdoor experiences are used deliberately for a variety of outcomes, including discipline-specific skill development, personal growth, environmental awareness, therapeutic outcomes, and instructional strategies.

For our purposes in this book, *administration* is defined as the identification of an organization's objectives and the effective acquisition, allocation, and maintenance of resources to meet the objectives. Resources used in pursuit of an organization's objectives include human labor and talent, financial assets, physical property, equipment, intellectual property, and public image. Among the most significant resources are the knowledge, skills, and abilities of the organization's outdoor program administrator.

# OUTDOOR PROGRAM ADMINISTRATOR DEFINED

As we have stated, the diversity of program types within the field of outdoor programming is extensive. Depending on the organization, administrative positions include full-time, part-time, and seasonal work. Although titles and job descriptions vary across organizations, the scope of responsibilities among outdoor program administrators remains fairly consistent. An outdoor program administrator is responsible for establishing desired outcomes that support an organization's mission and then managing and maintaining resources to meet these desired outcomes. Based on the size and needs of an organization, this might require working both in the office as an administrator and in the field as an instructor.

To distinguish the physical locations in which an outdoor program administrator's duties take place, we'll use the terms "administrative" and "field." *Administrative* time is spent in an office environment focused on administrative and management duties necessary to maintain operations. *Field* time is spent working outdoors in a capacity directly related to providing a recreational experience to staff or participants. Field-time duties and responsibilities might include assessing staff competency, instructing adventure-based activities, and managing the logistics of a field program. Many positions require outdoor program administrators to spend an immense amount of time in the field. Depending on an organization's needs, field time may be either in addition to or in lieu of administrative time.

An effective outdoor program administrator requires foundational outdoor skills developed through formal education coupled with additional training, personal and vocational practice, ongoing personal reflection, and access to professional assessment and feedback. Because of the onsite or offsite nature of the job, the outdoor program administrator must be able to work effectively both in the office and in the field.

# SKILL SETS FOR OUTDOOR PROGRAM ADMINISTRATORS

The road to becoming an effective outdoor program administrator is challenging. With responsibilities ranging from paddling a class III river in a dry top to donning a tie for a meeting with upper management, the position of outdoor program administrator is arguably one of the most complex positions in the recreation industry. Paul Nicolazzo's seminal work *Effective Outdoor Program Design and Management* (2007) states that "program administrators must have a strong field based background, and should develop human, educational, and outdoor skills concurrently to be a quality field leader." Thus, prior to becoming an administrator, appropriate field experience—as a participant, as a leader, and as a personal adventurer—is a requisite. An outdoor program administrator should be competent in all three areas before advancing to an administrative role.

The three skill sets identified by Nicolazzo (2007) represent the essential skills of an outdoor field professional. However, to account for the transition from field-based work to administrative work, we have added a fourth skill set—management skills. This book focuses on the management skills necessary for effective outdoor program administration.

Isolating skills into a category can be challenging; many times there is significant overlap. Figure 1.1 indicates the interdependent relations among the four skill sets that make up outdoor program administration.

Complex abilities such as leadership, decision making, and judgment are represented by effective integration and application of each skill set. The more the skill sets overlap, and are applied in coordinated unison, the better an administrator will perform.

## Outdoor Skills

Outdoor skills comprise the unique job qualifications required for positions in the outdoor recreation industry. The discipline-specific competencies needed to effectively guide, lead, and train others are becoming increasingly complex because of the endless variety of adventure-based activities offered to customers. For example, an outdoor program administrator might offer trips that demand instructor skill in rock climbing, mountaineering, skiing, caving, bicycle touring, canoeing, whitewater rafting, and sea kayaking.

Although administrators need not be competent in all activities, they must be able to make accurate program assessments for each outdoor activity their organization offers. Ultimately, these assessments will form the basis for risk-management strategies, training plans, and program offerings.

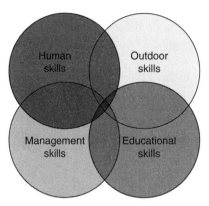

**Figure 1.1**  Outdoor program administration requires professionals to integrate four areas of skill competency. The intersection of the skill areas indicates effective leadership, experience-based judgment, critical and creative thinking, and decision making.

Nearly all of the aforementioned discipline-specific skills have a common set of basic outdoor skills that are needed to facilitate successful outcomes. Thus, at a minimum, competency in basic outdoor living skills is essential to being an effective outdoor administrator. However, identifying a concise and complete list of essential outdoor skills has been a subject of debate among outdoor professionals, with no uniform agreement. See figure 1.2 for the authors' listing of minimum outdoor skills required to be an effective outdoor program administrator.

## Human Skills

Human skills are complex and not limited to outdoor programming. Rather, effective human skills are required for employment in any industry. These skills are the essential intrapersonal awareness and interpersonal relationships skills necessary to engage and lead others. Engaging supervisors, staff, and participants requires an ability to recognize how others are interpreting situational factors and then to react appropriately. Figure 1.2 includes a list of the minimum human skills needed to be an effective outdoor program administrator.

Additionally, human skills include the development of ethics, or morals. Developed through life experiences, ethics drive individual behavior and decision making. Effective human skills allow

---

**Human Skills**
- Effective self-leadership
- Self-awareness
- Accurate assessment
- Developed personal values and ethics
- Ability to connect with others
- Humility
- Effective interpersonal communication skills

**Outdoor Skills**
- Incident prevention
- Equipment selection and use
- Equipment maintenance
- Health and sanitation
- Navigation
- Minimum impact techniques
- Meal planning
- Campsite selection and setup
- Hazard recognition
- Incident response
- Wilderness medicine treatment
- Rescue and extrication

**Management Skills**
- Program design
- Risk management
  - Incident prevention
  - Incident response
- Staff training and assessment
- Curriculum development
- Marketing
- Facility management
- Fiscal and resource management
- Technology use and management

**Educational Skills**
- Content mastery
- Educational methodologies
- Designing progressions
- Trip and lesson planning
- Articulate presentation and instructions
- Effective time management
- Ability to mentor others
- Ability to provide developmental and reinforcing feedback

**Figure 1.2** Minimum skill competencies—human, outdoor, management, and educational.

administrators to construct a workplace environment that honors individual differences by creating a culture supportive of civil dialogue.

## Educational Skills

Similar to human skills, the educational skill set is not limited to outdoor recreation. Educational skills are essential for effectiveness in any workplace setting. Outdoor program administrators need educational skills so they can effectively adapt teaching

Bruce Saxman

Outdoor program administrators must possess educational skills so they can select appropriate course content to meet the competency levels of their participants.

styles and selection of course content to meet the competency levels exhibited by participants. Educational skills include the ability to demonstrate detailed content knowledge of the topic, design appropriate lessons, verbally articulate information, design a logical progression, and either formally or informally mentor others.

Many times, educational skills represent the difference between success and failure on a trip or program. Whether the administrator is teaching a participant, a subordinate, or a superior, the ability to effectively deliver information to others is essential. Educational skills require content mastery, which can represent a significant challenge if an administrator is operating outside of his or her area of competency. Administrators should have content mastery in basic outdoor skills as well as in other technical skills such as climbing, kayaking, caving, or mountain biking. This is why past and present field time is important to the effective development and maintenance of outdoor skills. Figure 1.2 includes a list of the minimum educational skills needed to be an effective outdoor program administrator.

## Management Skills

Management skills include the business functions and duties that comprise the inner workings of outdoor administration. The nuts and bolts of outdoor program administration are not glamorous, but these skills are necessary for programs to be successful, financially viable, and incident free.

Common outdoor program business models require administrators to oversee a variety of onsite and offsite businesses, such as outdoor equipment rental centers, challenge courses, indoor climbing walls, retreat centers, trip and education programs, summer camps, and leadership development programs. Management skills are often grouped by their seemingly similar duties, but in practice they regularly require distinctly different approaches and applications (see figure 1.3).

Business acumen is key in this skill set. Administrators are responsible for managing an organization's resources and achieving goals and directives. Fiscal management must be an area of strength for an outdoor program administrator because the com-bined budgets of outdoor programs can easily range from under $20,000 a year to well over $2,000,000 a year. The varied facilities and equipment managed by the outdoor program administrator requires an understanding of facility design and maintenance, technical outdoor equipment, and vehicles. Administrators need competence in human resource practices to effectively hire and train staff. They must also be able to accurately assess their employees' skills because there is always a chance an employee will need to make critical decisions about the health and safety of participants. Competency in program design, developing policy and procedure manuals, and marketing are all skills that administrators should possess because they need to be able to develop programs that participants want and that their staff is competent to lead.

---

**Figure 1.3   Management Skills**

- **Program design:** The process of moving from concepts, anchored by the organization's macrostructure (vision, mission, values, and objectives), to deliverable products or services.

- **Risk management:** The design and implementation of plans, procedures, guidelines, and policies to eliminate, minimize, and manage exposure to loss while pursuing program outcomes.

  - **Incident prevention:** The practice of obtaining desired outcomes while avoiding the loss of resources (fiscal, physical, human, perceived). Incident prevention is the core priority of the outdoor recreation administrator.

  - **Incident response:** The prescribed and purposeful actions employed by the outdoor recreation administrator to manage an incident regardless of severity or where it occurs (office or field).

- **Fiscal and resource management:** The practice of maximizing effective use of resources while maintaining the financial records and procedures of the organization.

- **Staff training and assessment:** The process through which human, educational, outdoor, and (at times) management skills are imparted upon and measured to ensure that staff effectiveness and overall program quality meet desired outcomes.

- **Curriculum and program development:** The creation and implementation of course content and learning progressions that are combined to minimize risk and meet the desired outcomes of a program.

- **Facility management:** The process of managing a complete array of outdoor program resources, such as offices, rental programs, climbing walls, challenge courses, camps, water fronts, pools, vehicles, and trailers.

- **Marketing:** The activity, set of institutions, and processes for creating, communicating, delivering, and exchanging offerings that have value for customers, clients, partners, and society at large.

- **Technology use and management:** The process of applying specialized technical tools and equipment to improve services, provide new programs, and minimize risk of loss.

## ADMINISTRATIVE COMPETENCE

All administrators should possess basic administrative strengths, but outdoor program administrators must have a base level of competency in management skills to be able to effectively operate an outdoor program. Nicolazzo (2007) and Raiola (1990) have offered similar models to describe the development of skill competency. An understanding of levels of competence is important because an outdoor program administrator must be able to accurately self-assess personal competence and the competence of the staff working for the program. Figure 1.4 shows levels of competencies demonstrated by administrators.

The outdoor program administrator serves as program's caretaker. Intentionality is necessary when making decisions on behalf of the organization. These decisions must be deliberate and in alignment with the mission statement and desired outcomes of the organization. Unconscious behavior, whether competent or incompetent, makes an administrator's job more difficult and less rewarding and can endanger the lives of staff and participants. Although this book does not emphasize how to develop human, outdoor, and educational skills, it remains the professional's responsibility to acquire an appropriate amount of field time to effectively develop and maintain each skill set.

## ACQUIRING SKILLS

Unlike many careers, a career in outdoor recreation often has no direct path to becoming an outdoor program administrator. Professionals develop the four skill sets we have discussed through a variety of approaches. These approaches, discussed in depth in the following sections, include formal education and training experiences, personal adventuring and

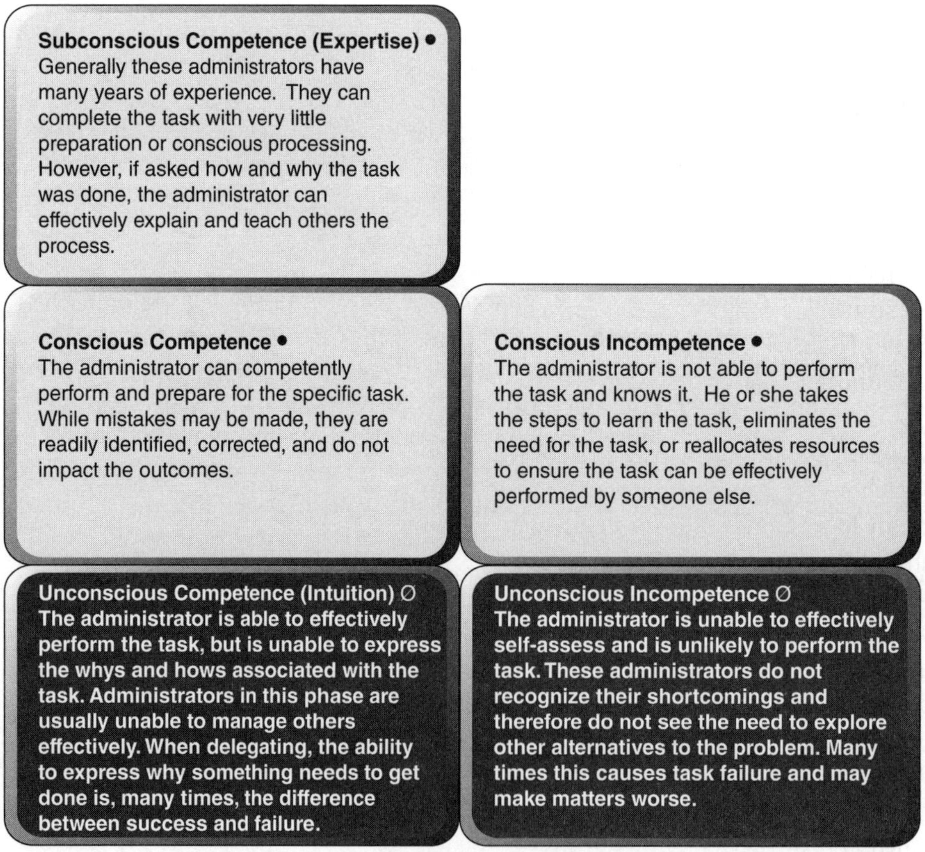

**Subconscious Competence (Expertise)** ●
Generally these administrators have many years of experience. They can complete the task with very little preparation or conscious processing. However, if asked how and why the task was done, the administrator can effectively explain and teach others the process.

**Conscious Competence** ●
The administrator can competently perform and prepare for the specific task. While mistakes may be made, they are readily identified, corrected, and do not impact the outcomes.

**Conscious Incompetence** ●
The administrator is not able to perform the task and knows it. He or she takes the steps to learn the task, eliminates the need for the task, or reallocates resources to ensure the task can be effectively performed by someone else.

**Unconscious Competence (Intuition)** ∅
The administrator is able to effectively perform the task, but is unable to express the whys and hows associated with the task. Administrators in this phase are usually unable to manage others effectively. When delegating, the ability to express why something needs to get done is, many times, the difference between success and failure.

**Unconscious Incompetence** ∅
The administrator is unable to effectively self-assess and is unlikely to perform the task. These administrators do not recognize their shortcomings and therefore do not see the need to explore other alternatives to the problem. Many times this causes task failure and may make matters worse.

**Figure 1.4** Adaptations of the competencies model to express the abilities of an administrator.

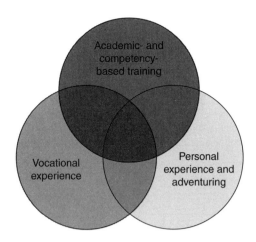

**Figure 1.5** Integrated professional development plan using a combination of academic coursework, vocational training, and personal outdoor experiences to improve effectiveness.

experiences, and vocational experiences (see figure 1.5). The sum of these experiences contribute to the effectiveness of an administrator.

## Academic Coursework and Competency-Based Trainings

Many professionals have both undergraduate and graduate degrees in subjects such as wilderness leadership, outdoor education, outdoor recreation administration, recreation and sport management, and natural resource recreation management. These programs of study provide professionals with a strong foundation of theory, knowledge, and practice.

Additionally, competency-based trainings from organizations such as the American Canoe Association, American Mountain Guides Association, Center for Outdoor Ethics, and Wilderness Education Association offer certificates indicating that a course in a specific skill area or outdoor discipline has been completed. Within any professional discipline, a wide variance in the areas of content knowledge, application, and emphasis may exist between providers of professional trainings. This being the case, it is critically important that outdoor program administrators research program providers and course curriculums to ensure offered programs provide the desired results.

Competency in the four skill areas can also be derived from experiences within other academic disciplines. Degree programs in philosophy, psychology, education, communication, and business administration provide the program administrator opportunities to further develop and maintain the skills required for outdoor program administration.

## Personal Experience and Adventuring

Educational opportunities should be complemented by extensive outdoor field experience derived from personal experience and adventuring. Field experience has three associated components: the time spent in the backcountry, the difficulty of the activity, and the leadership role. Commonly, outdoor programs offer instruction in discipline-specific outdoor activities such as rock climbing, ice climbing, mountaineering, kayaking, canoeing, rafting, backpacking, telemark skiing, cross-country skiing, surfing, and sailing. A serious commitment to personal training and adventuring is essential because many outdoor program administrators are expected to maintain technical and educational competency in at least three discipline-specific outdoor skill areas. All individuals pursuing a career in recreation should begin developing and maintaining their outdoor skills as early as possible. Learning a new skill by taking part in a whitewater kayaking class will not make one competent without the additional commitment to run a variety of rivers with different types of rapids at varying levels of difficulty. The need to maintain skill proficiency can become a pressing issue for an administrator who accepts a position that places him or her in the office more than in the field.

## Vocational Experience

The final piece of an integrated professional development plan comes from seeking vocational opportunities that place individuals in positions of increasing responsibility. The field of recreation offers many employment possibilities that range from part-time seasonal work to full-time administrative positions. Part-time or seasonal work opportunities to consider may include employment at park and recreation programs, YMCAs,

Geoff Harrison

Gaining field experience will prepare you for a career in outdoor program administration.

summer camps, climbing gyms, cruise ships, ski resorts, whitewater raft companies, bike touring companies, mountaineering guide services, and sea kayak guide services. Skills are best fostered through a combination of field experiences and administrative tasks such as planning, logistics, and customer service. Individuals may consider enriching employment experiences by volunteering for nonprofit programs focused on exposing youth to the outdoors. Programs like the Boy Scouts, Girls Scouts, Special Olympics, and Big City Mountaineers all offer volunteers a chance to work with youth in a variety of contexts.

When building a base of vocational experience, keep in mind that future potential employers will consider both the diversity and duration of an applicant's experience. An applicant who has a shallow but broad base of experience derived from seven distinctly different seasonal positions might not be as qualified as someone who has had only two positions but amassed significant experience within a narrow scope of duties. Conversely, individuals who have had fewer positions may not have the adaptability required to work for a company that will ask employees to work regularly in multiple areas of their program.

Individuals pursuing a career in outdoor program administration should create a professional development plan to guide them in the pursuit of personal and vocational opportunities to complement their formal education. They should allocate ample time for skill acquisition, practice, and refinement in all four skill areas. Those pursuing a career in outdoor programming should begin their personal adventuring and vocational training as early as possible.

## PROFESSIONAL MAINTENANCE

*Competency creep* is the slow degeneration of skill competency caused by lack of review, lack of practice, and lack of application. The best way to prevent competency creep is to commit time to maintaining each skill at or above the level required for a particular position.

Arguably, early in a professional career, skill development falls on the shoulders of the applicant. Skill development is not necessarily the responsibility of the employer because applicants obtain positions as part of a competitive process. Top candidates will have committed to the necessary skill development and will arrive possessing the required skills. However, once hired, skill maintenance becomes a shared responsibility between the employee and employer.

Outdoor program administration requires professionals to maintain an expansive and complex set of skills in a variety of disciplines. When working in the field or in the office, outdoor program administrators are responsible for positively representing their organization at all times. Positive representation includes dressing in professional attire both in the office and in the field, clearly articulating the vision and mission of their program to superiors and the public at large, and modeling expected behaviors at all times to staff and professional peers. It is the responsibility of each administrator to educate others about the complexities of the profession and to serve as an ambassador for the entire industry. There are tools available to administrators to help prevent competency creep. Regular involvement in professional affiliations and conferences, competency and certification courses, scouting trips and field-based staff trainings all help an administrator maintain and enhance human, educational, outdoor, and management skills.

## Professional Affiliations and Conferences

Many professional organizations serve the needs of outdoor program administrators. Although a professional might be an active member of an organization, such as the Association of Outdoor Recreation and Education (AORE), it is wise for him or her also to join other relevant organizations, or at least to periodically attend their meetings. Many organizations offer annual conferences and training institutes that bring professionals from around the country together to share information, learn new material, and network. A few of the relevant organizations are listed in table 1.1.

## Competency and Certification Courses

Continuing education through participation in competency-based trainings or recertification courses is an excellent means to maintain professional skills. Competency-based trainings offered by private companies and nonprofits should be considered as a method for skill review and enhancement. Organizations such as the American Alpine Institute, Colorado Mountain School, Outward Bound, and the National Outdoor Leadership School offer courses emphasizing skill acquisition and application. To stay engaged and passionate about their profession, administrators should consider taking discipline-specific courses in areas in which they feel their skills are lacking or need improvement.

Certification courses are another avenue for skill and knowledge development. Areas of development may include outdoor skill topics such as wilderness medicine, river rescue, or avalanche safety, or they

**Table 1.1**  Options for Ongoing Professional Development

| Recreation associations |
|---|
| Association of Outdoor Recreation and Education (AORE) |
| Association for Experiential Education (AEE) |
| National Intramural-Recreational Sports Association (NIRSA) |
| National Recreation and Parks Association (NRPA) |
| Wilderness Education Association (WEA) |
| **Technical training associations** |
| American Canoe Association (ACA) |
| Association for Challenge Course Technology (ACCT) |
| American Mountain Guides Association (AMGA) |
| Professional Climbing Instructors Association (PCIA) |
| **Higher education associations** |
| Association of College Unions International (ACUI) |
| Student Affairs Administrators in Higher Education (NASPA) |
| American Alliance for Health, Physical Education, Recreation and Dance (AAHPERD) |

can focus on areas of human development, such as conflict resolution and mediation. Certification courses can be expensive and should be researched to ensure they provide the expected quality, content, and consistency.

**>> Wilderness emergency medical training.** A minimum professional training requirement for most outdoor program administrators is completion of a Wilderness First Responder course. A host of quality organizations provide this training, including the Wilderness Medicine Training Center, Wilderness Medical Associates, SOLO, Aerie Backcountry Medicine, Desert Mountain Medicine, and the Wilderness Medicine Institute. The organizations listed here are private providers of wilderness medicine, and each offers a unique curriculum and approach for content delivery. Fortunately, the listed companies offer reciprocity toward each other—that is, they recognize each other's training as valid, and recertification is offered to graduates. Because each provider offers different training and has different strengths and education methodologies, individuals should consider diversifying their learning experiences by taking courses from several of the providers just listed.

**>> Discipline-specific skill certifications.** Certification courses offered through nonprofit entities are another viable avenue for continuing education. Courses and certifications are an excellent means to gain new knowledge and refresh existing knowledge. However, infrequent professional training is not enough to retain competence because ongoing practice is necessary for achieving and maintaining skills. Courses and certifications in technical outdoor disciplines are offered by the following associations:

- American Mountain Guides Association (AMGA)
- American Canoe Association (ACA)
- Professional Climbing Instructors Associations (PCIA)
- Wilderness Education Association (WEA)
- American Canyoneering Association (ACA)

**>> Center for Outdoor Ethics.** The Leave No Trace curriculum is managed by the Center for Outdoor Ethics. Minimum-impact outdoor adventuring is essential to sustaining the industry. All prospective outdoor professionals should consider becoming instructors qualified to teach the Leave No Trace Trainer and Master Educator curriculums. These courses are not certifications but rather completion courses sanctioned by the Center for Outdoor Ethics. Courses teach principles and practices for environmental stewardship.

## Scouting Trips and Field-Based Staff Trainings

Unlike building-based recreation programming, outdoor program administrators need to routinely scout activity sites prior to developing new programs. Content knowledge can come from third-party sources such as personal interactions, books, and the Internet, but the best knowledge always comes from firsthand experiences. Because of the risks associated with outdoor recreation, administrators should not send instructors and participants to unknown activity sites. Scouting trips are an effective means for an administrator to gain knowledge and familiarity with a course area, identify site hazards, and develop risk-management practices for each site. Scouting trips are also effective in helping a professional maintain field-based skill competence.

Staff training is another means for helping administrators to maintain skills. Field-based staff trainings need to occur on a regular basis so that administrators can make accurate assessments when considering who should staff their programs. Scouting trips, staff trainings, and leadership opportunities with other organizations are recommended ways to assist in maintaining skill competency.

## ADMINISTRATIVE CHALLENGES

As stated earlier, preventing competency creep is a consistent challenge for outdoor program administrators. The profession is different from other forms of recreation in that a professional may be required to spend an immense amount of time away from the office. To maintain educational and outdoor skill competency, the administrator should periodically work in the field as an outdoor leader. However, time spent in maintaining professional competency should be purposeful and efficient. Obviously, time in the field takes away from time in the office, and the expected office-based administrative duties must be completed.

Additionally, that time is taken away from personal functions such as spending weekends with family, attending kids' soccer games, mowing the lawn, playing golf, and so on. But the need to remain competent is essential to running quality, safe, and engaging programs, and maintaining competency takes time. Like individuals in other time-demanding careers, outdoor program administrators must find and maintain a healthy balance between the demands and rewards of professional and personal pursuits. To create sustainability within the profession, outdoor program administrators must have effective and open discussions with supervisors about how best to manage the demands of the position. For additional information, see chapter 13.

## SUMMARY

Outdoor program administration is a demanding but rewarding profession. The profession offers opportunities to work in challenging business environments similar to those found within any other corporate industry, but with the joys and opportunities provided by the outdoors. Outdoor program administrators are required to work in a variety of professional capacities and are regularly responsible for multiple business operations and functions, including

- program design,
- instruction,
- risk management,
- staff training and assessment,
- curriculum development,
- marketing,
- facility management,
- fiscal and resource management, and
- technology use and management.

The diversity of skills and experiences required to serve as an effective outdoor program administrator are vast and can be achieved only through a synthesis of personal experiences, formal education, professional trainings, and vocational opportunities. The responsibilities of outdoor program administrators are multifaceted and require a deep working knowledge of and ability to appropriately use educational theories, human psychology, administrative practices, risk management, and technical outdoor skills. We have introduced the four skill areas—human, outdoor, management, and educational—in this first chapter as a means of caching the required broad base of knowledge and abilities required of outdoor program administrators into four common-language categories.

Long and rewarding careers are available to those who aspire to be outdoor program administrators. The ceiling in the profession seems limitless; domestic and international employment opportunities exist within private businesses, universities, government parks and recreation programs, nonprofit agencies, and military welfare and recreation (MWR) programs.

# History of Outdoor Recreation in the United States: An Outdoor Program Administrator's Perspective

*Steven P. Guthrie, PhD, Bryan J. Cavins, EdD, and Jerome Gabriel, MEd*

The meaning of outdoor recreation varies among professionals in the field, but most textbooks share the standard definition we will use in this chapter (Ibrahim and Cordes, 2002; Jensen and Guthrie, 2006; Moore and Driver, 2005). Essentially, outdoor recreation is a form of leisure in which the natural environment (the outdoors) is essential to the leisure experience, involving interaction, appreciation, or an experience related to the natural environment. Under this definition, an outdoor leisure activity can be *experienced* indoors (e.g., through art, nature-based movies, museums, photographs, or on an indoor climbing wall). Further, not all activities (e.g., football, soccer, and other athletic competitions) that occur outdoors have the natural environment as an essential component, and thus are not considered outdoor recreation (Jensen and Guthrie, 2006, p. 9 ff.; Moore and Driver, 2005, p. 11 ff.).

In discussing the development of a national environmental consciousness, the rise of experiential education philosophy, and a cultural interest in outdoor recreational activities, this chapter documents the development of adventure recreation and adventure education programming as a subset of outdoor recreation. An outdoor program admin-istrator provides outdoor adventure programs to participants. The profession of nonprofit, university, municipal, and military outdoor adventure programming began in the 1960s, with substantial growth in the 1980s. Over 50 years, the profession has made tremendous progress toward creating a sustainable industry that supports the educational and recreational needs of our society.

Adventure, or outdoor, programming today "takes place with many different age groups in diverse settings including [K-12] schools, after-school programs, adventure clubs, outdoor schools, for-profit programs, not-for-profit programs" (Guthrie and Yerkes, 2007, p. 208). More specifically, outdoor programming occurs in environmental education centers or conservation not-for-profits; within governmental agencies at all levels (local or county parks and recreation; state parks and state fish and game agencies; and even sponsored by some federal agencies to generate income); in universities, both in academic and support services (campus recreation, student unions, first-year student orientation); and in military recreation (MWRs). Outdoor programming is popular among camping organizations throughout the world. Corporations, youth organizations, recreational clubs, and small businesses employ outdoor programming for health and fitness, leadership training, team-building education, and other endeavors. Additionally, outdoor programming is used as adventure-based counseling or adventure therapy to improve behavioral patterns for at-risk and adjudicated youths and for adults with drug abuse problems. Finally, outdoor programming is used in adaptive recreational therapy, or simply for recreation, for people with a variety of disabilities.

## THE BEGINNINGS OF ENVIRONMENTALISM AND OUTDOOR RECREATION: 1825 TO 1880

Members of the Lewis and Clark expedition (1804-1806) had brought back stories of the far West, awakening awareness of the vast potential resources, especially wildlife and land. Later, fur trappers roamed the Rockies, stumbling onto such wondrous sights as Yellowstone, the Grand Tetons, and the Great Salt Lake (Punke, 2007, pp. 49-51).

Around the same time, the industrial revolution set off tremendous economic growth, creating an economic middle class as well as wealthy aristocrats. As New York City became the dominant cultural city, a group of painters, the Hudson River School (1825-1880), introduced a new kind of landscape painting that celebrated American wildness and nature. The American landscape painting was primitive, fresh, wild, turbulent, and powerful, with nature predominant over humans. During the next 50 years, painters in the school traveled over the American West, bringing pictures of the glories of nature to the cultural urban elite (Howat, 1972).

In the 1850s, as the economic middle class developed, the concept of vacationing became increasingly popular (Aron, 1999; Paris, 2008, p. 22). In the 1860s and '70s, popular literature, both dime novels and magazines, began to be mass marketed to draw on the allure of nature and the West. The "out-of-doors" became "America's playhouse" (Punke, 2007, p. 116). In 1869, the completion of the transcontinental railroad allowed those with money and time to travel west to see for themselves the sights and to hunt big game, especially buffalo (Punke, 2007; Brinkley, 2009).

Prior to the second half of the 19th century, people spent much of their time outdoors; the idea of specifically seeking the outdoors in which to recreate was not in the purview of early settlers. The concept of outdoor recreation began only in the second half of the 19th century as the imaginations of urban Easterners in the United States were captured by fantastic stories of the West, with tales of cowboys and Indians, buffalo by the millions, and unimaginable hordes of other wildlife, geysers, giant trees, petrified logs, and alpine mountains. However, even by 1900 the term "outdoor recreation" was not widely recognized. It was another 25 years before the term was affixed into our national vocabulary (Leopold, 1925/1990b, pp. 113-114).

## THE BEGINNINGS OF A PROFESSION: 1880 TO 1920

As train tracks gradually opened up the Great Plains, sportsmen and hunters focused on the slaughter of buffalo to provide buffalo hides, and people began to settle the plains. By 1883, the last of the great buffalo herds were extirpated. Also in the 1880s, a huge wave of immigrants began to settle in urban areas. The 1890 census report announced the end of the western frontier. No longer were there any large patches of unsettled wilderness (Turner, 1893).

Beginning in 1890, a conflux of factors (recognition of our disappearing natural resources, immigration, industrialization, urbanization, end of the western frontier, the rise of sports, the club movement, more free time and wealth) led to a reform movement (the Progressive Era) over the next 30 years and the establishment of outdoor recreation. These in turn resulted in the protection of public lands, growth of the organized camping movement and youth programs, founding of numerous outdoor clubs, and the recreation profession.

By 1920, outdoor recreation had grown so much that the federal government in that decade arranged four national conferences to promote development of state parks systems, to recognize the role of recreation on public lands and especially in our national forests, and to discuss wilderness. As Leopold (1925/1990b) affirmed, outdoor recreation was now recognized to be of "indispensable" social value.

## The Rise of Sports

Prior to the Civil War, visitors to the United States were "impressed by our apparent lack of interest in amusements" (Dulles, 1965, p. 203). However, following the war, sports and active amusements became a craze. Many open-air sports, such as croquet, bicycling, roller skating, tennis, and archery were coed, providing an opportunity to socialize. Sports clubs were created to facilitate the activities, and popular sporting magazines helped spur the craze. Professional sports developed similarly, too. In the 1880s, an outdoor movement began as both sexes took to hunting and fishing, mountain exploration, and canoeing. Especially in the northeast, summer resorts offered fashionable, reasonably priced vacations in the mountains (Dulles, 1965, p. 202; Weaver, 1939).

## The Women's Club Movement

With the Industrial Era, families began to move into the cities, and the ranks of the poor, those unable to feed themselves through farming, increased. In the 1860s and '70s, a few social reformers, notably women, began to help the poor and become active in social causes. In 1858 in New York City, women created the first association to work with poor girls, a forerunner of the Young Women's Christian Association. Over the next few years, clubs for needy boys, employment offices, nurseries, boarding houses, and low-cost summer resorts were created by women for working women in several northeastern cities.

Women's clubs were created for a large variety of endeavors, including self-improvement, arts and literature, public service and social issues, and for political involvement. By the 1880s, thousands of clubs were formed; women's clubs could be found in every city. In the 1890s, many reform-oriented women's clubs were created as the reformist Progressive Era was ushered in (Blair, 1991; Price, 1999).

For example, women used clubs to mobilize the Audubon movement in 1896. At the time, women's hats made from birds were the rage; Audubons were created in different states to protect birds (Price, 1999). Women's clubs were instrumental in creating several national parks (Kaufman, 2006). They

helped create the Nature Study movement, designed to reform science teaching in the schools. This movement emphasized teaching natural science through experience-based, active learning activities (Kohlstedt, 2005; Russell, 1982).

## Education Reform, Experiential Education, and Recreation

Women were also very active in education reform. Until the mid-1800s, lower-class children had little access to formal schooling. Gradually, states begin to mandate education for all students in order to provide vocational training and to socialize immigrants into our American society. The philosopher John Dewey led the progressive education movement attempt to reform education to provide a more "meaningful" education for the working classes. Even more radically, he maintained that the three Rs (reading, writing, arithmetic), science, "formal" content, and especially thinking should be learned through the use of engaging "vocational" hands-on activities such as shop work, cooking, sewing, and nature-study (Dewey, 1897, 1900/1943, 1916).

Dewey's formulation of experiential education has been extremely important for adventure recreation and outdoor program administrators. It provided the philosophical underpinning and impetus for the Nature Study movement, the organized camping movement, and L.B. Sharp's later school-camp idea, which was an attempt to merge camp and school. This school-camp idea later evolved into outdoor education, conservation education, adventure education, and environmental education.

Recreation was also seen as an important tool for socializing immigrants (Brehony, 2001). The Playground Movement, viewed as a form of education, sought to develop trained recreation leaders to provide healthy, socializing physical activity to prepare immigrants for citizenship (Anderson, 2006). The burgeoning recreation profession also worked with public schools to create playgrounds because it was found that playgrounds helped students perform better in schools (Wood, 1913). The Playground Movement, along with the development of organized camping, marked the beginning of the recreation profession.

## Natural Resource Protection

Turner (1893) noted that the frontier helped determine our American character, and its loss marked a turning point. In 1890, the rapid disappearance of wildlife and wildlands, and the desire of easterners to see our natural wonders, prompted the railroad tourism industry and Congress to create three national parks, including Yosemite National Park, "the first reserve consciously designed to protect wilderness" (Nash, 2001, p. 132).

The following year (1891), the Forest Reserves Act allowed the U.S. president to create "forest reserves." President Harrison immediately created 13 million acres of forest reserves. By 1898, the nation added another 32 million acres to the reserves. Although labeled "reserves," these areas were essentially unprotected until the United States Forest Service was created in 1905 to provide protection and management of the nation's forest reserves (i.e., national forests).

In the years between 1890 and the establishment of the National Park Service in 1916, 14 national parks, 35 national monuments (many later to become national parks), approximately 60+ national bird reservations, and 4+ national game preserves were created. By that time, the nation also had 150 national forests, containing almost all of the 193 million acres of national forest land we have today.

Participants continue to enjoy the national parks today and they respect the resource by following instructions at the trailhead.

© Human Kinetics

And, beginning in the 1910s, states began to develop their own state park systems. This movement was accelerated in the 1920s and 1930s through the instigation of the National Park Service.

## From Youth Organizations to Outdoor Education

As the government began to enact laws establishing forest reserves and national parks, youth organizations, school camps, and outdoor clubs began to increase in popularity. In the urban northeast, with its wilderness resources mostly gone, a movement began to rediscover, to go back to, and to play in nature. A few early camps were established between 1861 and 1880. In 1881, the first camp that influenced the development of other camps was Ernest Balach's private camp for boys in New Hampshire, which began the organized camping movement (Gibson, 1936/1968a; Mitchell, 1938/1968). However, after 1890, the "organized camp idea caught the imagination of leaders of boy life" (Gibson, 1936/1968b, p. 98). As camping developed, so did the camping profession. The Camp Directors Association of America (for boys' camps) was formed in 1912, while the National Association of Girls' Private Camps formed in 1916. These would later unite into today's American Camp Association (Ball and Ball, 2000).

Additionally, John Dewey argued that nature study should be part of the life of a child (1900/1943). In 1912 the first camp that was part of a school education curriculum was opened. These programs came to be known as school camps. By 1925 educators more generally were beginning to consider summer camps for their educational values (Hammerman, Hammerman, and Hammerman, 2001).

L.B. Sharp, who coined the term "outdoor education" (Carlson, 2009), was a student under Dewey and applied experiential philosophy to camping in the 1930s and '40s. He and other advocates envisioned that camping and outdoor education would be an integral part of school curricula. In the 1940s, several school systems experimented with the school camp concept, and in the 1950s, resident school-based outdoor education camps and curricula became well established (Hammerman, Hammerman, and Hammerman, 2001).

During this period, "outdoor education" referred to education in the outdoors meant to further traditional educational curricula, especially nature or conservation studies, and to promote healthful living, meaningful work, and socialization into democratic values. In the 1950s, the term "outdoor education" began to take on expanded meanings. The physical educator Julian Smith advocated for fitness through traditional outdoor recreation such as hunting, fishing, boating and water safety, and hiking and as a component of outdoor education (Smith, 1957/1968). In the next decade (1960s), the concept of outdoor education would be expanded to include adventure-based programming.

# Conservation Organizations and Outdoor Clubs

Although a few outdoor clubs not related to hunting or fishing had been founded prior to 1890, the next 30 years saw many outdoor clubs and conservation organizations created. In 1892, a group of academics and scientists, along with John Muir, founded the Sierra Club to explore and enjoy the Pacific Coast mountains, to provide authentic information about them, and to enlist people and governments to protect them, especially Yosemite (Brower, 1960; Sierra Club, 1989). Figure 2.1 shows a timeline of

**Figure 2.1** Timeline of Conservation and Recreation Organizations and Outdoor Club Development of the 1900s

1876: The Appalachian Mountain Club (AMC) formed for exploration and science in the Appalachian Mountains.

1894: The Portland (OR) Mazamas was the first club devoted to the sport of mountain climbing.

1896: The Massachusetts Audubon Society was founded.

1900: AMC members were regularly canoeing whitewater in the Northeast.

1905: The National Association of Audubon Societies (now Audubon) was created.

1905: The National Ski Association was formed in Michigan (today the U.S. Ski and Snowboard Association).

1906: The Seattle Mountaineers formed.

1906: The Playground Association of America was founded and later merged to become the National Recreation and Park Association.

1906: The Boys Club of America was founded, which was one of the first national youth organizations.

1909: The Dartmouth Outing Club was formed. This was the first collegiate outing club that spurred the formation of other collegiate outing clubs. The club was later very influential in northeastern climbing.

1910s: The Appalachian Mountain Club (AMC) transformed from mountain exploration to mountaineering. Members traveled to the Alps to climb. They began to explore Canada, and to develop rock climbing in the East.

1912: The Colorado Mountain club formed.

1912: The Camp Director's Association of America for boys' camps was formed.

1914: The American Red Cross began its water safety program.

1916: The National Association of Directors of Girls' Private Camps was formed.

1920s: The American Red Cross began canoe instruction.

1922: The Adirondack Mountain Club was formed to promote protection and recreation in the New York Adirondacks.

1922: The Izaak Walton League of America was founded to protect natural resources and wildlife.

Late 1920s: Rock climbing as a sport was accepted by the AMC. The AMC also began snow and ice climbing.

1930s: In the west, technical rock climbing and mountaineering was occurring in the Tetons and in the far West, mostly under the auspices of clubs.

influential conservation and recreation organizations and outdoor clubs of the 1900s. In many cases, as organizations became more developed they used outdoor recreational activities as part of the educational process for conservation-based issues.

## Women in the Outdoors

Women were extremely active in adventure during this period, especially mountaineering and exploration. For example, the Appalachian Mountain Club encouraged women to join, and in the early days of the mountaineering clubs in the west, women made up half of the membership (Bialeschki, 1992). Women participants generally comprised one third of any club adventure (Kaufman, 2006). Waterman and Waterman (1993) note that women in the east were very involved in rock climbing as participants and leaders through the 1940s.

During early exploratory outings, women often took the lead in taking botanical field notes and naming new species. With their interest in field studies, and in their role as schoolteachers, women heavily influenced the Nature Study movement (1890-1930) to effect field-based nature study in the public schools (Kohlstedt, 2005; Russell, 1982). By 1920, Enos Mills, the father of the interpretation profession, encouraged women to be "nature guides" who guided trips and explored nature in the Rocky Mountain National Park. The early National Park Service also recruited women to be ranger naturalists. However, in the 1930s, nature study came to be seen as overly effeminate, and park ranger naturalists began to define their work as men's work (Kaufman, 2006). As a consequence of professionalization of conservation and club organizations, attacks by conservatives, and the Depression, women lost their unified focus, and membership in women's associations waned. Unfortunately, women were gradually phased out of leadership roles and involvement in clubs and professional scientific associations (Bialeschki, 1992; Blair, 1991; Glazer, 2005, p. 458).

It wasn't until the mid-1990s that women began to achieve greater representation in the National Park Service, although they have not yet achieved parity (Kaufman, 2006). The number of women park superintendents jumped from 16 percent to 25 percent; however, female rangers rose only from 30 percent (1993) to 32 percent (2003). On the other hand, women did make progress in salary equity by obtaining 84 percent representation in high-level administration, and 60 percent of curators (Kaufman, 2006).

# NATIONAL ENVIRONMENTAL CONSCIOUSNESS AND OUTDOOR RECREATION EVOLVES: 1920S TO 1960S

In the period following the emergence of outdoor recreation into public consciousness, federal and state governments responded to the increasing public demand for outdoor recreation and public recreation lands. More national parks were created, as were state park systems; the concept of wilderness protection developed. Hunting, fishing, and tourism remained dominant, but more people began to undertake hiking, backpacking, and other outdoor adventures. Although exploitation and development of our natural resources was the dominant resource-management theme, in the 1950s the tide toward resource protection began to change as outdoor recreationists gained political power.

On August 25, 1916, President Wilson signed legislation creating the National Park Service, which established a dual responsibility for the new organization. The organization was to preserve the area and provide enjoyment to visitors. Stephen T. Mather, the first NPS director (1916-1929), worked to expand public interest in parks by building the infrastructure to support tourism and to make the parks "national playgrounds." He supported the railroad companies as they developed hotels to ensure park visitor comfort (Unrau and Williss, 1983). Mather also encouraged road development, envisioning one major road into the backcountry of each large national park and promoting a 6,000-mile circle of roads connecting each of the large national parks (Sellars, 1997). Witnessing the development within national parks, wilderness advocates were disappointed.

Shortly after the creation of the National Park Service, whose primary role was recreation, the competing U.S. Forest Service began to support its recreation possibilities. During the 1920s, the federal government held three national outdoor recreation conferences, which assessed the outdoor recreation options, including the wilderness concept. In 1924, the first designated wilderness area was established, a result of the efforts of forest service employee Aldo Leopold. Later, a 1928 report from the national outdoor recreation conferences used Leopold's arguments to suggest establishment of wilderness areas as federal park and forest policy (Brown and Carmony, 1990; Lewis, 2006; Scott, 2004). In 1929, the forest service established "primitive areas" as the first official nationwide wilderness policy.

The first primitive areas had little real protection. Little progress in establishing protected wilderness areas was made until Bob Marshall, another forest service forester, worked outside of government channels to establish, in 1935, the Wilderness Society (with Leopold as a charter member) to advocate for wilderness. Working within the forest service, Marshall was able to convince the service to set aside 14 million acres—one percent of the United States (Scott, 2004; U.S. Bureau of Census, 1975, Series J 3-7).

World War II in the 1940s, an emerging baby boom, and increasing prosperity coupled with the development of suburbs in the 1950s led to an increased demand for wood and water, and an increasing push for tourist development in the national parks. Because primitive areas were protected only by administrative fiat, commercial interests threatened wilderness and primitive areas, and the national parks themselves. An emerging new threat was the dam builders, as America sought electric power and water for irrigation and drinking.

In 1950, a number of dams were proposed in various national parks, igniting the famous Echo Park wilderness battle in Dinosaur National Monument in northwest Colorado. The Sierra Club and the Wilderness Society worked energetically to mobilize support for wilderness. After a six-year battle, advocates succeeded in ending the plans for the Echo Park dam, and obtained a bill prohibiting dams in any national park. This victory marked the first time that convincing justifications for wilderness protection had been developed (Nash, 2001, p. 219), which in turn established the possibility of effective lobbying in the future (Scott, 2004, p. 46). In 1968, advocates again stopped a Grand Canyon dam project. However, it wasn't until the early 1980s that dam-building impetus ended entirely.

Several factors contributed to this success. The U.S. population had transitioned from a largely rural country to being urban centered, in that 66 percent of the population now lived in cities. As a result, outdoor recreation was recognized as clearly important to Americans; and wild areas were clearly diminishing. And because of the influence of Aldo Leopold, at this time a foremost ecologist and environmental philosopher, the country was developing an environmental awareness, which influenced legislators (Nash, 1967/2001).

In 1958, this increased awareness led the U.S. Congress to legislate the establishment of Outdoor Recreation Resources Review Commission (ORRRC) to study outdoor recreation and outdoor recreation natural resources. The subsequent reports, released in 1962, had profound impacts on natural resource planning and protection, and the growing outdoor recreation industry (Cordell, 2002).

When the ORRRC report emerged in 1962, the fight over the wilderness act had been undergoing extensive debate. The report confirmed that wilderness provided a significant recreation resource and recommended establishment of wilderness areas. Shortly thereafter the Wilderness Act (1964) was created, with the Wild and Scenic River System (1968) and the National Trails System (1968) soon to follow.

The ORRRC report also led directly to federal funding for state and local park lands and a law directing the Bureau of Land Management (BLM) to consider recreation in its planning. In addition, in the 1960s and '70s, other laws were passed to benefit outdoor recreation and the environment, including clean air and clean water acts. Additionally, ORRRC led to the passing of the Endangered Species Act, the creation of the National Wildlife Refuge System, and requirements that outdoor recreation be among all future federal planning considerations. Perhaps most importantly, it led to the creation of significant funding for federal and state outdoor recreation (Crandall, 1994; Olson, 2010).

# ADVENTURE PROGRAMMING EMERGES: 1960S TO 1990

Although in the 1950s, hunting, fishing, sightseeing, and motorized sports dominated outdoor recreation, in the late 1960s there began a sweeping movement toward outdoor adventure pursuits and nonconsumptive outdoor recreation. Data between a survey of 1960 and another in 1982-83 showed major increases in camping (200 percent), bird watching (295 percent), canoeing and kayaking (475 percent), and snow skiing (350 percent). In 1960, backpacking and climbing were too insignificant to be measured, but by 1982-83 backpacking was half as popular as skiing and canoeing and kayaking (Jensen and Guthrie, 2006, p. 34).

As participation in outdoor recreational activities increased, visitor use data for national forests and national parks showed similar increases. Between 1950 and 1960, visitation increased about 200 percent, with much of the increase occurring during the later five years. During the same period, visitation to national parks increased 128 percent. Between 1960 and 1964, national forest visitation increased about 10 million each year (a 45 percent increase); national park visitation increased 42 percent. Between 1967 and 1980, yearly visitation to both forests and parks increased by about 57 percent, far outstripping population growth.

In the 1950s and early '60s, the outdoor adventure movement had been greatly assisted by a wealth of World War II camping and outdoor equipment. Then, from 1960 to the 1980s, a number of technological developments revolutionized outdoor pursuits. Nylon and aluminum allowed for strong, lightweight equipment. Synthetic and Gore-Tex clothing was invented. Strong, lightweight skis were developed, and durable canoes and kayaks were manufactured in the United States. The lightweight hiking shoe captured the boot market (Jensen and Guthrie, 2006, p. 33).

## The Emergent Outdoor Leadership and Programming Profession

With the growth of outdoor pursuits came the development of outdoor adventure programming, for educational and recreational purposes, to help people in their outdoor passions.

## Outward Bound (OB) and NOLS

The first and most influential outdoor adventure education program was Outward Bound, which was founded in Great Britain. In 1961 Outward Bound USA (OB USA) was founded as an outdoor pursuits–based form of outdoor education. The program originally focused on taking people on extended wilderness expeditions for character development, cooperative leadership development, and community responsibility (Outward Bound, 2010). Outward Bound (OB) became the model for adventure programming. Many of its early instructors were schoolteachers, and because its goal was to affect education, it offered courses specifically for teachers. It became a model for physical education programs, which strongly pushed outdoor pursuits; led to the development of the challenge course industry, which had its start as alternative cooperative-based physical education; and spurred the creation of the National Outdoor Leadership School. Many teachers were inspired by OB and sought to put its teachings into the classroom (Cole, 1976/1980).

Throughout its history, OB had been, and continues to be, a leader within the profession, providing a high-quality education. From its beginning, OB sought to integrate its programs into schools. The OB concept is also popular for youth-at-risk programs. In 2007, OB USA went through a major restructuring to have a greater presence in cities, setting up urban centers in four large cities (Outward Bound, 2008).

Because OB was relying on schoolteachers untrained in the outdoors, shortly after the first U.S. Outward Bound school was set up in Colorado, its chief instructor, Paul Petzoldt, saw a need to produce outdoor leaders for Outward Bound and community outdoor youth programs. Leaving Outward Bound, Petzoldt formed the National Outdoor Leadership School (NOLS) in 1965. The focus of NOLS was to be outdoor skills, outdoor leadership and teaching, and environmental ethics (Bachert, 1999; Ringholz, 1997). Like OB, NOLS uses the several week wilderness expedition format. NOLS is today considered one of the leading wilderness-based outdoor or adventure education organizations in the country.

Bruce Saxman

Programs like Outward Bound and the National Outdoor Leadership School provide educational outdoor adventures.

## College and University Outdoor Programs

Although college outing clubs had been very common in the northeastern United States, especially in private colleges, with the advent of Outward Bound, a growing interest in outdoor pursuits education by physical educators, and the general growth in outdoor pursuits recreation in the 1960s, recreation-based cocurricular outdoor programming began to expand within higher education.

In 1967 to 1969, a few western universities established student union–centered outdoor programs in the western states. From those universities, a core of dedicated outdoor programmers spread the recreation-based adventure program concept to other universities. Through the 1970s, student union sponsorship of outdoor programs emerged (Grimm and Hilbert, 1973; Simmons, 1985; Watters, 1985). Over the next 10 years, at least another 80 universities established outdoor programs. Also in the early 1970s, the concept of campus recreation began to grow, with many of these new university outdoor programs being housed in campus recreation rather than in student unions. By 1991, one source (Webb, 1991) had a confirmed list of 160

university outdoor programs (and an unconfirmed list of another approximately 375 of such programs). Outdoor programs surged again in the 1990s as new student-orientation university outdoor programs were created. Today there are likely 400 such programs in the country (Poff and Webb, 2007).

## Adventure Leadership Degrees

Also in the 1970s, the first adventure leadership or outdoor education degree programs were developed, coming under such names as outdoor education, outdoor recreation, outdoor physical education, outdoor adventure, outdoor leadership, adventure recreation, outdoor pursuits, and experiential education. The outdoor programs at Mankato State University and Prescott College (both programs founded in 1971) were probably the first. Between 1971 and 1990, at least 23 colleges and universities created degree programs (Canberg and Daniels, 2004).

## Community and Military Outdoor Recreation Programs

During the 1960s, and especially the 1970s, community recreation centers expanded their concept of outdoor education as they began to embrace adventure recreation. One of the earliest was the municipal outdoor program in Eugene, Oregon, which offered backpacking, survival training, and mountaineering in 1966. Today, numerous community recreation programs across the country offer adventure programs, and such programming is embraced by many government agencies.

Within the military, historical roots of their recreation programs are traced back to the Revolutionary War (Military Homefront, n.d.). After World War II, the army set up "rest and recreation" areas. At that time, the emphasis on these programs was more facility based than recreation. In the 1960s, morale, welfare, and recreation (MWR) programs began to include soldiers' families, but it wasn't until the 1980s that they began to accept that a soldier's family was important (U.S. Army MWR, 2010).

In general, outdoor recreation is an integral part of the overall armed forces recreation program, which intends to achieve "fitness . . . cohesion, family well-being and quality of life outcomes" (Heeg, 1996, p. 122). As Heeg pointed out, outdoor recreation is "positioned to contribute more to mission support" than other recreation programs (p. 125). Today, support of families is integral to MWRs. All branches of the armed forces have MWRs, and they employ 61,000 persons, mostly civilian (U.S. Navy MWR Headquarters, 2010).

## Challenge Course Programs

In 1961, the Colorado Outward Bound (OB) School had made extensive use of a ropes (challenge) course (Wagstaff, 2003). In 1970, a Massachusetts principal who had been involved in setting up the 1962 Minnesota OB school decided to attempt to apply the OB concept within a traditional school setting. He involved teachers who had OB experience to develop a physical education curriculum called Project Adventure (PA), which used initiatives and low and high elements.

The purposes of this curriculum were to develop creative group problem solving and to overcome barriers to increased achievement. These two goals were incorporated with similar goals into academic subjects. Although the program was successful for several years, because of the conservatism of the 1980s, innovative educational programming was no longer supported, and Project Adventure separated

from the school to form its own business in 1981 (Prouty, 1999). Since then, Project Adventure has been a major leader in the challenge course industry, providing leadership training to thousands of challenge course professionals. Today, PA certifies challenge course practitioners and challenge course managers.

## Adventure Therapy

Several terms for adventure therapy exist, including adventure-based counseling, therapeutic adventure, therapeutic camping, wilderness therapy, wilderness-adventure therapy, and outdoor behavioral healthcare (Gillis and Ringer, 1999; Russell and Hendee, 2000). Essentially, adventure therapy is "programming aimed at changing dysfunctional behavior patterns, using adventure experiences as forms of habilitation and rehabilitation" (Priest and Gass, 1997, p. 24).

Much of the impetus for the camping movement of the late 1800s was for children who today might be termed "at risk." In the early 1900s, doctors at the New York Asylum for the Insane prescribed "tent therapy" to a few of their psychiatric patients and found positive results. These early results led to increased research on the benefits of natural environments. Later, the camping movement of the 1930s addressed, in part, the psychological needs of children. By the 1950s, therapeutic camping was a part of the organized camping movement. And in the same period, adventure programs for at-risk children increased (Jones, Lowe, and Risler, 2004). Adventure therapy also has its roots in Outward Bound and Project Adventure. Through the expansion of the Colorado Outward Bound School in the 1960s, and Project Adventure in the 1970s, the door for wilderness adventure therapy was opened and many programs emerged (Jones, Lowe, and Risler, 2004).

# OUTDOOR ADVENTURE PROGRAMMING TODAY (1990 TO PRESENT)

Being far more involved in physical activity and outdoor or adventure recreation than the previous generation had been, the baby boom generation embraced adventure activities in the 1960s, '70s, and '80s. By 1990, the adventure programming industry was well under way. Clubs and professional organizations in the standard outdoor pursuits (hiking and backpacking, rock and mountain climbing, downhill and cross-country skiing, whitewater kayaking and canoeing) had been established, and so had university outdoor leadership degree programs. In the 1990s, the children of baby boomers began also to embrace outdoor adventures. (Computers, the Internet, and cell phone technology were not yet readily available to distract children from the outdoors.) Furthermore, disposable income and the percent of income spent on recreation was rising steadily and significantly (Jensen and Guthrie, 2006, p. 72). The 1990s saw an even more significant increase in the number of participants jumping in to outdoor activities, and to a variety of new outdoor sports. According to the National Survey of Recreation and the Environment, in 1994, 37 percent of the population participated in outdoor adventures; by 2000, the number had increased to 57 percent of the population (Jensen and Guthrie, 2006, p. 52).

This growth in participation was also reflected in the growth of adventure leadership degree programs. From 23 programs in 1990, some 38 additional four-year and two-year certificate, undergraduate degree, and graduate programs were added through 2001 (Canberg and Daniels, 2004). And in the 1990s, the number of university outdoor programs (cocurricular and academic) identified by Webb increased from 160 to 195, a 28 percent increase (Webb, 2000). Poff and Webb's 2007 program directory lists 236 adventure programs (Poff and Webb, 2007).

# The Emergence of Professional Associations

As the outdoor recreation profession developed, so came the rise of associations developed by professionals to represent their interests, distribute information, host conferences, and educate the membership. As the industry has grown and expanded, it has also seen the rise of very specialized associations. Between 1970 and 2010, many adventure programming nonprofits focusing on specific segments within outdoor adventure programming emerged, with 60 such programs identified in

2006 (Jensen and Guthrie, 2006). With the trend toward professionalization, organizations devoted to developing standards emerged. These standards take the form of certification (in which *individuals* demonstrate that they have met some minimum competencies) or accreditation (through which organizations demonstrate the meet specified standards). See table 2.1 for arguments for and against certification. In the following section we focus on the development of three influential organizations formed specifically to represent the larger field of outdoor pursuits and adventure programming. We also describe many of the associations representing specialized segments of the field.

## Association for Experiential Education (AEE)

Spurred by Outward Bound, in 1975, the First North American Conference on Outdoor Pursuits in Higher Education was convened, drawing 200 participants (Garvey, 1999). Out of this conference, a steering committee involving Outward Bound and representatives from different universities developed to explore developing a national association on outdoor experiential education. Over the next three years, four more conferences were held, ultimately resulting in the establishment of the Association of Experiential Education in 1977.

In the early 1980s, the organization moved to the University of Colorado. In its early years, the AEE's programs and conferences were strongly influenced by its OB roots. However, in the 1990s, its mission statement gradually eliminated reference to its outdoor roots. Nevertheless, it still maintains strong ties to adventure education—its membership comprises a strong contingent of outdoor, wilderness, adventure, camps, and challenge course professionals, and it accredits outdoor programs.

## Wilderness Education Association (WEA)

By the mid-1970s, people were becoming worried about the impacts of increasing numbers of wilderness-based users of the outdoors. Some were also concerned about the number of programs (clubs, youth groups, science teachers, and so forth) taking groups into the outdoors with leaders inadequately trained in planning, leadership, or minimum-impact techniques. At a 1976 NRPA

**Table 2.1**  Arguments For and Against Certification

| Pros | Cons |
|---|---|
| Certification makes people more employable. | Good judgment is the most important attribute of safe leadership, and it is not possible to certify good judgment within the constraints of a certification course. |
| Certification establishes that a person has a minimum set of skills and sets a higher standard of leadership. | Certification is only as good as the certifying body, and no person or agency will regulate or certify the certifiers. |
| Certification makes the profession safer. | Who does the certifying? What qualifies any agency or person to certify? |
| Government agencies and insurance companies are trending toward requiring certification; certification will be needed to meet standards of outside agencies. | The criteria for certification are not yet established. |
| Developing our own certification standards precludes the government from stepping in for safety reasons to set standards. | A leader can be competent even if uncertified. Due to expense or time constraints, good leaders, if part-time or volunteer, may not be able to become certified. |
| Certification and standards are marks of a true profession. | Certification takes away the freedom of leaders. |
| Certification and standards are needed to protect the environment. | The standards used may not adjust to changing conditions, and a "certified" person following outdated standards might not be safe. |
| | Given regional geographical differences, a national standard may be inappropriate for a given area. |
| | Certification is expensive. |

Cain, 1985; Cockrell, 1987; March, 1985a; 1985b; Miles, 1987; Wilkinson, 1985; Yerkes, 1985.

student conference, Paul Petzoldt happened to meet with Frank Lupton, a Western Illinois professor of recreation. In 1977, they and other Midwestern professors discussed the need for a wilderness leadership curriculum and a certification program. A few months later, in 1980, the Wilderness Use Education Association was founded, later to become the Wilderness Education Association. From the WEA's beginning, it developed a core of outdoor leader competencies to certify outdoor leaders (Teeters and Lupton, 1999).

Unlike OB and NOLS, which are actually outdoor schools, the WEA does not offer outdoor programming. Rather, it relies on approximately 40 affiliates to deliver its curriculum, mostly within a college or university setting. In 2010, the WEA began to transition from a certifying body to an accreditation model. Under this model, it would accredit institutions who in turn would certify outdoor leaders.

## Association of Outdoor Recreation and Education

By 1980, many colleges and universities around the country had cocurricular outdoor programs, but they were housed in a variety of settings and affiliated with a variety of professional associations. Program affiliations were spread across a number of associations, such as the Association of College Unions International (ACUI), the National Intramural-Recreational Sports Association (NIRSA), the American Alliance for Health, Physical Education, Recreation and Dance (AAHPERD), and the National Association of Campus Activities (NACA). Within each of the organizations, outdoor programs were a small minority, and it was difficult for outdoor professionals to link with, learn from, and associate with other professionals.

In 1984, university outdoor professionals organized a Conference on Outdoor Recreation hosted in Bozeman, MT, which was attended by some

180 participants from approximately 20 states and Canada. Some of the important themes of this conference were leadership standards and the certification debate, public lands access and wilderness management, outdoor programming for people with disabilities, networking, and developing outdoor programs. From 1984 to 1990, conferences were held every two years. Since 1991, a conference has been held annually.

The 1991 conference in Moscow, Idaho, was called the International Conference on Outdoor Recreation (ICOR) to reflect the fact that Canadians were attending the conference. At the 1992 ICOR, the decision was made to create a national association (Guthrie, 1992). A committee was formed to create a mission statement and by-laws. Members of this committee included many founding members, including Tim Moore, Jim Rogers, Steve Guthrie, Ron Watters, Georgi Baird, and others, with Moore taking a lead role over the next year.

Prior to the 1993 Corvallis conference (that year, the International Conference on Outdoor Recreation and Education), a group of about 15 professionals met for several days to draft the mission, goals, and by-laws for the new association. The Association of Outdoor Recreation and Education was created (Guthrie, 1993, 2001). However, until 2005, the ICORE (International Conference) remained independent of the AORE when it was renamed the AORE Annual Conference (AORE, 2006; Guthrie, 1993).

Today, the AORE Annual Conference draws over 500 participants a year from all across the United States and international locations. In 2009, AORE began to coproduce a new journal (*Journal of Outdoor Recreation and Leadership*), and work was under way for this textbook. Though the largest professional association devoted solely to outdoor adventure programming, they do not certify leaders or accredit organizations.

## Additional Associations

Within the adventure recreation industry, several associations provide accreditation or certification, education, and other resources, including the following:

**»» American Camp Association (ACA).** The ACA is composed of organized camping professionals concerned with providing a camp experience to all youth. The ACA disseminates information and research about the association and accredits camps. Of the approximately 12,000 camps in the U.S., about 2,600 are affiliated with the ACA, and 2,400 are accredited (American Camp Association [ACA], 2009, 2010, 2011). It has about 7,000 members. In the past several years, adventure programming has been the focus of new programs. About 50 percent of accredited camps provide ropes courses or other adventure programming, with 22 percent offering wilderness trips (American Camp Association [ACA], 2010).

**»» American Canoe Association (ACA).** Founded in 1880, the ACA supports recreational paddling and provides curricula and certification of instructors for canoeing (touring, whitewater), kayaking (whitewater, coastal, and surf kayak), oar and paddle rafting, and swiftwater rescue. The association provides certificate endorsements for adaptive paddling, rolling, canoe camping, and other activities. In addition to certifications, the ACA is actively involved in waterway conservation and public policy. The ACA has about 30,000 members, mostly recreational paddlers (ACA 2008; American Canoe Association [ACA], 2010).

**»» Leave No Trace (LNT).** Interest in minimum impact began in the 1970s and was fostered by the U.S. Forest Service and other federal agencies. In the early 1990s, NOLS and the U.S. Forest Service developed a curriculum. In 1994, Leave No Trace was established as a nonprofit organization to teach principles and practices to greatly reduce the impact of visitors in natural resource areas. LNT trains instructors who in turn teach LNT workshops to outdoor users and provide certificates to graduates of their workshops. Many governmental outdoor recreation agencies endorse and promote the LNT program (LNT, 2008).

**»» American Mountain Guides Association (AMGA).** Founded in 1979, the AMGA began its certification program in 1987. Today it provides guide training and certification in rock and alpine climbing and ski mountaineering and climb instructor certification for climb walls and single pitch sites (AMGA, n.d.).

**»» Professional Climbing Instructors Association (PCIA).** Founded in 2007 by former AMGA members who wished to focus on climb instructors for groups, the PCIA provides a belay certification curriculum, certifications as instructor for top rope and climb wall sites, and traditional leading instructor certification. The PCIA also accredits organizations that provide rock climbing (PCIA, 2011).

>> **Professional Ski Instructors of America–American Association of Snowboard Instructors (PSIA-AASI).** Founded in 1961 to formalize a ski instructor curriculum for U.S. instructors, by the 1970s this association was providing instructor certification for alpine and Nordic skiing. In the late 1980s, it began to include snowboard instruction. Today the PSIA-AASI certifies instructors in alpine, Nordic track, Nordic downhill, snowboarding, and adaptive skiing and snowboarding. The association has over 31,000 members (PSIA-AASI, n.d.).

>> **Association for Challenge Course Technology (ACCT).** The ACCT was founded in 1993 to establish standards for challenge course facilities (including installation, operation, and inspection). The association evolved from a series of ropes course builders' conferences. In 2007, they set practitioner certification standards for challenge course managers and facilitators. However, the association does not directly certify people or courses; rather, it accredits professional vendors who, in turn, can certify practitioners or inspect course facilities for safety. The ACCT has over 1,700 members (ACCT, 2010).

>> **Professional Ropes Course Association (PRCA).** The PRCA was founded as an alternative standards-setting body to the ACCT. It sets standards for challenge courses and canopy or zip line tours and provides a peer review of challenge courses. However, this association does not accredit organizations or certify facilitators or managers (PRCA, 2011).

## Climbing Walls

Artificial climbing walls grew out of a desire to have a nearby area to climb and for year-round training. The 1990s saw a surge in climbing wall technology, construction, and visibility. Indoor rock climbing also started to attract the recreationalist looking for new ways to exercise and stay fit. Climbing gyms developed, and soon the climb wall became a part of many recreation centers.

With the advancement of the artificial climbing wall industry came the need for common industry practices and construction standards. In the early 1990s, the Climbing Wall Industry Group (CWIG) and the Climbing Gym Association (CGA) were formed to fill the need for industry standards and practices. The engineering standards they established for the construction of climbing walls remain in use (Stiehl and Ramsey, 2005, p. 10), but the trend is to also meet ASTM (formerly American Society for Testing and Materials) standards. Although the Climbing Wall Industry Group and Climbing Gym Association dissolved, in 2003, the Climbing Wall Association (CWA) was formed. That year, the association published climbing wall operations standards. In 2009, the CWA published a manual of climbing wall engineering practices to supersede the CWIG standards. In 2011, the CWA announced a certification process for climbing wall instructors (CWA, 2011). Currently, the CWA is the primary climb wall standard setter in the United States.

# Wilderness First Aid, Medicine, and River Rescue

Skiing was one of the earliest outdoor pursuits, and the National Ski Patrol (NSP) was founded in 1938 to provide first aid and rescue to skiers. Today, the NSP provides skiing-based wilderness first-responder training and certification as well as other educational programs. Though not the only ski patrol organization, the NSP is the largest, with 26,000 members (NSP, 2011). Some ski patrols are professional units, and others are comprised of volunteers. Ski patrol training provides a great way to acquire first-aid experience.

In the early 1970s, the Seattle Mountaineer's *Mountaineering Medicine* was perhaps the only source of information for wilderness first aid published in the United States. Then, in 1975, Frank Hubble began to teach a basic mountain or woods first-aid course in New England. Two years later, he established the first wilderness first-aid school, SOLO, teaching courses for Outward Bound, the AMC, and college groups (SOLO, n.d.). In 1981, Wilderness Medical Associates was founded to teach first aid for Outward Bound schools (WMA, 2010).

In 1983, three physicians involved with outdoor recreation established the Wilderness Medical Society. In 1987, they began to publish position papers on wilderness medicine practice, and in 1990, they initiated efforts to get wilderness practice guidelines accepted by the medical community (Barry and Erb, n.d.). Today, along with wilderness first aid, many organizations provide certifications and rescue and leadership training. Wilderness first aid has become a standard requirement for outdoor leaders.

In 1980, in response to the deaths of several of its professional rescuers, the Ohio Department of Natural Resources (DNR) developed river rescue techniques and curriculum for professional rescuers (Elverum and Smalley, 2008). With thousands of low head dams in the East and Midwest, other eastern state DNRs soon adopted the Ohio DNR practices. Since then, the American Canoe Association and Rescue 3 International have researched and refined river rescue techniques and are now the primary service providers of the river rescue knowledge and skills for both river guides and private boaters.

# Wilderness Search and Rescue

Except in national parks, mountain rescue has traditionally been performed by volunteer rescue groups, though their rescue efforts are coordinated by local government agencies. The Mountain Rescue Association (MRA) was founded in 1959 in the Pacific Northwest and focuses on mountain rescue in the West, including Alaska. Its members are members of mountain rescue units, and most are volunteers. The MRA has 90 government-authorized mountain rescue units. The MRA established national standards and qualifications for, and accredits, mountain rescue units (MRA, n.d.).

Founded in 1972, the National Association for Search and Rescue (NASAR) operates nationally and in all environments, including searches and rescues for plane wreckage, hurricane victims, and people lost at sea. The NASAR is comprised of 14,000+ volunteers and professionals. The professionals are typically government employees involved in search and rescue for their governmental unit. The NASAR has developed SAR standard practices, and they train and certify SAR professionals (NASAR, n.d.).

# SUMMARY

The field of outdoor recreation is extremely diverse, with a rich, albeit recent, history. The range of outdoor recreation activities is very broad, encompassing human-powered adventure activities that range from hiking to kayaking; consumptive activities, such as four-wheeling and hunting; passive outdoor recreation, such as scenic driving and wildlife viewing; and outdoor education and interpretation.

Within the category of outdoor recreation lie many ways of interacting with the environment. Earlier endeavors within the history of outdoor recreation focused on geographic and nature exploration, along with hunting and fishing. This mode was predominant in the United States in the 19th century. Historically, because of the perception of inexhaustible natural resources, settlers had little concern for protecting our resources. As our country became more urban, and a middle class emerged with money and time, tourism became a powerful force for the protection of resources. The second half of the 19th century witnessed the emergence of conservation efforts to protect our natural resources. With immigrants moving to the cities, and the wealthier classes seeing a need for enculturation of immigrants, organized camping and outdoor education and the recreation professions were established.

In the early 20th century, as some sportsmen developed an environmental consciousness, the natural resource profession emerged to protect game, then game habitat. With the development of wealth, the automobile, and increasing urbanization, new forms of outdoor recreation captured people's interest. These included motorized touring of natural areas, camping and hiking, and nature study.

Although hunting, fishing, and motorized outdoor recreation were long the dominant forms of outdoor recreation, World War II and the subsequent availability of cheap and lightweight camping equipment quickly led to nonmotorized outdoor pursuits, such as backpacking, climbing, skiing, and canoeing and kayaking as the predominant forms of outdoor recreation. With the advent of Outward Bound, and the use of outdoor pursuits for educational purposes came the development of the outdoor leadership and adventure programming profession.

Professional employment exists in natural resource management, outdoor education and environmental education, and adventure education and adventure recreation. However, a potential problem for our profession is the large diversity of activities and pursuits in outdoor recreation, and even in adventure recreation.

It is hard for professionals to stay abreast of all the changes. This is where professional associations, especially the AORE, AEE, and the WEA, and related associations, play important roles in the development and maintenance of professional skills and knowledge possessed by those serving the profession.

# Chapter 3

# Dimensions of Outdoor Recreation Programs

*Todd Bauch, MEd, and Steve Hutton, MA*

*Outdoor recreation* is a recreation activity done outside (Miles and Priest, 1999). Such activity might include motorcycling, bicycling, fun runs, skiing, climbing, or watching a professional football game at an outdoor stadium. Outdoor programs often employ full- or part-time administrators to offer a distinct set of outings to participants. Many outdoor recreation programs focus on human-powered activities in a natural outdoor environment, and are alternately referred to as outdoor pursuits. Outdoor recreation programs are administered in a wide variety of physical and organizational settings and may function under different operational models or philosophies. In this chapter we discuss various dimensions of outdoor recreation programs used in a variety of organizational settings. Based on organizational structure, expectations, and desired outcomes, outdoor program administrators choose which dimensions are best for their programs.

The structural aspects of outdoor programs depend on the organizational setting. Many outdoor programs are part of a larger organization—college or university, military, or community recreation program—and, as such, support and serve the mission of the parent organization. In this chapter we identify three service sectors under which outdoor recreation programs operate, common outdoor recreation programming types, facilities and resources commonly managed by outdoor recreation programs, and traditional administrative structures and models used by outdoor programs.

## THREE SERVICE SECTORS OF OUTDOOR RECREATION PROGRAMS

Outdoor recreation programs operate in one of three sectors providing public and private services: nonprofit, commercial, and government. Differences across sectors are represented by differences in the mission, vision, and desired outcomes of individual programs. For example, regardless of the service sector, outdoor programs are influenced by economic shifts, fluid industry trends, consumer demands, and current events. Given the differences among sectors, the administrator must select the most appropriate strategies needed to operate successfully within the existing organizational framework.

## Nonprofit Outdoor Recreation Programs

Nonprofit outdoor recreation programs are organizations that serve either their own members (addressing the needs of only a select number of individuals) or the public (serving the greater community without regard to membership requirements) and do not expect to make a profit that goes beyond operating costs, service enhancements, and reserve capital.

Many nonprofits with an educational mission are eligible for either 501 (c)(3) or 501 (c)(4) status.

Businesses operating under a nonprofit status represent a legal entity authorized by federal law to operate for the benefit of their membership (clubs, associations, organizations) or for a greater public good (such as a hospital, environmental organization, or literary society). For example, the Sierra Club has an extensive outing program and is a nonprofit. Part of its mission is "To practice and promote the responsible use of the earth's ecosystems and resources; to educate and enlist humanity to protect and restore the quality of the natural and human environment; and to use all lawful means to carry out these objectives" (for more information on the Sierra Club's mission and policies, see www.sierraclub.org/policy/default.aspx).

Volunteerism is an economic driver of nonprofit organizations. Many times, nonprofit outdoor programs, despite the term "not-for-profit," need to generate revenue, but rather than returning profits to shareholders, they use profits to enhance services and benefits for their membership. Many nonprofit outdoor recreation programs generate some annual revenue from donations, but most income comes from the provision of products and services.

## Commercial Outdoor Recreation Programs

Commercial outdoor recreation programs offer adventure experiences to paying customers and expect to financially profit from their offerings. Outdoor programs that operate on a for-profit status are viewed as commercial businesses. These outdoor programs generally operate in the form of a privately held business, a partnership, or a publicly held corporation. Examples include private guide services throughout the United States. This includes famous companies such as the American Alpine Institute, Exum Guides, Mountain Sobek Travel, and many other commercial adventure-based guide services. Unlike nonprofit organizations, a commercial outdoor program is trying to make a profit to benefit company owners or a group of investors. Success might be measured in monetary profit, and commercial owners might rely on the revenue for income.

## Government Outdoor Recreation Programs

Government outdoor recreation programs are run by governmental agencies and include any outdoor recreation program that uses government (federal, state, or local) infrastructure or funding to serve the public at large. Membership might be required. These programs include those run by military recreation, state and local parks and recreation departments, and public universities and colleges. Outdoor recreation programs operating in this classification bear similarity to nonprofits in that funding for programming might require the program to make enough revenue to cover operating costs, service enhancements, and reserve funds. Revenue expectations will vary based on subsidies, endowments, donations, and organizational expectations. Here is an overview of common organizational hosts in government outdoor recreation programs:

>> **Municipal park and recreation programs.** Many cities and towns in the United States have some type of a recreation department or program that is funded through local taxation and overseen by a municipal or regional government. Traditionally, these programs have provided citizens with baseball leagues, city parks, swimming pools, and playgrounds. As concepts of recreation and leisure have evolved, so too have many of these municipal recreation programs. A growing number now offer some forms of outdoor (adventure) recreation through one of the models described elsewhere in this chapter. Programs range from adult outdoor adventure pursuits to children's adventure education camps.

>> **Educational institutions.** Both public and private universities and colleges recognize the value of outdoor recreation programming to student life. Although private universities aren't part of a government agency, they play a role similar to public universities. Additionally, high schools and primary schools offer outdoor recreation programs as ways to enhance student experiences. This has manifested in a variety of program types, ranging from student-run clubs to highly structured programs.

Universities have provided some of the oldest and largest outdoor recreation programs and clubs in the United States. Historically, these programs and clubs have existed in a number of different departments on college or university campuses, including Student Activities, Campus Recreation, Athletics, and Physical Education departments. Colleges and universities offer many of the program types explained in this chapter, including outdoor adventure pursuits, adventure education, environmental education, and even adventure therapy. A recent example of adventure education in higher education is wilderness orientation programs. These programs use the shared experiences of trips and outings as well as specific activities to deliberately foster healthy choices and develop a community.

**>> Military bases.** United States military bases throughout the world hire civilians to provide recreational programming for enlisted men and women, as well as for officers and their families. These morale, welfare, and recreation (MWR) programs are likened to university recreation programs in that they use similar methods to serve populations with comparable demographics. Typically the employees of MWR programs are civilians, and the funding is from the federal government. These programs range from outdoor adventure pursuits to adventure therapy. Current events, namely military conflicts, influence the services being offered to those stationed at the base. Many bases benefit from being located in areas with strong potential for outdoor recreation activities, such as near large bodies of water, deserts, or mountains.

Although outdoor recreation programs have different core values and organizational expectations, they share many similarities. They require highly trained staff; they require administrators to manage permits, staffing, and budgets; and they entail access to natural outdoor environments.

# COMMON PROGRAMMATIC TYPES

Regardless of sector, organizations typically define themselves through mission, vision, goals, and objective statements. In combination, these documents convey not only an organizational philosophy but what the program aspires to become. In general, outdoor recreation programs provide many types of services to clients, including outdoor adventure pursuits, outdoor skill instruction, adventure education, adventure therapy, and environmental education. The following list of program types is not comprehensive but provides a framework for discussion. Most administrators recognize that outdoor recreation entities are made up of a mixture of programming elements.

**>> Outdoor adventure pursuits** have two desired outcomes: to provide leisure experiences for participants, and to provide opportunities to participate in an adventure activity. Motivation for participation in adventure programs might relate to novelty seeking, an interest in personal growth, a need to connect with the natural environment, or a desire to build social connections (Goldenberg, McAvoy, and Klenosky, 2005). Participants may or may not want to engage in a given activity as a lifelong pursuit. Whatever their interests and motivations, participants are given opportunities to enjoy outdoor recreational activities through the program's resources, including staff expertise and knowledge, transportation, access to outdoor sites, and the provision of appropriate equipment. Often participants must be taught at least rudimentary skills, which means program staff must be skilled in educating. The skills taught are generally limited to essential knowledge and abilities the participant requires to safely enjoy the experience.

**>> Outdoor skill instruction** teaches participants about a specific discipline so they can begin to take part in the activity independently. Many times, outdoor instructional opportunities provide participants with an outdoor experience *and* specific skill instruction. If the desired learning outcomes are achieved, and participants become proficient at the skill, they will often pursue the activity independently. In the best of cases, instructors design skill progressions that help participants learn new information, test newly developed skills and abilities, and share constructive feedback for improvement. For example, the American Canoe Association provides instruction courses in all aspects of paddling.

Mat Erpelding

Students learn about glaciers as part of their outdoor skill instruction.

The primary emphasis in many of these courses is skill improvement, such as helping participants become proficient paddlers.

**>> Adventure education** uses adventure activities (typically outdoor, but not exclusively) to develop and enhance human skills, including intrapersonal awareness and interpersonal relationship skills. Common activities include rafting, challenge courses, climbing, and backpacking. These activities provide the learning environment for interpersonal growth and are the medium to achieve human skill development. For instance, Outward Bound uses adventure programs to "inspire character development, self-discovery, and service" (see www.outwardbound.org/index.cfm/do/exp.about for more information on Outward Bound).

**>> Adventure therapy** uses adventure activities as part of a treatment program for the emotional, psychological, physical, or social problems of participants. Therapeutic goals are facilitated by a combination of staff, including field instructors, licensed counselors, and program administrators. As an example, Gateway Academy in Salt Lake City, Utah, is a residential therapy program for adolescent boys. The weekend outdoor program uses adventure activities to engage the boys in eustress and, at times, distress. Later, staff therapists use these experiences as a context to address treatment goals.

**>> Environmental education** focuses on the relationship between humans and the natural environment. This might include adventure activities, but not necessarily because its emphasis is to teach others to recognize the impacts and influence that human society has on the natural environment.

Optimal programming often blends multiple program elements. Historically, the term "outdoor education" encompasses a combination of adventure education and environmental education. Finding the right mix of program elements is the key to a successful ongoing operation. As it is, outdoor program administration is an intentional process designed to enhance participants' lives and experiences. Many times, this process is guided by the organizational setting the program takes place in. Additionally, each outdoor recreation program will use the different resources and facilities available to them to accomplish desired outcomes.

## COMMON FACILITIES OR RESOURCES OF OUTDOOR PROGRAMS

Although programming elements are the most often considered components of an outdoor program, many programs also incorporate and benefit from the management or use of a variety of facilities. Here we describe a few examples of facilities routinely managed by outdoor program administrators.

>> **Equipment rental centers.** Outdoor programs have recognized that a significant barrier to participation in certain outdoor activities is the large expense of specialized or technical equipment. By providing the rental of items such as tents, canoes, rafts, and skis, these programs can dramatically broaden appeal and service to people who have not yet invested, or may never invest, the financial resources required to own such equipment. For some agencies, rental centers are essential to the operation of the program as a whole—serving not only to outfit a program trip but also to provide significant subsidy to other, less profitable, components of the program.

As a spinoff of the equipment rental center, some programs operate onsite boat rental facilities that provide access to rental sailboats, canoes, and kayaks, as well as a destination for the equipment's use. This convenient option avoids logistical challenges of transporting large or cumbersome vessels that might deter users. Onsite facilities are particularly valuable to outdoor recreation programs with waterfront access.

>> **Climbing and bouldering centers.** Rock climbing and bouldering walls have gained popularity across the country and are typically a resource managed by outdoor programs. Once used only to substitute for a missing resource (rock cliffs), climbing walls are now seen as training areas, teaching resources, and convenient recreational options for participants. Outdoor programs that have the resources to build and operate such structures use them for program offerings that vary from birthday parties to emergency rescue and climbing clinics.

>> **Challenge courses.** Challenge courses are available throughout the country. Simple or complex, and built from rope, cable, lumber, and trees (or power poles), challenge courses and challenge structures are used by trained facilitators to provide a series of sequenced, condensed adventures that test the problem-solving skills of individuals and groups. Backed up by safety equipment or safety techniques, challenge course elements may be 2 feet (.6 m) or 50 feet (15 m) off the ground, and are designed to quickly remove participants from their

typical, comfortable life and place them in position of disequilibrium to elicit change or learning.

>> **Resource libraries.** Prior to the Internet and search engines, outdoor program resource libraries were full of maps, guidebooks, and government agency brochures. In addition to maintaining a library and resources, the program staff usually possessed a great deal of personal knowledge about local areas. Today, an assortment of guidebooks are still found in many program offices, and some popular maps still hang on the walls. It still helps to have a great amount of local knowledge, but staff must also understand the complexities of the computer-based resources available. Program administrators should know how to use websites, blogs, list-serves, Facebook, Twitter, and search engines effectively. Often the resource library complements the equipment rental center. In addition to a snowshoe rental, customers might request information on places to go snowshoeing, directions to a trailhead, and difficulty ratings.

# OUTDOOR PROGRAM ADMINISTRATIVE STRUCTURES AND MODELS

An administrative structure, also known as the program delivery method, includes aspects such as how much oversight is afforded to the outdoor program administrator, how fees are paid to the organization, and how much responsibility trip leaders have while in the field. An example of an administrative structure is a club, which is run by elected officers and guided by a club constitution. Another example of an administrative structure is an institutionally directed operation in which the outdoor program is a department within a college or university.

Within the administrative framework, outdoor program administrators have a choice of several models to employ to accomplish the goals and mission of their program. Which model works best depends on the program's clientele and the overarching needs of the parent organization. Further considerations depend on programming budgets, availability of nearby outdoor resources, and the skills and knowledge of the staff. Outdoor program administrators often use a blend of models. Creating just the right blend is key to a successful program.

## Outdoor Clubs

Note that Guthrie (1999) argues that the club model is not really a model at all. It's an administrative structure—a delivery method. Clubs can use one or more models in how they offer trips, choosing from common adventure, instructional adventure, and guided adventure. Outdoor clubs operate under an organizational charter, and club decisions are made by members or elected representatives. See figure 3.1 for a brief history of clubs. Outdoor clubs serve as mechanisms to organize people to participate in outdoor activities and as long-term social networks. Actual club membership might be open to anyone or restricted, as decided by the organization. Volunteers or elected officers, or a board of directors, conduct the business of the club. These representatives rely on bylaws or a constitution to guide their actions. Depending on the articles of the organization's constitution, funds may or may not be used to actually get people outdoors to enjoy themselves. The actual cost of participating in an activity might be an additional fee.

Membership dues typically finance the operations of a club, but some college or university clubs, such as the Dartmouth Outing Club and the Kayak Club at Boise State University, receive institutional support (that comes with limited oversight). Some clubs might have local chapters that have some autonomy but still answer to a larger organization; much of the chapter's energy is put toward maintaining the club's membership and direction of purpose. As the club grows in size, it might decide to hire an executive director and staff to monitor the business operations of the club. Although this staff can become essential, they still serve at the pleasure of the organization's board of directors, and ultimately of the membership. For example, the Mountaineers Club has over 10,000 members, an executive director, and local chapters around the country. The Mountaineers provide outing opportunities to club members all over the country. Outdoor program administrators generally act as advisors to clubs, with limited direct oversight.

---

**Figure 3.1   An Abbreviated History of Outdoor Club Programming in Higher Education**

1909: The first collegiate outing club, the Dartmouth Outing Club (Dartmouth College), was formed in New Hampshire, primarily to promote skiing and snowshoeing.

1911: The Dartmouth Outing Club held the first Winter Carnival, which included intercollegiate ski and snowshoe races and ski jumping.

1915: The Williams Outing Club (Williams College, MA) was formed. Though modeled after the Dartmouth Outing Club, it expanded activities to include hunting and fishing, camping, and caving.

1932: Fourteen college outing clubs formed the Intercollegiate Outing Club Association.

1932–1945: Outing clubs in private colleges, especially Dartmouth and Harvard, were very influential in climbing and skiing.

1950s: Several other clubs added climbing and caving.

1960s–1970s: The number of college outing clubs peaked.

1980s–2000s: With a greater availability of cars, a "do your own thing" mentality, and the later growth of more structured campus recreation and student union outdoor programs, outing clubs became less common.

2011: The Intercollegiate Outing Club Association lists 190 clubs as members, mostly in the northeast United States.

Dudley, 1935; Hooke, 1987; Intercollegiate Outing Club Association, 2011; Sacks, 2002; Waterman & Waterman, 1993; Webb, 2001.

# Common Adventure or Shared Responsibility Model

The shared responsibility model is also known as common adventure (Wyman, 1972; Grimm and Hilbert, 1973) or cooperative adventure (Guthrie, 1999). Watters (1999a) defines a common adventure trip as "two or more individuals working cooperatively for common goals, and sharing expenses, decision making, and responsibilities as equitably as possible" (p. 99).

A common adventure program is generally managed by an outdoor program administrator, but trips are not organized in the sense that the outdoor program organizes and conducts the trip. On a common adventure trip, everyone is expected to share in the trip's responsibilities. The trip initiator (many times a volunteer for the outdoor program who posted the sign-up sheet) simply gets the ball rolling. The rest of the group is expected to help plan, organize, cook, wash, load and unload vehicles, buy food, clean up equipment, and so on.

One of the big misconceptions about the shared responsibility model is that there are no leaders. Common adventure trips *do* have leaders. In almost all cases, the leader is the person who puts the trip together, and this individual will probably continue in the leadership role throughout the trip. Outdoor program administrators may or may not have significant experience with the person who posted the trip, and may or may not have provided training for the trip initiator. In many cases, the trip initiator functions in a volunteer capacity on the trip and shares expenses with the other participants.

Watters (1999b, p. 91) further distinguishes common adventure programs as being either assisted or unassisted. Unassisted common adventure is the purest form, in which two or more individuals combine together for an outdoor trip and share expenses and responsibilities. No outside body (such as a club or institution) is necessary. On the other hand, the assisted forms of common adventure are subsidized in one or more ways: by organizations providing resources, volunteers, or even paid personal to help initiate trips. As long as the other tenets of common adventure are involved (shared decision making and shared responsibilities), the trip remains essentially a common adventure trip. The outdoor program administrator

Kayak Club members on an outing on the Oregon coast.

manages the subsidies and might provide a forum or training for trip initiators.

Watters (1999a, p. 106) draws a line between common adventure programs and other administrative structures and models if the program's organization charges participants and makes money from the trip. At this point, according to Watters, the trip becomes a guided enterprise. This line of demarcation that separates models is the same that the National Park Service (2010) uses to distinguish between noncommercial and commercial trips—to wit: "Trips may be considered noncommercial even though a member of the trip receives a salary, under their normal scope of employment, from an educational institution or non-profit organization, but not directly through fees contributed by members of the party" (p. 2). This is an important distinction for an outdoor program administrator because it might change the type of permit or the need for a permit when offering trips.

## Institutional Directed

Institutionally directed outdoor programs provide risk management, structure, and training to support operations. Institutional support varies significantly based on the resources provided to the outdoor program administrator. In most institutional outdoor programs, participants don't have to pay a membership fee or make a long-term commitment as they would to join a club. Nor do they have to pay to cover the profit margins typical of a commercial company. Participants might pay a fee to participate and to cover direct costs such as transportation and food, whereas operating and overhead expenses are subsidized by the larger organization.

Paid outdoor program administrators who report to a larger organization manage institutional directed outdoor programs. The administrator operates the program according to policies and procedures created with approval of the larger organization or provided to them by the organization.

The amount of subsidy provided to the program can vary significantly. Sometimes subsidy is as little as paying all or a portion of one professional staff person's salary, which may or may not be full time. Other times, the funding organization is willing to cover operational expenses such as electricity, space leasing, and vehicle maintenance. However, many outdoor programs are expected to have a revenue stream of some sort. Employees of the organization receive varying levels of training based on how much institutional support is provided to the program.

## Guided Adventures

Guided adventures go back a long time, and are typically well understood by the general population. In this model, a client hires a guide who is paid for his or her expertise. In guided trips, participants might actively be involved, such as paddling, setting up their own tent, or carrying out a deer on a hunting trip. In other guided trips, clients might just go for the ride, participating only in a minor way. Clients on oared or motorized river trips might have their tents set up for them and their dinner cooked and served to them by guides. Most certainly, they will not do any of the oaring. Primary decision making in this model, of course, is the domain of the guide.

A number of universities and nonprofit entities successfully incorporate guided and packaged trips into their program offerings. In many cases, most trips offered by the organization are simply recreational, and leadership is designated to paid outdoor program staff members. Packaged ski trips are common, but offerings also include climbing,

rafting, canoeing, backpacking, and other adventures. Outsourcing to a commercial guide service might be a particularly attractive way of offering specific technical trips if the program administrator does not have appropriately trained staff. Guided operations are eager to work with nonprofits and will structure trips so participants can be more actively involved; they will even provide instruction services when appropriate.

## Instruction Model

In this model, the primary purpose is to teach participants skills and knowledge. This model is the main purpose of educational programs in the nonprofit sector. Some municipal recreation departments and many colleges and universities offer courses in outdoor activities. In the college setting, physical education or recreation departments might offer a class or two in activities such as backpacking, cross-country skiing, and the like. Or they may offer a degree program made up of an extensive series of classes in outdoor recreation, education, and leadership.

Educational offerings are not limited to universities. They are also the purpose of a number of noninstitutional nonprofits. The oldest nonprofit outdoor school is Outward Bound. Thousands of individuals have been introduced to the outdoors and have learned skills and knowledge through the many Outward Bound course offerings. Other examples of nonprofit schools that use the outdoors as a classroom include the National Outdoor Leadership School and the Alzar School.

## SUMMARY

Outdoor recreation programs operate in a wide variety of organizational settings and are governed by diverse philosophical views. Despite these differences, many similarities exist in the skills required of professional outdoor program administrators. These skills must be carefully nurtured within the context of the parent organization's mission and available resources. Effective outdoor recreation professionals understand that they have a variety of tools and models from which to select, and are able to derive the greatest benefit for their programs and participants through appropriate use and a careful blend and mix of those resources.

# Chapter 4

# The Future of Outdoor Program Administration

*Laurlyn K. Harmon, PhD, and Susan L. Johnson, MS*

A plan by Virginia's Department of Conservation states that "Outdoor recreation promotes health and wellness by providing open space and natural areas for public access, and by offering recreational programming that contributes to active lifestyles and vibrant communities. The significance of outdoor recreation in creating healthy lifestyles should not be underestimated" (2007, p. 194). Agreeing with these statements is to acknowledge the significance of outdoor program administrators and the importance of their roles in the future of outdoor recreation.

The issues we discuss in this chapter include the need to understand changing demographics and generational cohort characteristics of outdoor participants, the impacts of an increasing external emphasis on professionalization, technological effects on outdoor participation and operations, sustainability, staffing, collaboration, outdoor ethics, public land pressures, and outcome assessments. We also present a case study (see p. 48) of one exemplary organization.

Outdoor recreation and the administration of programs and services are continually evolving. Agencies and organizations are being asked, for example, to become increasingly creative in their funding efforts and more sophisticated in their use of technology-related resources. Administrators are responding to increased expectations of professionalism for outdoor leaders, including the accreditation for agencies and multiple certifications for staff. Simultaneously, outdoor program administrators find they must respond to participants' needs for traditional recreation activities—hiking, biking, fishing, picnicking—while addressing new requests for locales in which clients may engage in high-adventure and nontraditional activities, such as zorbing, geocaching, and kite surfing.

Subtle shifts in climate and outdoor recreation participation are having slow but lasting impacts on the venues for outdoor recreation activities (*An Inconvenient Truth*, 2006). Some multiseasonal facilities, for example, are finding it increasingly difficult to provide quality snow-supported activities (e.g., skiing and snowmobiling); other facilities are experiencing temperature extremes such as excess heat, rain, and wind. The number of glaciers in parks such as Glacier National Park has decreased (National Park Service, 2011), and tropical locales such as Florida are experiencing increased bleaching of their coral reefs. Participants, too, are changing, not only in the activities in which they participate but in their motivations for participating. To address the issues associated with such a range of changes, outdoor program administrators must first understand them.

# EVOLVING PARTICIPANT CHARACTERISTICS

One of the primary drivers of any outdoor recreation agency is the clientele it serves. Thus administering appropriate programming requires an understanding of population demographics as well as individual and group needs.

## Changing Demographics

In 2008, the U.S. population reached 300,000,000 and shows no sign of decreasing. In addition, there is a greater diversity in terms of age, race, education, residence, and cultural backgrounds among the people who participate or could be participating in outdoor recreation. Population projections in the United States suggest several key changes to which outdoor program administrators must respond and understand (see table 4.1). According to the National Center for Health Statistics (2011), males and females will continue to be relatively equally represented, although as the population ages there

will tend to be more females than males. An important change in ethnic diversity is expected to occur over time as individuals of Hispanic ethnicity are projected to represent approximately 25 percent of the U.S. residents in 2050, and there is projected to be a wider overall range of racial diversity within U.S. society. Age distribution of U.S. residents will also change significantly, with the most dramatic change in the age category of 65 years and older. This category is projected to increase from representing 13 percent of the population in 2010 to representing over 20 percent of the population in 2050.

## Cohorts

The first step in understanding our participants is to understand the characteristics of generational cohort. Generational cohorts are groups of individuals identified by the range of years in which they born. To further understand generational cohorts and their expectations, it is necessary to provide the societal frame of reference for each generation. Their descriptive characteristics and behaviors

**Table 4.1**  Population Projections by Age, Race, and Ethnicity

| Year | Age | % | Race | % | Ethnicity | % |
|------|-----|---|------|---|-----------|---|
| 2010 | 0-19 | 26.9 | White alone | 79.3 | Hispanic (of any race) | 15.5 |
|      | 20-44 | 33.8 | Black alone | 13.1 | | |
|      | 45-64 | 26.2 | Asian alone | 4.6 | | |
|      | 65-84 | 11.0 | All other races | 3.0 | | |
|      | 85+ | 2.0 | | | | |
| 2030 | 0-19 | 26.2 | White alone | 75.8 | Hispanic (of any race) | 20.1 |
|      | 20-44 | 31.6 | Black alone | 13.9 | | |
|      | 45-64 | 22.6 | Asian alone | 6.2 | | |
|      | 65-84 | 17.0 | All other races | 4.1 | | |
|      | 85+ | 2.6 | | | | |
| 2050 | 0-19 | 26.0 | White alone | 72.1 | Hispanic (of any race) | 24.4 |
|      | 20-44 | 31.2 | Black alone | 14.6 | | |
|      | 45-64 | 22.2 | Asian alone | 8.0 | | |
|      | 65-84 | 15.7 | All other races | 5.3 | | |
|      | 85+ | 5.0 | | | | |

Data from the U.S. Census Bureau.

have a connection to significant broad events that occurred during their lifetimes (Schuman and Scott, 1989). In the United States there are four primary cohorts affecting future outdoor recreation program participation: baby boomers, Generation Xers, millennials, and Generation Zers.

## Baby Boomers

Baby boomers—individuals born between 1945 and 1965—remember a time of political unrest. During their formative years, John F. Kennedy was assassinated, the Vietnam War occurred, and the civil rights movement was just gaining momentum. As the baby boom generation moves into retirement age over the next 20 years, these individuals are increasingly interested in and able to participate in outdoor recreation programs (Cordell, 2004). As this large percentage of the population ages, they influence the overall age distribution of the population (the median age of the U.S. population is expected to increase from 35 to 42 in 2020). Boomers are highly active and tend to participate in a wide range of programs, including Outdoor Adventure Travel (OAT), Elderhostel, Sierra Club, and Outward Bound. As a group, individuals in this cohort are interested in outdoor pursuits that engage their mind as well as their body and spirit.

## Generation X

Individuals categorized within the X Generation—those born between 1965 and 1978—are also interested in the outdoors. Generation Xers remember the space shuttle Challenger explosion and the Iran Contra Scandal, were introduced to mass-produced computer technology, and tended to have working parents during their formative years of development, which meant they often spent significant time after school without supervision. They are, generally, independent, technology literate, adaptable, not intimidated by authority, and creative. When designing outdoor recreation programs for Generation Xers, it is important to remember some of their key motivations (Burmeister, 2008).

1. Mentorship: Generation X individuals tend to appreciate gaining knowledge from skilled colleagues.
2. Coaching: Separate and distinct from mentorship, coaching occurs at a deeper level and

helps Generation X individuals understand who they are and what experiences they need to develop. Coaching can come from external or internal sources; coaches should be familiar with generational characteristics of X individuals.
3. Individualized plans: Generation X employees tend to appreciate and desire having personalized plans for learning outdoor recreation activities.
4. Empowerment: Empowering Generation X employees by asking them to participate in creating their plan for learning can increase their likelihood to participate.
5. Flexibility: Identify and encourage the values of Generation Xers. These individuals will look for programs that allow for flexible participation. They might want to choose nontraditional hours, vary when they participate, and travel extensively to participate in their chosen activities.

## Millennials

Sometimes called the Net Generation or Generation Y, Millennials—individuals born between 1978 and the early '90s—are new entries to the outdoor recreation world. Millennials are growing up in an era of social change influenced by events such as the September 11, 2001, attack on the World Trade Towers, high-speed information access in the form of the Internet, and a second environmental revolution. They are better educated and have traveled more than any prior generation. Millennials also believe in inclusiveness, have a strong sense of community, and are connected with social issues of the day (Carlton, 2009). Because they have also grown up during the revitalized green movement, taking care of the environment will be a part of their value system and they will seek outdoor recreation programs exhibiting sustainable values and processes.

Millennials are extremely technology literate and savvy, and are eager to learn. They can be differentiated from baby boomers and Generation Xers by their combination of seven primary traits (Howe and Strauss, 2000): high confidence, team orientation, sheltered living, conventional behavior, pressured throughout life-development stages, high achievement, and highly specialized. They have never known a time without the Internet and can bring this knowledge and skill to the outdoors. Many enjoy bringing a host of electronic gadgets with them to enhance their outdoor recreation activities. Items such as altimeters, GPS units, cell phones, satellite phones, weather monitors, and other communication devices have been added to their standard list of outdoor items. Many of these items are staple items in the backcountry for Millennials, who also have a heightened sense of fear compared to previous generations. It is intriguing to consider, though, that many of these items can be nonfunctioning in the wilderness and might offer users more of a perceived safety net than actual safety.

Individuals in the millennial generation are confident, high achieving, and specialized.

Laurlyn Harmon

## Generation Z

Generation Z individuals—born between 1994 and 2004—are the technology generation; they are sometimes called Generation Net because their lives are spent connecting to friends, families, and the world using social media such as Facebook, Twitter, Skype, and Facetime on their computers or handheld devices. Needless to say, they are extremely Internet savvy.

Because both parents were working, Generation Z was often left alone to find their own way (Cross-Bystrom, 2010). They have developed a sense of individualism and independence. That said, they also believe in traditional values, are connected with their families, and value giving back to their communities.

This generation will lead the "go green" movement. These individuals are extremely aware of environmental issues such as global warming, habitat sustainability, and the importance of clean water and air. They have been taught about these issues throughout their lives in school.

It is believed that Generation Z will be a transient workforce, unlike their grandparents who worked the same job from the start of their careers to finish. Some say Gen Z will not be team players, but others believe they will be because they will be taught by Gen Y teachers, who are known for being obsessed with team and group development.

Research has proven that spending time in nature benefits everyone and that we become healthier individuals in every way—intellectually, emotionally, spiritually, and physically (California State Parks, 2008). That's why what outdoor recreation provides is so important to future generations.

Knowing what we do about Gen Z, outdoor program administrators need to pay attention to the forthcoming research on the trends of this group. Little is yet known about how this generation will affect the outdoor recreation field; they could be a huge benefit or a possible liability—perhaps even a detriment to the workforce.

## Age

Beyond understanding generational cohorts, outdoor program administrators will also need to consider general trends in age distribution

The overall population increase in the United States means more older individuals will be participating in recreation activities.

and longevity. The average life expectancy in the United States increased from 47.3 years in 1900 to 68.2 years in 1950, 75.4 years in 1990, and 77.8 years in 2004. The trend is a steady increase in longevity, which means retirees, who may have additional discretionary income, are increasingly able to participate in traditional outdoor recreation activities (USDHHS, 2008). Older individuals may also be more physically able to participate in outdoor activities than their counterparts from earlier generations because they smoke less, are increasingly likely to become vaccinated against disease, and are more likely to get basic health care needs met (Federal Interagency Forum on Aging-related Statistics, 2008). Though we will continue to see approximately 20 to 25 percent of individuals over 65 participating in leisure activities (FIFAS, 2008), the overall population increase in the United States means more older individuals will be participating in recreation activities.

## Race and Ethnicity

In addition to age, the racial makeup of our citizenry, as well as the cultural framework, will continue to shift. Individuals of Asian American descent are expected to more than double from 2000 to 2050, whereas persons of African American descent will increase by approximately 71 percent (U.S. Census Bureau, 2004). In addition, we can expect to see a greater increase in persons of Hispanic ethnicity—an increase of approximately 18 percent. This shift in racial and ethnic background suggests programs and activities will need to be reconsidered to meet evolving cultural needs such as increased family-oriented activities. However, it is necessary to accurately understand the needs of people from varying cultures before making assumptions. To do this, programs will need to rely on needs assessment studies targeted specifically to individuals who may or may not have traditionally frequented outdoor recreation facilities.

As population demographics in the United States continue to change, the diversity of outdoor recreation participants will broaden. Participants will be increasingly multilingual, will include aging adults, will represent a wider range of racial diversity, and will have increasingly diverse activity interests. Although many outdoor recreation activities will continue to rely on wilderness or wilderness-type areas, many potential participants are interested in both urban and nonurban outdoor experiences; outdoor program administrators will need to offer opportunities providing experiences that meet this emerging market.

## STAFFING

"Staffing is perhaps the greatest single challenge for administrators of outdoor programs" (Ford, Blanchard and Blanchard, 1993, p. 219). Part of an administrator's responsibility in outdoor recreation is to build a sense of agency among employees so they may best represent the organization as well as the profession. To do this, it is imperative to understand and consider the driving forces behind current as well as incoming staff. Encouraging personal responsibility and engagement can be as important as compensation, education, professional development, and knowledge levels. Identifying differences between generational cohorts with respect to employment goals can provide a basis for understanding and addressing the dynamic needs of employees.

The current outdoor recreation facility staff is well represented by the generational cohort identified as the baby boomers—individuals born between 1945 and 1965 (Easterlin, Schaeffer and Macunovich, 1993). Boomers are just beginning to reach retirement, particularly since retirement is often earlier than the traditional 65 years of age. As boomers retire, many positions will be filled with Generation X employees advancing from entry level or similar positions. As the entry level positions become available, the Millennials will enter the workforce. When Boomers entered the workforce, they were looking for career jobs they could hold for a long time. They have been service oriented, driven, willing to go the extra mile by developing professional relationships, eager to please, and strong team players (Burmeister, 2008).

Incoming Millennial employees are seeking employment at organizations where mentorship and professional development is provided. This is where baby boomers can be used to advantage. Boomers can pass on their institutional knowledge and skill by having the Millennial generation employees shadow and observe them in action while providing critical and thoughtful mentorship. Ensuring institutional knowledge is already passed on to individuals who represent Generation X is also critical.

Before the baby boomers cycle out of the workforce, it is prudent for organizations to implement a system for collecting and preserving the institutional knowledge of these seasoned employees. Most boomers in the outdoor recreation profession, or a related field, have been there for over 30 years. They have been an integral part in the developmental stages and growth of outdoor recreation.

Organizations would benefit by adopting a knowledge management system that ". . . captures and stores the knowledge and experiences of employees and makes this information available to others in the organization" (Virginia Department of Conservation and Recreation, 2007, p. 185) In particular, information such as historical development of the organization, milestones, strategic plan formation, challenges negotiated, program history, and notable accomplishments are integral in planning for the direction and continued success of any unit.

In his description of how to move an organization from satisfactory to outstanding, Collins (2001) states, "If we get the right people on the bus, the right people in the right seats, and the wrong people off the bus, then we'll figure out how to take it someplace great" (p. 12). Outdoor program administrators frequently make personnel decisions. It is just as important to get the wrong people off the "bus" as it is to hire the right people to join. The right combination of staff members is an integral component of any successful organization.

"The most successful companies will be those who can attract [employees], create an environment in which they can thrive, and learn to leverage their differences into assets for the company," (Burmeister, 2008). The relationships created among administrators and employees by using the strengths of Generation X and Millennials along with the core knowledge of baby boomers will need to be a priority in order to hire and retain the best outdoor recreation professionals in this new generation of employees. Knowledge management will be an important consideration, as will staff development and retention. Acknowledging and embracing these changes will greatly enhance outdoor recreation organizations.

## PROFESSIONALIZATION OF THE FIELD: STANDARDS, CERTIFICATIONS, ACCREDITATION

Another facet of outdoor program administration to be considered in planning for the future is the increased need for meeting standards, providing certified staff and programs, and attaining accreditation. Over the last 25 years, practitioners have been developing and instituting certification and accreditation standards for many outdoor recreation programs, including residential and day camps, adventure programs, and community recreation programs.

Certifications and accreditation standards represent best practices gained over years of experience by leaders in various aspects of outdoor adventure industries. They should be seen as the minimum standards by which an organization operates. When a practitioner (individual or organization) follows the standards and procedures through which it was certified or accredited, little question remains about what was done and why. Our society has become increasingly litigious, and projections suggest no change in this regard. Outdoor recreation agencies, in order to continue providing services, must keep this issue forefront in their considerations. Program safety must be stressed for all participants. Outside agencies, such as insurance companies, often require certifications and accreditations as a condition for service. In the event of an accident or a legal suit, the practitioner will need to have reasonably met industry standards.

Certification standards cannot always be universally applied, however. Accidents occur even in the best designed and safest recreation programs. Incident prevention and response skills learned through certification trainings (e.g., CPR, basic first-aid, and first-responder skills) are essential in preparing for and managing accidents and incidents. All staff must understand the risks and prepare for them. If staff members are not provided with the opportunity and time to practice, these skills will fade over the course of a typical three-year certification. Every program and situation has its own unique characteristics. Thus each organization should develop its own operating procedures that augment and do not bend the broader standards of certification.

Organizations are responsible to diligently train their staff in operating procedures and to regularly audit the certified skills of their staff so that incidents are handled with practiced consistency and understanding. Incident response is very important, but preparation to avoid incidents is top priority for outdoor recreation agencies. Agency accreditations provide the system and structure to facilitate this

preparation. Looking into the future, accrediting bodies will increasingly be the avenue for ensuring organizations are using best and appropriate practices to develop, monitor, and maintain employee skills and certification programs.

# YOUTH AND THE OUTDOORS

The current political climate holds a clear interest in getting people outside. In 2005, several seminal events took place. The Connecticut Department of Environmental Protection successfully developed the powerful statewide initiative of No Child Left Inside. Almost simultaneously, the first edition of Richard Louv's publication *Last Child in the Woods: Saving our Children from Nature Deficit Disorder* was released. Faced with increasing obesity rates among adults and children, instances of emotional health problems, and reliance on electronic media for entertainment, the nation is responding.

One of the key outcomes of this movement was the legislative effort to introduce environmental education into the core curriculum of the K-12 public school system nationwide. The No Child Left Inside (NCLI) Act (H. R. 3036) was not adopted by Congress in 2008 but was reintroduced in 2011 as a bill to amend the Elementary and Secondary Education Act of 1965 regarding environmental education. NCLI is intended to support direct experiences for environmental education of K-12 students and provide training opportunities to educators to conduct these programs (Chesapeake Bay Foundation, 2010) for the overarching purpose of developing environmental literacy among young people. The North American Association for Environmental Education (NAAEE) is one of the key organizations collaborating to advocate for congressional support of the NCLI legislation. However, other organizations, such as the Children and Nature Network (CNN) and the National Recreation and Park Association (NRPA) are also providing active support. In addition, multiple agencies have initiated programs designed to get people outdoors (see table 4.2).

The effect of this movement to engage young people in the outdoors is widespread. Many parents are making conscious choices to spend increased time outdoors with their children. As increased instances of systematically collected data

**Table 4.2** Programs Promoting Outdoor Recreation Participation

| Agency or organization | Program | Contact information |
|---|---|---|
| Children and Nature Network | Multiple programs and research | www.childrenandnature.org |
| Get Outdoors USA | National Get Outdoors Day | www.nationalgetoutdoorsday.org |
| North Carolina Museum of Natural Sciences | Take a Child Outside Week | www.takeachildoutside.org |
| National Park Service | Junior Park Ranger, Web Rangers | www.nps.gov/learn/juniorranger.cfm |
| National Wildlife Federation | Great American Backyard Campout | www.nwf.org/BackyardCampout/ |
| Outdoor Recreation Coalition | Multiple events (clearinghouse of information) | www.funoutdoors.com/events |
| U.S. Department of Interior | Take Pride in America | www.takepride.gov |
| U.S. Fish and Wildlife Service | National Wildlife Refuge Week | www.fws.gov |
| USDA Forest Service | More Kids in the Woods | www.fs.fed.us/recreation/programs/woods |

are shared showing the benefits of spending time outdoors, and more important, this information is shared with politicians, educators, primary care-givers, and health professionals, we anticipate an increase in time spent outdoors. Outdoor program administrators have an opportunity and obligation to capitalize on this social movement of getting children outdoors.

Slacklining is a creative outdoor activity that young people enjoy, partly because of its perceived adventurous quality.

Laurlyn Harmon

# TECHNOLOGY AND THE OUTDOORS

The speed with which technological applications are introduced today is phenomenal by most standards, and the life of electronic technologies is short. Laptop computers are expected to remain useful for only two years, software is updated annually, and cellular phone technology is upgraded at least every six months. Such trends will continue. Increasingly sophisticated technology is the wave of the future. This being the case, outdoor program administrators should strive to stay on top of current practices and be familiar with the technological tools available to them.

In 2010, the Kaiser Family Foundation (Rideout, Foehr, and Roberts, 2010) reported, ". . . young people have increased the amount of time they spend consuming media by an hour and seventeen minutes daily, from 6:21 to 7:38—almost the amount of time most adults spend at work each day, except that young people use media seven days a week instead of five" (p. 2). In his book, *Last Child in the Woods*, Richard Louv (2008) identified a condition, nature deficit disorder, describing the current state of young people that has resulted from too much time with technology and too little time with nature. Louv's publication, along with reports of increasing media use and rising rates of obesity among young people (CDC, 2010) has brought attention to the nation's lack of connection with the outdoor world. As a result, federal, state, and local agencies, in addition to not-for-profits, private, and public education groups, have come together to promote participation in outdoor recreation activities as a path toward healthy living. Many programs have been created to engage youth, adults, and families in outdoor activities. In a time when obesity is a critical health issue for Americans, particularly among youth, outdoor program administrators are important providers of opportunities for children and their families to hike local parks, climb mountain trails, canoe rivers, explore wilderness areas, and develop a closer relationship with the outdoors.

Outdoor program administrators should consider technology from two perspectives: facility driven and user driven. Facility-driven technologies include management and design software, environmentally friendly products and actions, and program equipment. For example, as outdoor recreation facilities are seeing an increasing demand for accountability, they can take advantage of sophisticated recreation organization management software such as ReCPro and Rectrac. This software is used for sales tracking, league scheduling, facility rental, on-line registration, and to process payments at recreation facilities.

User-driven technologies refer to items outdoor recreation participants find increasingly useful, interesting, or important and may bring with them on trips. For instance, new materials and designs are allowing outdoor gear distributors to provide lighter and stronger tent materials, more options for waterproof gear, and clothing with sun protection. In addition, each generation of communication devices provides services not previously available that can affect not only the comfort and enjoyment of outdoor experiences but also user safety. Handheld global positioning satellite (GPS) units are replacing the standard compass units, satellite phones are providing service in areas previously isolated from electronic communication, and handheld weather monitoring units allow outdoor enthusiasts to be prepared for even the subtlest of weather shifts.

Another user-driven technology available is robotics. Available for land or water use, remotely operated vehicles (ROVs) allow individuals to observe wildlife and habitat or collect data as part of an outdoor education program with minimal site disturbance (Harmon and Gleason, 2009). The units can be small (about the size of a football) and are connected to the surface operating system via a tether that transmits power and images. The operator can guide the robot from the deck of a boat or from shore while the unit flies silently in the water, transmitting video to the surface monitor from depths of 2 to 2,000 feet. Sophisticated units can be purchased for $10,000 or more, but make-your-own kits are available for under $500. The assembly of these units can be an integral part of engaging individuals in discussions regarding the future of the outdoors.

The tendency may be to shy away from technology when thinking of outdoor education. After all, young people are spending almost 50 percent less time outside than they did 10 years ago, opting for video games, computers, and televisions instead (Roberts, Foehr, and Rideout, 2005). But the future holds many opportunities for using technology to draw people outdoors, and outdoor program administrators will be increasingly expected to take advantage of these opportunities.

## SUSTAINABILITY

Acknowledgment of the effects of climate change is resulting in increased attention to addressing impacts at an organizational level. Lowering carbon footprints, LEED-designed facilities, and sustainable operations are also becoming hallmarks of the outdoor recreation industry. Facilities managers must be cognizant of the impact that upgrading their facility with the latest in eco-friendly products has on the community as well as the profession. Replacing wooden boardwalks with newly designed composite boards manufactured from postconsumer plastics, for instance, or converting energy sources to wind or solar, illustrates a commitment to the future of the planet and demonstrates an organization's outdoor ethics. Engaging in and advocating for environmentally responsible behaviors, emphasizing outdoor ethics, addressing impacts on public lands, and promoting public participation

## CASE STUDY: NORTHBAY ADVENTURE CAMP: LOOKING TOWARD THE FUTURE

One organization successfully using some of the strategies and methods discussed in this chapter is NorthBay Adventure Camp in northeast Maryland. Founded in 2005 by philanthropist John Erickson, NorthBay is an environmental education camp designed to house up to 450 people at a time. Participants spend their days addressing a variety of research questions while hiking, exploring natural areas, and collecting scientific data in the Chesapeake Bay and adjacent areas. The primary purpose of these activities is to help students identify a situation or event, instigate discussion, and generate different investigative approaches. Evenings are spent sharing the approaches students have used to solve that day's research problem. To provide an educational experience, each program is guided by two overarching questions: "To what extent do your choices affect your future and the people around you?" and "To what extent do your choices affect the environment?" According to Keith Williams, director of education at NorthBay, grappling with these questions teaches students ". . . how to look at environmental and social problems through that lens—they can use this approach when they return to their own communities and be better prepared to handle differences of opinion" (personal communication, June 5, 2008).

The multi-day programs for sixth graders that are conducted during the academic year were designed and are regularly modified in partnership with the Maryland Department of Education (MDOE) to ensure curricula meet the state's current learning standards. In this way, the outdoor environment becomes a platform for learning language, arts, and mathematics, which helps students perform better on the standardized exams required by the state.

Staff development is a priority at North-Bay. Hiring is based on a love for working with kids and a willingness to learn, coupled with professional credentials. Education staff are encouraged, via personal development and monetary incentives, to attain state teaching certification. They are provided with two weeks of training, paired with a senior educator for mentoring, and participate in peer observation throughout their time at NorthBay. Individuals are allowed to adapt the curriculum based on context and personal expertise while retaining the core standards. The high-trust, collaborative opportunities among staff have resulted in excellent programming and high retention rates.

Laurlyn Harmon

Sixth grade girls from the Baltimore Public Schools try their hand at running an underwater robot as part of their bivalve science program in the Chesapeake Bay.

Funding for initial programming was provided by Erickson, but the Maryland Department of Natural Resources offered a 30-year lease to NorthBay and maintains a continual partnership by working together to develop courses (e.g., Bay Grasses in Classes), bringing experts to share knowledge with the education staff, and holding regular meetings at the facility.

Partnerships with university researchers have resulted in unique opportunities for students as well as alternative program funding. In summer 2008, 11 groups of sixth graders from inner Baltimore operated underwater robots as part of their bivalve study in the Chesapeake Bay. Funded by George Mason University, the research was designed to assess the perception young people have of new technologies and how they affect learning.

NorthBay has embraced several creative approaches to funding, staff development, and programming—all key components of this successful organization.

regarding sustainability are all practices embraced by outdoor program administrators.

**>> Outdoor ethics.** The impact of the sustainable movement on the future of employee stewardship and perceptions of visitors or clients is necessary for any outdoor program administrator to consider. Sustainability and outdoor recreation are inextricably linked, and administrators have an opportunity to lead by example through their advocacy for and engagement in a specific set of outdoor ethics. What does this mean to an agency? In some cases, it can be as straightforward as recycling; in other cases, using nontraditional fuel sources such as wind or solar energy is an example. However, agencies must take the additional step of making their program visible by sharing the sustainable methods they have implemented with their clients, community, and other professionals. Of course doing so takes additional resources. Here is where creative administrators could incorporate sustainable activities into existing programs, distribute stories to the media, and share information at conferences. Outdoor program administrators may also find it useful to partner with existing outdoor ethics programs such as Leave No Trace, which provides small grants to support materials and training to agencies interested in developing new (or expanding existing) outdoor ethics programming.

**>> Impacts on public lands.** Accompanying increases in the population has resulted in increased visitation to public recreation lands. At the same time, external pressures are on the rise from organizations and individuals who want to extract resources from the land or build additional housing.

Meanwhile, land managers are seeing a decrease in annual budgets, making it difficult to maintain and improve trail systems and facilities and to minimize impacts from increased usage demands. Activity conflicts are rising in high-density population areas as well as in open areas. For example, new activities such as geocaching, while potentially drawing more people outdoors, can also create a network of unplanned social trails, cause soil compaction near cache areas, and distract users from respecting the natural environment in which the activity takes place. In the western states, an excellent example of user conflict on public lands is the increasing number of encounters between motorized and nonmotorized visitors (e.g., ATVs and hikers). These challenges are leading to implementation of new policies for public lands that often result in limiting overall use.

**>> Economics.** A nation's economy plays a huge role in outdoor recreation. Discretionary income levels affect purchases of outdoor-related gear and decisions to engage in outdoor trips and activities. Having less money to spend on activities identified as leisure activities affects purchases of associated equipment, participation in outdoor programs, and willingness to travel to distant locations. What is not clear is how each generational cohort (baby boomers, Millennials, Generation Xers and Zers, and beyond) will respond to economic trends. Will Millennials prioritize their discretionary income differently from the way that baby boomers have? If so, what impact will this have on participation in outdoor recreation programs and related activities?

**»> Public participation.** To address conflicts and engage individuals more directly with management issues affecting outdoor recreation agencies, many organizations are increasing public participation efforts. National Public Lands Day, which occurs on the last Saturday of September each year, offers free access to all federal public land holdings while providing opportunities in invasive species removal, trail maintenance, and other outdoor-management projects. Other programs engaging the public include Take A Child Outside Day (September 25), the National Audubon Society's Project BudBurst (early Spring), U.S. Fish and Wildlife's National Wildlife Refuge Week (second week in October), and National Get Outdoors Day (mid June). Outdoor recreation agencies can coordinate their own events with national events to increase public exposure and positive impact on the environment.

## COLLABORATIONS AND PARTNERSHIPS

One of the most important concerns for outdoor program administrators is to build relationships and make connections with individuals and organizations outside the field. This is important because doing so allows for a more free-flowing exchange of information, gives outdoor recreation increased opportunities for sharing benefits of programs, and creates partnerships that can allow for additional funding opportunities.

Many outdoor program administrators are feeling increased pressures to be self-sufficient and creative in terms of funding. Though the national economic situation fluctuates, it is unlikely recreation agencies will see a resurgence of support from the federal government because of spending pressure from health care services, the military, education, and the environment among others. Increasing fuel, travel, and equipment costs, especially when coupled with economic downturns, will lead to more local travel for families rather than the traditional long trips. These developments will provide occasions for outdoor professionals to collaborate at a local level and, ideally, will present increased opportunities for individuals to participate in previously unavailable outdoor recreation programs.

An excellent example of collaboration is the partnership formed among Outward Bound, the Sierra Club, and the U.S. Military. In 2008, Outward Bound received a $3.5 million grant through the Sierra Club as part of the Military Family Outdoor Initiative Project. This money is being used to fund five- to seven-day trips in the backcountry designed specifically for returning veterans from Iraq and Afghanistan. The programs, which include rock climbing, backpacking, and canoeing ". . . help participants gain self-confidence and skills for re-integration into civilian life and non-combat zone redeployment, as well as strengthened communication and relational skills in a supportive environment that builds trust and camaraderie" (Outward Bound, 2008).

How, though, can an outdoor recreation agency get involved with nontraditional partners? Once the desire to pursue partnerships is initiated, getting the staff personally involved is paramount. For example, if an agency wants to work with health professionals and, perhaps, offer recreation as preventive medicine, the outdoor program administrator should meet with staff and ask them to generate their best ideas for initiating contact.

In addition, having a plan to bring to potential collaborations is important. Such a plan could be a "boxed presentation" to be used in schools or with public groups (e.g., property owner associations) or potential funding partners. Collaborators are interested in what they can do for (and with) potential collaborators as well as how others can help them. Identifying common interests and goals creates a sense of camaraderie, whereas discussion of the outcomes unique to outdoor recreation allows agencies to understand the value of working together.

Outdoor program administrators should attend meetings and conferences outside of the outdoor recreation profession and offer to speak at public engagements. When doing so, they should bring well-documented effects of outdoor recreation program outcomes. Nonprofit groups such as the Children and Nature Network (www.childrenandnature.org) can be excellent sources for this information.

## OUTCOME ASSESSMENT

A final consideration, yet one of the most necessary for managing a strong future for outdoor recreation, is assessing user feedback and measuring outcomes.

Most administrators, programmers, and facilitators intuitively recognize the value of participating in outdoor programs; however, they have been less than rigorous in measuring the impact of their programs on participants. In the instances where research has been implemented, results suggest participants exhibit increased creativity, decreased stress, increased attentiveness, and an overall increase in physical and emotional well-being. Assessing these outcomes, as well as education-related outcomes, is imperative if recreation agencies wish to compete for external funding, validate outdoor professions to the public, and increase participation.

## SUMMARY

Outdoor program administrators are increasingly pressured to be multitalented, professionally savvy, and creative in the management of their agencies and organizations. The demands of clientele will change in the coming years, and the resources on which programs rely will continue to evolve. Some of the critical facets to address include the increasing reliance and availability of a plethora of technological tools, for operations as well as participation; the need for securing funding in nontraditional ways; meeting the needs of a diverse staff; and engaging in multiple and increasingly sophisticated partnerships.

The need to address these critical concerns while maintaining and developing new, well-designed, and outstanding outdoor recreation programs drives the future of outdoor program administration. By acknowledging these changes and capitalizing on the opportunities available, administrators will be able to proactively meet or exceed client, community, and employee expectations and exemplify leadership in our profession.

PART

**II**

# Program Design and Implementation

Chapter **5**

# Administrative Risk Management

*Mat Erpelding, MA, and Geoff Harrison, MS*

Outdoor recreation programs purposefully use risk as a medium for facilitating an experience for participants. The outdoor program administrator provides a service to clients that often has inherent risk that cannot be eliminated from the experience. *Risk* is the threat of loss. The reason people participate in risk-taking pursuits, from gambling to mountaineering, is because of the opportunity to gain something of value, such as reaching a goal (Arenas, Tabernero, and Briones, 2006). Many argue that eliminating risk removes the intrigue, value, and permanence of outdoor pursuits, and consequently may devalue the experience (Gregg, 1999).

Accepting that risk is inherent in adventure programming, the outdoor program administrator is often expected to explain how safe and well prepared the trips are to clients and supervisors. This dichotomy can be very difficult for the administrator to articulate to other stakeholders. Especially when risk is realized, the loss may include money, clients, staff, relationships, and reputations. To a person loss could be physical, emotional, social, or financial (Priest and Gass, 2005). Because risk in many outdoor pursuits is part of the pursuit's inherent value and important to clients, a systematic and thorough approach to administrative management is warranted.

Administrators should manage risk holistically. A holistic approach purposefully sees all aspects of an outdoor program as related and necessary to the entire system; each part of the program depends on the effective operations of all other parts. This includes understanding and designing policies and procedures, effective program design, financial management, marketing, staff hiring, training and assessment, legal issues, access and permitting, and specific planning for challenge courses, rental programs, land-based activities, water-based activities, and special events. A decision made in one area might directly or indirectly expose another area of the program to risk. The decisions made by an administrator must be carefully considered and intentional to maximize positive outcomes. In this chapter we identify the essential components associated with administrative risk management, reviewing risk definitions and types of risk, discussing four strategies to manage risk, and describing how to develop a holistic risk-management plan.

## TERMS AND DEFINITIONS OF RISK MANAGEMENT

In outdoor programming, risk is subdivided into two categories: actual risk and perceived risk. *Actual risk* is the genuine level of risk present in a given endeavor. *Perceived risk* is the amount of risk believed to be present by participants and the general public for a given endeavor. *Inherent risk* is the level of actual risk present in an endeavor that cannot be eliminated without changing the nature of the endeavor (Gregg, 1999), which may or may not be manageable. Risk is believed to be a necessary component of the outdoor experience, and it is the administrator's responsibility to manage it effectively using a variety of tools and techniques to pursue success (Gregg, 1999).

*Risk management* is the design and implementation of plans, procedures, guidelines, and policies to eliminate, minimize, and manage exposure to loss while pursuing reasonable program outcomes (Hansen-Stamp, 1999). Risk management is an extensive process that should be part of an organization's culture. It needs to be included as a consideration in all decision-making processes, whether in the field or in the office. Risk management should be systematic, extensive, and based on as much information as possible from current industry trends, past industry incidents, and best practices. As a result, outdoor program administrators should craft an extensive and systematic risk-management plan to help guide decisions.

Risk management can be divided into two classifications: incident prevention and incident response. *Incident prevention* is devoted to minimizing risk to all aspects of an organization; *incident response* is a predetermined plan created to respond to injuries, damages, or losses.

Incident prevention is the practice of avoiding the loss of resources, and is the priority of every outdoor program administrator. Resources include both the tangible and intangible aspects of an organization. Tangibles include staff and participants, financial assets, property, facilities, vehicles, equipment, and land access. Intangibles often include customer loyalty, business relationships, and public perception. Intangibles are difficult to measure and manage because of their broad scope. However, a well-managed and professional operation that participants benefit from will aid in the positive development of intangible resources.

Even the most prepared administrators eventually experience accidents or incidents—because inherent risk is not entirely avoidable. As part of the risk-management system, incident response is the prescribed and purposeful actions employed to manage an incident regardless of where it occurs (office or field).

## CREATING A COMPREHENSIVE RISK-MANAGEMENT PLAN

When considering the uses of risk-management techniques, many automatically think of avoiding accidents and incidents during field-based programs. However, in this section we will generalize risk to include all aspects of outdoor program administration, both in the office and in the field. Overwhelmingly, the effectiveness of the internal operations of a program dictate the external successes as measured by participation, accident rates, referrals, return customers, and financial stability. Figure 5.1 indicates the important internal operations necessary for either external success or struggles. Administrative risk management is not limited to maintaining an incident-free field experience. Rather, it is the gestalt (whole) process of maintaining an outdoor program to support the mission, meet expectations, minimize loss, and provide positive experiences to staff and clients. Losses incurred through poor customer service from a staff member, or from providing low-quality rental equipment to a client, or from terminating a staff member because of too many infractions are losses and can be financially detrimental, time consuming, and create a poor reputation for the program. Though these examples may not seem serious in terms of immediate outcome if losses are rare, regular losses can eventually cause an organization to decrease program offerings and core services or, in a worst-case scenario, to fail financially.

Thus the process of developing a risk-management plan must be intentional. The process involves identifying risk factors, integrating staff and site

Identify risk factors

Integrate assessment data and select appropriate risk strategies

Manage risk

Monitor and review strategies

**Figure 5.1**   The steps for developing a risk-management plan.

assessment information, choosing appropriate risk-management strategies, and monitoring and reviewing for changes in risk after the development of the plan.

## Identify the Risk Factors

When outdoor program administrators elect to use activities that involve risks as educational or experiential tools, they must identify the risks and ensure they are managed effectively. This process can be accomplished by breaking down the bull's-eye in figure 5.1 into four categories that serve as a platform to assess risk variables associated with an organization. The four categories are *strategic risks, financial risks, operational risks,* and *field risks.* Identifying risks, their severity and probability, and effectively managing them is essential to effective outdoor program administration. An analysis of each program should be conducted to determine what, if any, potential losses the organization is willing to absorb. Outcome-focused risk identification is the process through which risks that might impede an organization from achieving desired outcomes are identified and managed. This includes modifying desired outcomes if available resources are not adequate.

Strategic risks, financial risks, operational risks, and field risks can all negatively impact an outdoor program. These risks are related, and if loss occurs in any of the four areas, a ripple effect is felt throughout the organization (see figure 5.2).

## Strategic Risk

Strategic risk is anything that might affect one or more aspects of an organization's future operations, including its vision, mission, desired outcomes, service sector, scope of services, program design, external partnerships, regulatory or political concerns, future customer expectations and needs, reputation, and industry trends. Strategic risks affect the long-term trajectories an outdoor recreation program will follow. These risks include lack of direction, limited access to land, and a lack of clearly defined goals. Additional strategic risks exist for programs residing within larger organizations, including the risk of program isolation. Program isolation occurs when a program does not actively work to bring its vision, mission, and outcomes into alignment with the parent organization.

**Program Design and Development** Program design and development must be purposefully anchored to a program's vision, mission, and goals

**Figure 5.2** Risk can be broken down into four different factors: strategic, financial, operational, and field.

(see chapter 6). The process begins with developing an understanding of relevant outdoor recreation history. Once a program establishes a vision statement to aspire toward, a mission statement to build off, and clearly desired outcomes for the organization, then the formal process of administrative risk management can begin. A clear and concise understanding of what the program does, who its constituents are, its desired outcomes, and how it plans to accomplish them represents the scaffolding or skeleton for a functional administrative risk-management plan.

Consider the following example of two separate businesses that use Mt. Everest as a backdrop to meet program outcomes. One is an international guiding company, and the other a challenge course provider. The guiding organization has set its vision as "to help more clients reach the summit than any other guide service has done." To accomplish this, the company has established a comprehensive risk-management plan that revolves around the risks associated with climbing in a foreign country, climbing in the "death zone," moving through dangerous ice falls, being on the mountain with nonassociated parties, and many, many more concerns. Meanwhile, the vision of the second company (challenge course provider) is "to be the leading challenge course provider in Nevada by helping clients reach personal summits," so this company might elect to use climbing Mt. Everest in a different context. Instead of setting out to climb the mountain, they highlight the metaphorical association of success during a challenge course program with that of climbers vying to reach the top of the world. To build on the metaphor of success, the company organizes a slide show and motivational speaker series to share the challenge and success of climbing Mt. Everest. Clearly, the risk-management plans will be far different for each company, but what is important to note is that both plans are directly linked to their organization's overall vision.

**Legal Considerations**    Topics such as liability, negligence, releases, and insurance represent the legal aspects of an effective risk-management plan. The need to maintain legal counsel is prudent and should be a key process in the development, review, and revisions of any risk-management plan and other administrative functions. To explain program operations to the organization's legal team, the outdoor program administrator must have more than a common understanding of liability and be aware of how a legal professional looks at activities that an outdoor professional may take for granted. See chapter 7 for a foundation of knowledge and common language for recreation law.

**Permitting**    Working with land managers is an essential aspect of strategic risk management. Land managers are charged with maintaining recreational resources for all people, not just a few select programs or outfitters. Thus they see land use differently from the way an outdoor program administrator sees it. Consequently, finding business practices that support the land manager and the outdoor program are essential to maintaining access to public lands. Loss of access is one of the single biggest concerns affecting the outdoor programming industry. Chapter 10 discusses the extensive process required of outdoor program administrators to work with private landowners, as well as local, state, or federal agencies to ensure legal access to land. Proactively managing this strategic risk ensures long-term access to the sites an outdoor recreation organization needs to offer quality programs.

## Financial Risks

Financial risks are those risks that might impact the financial status of the organization. They include decreased revenue, an increase in operating expenses, unidentified expenses, and decreased access to credit. Outdoor program administrators must have a detailed understanding of their organization's financial needs because this is essential information for budgetary planning and implementation. Financial considerations are related to program design because program goals and expectations must address revenue generation. Many times, goals must be placed on hold because of financial constraints and implications. It is essential that accounting procedures, forecasting, and revenue expectations be accurate so that unnecessary risks are not created.

Losing, misappropriating, or mismanaging an organization's finances is one of the clearest examples of a concrete loss. Protecting against financial loss is a core responsibility of most outdoor program administrators. Whether a program is commercial or nonprofit, money management is directly related to risk-management plans. Consider a program that cannot make its revenue projections for the year and is forced to forgo plans to purchase new kayaks to replace a current fleet of older-model whitewater kayaks they have been using for over five years (table 5.1).

Most outdoor program administrators are required to prepare and manage budgets for their departments or programs. Although expectations for profit, loss, and subsidy are generally determined by the nature of the parent organization's mission, all programs should expect to operate within an approved budget. Thus administrators are responsible for knowing and understanding the budget process, tracking expenses and revenues to operate within the current budget, and to project changes needed for future fiscal years. An overview of fiscal management practices for outdoor programs is presented in chapter 8.

## Operational Risks

Operational risks include any part of business involved in producing the service or product, including human resource concerns, staff training and assessment, facility maintenance, and marketing. Outdoor program administrators must define each operational consideration clearly, ensure

adequate time is spent on each variable, and make certain plans are established to ensure a thorough vetting. Administrators must market the program, effectively hire and train staff, work with field instructors to design consistent curriculums, and maintain equipment and facilities. Operational risks are managed beginning with the selling of the adventure and ending with the post-course evaluations.

**Marketing: What Is Promised? What Is Provided?**  Selling programs and services is an essential skill for the outdoor program administrator, and a detailed understanding of the marketing process is necessary to meet financial and program goals. Straddling the line between making sure that a program is attractive to potential customers, but not painting an unrealistic and unattainable expectation for clients, is a difficult task. Marketing programs inevitably brings into question the amount of actual and perceived risk associated with a program. Inherent risk is present in all recreational activities, and the marketing materials must accurately represent the risk either through photos, text, or customer service interactions. Do photos used for marketing show smiles, dry environments, and students in short-sleeved shirts or swimming suits, even though the organization runs the majority of its

**Table 5.1**  Case Example of a Financial Risk: Use of Older Model Whitewater Kayaks (Five Years or Older)

|  | High risk | Low risk |
|---|---|---|
| Actual physical risk to participants |  | Generally, older model kayaks that are maintained do not pose a significant safety risk to participants if quality site choice and quality leadership and education are present. |
| Marketing risk | Using older model kayaks may imply that the program is behind the times in both equipment and instruction. This perception may not instill confidence in the consumer and move them to seek instruction from another vendor that offers courses using modern equipment. |  |
| Financial risk | All equipment depreciates over time. Using equipment for too long can significantly decrease resale value and thus limit a program's ability to recoup costs and purchase new kayaks. |  |

programs on the Olympic Peninsula in Washington? Is the client told that the company provides safe programs, even though inherent risk is an accepted and desirable aspect of outdoor adventure? Figure 5.3 shows two very different promotions for the same trip.

Depending on resources available, outdoor program administrators may be solely responsible for all aspects of marketing for their respective programs. Given that many programs and administrators are evaluated based on program participation, program revenue generation, or a combination of the two, the importance of marketing what the program offers cannot be overemphasized. Finding a balance between painting a perfect picture and a realistic picture is essential to the administrative risk-management plan.

**Staffing Considerations** A challenging aspect of an effective risk-management plan is addressing the human factors. At its core, effective hiring, training, and evaluation are integral to the safety of clients. Competent field staff represent the front line against field risks, whereas competent office staff represent

the front line against operational risks. Field staff are responsible for the physical, emotional, and mental safety of participants from the time they leave the building until the time they return. Office staff tend to be responsible for customer service, equipment management, and logistics. The outdoor program administrator must have an accurate assessment of the human, outdoor, and educational skills associated with each staff member to appropriately assign staff to the right position. Thus hiring processes should be purposeful and designed to maximize staff competency. This might include a field-based assessment to ensure that the written documentation provided by the applicant is actually demonstrable in the field.

Staff retention and termination are other key concerns for the outdoor program administrator because staff who *want* to be at work tend to be more invested in the program's outcomes. Opportunities for advancement, professional development, reasonable salaries, and staff involvement are essential to recruiting and retaining staff members. Additionally, an understanding and willingness to remove

**Figure 5.3** Comparing promotions: technical canyoneering in the canyonlands in the winter. Which promotion is more accurate?

ineffective staff is the responsibility of the administrator. Retention of quality staff is usually less expensive over time and less risky than constantly investing in new staff.

**Facility Management** Outdoor program administrators manage facilities that often employ perceived risk to provide experiences. Facilities represent operational and field risks in the same location at the same time. Whether your organization is a rental center, challenge course, climbing wall, or whitewater park, extensive facility planning and risk-identification processes are necessary to prevent losses. Using a standardized or global plan applied to each and every facility is not prudent. Each facility has intricacies unique to its type and function. Thus a slightly different risk-management plan is required to be written to address different desired outcomes, acceptable risk, and client expectations for each particular facility. See table 5.2 for an example of common differences in risk-management considerations at two similar facilities.

Many outdoor facilities—rental centers, challenge courses, whitewater parks, and many more—are expensive to operate, so mitigating all forms of loss is essential. A working knowledge of each area is essential to effectively manage and develop an outdoor program. Many times, a facility such as a climbing wall expands the clientele being served beyond its core constituents, which in turn helps broaden other aspects of the program. Thus a well-managed facility is essential to effective administrative risk management.

## Field Risk

Field risks are conditions that heighten the chance of an accident or incident within an organization; these risks tend to be most commonly associated with programs in the field. The outdoor program administrator should address field risks by developing concise policies, procedures, and guidelines. Additionally, operational, financial, and strategic risks must be effectively managed in order to manage field risks, including having

- the vision, mission, and desired outcomes of the organization be understood and supported by the entire staff;
- appropriate program designs for available financial resources;
- organizationally supported and effective staff training; and
- regular equipment maintenance.

Managing field risk requires an emphasis on effective staffing and staff training. Customary-risk reviews occur when a list of common risks are reviewed before completing a task. For example, as a trip leader for a backpacking trip in the North Cascades in March, a series of existing hazards are reviewed and managed, including equipment selection; participant recruiting, screening, and education; route selection; and weather forecasts.

Understanding accident theory is essential to creating and effectively conducting a customary-risk review. In this case, hazard risks are being identified and mitigated to effectively avoid an accident or incident. According to Priest and Gass (2005), accident potential is created when field risks are present caused by the environment, participant behavior or actions, or leadership errors (see figure 5.4). Many times, environmental, participant, and leadership hazards combine to create extremely dangerous situations and increase accident risk (Meyer, 1979). Risk of an accident is minimized if a vigilant field risk review is performed and identified hazards are immediately managed.

**Table 5.2** Facility Differences

|  | Climbing wall | Challenge course |
|---|---|---|
| Common outcomes | Recreation | Education |
| Common equipment variance | Aluminum carabiners | Steel carabiners |
| Most common clientele | Individual users | Organized groups |
| Employees | Facility supervisors | Facilitators |

---

**Figure 5.4**  Examples of Leadership, Participant, and Environmental Hazards That Require Management Strategies

### Environmental Hazards

Cold or hot temperature

Rain, sleet, or snow conditions

Snow conditions (snow pack depth, quality of snow)

Avalanche conditions (weather, terrain, snow pack, recent activity)

Water currents (wind produced, gravity induced, or tidal)

River conditions (deep, flooded, strainers, cold)

Trail conditions (icy, muddy, slick, uneven)

Rock conditions (falling, loose, icy)

Road conditions (deer, ice, rain, snow)

Animals (bears, raccoons, skunks, snakes)

Insects (hymenoptera, spiders, mosquitoes, fleas)

### Participant Behavior or Actions

Misuse of equipment (stoves, axe, crampons, lifejacket)

Exceeding competence level (hiking too fast, misuse of technical skills)

Poor hygiene (fecal contamination, food management, waste management, etc.)

Falling (snow, rock, into river)

Time stress (tired, rushed, late)

Becoming lost

Communication (disregarding, not hearing, or misunderstanding leader instructions)

### Leadership Errors

HALTT (hungry, angry, lax [apathetic], tired, thirsty)

Inaccurate assessment (self, coleaders, participants, hazards, equipment, site)

Poor instructional progressions

Poor site choice

Incompetent human skills

Incompetent educational skills

Incompetent outdoor skills (basic living skills, specific technical skills)

Ineffective supervision of participants

Desired outcome confusion (disregarding, misunderstanding, or not knowing)

---

### Developing Field Policies and Procedures

Common practices or industry standards become a measuring tool for all outdoor programs when risk-management practices are called into question. Policies and procedures are tied to staffing considerations because staff must understand policies and procedures to operate within their abilities. The outdoor program administrator is responsible for maintaining information on the policies, procedures, and guidelines for conducting activities. In developing field policies, procedures and guidelines, administrators are not attempting to stifle the creativity and autonomy of individual staff members but rather to create predictability and consistency within the program. This is why the administrator is also responsible for determining what items

Effective staff training, such as the canoe over canoe rescue shown here, is one aspect of managing field risk.

need to be included within the policies, procedures, and guidelines. These items should be customarily reviewed by all members of the community.

Policies, procedures, and guidelines should be reviewed, changed, and adapted consistently. Adherence to procedures established by other recognized bodies external to the program is a common and wise practice. Curricula provided by outside organizations such as the American Canoe Association, American Mountain Guide Association, Wilderness Education Association, and the Center for Outdoor Ethics are great assets to program administrators attempting to ensure that their programs are operating in accordance with common practices. Several professional associations provide best practices manuals for further administrative use.

Finally, policies, procedures, and guidelines cannot cover all the occurrences that staff will experience while leading trips. At some point, outdoor program administrators must rely on the judgment of staff, and methods for encouraging responsible decisions in ambiguous situations is an essential component of a policies manual. Cline (2004) encourages administrators to teach staff to make decisions based on the mission and desired outcomes of the program. This changes the dynamic of the decision-making process away from "will I get in trouble with the boss?" and moves it to the process of "will my students get the desired outcomes

of the course without taking this risk?" See chapter 12 for detailed information on preparing policies, procedures, and guidelines for both incident prevention and incident-response situations.

## Integrating Staff and Site Assessment Information

Accurate staff assessment and site assessment is essential in outdoor programs. Outdoor program administrators must be sufficiently knowledgeable of the site being used for both water and land programming. This means that program administrators need to schedule enough time to periodically be in the field scouting programs. Additionally, as mentioned in chapter 1, avoiding competency creep is important for the outdoor program administrator to effectively maintain accurate site assessments. For more information on location and site assessments, see chapters 19 and 20.

Staff assessment and evaluation systems are viewed as opportunities to improve program services and assist in the employee's growth and development. Site assessments and staff assessment may often occur simultaneously as part of a staff-development program. Coupling sites with appropriately trained and developed staff is an essential risk-management component. See chapter 15 for information on staff-assessment techniques.

## Choose Risk-Management Strategies

Identifying the acceptable level of risk exposure for an organization, a given department, a specific trip, or a specific program is the next step to be taken by outdoor program administrators. Identifying risk can be an extremely slippery slope, and striking a balance between probability and severity associated with each risk factor is essential. Upon integrating and assessing the significance and likelihood of strategic, financial, operational, or field risks, they must be prioritized and managed. According to Van der Smissen (1990), four strategies to manage risk are *risk elimination, risk transfer, risk retention,* and *risk reduction.* Outdoor program administrators commonly use all four strategies to manage risk.

### Risk Elimination

Risk elimination is the complete removal of the risk from the organization. A program must choose to either offer or to discontinue offering an activity because the risk associated with it is not acceptable as determined by the program mission and vision, or not manageable because of a lack of resources. A few (not all) factors to consider when focusing on risk elimination are staff competence, equipment available, likelihood and severity of an incident, and trip purpose (e.g., traverse a horizontal cave or learn to do free rappels in a vertical cave). An outdoor program that has historically offered extensive caving programs but experiences a string of minor incidents that could have been major accidents must make a decision on whether to continue or discontinue the program. Canceling the caving program would be an example of risk elimination.

### Risk Transfer

Risk transfer is the process through which a person, organization, or entity may choose to transfer all or partial responsibility for the risk to another party. For example, an organization that chooses to stop offering its caving program internally might elect to outsource the facilitation of the program to a commercial guide service. Contracting with a third party provider is a means of contractually transferring a portion of the risk away from the outdoor program and onto another entity. Another common technique is to transfer risk to participants by informing them of the many risks associated with the activity and having them sign an assumption-of-risk document. Assumption-of-risk documents are written documents that express the risk present in the activity, and details the responsibilities of the participant. After reading the document in depth, participants may choose to agree to the contents and sign the agreement. Administrators and staff must ensure that the risk is actually understood by participants, which is achieved through effective participant education and accurate trip materials.

### Risk Retention

Risk retention means that the risk of loss is acceptable or manageable. The risk is deemed acceptable or manageable if the loss will not significantly impact the organization. If risks associated with the caving program, for example, were deemed manageable, the outdoor organization might elect to continue offering its caving programs. Other examples of risk retention include sending a customer away unhappy and risking a negative customer evaluation because of a need to support a staff decision, and to directly pay for repairs on a vehicle hit by a company car to avoid further financial risk through an insurance claim.

### Risk Reduction

Actively taking steps to reduce risks associated with a particular activity is risk reduction. Caving operations could continue to be internally managed and offered if the outdoor organization elected to increase staff training and assessment, reviewed and updated the design and progression of its caving trips, refined the caving curriculum, and more effectively informed participants of associated risks during pretrip meetings.

## Monitor, Review, and Update

Risk-management plans should clearly address ambiguity, and should account for human differences. Administrators should recognize that the more minds involved in designing and implementing a risk-management plan, the better, and that risk-management plans vary significantly based on the contextual variations of outdoor programming. The collective organization will create effective standards and expectations if the culture has been developed effectively. Open communication channels that engage all stakeholders within the organization can ensure this process, which leads to clarity of vision and actionable purpose for all involved. Administrators should tread cautiously when requesting assistance in developing a culture among constituents and be prepared to mediate differences and potentially accept outcomes that meet the organization's needs and might not be in alignment with the administrator's personal vision.

A risk-management plan is a living document, and the outdoor program administrator is charged with maintaining its health. Living documents are evolutionary in nature and should improve over time. This allows risk-management plans to be responsive to new developments, changes, and required adaptations. In essence, it is incumbent on outdoor program administrators to take responsibility for understanding the specialized contents identified in this book. Armed with this knowledge, administrators should strive to effectively allocate resources to maximize program safety and improve program value.

## SUMMARY

The outdoor program administrator serves as a specialized risk manager responsible for protecting resources and mitigating loss. As a result of the complexities of being a risk manager, making the shift from a field instructor to an administrator can be a daunting task. At a minimum, the outdoor program administrator should understand the systemic nature of risk management and recognize its application to all facets of the field. Because risk-management plans are living documents, adequate time and resources should be dedicated to creating risk-management plans that are customized to the program's unique needs. The four areas of administrative risk management are strategic risks, financial risks, operational risks, and field risks. The outdoor program administrator must identify and understand risks in all areas and develop policies and procedures that support the organization's risk-management plan. As in a pyramid, instability problems at the top are often indicative of foundational problems; thus the outdoor program administrator should periodically review and reassess the risks existing at all levels and act appropriately to mitigate the potential for loss.

# Chapter 6

# Designing and Developing Outdoor Recreation and Education Programs

*Todd Miner, EdD, and Heidi Erpelding-Welch, MS*

Outdoor program administrators constantly hear about the value of preparation and planning in many aspects of outdoor recreation. The first principle from the Leave No Trace Center for Environmental Ethics is "Plan ahead and prepare." The Boy Scouts of America go by the motto "Be Prepared." And you might have heard of the seven Ps of preparation: Prior proper preparation prevents pathetically poor performance. Preparation is important.

Outdoor program administrators are often consumed with day-to-day operations and stomping out reactionary brush fires. The pressure and desire to get participants out into the field can sometimes push the important practice of administrative preparation to the sidelines. Without taking the necessary steps to prepare the organization, the programs provided might not actually serve the purpose intended. In this chapter we describe the crucial organizational preparation that needs to occur to design and develop outdoor recreation and education programs for long-term success.

## VISION

No matter how long an organization has existed, a strong, compelling vision is a critical component for success. A *vision statement* inspires one toward a future organizational state or goal. It paints a picture of higher planes, a better future world. This statement often implicitly suggests an organization's values, as opposed to simply an economic bottom line.

A mission statement describes what an organization does; a vision statement describes the significance of that work, the difference the work makes, or ultimate possibilities. A mission statement is safe; a vision statement is daring. A vision statement takes a leader and an organization out of the comfort zone and deep into the learning zone.

An excellent example of a compelling vision is NASA's statement from the early 1960s: "A man on the moon this decade." The message is simple and engaging; it captures the imagination. At the time, when President Kennedy made the declaration and NASA adopted it, no one knew if it was truly possible, but that was beside the point—the vision of that huge step for humanity inspired a massive governmental bureaucracy and a whole generation.

A vision statement is generally not a measuring stick. When Microsoft said, "A PC in every home running Microsoft software," there was no need for employees of the company to try to determine how close they had come to achieving this goal; rather, the vision inspired them to create one of the world's biggest and most successful corporations.

Bringing the example home to the outdoor recreation and education world, Cornell Outdoor

Education (COE), as part of its 2008–2012 strategic plan, developed a vision of expanding its programming to "touch every Cornell student." With 13,000 undergraduates, the program's administration didn't expect that every single student would participate; 80 or 90 percent was probably much more realistic. But how motivating is the statement "COE will serve 85 percent of its undergraduates?"

COE's administrators weren't even sure how they'd know if they were successful in touching every student. What they did believe was that the vision would help point the organization in the right direction and would inspire staff and donors.

The important part of a vision statement is not how realistic it is but how inspiring it is. As Michelangelo said, "The greatest danger for most of us is not that our aim is too high and we miss it, but that it is too low and we reach it." A good vision statement helps set the aim high for everyone in an organization.

Vision statements can be inward or outward directed. Inward-directed vision statements are aimed at staff or other program personnel. Cornell Outdoor Education and Microsoft's vision statements were written to motivate staff and board members—they don't mean a lot to the public, participants, or customers.

Outward-directed vision statements are usually written in terms of a better world. Nonprofits often go this route, as their ultimate purpose is the public good. An example is that of a food pantry with the vision, "A world (city, county, region, etc.) without hunger."

When developing a vision statement, it would be wonderful if the statement were simply organically developed, to be embraced by all. But that seldom happens. The reality is that a truly compelling vision statement takes some work. It might not be romantic to sit down and explicitly put into words a vision statement, but it is critical to do so. And lest it feels that an intentional development of a good vision statement is too "corporate," remember that one is likely tapping into latent dreams that already exist but have yet to be fully fleshed out and written up. The effort isn't in making up something new so much as in articulating existing yet unarticulated dreams.

To get to that compelling vision statement, consider taking the following steps:

1. Decide whether an internally or externally directed vision statement is best.
2. Based on your decision, gather appropriate constituencies (if internal, probably just staff; if external, a broader base including participants and members of the larger public is probably called for).
3. Brainstorm a perfect world—"If we could wave our magic wand, our program would _____" or "Students [participants] in our program would _____." As with any brainstorming, don't worry about practicalities, and don't let negatives into the conversation—just let it flow.
4. Refine, using vivid language, action verbs, inspiring text. Put the statement in human terms, emotions, and values.
5. Develop several competing statements; write them up for all to see and toss them around for a period of time. See what sticks and what doesn't.
6. Choose one statement and use it . . . until a new dream is needed.

A vision statement only works if it is used. A perfectly crafted vision, if not truly embraced and commonly used, simply gathers dust. Many vision statements are timeless ("a world without hunger"); others might need review and ultimately retirement as new visions and dreams develop. Particularly in this increasingly fast-changing world, vision statements might need regular updates.

A vision statement provides an inspiring picture of a better, even perfect, world. The statement is a tool to help an organization aspire to that higher future state. If your organization doesn't have a vision statement, now is the time to create one. As the past president of Notre Dame, Theodore Hesburgh, put it, "The very essence of leadership is [that] you have a vision. It's got to be a vision you articulate clearly and forcefully on every occasion. You can't blow an uncertain trumpet."

## MISSION STATEMENT

A vision statement points an organization in the right direction; it provides a target or idealized future state. But a vision statement says little about an organization's purpose, what it does, or who it serves. Without a clear definition of who and what an organization is today, it will have trouble realizing that idealized future. A *mission statement* provides the succinct definition of an organization's purpose. It clearly states the raison d'être for the organization and its charge.

Tom O'Rourke, Executive Director of the Charleston County Park and Recreation Commission, says of his organization's mission statement, "It focuses our minds. It is the second slide of every PowerPoint presentation I make. It explains why we get up in the morning and what we stand for" (O'Rourke, personal communication, March 26, 2010).

Before effective plans can be made for the future of an organization, a program needs to decide the purpose and the immediate direction of the program. It needs to know where it is before it can move forward. To start this process, the program must have a clear vision of how it hopes to serve and change the world. Beyond that, a successful program should have an understanding of the populations served and the wishes of those populations—a needs assessment. Once armed with this information, a mission statement can then be developed.

## Needs Assessment

To ascertain a populations' needs, a needs assessment might be necessary. A needs assessment is just as it sounds—a study used to project the programmatic requirements of the populations the organization serves or hopes to serve. A needs assessment is a very fluid concept. Often, the information desired from a needs assessment is specific to a particular program.

The first step in creating a needs assessment is determining what data to collect. At this point in the process, program administrators should get together to discuss what is already known about the populations the organization will serve and the programs available to those populations. New programs might need to get a general idea of the desires of an entire community. Programs that have been in existence may use a needs assessment to identify the needs of specific populations or to find gaps in programs already being offered. Each of these topics can be covered in a needs assessment.

When creating a needs assessment, be realistic with the options provided in the survey. If it is not feasible to offer a specific service, do not list it as an option in a needs assessment. The content of the assessment should be focused on finding needs that match the strengths and abilities of the organization.

The assessment should be short and to the point. As with any type of survey or study, participants will not spend a lot of time answering questions. It is better to keep questions to a minimum and focus on the information the organization really needs to know. Incentives for participation in the survey, such as drawings for an iPod or a certificate for future programs or services, might prove helpful as well.

If a program is a part of a larger organization, other departments within the institution might have already explored different methods of performing a needs assessment. Larger institutions might have offices of institutional research that can be of assistance. It is probably worthwhile to at least check in with colleagues to see if they have ideas on efficiently reaching the identified populations.

Once a vision statement and a needs assessment have been completed, it is time to tackle writing a mission statement for the program. As mentioned, a mission statement is a declaration of an organization's current purpose. It might be the single most important document of a program because it defines the program's purpose for being.

Writing a mission statement can be a challenging but rewarding process. Condensing everything an organization does into one or two well-worded sentences can take time and a lot of buy-in from everyone involved.

## Necessary Components

For a mission statement to be successful, it must contain at least the following three components: what the program does, how it does it, and the populations the program serves. Take a look at the mission statement of Outward Bound:

The mission of Outward Bound "is to inspire character development and self-discovery in people of all ages and walks of life through challenge and adventure, and to impel them to achieve more than they ever thought possible, to show compassion for others and to actively engage in creating a better world." This statement can be broken down into the three components of a successful mission statement.

- *What does the program do?* Outward Bound inspires character development and self-discovery. It impels participants to achieve more than they ever thought possible, to show compassion for others, and to actively engage in creating a better world.
- *How does it do it?* It does it through challenge and adventure.
- *What population does it serve?* It serves people of all ages and walks of life.

Every word in Outward Bound's mission statement serves a purpose and answers the questions needed to define an organization. The statement is clear and concise and contains no fluff. Now let's look at a mission statement lacking these attributes:

*"The department of athletics provides the students, faculty, staff, alumni, and community of Nowhere University with the opportunity to participate in physical, outdoor recreation, club sports, intramurals, individual exercise, and intercollegiate athletic teams that support the overall health and well-being of those individuals.*

*Nowhere University strives to provide opportunities for experiential learning, competition, and leadership development that instill a commitment to lifelong pursuits of healthy living focused on the physical, emotional, character development of the individual. We cultivate the values of discipline, character, teamwork, and sportsmanship within individual participants.*

*The department of athletics recognizes its role in promoting school and community pride within the university and local community. The department uses this role to draw support for the university by maintaining and showcasing the high standards of Nowhere University."*

*What does the program do?* It does a lot. This mission statement fails to identify the core function of its division. This mission statement clearly identifies every type of outcome that might come from participating in any of the programs available within

the department. The mission would have been more successful if it focused on the overall objective of the department and allowed each of its programs to write a mission statement that defines the purpose of that program.

*How does it do it?* In a whole bunch of ways. Although it is important to make sure that all programs within a department are represented in a mission statement, there are many other inclusion methods beyond naming each program. This statement would be more successful if it focused on the common ground among all programs.

*What population does it serve?* According to the mission statement, this organization has every population known to man as its core population served. One could argue that in a university setting it is doubtful that all of the populations mentioned belong in the mission statement. The mission statement is an opportunity to truly focus energy on the population the department is intended to serve. Many outdoor recreation programs use alumni or community members to offset the cost for students. If other populations are served in the process of serving the core population, that's great, but it does not belong in the mission statement.

Though this mission statement clearly defines every population that may be touched by this organization and plainly describes what it does and how it does it, it does not provide a focused or concise vision of the organization. It would be difficult for anyone to use this mission statement as a constant reminder of purpose.

## Writing a Mission Statement

Before undertaking the task of writing or reviewing a mission statement, gather as many relevant perspectives as possible. Administrators, staff, volunteers, board members, and individuals from within the community served should all be involved in the process. A mission statement will have a lasting impact on the organization it represents. It is essential that stakeholders of the organization support the final product of this process.

When creating a mission statement, remember that the statement serves to define the current purpose of the organization. It is important to keep the mission statement as a working document and to revisit the statement often. The mission of an organization might change as goals are accomplished, trends change, or even when staff members with specific skills and interests depart (Drucker, 1990). An organization will falter if it fails to adapt its mission to its strengths and the needs of its supporters.

The mission statement should serve as a constant reminder of what is important to the various stakeholders of the organization. It should be a statement that individuals can return to when making decisions on whether or not to take on new initiatives (Carver, 1997).

A quality mission statement will not double as a slogan, tagline, or motto. Instead, a quality mission statement consists of real language that anyone can understand and should be devoid of fluff. If an organization's mission statement refers to the roots of a tree (unless the organization is an arborist company) or planting a seed of any kind (unless the organization is a gardening program), it will not serve the purpose it intends (Carver, 1997).

A well-written mission statement has the potential to provide clarity to staff members and to motivate and excite potential participants and stakeholders. The time and effort spent in writing a quality mission statement will be appreciated when the organization is able to move forward with a clear idea of purpose.

# STRATEGIC PLAN

It is assumed that outdoor recreation programs don't want to be like Alice in Wonderland—they *do* care where they are going, they *do* care about their future. A strategic plan helps an organization to better serve its participants by proactively charting its near future and specifying that destination. It also can serve as a rallying point or motivator internally to the outdoor program and a tool for recruiting support from outside the program. In this section we look at Drucker's model of strategic planning, the critical role of customers or participants, the product or services delivered, and, finally, the process of putting together a strategic plan.

## Drucker's Model

There are many different approaches and models for strategic planning. The noted management consultant and writer Peter Drucker (1999) recommends

asking the following four questions as part of any strategic assessment or plan:

- What is the mission?
- Who is the customer?
- What does the customer value?
- What are the results?

## What Is the Mission?

Fundamentally, the strategic plan must be based on and tied directly to an organization's mission. Questions about directions, priorities, or strategies all should be viewed through the lens of the program mission.

In addition to the outdoor program's mission, the mission of the larger institution (if any) should be considered and integrated into the plan. And if the larger institution has a strategic plan, the outdoor program's plan should probably closely support or relate to it. This is particularly true if additional or outside support for the program's plan will be sought.

## Who Is the Customer?

The question of who is the customer gets a little more complicated. Sure, the customer is an organization's participants, but it shouldn't stop there. If the organization has students, what about the students' parents? If the organization is part of a larger organization (a city or county government, a military base, a university or school district), what about that larger organization's upper administrators? Does the outdoor program serve them in some way, too? How about the greater community? Does the organization, or should it, serve them and thus see them as a customer? What about other units in a larger organization? Are they sometimes customers? Really stretching things, should staff members be considered customers?

A similar concept, one that might be a bit more palatable to those working in the nonprofit world, is stakeholders. Stakeholders are groups that have a vested interest in the organizations' success. They can be students, a board of directors, community members, staff, alumni, taxpayers, or others.

For example, for a Morale, Welfare, and Recreation (MWR) program on a military base, the primary "customers" are the men and women in uniform. But their families are also stakeholders.

Mat Erpelding

On a field-based program, customers and stakeholders include the participants, staff, organization, and those affiliated with these individuals and entities.

Other stakeholders are the base's brass as well as the program's staff—the people who deliver the outdoor activities.

For a private guide service, it seems clear that the primary customers are the clients who pay the bills. But there are other groups that have an interest in and influence on the company, including guides, local land agencies and their managers, and community members.

At Cornell Outdoor Education, the primary customers or stakeholders are undergraduate students, but there are also graduate students and the parents of students. There are participants who take classes who are university staff members, alumni, and folks from the community. Customers are sometimes advisory board members, and they are definitely important stakeholders. Other units across campus who are served are also stakeholders, as are local community groups.

Considering who the customers are, or who the prime customer is, has important practical ramifications. Looking at many collegiate outdoor programs, there is an important distinction to be made. Is the focus on the general student body or on the student staff who lead most of the programs? This distinction can be critical to such questions as the amount of resources that are put toward train-

ing staff as compared to the resources put directly toward programming.

## What Does the Customer Value?

The question of what customers value is even more complicated than who the customer is. How can it be determined what customers value? A needs assessment might provide a partial answer, but a strong program will recognize that it needs to consistently hear from the customer on an ongoing basis.

Surveys are commonly used to assess customers' wants and have a number of advantages. When they are distributed to participants either immediately before or after a program they tend to be simple to administer and cost effective, they provide immediate feedback, and response rate is strong. Surveys can also be easily posted on the web on sites such as Survey Monkey, though response rates tend to be low.

Other ways of determining customer values are through focus groups, interviews of key stakeholders, and public meetings. These methods tend to be time consuming, expensive, and can take a certain amount of expertise. However, these more in-depth methods can provide a richer and more robust response than a simple survey.

When asking questions, it is important to be objective to avoid skewing results toward a preferred or assumed outcome. It is also critical to ask open-ended questions that invite customers to provide information on what they value that might not be derived otherwise.

## What Are the Results?

In answering this final question, it is important to distinguish between means and ends. The means may be backpacking trips, leader trainings, expeditions, rentals, first-aid classes, and so on, but the ends are probably quite a bit deeper. For instance, at Cornell Outdoor Education, the mission statement is "Teamwork, leadership, and growth through outdoor experience." The means are outdoor experiences, but the ends—the real results that are sought—are teamwork, leadership, and growth. The university and its funders view leadership and teamwork as important values, whereas support for mere adventure and the outdoors will likely be limited.

Interestingly, the results listed might not be what most participants want. Many undergraduates participate in outdoor programs not for personal growth but for the thrills and spills. Program administrators have added the leadership or teamwork or personal growth component not because the participant necessarily believes in these lofty goals but because *they* believe in them. (Of course other "customers" such as parents, upper administration, and society also value these results, so it is not a black and white issue.)

To best determine its bottom-line results (ends) the Charleston County Park and Recreation Commission, one of the leading park districts in the country, sat down all 163 of its employees with one sheet of paper and one question: "What do you do to improve the quality of life in Charleston County?" An employee focus group then took the responses and distilled them into several synthesized one-word value statements that remain important tools to the organization's leadership (O'Rourke, personal communication, March 26, 2010).

Focusing on the correct bottom-line results is crucial as that is likely how an organization will ultimately define the strategic plan and evaluate its progress toward implementing it. Although it is important to know basic rental program statistics (such as how many stoves were rented), perhaps a better measure is how many leaders were trained, or how many clients describe participation in the outdoor program as an important part of their community experience, or how many fewer referrals there were to the mental health clinic.

## Process and Task

President Dwight Eisenhower has been quoted as saying, "Plans are worthless. Planning is essential." There might be some hyperbole in this statement, but the point is that the process is as important as the task. Simply going through the process of planning can be very beneficial all by itself.

In terms of process, a comprehensive strategic plan takes a certain amount of planning. Perhaps the first consideration is the time period to be covered. Most strategic plans cover a time period of several years. There are also annual strategic plans. In our rapidly changing world, reaching much beyond five years is not recommended because many unknowns will be impacting the external environment.

A fundamental consideration is whether the process will be facilitated by others or led in house. Involving a professional facilitator experienced in strategic planning can be a smart investment, considering that this plan will guide the organization for years to come. However, such services do not come cheap. If there are internal resources, these should definitely be investigated. Even a preliminary meeting with a professional could help provide direction.

The next question to ask in terms of the process of writing a strategic plan is who will be involved. This question is important even for a small outdoor or adventure program with one or two staff members. Are students or clients included? If so, how many and which ones? Are other staff from the larger institution involved? Perhaps the program's supervisor or a member of upper administration? What about including outsiders for an objective perspective? Whatever criteria for membership are decided on, broad and diverse perspectives should be represented.

In terms of how many participants should be involved in writing the plan, there is no ideal number. A half dozen to a dozen participants allows, at the lower end, a minimum of diversity and, at the upper end, nearing a maximum number provides for good dialogue and participation by all. That participation, particularly for larger numbers, can be enhanced by the use of subcommittees. This can make for more efficient operations at the same time.

Writing a comprehensive, multiyear, strategic plan is time consuming. It took Cornell Outdoor Education over a year and a half to write its most recent strategic plan (Cornell Outdoor Education, 2008). It doesn't have to take that long, but it is probably wise to allocate at least a year.

## Organizational Analysis Tools

Many tools or techniques are helpful in assessing a program's situation and near future. One of the most popular is SWOT, which stands for **s**trengths, **w**eaknesses, **o**pportunities, and **t**hreats, developed by Albert Humphrey. Appreciative inquiry is a technique that focuses on what an organization is doing right and building from there (Cooperrider et al., 2008). Another technique for analyzing an organization is PEST, which stands for **p**olitical, **e**conomic, **s**ocial, and **t**echnological (Aguilar, 2006).

These tools can be helpful in giving a team developing a strategic plan a different view of the organization. There still remains the hard work of taking the findings and using them to develop goals and objectives of an organization's strategic plan.

## Format

In terms of a strategic plan format, there is no sense in reinventing the wheel. We recommend that a number of other units' strategic plans be reviewed and a favored format used, or that a blended format be adapted from several favored versions.

When Cornell Outdoor Education wrote its most recent strategic plan, three different formats for three different audiences were developed. A basic one-page version was developed for shorthand use and to post on staff members' desks. A second glossy version was drafted for upper administration, fund-raising, and outside audiences. A third very detailed version went into great detail in terms of implementation. This version included a table indicating measurable outcomes, the responsible party, needed resources, and notes. This version was designed for staff use and for evaluating progress in implementation.

No matter the format, a detailed strategic plan document is most likely going to include the following information:

- Title page with dates
- Program mission
- Executive summary
- Goals (general)
- Objectives (specific, measurable outcomes, listed as subtopics of goals)

In terms of numbers of goals, it is likely that less is more. Having three to five main goals as opposed to a dozen is more realistic and will focus the work. Goals must be achievable. A vision statement is for those lofty, perhaps unattainable dreams. Keep strategic plan goals doable so that the plan becomes an affirmation for the program.

## Implementation

Too many strategic plans, once written, promptly go onto a shelf to lay ignored and gather dust. As management guru Peter Drucker has said, "Plans are only good intentions unless they immediately degenerate into hard work."

There are many strategies to ensure that a strategic plan is used and followed. To begin, print a number of one-page summaries and post them on everyone's bulletin board or wall. Make strategic plan check-ins a normal part of staff meetings. Individual staff members should have their annual goals tied to the strategic plan. The strategic plan goals for which individual staff members are responsible should be a significant part of their annual evaluation. Another strategy to make the plan more likely to be put to use is to post the plan on the organization's website. Public proclamation holds a program accountable.

Over 2,000 years ago, at a time when the world was changing at a far slower rate, Roman poet Publilius Syrus wrote, "It's a bad plan that admits of no modification." Today, in a world that is changing at a dizzying rate, changes that couldn't be foreseen at the time of writing are going to significantly impact the plan. A strategic plan is not written in stone; be ready to adapt it, letting go of goals that are no longer relevant or practical and adding ones that become so.

Writing a strategic plan is a lot of work; for administrators who have never done one before, the task can be intimidating. However, the payoffs in terms of focusing energy and resources and gaining alignment are well worth the effort. A leader or organization should not get hung up on developing a perfect process or plan, especially when doing it for the first time. General George Patton once advised, "A good plan today is better than a perfect plan tomorrow." Get started, develop a plan, and put it to work.

# SUSTAINABILITY

Most outdoor professionals want to make a lasting positive impact on the world. They want to create or be part of something bigger than themselves that outlasts their brief time tilting with windmills. The key is to think like an environmentalist and think *sustainability*. Sustainability means thinking for the long haul. It means building a strong foundation to ensure viability in a world that is changing at an ever and ever faster rate. This is no easy feat. Sustainability, for our purposes in this chapter, includes becoming mission central, building relationships, developing multiple revenue streams, nurturing advisory boards, and writing grants.

## Mission Central

Many outdoor programs complain of lack of support from their larger organization. Part of the problem is that the programs are perceived as being too risky, or that benefits are not substantiated, or that they are seen as simply being frivolous. However, the real reason is more likely that outdoor adventure programs are not seen as central to the larger organization's mission (Miner, 1993).

Outdoor and adventure programs must remember the core mission of the larger institution and keep that central in their planning and operations. More specifically, successful programs determine which challenges the institution or larger unit is facing, and how they can be part of the solution. To modify Kennedy's famous challenge: "Ask not what the institution can do for your program, but what your program can do for the institution." In other words, in the long run, to be most successful, and ultimately sustainable, a program must be counterintuitive and do the opposite: Don't expect the institution to support the program; rather, figure out how the program can support the institution. Once the program is perceived by the institution's power brokers to be reinforcing the needs of the institution, the support will start to flow.

At many institutions of higher education, student retention is a huge (and expensive) issue. Many outdoor programs at these schools have started wilderness orientation programs to help students adapt to collegiate life. These programs assist students in making the crucial transition, and in doing so they increase retention.

In sum, there are two questions to ask: (1) What keeps the dean and vice president (or other administrators) up at night? (2) How can the program help them sleep better? Answer these questions, and a program will move closer to mission central. Move closer to that central mission, and the program will much more likely be supported and sustained in the long run.

## Collaboration

When it comes to teaching or leading students and participants, outdoor programs emphasize teamwork and collaboration. Given today's competitive and fast-changing world it is high time outdoor programs took some of their own medicine. Not only does teamwork and collaboration need to be practiced in the woods and waters, it must be practiced in the organizational and business environment. Teamwork, even at the organizational level, is the name of the game for programs seeking to sustain and potentially extend their influence within their organization and the communities in which they reside.

The days of going it alone are gone. Such a mentality isolates outdoor programs from the power and influence their greater community can have on the success of the program. Outdoor recreation programs need to build and maintain relationships with a variety of players and units inside and outside of their organization. Be it for program support, grant writing, or new program development, partnerships are key to program viability. Eventually long-term or strong partners grow into allies, which means more support across the institution.

## Internal Collaboration

Collaboration builds understanding. When we work with other programs they see the power in our work, and we can get beyond the stereotype that we are just fun and games in the woods. Likewise, collaborations also provide an opportunity for outdoor program administrators to better understand our partners and their strengths, needs, and challenges. Through collaborations we can learn how others handle marketing, hiring, logistics, and so on, thereby bettering our own programs.

Collaboration can help an outdoor recreation program become sustainable by building social capital. Just like financial capital can be developed and saved, so can social capital. Social capital is the intangible good will, positive perceptions, and networking accumulated by an individual or an organization (Fields, 2003). A wise program will accumulate social capital when it can so that it can be spent when needed.

Building partnerships and social capital with the institution's infrastructure and auxiliary services is an important part of collaboration. Having good relationships with business offices, human resources, risk management, public relations, and marketing units can pay off big time in the long run because all outdoor programs need to (or should) interact with these other offices at some time.

In addition to building allies, understanding, and social capital, partnerships tend to be more efficient than going it alone. It is much more efficient to work with another unit that best knows its members and how to reach out to them and let them market and fill programs than it is to try to run an open enrollment program from the outside. Units can join forces to design, market, register, and ultimately deliver programs in a more efficient manner.

Building and maintaining collaborative relationships can be critical to effectively managing threats before they appear. For 10 academic years, the outdoor program at Boise State University offered a successful battery of wilderness orientation programs that complemented and supported the greater university's orientation goals. Because of a reorganization of the orientation programs, institutional knowledge of the collaboration between the orientation program and the outdoor program was lost, which equated to the wilderness orientation programs being initially removed from key market-ing publications. Thankfully, the outdoor program had collaborated with individuals from other preorientation programs who were able to help educate the new orientation administrators about the historic value and success of the wilderness programs. Had just one small program tried to fight the deletion, it is unlikely it would have been successful. But when directors of multiple programs advocated for the program there was strength in numbers, and the wilderness orientation programs were again highlighted in key marketing publications.

Internal collaboration is a key strategy to sustainability. It develops understanding, allies, and social capital. Successful outdoor programs are going to spend significant time serving not just their immediate participants but also a broader range of constituents across the organization.

## External Collaboration

Building partnerships outside the larger institution is also important to an outdoor recreation program's long-term viability. Outside voices can be seen as being more objective and thus carry more weight than internal ones. When support is needed, such external partners can be very helpful. Collaborations can be made with local youth groups, guiding concerns, school districts, land managers, or outdoor clubs. Through these collaborations, an outdoor program can extend the institution's resources out to the community and thus better serve the public. They also help the outdoor program to better understand its community.

External collaboration can also lead to more efficient operations. Partnerships with local youth organizations, municipal recreation programs, and university programs can yield access to additional resources and support. An example of this would be if a program negotiated a discounted rate for use on its ropes course in exchange for access to another program's canoes during peak programming time. Both programs, and the programs' participants, would potentially benefit from this relationship.

## Building the Brand

Jim Collins, a Stanford professor and now independent management consultant, has written extensively on organizational excellence and sustainability. In *Good to Great and the Social Sectors,*

Collins (2005) focuses on nonprofits and how they achieve excellence and enjoy long-term success. He describes five principles, but the one that is key to sustainability is what he calls "building the brand."

By "brand" Collins means reputation of the organization, what its name means to people. He suggests that the amount of support for an organization will follow proportionally to the success of its long-term reputation, or brand. Think about the power of certain brands in the outdoor field. NOLS, Outward Bound, Project Adventure—these organizations have been successful for many decades because they have established strong brands. Because of their strong brand they are the programs students or young instructors are referred to if they want or need more training or work experience. They are where friends and family are freely referred if they have a young person who is looking for adventure.

An outdoor program that wishes to go from good to great wants to build its brand. According to Collins, the key to doing so involves, first, demonstrating results. Collins suggests demonstrating success by a relentless focus on key metrics. Considering the concept of collaboration, these key metrics should be important not only to the outdoor program but to the larger institution as well. This doesn't happen quickly. However, year after year of demonstrating success on these key metrics will begin to build

reputation, and momentum develops. Assuming that these successes are leading to participants' valuable and positive experiences and even changed lives, the organization begins to build an emotional connection with participants, key stakeholders, and the community. This strong reputation, turning into an emotional connection, evolves into a brand that transcends a particular service or program or year—it becomes attached to the outdoor organization.

The resulting brand, with its strong reputation and emotional attachment, attracts support. People, be they upper administration, donors, funders, or participants, want to support success and winners. Success breeds success and moves an organization toward long-term sustainability.

## Advisory Boards

Advisory Boards have many advantages in terms of building a sustainable outdoor or adventure program. These primarily include developing allies, new revenue streams, and getting advice.

Miner (2003) has described a different kind of advisory board that he claims is more beneficial than the traditional version. This "triple C" approach focuses on clout, cash, and counsel. Traditionally, outdoor program advisory boards have consisted of fellow expert outdoors folks such as guides,

By providing participants with valuable and positive experiences, an organization begins to build a strong reputation with those participants, which eventually evolves into a brand for the organization.

wilderness medicine experts, park management, or other outdoor program professionals. In general, outdoor recreation programs are run by competent professionals who possess strong outdoor skills; thus an advisory board can fulfill a more valuable need by bringing clout, cash, and counsel to the table. To stay focused on its charge, the "triple C" board purposefully elects to ignore outdoor professionals and focuses its energy on those who can help with political influence, financial gifts, and business or organizational advice.

By "political influence" we mean not the mainstream or even local political arena but the politics at the institution's core. This might include trustees or regents, influential alumni, local movers and shakers, big-time donors, maybe even a top administrator. In addition to simple raw firepower, it is ideal if the program can recruit a diversity of those with influence so that a wide array of political clout can be applied.

Resources, be they human, financial, or physical, ultimately equate to money for an outdoor program, and advisory boards can help obtain these resources. Cornell Outdoor Education has maintained an effective advisory board for the past two decades. Though both unique and ambitious, the program is upfront about its financial expectations for board members. Individuals serving on the advisory board are responsible for either personally donating or raising $3,500 a year for the program. Though this model might not work for every outdoor program; the idea behind the model is sound because it can provide a program with a whole new revenue stream that's independent of the rest of the institution and its funding. Be it money, time, expertise, or labor that you seek from advisory board members, the expectations and corresponding commitment you seek should be upfront and transparent so you can engage them for the long run.

The final benefit a triple C board member makes is in terms of business or organizational advice. Board members can provide outdoor program administrators with financial savvy, knowledge of the inner machinations of higher education or governmental bureaucracies. Thus a board stocked with business leaders can be extremely helpful in developing strategy, marketing, business plans, and so on.

There are a few tricks to identifying and recruiting top-notch advisory board members. By far the most effective method for schools and colleges is to work closely with an alumni office. This office often controls access to key alumni, so getting them involved is crucial. One way to get the alumni office involved is to volunteer to do programs for visiting alumni VIPs. This also exposes the program to alumni who are preselected (by the alumni office) to enjoy outdoor adventures. Running alumni invitational adventure trips is a great way both to reward standing members and to recruit new ones.

For organizations such as guiding companies, parks and recreation agencies, and MWR programs, a little more ingenuity might be needed to recruit politically savvy advisory board members. The first people to look at are former participants (alumni) of the program. Which recent or loyal participants had an amazing experience *and* have influence, strong networks, and positions of power? Local chambers of commerce, convention and visitor bureaus, or fraternal organizations (Kiwanis, Rotary, etc.) can also be fertile ground for connecting with and recruiting effective advisory board members.

Of course advisory boards are not without their downsides. Recruiting board members can be expensive because the process likely involves human, fiscal, and physical resources. Once an advisory board has been secured, efforts will be shifted toward retaining and rewarding their involvement. Outdoor program administrators must recognize that each advisory board member will give clout, cash, and counsel to an outdoor program for different reasons, so it can be difficult to meet their unique expectations and keep them all happy.

# Financial Sustainability: Multiple Revenue Streams

In the long run, sustainability depends on firm political support and a robust economic base. In the preceding sections we have discussed political support; we now turn to the importance of finances to sustainability.

Few programs are blessed with one strong and unwavering stream of revenue. When this does occur, it generally is a direct appropriation from the institution, or activity fees levied on students or members, or some kind of tax base, as in MWR programs. However, such programs are becoming fewer, and they are always subject to financial disruption if that one revenue stream is blocked or even partially stemmed. Developing multiple streams provides financial insurance against such disruptions. Multiple revenue streams allows outdoor programs to prosper even when part of their income falters.

Imagine an outdoor recreation program with four revenue streams (user fees for instruction programs, team-building contracts, rentals and retail sales, and a dedicated appropriation of some sort from a parent organization—taxes, student fees, etc.). If over the years the appropriation from the parent organization either remains flat or is decreased, the program will need to rely on the other streams of revenue to manage significant growth in services. The sole reliance on an appropriation can cause a program to curtail services if it did not manage its other streams of revenue. A program with multiple revenue channels can maintain services when one is reduced because there are others to rely on. Outdoor programs become more adaptable to a changing world by not relying on any one stream of revenue.

The Charleston (SC) Parks and Recreation Commission has diversified in this way. The commission's revenue comes from an amazing variety of sources, including rentals, corporate teambuilding, campgrounds, park pass sales, a huge selection of guided adventures, a climbing wall, and special events. By taking an entrepreneurial approach, the agency has insulated itself from inevitable reductions in tax monies, the main revenue stream for most park and recreation districts (O'Rourke, personal communication, March 26, 2010).

Financial sustainability through multiple revenue streams builds trust and respect from the institution. It also develops at least some independence because not all streams flow from the larger institution. The trust and respect earned with the business offices is a kind of social capital that can be used when a new venture is planned or when times get tight.

# Writing Grants and Proposals

Generating serious funding through writing proposals is a *lot* of work. This money is not "easy" or "free" money. It means putting on paper everything—and then some—of what is floating around in one's

head. It means getting letters of support, writing budgets, and jumping through a lot of someone else's bureaucratic hoops. It means tracking and reporting of details. It might mean "paying" overhead, or a large percentage of the funding to the institution of which one is part. However, there is money out there, and there is every reason why the great work of outdoor and adventure education and recreation programs should be funded by grant or foundation sources. Whether an organization is looking to build new facilities, hoping to establish a scholarship, or starting a whole new program from scratch, new funding sources can be critical to success.

## Principles

All proposals must be tailored to the funders' requirements and purpose, but some general principles of proposal writing are always important to consider:

- Set aside plenty of time to research, gather documentation, recruit letters of support, and write the proposal.
- Clearly define the need or the problem being addressed in the proposal.
- Clearly describe how the funding will address or solve the problem or need.
- Ensure that there is a good match between the funding organization and with the need or problem, as well as with the request.
- Write well, using clear, concise language. Use active verbs that jump out and grab attention. Be rational, logical, and factual.
- Set a hook. Why is this need so critical? Why is the solution so unique? Write so that this funder will find the idea irresistible. Write creatively, painting a picture of a better world that will come about only through this proposal's funding.
- Ensure that all of the funding organization's guidelines and requirements including forms, format, deadlines, attachments, and so on are exactly followed.
- Don't be discouraged by rejection. Get feedback and incorporate it into the next round or version of the proposal.

## Parts of a Proposal

Every funding source will have its own list of requirements, but again, there are some general parts that will be common to most, if not all, of them. Also, if seeking funding from an internal (to one's organization) source, or a private individual, there might not be a form; the following can be a good outline to follow in these open-ended cases.

>> **Executive summary.** This three- to five-sentence synopsis provides a big picture overview of the request. Narrowing a proposal to a couple of sentences is hard but has the benefit of honing in one's thinking and the "ask." This synopsis must be clearly, even eloquently, written to lure the funding organization into reading further.

>> **Problem or need statement.** This is where the need or problem is laid out in clear yet concise language, demonstrating the significance (both depth and breadth) of this issue. Be sure to specify who is going to be served. Use quantifiable data from reputable sources. If possible, paint a picture from a human interest perspective (tell a story). Keep in mind that an absence of the solution is not the problem or need. The problem is not that there isn't a climbing wall; the problem is that students are becoming obese, they are getting involved in socially unacceptable forms of risk taking, they are climbing on the library walls.

>> **Goals of the funding.** What difference will there be after the funding and the program or project? How will the problem or need be solved? What are the impacts and the outcomes, in measurable terms?

>> **Methods.** How will the goals be achieved? What programming, building, services, and so on will be offered? Use language that a lay person (or one's mother) would understand. Avoid jargon or technical terms that we easily throw around, such as carabiner, bouldering mat, belayer, and the like. Quantify whenever possible. Provide a timeline.

>> **Evaluation.** In what ways will progress and goal achievement be demonstrated? What metrics will be used? When will evaluation(s) take place?

>> **Budget.** How will the money be spent? Provide a detailed accounting of proposed expenditures, as well as revenue sources beyond what is being requested in the proposal. How will the program, service, or facility continue after the money being requested is spent?

>> **Organization qualifications.** Describe the organization and why it can be trusted to effectively use the funder's money. Who does the organization serve, and how does it do so? What is the organization's mission, history, values, philosophy, and track record (if any) with previous grants or gifts?

>> **Summary and conclusion.** Provide a succinct summary of the main points of the proposal: the problem, the proposed solution, the "ask," and the organization. There might also be attachments or appendices that the funder has requested.

## Sources of Funding

There are five main sources of funding for which proposals could be written. Although there are many commonalities to writing proposals to these various sources, there are also clear differences. Depending on the funding need or request, the following sources will vary in their suitability.

>> **Private foundations.** Private foundations provide the most varied source of funding, with thousands of different foundations ranging from small family foundations giving away hundreds of dollars per year to major players giving away millions each year. Some foundations will have very formal and detailed applications; others will be brief and informal. Some foundations fund fairly generic proposals, but many are fairly to very specific in their focus.

>> **Government sources.** Not surprisingly, government funding sources generally require the most lengthy and complicated forms and proposals. There are local, state, and federal grants, with by far the most funding coming at the national level.

>> **Corporations.** Many larger corporations have an associated foundation that supports nonprofit and philanthropic endeavors. These are no different than other private foundations; they are just funded largely by the for-profit corporation. Corporations can also be sources of "in kind" funding—equipment, supplies, or services that can greatly assist in meeting the organization's needs or challenges.

>> **Internal sources.** For programs that are part of a larger organization (e.g., college, university, local government, military), there is always the opportu-

nity to propose a new or expanded program. There might be competitive grants, or the proposal might be totally out of the blue. If the latter, aligning the ask with institutional or key players' priorities or strategic plans is critical to success.

>> **Private individuals.** Particularly for those in higher education, there are alumni who might be convinced of the merits of a specific project or program. A key is keeping good relations with the institution's alumni affairs office because they are usually the gatekeepers to alumni and requests for support.

See the resources listed in the References and Resources section at the back of the book.

## General Suggestions

No matter the funding source, some general principles will increase the chances of getting funding. Following these principles is no guarantee of getting funding in this very competitive world, but ignoring them certainly makes it less likely.

>> **Timing.** Writing a grant or proposal always takes far longer than one ever wants or expects. In addition to the general forms, there are letters of support, signatures, and information needed from other people and organizations. To get this external support for the grant or proposal takes considerable lead time, reminders, and sometimes outright begging or badgering. Even when a deadline for submission seems far in the future, there is often a last-minute scramble that can affect quality. The bottom line is to start early and provide plenty of cushion time wise.

>> **Know the grant or funding source.** As in any writing, a key to writing good proposals is to know your audience—in this case the funding source. What is their mission, vision, philosophy, and clientele? One of the best ways to learn about a source is to research proposals they have funded in the recent past. These are often available online; if not, they can be requested. Speaking of which, making personal contact with the grant officer or other decision maker(s) at the funding source is a very wise move.

>> **Writing assistance.** Even the best ideas or the most critical needs are not going to get funded if a grant is poorly written. At a minimum, get mul-

tiple sets of eyes to review and critique the proposal before submission. Have a colleague proofread the proposal or, if feasible, pay for professional grant-writing assistance. For units of a larger institution, particularly in higher education, there will likely be a grant writer or office that provides internal assistance.

>> **Professional grant writers.** Whatever the size of the organization, professional grant writers can provide a valuable service. Professional grant writers provide extensive experience in navigating the often arcane and complicated grant world. They know the game, including the most effective language to use and how to best leverage letters of support. Of course this expertise comes at a cost (likely much more per hour than most outdoor educators are paid!). Also, adding one more player adds time and complication to the writing process.

>> **Matching funds.** Funding sources are generally going to expect the organization or institution to put its money where its mouth is and demonstrate financial investment in the proposed project or program. Matching funds can also be sought from other funders or external organizations. Such collaborations are seen by funding sources as additional validation of the request, and thus they strengthen a proposal.

>> **Collaboration.** These days grantors are looking more and more to collaborations between organizations. Funding sources are looking for multiple organizations, each bringing in their particular strengths, to best address needs or problems. Partnering is the name of the game.

>> **Sustainability.** Funding sources want to know that their investment will continue after their funding is over. They want to know about long-term impact. Demonstrating that their initial funding is the start of long-term positive change will significantly increase the chance of funding.

>> **Evaluation.** The ability to demonstrate effective use of funding is becoming increasingly important to successful proposals. Clear outcomes and solid metrics are critical, if often challenging, to developing a strong evaluation component.

## Grant-Writing Conclusions

New projects or programs often require funding beyond current fees or budgets. Without new sources of funding, new initiatives, new responses to serious challenges, will not become reality. One of the most effective ways to find new sources is through grant or proposal writing. Such efforts involve considerable research, writing, and often collaboration, yet no guarantee of funding. However, for those willing to make the effort, the organization and clients can take giant strides forward with help of new monies. And there is only one way to find out about funding, and that's to write a proposal.

## DEALING WITH CHANGE: EVOLVE TO SURVIVE AND THRIVE

One thing is for certain—if a program is to make a long-term positive difference in students' or participants' lives, it will need to change and evolve. This doesn't mean that core values or the mission change (Collins, 2005) but that practices, tactics, and strategies, as well as services and programming, must all be adaptable.

A good example of the need to adapt in the outdoor world is programming length. As our participants' available time and attention span have dwindled, we have adapted by running shorter programs. This hasn't necessarily been good, nor has the change been easy, but programs that haven't evolved to respond to the reality of participants' time frame have suffered or not survived.

Change is coming at us at an ever-increasing pace. Be it economic, social, or political, change is exploding. In the future we are going to need to become even more adaptable. Peters (1988) suggests we need to embrace and thrive on the resulting chaos of fast-paced change. Outdoor programs that refuse to adapt and evolve will not survive. In the long run, a key to sustainability is staying true to core values and principles while riding the waves of inevitable change.

## SUMMARY

Today's economic realities require that outdoor organizations be politically astute and be run effectively and efficiently. Outdoor organizations need indoor skills. Too many outdoor programs have gone under not because their leaders lacked excellent outdoor skills but because they struggled with the indoor skills of running a complicated organization in a tough organizational environment.

The skills of developing a powerful vision, creating a strong mission statement, designing a successful strategic plan, writing a rewarding grant proposal, or building an effective advisory board are not sexy. The political skills of developing collaboration and building social capital are not easy. Such competencies aren't learned in the field, and they often are not emphasized in outdoor education curricula. However, without these skills an outdoor program is going to suffer in this storm-laden economic environment. Think of developing such organizational proficiencies as just another form of adventure. And, remember, as Helen Keller said so eloquently, "Life is either a daring adventure, or it is nothing at all."

# Chapter 7

# Legal Considerations in Outdoor Recreation

*Brent Wilson, JD, and Tracey Knutson, JD*

In this chapter we address the law and basic legal issues that affect outdoor recreation programs. Understanding the fundamental legal principles that most often influence outdoor programmers will assist leaders in analyzing and mitigating risks associated with legal liability. The reader should keep in mind, however, that the law evolves and changes over time, and may differ from state to state. Application of the law depends on the unique circumstances of each case and how the courts of a particular state construe and apply the law. Although the law may dictate a certain outcome in one case, a change in the facts or a difference in the applicable law might require an entirely different outcome in another case.

This chapter begins with a discussion of negligence and the basic legal concepts that most often affect outdoor recreation programs. Defenses against negligence and liability limiting agreements (release and waiver documents) are then addressed. The chapter closes with a discussion of insurance and the role of insurance in legal matters. To assist the reader in understanding the legal concepts discussed in this chapter, four factual scenarios from actual court cases are provided here for review. These factual scenarios will be referred to throughout the chapter to illustrate the legal principles discussed and to assist with learning the process of analyzing legal issues. Other court cases will also be discussed in the chapter to highlight or illustrate the legal concepts presented.

## Fact Scenario I

*Regents of the University of California v. Roettgen, 41 Cal.App.4th 1040, 48 Cal.Rptr.2d 922 (Cal. Ct. App. 1996).*

In this case the widow of a student who was killed during a rock-climbing class offered by the University of California at San Francisco sued the school. Prior to his fatal accident, the student had participated in several rock-climbing classes offered through the university. These classes included Introduction to Rock Climbing, Advanced Beginners, and Instructor's Training. The student had learned top-roping, belaying, and setting anchors from these classes. The student died after falling during an intermediate rock-climbing course.

The purpose of the intermediate course was to teach climbers, among other things, to place protection while climbing. On the morning of the fatal accident, the instructor and the student, who was designated as an assistant instructor, set up a top rope anchor in one crack feature. A second instructor and assistant instructor team set up a separate top rope anchor in a second crack feature. Normally, such a setup is considered safe as long as the anchors within each system are set in separate crack features. After completing the protection placing activity portion of the class, the student was belaying down the rock face on the system set up by the second instructor or assistant team when a large piece of the rock shifted, causing the anchor devices to let loose. The student fell over 90 feet to his death. The anchors installed by the second instructor or assistant instructor team were installed in one crack feature instead of separate cracks. When the rock shifted, the anchors failed.

The second instructor or assistant team had significant experience in setting anchors. They both believed that their anchor system was safe as set that morning. In fact, they had considered a different location for the second anchor system but ultimately rejected it because they determined that it was less safe and the system that they chose was better for the intermediate class climb that morning. Before the decedent's fatal fall, both the second instructor and his assistant belayed down on the system that eventually failed, as did another student who successfully completed the protection-setting exercise before the fatal fall.

## Fact Scenario II

*Murphy v. North American River Runners, Inc., 412 S.E.2d 504 (Ct. App. W.V. 1991).*

In this case, a participant was injured during a commercially guided whitewater river trip. During the trip, one of the rafts lodged on some rocks in the river. The guide in the injured participant's raft attempted to rescue the stuck raft by intentionally bumping into it with his raft. The injured participant in the rescuing boat was forcefully thrown from her raft into the river while her guide was bumping the stuck raft. The participant thrown into the river suffered serious knee and ankle injuries. According to the injured participant, the guide did not warn anyone in the raft that he was about to bump the stuck raft or that he was attempting to rescue the stuck raft. The participant sued the rafting company, claiming negligence caused her injuries.

## Fact Scenario III

*Lesser v. Camp Wildwood, 282 F.Supp.2d 139 (S.D.N.Y. 2003).*

In this case the parents of a 12-year-old boy sued the owners and operators of a private overnight camp where their son attended summer camp. The boy was injured when a tree fell on him during a thunderstorm. The boy and his fellow campers had been enjoying a July Fourth fireworks display at the camp's waterfront when a sudden thunderstorm overtook the camp. The summer camp was accredited by the American Camping Association (ACA) and licensed by the state of Maine.

As a member of the ACA, the camp was required to have procedures in place for emergency situations, including for severe weather conditions. According to the camp's procedures, a local police department was to notify the camp of forecasted severe weather. Upon notice, the campers and staff were to be brought to a part of the camp away from the water and trees and placed along the walls of the camp's gym until the severe weather passed. Only after inspection for hazards and damages were campers to be excused from the gym after a severe weather event. In the case of an unexpected storm, the camp's policy was to immediately evacuate campers from the waterfront and escort all campers to the gym. The camp also had a policy in place that required maintenance personnel to inspect trees and bushes within the camp, and to call a local arborist for service in case any problems were discovered.

On the day of the storm, the National Weather Service forecast storms in the area. It was disputed whether anyone at the camp actually checked or verified the weather forecast for the evening of the fireworks display. When the fireworks started after dark there was no wind or rain, though the sky had become overcast before the display. Soon after the fireworks began, rain started to fall, quickly intensifying. Camp counselors and staffers immediately began to shout instructions to evacuate the beachfront and seek shelter in the nearby bunks. The injured boy heard these instructions and headed to the bunks, but he became lost and confused. While searching for the bunks, the boy was struck by part of a tree that snapped at the trunk approximately 15 to 20 feet above the ground. The injured boy's parents sued the camp, alleging negligence, negligent supervision, and negligent failure to follow the camp's own policies and procedures regarding severe weather events.

## Fact Scenario IV

*Harmon v. United States, 532 F.2d 669 (9th Cir. 1975).*

In this case two people drowned while on a week-long commercially guided river rafting trip on the Middle Fork of the Salmon River in Idaho. The Middle Fork runs through four different sections of U.S. Forest service land and is congressionally designated as a wild river under the federal Wild and Scenic Rivers Act. The Middle Fork includes rapids rated from class III to class V. The float trip began in late June 1970 during a time of extraordinarily high water. Spring and early summer that year had been cooler than usual, slowing snow melt in the higher elevations. Temperatures during the first few days of the trip, however, warmed considerably, creating significant melt runoff and high water. The river's water level increased each day as the weather warmed. The river crested twice during the week. At some point, the party discussed "lining" their boats by floating them through the most dangerous sections of the river using ropes from the shore, but ultimately they decided not to line the boats. During the trip, two rafters were thrown from their boat in the middle of a particularly difficult rapid and drowned.

The survivors of one of the rafters sued the United States Forest Service, alleging the federal public land administrator was aware of the high water conditions, had a duty to inform the public of this condition, and had negligently failed to warn the rafters of the increased risks associated with high water. The lawsuit additionally alleged that the drowned rafters did not have the experience to understand the dangers involved in rafting the river at such high water levels.

## NEGLIGENCE

Discussions about the law and outdoor recreation programs focus on *negligence,* a type of legal claim, because questions about liability most often arise in the outdoor recreation setting because of accidents that cause physical injury to a participant. When this happens, the injured person may turn to the legal system to recover damages allegedly caused by the negligence of the recreation program. Negligence is a subset or type of a broader set of legal claims called torts. Outdoor recreation programmers may face various types of legal claims in the event of an accident and injury to a participant, but the overwhelming majority of legal claims against programmers involve allegations of negligence.

## LEGAL DEFINITION (ELEMENTS) OF NEGLIGENCE

Negligence is commonly thought of as carelessness. Negligence under the law is generally defined as the failure to use ordinary care—that is, failing to do what a person of ordinary prudence would have done under the same or similar circumstances. Essentially, the law looks to determine whether an operator, educator, or land administrator could or should have recognized an unreasonable risk and did nothing to warn the participant or to reduce or eliminate the unreasonable risk. To examine negligence in behavior or conduct, look to answer two questions: Was the risk foreseeable? and Was the risk unreasonable? These questions are discussed in more depth below.

Negligence has specific legal meaning and (like many legal claims) is defined by specific elements. The elements of negligence are (1) a *duty of care* owed to another person; (2) *breach* of that duty of care; (3) the breach of the duty of care was the proximate and actual *cause* of harm to the other person; and (4) the *damages* suffered by the person to whom a duty of care was owed. The shorthand negligence analysis is "duty, breach, cause, damages." These elements taken together are referred to as a "cause of action" sounding in negligence. To win a negligence claim, a complaining party must have (admissible) evidence of each of the four elements; failure to prove even one of the four elements defeats a negligence claim or cause of action.

## Element One: Duty of Care

*Duty* generally refers to one party's responsibility to take reasonable care for the protection of another party. Everyone has a general duty to act reasonably and prudently in their daily activities relative to other people. This general duty is often referred to as the "reasonable and prudent person" standard of care or the "general standard of care." Duty has three primary origins: (1) from a relationship inherent in the situation; (2) from the voluntary assumption of a duty; or (3) from a duty mandated by a statute or regulation of some sort. So, in determining the existence of a duty of care, the threshold question is whether the claimant and another person had the type of relationship that placed a duty on the first person to prevent or avoid an injury to the second person. For example, bus drivers have a client relationship with their passengers and so have a duty to act reasonably while driving and to avoid accidents. The context of the relationship creates a duty to avoid foreseeable accidents.

Once the existence of a duty has been determined, the next question involves the extent or scope of that duty of care; asked another way, what is the "standard of care" owed given the circumstances? The relationship creating a duty may arise from a legal relationship such as a contract between an outdoor recreation program and a participant, or may arise when a person's conduct creates a foreseeable risk of harm, such as a skier crossing an avalanche prone slope while other skiers are exposed below to the avalanche hazard. Although the relationship dictates the standard of care, the actual standard may vary. For example, a professional guide will have a different and higher standard of care than a lay person.

© Human Kinetics

Parties have a general legal duty to act reasonably and carefully with one another.

Consider fact scenario I. Did the instructor who set the belaying system owe a duty to the deceased student? What about the assistant instructor who helped set the system? Was there any difference in the standard of care owed by the instructor and the assistant instructor? What about the duties of the deceased climber who was also experienced and was designated as an assistant instructor that day? In fact scenario II, did the rescuing guide owe a duty to the people in his own boat before he attempted the rescue, and if so, what was that duty? As for fact scenario IV, did the Forest Service have a duty to warn the rafters of high water conditions?

## Element Two: Breach (of Standard of Care)

If circumstances suggest that one person owes a duty of care to another person, the next question in a negligence analysis is whether the person breached his or her duty by failing to exercise the necessary amount of care. Think of this as the "act or omission"—what was done or not done. For example, look at what a guide or instructor did or failed to do to protect a participant that was not in accord with what a reasonably prudent guide or instructor should do under those circumstances.

Generally, determining what a reasonable person would have done under the circumstances is establishing the "standard of care." Standards may be set by statute, ordinance or regulation, or by the profession. A standard of care will take into account who is delivering the service and what his or her level of knowledge should be—in other words, the standard will be what would be expected of a reasonable and careful person carrying out the same activity.

The standard of care for a professional person is that degree of care that is shown by a reasonably prudent practitioner operating in like or similar circumstances. So, it becomes crucial to understand established professional customs and practices in your field. And again, it is important to look at the issue of the foreseeability of the risk that was encountered. Would a reasonably prudent person have recognized an unreasonable risk of harm under the circumstances?

Consider fact scenario II. Did the commercial guide breach any duty to the participant by attempting to rescue the other raft by bumping it? Consider fact scenario I. Were any duties breached when the anchor system that should have protected the decedent failed?

## Element Three: Causation

Proof of a duty and breach of that duty constitutes negligence *if* a claimant can prove that he or she suffered damages *caused* by the breach of the duty. This is the foundation of our fault-based legal system. The idea is that the negligent person's misconduct (act or omission) must be connected to the claimant's injury. Duties are breached routinely, but the law does not allow recovery in those situations unless the breach has caused damages. Think of the tailgater who follows too closely to the car in front. Tailgating is generally unreasonable and is likely a breach of a duty to drive safely, but aside from annoying the driver in front, has the tailgater caused any real damage? The law requires proof that the breach of a duty caused some loss or damage to the claimant.

There are two types of causation, both of which must be present to prove that a breach of a duty caused damages. These two types of causation are *actual cause* (also known as *cause in fact*) and *proximate cause* (also known as *legal cause*). Actual cause asks whether the allegedly negligent person's conduct, in fact, caused the damages the complaining person alleges. If actual cause is present, then further proof of proximate cause is required. If the harm or the kind of harm caused by the negligent act was unforeseeable, then the defendant's act, in a purely legal sense, is not the proximate cause of the plaintiff's injury. In other words, proximate cause is a limitation on negligence if a negligent person's act or conduct is too far removed from the claimant's injury.

## Element Four: Damages

Even assuming that a person making a claim against a program can prove the first three elements of a negligence cause of action—duty, breach of that duty, and causation—there must be some type of compensable bodily injury or emotional or economic harm (damages) for that person to prevail in a legal action. Generally, there are two types of damages: *special damages* (also called actual damages), which reflect actual economic loss to the injured person for things like lost wages, medical care costs, custodial care costs, and costs arising from physical impairment, and *general damages* (also called noneconomic damages), which reflect noneconomic loss for things such as physical pain and suffering, emotional distress (fright, anxiety, loss of peace of mind or happiness, humiliation or embarrassment), and loss of consortium or association. Together, special and general damages may be referred to as *compensatory damages* because they are aimed at compensating the injured person for her or his loss. Damages must be proven in court with admissible evidence.

Under certain highly egregious circumstances, an injured person may be awarded punitive damages. Punitive damages are not meant to compensate the injured person; they are meant to punish the liable party and to deter similar conduct by others. Punitive damages are awarded only in cases of gross negligence—when the negligent person's conduct rises to the level of being oppressive, malicious, or outrageous.

Compare fact scenarios I and IV with scenarios II and III. What are the common sources of damages, and how may the damages differ in the cases involving fatalities? Are significant damages more or less likely in fact scenario III? Does the answer change if the young man suffered a significant or paralyzing injury? Consider the facts presented in fact scenarios I and IV. Does the fact that these cases involved a death of a participant suggest punitive damages may be more likely?

# NEGLIGENCE AND RELATED THEORIES OF LIABILITY

Liability for negligence arises in a variety of circumstances, may involve a variety of actors, and will involve varying complaints. Legal practitioners examine these changing contexts and circumstances and use them to create or defend against "theories" of liability. In the following sections we discuss some common theories of negligence or tort style claims of liability that outdoor program administrators might face.

## Vicarious Liability

Vicarious liability involves a situation in which one person may be held legally responsible (i.e., vicari-

ously liable) for the negligence of another. Under a theory of vicarious liability, the "superior" (usually an employer) becomes responsible for the acts of its "agent or subordinate" (usually an employee) based on the relationship between the superior and the subordinate. As suggested, the most common context for vicarious liability is employer liability for employee negligence. An employer such as a university recreation program may become liable for the negligent conduct of its employee(s) if an employee causes an injury to another person.

The key issue in vicarious liability cases is whether the employee was acting within the "course and scope" of his or her employment duties when the negligent act or omission occurred. If the employee was carrying out an assignment from the employer or furthering the employer's interests, then the employee is generally thought of as acting within the scope of employment, and the employer may be responsible for the employee's conduct. If the employee was engaged in purely personal matters or was off duty when the negligent act occurred, the employer likely will not be legally liable for the employee's conduct.

An issue that often arises in vicarious liability cases is determining whether the negligent person was (legally speaking) an employee or an independent contractor. Some companies try to classify their hired help as independent contractors rather than employees. There are legal tests, which vary from state to state, to determine whether a person is an employee or an independent contractor. The relevant factors often include whether the alleged independent contractor controlled the means through which she accomplishes her work, sets her own work schedule, provides her own tools, the method of payment and tax withholding, the nature of the work performed and other similar factors. In very general terms, a person is likely an employee and not an independent contractor when the employer or superior controls the work and the schedule or timing of the work and how the work is accomplished. If the employer or superior controls the end result only, but not the method for reaching the result, the worker likely is an independent contractor. It is important to note that merely classifying a worker as an independent contractor does not make that worker an independent contractor for purposes of the law. The legal ramifications for misclassifying employees as independent contractors may be significant. An employer who misclassifies an employee as an independent contractor may be vicariously liable for the acts of the employee. The employer may then find itself in a situation in which it lacks appropriate insurance coverage. True independent contractors, on the other hand, are generally liable for their own actions.

## Products Liability

Products liability is an area of tort law concerning the liability of manufacturers and people or entities who sell products for harms caused by defectively designed, produced, or marketed items. There are two main types of product liability claims: those arising from design defects and those arising from manufacturing defects. A design defect is one in which the design of a product creates an undue risk and the defect exists in all products of the same kind. A manufacturing defect involves a product that is defective because of the manufacturing process. Because parties throughout the chain of distribution may face liability for defective products, a potential products liability claim exists for recreation programs that distribute or sell manufactured products. For example, if a product fails while a recreational program is using the product, the program may be sued. If this is the case, the program may bring the manufacturer into the lawsuit as the real party subject to legal liability for failure of the product. Although product manufactures are generally and most often the target of products liability lawsuits, programmers should be aware of the issues and acts that might expose them to a products liability or similar claim. For example, legal issues may arise when a program maintains or repairs equipment, particularly in lieu of returning it to the manufacturer under a warranty or in light of a recall. Operators or other providers may also be sued for improper fitting or noncompliance with the manufacturer's instructions or representations for use of the product.

Also note that if a programmer alters equipment or uses it against the manufacturer's suggestions, the warranty may be voided by such improper use. Altering or modifying equipment may absolve the manufacturer from liability exposure for any claims based on the equipment's failure, and in turn may create liability for the program. Modifications to any

outdoor recreation equipment should be done only by trained personnel. Programs should also make timely inspections of equipment and document inspections and maintenance so that damaged or overused equipment is repaired by qualified persons, or replaced. Equipment should be inventoried and numbered or labeled, and programs should keep all manufacturer warranties and make sure the warranties are registered. Although a failure to properly inspect and repair or maintain equipment generally will not result in a products liability claim, such omissions may result in a different claim of negligence against a program.

## Premises Liability

Premises liability arises when an owner or person in control of land or a facility is liable for an injury caused by conditions on the property. A slip-and-fall accident on the floor of a rock-climbing gym is an example of potential premises liability claims. In the scheme of premises liability, the "status" of the person entering the land dictates the scope of the duty the landowner owes to the person. These statuses generally include "trespasser," "licensee," or "invitee."

A trespasser is anyone occupying or entering property without the permission or consent of the landowner. A landowner's duty to a trespasser is to avoid intentionally causing injury or refrain from a willful act that may cause injury. Once the landowner knows of the trespasser's presence on the land, however, his duty to the trespasser becomes one of ordinary care. A licensee is a person entering or occupying property with the consent of the landowner, but is there for the licensee's own purposes—unguided hunters using a rancher's property, for example. A landowner's duty to licensees is to warn the licensee of known dangerous conditions or activities on the land. An invitee is one who is invited to enter the land as a general member of the public or in connection with a business dealing with the landowner or the party possessing the land—a client participating in a commercial horseback ride through a stable or ranch, for example. The duty owed to invitees is to keep the premises in a reasonably safe condition or to warn of hidden or concealed dangers. Courts in some states have handed down rulings that do away with these "status" categories and instead simply apply an ordinary duty of reasonable care in all premises liability cases regardless of the plaintiffs status.

Recreational use statutes put another twist into the question of premises liability. Recreational use statutes are based on legislatively announced policies that encourage private and public property owners to make their land available for recreation. These statutes immunize or protect landowners or occupiers of land from some types of liability when they open their land to the public, free of charge, for recreational use. The scope and coverage of recreational use statutes vary significantly from state to state. Some recreational use statutes specifically identify the type of land and recreational activities covered, and some speak to the issue in very general terms. Some statutes place a duty on landowners only to avoid causing willful injury to recreational users, whereas other statutory schemes require more of the landowner in terms of the duty owed to recreational users. The recreational use protections in some states apply both to private and public land, and in other states they apply only to privately owned land. Thus the application of a recreational use statute protecting a landowner from liability depends entirely on the recreational use statute of the state in which the land is situated.

## Coparticipant Liability

In general, a person participating in an outdoor recreation activity is not legally liable to another participant except in cases in which reckless or intentional conduct is involved. This legal rule arose from a landmark decision made by the California Supreme Court in the case *Knight v. Jewitt*, 3 Cal. 4th 296 (1992). In this case Knight sued Jewitt after Jewitt stepped on Knight's hand in a game of touch football. Knight had warned Jewitt that he was playing too rough before the injury. At some point after this warning, Jewitt ran into Knight, knocking her down and stepping on her hand. Knight's hand was injured to the point that after three operations failed to restore functioning to her little finger, it was amputated. After a significant review of existing case law and legal doctrine regarding Knight's voluntary participation in the game and assumption of certain risks related to playing a game of touch football, the court determined that a participant

in an active sport breaches a legal duty to another participant only if he or she intentionally injures another participant or his or her conduct is so reckless that it falls outside the scope of what would be considered reasonable under the circumstances. In this case the court determined that although the defendant's conduct may have been negligent, it was not intentional or reckless.

This legal rule is illustrated in the case of *Distefano v. Forester*, 85 Cal. App. 4th 1249 (2001), which involved two motorcycle drivers who were "offroading" and collided as they approached the crest of a hill from opposite directions. One driver sued the other for negligence. The court cited the *Knight* case and determined that the other driver's conduct, although perhaps careless, was not so reckless as to be totally outside the range of the ordinary activity of the sport. In fact, the court found that the careless conduct of others is treated as an inherent risk (a concept discussed in depth later) of the sport, thereby preventing the recovery of damages. The *Distefano* court cited public policy, stating that promoting vigorous participation in sports and avoiding a floodgate of litigation were both furthered by this legal rule of not holding coparticipants liable for injuries to each other unless reckless or intentional misconduct is involved. Note that although a majority of courts follow the intentional or reckless conduct rule on coparticipant claims, not all courts do. Some courts apply rules governing ordinary negligence in coparticipant claims. This was the case in *Crawn v. Campo*, 630 A.2d 368 (N.J. App. Ct. 1993), in which the court determined that a claim by a catcher in a softball game for an injury caused by a collision with a base runner should be determined based on ordinary negligence, not on an intentional or reckless conduct standard.

## Negligent Medical Care or Rescue

Recreation and adventure programmers must be prepared to provide an adequate response in the event of an incident involving a participant, whether the incident involves a physical injury to the participant or a medical emergency. When improper or inadequate rescue or response occurs, or when a provider has no procedure for emergency response in place, the participant may argue that an accident of some sort was certainly foreseeable and that the provider's poor response exposed the participant to an unreasonable or increased risk of harm.

This type of claim is exemplified in the case of *Jaffee v. Pallota Teamworks*, 276 F. Supp. 2d 102 (DDC, 2003). In this case, Jaffee died after participating in a charity bike ride sponsored by Pallota to raise money for AIDS research. The event involved a four-day ride. One afternoon while riding, Jaffee approached a medical aid station and complained of dizziness and nausea. Volunteers gave her IV fluids, and when her condition failed to improve and she began vomiting, they gave her more IV fluids. When her blood pressure dropped and she collapsed, she was transported to a hospital. Jaffee died the next day of a brain hemorrhage. Jaffee's parent and estate sued the race organizer, claiming that they negligently trained and equipped the aid stations, and then negligently failed to diagnose, monitor, treat, and care for Jaffee. Jaffee had signed a release before the event, however, that acknowledged the risk of injury or death, that stated she was physically capable of participating, that her medical care provider had approved her participation, and that included medical care personnel in the list of persons or parties to be released. The court upheld the release and specifically found relevant the fact that Jaffee had participated in another like race so that she likely understood the type of care available during this charitable event. Please note that although the claims of Jaffee's survivors were dismissed based on a release she had signed, the exposure to the risk of liability for inadequate response to an injury or medical emergency remains a prominent risk for outdoor programs.

# Negligent Supervision or Instruction

Programmers and commercial operators have a duty to supervise, instruct, and oversee their students, clients, or participants. When appropriate attention or instruction is not given, a program may be sued for breaching this duty. The legal doctrine of *in parentis loci* is closely related to the concept of negligent supervision. Entities such as camps, schools, or other similar organizations entrusted with the care of minors have a duty to exercise the same degree of care as a reasonably prudent parent under the same circumstances. As a result, care of children usually implicates a higher degree of care and thus a heightened duty. This does not mean recreation providers are legally obligated to ensure the absolute safety of minor participants. Consider fact scenario III. Does the concept of *in parentis loci* create an increased or enhanced standard of care owed by the camp to the young man? If so, did the camp breach the standard when the instructors failed to follow established procedures during a storm?

The concepts of negligent supervision and the related doctrine of *in parentis locus* are easily illustrated in various court cases. In the case of *Dunn v. Southern Calif. 7th Day Adventists*, San Bernadino Sup. Ct. 1998, a 14-year-old boy fell while rock climbing on a church-sponsored camping trip and suffered severe brain injury. The plaintiffs asserted claims for negligent supervision and undertaking a high-risk activity without sufficient experience. The parties settled the claim for the negligent supervision of a minor for a reported $4.4 million dollars. In *Voight v. Colorado Mountain Club*, 819 P. 2d 1088 (Colo. App. 1991), the plaintiff suffered frostbite and amputation while on a hike. The plaintiff became separated from the hiking group and alleged that the designated leader failed to properly monitor and supervise the group, allowing her to become separated. Expert witnesses testified that it was the designated leader's duty to keep the group together. A jury found the club 70 percent negligent and the plaintiff hiker 30 percent negligent. In *Bendik v. Crossroads School*, a 15-year-old girl was killed on a school outing when she slid down a mountain snow slope after a brief hike to a scenic overlook. Her parents sued the private school and guide service hired by the school to take the group on the outing, alleging negligent instruction (snow sliding) and negligent supervision. The jury found in favor of the school when some of the testimony revealed the girl did not follow instructions. Finally, in *Fintzi v. New Jersey YMHA-YWHA*, 2001 NY Lexis 3791 (NY 2001), 10-year-old Fintzi participated in a relay race on a grass field that was wet with morning dew and fog, slipping twice and breaking his arm on the second fall. Fintzi's parents sued, claiming negligent supervision of their son. The court stated that merely allowing children to play on wet grass does not constitute negligent supervision. The court specifically stated that organizers of sporting activities owe a duty to exercise only reasonable care to protect participants from risks; where there was no evidence the camp had increased the risk of playing on a naturally and obviously damp field, the court stated that to find the camp liable under those circumstances would unnecessarily sterilize camping into a sedentary type of activity.

## Negligent Hiring or Inexperienced Guides or Employees

Guiding or working with people involves decision making and judgment; so too does hiring, supervising, and retaining the right people. The success or failure of a program (and whether participants have good or bad experiences) will be significantly impacted by the judgments made by staff as they inform participants of the risks associated with the outdoor recreation activity, deal with them as clients, and make critical judgments made in the field. Liability for negligent hiring, supervision, or retention is based on the relationship between an employer and an employee, and arises from harm caused to a third party by the employee.

Negligent hiring usually is alleged when an operator or program has failed to act reasonably or prudently in ascertaining an employee's qualifications or fitness to guide or instruct. Negligent supervision usually involves situations in which the employer fails to review or oversee an employee, and fails to ascertain whether employees are following the program's policies or procedures or industry standards. Negligent retention usually involves a situation in which an employer retains an incompetent or unfit employee, and the employer knew that the employee's incompetence presented an unreasonable risk of harm to clients, students, or participants. Consider fact scenario III. Do the facts give rise to potential negligent supervision or hiring claims if camp leaders failed to follow the camp's procedures? Also consider the case of *Shaw v. Rivers Whitewater Rafting*, 2002 U.S. Dist. Lexis 23575 (Michigan, November 2002). In this case, Shaw was injured on a whitewater rafting trip in Virginia. Shaw alleged that the rafting company allowed an inexperienced and inadequately trained rafting guide to take the clients out on the trip in question. Specifically, Shaw alleged that the guide was not wearing her helmet even though passengers were required to wear helmets. According to Shaw, upon entering a set of class IV rapids, the guide let go of the rudder to put her helmet on, at which point the raft struck a rock and overturned, causing injury to Shaw. As this case illustrates, judgments made by employees or guides in the field may reflect on the employer, which in turn may lead to legal action over the employer's allegedly negligent hiring, training, or retention of employees.

## Failure to Warn and Reducing Risk by Warning

Outdoor professionals or programs must appropriately inform guests of the risks that they are taking by participating in a given activity. This duty to warn is usually accomplished by the following: setting good event policies and procedures or rules, posting warnings on equipment or facilities, oral warnings (e.g., safety briefings and ongoing instruction or guidance during the activity), encouraging safe participation, and making sure all participants and spectators are aware of the inherent and other risks of the sport. An effective warning is specific, obvious, direct, unambiguous, easy to understand, simple, and complete. After providing information on the risks involved in the activity, a guide or instructor should confirm that participants appreciated and understood the warning.

Beyond use of appropriate release and waiver documents (discussed later), guides, instructors, and staff should conduct safety talks as a standard part of the program's policy or procedure for conveying information about risk. An appropriate safety talk will not only fully inform participants about the risks involved in the activity but also provide evidence supporting the assumption-of-risk defense and evidence that may potentially defeat a claim for failure to warn.

## Industry Standards or Practices

Existing industry standards or practices might affect the duties that a court or jury determines a program owes to participants; as a result, industry

---

### SAFETY TALK

The basic outline of a good safety talk should include the following:

» *Specifics about the activity:* the area in which the activity will take place; the forecasted or predicted weather; what may be expected on the trip; inherent dangers and risks most commonly involved in the activity; the equipment used in the activity and proper use of the equipment; demonstration of proper techniques for equipment use; and procedures in the event of an emergency.

» *Participant responsibilities:* the common level of physical involvement; confirm that no participant has a medical or physical condition that will prevent participation or ability to help in the event of an emergency; explain that no drugs or alcohol may be consumed during activity; explain that participants must notify guides of any problems with equipment or other guests; explain that participants must report all incidents or accidents; explain that participants must follow the guide's or instructor's directions at all times.

» *Closing:* ask participants if everyone has signed the release form or other forms the operation or program requires as a condition of participating; ask for questions participants may have; arrive at consensus that the group understands and agrees to what is required of them for participating in the activity, and that they acknowledge, understand, and accept the risks of the activity; provide an out for participants who decide not to participate so that participation is voluntary.

---

standards or practices affect the ultimate liability assigned to both the operator or the participant. Industry standards or practices generally include what most other programs or operators do in similar situations. Participants suing programs use industry standards as evidence of what the appropriate standard of care—ergo, duty—should have been (with regard to just about any policy, procedure, method, or matter for which there is a custom or standard of practice within the relevant outdoor recreation industry) when they bring claims or lawsuits against programs or operators.

It is thus wise to be aware of the professional, trade, or commercial associations or other programs in your outdoor recreation activity or area of concentration, as well as any standards or practices that they may articulate, encourage, or use in the industry. This level of awareness and understanding is important so that a program may evaluate standards, practices, or customs and explain why or why the program has not adopted these standards or practices. The case of *Rendine v. St. John's University*, 289 A.D.2nd 465 (NY, A.D. 2001), provides a good example of how industry

standards can impact liability. In this case, a college cheerleader was injured after falling to the ground while attempting a stunt with her partner. The cheerleader sued the university, claiming that her coach was negligent for failing to provide her with a spotter when she requested one. The coach denied that the cheerleader asked for a spotter. The university asked for dismissal on the basis that the cheerleader had assumed the risks of the sport. The court agreed that the cheerleader assumed an inherent risk of cheerleading—that she might fall performing one of the stunts in the sport. The court specifically addressed a safety manual from the American Association of Cheerleading Coaches and Advisors requiring a spotter when practicing the stunt in question only if participants are high school age. The court determined that because this nationally recognized association prescribed a protective standard only for high school students, the manual was evidence that the university and its coach had not breached a recognized standard of care or duty so that negligence could not be proven. The court's discussion of the association manual and the standards that are often articulated by professional or trade associations provides a cautionary note with regard to adhering to well-known or established industry practices or customs. Programs and operators should be aware of local, regional, and national standards, who is articulating those standards, and why. If a program is going to deviate from common practices in their activities or offerings, they should be able to articulate why they are deviating; in other words, a program must act reasonably and prudently in their risk-management practices in thinking through and being able to discuss why their practices are different from the norm—if they are, in fact, deviating from known standards.

# DEFENSES AGAINST NEGLIGENCE

Even if a person or entity is found negligent, one or more legal defenses to that negligence may relieve or absolve the negligent party from liability. Simply denying the truth of the factual allegations made by the plaintiff (injured participant) or introducing evidence that demonstrates that the facts are not as they are represented by the plaintiff can negate the plaintiff's legal claims. An operator or program may also attempt to share or shift liability to the claiming party by proving that the claimant is "comparatively negligent." An operator may also attempt to avoid liability completely by proving that the claimant "assumed" the risk of the activity, signed a contractual release and waiver document, or encountered an inherent risk of the activity. These are all valid defenses to a claim of negligence.

## Comparative Negligence or Contributory Fault

Just as guides, operators, or programs have a duty to act reasonably, participants have a duty to take reasonable care to prevent injury to themselves. When participants engage in conduct that is unreasonable and contributes to their own harm, they are contributorily negligent. If a participant engages in the activity in an unreasonable manner, any award or finding of liability is either reduced by the percentage of the plaintiff's own fault (comparative fault) or may be a complete defense to the claims (contributory negligence). In other words, if a participant's own conduct falls below the standard of what a reasonably prudent person would do in similar circumstances, the participant has acted negligently on his or her own behalf.

Geoff Harrison

When a participant acts unreasonably in an outdoor recreation activity, the participant may be found negligent in causing his or her injury.

With a comparative negligence or fault defense, the focus is on the participant's own conduct. When an operator asserts a comparative negligence defense, the court or jury will be asked to assess the conduct and the negligence of both parties, and assign a percentage of fault to each party. Remember that in any situation there can never be more (or less) than 100 percent liability. The inquiry, therefore, will be to decide what percentage of fault (liability) to apportion to the claimant (the participant, student, or client) and what percentage of fault to apportion to the party being sued (the commercial operator, camp, university, employer, or program). If the judge or jury finds that the claimant acted negligently (in other words, acted unreasonably given the circumstances), the claimant's damages are reduced by the percentage of fault assigned to their own malfeasance or misconduct.

Comparative negligence laws vary from state to state. In some states, if the participant's negligence is equal to or greater than that of the negligent party, the claimant or participant is completely barred from recovery. In other states, the courts will take a purely comparative view and the claimant or participant will recover damages according to the percentage of fault assigned to the operator or program. Consider the facts from fact scenario I. The deceased student had rock-climbing experience and was an assistant instructor for the class. Was he comparatively negligent if he failed to check the belay system setup by the other instructor before using it? Similarly, in fact scenario IV, were the rafters comparatively negligent because they discussed lining their boats because of the high water but apparently chose not to?

# Inherent Risk

Every outdoor recreation activity involves certain inherent risks. Backcountry skiing involves the risk of avalanche, whitewater river rafting involves the risk of drowning, rock climbing involves the risk of falling, and so forth. Inherent risks are those risks that may subject participants to harm or physical injury but are so fundamental to the activity that if changed, removed, or controlled, the activity would be changed in character or nature.

The key to the concept of inherent risk is that a recreational provider *has no legal duty* to protect a participant from inherent risks or to control an inherent risk. In other words, where we already know that an injured party must prove all four elements of a claim for negligence (duty, breach, causation, and damages), this means that the duty element fails so that no liability can be found or assigned when a participant encounters and is injured, harmed, or suffers damages caused by an inherent risk of the activity.

Generally, the law says that participants consent to or assume (take upon themselves) the responsibility for all obvious or observable inherent risks of an activity and the potential for injury caused by those inherent risks. The courts vary on whether the participant must be aware of the inherent risk to have effectively assumed the risk. Given this conflict, a prudent operator will warn participants (in the release, during the safety talk, and throughout the activity) of known inherent risks. It is critical to note, also, that if a program enlarges or increases the risk of harm from an inherent risk, the operator may still be held liable. For example, avalanches in uncontrolled backcountry settings are an inherent risk of that activity, but if an operator takes a client or group into this kind of setting without safety equipment such as beacons, shovels, or probes, then the operator has enlarged the risks associated with encountering an avalanche and can be held liable.

Thus it is important to know and understand what risks are inherent in the relevant outdoor recreation activity. It is also important to know and understand what programs can do to avoid enlarging or enhancing inherent risks. Consider fact scenario II. Falling from a raft is likely an inherent risk of whitewater rafting. Is falling from a raft after a guide intentionally bumps another raft an inherent risk, or did the guide enlarge or increase the risk of whitewater rafting by intentionally bumping the other raft? Does it make a difference if the guide forewarns the rafters that a rescue maneuver is necessary and explains the maneuver beforehand? Does it make a difference if the lives of the rafters in the stuck raft are in danger and the guide has no time to explain the rescue maneuver?

# Assumption of Risk

Assumption of risk is one of the more important legal concepts for outdoor programs to understand

Outdoor recreation activities often include risks that may cause physical harm to the participant.

and apply. Assumption of risk is also, unfortunately, confusing, controversial, and an often misunderstood legal doctrine, even among legal professionals and courts. Adding to the difficult nature of assumption of risk is that, unlike negligence, which is understood and applied fairly consistently among courts, the actual rules, and even the terminology, regarding assumption of risk vary from court to court and from state to state. Thus it is not only important to understand assumption of risk as a legal concept but to also understand how the courts in the state or states where the program operates apply assumption of risk.

Assumption of risk is discussed as being either "implied" or "express." Express assumption of risk usually involves a written and signed document referred to as a waiver or release agreement. An implied assumption of risk exists when the participant orally agrees to participate or simply goes along and participates, and thereby implicitly agrees to the inherent risks of the sport. Assumption of risk is a defense to negligence that usually results in either a decrease in the program's liability (i.e., a comparative negligence analysis) or completely shields the operator or program from liability. Assumption of risk applies to situations in which

a program owes a duty to the participant, but the participant voluntarily and knowingly encounters the risk, thereby assuming liability for the results of encountering that risk. Thus the focus in an assumption-of-risk analysis is whether the participant knowingly accepted or consented to a risk related to the program activity.

## Implied Assumption of Risk

When participants decide to go along on recreational trips or endeavors after they have been warned about the inherent risks involved (through appropriate marketing, safety briefings, instruction, or when a risk is open or obvious) they are (legally speaking) thought to have implicitly assumed the risks of the activity. In other words, a programmer or operator may imply or infer through the participant's conduct or voluntary participation that he or she decided to assume the risks of the activity, thereby absolving the operator or program of liability or reducing the program's liability. Consider the fact scenarios introduced at the beginning of the chapter. In scenario I, what did the student instructor's conduct imply, if anything, about his assumption of the risks involved in the rock-climbing activity? In scenario III, did the camper implicitly assume the risk of getting hit by a falling tree by participating in the camp? In scenario IV, did the rafters engage in conduct that suggested they implicitly consented to the risks inherent in whitewater boating? Does it matter if their guide or the forest service did not warn them about the risks involved?

The legal concept of implied assumption of risk has been the focus in many written legal decisions. In the case of *Fairchild v. Amundson*, 2001 Washington App. Lexis 149 (January 2001), the plaintiff, Fairchild, and his church went on a whitewater rafting trip. The group stopped to scout a rapid, and after doing so the raft group re-entered the river and were sucked into a "reversal." All the participants were thrown from the raft into the river. Fairchild was rescued but sued for injuries he suffered as a result. The courts dismissed Fairchild's claims on the basis of implied assumption of the risk, finding Fairchild voluntarily chose to encounter the risk. Factually, it was proven that Fairchild had read the guide's brochure, that he knew being thrown in the river was a risk of rafting, that he had received a safety briefing, and that he had signed an acknowledgment of risk form prior to the rafting trip. In *Tremblay v. West Experience, Inc.*, 745 N.Y.S. 2d 311 (NY App. Div. 2002), Tremblay, the plaintiff, was injured while snow tubing. She hooked snow tubes with a partner and descended a 1,000-foot run. She was not able to unhook from her companion's tube at the bottom of the run, causing her to spin out of control and hit a retaining barrier. Tremblay sued, claiming the park was negligent in designing and constructing the course, as well as negligent in supervising and instructing. The court dismissed her claims on grounds that Tremblay had assumed the inherent risks by her participation. The appeals court agreed, finding that voluntary participants assume the commonly appreciated risks that arise out of a sport and generally flow from participation in the sport. The *Tremblay* court determined that the inquiry is not dependant on the individual plaintiff's subjective beliefs about the risks, but rather on whether the risks assumed were known, apparent, or reasonably foreseeable.

*Morales v. New York City Housing Authority*, 187 A.2d 295 (NY App. Div. 1992) provides another example of how implied assumption of risk factors into legal claims. In this case, Morales decided to play football with some buddies on a grassy area behind a building owned by the housing authority. Water that was flowing from the building made the ground wet and muddy, but the participants, including Morales, decided to play anyway. During the game, Morales slipped and fell while going out for a pass and broke his ankle. Morales sued the housing authority, alleging that it was negligent for allowing the water to flow from the building and out onto the field. The court rejected his allegations and determined that Morales had assumed the risk of falling and injury when he decided to play when he knew the field was wet, muddy, and slippery, and that these dangers were open and obvious.

It's important to note that even children, when appropriately warned, can be found to have (legally) assumed risks. In the case of *DeLacy v. Catamount Development Corporation*, 2002 W.L. 31992955 (NY App. Div. 2003), a seven-year-old fell from a chair lift at a ski area, sustaining serious injury. The child's mother filed a lawsuit, and the ski area defended on grounds that the child had assumed the risks of skiing and riding a chair lift. The appellate court determined that implied assumption of the risk must be assessed against the skill and experience of the participant. There was a question of fact whether the child in this case fully appreciated the risks of using a chair lift, so the appellate court referred the case back to the lower court for the parties to present evidence with regard to assumption of the risk. In *Spooner v. City of Camilla*, 568 S.E. 2d 109 (GA Ct. App. 2002), a 13-year-old child drowned in a mining pit pond on land purchased by the city for industrial development. The child's parents sued the city, claiming negligence for failure to post warning signs or erect barricades. The city defended on the basis that the child had assumed the risks of playing or swimming in the pond. The court found for the city. The evidence offered at trial proved that the thirteen-year-old decedent, who was bike riding with friends at the time, had been warned beforehand by his aunt and guardian about not swimming in the pond because he did not know how to swim. The evidence further established that as the boys approached the pond, the decedent got off his bike and went to the pond despite the other boys yelling at him not to jump in. The boy proceeded to jump in anyway, and then the others tried to save him.

The court determined that this child had actual knowledge of the danger, understood and appreciated the risks, and nevertheless exposed himself to the risks and dangers.

## Express Assumption of Risk

Parties can generally (legally speaking) agree in advance and in writing to "expressly" assume the risks associated with participating in a given program or activity. This usually involves a written release and waiver document, which creates an interesting intersection between tort and contract law in outdoor recreation. The act of contractually "assuming" or "shifting" risk is called express assumption of risk.

The law generally allows parties to agree ahead of time that one party will not be legally liable to the other. As a result, an outdoor recreation program and a participant may agree to contractually limit the program's liability or "exculpate" the program, and shift the risk of injury or liability to the participant. This contractual limit on liability may include not only injury caused by an inherent risk (for which the program has no "duty of care"), but also for an injury caused by the provider's simple negligence.

These agreements (which are contractual in nature) are usually referred to as waivers, releases, release of liability and waivers, or voluntary assumption-of-risk agreements. Release and waiver agreements may take various forms, depending on the provider's needs, the circumstances, and any rules or regulations related to involved third parties, such as public land administrators. Regardless of how the contract is formatted, an essential characteristic of a waiver agreement is that the participant acknowledges and assumes inherent risks, waives any legal claim against the provider, and releases the provider for conduct or omissions that may otherwise be negligent.

To be binding, a contract must meet some basic legal requirements. A legally enforceable contract generally requires a written agreement that is clear and unambiguous in its terms, signed or acknowledged by the party who will be bound (i.e., the participant), and supported by what the law calls "consideration." In a recreational context, legally sufficient consideration is usually present when a party agrees to do or provide something (e.g., a raft trip or a ropes course) that the party is not otherwise legally obligated to do or provide, and in exchange the recipient agrees to give something for that service—usually the payment of money *and* an agreement to release the provider from certain liabilities by signing a release and waiver agreement.

The legal right of parties to contractually agree to shift risk before an activity notwithstanding, courts have formulated a number of limitations on the enforceability of release and waiver agreements. One of these limitations on enforcement is based on the nature of the provider's conduct. Courts in virtually all states refuse to acknowledge or enforce release and waiver agreements against a program operator's gross negligence, or for intentional, willful, or reckless misconduct on the part of the operator. Gross negligence may be thought of as another term for recklessness or a willful and conscious disregard for the safety and well-being of others. Whatever the name, liability for conduct well above that of ordinary or "simple" negligence generally cannot be contractually released or waived in advance of the activity by the participant.

Another potential limit on enforcement of release agreements is that courts will "strictly construe" the language used in the contract document against the party who drafted it—usually the program or operator. For this reason, certain drafting "rules" apply to release and waiver agreements. Liability limiting provisions must be stated in clear, unambiguous language. Recreational release contracts should avoid confusing and unnecessary legalese and should use plain, everyday language to explain the concepts. A release and waiver will not be inferred from larger, mixed, or more confusing documents. Release and waiver provisions should be set forth separately from all other written materials, such as registration information. Related to this, participants should not be allowed to strike provisions from the release agreement or to participate without signing the release agreement. Release and waiver agreements should be used and administered uniformly and consistently.

Another hurdle to enforcement of a release agreement is that courts will consider the issue of whether the participant signing the release had an option not to participate at the point the waiver is presented for signature. This is particularly true of multiday trips in which participants travel long distances to a departure point and are then told for the first time that, in order to participate, they will have to sign an exculpatory contract waiving their legal rights. A potential key to overcoming this issue is to make clear to all participants in advance of the activity that the participant will be required to sign a release agreement as a condition to participating. Another good practice that creates evidence of express and implied assumption of risk is for programs to conduct detailed safety briefings that provide an opportunity for dialogue and in which participants can expressly state (verbalize) that they understand and agree to the rules and risks. The participant can then be said to have made an informed decision on whether to continue and participate in the activity.

In some states, lawmakers have enacted liability limiting statutes for the benefit of certain outdoor recreation providers, such as commercial outfitters and guides, whitewater operators, or equine operators. These statutes are intended to benefit programs by restricting the legal claims of participants. A likely unintended consequence of these statutes is that courts, when faced with a lawsuit filed by a participant for injury, have determined in some cases that the outdoor recreation provider, as the beneficiary of the statutory grant of limits on liability, owes a "public duty" to participants in general. As a result, outdoor recreation programs may not enjoy the benefit of a contractual limit on liability, no matter how well the contract is drafted, because these providers owe a public duty to protect participants. This public duty arises from the same statutes that purport to limit the program's liability to participants, and further limits the ability of operators or programs to contract with participants regarding liability.

Related to this public policy prohibition on the use of waiver agreements are the rules and regulations of certain government regulatory agencies, which may render waiver and release agreements unenforceable. For example, certain forest service regulations may prohibit the enforcement of waiver and release agreements when the provider or program (usually commercial providers) is permitted to operate on federal land managed by the forest service. The same may be true of commercial providers operating on National Park Service lands and Bureau of Land Management lands. These federal agencies may allow commercial operators to use voluntary assumption-of-risk forms but may otherwise prohibit the use of general release and waiver agreements as a condition to granting special use permits that allow the provider access to the public lands.

Outdoor programs that cater to minor children (in most states, under the age of 18) or allow minor children to participate face some additional and unique issues with the enforceability of liability limiting contracts (releases). In most states, a person must be an adult to legally enter into a contract. Thus a minor child cannot directly contract with the provider to absolve the provider from liability. Additionally, minors usually cannot file a lawsuit; they may pursue legal action only through a parent or guardian. For these reasons, parents or legal guardians are usually required to sign a release and waiver along with their minor child.

The laws regarding the enforceability of waiver agreements signed on behalf of minor children vary widely from state to state. In a few states, the outdoor industry has successfully lobbied lawmakers to pass statutes that allow a parent or guardian to release or waive the legal claims of a minor child. The policy behind such statutes is that a parent or legal guardian is entitled to make choices and decisions for the minor child, which includes waiving claims against the provider in consideration of the program allowing the child to participate. These statutes also recognize the value of making children's recreational programs available to participants. Courts in other states, however, have ruled that the legal right to make a claim for an injury belongs exclusively to the minor child, and a parent cannot waive the child's claim or release another party from liability to the child. The reasoning behind these types of court decisions is often based on a public policy that seeks to protect the legal rights of minors.

Actual court decisions help illustrate the various ways in which courts address release agreements involving minor participants. For example, in *Scott v. Pacific West Mountain Resort*, 834 P.2d 6 (WA 1992), Scott, a minor, filed a negligence claim against a ski resort for injuries he suffered while taking a ski lesson. Scott's parents also brought claims for their alleged losses. Before the lessons, the minor's mother, with the knowledge and approval of the father, signed a release and waiver agreement on behalf of the parents and their minor son. The Washington Supreme Court specifically addressed the issue of whether one parent can waive the other parent's claims arising from injury to the child. The court affirmed dismissal of the parents' claims based on the release signed only by the mother but overruled dismissal of the minor child's claims, deciding that public policy prohibited a parent from releasing and waiving the claims of a minor. In *Childress v. Madison County*, 777 S.W.2d 1 (TN App. 1989), a 22-year-old mentally handicapped boy was accidently injured while swimming at a YMCA pool. The boy's mother had signed a release for him to participate in a Special Olympics program. The court barred the mother's claims based on her signature on the release, but the court did not dismiss either the son's claims or the nonsigning father's claims. The *Childress* court also found that the indemnity provision of the release required the mother to indemnify the pool for any claims brought by father. Contrast the above two cases with the case of *Fisher v. Rivest*, 2002 Conn. Super. Lexis 2778 (August 2002), which involved a child injured while participating in a youth hockey game. The injured child's parents had signed a prerecreational release on behalf of the minor child. When the parents sued their child's hockey league after the child was injured while playing hockey, the court upheld the release signed by the parents. The court specifically reasoned that if it did not uphold this type of release, individuals who volunteered as coaches and leagues that provide this type of activity may well decide the legal risk is too great and that children would thereby be deprived of opportunities to participate in these valuable activities.

These limits on enforcement notwithstanding, release and waiver agreements are legally enforceable contracts under appropriate circumstances. Where permitted by state law or by the policies of public land administrators, programmers should always utilize a release and waiver agreement. The worst consequence of utilizing the agreement is that a court of law may refuse to enforce the waiver and release provisions of the agreement. The agreement may still be used as evidence of the operator's warnings or of the participant's assumption of the risks. Another reason for always using waiver and release agreements is that they are effective tools for teaching participants about the activity and for

facilitating a dialogue between the provider and participant regarding the inherent risks and other risks of the activity.

Finally, it is important to address some of the criticisms leveled at the use of waiver and release agreements by outdoor recreation providers. Critics of waiver and release agreements often argue that such agreements are inappropriate because providers become less concerned with safety when they believe a client has waived his or her claims. The reality, however, is that programs that experience accidents expose themselves to loss of their insurance and loss of permits they may hold to operate on public lands or other properties. Programs with poor safety records also risk loss of funding from universities or other sponsors. Thus the reality is that programmers are motivated to do everything within their power to manage risk and minimize or mitigate the risks to their clients. In the free-market economy, reckless or unsafe programmers likely will not remain in business because clients will choose programs with solid safety records. There is also peer pressure within the recreation and programming industries to operate safely because the general reputation of all outdoor providers and programs are called into question by the risky practices of poorly run programs. All of these factors negate the legitimacy of the arguments generally made against the use of waiver and release agreements. Exculpatory contracts containing appropriately drafted waiver and release provisions are an effective tool for outdoor recreation providers not only to hedge against legal liability risks but also to inform and convey important information to participants that help them make informed choices. For these reasons, operators and programmers should view waiver and release agreements as valuable tools in managing and mitigating risk.

**Contents of a Release and Waiver Agreement**  Program operators commonly ask about the contents of a well-drafted release and waiver agreement. There is no one-size-fits-all approach to release and waiver agreements. Each program and operator is unique, and the specific risks involved with the program or operation are unique. A written release and waiver agreement is a contract and, if properly drafted and entered into, is legally binding. Thus an attorney familiar with the outdoor recreation industry and the relevant laws, rules, or regulations of the state or states and public lands upon which the program operates should draft and regularly review and approve the agreement. As a matter of course, however, most well-drafted release and waiver agreements should contain the following:

**>> Clear, easy-to-read, and unambiguous language.** As an initial matter, if a court is asked to interpret a release and waiver agreement, the agreement must be unambiguous and easy to read if it is to be enforced. The typeface should be sufficiently large, easy to read, and written in a common type face or font. The agreement must also be clear and unambiguous without conflicting language.

**>> Disclaimer language.** Such language is often found at the beginning of the agreement and also at the end just before the signature lines; it may be set forth in bold or larger than normal font. Disclaimer language indicates that the participant, by signing, agrees to give up important legal rights and that, by signing, acknowledges that he or she is voluntarily signing the agreement and voluntarily participating in the activity offered by the operator.

**>> Acknowledgment and assumption of risk.** This provision should identify all prevalent inherent risks and state that the risks "include but are not limited to . . ." the risks identified. Include language clarifying that the participant understands and acknowledges the risks involved, and agrees to assume those risks and the injuries or damages the risks might cause. Also include language indicating the participant is affirming that his or her participation and assumption of risk is voluntary.

**>> Consideration language.** Consideration is necessary to form a legally binding contract. The consideration from the participant to the program or provider includes the participant's willingness to assume inherent risks and waive legal claims and to release the program or provider from legal liability. The contract should clearly recite this consideration.

**>> Waiver of claims and release of liability.** Do not bury this part of the agreement. It must be set out and clearly identifiable in the agreement. Language in this provision requires the participant to agree to waive all legal claims against the provider or program for injury, death, or property damage and release the provider or program from all legal liability, *including* that arising from the provider's or program's negligence.

**>> Identification of everyone the participant is releasing from claims.** This includes the program or provider, guides, staff, contractors, owners, directors, members, and so forth. Likewise, identify all parties other than the participant who are waiving their rights to sue as a result of the agreement, including spouses, children, parents, estate, and any others.

**>> Indemnity and hold-harmless provision.** This usually includes a promise from the participant not to sue the provider or program for injury, death, or damages (hold harmless) and to bear the costs or reimburse the costs (indemnity) resulting from any legal claim brought by anyone against the program as a result of the participant's involvement in the outdoor activity. In essence, the participant agrees to assume the financial responsibility for all legal actions arising from the participant's conduct or injury, death, or damage to the participant.

**>> Consent to medical treatment provision.** This sets forth the participant's consent for the provider or program to call for or administer medical treatment, first aid, CPR, or AED when deemed necessary after an accident, injury, or other medical event. This provision may also include an authorization by the participant to allow the provider to release or share medical information about the participant with medical care providers.

**>> Participant representations.** Representations may include any information about the participant that is important to the program. This typically includes a representation from the participant that he or she (1) has no health problems, physical disabilities, or mental impairments that preclude participation; (2) has sufficient skill and fitness to participate; (3) is not under the influence of drugs or alcohol, and that there are no other reasons the participant would lack the rational understanding required to sign the agreement; and (4) has insurance to cover the costs of medical treatment and transportation or is willing to personally bear the costs.

**>> Miscellaneous provisions.** These provisions are often found at the end of a written contract and may include requirements such as (1) a "forum selection clause," which sets forth where the participant is required to bring a lawsuit (usually in the city or county where the program's headquarters are located) in the event of legal action; (2) a "choice of law clause," stating which laws apply to a lawsuit (usually the laws of the state where the program is headquartered); (3) a statement that the written agreement is the entire agreement between the participant and program and cannot be modified or amended without an additional written and signed agreement (i.e., the participant cannot cross out parts of the release and waiver agreement, nor can an unsuspecting guide nullify the agreement by stating that the activity is "safe"); (4) a "severability clause" stating that if any part of the agreement is found unenforceable by a court, all other parts will remain in full force and effect and will be given the broadest construction possible; or (5) an "attorney fees" provision stating that in case of a lawsuit, the program is entitled to a payment from the other party for its attorney fees and costs incurred in defending the lawsuit.

>> **Signature line.** State the disclaimer language conspicuously, placing it directly above the signature line. Include spaces for names, addresses, e-mail, and phone numbers. If the participant is a minor, include a signature line for both the parents and the minor (making sure the agreement is consistent with the relevant state law about a minor signing a waiver and release agreement). Require that each participant sign a single agreement—do not have multiple participants or clients sign the same agreement.

Our disclaimer to you: This information provides only a general rule of thumb for the basic provisions in a well-drafted release and waiver agreement. State or federal law or regulations or circumstances under which a program operates (i.e., public land or special use permits) may dictate different terms and different legal consequences. A program must ensure that its waiver and release agreement is properly drafted and includes all of the necessary content. Do not simply copy or cut and paste from a friend or other program's or operator's agreement. Retain competent legal assistance to prepare or review a release agreement. The process of preparing your agreement should not be taken lightly—it may serve as the primary or even sole defense in the event of participant injury and litigation.

**Procedures for Properly Administering Release-Type Documents**  Once a program or provider identifies the appropriate scope and contents of its release and waiver agreements, then policies and procedures for administering the waiver document and for document retention should be created. One primary issue with release-style contracts relates to when and how to disseminate the information that all participants will be required to sign such an agreement before participation. Ideally, participants should be told in advance that the program will require them to sign a release of liability agreement rather than at a point when the participant has no choice but to participate in the activity. The best practice for obtaining signatures is to acquire them and have them witnessed at the time of the trip. Other measures to ensure releases are properly administered can be reviewed in figure 7.1.

## Some Final Thoughts on Participants "Assuming" the Risks of the Activity

Marketing and advertising are critically related to accurate depiction of the activity and, therefore, to dissemination of risk information. Program advertisements, brochures, websites, and other marketing materials should accurately reflect the risks involved (in other words, not negate or mislead participants about the actual risks) and should make clear that clients will be required to follow the program's policies and procedures and to sign a release agreement as a condition of participating in the activity. Inexperienced participants might erroneously believe the activity is completely safe simply because the program offers the activity or because the program accepts beginner or inexperienced participants. Outdoor programmers, of course, must seek the appropriate balance; there is an obvious tension between effectively marketing the activity and identifying and discussing the risks involved. The primary legal concern with marketing materials is that a participant may overcome a defense to a negligence claim or conceivably base a legal claim against the provider on alleged or express representations or misrepresentations if marketing materials or program descriptions are misleading. And while it may be tempting to tout a program's safety record, safety cannot be guaranteed, and participants must be aware of this fact.

> **Figure 7.1**  Beyond Getting a Signature, Outdoor Program Administrators Should Also Follow These Procedures
>
> - Allow participants sufficient time to read the document.
> - Nonreaders should have the agreement read to them and account for language barriers for nonnative speakers or foreign participants.
> - Educate your staff so they do not render your release meaningless by using inappropriate words or language that has the effect of nullifying release and waiver provisions.
> - Do not allow participants or clients to cross out words on the release—they either sign the agreement as is or are given a clean one to sign.
> - Consider having a staff member witness the participant signing the release agreement, and then have that staff person initial the back of the release so you have an identifiable witness to the validity of the signature.
> - Do not allow intoxicated individuals to sign a release agreement; they lack the legal capacity to understand or to bind themselves to the contract.
> - Retain the agreements! This point cannot be overstated. All signed release agreements should be kept at least as long as the statute of limitations in the state in which you operate or the activity took place. You may choose to retain and organize all waivers by trip because the documents provide names and addresses of other witnesses in the group from the time of the incident.
> - Organize documents and store them in a secure, fireproof cabinet or storage container. Consider scanning the originals so electronic copies are available. Courts usually will not consider or uphold lost or destroyed waivers.

As discussed earlier in the Failure to Warn section, both the provider and the participant also benefit from the oral discussions and safety briefings about risk. Again, informing the client or participant of the risks and requirements of the activity in a safety briefing format provides both she and the provider an opportunity to exchange information regarding risk and regarding the participant's tolerance for risk. Participants will likely feel empowered by greater knowledge and understanding of what the activity actually entails and, in turn, may be less likely or able to pursue a claim against the provider in the event of an accident or injury. This dialogue also allows the provider an opportunity to assess the client's fitness for the program, which is especially important with programs that involve more strenuous activities, multiple-day travel, or remote locations. Openly communicating about risk might dissuade some clients from participation, and this should be an acceptable result of the information dissemination process for any program or provider. Getting a good match between activity and participant is a goal of good advertising and risk communication.

## Postaccident Procedures

In the event of an accident and injury to a participant or client, operators must act reasonably in responding to a situation or incident both with respect to the client or participant and with respect to their program or operation. Postaccident conduct may have a lot to do with whether a program is sued. One of the best pieces of legal risk management advice for the program is to have a good relationship with its participants. The old maxim "it's harder to sue your buddy" is actually true in most cases. A lot of the anger from injured participants or clients can be dissipated by how they are dealt with after an incident.

In the event of an incident or accident, programmers should not assume that an injured client is getting appropriate medical care. Follow up with the participant to help ensure that medical needs are being met. Make sure to notify your insurance company right away to get advice on your conduct and what the insurer may be willing to pay for. Notify the relevant public land administrator and make sure reporting to the administrator is timely to avoid jeopardizing permits. If there are press inquiries regarding the incident, one central person from the program or operator should act as the designated spokesperson. Finally, develop a file on the incident that includes the following:

- Witness statements, complete lists of participants and addresses, staff and guide statements, and addresses
- Law enforcement files and contacts (again, notify your public land administrator)
- Photographs or videos—find out whether clients or others took photographs of the incident or scene and whether you can obtain them
- Participant agreements, including releases and exculpatory agreements and registration documents
- Radio logs or trip manifests
- Media reports

In addition to these, it is imperative that the program designate one person to communicate with the injured participant including, under the appropriate circumstances, sharing concern and empathy for the injured participant. Be careful, however, to avoid accepting responsibility for what happened because such statements might be considered "admissions" under the law and may negate defenses to any legal claim resulting from an incident. Finally, an important piece of the legal risk-management process postincident is anticipating how the participant may assemble evidence against you to prove a case of negligence, and then investigating the incident and gathering information for an appropriate response. This will require administrators to assess their incident file, identify witnesses and other evidence (such as photographs, written statements, video, and so forth), and consider how those factors may affect legal action against the program.

# ROLE OF INSURANCE IN LEGAL LIABILITY MATTERS

Insurance is a necessity. The costs related to an injury or accident involving a participant, particularly if a serious injury or multiple participants are involved, may be staggering and well beyond what most programs can afford to pay. Insurance is another method for parties to contractually shift the risk of liability and loss from one party to another, in this case from the outdoor program to the insurer. Insurance provides a means for programs to pay for the costs, including legal fees and damages, in the event of an accident. Some states require by law or regulation that commercial providers carry certain types of insurance with specified minimum liability limits. Public land managers also require insurance as a condition to obtain a special use permit to operate on public land. Insurance comes in many different forms, from standard liability insurance to specialty policies directed at particular types of outdoor recreation activities. The best insurance for a program depends on several factors but will primarily be driven by cost and the actual coverage provided by the policy.

Insurance companies have two primary duties to their policyholders when they issue policies of insurance. The first is the duty to defend the insured against lawsuits. If a participant sues a program following an injury, the program's insurer, pursuant to the contract for insurance, bears the costs of defending the participant's lawsuit. The insurer's duty to defend the insured in a lawsuit is broad and is triggered even when coverage for the claim may be questionable (though the duty to defend does not include claims in which the allegations are simply not covered under the policy). This duty to defend is important because of the extreme costs involved in defending a lawsuit.

The insurer's second duty under the policy is to 'indemnify' the insured for amounts, up to the limits of the insurance policy, that the insured becomes legally obligated to pay to a third party. The insurer's duty to indemnify the insured is narrower than the duty to defend, and applies only if the liability arises from the type of event or occurrence expressly covered by the insurance policy. When a claim exceeds coverage amounts, the insurer's obligation to indemnify, and to pay defense costs, ends when coverage amounts are exhausted. For this reason, administrators must be aware of insurance policy limits and purchase sufficient insurance to cover potential losses. Otherwise the program itself will become responsible to pay amounts above and beyond its insurance coverage.

## Standard Form and Specialty Insurance

The basic liability insurance policy available to any business, including outdoor recreation programs, is referred to in the insurance industry as the commercial general liability (CGL) policy. The CGL is a comprehensive insurance policy primarily covering bodily injury and property loss liability with certain conditions and exclusions to coverage. In addition to CGL policies, specialty insurers or underwriters may offer policies for specific and discreet outdoor activities. For example, a specialty insurer may provide a policy specifically for whitewater boaters, hunting clubs, or equestrian programs. Specialty insurers often provide more comprehensive coverage based on the insurer's familiarity with the exposure to risk.

Other types of general liability insurance, in addition to CGL or specialty insurance, include excess and umbrella insurance coverage. Excess insurance is an insurance policy that covers the same types of losses as the underlying CGL or specialty insurance policy except that it pays for losses in excess of the limits of the underlying policy. Umbrella insurance, on the other hand, is a broad excess insurance policy that comes into effect and pays for defense costs and losses not covered by any applicable underlying insurance policy. Most insurers offer only excess insurance as opposed to a true umbrella policy, which were more common in the past. Excess and umbrella insurance policies are insurance costs above and beyond the costs of standard form CGL insurance and specialty insurance. A program administrator must evaluate the overall risks and exposures to legal liability as well as the potential fiscal consequences of liability beyond insurance coverage to determine whether these additional insurance policies and associated expenses are warranted. Depending on the circumstances, an excess or umbrella insurance policy might be more affordable and be a financially better option for a provider to insure against damages arising from severe accidents.

An outdoor program that offers activities such as whitewater rafting should have specialty insurance in addition to a CGL policy because of the additional exposure to risk.

## The Concept of an Additional Insured

An "additional insured" is a person, entity, or party who is not specifically identified as insured under the policy but to whom the policyholder wishes to extend some measure of coverage under the policy. Status as an additional insured under another's policy generally arises because of a close relationship with the insured party or because of a contractual relationship with the insured party that requires the insured party to name the other party as an additional insured. If the language of the insured's policy itself does not grant additional insured status to certain other persons or entities, an *endorsement* to the policy will be required in order for the intended additional insured to become covered under the policy.

Additional insured "coverage" applies only to joint liability created by the insured and additional insured; the insurance never provides primary coverage for the additional insured. The additional insured does not have the same rights as the insured party under the insurance policy. A party named as an additional insured needs his own primary insurance to cover his own liabilities and to cover joint liabilities he might face with other vendors or programs.

When contracting for services with other programs or providing services on behalf of other programs, it may be desirable to be identified as an additional insured under the other program's insurance policy. It is imperative that the contracting parties take care to identify the circumstances under which one or the other should be identified as an additional insured under the relevant insurance policy. A review of the relevant insurance policy or endorsement is also necessary to ensure that additional insured status is actually achieved. Many insurance companies require evidence of a written agreement obligating the insured party to name another party as an additional insured before an additional insured endorsement is valid. Also, many insurers will not provide or extend additional insured coverage after completion of the work or services identified in the contract, which effectively terminates the additional insured status.

## Professional Liability and Other Insurance Coverage

Another type or category of insurance coverage that might be necessary for some programs is a coverage known as professional liability errors and omissions, or E&O insurance. E&O insurance provides coverage for professionals and professional liability or malpractice. Professionals are generally individuals who possess specialized, technical knowledge, training, and skills. An important difference between professional liability insurance and a standard CGL policy is that professional liability insurance usually applies only to losses that result directly from professional negligence, not for bodily injury or property damages. Thus E&O insurance is not a substitute for general liability insurance.

Another type of potentially relevant insurance is director and officer (D&O) liability insurance. This insurance protects directors and officers of formally organized corporate entities. D&O insurance protects corporate officers and members of the board of directors from the decisions they make and actions they take connected to their corporate duties and in setting policies, procedures, or business direction for the program. Generally, D&O coverage applies when directors and officers act in good faith in carrying out their duties but something still goes wrong. This insurance will usually not provide coverage to legal claims arising from malicious or intentionally wrongful conduct. Some programs, particularly nonprofit entities that are incorporated, might wish to protect the officers and directors who oversee or administer the program. Typically, D&O insurance incorporates "pay on your behalf" language in the policy for defense costs, which means the insurer will pay out those costs on behalf of the directors and officers after liability has been established. As a result, payouts under such a policy are typically to cover defense costs.

Employment practices liability (EPL) or fidelity insurance is another potentially necessary insurance coverage. EPL provides coverage to formally organized entities for lawsuits filed by employees or former employees for specified employment practices, including discrimination or harassment. Programs should also consider policies that provide commercial automobile and worker's compensation coverage so they are protected against claims deriving from car accidents and employee injuries. Circumstances such as cost, exposure to liability, and formal organization of the program often dictate the need for these types of coverage.

## Self-Insurance Versus Private Insurance

Many public universities (and some private ones) that run outdoor recreation programs are self-insured. Large commercial outfitters may also be self-insured. The concept or fact of self-insurance might affect the insurance-related services available to a program or provider, and how a program or provider ultimately views and analyzes exposure to risks and liability. Institutions or businesses that are self-insured basically set aside a certain amount of money to cover liabilities and defense costs.

Typically, even large institutions such as public universities self-insure only up to a certain amount. Self-insuring might help an entity avoid the high costs of primary insurance, but it becomes too risky when the costs-savings outweigh potential exposure to liability. For this reason, self-insuring entities often carry regular or standard form liability coverage for amounts greater than the self-insurance limits, or the "self-insured retention." For example, a university might be self-insured up to one million dollars and then purchase commercial or other insurance to cover damages in excess of the self-insured retention amount.

## Practical Considerations

As a practical matter in obtaining insurance, outdoor recreation programs and providers should seek out an insurance broker and company or underwriter that specializes in outdoor risks or has experience with insurance in the outdoor industry. The broker or insuring agent's experience with recreational programming is necessary so that they understand what programs and commercial providers deal with in terms of actual risk and exposure, and so the insurer can provide appropriate risk-management and loss-control services when necessary.

In the process of obtaining insurance, operators should be proactive on their own behalf and demonstrate that they are a good risk for the insurance company. This may be accomplished by demonstrating to the insurer that the program or operation has an active and comprehensive risk-management program in place. Programmers and operators should approach insurers as if they are "selling" their operation to the insurer. Complete all applications for insurance in a comprehensive and professional manner. Invite brokers to visit the business and see how it is operated. Have waiver and release agreements available for review and comment. Have policy and procedure manuals available for review; maintain employee-training manuals and employee files, including criminal background checks; have equipment checks and safety reviews cataloged and regularly scheduled on an ongoing basis; and demonstrate that the program makes a consistent effort in following and enforcing stated policies and procedures. These efforts will help the insurer understand the program or operator's risk profile, and will likely result in better and more affordable insurance coverage.

## SUMMARY

Administering an outdoor recreation program naturally involves significant legal considerations because programs often undertake or offer activities that involve unique risks for injury or accidents. Understanding the relevant legal issues assists program administrators in conducting appropriate risk management for both the delivery of the actual outdoor activity and for the potential legal consequences of delivering the program or activity. Knowledge of the elements of negligence will better prepare a program to identify and satisfy its duty of care to participants, or avoid breaching the duty of care. Understanding the role of inherent risk and legal defenses to negligence, such as assumption of risk, also helps programs proactively identify and approach risks in a professional manner. Proper formation and implementation of release and waiver agreements enhances communication with participants about risk and helps educate participants so they can decide for themselves whether to assume the risks involved in an activity. Finally, insuring against the risk of liability not only satisfies the usual legal requirements of state licensing boards and federal land managers but also provides an administrator with a relatively affordable way to shift the risks and costs associated with accidents to the insurer.

# Chapter 8

# Budgeting and Financial Operations of Outdoor Programs

*Tim J. Moore, MS, and Geoff Harrison, MS*

Outdoor program administrators are responsible for using sound fiscal management practices. Because many outdoor programs are nested within larger organizations, it is critical that each program's administrators ensure that business plans and practices are in alignment, congruence, and support of the mission statements and core values of the parent organization. Once the objectives for the business are identified in the business plan, the outdoor program administrator is responsible for developing and managing a financial budget that attains the stated goals.

In thinking through the processes and systems of budgeting and financial operations for an outdoor program, one must consider the potential market, resources, program opportunities, related expenses, and potential revenues. Through this analysis an appropriate mix of programs and services can be created to maximize opportunities, efficiency, effectiveness, and ultimately participant satisfaction and learning. Specific budgets for the identified mix of programs and services can then be developed, administered, evaluated, and adjusted to ensure ongoing program success.

Outdoor program administrators are charged with the fiduciary responsibility to provide programs and services to stakeholders in their community. Depending on the program mission, stakeholders can include groups such as military personnel and family members; university students, faculty, staff, alumni, and associated family members; and residents of a particular state or local municipality. Prudent fiscal oversight and management of programs and services is a primary responsibility of outdoor program administrators; however, their duties also encompass the need to ensure that ample and available programs and services exist to meet the needs of their stakeholders. To strike a balance between fiscal constraints and programmatic needs across time, administrators should develop a plan that addresses the outdoor recreation and education needs of the community they serve and then work to find resources to fund them. This is preferable to first identifying available financial resources and then developing programs and services that fit within the constraints of these resources. The design-first, fund-second approach offers administrators a greater chance of obtaining program success because it allows the opportunity to identify creative solutions for cultivating and developing the financial resources needed to serve their community.

However, outdoor program administrators will also find it helpful to ask themselves and their staff other important questions when creating or evaluating their outdoor program business plan and subsequent budget plan. These questions include but are not limited to the following:

- Is the outdoor program business plan congruent with institutional, divisional, departmental, and program mission statements and core values?

- Does the outdoor program business plan address divisional and departmental strategic plans?
- Does the outdoor program business plan meet industry standards related to staffing and supervision, safety, education, and environmental stewardship?
- Does the outdoor program business plan meet the desires and needs of the community that it aspires to serve?

Departmental directors, business managers, and participants expect outdoor program administrators to make sound business decisions that maximize the availability of programs and services, enhance leadership and employment development opportunities, and generate participant satisfaction—all at the best possible value to the organization.

A key task for the outdoor program administrator is to efficiently develop financial systems and structures that will ensure careful and efficient fiscal management, offering programs and resources that serve the needs of the community, and the time to do the work they enjoy. An entrepreneurial spirit combined with careful fiscal management can provide more opportunities to grow a business capable of better serving the needs of its community.

In this chapter you will learn concepts and techniques related to program and budget development, forecasting, daily financial operations, reconciliation, and budget analysis.

# BUDGET COMPONENTS

In general, the process of budgeting can be thought of as the art of identifying and managing costs associated with producing a desired outcome.

*The Statement of Federal Financial Accounting Standards #4, Managerial Cost Accounting Concepts and Standards for the Federal Government states that "cost" is the monetary value of resources used or sacrificed or liabilities incurred to achieve an objective, such as to acquire or produce a good or to perform an activity or service. Costs incurred may benefit current and future periods. In financial accounting and reporting, the costs that apply to an entity's operations for the current period are recognized as expenses of that period. (FASAB, 1996, p. 15)*

When developing a program budget, a professional must consider both available resources and related expenses. Budget methods vary from organization to organization, but common budget items include personnel, equipment, transportation, program operations, physical facilities, and capital expenditures. Each of the aforementioned items may reflect a cost category that will be further detailed by specific line items to denote exactly how a cost is being generated. See table 8.1 for an illustration of how categories and line items can be documented in a budget.

Four common terms used to illustrate levels of relations within an organization are institutional, divisional, departmental, and program.

**Table 8.1** Example of a Budget Category and Line Items Within the Category

| Category type | | | Category total | |
|---|---|---|---|---|
| Communication services | | | **$6,960.00** | |
| | Account code | Line item description | Line item cost | Comment |
| | 503000 | Phone or fax—local and equipment | $5,400.00 | Office phones |
| | 503300 | Cellular or wireless phone services | $360.00 | Professional staff cell phone subsidy |
| | 505000 | Other communication services | $1,200.00 | Satellite phone rental and spot device service charges |

- *Institutional example:* University of Nebraska Lincoln (UNL) or the United States Army
- *Divisional example:* A unit within the greater institution, such as UNL Student Affairs or Fort Carson Army Base
- *Departmental example:* A department within a division, such as UNL Campus Recreation Directorate or Fort Carson Family Morale Welfare and Recreation (FMWR)
- *Program example:* A program within the department, such as UNL Campus Recreation Outdoor Adventures or the Fort Carson FMWR Adventure Programs and Education

In addition to the identification and management of costs, potential sources of funding and revenue must also be considered to either offset or reduce the debt-to-revenue ratio of the overall budget. In developing a budget, the outdoor program administrator must first assess the size and scope of the program based on the assessed needs of the community to be served, develop an outdoor program business plan to serve those needs, and then formulate a budgetary plan based on available and potential resources. Outdoor program administrators must understand that budgeting is not an exact science; however, through careful construction, planning, management, analysis, and adjustment, a budget can become an accurate and powerful management tool.

## Personnel

The most important and expensive resource for any outdoor program is personnel. Personnel costs include recruiting, salary, benefits, and training costs. Understanding the availability and skills of potential staff are key elements in the budgeting process. From financial and operational perspectives, outdoor program administrators must evaluate the availability of staff resources in the local area, the training and certification one can expect to require as a condition of employment, the cost to provide necessary training for staff, and the availability and cost of outsourcing program leadership. Institutional staffing requirements may also affect staffing decisions that can ultimately shape programming possibilities.

## Equipment

Outdoor program equipment generally falls into one of two categories: capital equipment or operational equipment. Capital equipment is usually considered by organizations to be large ticket items in excess of a certain dollar amount (e.g., $1,000-$5,000 or more per unit) that will have a scheduled life of service, after which they may be liquidated for either a predetermined value or an undetermined public auction price. Capital equipment for an outdoor program might include facilities, machinery, vehicles, and other costly items such as whitewater rafts. Capital equipment will often have maintenance expenses that will be incurred over the life of the product. Operational equipment involves items that cost less than the institutional minimum requirement for capital equipment, have potentially a shorter service life, and are more likely to be consumed (lost, damaged, or destroyed) in the process of delivering programs and services. Most organizations have specific definitions, requirements, and procedures for capital equipment and operational equipment purchases.

For many outdoor programs, capital equipment may be provided, procured, or maintained by other organizational departments (transportation services, grounds, or physical facilities). However, some programs might be required to procure and maintain their own capital equipment. In these cases, outdoor program administrators should meet with appropriate parties (project managers, purchasing agents, etc.) to learn institutional requirements for developing and funding capital plans; developing, evaluating, and selecting requests for proposal or bid quotes; or other activities related to capital equipment purchases.

The appropriation of resources for the procurement of outdoor program operational equipment must be focused on core programmatic needs. During the start-up phase of a new program, equipment purchases are regularly targeted at general camping categories rather than a sport-specific equipment inventory because these items can support all types of customer activities. General camping items such as tents and sleeping bags can be used for any type of overnight activity. Another common equipment purchasing scenario is for a program to acquire equipment that targets popular local activities that in time could support the development of other programs and services. An example of this approach is the purchase of snowshoes and cross-country skis for a program located in an area of abundant local snowfall. After the initial rental inventory has been purchased, the program may elect to start using the equipment for instructional programs. Over time, the gathering of data on program participation and participant feedback can help an administrator refine the program vision and aid in developing a more comprehensive rental equipment inventory that meets the needs of their customers.

Rather than maintain an exhaustive inventory of sport-specific equipment, an administrator might elect to develop reciprocal agreements focused on equipment sharing with other organizations. Reciprocal agreements for the use of sport-specific equipment can help an administrator offer instructional programs with equipment that cannot initially be afforded by the program. Boise State University, for example, works with other universities to rent surfboards and sea kayaks for beach-based trips and regularly provides mountain and river equipment to schools interested in offering programs in the mountain states. More information concerning the development, purchasing, and liquidation of program inventories and rental program operations can be found in chapter 16. Specific trip and instructional program equipment inventories are addressed in chapters 19 and 20.

## Transportation and Travel Expenses

Another major area of any outdoor program budget is transportation and travel expenses. Program transportation includes travel-related costs for reconnaissance of future activity sites, transporting participants to activity sites, and the costs of travel for staff who attend professional conferences, trainings, workshops, and seminars. The rising cost of fuel and vehicle maintenance and increased risk-management concerns surrounding transportation have all complicated the landscape of travel programs by escalating costs of transportation and personnel.

An analysis of transportation and travel expense options and related costs is critical to the overall success of any outdoor program. Because of the complexity and expense of transportation, it might be helpful to isolate these expenses in an outdoor program budget to monitor costs and ensure efficiency and effectiveness of program operations. Regular questions that should be considered by administrators include the following:

- Based on travel patterns, overall program operations, and availability of vehicles, is it better to outsource, own, lease, or rent vehicles?

- What types of vehicles are required? (It might be better to have a mixed fleet of fuel-efficient cars for day hikers so you don't use the organization's 10-ton truck for every trip.)

- Are there institutional arrangements that can help reduce the costs of travel, lodging, or related travel expenses (e.g., institutional hotel rate contracts, rental rate contracts, or airfare contracts)?

- Are there proximate resource areas that can be used to provide affordable opportunities to all members of the community being served?

## Operational Expenses

General expenses related to conducting the routine business of an outdoor program fit under program operations and might include items such as telephones, computers, software, copiers, office supplies, marketing and printing expenses, utilities, and cleaning and maintenance supplies and services. This area may initially be a catch-all for expenses that do not fit neatly under other areas, but over time an administrator can identify operational expenses that may require special attention or monitoring and move these to a separate or subordinate line item in the budget. For example, operational expenses might have several subordinate budget lines that include categories such as supplies and materials, services, computers, printers, communications, and marketing. Additionally, expenses attributed to credit card fees, taxes, refunds, coupons, and complimentary programs or services should be considered operational expenses.

## Physical Facilities

The size and location of physical facilities for outdoor program operations and the program's proximity to participants and outdoor recreation resource areas will affect the size and scope of program operations, staff, transportation, equipment, and potential program fee structures. Facilities must be large enough to store and manage appropriate equipment inventories and conduct the operations of an outdoor program. Common facility space needs for an outdoor program include areas for administrative functions, rental and retail operations, meeting spaces, vehicle storage, classrooms, climbing wall, team challenge courses, rope courses, boat storage facility, and trip preparation and staging areas. Additional facility needs might include proximal parking and loading zones for customers to pick up and return rental equipment. From a fiscal management standpoint, it is critical for the outdoor recreation administrator to understand if costs related to physical facilities will be included in the outdoor program budget. Items such as utilities, routine facility maintenance, facility modifications or renovation, and debt retirement can all significantly affect the program business plan.

## Revenue

For many outdoor programs, revenue sources include institutional support, student fees, user-generated program fees, and possible endowments, gifts, and grants. Each one of these sources can play a unique role in the development and operation of an outdoor program.

Each parent organization, be it a municipal township, university, or military base will have a model or method for the allocation of funds to outdoor program areas. Program areas that are viewed by a parent organization as less traditional or mainstream might receive a smaller funding allocation. Disproportionate funding can be attributed to factors such as program visibility, participation numbers, and a perception that user fees are an appropriate source of revenue for outdoor program operations. Disproportionate funding might also be related more to the philosophical background of the leadership of the recreational sports department or the historical development of the department than to the actual needs of the community.

Climbing walls are an example of a physical facility commonly operated by an outdoor program.

Justification for allocation of institutional support or student fees might also be related to participation numbers. For example, by virtue of the type of program offerings, intramural sports and group exercise fitness programs can generally claim higher participation numbers than outdoor programs. Counting participation numbers is a common strategy used to develop requests to receive a greater share of the available institutional or user fee support. Unfortunately, use of participation numbers to compare programs is like comparing apples to oranges. If outdoor professionals look at an equalized unit of participation, such as "participation hours," all recreational sports programs could vie for institutional and user fee support on equal footing. Each institution defines how participation should be reported. Because there is not one standard method for reporting participation, an example is to calculate the number of participants times the number of contact hours of each program. For a weekend climbing trip with a three-hour pretrip skill workshop and pretrip meeting, the number of participation hours might look something like this:

$$12 \text{ participants} \times (3 \text{ hours workshop} $$
$$\text{and meeting} + 51 \text{ trip hours}) = 648$$
$$\text{participation hours}$$

Similarly, rental program participation hours could be calculated by asking renters how many people will be using the equipment listed on their contract, or calculating use of the item by the highest possible number of users times the length of the rental contract. For example, if the rental contract includes six sleeping bags for a weeklong rental, the participation hours could be calculated at:

$$6 \text{ participants} (1 \text{ per sleeping bag}) \times 56$$
$$\text{hours} (8 \text{ activity hours per day}) = 336$$
$$\text{participation hours}$$

With the current emphasis on the cocurricular learning experience and learning outcomes, outdoor recreation and education programs may have an opportunity to challenge disparate funding models by demonstrating the unique ability to design and develop programs and services that meet institutionally driven agendas. Outdoor program administrators who work to support institutionally driven agendas stand to have their programs benefit financially during budgeting cycles that allow for the redistribution of institutional and user fee allocations if they accurately document the use of offered programs and services.

Other opportunities to develop institutional support include collaborative efforts with academic and administrative departments and programs. Collaborative programming can help build bridges and provide funding and support for other outdoor program operations. Examples of collaborative programs include orientation programs, credit-bearing expeditions, field study programs, group and leadership development programs, service learning, civic engagement, and alumni programs.

Some outdoor programs operate solely on a fee-for-service basis, and for most collegiate, municipal, and MWR outdoor programs, fees charged for participation in trips, workshops, and seminars are the largest resource for program revenues. For this reason, it is critical that program fees are carefully assessed, monitored, and adjusted to maximize the opportunities for programming and service.

An accurate knowledge of the fair market values or average prices for similar programs and services in the local market is critical during the assessment and development of program fee structures. Understanding and structuring how the allocation of institutional support and student fees influences this equation is equally important. An example of this concept would be looking at the fees for competitive sports and outdoor programs at other public entities (schools and municipalities) and private entities (schools and private businesses) in the local market and comparing them to the intramural and outdoor program fees at one's own institution. This analysis might assist the outdoor program administrator in garnering a greater share of institutional support or student fees and justify the assessment of program fees.

Another strategy for determining fee structures is activity-based budgeting, which combines the direct and indirect costs of providing programs and services and establishing fees. Specifics related to how this strategy can be employed is included in the following segment on budget development strategies under activity-based costing.

Endowments, gifts, and grants can also provide important revenue support for an outdoor program. The bonds made with outdoor program participants can lead to a lifetime of parent and alumni giving. More information on developing endowments, gifts, and grants was provided in chapter 6.

# BUDGET-DEVELOPMENT STRATEGIES

A budget can be viewed as a purposeful plan for tracking revenue and expenses. Once crafted, a budget serves as a mechanism by which an outdoor program administrator can measure the fiscal performance of his or her organization. A well-crafted budget serves as a plan of action for business decision making, a measure for organizational performance, and a touchstone for identifying and managing adverse economic conditions.

The process for developing a budget will vary from institution to institution; however, key components of all budget formats offer the ability to track revenue and expenses, help identify areas for improvements, and serve as a platform to influence policy making and overall business development. Budget formats will vary from program to program and can be incredibly varied and unique. Most programs ultimately develop a blended format that applies the strengths and minimizes the weaknesses of each budgeting style. The following summary of budgeting methods will help outdoor program administrators understand contemporary approaches to budgeting so they may obtain better information for effective decision making and

programmatic success. A complete and accurate budget assists the outdoor program administrator in working more effectively to report program performance, analyze program financial viability, develop fee structures, and create and maintain a mix of programs and services that ensure program sustainability. See table 8.2 for a comparison of strengths and weaknesses of the four budgeting methods covered in the following section.

**Table 8.2** Budget Comparison Chart

| Budgeting method | Strengths | Limitations |
|---|---|---|
| Incremental line item budgeting | • Simple and time effective method of budgeting<br>• Easy to train new fiscal managers the methods used to develop budgets<br>• Does not compare program to program within a budget but rather looks at each line in the budget independent of the other lines<br>• Easy to compile master budgets that include budgets of lesser programs because line items remain relatively static and can be tracked from year to year | • Assumes historical expenditures are valid and that any future increases are automatically accepted<br>• Inaccuracies of the past automatically moved forward with a higher financial authorization<br>• Does not account for variables outside the control of the organization (rising fuel costs, saturation of consumer markets by other vendors, staffing changes, etc.), which can lead to huge miscalculations of budget<br>• Administrator has very little discretion on how money is spent because it is allocated to particular lines and in general is not transferable between categories or line items |
| Performance-based budgeting | • Uses a mission-driven budgeting strategy to assess attainment of performance goals and expectations<br>• Is by design results-oriented and provides clear measures for assessment<br>• Is inherently flexible in design because it allows for multiple means to achieve stated goals | • Requires administrator to link performance measures or indicators to particular resources within the greater budget<br>• Requires detailed tracking of resources to accurately track true allocation of resources to the attainment of the stated goals<br>• Requires administrators who are deeply knowledgeable of the organization, its mission, how it operates, recognize its efficiencies and inefficiencies, and are committed to the overall improvement of the organization<br>• Is difficult to train to new staff on PBB method because it requires some level of institutional knowledge |

*(continued)*

**Table 8.2** *(continued)*

| Budgeting method | Strengths | Limitations |
|---|---|---|
| Performance-based budgeting *(continued)* | | • Does not account for intangible benefits of programming, such as feeder programs that might not be financially viable but might serve as doorways to other programs that might cover the feeder program shortages |
| Zero-based budgeting | • Requires detailed understanding of specific programs and services<br>• Requires administrator to honestly evaluate each program and service on its ability to achieve stated goals<br>• Can promote efficiency in overall operation by identifying costly obsolete systems | • Has a high probability of creating conflict within an organization because programming units fight to be perceived as a high-priority candidate for funding<br>• Allows one program to go underfunded or entirely unfunded while another may receive an increase in funding<br>• Extremely time consuming and requires administrators who are deeply knowledgeable of the organization, its mission, programs and services, and overall historic fiscal and programmatic performance of the organization |
| Activity-based costing | • Requires administrators to consider outdoor programs as complete business units rather than a series of programmatic service islands (climbing gym, rentals, education and trips, etc.)<br>• Tracks both direct and indirect costs associated with any program or service<br>• Assists with assessing the viability of programs before they are offered<br>• Aids in the refinement of the fee structures for programs and services | • Possible resistance from administrators to honestly track expenses for pet projects<br>• Requires detailed tracking systems to accurately assign a portion of consumed resources across budget lines<br>• Requires administrators who are deeply knowledgeable of the interconnectedness of programs and services<br>• Must be done in combination with activity-based accounting and management practices |

# Line Item Incremental Budgeting

Incremental budgeting is a method that groups costs into broad categories and then details each type of expense down to a particular line item. This simple budgeting strategy is commonly used to develop institutional budgets. In incremental budget development, the current year's budget is used as a base, and a percentage increase can be

electively added to account for rising costs of doing the same amount of business for the next year (see table 8.3 for an example). This is a quick and useful process for budgeting several years ahead for stable, established programs in which no changes in programs or services are planned for the years being projected. However, using incremental budgeting as the sole strategy can lead to numerous problems and errors because this system takes for granted that last year's budget and program were appropri-

**Table 8.3**  Incremental Budgeting Example

| Expense category | Previous fiscal year | Current fiscal year | Next fiscal year |
|---|---|---|---|
| Base professional staff salaries (3% increase per year) | $84,000 | $86,520 | $89,116 |
| Benefits (40% of base salaries) | $33,600 | $34,608 | $35,646 |
| Student staff salaries (2% increase per year) | $46,000 | $46,920 | $47,858 |
| Benefits (4% of student salaries) | $1,840 | $1,876 | $1,914 |

ate and that needs and trends will not change in the coming years.

# Performance- or Target-Based Budgeting

Performance-based budgeting operates on the premise that budget allocations should favor the high-performing business units within an organization rather than broadly funding all programs and initiatives (Blanchard, 2006). When outdoor program administrators use performance- or target-based budgeting, they focus on specific financial or programmatic goals rather than on direct allocations. Operating with a focus on goals and subsequent performance measures is one of the key defining characteristics between performance-based budgeting and traditional budgeting approaches. Performance-based allocations offer incentives to administrators to improve performance within their programming unit in an effort to be awarded a higher allocation of the institutions finite resources (Blanchard, 2006). For example, administrators might set a goal for the annual average number of use days for specific pieces of equipment before expanding inventory. By establishing benchmarks for rental performance, an administrator can make sure that the cost to acquire, house, maintain, and replace equipment is factored into the decision making for purchasing additional equipment and removing items from the inventory. Another example would be to set a net revenue goal for fall adventure trips that is tied to decisions for offering a slate of trip programs planned for the spring of

the fiscal year. As a result, if the program does not meet the participation and revenue goals for the fall season, they may stipulate in the budget that certain programs or events may be canceled or expenses reduced in the spring program in an effort to balance the budget at the end of the year.

A performance-based budget lists what each administrative unit aspires to accomplish, how they anticipate accomplishing the goals, what resources will be needed to accomplish the goals, and what the measures for success will be (Rubin, 2000). Performance budgeting also reviews prior performance to help project future ability to meet current goals and expectations.

The federal accounting standards advisory board details the five core accounting standards for performance budgeting (FASAB, 1995):

- Accumulating and reporting costs of activities on a regular basis for management information purposes
- Establishing responsibility segments to match costs with outputs
- Determining full costs of government goods and services
- Recognizing the costs of goods and services provided among federal entities
- Using appropriate costing methodologies to accumulate and assign costs to outputs

Benefits to using a performance- or target-based budgeting strategy include (1) staff staying focused on and invested in financial success, because they are rewarded for their accomplishments and (2) outdoor professionals maintaining flexibility in programming based on attainment of performance goals and expectations. To some extent, many programs use performance-based budgeting when they establish a minimum registration number as a factor for deciding whether a trip will go out or be canceled.

## Zero-Based Budgeting

Instead of justifying increases over the previous year, as done in incremental budget preparation, administrators preparing zero-based budgets are required to methodically analyze all program needs and operations. The method assigns costs to all levels of an operation (programs and services) and then prioritizes all the available options from high to low. Top-priority items are funded first, and then lower priority items are funded based on available resources. In zero-based budgeting, administrators must be able to explain and defend the entire budget allocation request through a line-by-line analysis and justification.

In concept, the advantages of this type of budgeting are that administrators must honestly evaluate programs against predetermined criteria and develop a very accurate budget based on previous years' performance and outcomes and the stated goals for the next year. Through this process, outdoor program administrators can identify areas in which budgets might be inflated from incremental increases, inefficiencies in program operations, and obsolete systems, programs, or services. This strategy allows the program administrator to make scientific decisions on program vitality, efficiency, and effectiveness.

Using a zero-based budgeting strategy may be helpful to fully investigate programs that have financial or operational issues or programs that might be experiencing major changes, such as new facility development. Zero-based budgeting is an extremely time-consuming process and is rarely used as a wholesale budget format for an entire organization because it can create internal vulnerabilities for particular programs, services, and business units. Because funding allocations are based from high priority to low priority there is a possibility that an entire business unit might not be funded for a particular year. This uncertainty can make it difficult to ensure that multiyear projects are adequately funded for the duration of the project.

To minimize the few negative aspects of zero-based budgeting, many businesses elect to use a modified version of performance-based or target budgeting. This method follows a similar process as zero-based budgeting, but when it comes to the assessment and allocation process, it allows only 5 to 10 percent of a department's budget to be at risk for reallocation (Rubin, 2000).

## Activity-Based Costing

Activity-based costing (ABC), also called activity-based budgeting, is a relatively modern approach to fiscal management that attributes the appropriate portion of all operational costs to each program or service function. See table 8.4 for an example. This model allows the outdoor professional to better understand the total cost of doing business in each business unit because it assigns a portion of the overall organizational support costs (administrative staff, marketing, office supplies, etc.) to each specific programming area (e.g., climbing wall, rental shop, challenge course, trips, education program) and then more specifically to each step of the process required to produce a particular product or service. Administrators using this model will assign costs down the line to each specific program function (e.g., weekend backpacking trip, rental equipment purchasing, climbing wall basic skills clinic, participant registration, fueling vehicles, packing equipment). ABC models can be useful for outdoor professionals who strive to improve program efficiency and effectiveness because it helps them understand the impa ct of direct and indirect costs in program operations, helps them accurately appropriate resources, and aids them in making decisions on program viability and fee structures (Blanchard, 2006).

*Direct costs* are those that can be readily attributed to a program, such as instructional staff, transportation, and consumables. Some programs consider direct program costs only when developing a budget or evaluating the financial success of a specific program.

*Indirect costs* are expenses not directly traceable to the development and execution of a program or service. Indirect costs are harder to quantify but are critically important to developing an ABC model. Once direct costs are assigned to programming units, then administrators using the ABC method allocate the remaining indirect costs via a method of prorating a share of the costs to each program through the use of key cost drivers (Blanchard 2006). Cost drivers are any factors that cause a change in the cost of an operation. As an example, an educational trip can have multiple cost drivers, such as labor, transportation, personnel expenses for administrative support, office supplies, marketing, data and phone equipment, and lighting, heating, and cooling of the office space. Businesses often develop strategies to prorate or portion out indirect expenses across an entire budget to ensure that the resources spent to support a particular program or service are tracked and reconciled in the master budget. By calculating indirect costs such as administrative salaries, facility maintenance, or marketing expenses attributed to specific programs, administrators can truly quantify the resources being used to provide specific programs and services, assess the accuracy of the current fee schedule, and evaluate the viability of any particular program. For example, if a program offers extended (15 to 30+ days) or international trips

Geoff Harrison

The cost a participant pays for a trip or activity may not cover all of the direct and indirect costs.

rather than weekend trips, the amount of administrative time per trip for managing logistics increases

**Table 8.4**  Activity Based Costing (Direct Costs + Assigned Organizational Costs + Assigned Administrative Costs)

| Type of cost | Description | Examples |
|---|---|---|
| Direct costs | • Supplies and personnel costs specifically for program | • Participant meals<br>• Land use permits<br>• Gasoline for vehicles<br>• Instructional staff wages<br>• Consumable program-specific recreation equipment such as water purification tablets, etc. |
| Assigned organizational costs | • Costs that change in direct proportion to output. The addition of 10 new revenue-generating programs midsemester would be included in this category because their addition will increase the pressure on finite administrative, fiscal, personnel, and physical resources. | • Professional staff salaries and benefits<br>• Marketing materials produced specifically for the program<br>• Labor to staff booths to promote programs for an entire semester |
| Assigned general administrative costs | • Costs incurred regardless of the size and scope of the operation. These are the costs that cannot be reasonably attributed to one particular program or service but are required to support the functioning of the entire operation. | • Office operations costs such as phone, fax, copier<br>• Marketing materials to promote overall program<br>• Depreciation of equipment regardless of use<br>• Vehicle maintenance |

exponentially, which in turn affects the administrative time that could be spent in other program areas. This administrative resource is important to ensure program success, but if these costs are not attributed to the specific program(s), then program fees cannot be accurately set to cover the full cost of the program.

Initially, developing an ABC model is an arduous and painstaking process. It is critical to develop templates that can be used and modified for different program areas.

Because of the nature of outdoor program operations, ABC is useful in allocating expenses and thus is used as an example for the subsequent section on developing a budget.

# FORECASTING EXPENSES AND REVENUE

Whether an outdoor program administrator is developing a new outdoor program or working to redevelop budgets to identify efficiencies, it is helpful to develop outdoor program budgets from the ground up (see table 8.5). To this end, using standardized small business software or spreadsheet templates that roll up into the overall program budget can be helpful. In this way, outdoor program administrators can see specific details and make changes in individual program budget lines or program area budgets and readily see the impact they have on the overall program budget.

**Table 8.5** Trip Program Budget vs. Actual

| Activity period and description | Rev. (exp.) | Revenue | Expense | Labor | Promo | Vehicles | Meals | Camp fees | Permits | Misc |
|---|---|---|---|---|---|---|---|---|---|---|
| *Projected fall budget based on a minimum of 6 participants per trip (maximum participants 10 per trip)* | | | | | | | | | | |
| Intro to outdoor climbing | $154.70 | $510.00 | $355.30 | $200.00 | $25.00 | $55.00 | $60.00 | $– | $15.30 | $– |
| River raft or cave combo | $72.50 | $750.00 | $677.50 | $300.00 | $25.00 | $125.00 | $150.00 | $40.00 | $22.50 | $15.00 |
| Intro to backpacking | $61.10 | $630.00 | $568.90 | $300.00 | $25.00 | $105.00 | $120.00 | $– | $18.90 | $– |
| Intro to canoeing | $36.80 | $690.00 | $653.20 | $300.00 | $25.00 | $140.00 | $120.00 | $40.00 | $20.70 | $7.50 |
| Advanced climbing | $17.90 | $570.00 | $552.10 | $350.00 | $25.00 | $100.00 | $60.00 | $– | $17.10 | $– |
| **Program total** | **$346.70** | **$3,360.00** | **$3,013.30** | **$1,550.00** | **$150.00** | **$570.00** | **$540.00** | **$80.00** | **$100.80** | **$22.50** |
| *Actual fall budget* | | | | | | | | | | |
| Full moon night hike | $41.55 | $315.00 | $273.45 | $150.00 | $25.00 | $52.00 | $37.00 | $– | $9.45 | $– |
| Intro to outdoor climbing | $177.15 | $595.00 | $417.85 | $225.00 | $25.00 | $75.00 | $55.00 | $– | $17.85 | $20.00 |
| River raft or cave combo | $495.50 | $1,250.00 | $754.50 | $400.00 | $25.00 | $125.00 | $127.00 | $40.00 | $37.50 | $– |
| Intro to backpacking | $85.95 | $735.00 | $649.05 | $325.00 | $25.00 | $140.00 | $137.00 | $– | $22.05 | $– |
| Intro to canoeing | $308.95 | $1,035.00 | $726.05 | $300.00 | $25.00 | $140.00 | $155.00 | $40.00 | $31.05 | $35.00 |
| Advanced climbing | $285.35 | $855.00 | $569.65 | $350.00 | $25.00 | $100.00 | $69.00 | $– | $25.65 | $– |
| **Program total** | **$1,394.45** | **$4,785.00** | **$3,390.55** | **$1,750.00** | **$150.00** | **$632.00** | **$580.00** | **$80.00** | **$143.55** | **$55.00** |

However, an outdoor program budget may also be developed from the top down by defining operational parameters such as program participation levels, operational hours, employee pay rates, staffing levels, travel distances, and other factors. For example, a program professional may define parameters for developing a full cost expense budget for weekend trips to include the following:

- Trips that leave Friday or Saturday and return Sunday
- Travel distances of 250 miles or less
- A conservative daily vehicle and mileage charge
- Participation levels at 8 to 16 depending on the type of trip, permit group size limits, vehicle limits, and other factors
- Rates of pay at the area wage per hour times a certain number of hours for leaders, and the area wage per hour times a lesser number of hours for assistant leaders
- A per-day expense for equipment, physical facilities, and program operations per type of trip or use of resources
- Marketing expenses based on the average cost of promoting weekend trips per type or length of trip

With this information, the administrator could then decide on the types and number of trips to be offered and develop an approximate ABC weekend trip program expense budget. Similarly, parameters could be developed for extended trips, instruction workshops, a rental program, climbing wall, and challenge programs, and budgets could be built for these program areas as well.

Expense budget template worksheets created by the outdoor program administrator can then be saved as documents for that particular year, and rolled up into the major heading areas previously discussed, including personnel, equipment, transportation, program operations, physical facilities, and revenue (see table 8.5). Once the exact trip locations are selected, and after trips are administered, more exacting or actual expenses can be used to reforecast the annual budget.

## Forecasting

Forecasting is the practice of estimating expenses and revenue that will occur in a future period of time. Commonly, that period of time is a fiscal year or biennium, but this depends on institutional practices and the intended purpose of the forecast. Forecasting allows outdoor program administrators to plan ahead for known program changes and developments, establish financial and program goals and objectives, and ultimately evaluate the plan against actual program performance. Incremental budget formats are routinely used to forecast multi-year budget projections because they are a quick method of long-range planning (see table 8.3). Although this type of budget format is commonly used by municipal, university, and MWR programs, an outdoor program administrator might be better served to use a budget format that regularly reassesses the validity and priority of all items on the current budget and then include anticipated program changes. Anticipated changes might include items such as facility additions, new program opportunities and developments, anticipated organizational mandates, or other financial dynamics that are not identified through an incremental budget forecast.

Developing an expense forecast for an established program could involve a simple process of evaluating the changing needs of the community being served, the success of the previous year's program, changes in the market, and then making budget decisions and adjustments based on these evaluations and actual financial data. However, outdoor program administrators should continue to watch their local market for new resources and opportunities that may help minimize expenses and maximize participant satisfaction and revenues. Many functions of an outdoor program can be done either internally or outsourced, and the cost benefit ratio of each function should be assessed against the overall goals of the program. Inherent savings can be had by outdoor programs when they choose not to simply maintain a status quo style of business but rather consider the availability and cost effectiveness of using new options for transportation, outfitters or guides, facilities, and means of access to public or private lands.

Creating an expense forecast for a new program involves gathering more comprehensive data on the needs of the community, including resources and opportunities in the local market, pricing and fee structures of similar programs in the local market, and then developing creative solutions to shape an outdoor program. Data that could be useful for this exercise might include demographic data from the university institutional research department, or local census bureau, conducting a needs assessment for the community to be served, and using resources available through OutdoorEd.com, the AORE listserv, The Outdoor Programmer's Directory and Data Resource Guide, and program guides and information from similar public or private outdoor programs.

Developing a revenue forecast is equally important and can be accomplished by calculating the average or expected participation for each program or service area and multiplying average participation × the fee schedule established for each program or service. For new programs, an educated estimate based on proposed program expenses, market trends, and competitor participation rates can easily be made and then extrapolated to fit the financial needs of the outdoor program budget.

Outdoor program administrators should work to develop realistic expense budget forecasts that consider a multitude of factors including, but not limited to, inflation, program capacity versus average registration numbers, and the financial impacts of weather cancelations, vehicle breakdowns, risk management, and other factors. The probabilities and costs of these potential expenses can also be quantified and factored into the overall budget.

When budget forecasts are completed, outdoor program administrators can then analyze projected revenues against projected expenses and make adjustments to ensure that the overall program plan is fiscally responsible and balanced in a way that generates the greatest return on investment while still meeting the expectations of the outdoor program community.

Over time, administrators can become very accurate in forecasting budget trends. With experience in a particular program and armed with actual budget records, the budget forecasting process can become very accurate. Developing accurate forecasts provides a deep understanding of budget details and market forces that can help an outdoor program administrator make sound decisions and improve their efficiency and effectiveness of program operations. Accurate forecasts help develop credibility among upper level administrators and can open the door to new opportunities for the outdoor program.

# Revenue Management

Outdoor programs generally operate on some ratio of revenue generation that includes fee for service programs and partial subsidies from either user fees or institutional support. Fee for service revenue generation can come in the form of hundreds of cash handling exchanges, whereas institutional support will regularly be transferred into an outdoor program account as a lump sum amount. The revenue ratio will vary from institution to institution, but all outdoor programs need to develop policies and procedures for accurately managing the revenue that it generates.

## Daily Cash Management

Accurate financial management starts with strict daily cash management policies and procedures (see figure 8.1). Because most outdoor programs charge fees for the services they offer, it is regularly necessary to maintain a certain amount of daily operating cash to make change for cash transactions.

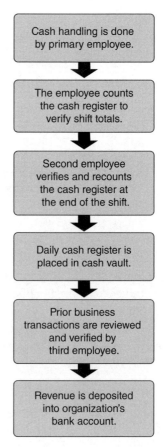

**Figure 8.1**   Multistage cash-handling process.

Outdoor program administrators should work with departmental or organizational business managers to establish approved cash-management procedures that increase accuracy and prevent potential losses caused by employee error or intent.

One standard method for managing cash is to separate cash handling and reconciliation; responsibilities are assigned to separate individual employee roles such as cashiers, program leadership, and business managers. Separating duties

- ensures each procedure is verified by two parties,
- ensures there is a paper trail at each step, and
- ensures no one individual has the opportunity to receive and reconcile income at multiple steps of the accounting process.

Overages and shortages to operating cash should be documented, investigated, and reported to the business office immediately. On most occasions a review of shift transactions will reveal the reasons for any overage or shortage. However, there might be other situations, such as an employee making change for a check written in an amount greater than the amount charged, that could cause a shortage in operating cash. In these situations, shortages should also be documented, reported, filed, and stored for future reference by auditors. Structured properly, an effective daily cash-management process can greatly reduce the chance of losses and other accounting or programmatic errors and help to reduce employee theft of institutional funds.

In terms of refunds and price changes, it is also advisable to have designated program leadership staff approve such transactions during the course of daily business. An example of this approval process is for a primary cashier to request a shift manager to authorize any refunds or price changes prior to completing a transaction.

These simple verification processes ensure the protection of revenues, inventory, and related services. Multistage verification processes for frontline cash management help to quickly identify discrepancies in cash handling, document their occurrence, explain where they occurred in the cash-handling process, and explain how they occurred and by whom; they can also help a financial officer modify processes to ensure that problems do not persist.

Organizational business officers or managers can assist an outdoor program administrator in establishing appropriate cash-management procedures for the program. Outdoor programs using rental and program registration software might have access to a variety of reports that can assist with managing sales, inventories, and revenues. It is important for cash-management procedures to be clearly defined, documented, and included in appropriate staff-training manuals to ensure compliance and accountability.

## Managing Deposits and Conducting Reconciliations

The next level of cash management is compilation of shift income into daily deposits (see figure 8.2).

RecTrac  Page: 1

**CASH JOURNAL**

Run Date: 06/22/11
Run Time: 10:21A

User: NGALLAHER

| Date | Time | Rcpt # | Drwr | Mod | D/C | Type | User | House/Other | Payment Reference | Amount |
|---|---|---|---|---|---|---|---|---|---|---|
| 06/17/2011 | 11:16A | 205873 | 1 | POS | C | Check | JDYER | Clark, Christian | check 1000 | 315.00 |
| 06/17/2011 | 11:30A | 205875 | 1 | POS | C | Visa | JDYER | Marino, Robert | VISA 1234 | 26.50 |
| 06/17/2011 | 12:41P | 205884 | 1 | POS | C | Visa | JDYER | Sanchez, Daniel | visa 8005 | 116.60 |
| 06/17/2011 | 1:01P | 205886 | 1 | POS | C | Visa | JDYER | Rogers, Melissa | VISA 6723 | 8.48 |
| 06/17/2011 | 2:24P | 205893 | 1 | POS | C | Cash | MTUSTIN | Gibson, Trevor | CASH | 3.71 |
| 06/17/2011 | 3:29P | 205897 | 1 | POS | C | Visa | JDYER | Porter, Sydney | VISA 8910 | 1,076.96 |
| 06/17/2011 | 4:15P | 205899 | 1 | A/R | C | Visa | JDYER | Fisher, Brandon | visa 2323 | 30.00 |
| 06/17/2011 | 4:19P | 205900 | 1 | POS | D | Visa | JDYER | Venu, Rhea | visa 1122 | 66.25 |
| 06/17/2011 | 4:53P | 205904 | 1 | POS | C | MC | JDYER | Bruno, Paul | MC 4589 | 20.00 |
| 06/17/2011 | 6:08P | 205909 | 1 | POS | C | Visa | JDYER | Shields, Anna | visa 6712 | 13.25 |
| 06/17/2011 | 6:25P | 205911 | 1 | POS | C | Cash | JDYER | Phillips, Sean | cash | 42.40 |

**Figure 8.2** Cash journal example.

If the cashiers and management staff who verify cashier shift deposits have appropriately managed the income and receipts from each shift, the work of the program professional or business manager is much easier. This work begins by verifying all shift deposits, cash register tapes, shift cash balance reports, and any other related contracts or receipts. Unexplained discrepancies and overages or shortages should be documented and discussed with cashiers and verifying management staff as soon as possible.

Shift deposits can then be compiled and a daily deposit prepared. Note that checks are listed by the customer's name and check number, and cash is listed by denomination to ensure accuracy and verification at the point of bank deposit and ease in reconciliation. Credit card income should be recorded by the amount of batch total for the shift. All shift and daily deposit documents should then be compiled and filed by date. Files should be kept organized for quick retrieval for customer service, risk management, and auditing purposes. Normal storage for financial and risk-management documents is seven years, but administrators should check with their institution to see if it has other requirements for record storage.

It is appropriate to report daily income with gross sales, refunds, overages or shortages, and net deposit. The daily summary provides a quick overview of financial operations and allows program professionals or business managers to identify potential problems in frontline training or accountability. Daily income should then be reconciled against monthly bank and credit card statements to ensure proper handling of deposits by banking agencies. Once again, if the preceding work by cashiers, designated program leadership staff, and outdoor program administrators has been done accurately, and with appropriate documentation, the work of reconciliation will be an efficient process. Any discrepancies in the reconciliation process that are found should be mitigated with the appropriate individual or agency and documented. Common losses that occur at this level include bad or lost checks and problems that arise with the processing of credit card charges. Institutional collection procedures should be employed to address these issues.

## Using Credit Cards

Electronic payments via credit and debit cards are increasingly becoming the standard means of payment for products and services offered by outdoor programs. This type of transaction requires compliance with the conditions established by the Payment Card Industry Security Standards Council (PCISSC). The council is comprised of representatives from the major credit card companies, and the data security standards established by the group serve to protect the consumer from having their personal data and financial information from falling into criminal hands.

Each institution has policies and procedures for managing credit card transactions, but the following points from the PCISSC highlight the core areas of concern and action:

- Build and maintain a secure network by using firewalls to prevent intrusion to the institution's computer network from external sources, and internally create and update passwords.
- Ensure cardholder data is protected from outside sources by using systems for encrypting cardholder data when transmitted across the Internet.
- Maintain a vulnerability-management program by using and regularly updating antivirus software to maintain secure systems and applications.
- Implement strong access control measures by restricting access to cardholder data to a "business need-to-know" basis that limits access to cardholder data by assigning unique user IDs for all computer users.
- Regularly monitor and test all network security systems and processes that allow access to network resources and cardholder data.

## Managing Petty Cash Advances

It might sometimes be necessary to obtain petty cash advances to conduct trip programs. Request forms and receipts for petty cash advances should be kept in separate files so they can be easily retrieved for auditing purposes. All records, reports, and copies of receipts for the disbursement of these funds should also be kept in these files.

Cash advances require careful management because the opportunity for fraud and embezzlement exists, as does the potential for simple unintentional human accounting errors that can easily occur during cash transactions. Policies on accountability and disbursement of funds must be clearly written, and staff should be trained and regularly evaluated on their performance in following departmental and institutional procedures. Requiring staff to verify and sign out cash advances is an important first step. It might also be helpful to provide staff with a cash transaction report that they can complete as they make purchases in the field. Requirement of receipts for all cash transactions is a generally accepted accounting practice, and further fiscal controls such as requiring employees to have cashiers sign and date receipts to verify they received payment from the outdoor program employee can also be employed. Providing a receipt book is often helpful for operating in remote areas. Cash advances should be reviewed and reconciled as a part of the reporting and debriefing process for each program in which they are used.

## Unrelated Business Income

Some of the income received by an outdoor program at a college or university or other tax-exempt organization might qualify as unrelated business income (UBI). "Tax on unrelated business income applies to most organizations exempt from tax under section 501 (a)" of the Internal Revenue Service Code. The IRS defines "unrelated business income as a trade or business that is regularly carried on and is not substantially related to an organizations tax exempt purpose." An exempt organization must file a report on UBI if income received from these sources is $1,000 or more.

Some examples of UBI for an outdoor program might be income received from pro shop retail sales or used equipment sales, proceeds from special events such as film festivals or speaker engagements, or facility rentals and memberships from external sources. Even if an outdoor program routinely conducts an unrelated trade or business to provide funding necessary to conduct activities related to the exempt purpose of the organization, the income received through unrelated activities may be subject to tax. Some other activities such as corporate training programs may be interpreted as substantially related to an organization's educational purpose. Administrators should regularly check with their organization's accounting office to keep abreast of current guidelines for tracking and reporting UBI.

Outdoor program administrators can work with their organization's business office to identify programs or services that might be considered unrelated business. Once these activities are identified, administrators can set fees to account for the tax expense and develop systems for recording revenues and expenses related specifically to these activities.

## Budget Management

The arrival at a balanced budget takes a lot more time than building an equalized climbing anchor. Though equally technical in nature, budget management is structurally linked to the larger issues encompassing the scope of the organization, and the attainment of balance requires accurate decision making as it pertains to raising user fees, maintaining the scope of the operation, or addressing and acting on the need to cut spending or reduce the scope of operations (Rubin, 2000). Similar to the need to regularly assess the physical, emotional, and cognitive abilities of participants while working with groups in the field, administrators must pay an equal amount of attention to the budget-reporting process. In both instances, errors in decision making can be catastrophic to the organization.

At a minimum, budget reporting should be conducted quarterly and annually. Outdoor program administrators might find it easier to complete monthly budget reports to minimize the amount of time spent on reporting. In the reporting process, administrators can update the annual revenue and expense budgets with actual financial data that will then provide a new forecast for the year. Through this process, the financial viability of each program or program area can be assessed, and decisions and plans for the remainder of the year can be made.

A simple, one-page executive summary or overview indicating approved budget projections, actual revenues and expenses, amount over or under projections, and the percentage over or under can serve as an effective means of providing a simplified understanding about outdoor program operations to financial administrators and key decision makers working within the parent organization. Additionally, an accompanying, one-page synopsis explaining period highlights and decisions that will be made for the remainder of the year based on budget performance will demonstrate the outdoor program administrator's overall understanding of their budget, how their budget affects other aspects of the organization, and how their current actions will help meet budget targets (see table 8.6).

Through the process of budget reporting and reforecasting, decisions can be made at the end of each reporting period. Adjustments that might be useful to consider in some situations include the following: redirecting marketing efforts, changing fee schedules, changing the program plan, freezing operational spending, deferring capital expenditures, adjusting operational hours, adjusting staffing, and freezing hiring or salary rates. The importance of building credibility by meeting annual budget goals should not be underestimated by outdoor program administrators. Upper-level administrators are more likely to trust plans and proposals from program administrators who have a demonstrated track record of sound financial management.

## SUMMARY

In this chapter we have presented an overview of program and budget development, forecasting, daily financial operations, reconciliation and

**Table 8.6** Profit Loss

| Outdoor rental 863L101060 As of August 31, 2010 | | | | | | |
|---|---|---|---|---|---|---|
| | Annual plan | July | August | Year to date actual | Remaining plan | % remaining |
| Total revenue | $69,400.00 | $18,093.00 | $11,892.00 | $29,985.00 | $39,415.00 | 56.8% |
| Total expense | $138,507.00 | $11,879.00 | $9,682.00 | $21,561.00 | $116,945.00 | 84.4% |
| Net income (loss) from operations | ($69,107.00) | $6,214.00 | $2,210.00 | $8,424.00 | ($77,530.00) | 112.2% |
| Capital outlay | — | 0 | 0 | — | — | NA |
| Period net income (loss) | ($69,107.00) | $6,214.00 | $2,210.00 | $8,424.00 | ($77,530.00) | 112.2% |
| Fund Balance Summary Surplus (Deficit) | | | | | | |
| | Annual plan | July | August | Year to date actual | Remaining plan | % remaining |
| Surplus transfers | $70,000.00 | 0 | $20,000.00 | $20,000.00 | $50,000.00 | 71.4% |
| Carry forward and transfers | $70,000.00 | 0 | $20,000.00 | $20,000.00 | $50,000.00 | 71.4% |
| Period net income (loss) | ($69,107.00) | | | $8,424.00 | | |
| End of period fund balance | $893.00 | 0 | $20,000.00 | $28,424.00 | | |

Run: 09/14/2010 at 11:26 a.m.

budget-reporting, analysis, and related decision making as a means to provide outdoor program administrators with a general working knowledge of these concepts and techniques. As with many other areas of outdoor program operations, institutional or organizational policies and procedures concerning budget development, accounting procedures, and reporting may be established that impact short- and long-term decision making. Outdoor program administrators should work to develop and hone the skills and develop the relationships with business managers that are necessary to develop systems to effectively manage program business operations.

# Chapter 9

# Marketing Outdoor Programs

*Geoff Harrison, MS, and John McIntosh, PhD*

**M**arketing is the art of building relationships among producers of products or services and intended customers. The often demanding process of designing and developing a service or product for the public is hardly a guarantee that it will be purchased by a consumer. Many great services and products have fallen by the wayside because they were not properly marketed to the intended consumer base. The outdoor program administrator must maintain a strong working knowledge of marketing practices and methods to be able to effectively bring potential customers from a point of nonpurchase to one in which they are purchasing their offered products and services. The diversity of products and services offered by most outdoor programs can create a difficult, tenuous, and trying marketing challenge for the administrator because marketing methods must often vary dramatically across goods and services available to consumers. Clearly, a generic marketing method will not work for promoting both outdoor equipment rentals and 30-day international adventure travel programs.

Outdoor programs commonly report to larger departments within university, municipal, or MWR organizations. This being the case, many of these organizations employ marketing and graphic design professionals to assist with the development and delivery of products and services produced by the organization. These marketing and graphic design professionals are obviously useful and should be taken advantage of, but the outdoor program administrator must also be well versed in the concepts and applications of marketing practices because there is often a fine line between the financial success and failure of any product or service. In this chapter we provide readers with an overview of the following aspects of marketing:

- Marketing terminology
- Market segmentation strategies
- Market research practices
- Marketing strategies
- Marketing delivery methods
- Product branding practices
- Standard life cycles of products

Having completed the chapter, readers will be able to confidently develop an independent marketing strategy for their outdoor program or to collaborate with marketing and graphic design professionals within their organization.

## MARKETING BASICS

Be it the bartering of a goat or selling the locking mechanism for a newly designed carabiner, there has always been a need to communicate value of a product or service being offered to others. Marketing is defined as the activity, set of institutions, and processes for creating, communicating, delivering, and exchanging offerings that have value for customers, clients, partners, and society at large (AMA, 2004). In sum, marketing is anything you do to attract your customers to the products and services you offer, and then to retain them there. To be successful, all organizations must employ marketing principles and practices to establish, nurture, and maintain a consumer base for the products and services they offer.

Let's first define products and services. *Products* are considered tangible because they can be seen, touched, and retained for future use. The tangible physical traits associated with a product can make it easy to compare one product to another. A whitewater kayak made by one manufacturer can easily be compared to a competitor's based on physical features, such as length, volume, outfitting, and safety features. A pair of rental snowshoes is considered a product because the item is tangible; however, the rental transaction process is a service.

*Services* are generally identified as intangibles that are consumed during one use. Services vary from provider to provider and can be difficult to accurately compare because of the inherent variables such as cost, duration of activity, location of activity, type of equipment used for activity, weather, quality of instructors, mood of instructors, and the engagement or skill of other participants. Items like tents, kayaks, and carabiners are products, whereas a day of whitewater rafting or climbing instruction is a service.

Under most outdoor program business models, a mix of products and services are offered to customers, but with a significant emphasis on services, which are the primary means of revenue generation. However, in a marketing context, the terms "products" and "services" can generally be used interchangeably, so for simplicity's sake we'll use the term "product" in this chapter to cover both products and services.

## IDENTIFYING THE MARKET

University, municipal, and MWR outdoor programs often serve a predetermined population or market. The term "market" represents all the potential consumers of a product. Residents of a community, students at a university, or soldiers from a particular base can all represent markets. Markets are incredibly broad and do not represent those individuals who will actually consume a product but rather those *who have the ability* to purchase or use the product. Offering a product to the entire market can be costly and ineffective; thus market research is commonly done to narrow the scope of possible consumers and to more accurately identify their needs and wants.

## Marketing Research

As defined by the American Marketing Association, market research is . . .

*the function that links the consumer, customer, and public to the marketer through information— information used to identify and define marketing opportunities and problems; generate, refine, and evaluate marketing actions; monitor marketing performance; and improve understanding of marketing as a process. Marketing research specifies the information required to address these issues, designs the method for collecting information, manages and implements the data collection process, analyzes the results, and communicates the findings and their implications.*

The level of market research necessary for the introduction of a product will vary dramatically from organization to organization because of the demographics of the targeted consumers. Market research helps to identify consumer needs, desires, and expectations from a particular product category. The key driver in completing market research is the need to identify the motivators and barriers to purchasing a particular product.

Generally, two types of market research can be done: primary and secondary. *Primary research* is a process done by or on behalf of a company to get information directly from a representative population of consumers. This type of research generally entails the use of questionnaires and surveys, direct interviews, and focus groups. After the results from primary research have been compiled and analyzed, the outdoor program administrator can assess how people reacted to the questions. The results should always be perceived as valuable insights into the minds of your customers regardless of whether they support the direction of the current business model. Results can be used to guide decision making pertaining to the modifications to, development of, and possible elimination of products and services.

The analysis of information gathered or created by others that is available in the public domain is termed *secondary research*. Secondary research can often be acquired for free on the Internet, from trade associations, at the library, or from other organizations. This source of research can be used to identify macro trends in the economy, purchasing behaviors of customers, and what other organizations and competitors are doing. Secondary information is useful for gaining a big picture perspective; however, primary research derives the useful information for the outdoor program administrator because the information gathered has been designed specifically to assess the needs of the organization.

## Questionnaires

Questionnaires (or surveys) give the outdoor program administrator an opportunity to gain constructive feedback from existing and potential customers. The key to successfully using a questionnaire is to "start with the end in mind," or knowing upfront what type of information that you are seeking to gain from the process. Questionnaires should be brief in nature, move from general to specific, use multiple-choice questions, avoid open-ended and leading questions, maintain a consistent rating scale, and be tested on multiple parties and modified as necessary before broad distribution.

Questionnaires are popular and effective tools to discern customer preferences, desires, and patterns of resource use. They can be short or detailed, depending on the method used to implement the instrument, the expected time pressures on potential respondents, and the depth of information required. On one pole of the continuum of survey types is a quick questionnaire finely targeted to end users who have consumed a particular product. These are often very short and do not require the planning and permissions of a more comprehensive instrument. The harvest reports that many state fish and wildlife agencies use exemplifies this simple type of survey. Such surveys allow quick collection of narrowly defined data and often receive very high response rates. Straugh, Converse, and White (2004) report a 60 percent response from deer hunters surveyed in 2003.

Typical elements of these surveys include the following:

- The hunter or angler's zip code, which proxies their residence
- Species pursued
- Number of days spent in the field
- Locales where their activities took place
- Level of success—did they harvest or catch targeted species?
- Dates of activities or number of days spent in the field

On the other end of the survey continuum are marketing research surveys. These are comprehensive undertakings that require significant preparation and planning. The detailed information possible through a research survey potentially garners keen insight into target customer groups. Research surveys require the following steps:

1. *Determining the objectives of the survey.* What demographic groups are of interest? What type of information is sought? What is the mode of survey distribution? Surveys can be distributed by mail, e-mail, online, or in person. The requirements of "pen and paper" surveys are very different from face-to-face or in-person surveys.

2. *Create draft questions based on the information desired.*

3. *Decide on a measurement scale.* Most surveys use a numerical scale with the extreme ends as anchors. For example, a 1 to 7 scale might be anchored with strongly agree = 7 on one end and strongly disagree = 1 on the other.

4. *Identify the population of interest and determine the optimal sample size.* Sample size is important because surveys typically yield between 10 and 35 percent response rates. The statistical significance of the survey hinges on the response rate. Statements safeguarding anonymity of respondents is especially importance when conducting surveys.

5. *Complete a pretest.* Pretesting surveys is necessary to ensure that the survey is both relevant and appealing to intended respondents. Pretesting is typically done by distributing the instrument to a panel of individuals who have knowledge or expertise in the area of interest. Feedback from the panel is used to refine questions and resolve inconsistencies.

6. *Implement the survey and compile the data.*

## Direct Interviews

One-on-one interviews can be an effective means of gaining a personal perspective on a current or proposed product because the interviewer can guide the participant through a free-form casual conversation. Direct interviews can happen just about anywhere but are best done in a defined location, such as table or booth in a building or in a commonly traveled campus location. Interviewers should have set questions they intend to ask and then thoroughly listen to the responses of the interviewees. At the close of an interview, the participant should be thanked, and if possible their contact information should be collected for follow-up questions or an invitation to a focus group or town hall meeting.

## Focus Groups

Focus groups provide an interactive opportunity to gain insights and opinions from your customers. Multiple focus groups should be hosted with 6 to 10 participants in each group to validate the information gathered. Participants should be a group of individuals that represents the community that you are serving or intend to serve. Each focus group should have the same moderator; the moderator should have a script of questions that are queried to all groups. The moderator should open the meeting by defining the purpose of the focus group and informing participants that their honest opinions are valued. Moderators should define the scope of the meetings and how much time they will take; they must stay neutral and not lead questions with their opinions. Notes should be taken at each meeting, and the focus group participants should receive some form of compensation (because they will be spending one or two hours of their time).

## Market Segmentation

Once the market research data has been compiled and reviewed, the information is used to narrow the market (market segmentation) to those individuals who have a common demographic: age, income, wants, needs, and interests (figure 9.1). Market segmentation is a means to better utilize fiscal and human resources that will be used to market a product; it can be very effective if the intended service population has the required size, purchasing power, and perceived need to sustain the product in the marketplace. A segment can be deemed viable if it will respond positively to the marketing efforts of the outdoor program. Further narrowing of possible consumers is done after a population representing a common demographic is identified. *Target marketing* is done to focus resources on the select group of consumers most likely to demand or want a particular product. Once an outdoor recreation administrator identifies a target market, she can begin to use a combination of marketing elements called the marketing mix. *American Demographics* magazine is a popular and comprehensive source of consumer information. Outdoor program administrators might also consider the following aspects of consumers in their search for target markets:

- Demographic characteristics such as age, gender, education, income, household size, and occupation
- Geographic location—this is especially useful because comprehensive demographic and marketing profiles are based on zip codes
- Psychographic information that stratifies consumers in terms of beliefs, attitudes, values, lifestyle choices, personality, and buying motives

Figure 9.1 illustrates these terms and how they can be used to narrow the market so that marketing resources are used effectively to generate participation in a semester-long whitewater kayak program.

## MARKETING MIX

In general, marketing can be broken down into four functional areas of development and delivery. The term "marketing mix" commonly refers to the elements that comprise the 4 Ps: product, place, price, and promotion. The development of a purposeful and well-planned marketing mix will benefit the outdoor program administrator because it will lead toward a maximum exposure of the product to intended consumers. The marketing mix will vary in intensity based on the type of product being brought to the marketplace. For instance, the addition of a new course to an existing outdoor program is dramatically different from the development and delivery of an entirely new outdoor program to a campus culture. Regardless of the scope, be it a

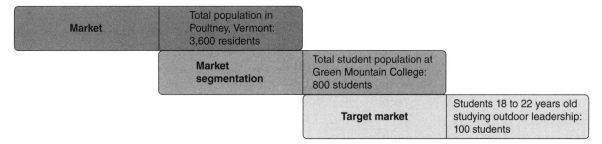

**Figure 9.1**  Segmentation example.

small addition or wholesale revision of a program offering, the 4 Ps are the foundation of the marketing mix.

## Product

The product piece of a marketing mix identifies the unique characteristics of the product or service being developed for sale and how these characteristics relate to the needs and wants of the intended consumer. Marketers focus on the features and benefits of the product or service. A rope manufacturer might focus on the durability and handling characteristics of a new lead rope being offered, whereas an outdoor program administrator might focus on the educational, health, and social benefits of a series of weekly hikes being offered. Both target the positive features of their product toward the perceived or stated needs of their customers.

## Place

Place relates to the ways in which a customer can access a product or service. Decisions regarding place need careful consideration because the ease with which a product can be accessed and the number of channels through which a customer can be found can have a huge effect on sales volume and revenue. In considering this element of the 4Ps, outdoor marketing managers can glean vital clues regarding the use of place by considering the question, Where do buyers seek outdoor products and services? The ability to go beyond a university campus, for example, and advertise outdoor recreation offerings in health clubs, community centers, and similar venues significantly increases the reach of a marketing program. Where do customers typically shop for outdoor experiences? Specialized venues such as enthusiast shops (e.g., REI),

online sites (e.g., Gorp), magazines (e.g., *Outdoor*), and electronic media (e.g., The Outdoor Channel) offer opportunities to use place to promote services.

In the modern business world, the delivery of products can occur in many ways. Product distribution might occur at an outdoor program office, on the side of a river, or through an electronic online consumer portal. Rental staff can issue equipment to a customer who is outfitting his own adventure, trip leaders can instruct a river safety program at the river, and an online consumer portal can offer retail equipment sales and trip registration opportunities.

As a whole, the outdoor industry distributes products to customers through both direct and indirect routes. An outdoor program that advertises, sells, and delivers climbing instruction at either an onsite or offsite location is a means of *direct distribution*. Manufacturers who sell directly to outdoor programs use direct distribution to maximize profits by removing middlemen from business transactions. An example of *indirect distribution* for a university outdoor program is the selling of a prepackaged selection of trips or services to a campus bookstore that in turn sells the package directly to students. Many organizations take advantage of both direct and indirect distribution methods to maximize their allocation of resources in the marketing mix.

## Price

Price is often the vague piece of the marketing mix because the value of a product is largely based on the perception of the customer and because prices can be set at, below, or above market value. Product and place are the expense-driven phases of the marketing mix. The process of identifying price is when potential revenues can be considered to offset development and distribution expenses.

Both direct and indirect expenses related to the development and distribution of products should be factored into the development of product pricing models. Direct expenses include the fiscal and human resources required to supply the product to a customer. Table 9.1 shows possible expenses in each category for an Air Force base caving trip.

When pricing a product, the outdoor program administrator must take into account the overarching business model of the program. When comparing programs to each other, it will become evident to an administrator that most programs use different budgeting and cost-recovery practices. Many municipal park and recreation services, university outdoor programs and MWR programs operate under a subsidy from a parent organization. Examples of direct and indirect subsidies include the following:

- Funding derived from property taxes
- Funding derived from student fees
- Utility expenses being paid by parent organization
- Facility space expenses paid by parent organization
- Administrative accounting and graphic design support paid by parent organization

Regardless whether the subsidy is derived from property taxes or student fees, these subsidies are often intended to reduce the direct cost of products to participants. Services such as informal recreation, intramural sports, and fitness programs are often included in operational or facility-based subsidies. Climbing during open hours might be free of charge, but a climbing wall rental for a club will often be priced on either a cost-recovery model or a profit-driven model. Another example of a directly subsidized program might be a six-day backpacking trip that has an actual cost per participant of $100 but is offered at a rate of $55 per participant. The $45 price discrepancy could be covered by a subsidy received by the program from the parent organization. Programs that operate entirely on a cost-recovery or fee-for-service model experience the same challenges as private organizations when they price their products.

Prices are also often structured to accommodate the widest range of consumers. An outdoor program equipment rental service might offer snowboard packages that include a rental board, boots, and bindings for customers who do not have their own equipment. The organization might also offer the rental of single items such as a board or boots for customers who might own some but not all the required equipment. Package deals are generally offered at a price lower than individually renting each piece of equipment. Bundling products and services can be an effective means of increasing a customer's perceived value of a product.

Price is not a fixed variable in the marketing mix. The price of a product may increase or decrease throughout the life of the product. Ultimately, the rate at which a product is consumed is based on

**Table 9.1**  Direct vs. Indirect Expenses

| Mountain Home AFB—Caving trip to Smith's Crack | |
| --- | --- |
| **Indirect expenses** | **Direct expenses** |
| Human labor expense to produce fliers | Production of 100 fliers |
| Human labor expense to post fliers on base | Staff labor expense for leading trip |
| Human labor expense to staff office to register participants | Fuel charges for vehicle use |
| Human labor expense to purchase and prepare participant meals | Participant meals |
| Utility expenses of administrative office | |
| Purchase and maintenance of program specific equipment | |
| Equipment depreciation | |
| Vehicle maintenance | |

the perceived value of the consumer. Thus, outdoor program administrators must actively manage the actual price and perceived value of their products to ensure they are attractive to participants.

## Promotion

Promotion, the last P of the marketing mix, is the dynamic through which the value of a product is communicated to the customer. Promotion can occur through many mediums, including print, web, radio, television, and word of mouth. Advertising, personal selling, promotional events, and public relations all fall under the umbrella of the promotion mix.

Figure 9.2, a print campaign for an annual climbing festival, represents the type of promotion routinely found in magazines that feature climbing and other adventure sports. The Red Rock Rendezvous is an annual event designed and hosted by Mountain Gear, an outdoor equipment retailer in Spokane, Washington. The annual climbing festival occurs at the world-famous climbing area located 20 minutes outside Las Vegas, Nevada. The event is envisioned to be a gateway for new climbers to experience the sport; proceeds from the event serve as a fund-raiser for the Access Fund, a national advocacy organization that keeps U.S. climbing areas open and conserves the climbing environment.

To further illustrate the complete range of possibilities for an effective promotions mix, let's look at examples adapted from "Promoting Issues and Ideas" by M. Booth and Associates, Inc.

1. It's *advertising* if Mountain Gear purchases ads in both *Rock and Ice* and *Climbing* magazines to promote the Red Rock Rendezvous.

2. It's *promotion* if the Mountain Gear staff puts up several display booths at regional climbing competitions to endorse the event.

3. It's *publicity* if a famous climber pledges to present a slide show at the festival and raffle off a day of climbing with them to one of the lucky participants.

4. It's *public relations* if the local newspaper, radio, and television stations cover the event as a news story.

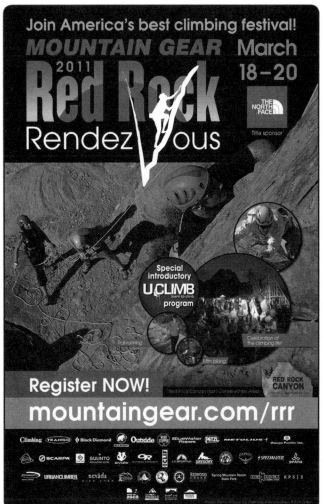

**Figure 9.2** Red Rock Rendezvous promotion example.

Courtesy of Mountain Gear.

5. It's *sales* if the Mountain Gear promotions mix gets the word out to members of the climbing and nonclimbing communities and ultimately sells tickets to the festival and sells lots of climbing equipment to new participants in the sport.

To build a successful promotional campaign requires an intimate knowledge of the value of any given product and an ability to effectively convey this information to prospective consumers. The outdoor recreation administrator will quickly find that value is easy to assign to a product, such as a pair of snowshoes, because they can be seen, touched, and compared with like products. However, the value of a service is difficult to quantify because it is basically intangible. The administrator will be challenged when she tries to identify the tangible and comparable aspects of a spring break climbing trip. When promoting services, administrators should consider communicating to participants the value of the program as being the desired program outcomes. Physical fitness, learning a lifetime sport, building social connections, and personal development are often desired program outcomes of services.

# Product Life Cycle

Within any marketing mix, each product will have a unique product life cycle. The *product life cycle* (PLC) is a series of discrete steps a product cycles through from its introduction to the market, to obsolescence, and eventual death. The PLC is important in product management because each stage of the life cycle requires specific action. Outdoor program administrators who understand the PLC can match their marketing resource expenditure more closely to anticipated sales. Without a clear understanding of the PLC, the administrator might either overinvest or underinvest in the four Ps and in promotion. For example, a newly introduced product such as a new style of autoblocking belay device for climbing might have significant sales potential, but if target consumers are uneducated about the product's benefits, sales will most likely be disappointing. An understanding of the product's position in the PLC would prompt large investments to educate prospective customers about the product's benefits and advantages. Failure to remedy this could lead to the product's demise. In contrast, a declining product is established in the marketplace. Consumers have detailed knowledge of the product's features and value—its price and performance characteristics. Such products tend to be commodity-like and essentially interchangeable with competition based principally on price. An administrator, lacking an appreciation of the product's location on the PLC, might make the tactical error of expending substantial marketing resources in an effort to boost sales. Given the commodity-like character of a declining product, such ill-timed expenditures will not likely yield a commensurate increase in sales.

Figure 9.3 depicts the four stages of the PLC—introduction, growth, maturity, and decline. Let's look at each step in turn, along with actions associated with the Four Ps.

## Introduction Phase

Products in the introduction stage are typically new, and the general public lacks awareness of them. Those with some awareness of the product are typically lead users or early adopters who are enthusiasts. These individuals possess esoteric knowledge of the product and typically are tolerant of product imperfections and glitches. Lead users, as the name implies, want to be "the first kid on the block" to own a particular product. In this stage, marketers pay attention to all four Ps of the marketing mix as they seek to educate the market and build sales. At the product level, efforts are made to establish brand awareness. This is often based on creating products with high quality, many features, and exceptional performance. Promotion is typically directed to lead users with the aim of creating awareness of the product's benefits. Pricing may be high to convey exclusiveness or high quality. This is especially effective with lead users who tend to be price insensitive. On the other hand, pricing may be low to achieve rapid, deep market penetration. The goal is to attract as many customers as quickly as possible. Place (distribution) of new products is often selective and confined to a small number of outlets. Luxury goods, for example, are distributed through exclusive outlets. As those goods mature, they migrate to mass market channels.

## Growth Phase

Products in the growth stage are established in the marketplace and competition, while growing, is limited. Their benefits, features, and performance are well understood by large segments of the popu-

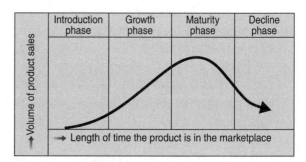

**Figure 9.3**  Product life cycle.

lation. Examples of these products are the spring-loaded camming devices (SLDs) used in climbing and the type III rescue vests used for kayaking and rafting activities. The goal of marketers is to sufficiently (but typically not dramatically) differentiate their offering from that of competitors in order to establish themselves as the brand of choice and to expand market share. In the growth stage, considerable research is conducted to determine the idiosyncratic needs of market segments that are desired by the organization, additional features are offered to appeal to profitable segments, and services are bundled to create additional value for end users.

Promotional campaigns are geared to reaching a larger number of demographic groups to build sales. Relatively less emphasis is placed on building awareness of the product's fundamental benefits, and more emphasis is placed on distinguishing the organization's products from those of competitors.

Decisions regarding place (distribution) are made with the aim of supporting higher volume sales as an increasingly broad set of customers purchase the product. New distribution channels such as the Internet are added to create incremental volume, while conventional brick and mortar channels might be enlarged.

Pricing decisions in the growth stage are not particularly difficult. The low competitive intensity of growing markets places few pressures on organizations to reduce price. As a result, prices are structured to promote high volume while increasing revenue. Undercutting rivals via low price is not vital because the market is burgeoning.

## Maturity Phase

In this stage the product is well established, and sales growth begins to taper off as new suppliers enter the market. Competitive rivalry increases not only from new entrants who field similar products but also from the proliferation of substitute products. Organizations, faced with many competitors, shift focus from growing market share to either maintaining or defending share while maximizing profits. Products created with Gore-Tex fabrics were early entrants to the waterproof or breathable clothing market. Now that that style of product is mature, many other products with similar features but at a lower production cost have entered the market place.

Product decisions are driven by a need to meaningfully differentiate offerings from competitors. This phase is marked by heightened consumer research to identify new features that may be incorporated into existing products or new applications of extant offerings. Large organizations may continue appealing to mass-market customers by offering products whose features satisfy a large group of customers. Alternatively, smaller organizations may retrench and seek small niches that were previously overlooked in the booming environment of the growth phase or that may not be profitably served by larger players. Promotion campaigns are now strongly oriented to emphasizing the differences between the organization's products and those of its rivals.

Pricing decisions are now made with the dual goals of maintaining sales volume while fending off competitors. In the mature phase, managers execute a delicate balancing act between offering prices that are sufficiently low to fend off rivals while at the same time maintaining revenue.

Place, or distribution, takes on a more important role in the maturity phase as emphasis is placed on channel efficiency. Paradoxically, this focus on conducting distribution at low cost is offset by the demand that distribution also encourages customers to choose the organization's products over rival offerings. This usually entails proffering highly motivational incentives, such as offering resellers substantial commissions for sales beyond a certain level, offering cash rebates on specific product models, and extending bulk purchase incentives to small retailers who typically could not afford to buy large quantities.

## Decline Phase

This stage of the PLC poses significant challenges for the administrator, who faces three fundamental options: discontinue the product, harvest the product, or maintain the product. Each strategic choice carries different implications for the four Ps. The decisions concerning price, place, promotion, and product are influenced by the selected course of action and the product's characteristics—tangible vs. intangible, low-tech vs. high-tech, mass market vs. niche market. The possible permutations are sufficiently large to exceed the boundaries of a book chapter, so we will discuss only the three major options open to the organization. Organizations choosing to discontinue a product remove it from the product line and liquidate any remaining inventory. These products are commonly seen being sold by online retailers such as Sierra Trading Post and Backcountry.com. In less common instances, managers may seek out a buyer who may continue producing and selling the product. An example of this was when Northwest River Supply temporarily secured the licensing agreement to produce and distribute the America's Cup Type V lifejacket. The decision to harvest a product entails substantially reducing production, distribution, and marketing costs while continuing to sell to a niche market. The decision to maintain a product is sometimes more challenging and riskier than prior strategic choices. An organization might attempt to rejuvenate a product by developing new features that appeal to potentially new customers. This entails research and development expenditures that might not be recovered. Alternatively, the organization might seek new applications for, or new customers for, a declining product. The latter often requires finding new markets and educating customers about the product's features, performance, and benefits. As with research and development efforts to rejuvenate a dying product, the costs of cultivating a new market might not be recovered.

# DEVELOPING A MARKETING PLAN

To successfully drive a product to market, the outdoor program administrator will need to develop a marketing plan that guides a consumer along a continuum from awareness to purchase. The administrator should have completed market research during the concept and development stages of bringing a product to market rather than developing a product or service and then determining if a need exists. Having identified a need early makes it much easier to develop a product that will be valued by prospective consumers.

The size and scope of a marketing plan will depend on the expected outcomes of the administrator. Getting a brand new outdoor program up and running will require a much more detailed marketing plan than when a 25-year-old program is introducing just one new program or service. In general, the content areas of a plan would be the same, but the plans would differ in the amount of resources required to develop and implement the plan.

The following information should clarify the common content areas regularly included in a marketing plan.

>> **Introduction.** The introduction serves as an overview of the marketing plan. It is an executive summary and anchors the content of the plan to the mission of the organization.

>> **Background.** The background provides the reader a chance to become apprised of the history of the organization, the product category, past marketing efforts, organization successes and challenges, and the reason for the development of the new product. The background can also include any consumer or market assumptions used to develop the product and plan.

>> **Review of research.** A summary of all primary and secondary research with a thorough analysis should be included to provide the reader with an understanding of the data incorporated in the development of the plan.

>> **Trade or organization climate.** This section details any cultural or business trends or phenomena that might exist within the greater organization or the industry as a whole. An example at a university would be an increased effort by the department of student life to engage students in healthy off campus cocurricular activities. A campus-wide climate focused on the development of healthy activities for students might offer an outdoor program administrator a variety of cobranding and collaborative opportunities to partner with other campus groups to promote a new or existing product. Within the greater outdoor industry, an example would be the push to educate all frontcountry and backcountry users on the Leave No Trace (LNT) principles. In this context, a manufacturer might choose to add LNT principles to a retail hangtag on a backpack.

>> **Consumer attitudes.** This is probably one of the most important pieces of any marketing plan because attitudes define current consumer buying patterns, needs, wants, motivations for participation, and barriers to participation in your service. The consumer attitudes section of a marketing plan is an appropriate place to highlight why your

product or service will fulfill, support, or enhance a consumer need.

**>> Marketing objectives.** This section answers such questions as, What will this program look like in three to five years? What will be its measures for success? (For example, is your program going to become the exclusive provider of outdoor educational opportunities for your campus, town, base, or region?)

**>> Product category.** This section details the entire scope of programs, products, or services that the proposed product will relate to so the reader can understand the broader context of the organization. A new whitewater kayak program might relate to and support a current whitewater rental business and instruction programs in rafting, canoeing, and river rescue.

**>> Brand name.** The name of the organization offering the product or service must be included in the plan. This might be the name of the municipality, university, or service provider. "Branding" is a term used for an organization's desire and attempt to have customers associate their product with their organization.

**>> Product name.** Simply stated, this is where the name of the new product is stated. If the name is intended to represent something broader, such as a concept, it should be fleshed out for the reader. An example is Eastern Washington University's Outdoor Program operating under the acronym EPIC (Experiential Programs Inspiring Confidence). Product name might also be the name of the program being offered, such as Introduction to Anchor Building.

**>> Product description.** A thorough description of the proposed product should be included in the plan. Beyond a curricular description, equipment specification, or service overview, the product description should also include a brief explanation of any risk-management assessments or findings made during the development of the product. Levels of perceived and actual risk should be considered during the concept and development stages of peripheral marketing materials.

**>> Target market.** A crucial part of the plan is determining which consumers you are going after. This is key to launching a successful marketing campaign because it minimizes the amount of

resources distributed into nonproductive advertising and publicity channels.

**>> Financial projections.** The plan should contain a clear summary of the product's return on investment (ROI), which goes beyond marketing and includes all expenses. ROI projections determine whether the product yields benefits to the organization. ROI analysis is a compelling tool to make a business case for a particular undertaking. Nonprofit entities might use ROI analysis to gauge how well they are using their resources. The bottom line is a primary driver as to whether you should bring a new product to market. If the potential financial gain does not significantly offset the anticipated investment, then it might be best to redirect resources toward another product.

**>> Pricing strategy.** Pricing strategy, another important piece of the marketing plan, is established through the development of solid financial projections and is affected by indirect and direct costs associated with the development and delivery of the product. The outdoor program administrator will consider information gathered through primary and secondary research to assess the perceived value of the product in the eyes of the consumer and the price of relevant competitors' products.

**>> Distribution methods.** The methods in which the product will be sold to customers must be included in the marketing plan. Most municipal, university, and MWR programs will sell products in person at an office and online through their organization websites. Some organizations also use third-party providers to handle transactions.

**>> Marketing channels.** There are many ways to market products to consumers, but the most commonly used channels for municipal, university, and MWR programs are print media, fliers, social media, press releases, and personal selling. From a financial perspective, the administrator must have clearly identified channels for marketing products to avoid devoting excessive resources toward product promotion.

**>> Resource commitment.** When bringing the product to market, the administrator should have an upfront plan for the resources that will be allocated to promoting the product. Human, fiscal, and physical resources can all be dedicated to marketing a product. Often the amount of money spent

## CASE STUDY: MICROMARKETING PLAN FOR HUMBOLDT STATE UNIVERSITY

Micromarketing, commonly known as niche marketing, seeks to appeal to individual consumers by crafting a message that is personally meaningful. This kind of marketing is useful for targeting small pockets of desirable consumers. Micromarketing is effective for small and medium-size operations that are resource constrained. Unlike their approach in large-scale marketing, micromarketers do not seek out already defined niches. Instead they create niches that can be served by their mix of products, services, and expertise by identifying customer desires and requirements and then tailoring products to those needs. Micromarketing seeks to make an organization a big fish in a small pond as opposed to a small fish in an ocean. Here is an example of a micromarketing plan:

- *Brand name*—Humboldt State University Center Activities
- *Product category*—Water sports
- *Product name*—Slammin' Salmon Rafting
- *Product description*—Whitewater rafting and camping on the Cal Salmon
- *Target market*—Humboldt State University first-year students
- *Financial projections*—Thirty percent return on investment
- *Price strategy*—Participant cost will be 5 percent above direct cost of program
- *Distribution methods*—Product sold in person at office and online via a website
- *Advertising and publicity methods*—Print media, fliers, social media, press release, personal selling at promo booths
- *Resource commitment*—Seven percent of gross revenue available to market program
- *Contingency plan*—Must obtain 60 percent of maximum possible enrollment; cancel for low enrollment

on marketing is a percentage of the expected gross revenue from the product. It will take more money to introduce a completely new product than it will to add one additional program to an existing program.

**» Contingency plan.** This part of the plan might be as simple as preestablishing a minimum enrollment number. Establishing a "go or no go" threshold beforehand makes it easier for an administrator to cancel a program for low enrollment before incurring the costs associated with running a program that will not generate the desired revenue.

## BRANDING

Moving from the vision of a marketing plan to its development and delivery can be the make-or-break moment for the promotion of a product. If an organization does not develop effective marketing concepts that link the organization to its product, chances are good that customers will buy a similar product from another organization down the road. Why? Because the customer does not associate the original organization with the product. This is a result of bad marketing. To set themselves apart from competitors, most organizations try to develop a brand to distinguish their products and services from others. A brand, as defined by the American Marketing Association, is the "name, term, design, symbol, or any other feature that identifies one seller's good or service as distinct from those of other sellers." A brand can be used exclusively for one product or a family of products.

An outdoor program, whether housed at a military base, university, or municipality, may choose to use its name as the primary brand but then also use a logo, select color palette, distinctive font, and consistent organization of key information on its marketing materials to help customers recognize the program as *the* service provider for a particular product. There are hundreds of retail outdoor equipment stores that may be recognized within a given region, but internationally recognized retailers like EMS (Eastern Mountain Sports), REI (Recreational Equipment Incorporated), and MEC (Mountain Equipment Co-Op) are recognized by outdoor enthusiasts because of the brand images they have developed, promoted, and protected. Building a successful brand requires the conscious, purposeful, and consistent action of arranging key pieces of information (who, what, when, where, and how) so that customers develop a familiarity with both the product and the organization. Familiarity leads to trust, which can ultimately lead to product loyalty and success for an organization.

## MARKETING METHODS

When developing marketing materials in support of a marketing plan's established advertising and publicity methods, the outdoor program administrator should be clear on how he or she intends to adhere to brand guidelines to increase *awareness* (A), attract *interest* (I), arouse *desire* (D), and initiate *actions* (A) from potential customers (AIDA; Strong, 1925). Moving individuals from a state in which they are unaware of a product to one in which they are purchasing the product is a not an easy task; however, there are some tried-and-true methods, including several common marketing delivery methods used by municipal, university, and MWR recreation programs. Each method discussed requires a different set of fiscal, logistical, or human resources and is intended to influence potential customers in different ways. Regardless of whether marketing materials are created in a print, radio, video, online, or social media format, they should be developed in a manner in which they will adhere to preestablished brand guidelines developed by the organization to ensure a level of consistency across all marketing materials.

### Printed Materials

Printed materials such as posters, fliers, table tents, handbills, and banners are commonly designed and produced with in-house resources. These items can be broadly distributed across campuses and at local businesses where an administrator expects to hit the target market. This form of marketing allows the administrator total creative control over the content of the promotional piece, but the breadth of information provided to potential customers is limited by physical space and cost. A flier obviously cannot share as much information about an event as a poster or can, but the flier is considerably less expensive to manufacture. Printed materials can be viewed as passive marketing tools because customer engagement with the information occurs only if the customer is interested in the content of the message. Because of the passive nature of printed materials, the marketing piece must clearly and concisely state everything the potential customer needs to know and also include a "call to action" to move the customer to purchase the product. Calls to action include details such as registration deadlines, price reductions, threat of price increases, and promotional incentives.

### Advertising

Advertising is generally a service purchased from a third party to promote both a product and the organization providing the product. Print, radio, television, and web formats are all common means for delivering advertisements. Whether an ad is a small box in a local newspaper or a 30-second television spot, it is purchased to run for a particular length of time. Because of the short duration of an advertisement, it must be timed to run at a peak moment that will alert and persuade potential customers to act. Paid advertising is expensive but can be very effective in broadcasting a message to the largest possible group of viewers in the total market. Global in nature, advertising will notify many people about an organization or product; however, these individuals may or may not be part of the target market identified in the marketing plan.

### Publicity

Publicity is any form of one-way communication with potential customers provided without payment by a third-party organization. Press releases are an effective publicity tool (figure 9.4). They help to get the word out about your event to a wide variety of media outlets. The editors and producers working for these media outlets are regularly in need of content for their newspapers, magazines, and newscasts and may consider developing a story about your product, service, or event if it is deemed newsworthy. This form of publicity can exceed the value of any other media because a story can be anywhere from one to four minutes in length on the television to a 1,000-word article in the local newspaper. When developing a marketing plan for a product,

---

**Figure 9.4**   Sample Press Release

**Boise State University**                **Contact: Cycle Learning Center**
                                          **208-426-RIDE**

**Media Release**

**For Immediate Release: 8/10/2011**

**Boise State University Cycle Center Grand Opening Block Party**

**Event:** Grand opening of the new Cycle Learning Center location

**Date:** 8/23/2011

**Time:** 11 a.m. to 1 p.m.

**Where:** Cycle Learning Center shop and patio area (Lincoln Avenue parking garage across from the Student Union)

**What to expect:** Speakers, music, food, prizes, and bike demonstrations

Join Boise State University in the opening of a newly constructed location for the Cycle Learning Center (CLC). The CLC serves as the university's centralized source for basic bicycle repair services, instructional clinics, and alternative transportation information.

The Cycle Learning Center is a partnership between University Health and Recreation Services and the Department of Transportation and Parking Services. CLC programs and services provide an excellent opportunity for the collaborative partners to combine efforts toward the complimentary goals of providing environmentally sustainable transportation options and promoting an active and healthy campus community. The CLC strives to create a hands-on learning environment that empowers campus users to explore sustainable transportation through educational programming and support services.

The Cycle Learning Center's new location, in the Lincoln Avenue parking garage, was selected due to its immediate proximity to the Recreation Center, Student Union, Transportation and Parking Services, Student Media, and the newly constructed Transportation Center.

**Schedule of events**

11 a.m.—Campus speakers

11:30 a.m.—Ribbon cutting

11:30 a.m. to 1 p.m.—Events

- Meet the mechanics and CLC tours
- Slow bike race
- Bike Barn demonstrations
- Valley Ride bus demonstrations: How to use the bike rack
- Zipcar demonstrations
- Free pizza and beverages
- Music
- Raffle prizes

1:00 p.m.—Group rides hosted by Boise State University's Cycling Club (2 hours)

---

Courtesy of Boise State University.

an administrator should consider sending a promotion packet to key media outlets to inform them of the potential for a story. In addition to a standard press release, the promotion packet should include event logistics, photos from past events, quotes from participants, the mission and history of the organization, event sponsor info, and website info to make developing a story easier for the editor or producer. This form of no-expense marketing can be very effective in getting information out to much of the local public. However, an administrator has no say in whether a story will be developed, or when it is run. Unfortunately, the media often choose to cover an event *after* it has occurred.

## Personal Selling

Personal selling represents both direct organization-to-customer communication and customer-to-customer communications about products or services. Personal selling supports two-way communication with the customer and often takes on a question-and-answer format. Personal selling can occur in both formal and informal contexts. Organization-to-customer selling will likely occur at promotional booths, on the telephone, and in the program office. Customer-to-customer selling can occur during nonstructured conversations that might occur, say, in the field on a backpacking program, in a bunkroom on a military base, during a van ride to a river, or in an college classroom. Past and current customers can serve as the best salespeople for a program. Word-of-mouth marketing can spread the word about an organization more effectively and less expensively than any other marketing effort.

## Promotions

Promotions are programs designed by an organization to provide additional value to a customer's interaction with the organization. Promotional campaigns are designed to help move the customer into a state of action in which they become a purchaser of the products provided by the organization. Promotional items might include free SWAG (stuff we all get) such as water bottles, carabiner key chains, and T-shirts. Promotions can also include incentives such as, "Buy five climbing day passes and get two additional sessions for free." Incentives are regu-

larly used to provide additional value to the base product and to drive people to purchase (because of the added perceived value) more items than they might have intended to purchase. All promotions should clearly tie the organization to the product (branding) so customers cannot forget how they received the benefit. Logos, website addresses, and phone numbers should be included on all give-away items. Because promotions are giving away financial resources, they must be well planned, with clear objectives, so the promotion can be measured for success.

## Social Media

Social media is a quickly evolving consumer-driven medium that uses the Internet and mobile-based tools for sharing and discussing information. Social media can take many different forms, including text, images, podcasts, and video and is quickly becoming one of the primary means of communication, especially in the youth culture. In a spring 2007 survey, Emory University found that 97 percent of freshman surveyed had a Facebook account for social media networking, and 24 percent of them stated they logged onto Facebook at least 18 times or more per day (Jacobs, 2008). Most social media sites are designed to allow people to interact instantaneously with others. Successful sites provide a forum for two-way dialogue that allows people to quickly share both their positive and negative moments from life. Sharing could be a text narrative with photos about the great hike they took in an outdoor program or a negative rant about the customer service they received. Social media is the newest available tool for the administrative marketing toolbox. At very little (or no) upfront costs, information about a program can be uploaded to Internet blog sites along with photos and videos from every outing and every program course. An outdoor program might also host a chat room forum that allows their target market of users to interact about outdoor-related topics. As with any new tool, the administrator must learn to use this technology properly to prevent it from becoming a liability to their program.

Social media includes, but is not limited to, the following:

- Web logs (blogs), such as Blogger and Word-Press
- Affinity group chat rooms, such as the Yahoo groups Cave Diggers and Backpacking Light
- Social networking Internet sites, such as Facebook and Twitter
- Business networking sites, such as LinkedIn
- Photo-sharing Internet sites, such as Flickr, Snapfish, Photobucket
- Video-sharing Internet sites, such as YouTube

## SUMMARY

Marketing is a critical duty of outdoor program administrators regardless of the mission, size, scope, and directives of the organization they operate. Successful marketing entails the use of conscious, purposeful, and consistent actions to develop, design, price, and promote products to a targeted group of potential customers. No matter how great a product or service an outdoor program produces, the organization will not be successful if it cannot effectively influence the buying actions of potential customers.

Building and maintaining a brand image that is easily recognized by consumers drives consumption of products and services and ultimately creates long-term consumer loyalty. This important process includes managing

- the public image of the organization through the type of marketing materials it produces,
- the accuracy of descriptions and imagery used to promote its products and services,
- the way the media portrays the actions of the organization and its employees, and
- how the organization publicly addresses and reacts to situations that arise during the course of normal operations.

Of course to extend the life cycle of the products and services that an outdoor program produces, the outdoor program administrator must accurately allocate human, fiscal, and logistical resources to the development, distribution, and marketing of these items. Marketing is among the most creative, challenging, and rewarding parts of an administrator's job. Good marketing can make a program; bad or even no marketing can break a program.

# Chapter 10

# Access and Permitting for Use of Public Lands

*Rachel M. Peters, MA*

Colleges, universities, community programs, military programs, and other not-for-profit outdoor recreation and education programs across the country have a long history of offering high-quality and safe educational experiences on public lands. Through the work of dedicated professionals from these programs, a shift in overall accountability for uses on public lands has emerged. A growing representation of land managers from all sectors has created an avenue of communication and education that goes both ways. In the 1970s and '80s these programs were able to offer courses on public lands with little to no communication with land-management agencies; today this is no longer an acceptable approach. Land managers face a perennial struggle in their efforts to achieve an appropriate balance between the competing mandates to preserve natural and cultural resources and to provide high-quality recreation use (Marion and Reid, 2001). Programs are now involved more than ever before in the policy- and decision-making processes governing land management of public lands. This involvement has been critical to the longevity of existing programs, as well as to new, emerging programs. The permitting process was developed to address ecological and societal needs for greater stewardship, responsibility, and accountability for the use of public lands. This process involves collaborating, communicating, and acquiring formal authorization and permissions with land-management agencies. Permitting has become a priority for

these programs, and as a result a new standard of involvement has been established for the profession. Visions for the future are being created by administrators who are actively investing time and energy to acquire, maintain, and sustain permitted use on public lands. This is done by researching, networking, and partnering with appropriate private landowners or land-managing agencies for sustaining use and enjoyment of specific program areas.

Many agencies manage land and water resources across the United States, but in this chapter we will look at the permitting process for three of the main federal land-management programs: the National Park Service (NPS), the Bureau of Land Management (BLM), and the United States Forest Service (USFS). In addition, there will be basic descriptions of the permitting process for accessing lands managed by the Bureau of Indian Affairs, Bureau of Reclamation, Army Corps of Engineers, municipal governments, and private landowners.

## OUTDOOR PROGRAMS ON PUBLIC LANDS

The research, acquisition, and maintenance of permits for multiple program areas is an invaluable investment toward the long-term sustainability of outdoor programs that operate on private and public lands. Permitted uses on public lands are tracked by visitor use days. This tracking is a numerical calculation to record the amount of use or visits any one area receives by a permittee. This number can then be compared to potential impacts an area might be receiving during high or low levels of visits. A user day is the actual number of days any one person visits public lands.

In the spring of 2007, the Association of Outdoor Recreation and Education's Access Committee did a survey of its members to determine use on public lands. Seventy outdoor recreation programs responded to the online survey, documenting over 145,639 annual service days on public lands. With an estimated 900 outdoor recreation programs in the United States, it is likely the cumulative estimated use on public lands for these programs is upwards of 2 million user days per year.

This staggering number of 2 million user days by outdoor programs has received growing attention by many federal employees working on permitting and allocation issues. The concern is that many of the uses of outdoor programs on public lands is unpermitted. When groups are using public lands without permits, there is no relationship or communication with the managing agency. This means the agency is unable to track impacts, and in some cases might be drawing conclusions, and making consequent managerial decisions, about a resource based on inaccurate data.

In 2008, there were over 672 million acres of public land—out of a total 2.3 billion acres in the United States—managed by federal agencies. This means approximately 30 percent of the United States has been set aside, valued, and deemed necessary to be managed for public use (Vincent et al., 2004). The majority of these 672 million acres are managed by three agencies: the Department of Agriculture's USDA Forest Service (USFS), the Department of the Interior's National Park Service (NPS) and, the Bureau of Land Management (BLM). Each of these agencies has developed departments and programs dedicated to the management of recreational activities that support public uses.

Bob Ratcliffe, Chief of the National Recreation and Visitor Services Division, Bureau of Land Management, spoke to a room of over 400 outdoor professionals at the annual AORE conference in Asheville, North Carolina, in November of 2007 and said, "Our population will continue to increase, but our public lands, they are finite. . . . If you want to

have a program in 10 years, get permits; the problem isn't going away." Ratcliffe's statements highlight an important point: As the population continues to grow, so will the public's interest and desire to seek out and experience nature. This will create a greater impact on the finite resources of our public lands. Thus obtaining permits to use the nation's natural resources will become increasingly more competitive. According to the Outdoor Industry Association's website (December 2008), 75 percent of Americans participate in outdoor activities. The continued growth of participation in outdoor recreation and education activities has created an increased burden on the public lands, and in response to the demand, land-management agencies have been forced to actively manage recreational impacts. Guidelines, policies, and regulations for private, organized, and commercial use have been developed to protect the resources.

Many of the administrative guidelines for permitting are interpreted differently from agency to agency and location to location. This exemplifies the importance of working directly with the agencies. Cultivating relationships requires more time and energy but allows for a greater possibility for collaboration, education, and overall understanding of the needs of a resource. Many of the nation's outdoor programs have strong educational missions and many are affiliated or sponsored directly by large land grant institutions, private colleges, military, or community recreation programs. The experiences offered on public lands by these organizations range from classes that are purely academic in nature (credit-bearing and in pursuit of an academic area of study), to extracurricular student-led and cost-sharing programs, to programs offered to the public for a fee, regardless of whether the service is offered by a for-profit or a not-for-profit agency.

This dynamic use spectrum represents institutional outdoor programs and the diverse students and participants served on public lands (see figure 10.1). It represents a myriad of program types that are equally as dynamic and diverse as the ecosystems that programs travel through, study about, and take pleasure in enjoying. This diversity of use requires flexibility in definition by the agencies and simultaneously in how a resource is managed. This flexibility can often seem burdensome, but it is a necessary approach to managing for a diversity

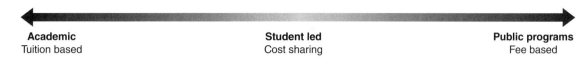

Academic | Student led | Public programs
Tuition based | Cost sharing | Fee based

**Figure 10.1**  Spectrum of recreational use of public lands.

of users. The land manager's job isn't an easy one, considering the delicate balance between managing public lands for either preservation or multiple use (or sometimes both).

Understanding the important role a program plays on public lands is a critical component of any outdoor program administrator's overall work model. Where does the program fit along this user spectrum? The way a program is designed and implemented has a direct effect on how it is viewed by the agency. The knowledge and skills required to effectively obtain and manage public land use permits is becoming an area of increased responsibility in the job descriptions of today's outdoor program administrators.

There continues to be momentum by federal, state, and municipal governments to create a system of accountability for organized groups offering a duty of care to their students, participants, or clients. Accountability exists regardless of an outdoor program's for-profit, not-for-profit, or cost-sharing business model. User-created impacts to public resources exist in both low use and popular recreational areas. Incorporating accountability begins with developing knowledge and understanding of the permit process and then weaving it into curriculum development and program delivery. The service of educating participants and students to understand the current state of our nation's public lands is another step toward embracing a stewardship ethic. Educators do a disservice by withholding information about or ignoring the current state of affairs on our public lands.

## PERMITTING DEFINED

The cycle of accountability starts with the outdoor program administrator beginning the permit research process with enough time to plan and execute all required steps prior to the date of expected use of a resource area. Partnerships, friendships, and working relationships take time to develop; thus

it's best for outdoor program administrators to start early and reach out to land managers prior to when they want to use public lands. Beyond developing a personal relationship, it is also important to develop an accurate understanding of differences between the permitting systems for each of the agencies highlighted in this chapter. Land-management agencies maintain disparate permitting systems that define users or visitors differently, including private, noncommercial, commercial, and institutional designations. There is some interest at the national level to develop more consistent guidelines and definitions so the systems in place are less ambiguous from agency to agency. Developing a culture of consistency among land managers offers a reliable way to do business and provides for a dependable level of customer service. Although consistency of permitting review, management, and oversight can lead to a more uniform and predictable process, there are certain situations and resource areas that require both land managers and users to be flexible in their expectations for a uniform and seamless process. Flexibility in the interpretation and administration of the permitting process allows regional land managers to develop mutually beneficial relationships with outdoor program administrators. Some administrators share that the flexibility of regional land managers has been an asset to the success of their programs because when a manager supports a program's work, or when projects are implemented that benefit the agency, the resource, and the community, it's possible to enter into agreements with the agencies (i.e., letters of agreement or memorandums of understanding) in lieu of attaining formal permits. Sometimes it is important to consider what your program can give versus what your program can get. This is a strategy to consider, especially in areas where land managers may require assistance or expertise in accessing or managing public lands. This kind of approach takes more creativity and energy than taking a status quo approach to permitting.

The conscious act by an individual or organization to not participate in the permitting process is commonly recognized as *permit avoidance*. Permit avoidance effectively leads to illegal access and use of the public lands. Because of the complexity of the permitting process, permit avoidance has been common in outdoor program administration. Unfortunately, the past behaviors of organized groups who elected to avoid obtaining permits to use public land have created an overall negative effect on land manager relations.

Permit avoidance is not an acceptable practice within the outdoor recreation industry, and outdoor program administrators must proactively work with land-management agencies to foster healthy and transparent relationships. Although many programs are in alignment with land conservation values and teach the Center for Outdoor Ethics' Leave No Trace curriculum, it is important to see the link between acquiring authorized permits and land stewardship values. Students, participants, leaders, and administrators alike must practice and apply the appropriate and current land-management policies to effectively participate in the public forums that influence and guide land-management decision making. Outdoor programs have the opportunity to educate participants and serve the general populace as advocates for the resource.

# MANAGEMENT AGENCIES AND REGULATIONS

Public lands are managed by a variety of federal, state, and local agencies. Each sector of land or water under the stewardship of these branches of government is managed to meet the predetermined goals of the agency that oversees it. When reviewing the distribution of public lands by agency, the federal government clearly manages the largest bulk of public resources. As such, outdoor programs predominantly work with federal agencies such as the Department of the Interior and Department of Agriculture to secure authorization for program trips and activities. Depending on the regional location, outdoor programs might find they are working more with municipalities and private landowners to gain access. The following section provides an overview of each agency and some of the management strategies that can be employed to gain access to public lands for trips and activities.

# Department of the Interior

The Department of the Interior (DOI), established in 1849, is the nation's key federal conservation agency. The DOI provides direction for seven land-management agencies: U.S. Fish and Wildlife, U.S. Geological Survey, Bureau of Indian Affairs, Minerals Management Service, Office of Surface Mining, Bureau of Reclamation, Bureau of Land Management, and the National Park Service (see figure 10.2). Each of these agencies has its own chartered responsibilities relating to managing our nation's natural resources. The National Park Service and Bureau of Land Management will be the focus of the DOI land-management agency section of this chapter. These two agencies within the DOI manage a total of 345.9 million acres (Vincent et al., 2004).

## National Park Service

Although Yellowstone National Park was established as the first national park in 1872, the National Park Service itself was not established under the DOI until the passing of the National Park Service Organic Act of 1916. The Organic Act states the foundational mission of the agency:

> *The service thus established shall promote and regulate the use of the Federal areas known as national parks, monuments, and reservations, hereinafter specified, by such means and measures as conform to the fundamental purpose of said parks, monuments, and reservations, which purpose is to conserve the scenery and natural and historic objects and wildlife therein and to provide for the enjoyment of the same in such manner and by such means as will leave them unimpaired.* (USDI/NPS, 1989, p. 6)

The national park system has grown to cover far more than just national parks. In addition to the 58 national parks, the NPS has authority over monuments, preserves, lakeshores, seashores, wild and scenic rivers, trails, historic sites, military parks, battlefields, historical parks, recreation areas, memorials, and parkways. The NPS manages 84.4 million acres and in 2004 had 276 million visits in 388 units (DOI, 2009). Each park unit is lead by

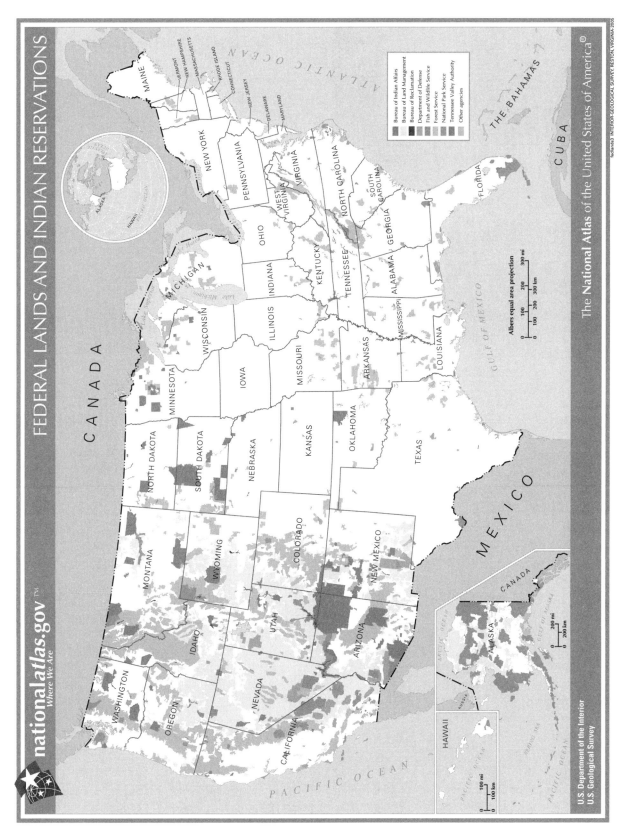

**Figure 10.2** Federal lands map.

Rachel Peters

The Colorado River, in the Grand Canyon National Park, in Arizona—one of the 58 national parks in the United States.

a superintendent who has the discretion to make decisions based on the management needs of the park's resources.

Each park maintains its own unique implementation and interpretation of policies, procedures, and regulations related to permitting for outdoor programs. The subjectivity of management practices from park to park is viewed as a persistent challenge by outdoor program administrators who seek to use public lands for educational and recreational programming. When applying for access, it's important to recognize that each ecosystem's carrying capacity is different, and as a result an attempt needs to be made to understand the complexity of the decision-making process for the land manager. Although it would be helpful for the application process to be similar for each agency, the protection needs and limitations vary across resource areas. For example, the decision-making process for granting access to Yellowstone National Park is very different from that for Chaco Culture National Historic Park. Access decisions often are based on factors such as visitation rates, geographic location, and the natural, biotic, and cultural resources of the parks.

In 1998, the 105th Congress passed the National Parks Omnibus Management Act into law. This law governs concession and outfitter activities in the national parks and introduced Commercial Use Authorizations (CUA) and policy that would require nonprofit organizations to be permitted but *not* require them to compete with commercial outfitters (this was done to solve the problem of commercial groups getting more permits). Section 418 C 3 of the National Park Omnibus Management Act of 1998 states

> *a non-profit organization is not required to obtain a CUA to conduct activities in a park area (even if the activities would otherwise be subject to authorization by a CUA) if the nonprofit organization does not derive taxable income from the activities.* (USDI/NPS, 2006a, p. 5)

The passing of this law has slowly but surely shifted the perception many parks have of outdoor programs. By knowing this law exists, each outdoor program administrator contacting a national park can reference this act and find out how it has been implemented into their permitting for the system and management of activities provided by nonprofit organizations. In February 2006, the director of the NPS sent memos to regional directors to begin the implementation of the commercial use authorizations (CUAs) and special-use permits (SUPs) for park uses:

> *Commercial use authorizations may be issued only to authorize services that 1) are determined to be an appropriate use of the park; 2) will have minimal impact on park resources and values; and 3) are consistent with the purpose for which the unit was established, as well as all applicable management plans and park policies and regulations.* (USDI/ NPS, 2006b, p. 150)

At this same time, the national parks began to phase out incidental business permits (IBPs). These IBPs were the old system of permitting the commercial outfitting and guiding use in the national parks. In lieu of IBPs, the parks initiated the CUA process.

Even after the passage of the Omnibus Bill, ambiguity and inconsistencies still exist among parks in the administration of the permitting process. However, in most cases this bill has allowed for the nonprofit community of park users to receive some clear definition of use for obtaining access. The new permitting structure within the parks doesn't require nonprofits to obtain a CUA, but it does include some requirements of nonprofit use. In place of the CUA, a special-use permit (SUP) is required. An organization's outdoor program administrator is required to contact the park and investigate the need to apply for the SUP. See table 10.1 for a summary of national park permitting. The park manager will likely ask if the activity the organization is proposing to offer meets these criteria:

- Provides a benefit to an individual, group, or organization rather than the public at large
- Requires written authorization and some degree of management control from the service in order to protect park resources and the public interest
- Is not prohibited by law or regulation
- Is not initiated, sponsored, or conducted by the service
- Is not managed under a concession contract (a recreation activity for which the NPS charges a fee, or a lease)

Each park has developed a specific application for the SUP process. The outdoor program administrator will need to call the park office or visit the park's website to view and download the application. It can take some time to find the right person at a park office, so preplanning is important. Calls

and inquiries serve as the first impression your program makes on the agency's staff and should be considered the prime opportunity to build a positive rapport with the park's employees administering the recreational and resource-management programs. Each SUP will be valid for the year it is issued, so consider the number of trips you will be interested in bringing to the park and prepare this information to submit with your application. Each SUP has criteria and supporting paperwork you will need to prepare to submit with your completed application (see "Permitting Tips" later in the chapter).

Most parks have set up opportunities for programs to apply for educational entrance fee waivers. The request for a waiver must be submitted at least 4 to 6 weeks prior to your arrival. These applications can be found online by going to www.nps.gov, selecting a park, and clicking on the "planning your visit" link. The parks' websites are becoming more and more user-friendly by providing one-click access to applications for waivers, permits, and basic visitor information. Most entrance fee waiver criteria require administrators to provide the following:

1. Documentation that you are offering credit for the class visiting the park
2. A curricular rationale for your visit that is founded on the resources of the park

**Table 10.1**   National Park Permitting

| Types of NPS permits | Commercial-use authorizations<br>Special-use permits (nonprofit organizations) |
|---|---|
| Educational fee waivers | Yes. Apply with specific park. Some parks may waive CUA or SUP for academic groups. |
| Advanced notice of request | Depends on park. Ideally, the November prior to the year you will visit. Most permits are granted January 1-December 31st. |
| Duration of permit | Maximum term for any commercial use authorization is two years. |
| Required operating plan? | Yes. Include itineraries, estimated camps, estimated numbers of user days, maps, resource protection plan, staff background, and risk-management plan. |
| Required certificate of insurance? | Yes |
| Actual use reports | Yes. To be submitted at the end of the year or 30 days after your last trip. |
| Fees | Yes. Depends on park ($150-$450). |
| Website | www.nps.gov |
| Permit-related resources | USDI/NPS management policies, 2006 |

3. Documentation of your tax-exempt, nonprofit status

National parks have a historical precedent in the support of educational endeavors outside the traditional walls of the classroom. Many national parks are interested in supporting and working with outdoor program administrators to support their work of getting students outdoors.

The fee structure for NPS permits vary from park to park. Most parks require a fee to apply for the umbrella special-use permit, and then another set of fees are associated with entrance fees, back-country permit reservation fees, and frontcountry camping fees. As mentioned earlier, the entrance fee can be waived if the published criteria are met. Most parks have a backcountry permit reservation system for overnight travel beyond any trailhead. These permits can be reserved in advance over the phone or by fax and are paid for separately from the special-use permit. Frontcountry camping is also an additional expense. Reservations can be made in advance. Check www.nps.gov for details.

## Bureau of Land Management

The Bureau of Land Management (BLM) was formed in 1946 by the merger of the U.S. Grazing Services and the General Land Office. The BLM currently manages about 261 million acres of public land and supports a multiple-use mission by managing diverse programs that range from resource extraction activities such as oil and gas production to motorized and human-powered recreation (figure 10.3).

The BLM mission is "to sustain the health, diversity and productivity of the public lands for the use and enjoyment of present and future generations" (DOI, 2009). Being the youngest of the four federal land-management agencies discussed here, the BLM is commonly known for getting the "leftover" public lands, whereas the perception is that the NPS received the nation's gems and the USFS received amazing forests and waterways. The truth is that the BLM has innumerable hidden jewels worth exploring and protecting; however, many of these jewels are currently being managed for resource-extraction activities, such as oil and gas drilling. Sadly, the after-effect of these extractive practices often destroys the outdoor recreational value of the resource area. Mining and drilling permits have become a strong focus of the BLM and a challenge for many of those employed by the bureau who are tasked to protect and manage the resources for outdoor recreation.

The task of stewarding our natural landscapes isn't an easy one. Whether you are employed by the agency or not, the wild landscapes of our planet need stewards, and the outdoor education and recreation field offers an avenue of experience that imprints a remarkable value on wild places and creates a connection worth advocating for. One of the many ways professionals working in the field of outdoor education and recreation can get involved with the agencies is to be a conduit of education, advocacy, and appreciation, even for those members of the public who will never visit these places. There is an opportunity and possibly even an obligation for the participants of our programs to understand the bigger issues our public lands face today and those they will face in the future. As professional outdoor educators and administrators, we can teach our participants through the civic process that they have an opportunity to comment on the following:

- Land management plans
- Environmental impacts
- How our public lands are being managed for outdoor recreation

**Figure 10.3**  BLM management areas.

- How our public lands are being managed for the future of our air and water quality

The BLM *Recreation Permit Administration Handbook* is available on the BLM website at www.blm.gov. Keep a copy handy and review it in depth as you are considering visiting BLM lands with your program. The handbook will assist you in navigating through the application process and help you predetermine your type of use and subsequent permit needed. Basically, the BLM issues special recreation permits (SRP) for multiple types of recreational use, including commercial, competitive, vending, special area, organized group activity, and event use. Regardless of whether a profit is made, the BLM permits most outdoor programs and organized groups under its commercial use category. Also see table 10.2.

The definition for commercial use is quite broad and applies to any "recreational use of public lands and related waters for business of financial gain" (USDI BLM, 2003, p. 8). The BLM goes on to define financial gain as "compensation . . . in excess of actual expenses incurred for the purposes of the activity, service, or use" as well as when "a duty of care or expectation of safety is owed participants by service providers as a result of compensation," (USDI BLM, 2003, p. 8). These financial gain definitions back up the bureau's decision to define educational use as commercial use regardless of nonprofit or for-profit status (unlike the NPS).

In 2008 the application fee for a special recreation permit from the BLM was $90.00. This is the fee submitted along with the permit application and supporting materials required by the field office issuing the permit. Upon issuance of the SRP, the permit administrator sends the final permit along with end-of-season paperwork. The end-of-season paperwork consists of an actual use report that is completed and sent back to the BLM documenting the gross revenue of the permitted use. The BLM sends an invoice for payment of 3 percent of the

**Table 10.2** Bureau of Land Management Permitting

| | |
|---|---|
| Types of BLM recreational uses requiring a SRP | Commercial use<br>Competitive use<br>Vendor use<br>Special area use<br>Organized group activity and event |
| Educational fee waivers | No. Although no permit is needed if you aren't providing a duty or care or a fee. |
| Advanced notice of request | 180 days prior to desired visit. |
| Duration of permit | Depends on permit type.<br>Commercial use permits 1-10 years. |
| Required operating plan? | Yes. Include itineraries, estimated camps, estimated numbers of user days, maps, resource protection plan, staff background, and risk-management plan. |
| Required certificate of insurance? | Yes |
| Actual use reports | Yes. To be submitted at the end of the year or 30 days after your last trip. |
| Fees | Yes. Depends on permit type.<br>Commercial-use permits $100 application fee plus 3% of gross revenue at end of year. |
| Website | www.blm.gov |
| Permit-related resources | USDA/BLM special recreation permit information: commercial, competitive and special events, 2006<br>USDA/BLM *Recreation Permit Administration Handbook* (Public) H-2930-1, 2006 |

Rachel Peters

The San Juan River is managed by the Bureau of Land Management, Monticello Field Office, Utah.

gross revenue or a flat $5 per person fee. For budgetary purposes, outdoor recreation administrators should consider the fee calculation in advance of the billing period.

## Bureau of Indian Affairs

The Bureau of Indian Affairs (BIA), operating under the Department of Interior, was established in 1852. The BIA oversees the administration and management of 66 million acres of land and serves over 1.7 million American Indians and Alaska Natives who are members of 562 federally recognized tribes (USDI/BIA, 2007).

The BIA mission is to ". . . enhance the quality of life, to promote economic opportunity, and to carry out the responsibility to protect and improve the trust assets of American Indians, Indian tribes, and Alaska Natives" (USDI/BIA, 2007, p. 9). Many tribes have parks and recreation departments with specific permitting guidelines for access and use of their lands by organized groups. Visit www.doi.gov/bia to find a contact for your regional or local tribal lands or for more detailed information.

## Bureau of Reclamation

The Bureau of Reclamation (BOR), under the Department of Interior, was established in 1902 and historically is best known for the construction of canals, dams, and power plants in the western states. Currently, the BOR declares that its mission is "to manage, develop, and protect water and related resources in an environmentally and economically sound manner in the interest of the American public" (USDI/BOR, 2003, p. I-1). There are 289 BOR project areas that have developed recreation facilities and opportunities available for public use, and within these areas there are over 90 million visits annually (www.usbr.gov/recreation/facts.html). Eighty-four of the 289 developed recreation areas are managed by another federal agency under an agreement with reclamation (www.usbr.gov/recreation/facts.html), which means the BOR owns the land, but other agencies such as the NPS, BLM, USFS, state, county, or city governments are the permitting agencies. Programs would then be permitted by those managing agencies, not the BOR.

## United States Army Corps of Engineers

The history of the United States Army Corps of Engineers (Corps) can be traced back to 1775 and to a time when their focus was on engineering armies. Three hundred years later, the corps continues to strive to meet the needs of a changing nation. With programs in civil works, navigation, flood damage reduction, wetlands and waterways regulation, recreation, emergency response, and others the Corps has attempted to stay up to date and provide stewardship of the lands and waters at their water resources projects. The Natural Resources Management Mission of the Corps is to manage and conserve those natural resources, consistent with ecosystem management principles, while providing quality public outdoor recreation experiences to serve the needs of present and future generations. The Corps has an interactive map available at www.usace.army.mil/about/Pages/Locations.aspx. Use this tool to research the relevant district office to contact and to determine the requirements associated with your proposed use.

# Department of Agriculture and the United States Forest Service

The USDA is a federal agency that oversees a mosaic of programs and initiatives. Agriculture, education, marketing, trade relations, natural resources and environment, and travel and recreation are all facets of the USDA. The United State Forest Service is one of the subagencies under the umbrella of the USDA and is responsible for the majority of lands used by outdoor programs.

The U.S. Forest Service was established in 1905 under the Reorganization Act and has since been placed under the Department of Agriculture. Early in the 20th century, the agency's primary concern was to protect the health of the forest for timber interests. In 1922 recreation was identified as an area of focus, and funding for public campsite improvements became a budgeted item. Recreational impacts on Forest Service–managed lands has since increased, raising the amount of attention and regulations placed on those using USFS lands for recreation. The mission of the USDA Forest Service is "to sustain the health, diversity, and productivity of the nation's forests and grasslands" (USDA/FS, 2006, p. 2).

The USFS currently manages 193 million acres with 159 forest units and 18 grassland units. In 2004 there were an estimated 34.8 million annual visits (USDA/FS, 2006) to our national forests.

Like the other agencies, the USFS determines the need to issue permits to outdoor programs by asking a series of questions related to the activity, duty of care, fees charged, salaries, and academic credits. Ideally, you will have your responses prepared for these questions and understand they are determining how to define or categorize your use and impacts. One common question asked regards the fee structure of the activity. The agency is interested in whether you charge a fee, regardless of whether you produce a profit. The NPS is the only agency interested in your program's not-for-profit status.

Although the type of permits the USFS issues are important, more important is how they define your program's use. How any agency defines your proposed usage will ultimately guide them into the permitting domain and, if a permit is available, the consequent fee structure. In many cases, outdoor programs and their activity on Forest Service lands are defined as commercial activities. Commercial use or commercial activity defined by the USFS is "any use or activity on National Forest System Lands (a) where an entry or participation fee is charged, (b) where the primary purpose is the sale of a good or service, and in either case, regardless of whether the use or activity is intended to produce a profit" (USDA, 1997, p. II-9). Commercial activity includes what the USFS refers to as "outfitting and guiding." The USFS defines guiding as "providing services or assistance (such as supervision, protection, education, training, packing, touring, subsistence, interpretation, or other assistance to individuals or groups in their pursuit of a natural resource-based outdoor activity) for pecuniary remuneration or other gain. The term "guide" includes the holder's employees, agents, and instructors (USDA, 1997, p. II-6). The agency then defines outfitting as ". . . providing through rental or livery any saddle or pack animal, vehicle or boat, tents, or camp gear, or similar supplies, or equipment, for pecuniary remuneration or other gain. The term 'outfitter' includes the holder's employees, agents and instructors" (USDA, 1997, p. II-7). This is the category most organized groups fall into.

The USFS has an additional definition of use called the institutional outfitter. Institutional outfitting is a definition of use on the Forest Service's own recreational use spectrum; it is not a type of permit. The USFS defines the institutional (semipublic) outfitter as an outfitter that "includes a variety of membership or limited constituency institutions such as religious, conservation, youth, fraternal, service club, and social groups; educational institutions such as schools, colleges and universities; and other similar common interest organizations and associations" (USDA, 1997, p. II-6). Institutional outfitters are required to get priority permits with the agency. The USFS definition of noncommercial use or activity is "any use or activity that does not involve a commercial use or activity" (USDA, 1997, p. II-10).

*Outfitting and guiding include but are not limited to packing, hunts, education, float trips, canoe or horse liveries, shuttle services, ski touring, helicopter skiing, jeep tours, boat tours, and fishing trips, and may be conducted by, among others, educational, rehabilitation, and interpretive ventures and outdoor institutional organizations, including both for-profit and nonprofit entities. (FSH 2709.11, ch40, sec41.53)*

Commercial and institutional users are required to get permission from the Forest Service for use and enjoyment of these lands. As of September 2008, there are two different types of permits for the USFS: priority use and temporary use permits. A priority use permit authorizes use for up to 10 years, and a temporary use permit is for short-term, nonrenewable use authorized in 50 service day increments up to 200 service days on the Forest Service lands.

The fee structure for these two types of permits are quite different. Similar to the BLM special recreation permit, the USFS priority use permit fee calculation is 3 percent of gross revenue. A flat fee is then charged for the issuance and use of the temporary use permits based on the range of service days allocated (see table 10.3).

The temporary use permit is a new model of permitting for the agency as of 2008. The 2008 policy change indicates that forests have until 2013 to create administrative systems to support temporary use permits. This model was adopted to accommodate users interested in gaining access for a short period, with the understanding the permit will not be renewed. In some cases this model will allow access into areas that have been closed to new permittees in the past.

Institutional outfitters who have acquired priority use permits with the Forest Service pay a fee of 3 percent of annual adjusted gross revenue. The Forest Service recognizes credited programs and noncredited programs within the institutional outfitting definition of use. These differences then translate to the fee calculation used for the permit.

**>> Credited programs.** Exclude tuition and other payments made by students that are unrelated to the use of National Forest System lands authorized for outfitting and guiding purposes if the program provided under the permit is recognized for credit toward graduation or a degree in a recognized school system or accredited educational institution.

**>> Noncredited programs.** Include all payments made by students for authorized outfitting and guiding services if the program provided under the permit is not recognized for credit toward graduation or a degree in a recognized school system or accredited educational institution (USDA, FSH 2709.11, Chapter 37.21k).

This direction is from the *Forest Service Handbook* (FSH) 2709.11, which contains policy direction for the administration of special-use permits. Chapter 40 in the handbook addresses the specifics of outfitter and guide permits. Outdoor programs that are academic and credit-bearing in nature still pay 3 percent, but they don't pay 3 percent of their tuition dollars as gross revenue. The calculation is based on activity fees or course-specific fees that are in addition to tuition dollars specific to the course using public lands.

It is important to discuss these definitions of use (commercial activity, institutional, and noncommercial) with the Forest Service permit administrator managing the resource area you plan on using. The way a program defines itself and the way the administrator defines it might not be the same. Plus, a permit administrator in one Forest Service area may define a proposed use one way, whereas the permit administrator in another Forest Service area in the same region may define the proposed use differently. This is when interpretation within an agency can seem inconsistent, confusing, and

**Table 10.3** Flat Fees for USFS Temporary Use Permits

| Number of service days | Flat fee | Maximum gross revenue for each bracket of service days |
|---|---|---|
| 1 to 50 | $150 | $10,000 |
| 51 to 100 | $300 | $20,000 |
| 101 to 150 | $450 | $30,000 |
| 151 to 200 | $600 | $40,000 |

challenging. Try not to get frustrated when dealing with the ambiguity of the permitting system; instead, actively engage the permit administrator by asking more questions and citing your understanding of the policy language. Not all permit administrators use the institutional definition of use or its related fee structure, so it is important to discuss these concerns with any Forest Service employee you are working with to be clear on their management plan and permitting system related to this category of use. This is the category that many outdoor programs fall under or best identify themselves with, so it's best to understand its use within the management plans of the areas used.

While the Forest Service uses slightly different terminology for the users of their public lands and the permits for the resources they manage, they too have a permit-focused guidebook. Similar to the NPS and BLM, the USFS has drafted a guidebook for public use—the *Forest Service Outfitter-Guide Administration Guidebook*. This is the best USFS permitting resource; you can find it online at www.fs.fed.us.

The handbook will assist you in preparing for the initial conversation, permit-assessment process, and follow-up stages of the permitting process. See table 10.4 for a summary.

## State Management Agencies

As you probably know, much of the nation's federal lands are west of the Mississippi. East of the Mississippi, the state governments tend to have the majority of oversight and management control of the natural resources. Outdoor program administrators might find they don't work with the federal agencies in their region, because of the lack of public land, but work predominantly with the state and county. Each region and state has its own thriving history with resource management as well as its own policies and regulations for governing public lands. Simultaneously, many states have very strong and active outfitter and guide associations and regulatory guide licensing boards. In states such as Idaho, Utah, and Colorado it's important to research their involvement in the management of that state's public

**Table 10.4** U.S. Forest Service Permitting

| Types of USFS commercial uses and activities | Outfitter<br>Guide<br>Institutional outfitter |
|---|---|
| Types of permits | Priority use permit<br>Temporary use permit |
| Educational fee waivers? | No |
| Advanced notice of request? | Depends. Many forests have application deadlines. Ideally 120 days prior to your desired visit. |
| Duration of permit | Special-use permit: 3 to 10 years<br>Temporary use permit: dates of intended visit to 1 year |
| Required operating plan? | Yes. Include itineraries, estimated camps, estimated numbers of user days, maps, resource protection plan, staff background, and risk-management plan. |
| Required certificate of insurance? | Yes |
| Actual use reports? | Yes. To be submitted at the end of the year or 30 days after your last trip. |
| Fees? | Yes. Depends on permit type.<br>Commercial use permits $90 application fee<br>plus 3% of gross revenue at end of year.<br>Academic courses pay 3% of course-related fees. |
| Website | www.fs.fed.us |
| Permit-related resources | *Forest Service Handbook:* www.fs.fed.us/passespermits/fee-legislation-qna.shtml |

Rachel Peters

Arkansas River, Arkansas Headwaters Recreation Area, is managed by the Colorado State Parks.

land. You might even find it beneficial to become involved with these boards to network, depending on the mission and vision of your outdoor program.

## County Parks and Recreation

County offices often have a Parks and Recreation Department to oversee parks, trails, and, in some cases, rivers. El Dorado County Parks and Recreation in Placerville, California, is a great example of an operation that manages whitewater recreation on one of the nation's most popular whitewater rivers: the South Fork of the American River.

In 2001, El Dorado County updated their River Management Plan and included a process for institutional users to apply for whitewater use on the South Fork. Considering the South Fork of the American currently has 32 commercially permitted outfitters, this has allowed other organizations who meet the criteria and definition established by El Dorado County to access the river.

The 2001 El Dorado County River Management Plan defines an institutional user as (1) a nonprofit organization that meets IRS tax-exempt requirements (river trips are one of the organization's programs) and (2) an accredited educational institution such as a school, college, or university (river trips are a component of the educational curriculum). This has created some challenges for the county because there was not a limit established for the number of daily launches for institutionally permitted groups. There are nonprofit organizations offering dozens of trips a year down the South Fork under the institutional permit. The county's concern is that many groups are not operating under the spirit of the institutional category on the South Fork of the American because they are being permitted as commercial entities on adjacent waterways. This is a perfect example of the complexities of the resource manager.

## Municipal Government

Each municipality also has differing views on permitting and access. It's best to start with the City Department of Parks and Recreation and begin to investigate from there. In many cases, municipalities have Open Space and Recreation Plans (OSRP). An OSRP "articulates a local government's vision of open space and recreation. It should establish a philosophical and practical justification for the protection and preservation of open space and recreation opportunities. The purpose of an OSRP is to provide a framework for implementation" (New Jersey Department of Environmental Protection, 2006, p.2). Check with the local city government for the most recent OSRP and inquire about permits for outdoor programs.

## Accessing Private Land

Crossing private property is a topic of importance. Many private landowners have privacy and liability concerns, so it is important to do your homework before entering private land. Visit the County Land office and investigate if they have an online Geographic Information System (GIS) for your county to find landowners and their contact information. This is a great tool. For example, Yavapai County in Arizona has an online database that can be searched by the owner's name or the township and range. This allows for research to be done on areas that may be private. A certain level of due diligence is required if your program is interested in crossing or using private lands for your programming. Once you have located the name and contact information of the owner, send a letter in the mail and then follow up with a phone call. Most private landowners are skeptical about allowing individuals or groups on their land because of unknown impacts to their resource and liability concerns driven by our litigious society.

Building a rapport with private landowners is done in a manner similar to working with public land managers. You are serving as an ambassador for your organization or institution by cultivating positive community relations. You might research your ability to add the private landowner to your insurance policy and provide them with a certificate of insurance. This often will be the piece of the permitting discussion that will create a formal partnership with the private land manager. You might even offer to work on a service project or report back on an area the landowner maybe hasn't been able to visit in a while because of an inability to access it. There is also the possibility that you won't hear back from a landowner. In this case, it is a good idea to consider your alternative plan while reviewing your proposed land use with your legal council until you make contact with the landowner. There are also access organizations in the recreation field that assist users in becoming educated (see table 10.5).

## PERMITTING TIPS

In this section there are clear guidelines for outdoor program administrators for preparing for the permitting process—from the initial conversation with the land manager to the actual use report and fees. Consider these tips when preparing the information you need to have before you even pick up the phone. With an understanding of the basic history of the agencies and how they view recreational uses, it is up to you to cultivate a relationship (be it over the phone or in person). These tips will help. Also see table 10.6 for how to start the permitting process.

## Drafting an Operating Plan

Land-management agencies require the submission of an operating plan that details how the outdoor program intends to facilitate activities on the public

**Table 10.5** Access Organizations

| Access organizations | Activity focus | Web contact information |
|---|---|---|
| Access Fund | Climbing | www.accessfund.org |
| American Whitewater (AWA) | Whitewater activities | www.americanwhitewater.org |
| International Mountain Biking Association (IMBA) | Mountain biking | www.imba.org |
| American Hiking Society | Hiking | www.americanhiking.org |

**Table 10.6**   Starting the Permitting Process

| Be prepared | Start making calls early | Ask questions | General information needed to begin to process a permit | Follow-up paperwork |
|---|---|---|---|---|
| • What is your rationale for visiting this area? Curricular? Is it a popular area? What day(s) of the week are you proposing? How many days? Particular routes? Do you have maps?<br>• Prepare yourself to be asked questions about what your students or participants are paying to participate. Are you being paid?<br>• Research local issues. Has the agency been working on a new management plan or recently put out a press release on closures or new facilities?<br>• Be inquisitive. Ask questions about the permitting process. Do they permit other groups like yours? Can you get a copy of their management plan?<br>• How are you defining your use? | • Pick up the phone 3 to 6 months in advance of your expected use date.<br>• Expect to play phone tag with at least one person.<br>• If the front desk transfers you, get the name and number of the contact.<br>• Keep a phone log with date, time, who you talked to, and basics of conversation.<br>• Have your maps ready, and ask lots of questions.<br>• They will interview you; and you will interview them. | • How do you permit groups like mine?<br>• Are permits available?<br>• When permits are available<br>• What is the timeline on applying?<br>• What kind of information do you need from me?<br>• When permits aren't available...<br>• Ask about the history of permitting there.<br>• Do they anticipate permits opening up?<br>• When is the next rewrite of the management plan? | • Cover letter<br>• Completed application form<br>• Operating plan (see operating plan section for more details)<br>• Certificate of insurance<br>• Application or administrative fee | • Keep track of your actual use while in the field. Create a user-friendly form for your staff to track who, what, where, and when.<br>• Sometimes what you have requested is different from what actually takes place, because of weather or other unexpected, uncontrollable circumstances.<br>• Submit actual use report.<br>• The agency will send you a bill based on your actual use, using their determined fee calculation. |

lands. Operating plans cover both the business and educational outcomes of the organization. Table 10.7 is designed to help an outdoor program administrator develop an effective operating plan. Many agencies will provide an operating plan template. Consider creating a program template that includes information that is synthesized from all the agencies you work with and is used consistently to acquire permits for your program.

## Obtaining Permits

Knowing how to navigate the permitting scene of any given federally managed area is an invaluable skill for an outdoor program administrator to have. Because of the differences among agencies, and even interpretations of policies within the same agency, there is no one best way to obtain permits. Do not expect an exact science. The best general approach is to research, communicate, and collaborate.

Being prepared is an essential part of the permitting process. Before calling an agency, a good amount of homework must be done. One of the most important aspects of permitting is determining if your program has sufficient rationale—in the eyes of the agency, that is—for visiting a given area. These rationale might include the goals for the trip, the relevance of the resource area to your trip's educational or recreational goals (why this area and not somewhere else?), the mission of your program, and in some cases even your educational objectives. Sometimes it can be helpful, for gaining credibility, to have a working knowledge of the land-management issues occurring in the resource area. The next step is to research exactly whom you need to contact to discuss permitting your planned activity.

Once you have established who you are going to speak with and what you want to say, call as much as six months in advance. Each agency has its own

**Table 10.7** Developing a Comprehensive Operating Plan

| History and description of your program | Area of operation | Fees | Qualifications |
|---|---|---|---|
| Are you an active permittee? Reference active (and expired) permits your program has used. | Location of proposed visit (trailheads and camps) | How much are you charging for your trip? | List trainings and other pertinent information of the staff. |
| Describe your historical use in the area. | Proposed parking location | Are you offering credit? | Attach copies of certifications. |
| Program mission and vision related to public lands | Submit a map with highlighted camps and route. | Is tuition being paid? | Insert risk-management plan. |
| Objectives of proposed use | Is your use in wilderness? | Is there a course fee or fee in addition to tuition? | Attach copies of program or organization accreditations. |
| Educational rationale for proposed use | | Are the leaders being paid or compensated in any way? | Explain interpretive and educational approaches. |
| Describe the activity. | | Ask about fee calculations so you can anticipate your budget. | If offering credit, attach course description and syllabus. |
| Document the total group size (students, participants, or staff). | | Be prepared to pay an administrative fee upfront. | Document the total group size (students, participants, or staff). |
| Submit an itinerary with specific dates. | | Create a form to track your actual user days. | Submit an itinerary with specific dates. |
| Estimate your user days. | | | |
| Describe LNT techniques used. | | | |
| Describe care handling and cooking of food. | | | |
| Equipment provided | | | |
| Contingency plan for an emergency | | | |
| Resource-protection plan | | | |

deadlines, so the sooner you can talk to someone, the better your chances of receiving the permit. Another important element of making contact is keeping a record of your phone conversations. Keeping a log of your calls, numbers you were transferred to, and a record of your conversation's highlights can make the application process easier when it comes time to renew permits or ask specific questions about the permit for which you are applying.

Once you are on the phone with the right person, make sure you have all the information you might need in front of you. This includes itinerary, maps, and any questions you might have about the area or permitting process. These people will be essentially interviewing you, so make sure you have the resources readily available to interview them back.

Cursory conversations like this help you determine the application timeline, the general mood of the particular agency employee you are talking with, and many other important details that will affect your chances of getting a permit. If permits are available, be sure to ask what step you need to take to submit a permit application. There are federal guidelines for submitting permits, but each office has its own preference when it comes to permit submissions, and you want to understand what those are before you begin gathering information.

If permits are not available, ask what the history of permitting has been in the area, and whether permits might be available in the near future. Also ask when the management plan for the area is up for revision. Getting this information is crucial if you are intent on running a program in this area in the future. If the resource area is currently not issuing permits, stay in communication with the permit administrator and ask to be informed of local projects, services, and updates on when and if they will be renewing their management plans. The management plan review process is when limits are set by each agency on the number of permits that will be granted for both high- and low-use recreation areas.

## SUMMARY

Outdoor programs using public lands have an obligation to cultivate a stewardship ethic among participants, clients, and students to understand the challenges our natural resources and land managers face. Marion and Reid (2001) state that "social and ecological impacts of use on public lands are unavoidable," and it is up to outdoor educational institutions to role model ways to reduce those impacts. One way this can be done is by playing an active role in the stewardship and management of public lands, by educating participants, students, and clients on the state of our nation's public lands. Whether designing an outdoor program or revisiting standard practices and procedures, programs in the twenty-first century must be willing to be part of the solution.

This chapter was designed to assist outdoor program administrators in navigating the landscapes of permitting on lands managed by federal, state, municipal governments, and private lands through research, communication, collaboration, and action. I hope you have found the resources you need to prepare yourself for the permitting process and to support your dreams and visions for your programs. The canyons, valleys, and vistas keep us motivated as a growing professional field while we are faced with an increasing population and finite natural resources. It is essential for the outdoor program administrator to be aware of the dynamic and changing world of permitting, and to be accountable for uses on public lands through permits and partnerships. Permits and accountable use are strong threads for creating sustainable programs and practicing stewardship.

# Chapter 11

# Environmental Stewardship

*Whitney Ward, PhD, and Will Hobbs, PhD*

Outdoor recreation professionals have long recognized their dependence on natural settings. These locations—rivers, lakes, seashores, forests, deserts, mountain ranges, and wildlands—offer an interaction with elements of nature and allow programs to take place without the physical distractions of human society. It is the interaction with the natural environment that sets outdoor recreation apart from other forms of recreation that occur out of doors (Clawson and Knetsch, 1966; Ibrahim and Cordes, 2002; Jensen and Guthrie, 2006).

Human-powered outdoor pursuits are generally considered less harmful to the environment than other consumptive forms of outdoor recreation; however, scientists have demonstrated that participation in even nonconsumptive recreation does indeed cause negative impacts to the vegetation, soil, water, and wildlife (Cole, 2004; Leung and Marion, 2000). This poses a unique problem for outdoor program administrators and other outdoor professionals because, unlike other recreation venues (such as community parks or playing fields), another mountain wilderness cannot be built, a wild, scenic river cannot be created, and a desert cannot be developed just because we need one. Once a pristine wild area has been affected, it can take generations to recover. Thus both direct and indirect interactions with the natural environment must be carefully managed. This is environmental stewardship. Environmental impacts are not just the result of an individual's actions but also those of program providers, organizations, and government entities. It is essential to have a collaborative effort across these levels of society to ensure successful stewardship of existing outdoor recreation resources—with the partners from the outdoor industry playing a leading role among key stakeholders. In this chapter we focus on developing a basic understanding of the impacts of outdoor pursuits on the natural environment as well as a framework for understanding the relationships across levels of society.

## HISTORY OF ENVIRONMENTAL STEWARDSHIP IN THE UNITED STATES

The stewardship heritage of the United States is filled with iconic personalities, divisive controversies, legislative boldness, and incredible disasters. An excellent summary of this history can be found in Hendee and Dawson (2001). However, there is evidence that elements of environmental stewardship have been practiced at all levels of society well into ancient history (e.g., the Hanging Gardens of Babylon, vast hunting estates of the Roman Empire, etc.). In most cases, the setting aside of tracts of land was intended to support some aspect of human life, such as agriculture, sport, or resources. In North America, the lifestyles of the early European colonists were similar to indigenous cultures following the natural cycles of the earth. Native cultures existed in clear connection and dependence on the land, seasons, and natural rhythms. Although these early cultures relied exclusively on natural resources for all aspects of life—shelter, clothing, food, medicine—the impacts of seemingly nonenvironmental practices (such as slash-and-burn agriculture and buffalo jumps) were mitigated because the human population remained within the carrying capacity of the land.

As European culture evolved into an American society, westward expansion and Manifest Destiny guided exploration and resource use. After the "discovery" of the vast resources in the New World, it was not long before the pressure from both domestic and foreign entities to exploit these resources increased significantly. Immense stands of white pine in the northeast—well suited for ship masts—were harvested to support the British navy (Klyza and Trombulak, 1999). Land in America was viewed as an endless supply of resources—wildlife and game, precious metals, timber, and space—and little care was given to how it was used, consumed, or occupied. Following the Civil War, the Industrial Revolution spawned a massive transition from a rural agrarian lifestyle to a fast-paced, urban industrial way of living. Subsistence living was greatly reduced as the urban population increasingly relied on others (including commercial agriculture) to provide for basic needs. This shift away from an agrarian culture caused many Americans to disconnect from the land and natural rhythms—a condition that is still prevalent today.

Overcrowding and poor working conditions in American cities worsened throughout the late 19th century. More and more natural resources were extracted from the West and shipped via railroad to the East for manufacturing. By the time newspapers heralded the "closing" of the frontier in 1890, Manifest Destiny had been fulfilled. With that declaration came a palpable feeling of loss for the American public. John Muir, Henry David Thoreau, Ralph Waldo Emerson, and other writers captured the country's attention with eloquent descriptions of wide expanses of land in the West and the romantic notions of a life not bound to industrial production. But even words could not describe the sublime landscape of the American West, and artists such as Thomas Moran, Albert Bierstadt, George Catlin, and others brought stunning paintings of Yellowstone, Yosemite, and other western territories back to the cities in the East. The social conditions exacerbated by the Industrial Revolution created tremendous demand for this Romantic ideal. Resource management soon emerged as a field of study at prestigious colleges engaging such notables as Gifford Pinchot (first chief of the National Forest Service) and Benton MacKaye (founder of the Appalachian Trail). The well-traveled president Theodore Roosevelt—utterly awed by the sublime views in California, Colorado, and Wyoming and absorbed by long conversations with Muir and Chief Forester, Gifford Pinchot—took decisive action with the help of Congress and set the United States on a course of stewardship policy that continues to this day. With the help of Congress and the Antiquities Act of 1906, Roosevelt designated some 15 million acres as national parks and monuments over the next four years. See figure 11.1 for more highlights of U.S. legislation and events.

---

**Figure 11.1** Historical Environmental Stewardship Legislation and Events

1872   Yellowstone National Park established.

1873   Adirondack and Catskill Forest Preserve established—the largest, publicly protected land in the contiguous United States, comprising about six million acres.

1876   Appalachian Mountain Club founded in Boston by Edward Pickering and other outdoor enthusiasts. It is the United States' oldest nonprofit conservation and recreation organization.

1892   The Sierra Club, founded by John Muir with 182 charter members, was established "to explore, enjoy, and render accessible the mountain regions of the Pacific Coast; to publish authentic information concerning them;" and "to enlist the support and cooperation of the people and government in preserving the forests and other natural features of the Sierra Nevada" (Cohen, 1988).

1902   First National Wildlife Refuge established—Pelican Island, Sebastian, Florida.

1905   U.S. Forest Service established—Gifford Pinchot, friend of Muir and Roosevelt, was the first Chief. National Audubon Society formed.

1906   The Antiquities Act gave presidential power to claim and protect areas of scenic wonder and natural beauty through Executive Order. Theodore Roosevelt created 17 national monuments under this Act.

1916   National Park Service established "to promote and regulate the use of the Federal areas known as national parks . . . to conserve the scenery and national historical objects of the wildlife and by such will leave them unimpaired for the enjoyment of future generations" (www.nps.gov).

1919   Arthur Carhartt recommended keeping Trappers Lake, Colorado, pristine, protecting it from development. This was the beginning of the wilderness preservation movement.

1921   The Appalachian Trail proposed by Benton MacKaye as a means of promoting wilderness. The trail, 2,175 miles stretching from Maine to Georgia, was not completed until 1937.

1924   574,000 acres in Gila National Forest, New Mexico, set aside for wilderness recreation.

1933   Civilian Conservation Corps established. The CCC built and improved outdoor recreation facilities across the United States.

1935   The Wilderness Society formed by Robert Sterling Yard, Benton MacKaye, and Robert Marshall as an organization that preserved "that extremely minor fraction of outdoor America which yet remains free from mechanical sights and sounds and smell."

1946   Bureau of Land Management (BLM) established.

1949   *A Sand County Almanac* published by Aldo Leopold.

1958   Outdoor Recreation Resources Review Commission (ORRRC) established by U.S. Congress; final reports issued in 1962 led to an expansion of outdoor recreation services at federal, state, and local levels.

1960   Congress passed the Multiple-Use Sustained Yield Act, which named outdoor recreation an official function of the U.S. Forest Service.

1964   Wilderness Act: It took nearly 30 years before this bill was finally signed into law, enabling Congress to immediately designate 9 million acres of national forest, parks, wildlife refuges, and other federal lands as wilderness, thereby protecting them in a "pristine" state. Today, there are over 107 million acres in the National Wilderness Preservation System.

1965   National Outdoor Leadership School (NOLS) founded in response for the need of qualified outdoor leaders.

1968   Congress passed the National Wild and Scenic Rivers Act and the National Trail Systems Act (which was amended in 1978).

1969   National Environmental Policy Act (NEPA) passed. It required environmental impact statements and public comment before implementing projects that might alter ecological relationships.

1977   Wilderness Use Education Association formed (the word "Use" dropped in 1978).

1980   Alaska National Interest Lands Conservation Act passed. Fifty-six million acres were preserved as national monuments and wildlife refuges (expanded NPS dramatically) and returned land to the native people.

1991   Leave No Trace outdoor ethics were developed through a partnership between the U.S. Forest Service and NOLS. Later, in 1994, became the Leave No Trace Center for Outdoor Ethics, a nonprofit organization.

2001   Roadless Areas Conservation Rule adopted by the U.S. Forest Service, designating about one-third of the national forest system's total acreage off-limits to virtually all road building and logging.

2007   No Child Left Inside Act proposed (passed by congressional House committee in 2008). Schools would be required to develop environmental education curricula that encourage a reconnection with the environment.

# MAJOR IMPACTS OF RECREATION TODAY

The people of the United States participated in 11.6 billion outdoor outings in 2006 (Outdoor Industry Foundation, 2007), a staggering number from an environmental impact perspective. Although walking, hiking, or backpacking are only a narrow slice of outdoor activities, even these have an impact; soil compaction and vegetative trampling are two of the most common negative impacts to the backcountry and can be seen after as little as one night of use in some areas (Cole and Monz, 2003). That is why it is essential to understand the full spectrum of impacts that outdoor recreation can have on the natural environment. Table 11.1 provides a summary of some of the most researched impacts related to outdoor recreation use. Simply put, impacts are inevitable with outdoor recreation, although they can vary significantly from one site to another. The rate of site recovery from outdoor recreation impacts also varies significantly; however, it is always much slower than the rate of deterioration (Cole, 1996).

The field of recreation ecology focuses on identifying, documenting, and mitigating the impacts of outdoor recreation to the wilderness environment. The biophysical components that make up this environment—soil, water, wildlife, and vegetation—are referred to as the resource (Buckley, 2002; Hammitt and Cole, 1998; Liddle, 1997). The research produced by recreation ecology since 1940 has increased the knowledge regarding recreation impacts to the point that it can now provide a scientific basis for management (Cole, 1996). More important, researchers have established that impacts on one component are often interconnected with all other components of the environment. We can use the single most significant direct cause of impact from outdoor recreation (trampling) to demonstrate this interconnectedness.

**» Vegetation.** Impacted vegetation holds serious implications for local ecosystems. Vegetation provides soil protection, shade, cover, and food for animals and is a vital contributor to the global nitrogen and carbon cycles. Trampling is the single largest source of groundcover damage, causing broken stems, torn leaves, and bruised or crushed plant parts. This impact can occur when we cut switchbacks, explore a pristine campsite for boundaries and hazards, visit bathroom areas, or use multiple trails to walk from kitchen area to camp. Trampling without death inevitably results in reduced photosynthesis and thus reduced growth. The issue of compaction plays a large role with trampled plants. Compacted soils reduce the ability of root structures to expand into areas with water and nutrients and also results in less available water and nutrients. Seeds are also less likely to be protected and nurtured on compacted soils, inhibiting new growth. Reduction in plant height, stem length, and overall leaf area are also concerns

**Table 11.1** Common Forms of Recreation Impacts

| Effects | Ecological components |
|---------|----------------------|
| Direct | *Soil:* Soil compaction, loss of organic litter, loss of mineral soil<br>*Vegetation:* Reduced height and vigor, loss of ground vegetation, loss of fragile species, loss of trees and shrubs, tree trunk damage, introduction of exotic species<br>*Wildlife:* Habitat alteration; loss of habitat; introduction of exotic species; wildlife harassment; modification of wildlife behavior; displacement from food, water, and shelter<br>*Water:* Introduction of exotic species, increased turbidity, increased nutrient inputs, increased levels of pathogenic bacteria, altered water quality |
| Indirect | *Soil:* Reduced soil moisture, reduced soil pore space, accelerated soil erosion, altered soil microbial activities<br>*Vegetation:* Composition change, altered microclimate, accelerated soil erosion<br>*Wildlife:* Reduced health and fitness, reduced reproduction rates, increased mortality, composition change<br>*Water:* Reduced health of aquatic ecosystems, composition change, excessive algal growth |

Adapted from Y.F. Leung and J.L. Marion, 2000, "Recreation impacts and management in wilderness: A state-of-knowledge review," *USDA Forest Service Proceedings* RMRS-P-15, vol. 5, p. 24. [Online]. Available: www.wilderness.net/library/documents/science1999/Volume5/Leung_5-4.pdf [September 7, 2011].

(Liddle, 1997). The susceptibility of damage from trampling varies from plant species to species. Herbaceous, nonshrub plants are typically fragile; trees and other woody vegetation tend to be more resilient. Native species are more susceptible to trampling and are eventually replaced by invasive species with higher levels of tolerance for trampling (LaPage, 1967). Removal of groundcover exposes the soil to wind and water erosion.

**» Soil.** Soil impacts begin with the removal of the litter layer, or duff. This removal occurs as a result of trampling, surface erosion or runoff, or deliberate removal by clearing or raking the site (e.g., clearing a campsite). These changes to the soil surface affect several soil characteristics, including aeration, temperature, moisture, nutrition, and living organisms, limiting the ability of the soil to support plant life. Trampling the litter layer results in a reduction of soil organic matter through simple removal of the leaf litter. Also, as traffic increases on a site, soil particles are forced together, reducing or eliminating pore space and breaking up aggregates, which leads to reduced water infiltration and increased runoff as well as increased stress on plants caused by lack of water in the soil. Increased runoff exacerbates surface erosion, which increases the removal of the litter layer (Manning, 1979). While all aspects are interrelated, vegetation and soil are the most interconnected and in most situations have the lowest resistance to outdoor recreation use (Cole, 1996).

Outdoor recreation impacts on soil.

**» Water.** Trampling also influences water quality. Water quality research at the Boundary Waters Canoe Area indicated that recreational use does indeed increase the water's phosphate concentration and coliform bacteria count near lakeshore campsites (Hammitt and Cole, 1998). Additionally, data collected during research on a semiwilderness lake in Canada indicated a causal relation between human trampling of the shoreline and an exceptionally high phosphorous loading (Dickman and Dorais, 1977). Compaction inhibits the absorption of precipitation, resulting in greater runoff and subsequently erosion, which increases sedimentation and turbidity, thereby lowering water quality (Cole, 2004). It has been estimated that 80 percent of the deterioration of water quality is caused by suspended matter (Anderson, Hoover, and Reinhart, 1976). By reducing penetrating light, turbidity reduces photosynthesis and contributes to reduced vision for fish and other animals. This is caused partly by swimmers, motorboats, and personal watercraft operating in shallow waters and stirring up sediments. Although water quality is a major concern for society, the impacts of outdoor recreation to water quality are not prevalent. The major impacts to lake and stream quality are logging, land clearing, and agricultural runoff.

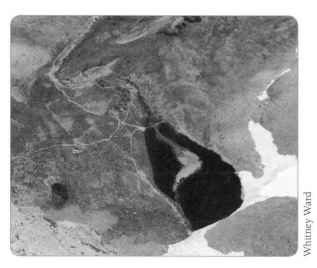

Outdoor recreation impacts on vegetation.

Outdoor recreation impacts on water.

**» Wildlife.** The loss of vegetative cover from trampling means a loss of a food source and shelter for many species of fauna. Increased turbidity in water sources reduces vegetation, shelter, and visibility for fish and other aquatic organisms. Habitat modification impacts can include destruction of tunnels, dens, and insulation in snow as a result of snowmobiling, off-road vehicles, and other factors, and the removal of vegetative cover in campgrounds and backcountry sites. Although recreation ecology has researched less on the impacts on wildlife than

Outdoor recreation impacts on wildlife.

any of the other aspects (Cole, 2004), there have been several studies on short-term disturbances caused by a recreation wildlife interaction. Current research is examining the long-term effect that outdoor recreation may have on wildlife communities. What is known is that outdoor recreation has influenced such things as predation, wildlife mating patterns, and movement through an ecosystem (Gutzwiller, Riffell, and Anderson, 2002; Knight and Cole, 1995).

# APPLIED ENVIRONMENTAL STEWARDSHIP

Looking at the full spectrum of individual and programmatic activities, patterns, and behavior through the lens of environmental stewardship can be daunting. However, a systems theory approach may shed light on possible solutions. This theory applies the ideology that all things are interconnected or interrelated and declares that these connections create different types of relationships. In other words, major impacts on the environment are often the cumulative result of an interconnected series of smaller choices made by individuals, society, or government—the "community of interdependent parts" (Leopold, 1968, p. 203)—in everyday life. Indeed, each choice "may appear to be small and of little consequence, but when multiplied by the number of times they are made every day, they have significant implications for the environment and the quality of life for everyone" (EPA, 2005, p. 3).

A parasitic relationship is characterized by one entity benefiting at the expense of another, whereas in a symbiotic relationship both entities live in a manner that benefits both. Too often, outdoor recreation has modeled a parasitic relationship with the land. Although participants proclaim they are "wise environmental stewards," actual land use practices often create long-term environmental damage. Fortunately, all it takes to change this situation to a symbiotic relationship are the everyday choices centered on collaboration between key players (see figure 11.2).

Take for example the issue of human waste, which can be found almost anywhere, from local forests to high-alpine environments, and can range from common household garbage along the roadside to the specific mountaineering waste left on remote peaks. Beyond aesthetics, human waste can also cause health concerns when not disposed of properly. The National Park Service (NPS) implemented regulations for both commercial and noncommercial river rafters as a result of health issues from years of improper disposal of human waste on the Colorado River through the Grand Canyon (NPS, 2009). As a result, the impact of human waste along the river corridor has been reduced, and the quality of the canyon float trips has improved greatly. Mt. McKinley experienced a similar human waste problem. A climber produces approximately 10 pounds of waste while climbing the mountain (Ward, 2005). Given the thousands of climbers that attempt the summit of Mt. McKinley annually, that means approximately 7,000 pounds of waste potentially left on the mountain each year (Ward, 2005). Much like the Grand Canyon strategy, the NPS implemented several rules and regulations supported by an education program that rewarded the actions of individual climbers—the result of a collaborative effort between government, organizations, and individuals. The end result is a cleaner mountain and a better experience for all.

Collaboration is combining the resources of two or more stakeholders to resolve problems that cannot be solved individually (Moore and Driver,

2005). Using a systems or holistic approach for collaboration has been successful in addressing environmental concerns. Government legislative efforts to regulate environmental stewardship have been successful in the past, yet they have been more effective when coupled with collaborative environmental stewardship efforts of all key players (Environmental Protection Agency, 2005).

# Key Players

The Environmental Protection Agency suggested that four segments of society play critical roles in stewardship (EPA, 2005). We have adapted that framework for outdoor recreation (see figure 11.2). The four key players in outdoor recreation are individuals, providers, associations, and government. Providers have the most power to effect change because they are in contact with each of the four key players. They work closely with individuals, are members of organizations, and as members of these organizations work to affect the legislative process of the government. An individual provider who wishes to be a wise environmental steward knows how to assert their pull in each of these arenas.

## Individuals

Outdoor recreation is primarily driven by individuals; thus this category comprises the largest and

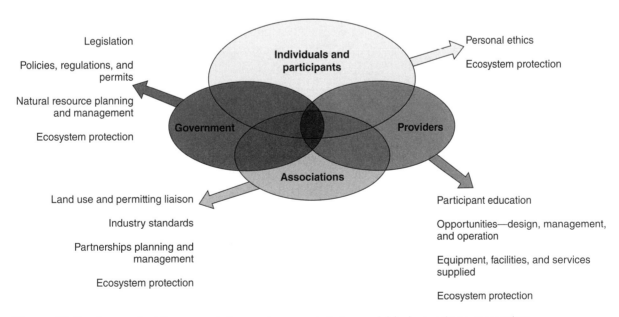

**Figure 11.2**   An applied framework for environmental stewardship in outdoor recreation.

Whitney Ward

Garbage where you least expect it—in the wilderness.

most diverse segment of key players. It includes individuals who participate in outdoor recreation opportunities independently, program participants, and outdoor program administrators and other outdoor professionals. Individual users determine location popularity, make clothing and equipment decisions, and are the "boots on the ground" in the backcountry. These choices directly impact the backcountry—by adhering to Leave No Trace principles while in the backcountry, making wise purchases, and traveling to remote locations efficiently. Individual choices are guided by personal ethics and other realities.

## Providers

Not all individuals feel capable of pursuing a wilderness experience on their own. Providers play a critical role in introducing inexperienced participants to the wonders and power of the natural environment. Program providers have an opportunity to introduce individuals to the twofold role of environmental stewardship. First, the responsibility

for ecosystem protection on an individual level, and second, the development of a personal outdoor ethic that leads to environmental stewardship. Research (Corbett, 2006; Ewert, Place, and Sibthorp, 2005; Louv, 2005) has established that individuals who are exposed to the outdoors earlier in life and with more frequent exposure possess a stronger connection to the environment. Providers help individuals realize this connection as they bring individuals into the outdoors. This is essential in the success of environmental stewardship, and providers have a unique opportunity and responsibility to consciously educate and help individuals develop a framework that guides their positive environmental behavior—an outdoor ethic. This is not an easy task but may be the only way to achieve lasting environmental stewardship.

For this to happen effectively, providers must ensure that their mission and goals are in line with the goods, services, or programs that they currently offer. Increasingly, participants and customers expect providers to address environmental stewardship; part of a provider's mission statement should address this need. A mission serves to dictate the everyday stewardship decisions providers make. Decisions such as the type of programs conducted, locations used, and equipment used and produced can all be made by referencing a mission statement that includes an environmental stance. At a minimum, providers should endorse Leave No Trace principles. However, it is imperative that providers commit to more than just the minimum. Service learning programs or volunteer days are excellent strategies for offering participants altruistic opportunities. Consider the Sierra Club's Inner City Outing, which helps inner city youth make a connection with outdoor resources (Outdoor Industry Association, 2008). Providers can plan something informal or enlist a service learning organization, such as Wilderness Volunteers, to run a service learning trip in cooperation with local land-management agencies.

A provider's mission must drive any stewardship decision. Most equipment providers have established green practices (e.g., Patagonia), and any provider wishing to establish a trend of environmental stewardship within their programs should do the same. But even micropolicies, such as paperless forms, can support a provider's environmental stewardship. Using local food co-ops and farmers markets for rations also reduces impact. Everyday choices regarding energy conservation also can be significant, such as rain water recycling, a hot-water-on-demand system, or energy-efficient lights and computer systems. Other, more nontraditional options such as biofuel vans or carbon offsetting for more environmentally sustainable travel are available at a greater cost. Because of their position as industry professionals, providers have the ability to significantly influence other key players. Providers can encourage individuals to buy gear made from recycled or sustainable materials or provide a dropoff point for individuals to participate in gear-recycling programs. Providers drive the collective industry by setting operational standards, best practices, and norms. Consider contributing a percentage of profits to environmental causes or collaborating with other providers to support outdoor products and programs with reduced environmental impacts (Business Wire, 2007). Government regulations are often set in response to needs identified by providers, either through direct communication or in response to emergent issues. Providers should have an active voice in professional associations and stay aware of current government issues. Each strategy alone might not have a significant impact, but taken together the culmination of actions can be significant.

## Associations

The professional networks of individuals and providers with similar views and priorities are essential for environmental stewardship. The association often acts as a voice or catalyst of the members, establishes operating norms or best practices, and serves as a liaison between individuals, providers, and government land managers on advocacy issues and critical issues such as permitting and policy development. This category can be subdivided into three types of organizations: educational, advocacy, and professional.

The Wilderness Education Association (WEA) and the Leave No Trace Center for Outdoor Ethics (LNT) are examples of educational organizations; advocacy organizations include the Wilderness Society, Nature Conservancy, and the Sierra Club. State and national professional associations such as the American Canoe Association (ACA), Associa-

tion of Outdoor Recreation and Education (AORE), the Association for Experiential Education (AEE), the National Recreation and Parks Association (NRPA), and the North American Association for Environmental Education (NAAEE) fall under all three areas because they offer opportunities for networking, professional development, and advocacy to providers and individuals. All of these associations provide a collective voice to many; those who take an active part in these organizations add power to that voice on advocacy issues and critical issues. For example, the Outdoor Industry Association represents retail and equipment manufacturing interests (OIA, 2007). The outdoor industry sustains a large and profitable retail segment providing gear, equipment, and gadgets in exchange for about $5 billion annually (see the GreenYour website in the reference list). Outdoor enthusiasts have not escaped consumerism! This amount represents a significant level of power and influence. When consumers start demanding equipment that supports environmental stewardship, manufacturers will listen.

Service learning program are excellent strategies for offering participants altruistic opportunities.

## Government

The government consists of land managers and policymakers at the local, state, and federal level. As the largest landowner in the United States, the federal government has traditionally served as the gatekeeper to natural resources by enacting key legislation and policies guiding protection and use. Individuals, providers, and organizations must abide by the use restrictions and regulations set by land managers, legislators, and other decision makers. Government regulation also controls industrial standards for human safety, environmental protection, and economic concerns. Programs such as Eco Cycle Zone help residents in Boulder County, Colorado, to network and reduce waste. The government must be proactive in collaborating with all key players. Organization and government programs can assist individuals and providers by supplying needed information, coordination and logistics, as well as participation incentives.

## Barriers

Each segment of key players has constraints or barriers that discourage positive environmental stewardship. There can often be a lack of accountability or responsibility for actions that can foster mistrust between, or within, a segment of key players. For example, government land managers overseeing heavily abused land areas might not trust individuals or groups to use a resource properly, so they implement policies to protect the resource. In response, individuals or providers do not trust the government because they sometimes appear to implement policies that inhibit their recreation without proper input from stakeholders. Individuals might be constrained by the belief that personal actions are inadequate or inconsequential and thus cannot make a difference in the overall picture. There might also be a lack of connection to the environment. Providers are often constrained by unclear mission and vision statements such that when available financial resources are limited, environmental stewardship is often sacrificed first in the pursuit of fiscal security. Organizational structure might require reporting to nonoutdoor managers who lack a basic understanding of stewardship principles or are otherwise unsympathetic. Associations are challenged by motivating member buy-in

and coordinating efforts of individual members in a manner that is productive, often with limited financial and personnel resources. Financial barriers often limit government environmental actions as well. However, the lack of alignment between stewardship and current regulations is more important. Positive relationships serve as the foundation for effective collaborations. It is important to remember that "environmental stewardship is a means, and sustainable natural resource systems and better environmental quality are ends" (EPA, 2005, p. 7).

# INTEGRATION OF ENVIRONMENTAL STEWARDSHIP AND RECREATION

Environmental stewardship has yet to become the hallmark of all key players in outdoor recreation. But when environmental stewardship is successfully integrated into outdoor programs, everyone benefits. L.L. Bean is a provider that has successfully integrated environmental stewardship into its mission. As an outdoor retailer and program provider, L.L. Bean has committed to green certified buildings, following green administrative practices, supporting numerous conservation partners, and supporting equitable labor rights (L.L. Bean, n.d.). Probably the most successful example of successful integration of environmental stewardship is the establishment of the Leave No Trace Center for Outdoor Ethics (see figure 11.3). The center's success is largely a result of the exemplary collaboration between key individuals, other providers, associations, and government agencies. Early attempts by federal land-management agencies to reduce outdoor recreation impacts varied in success over the years (Marion and Reid, 2001). It was not until the United States Forest Service and the National Outdoor Leadership School came together on minimum impact principles in 1990 that the Leave No Trace outdoor ethics and educational curriculum emerged. Since then, the Center for Outdoor Ethics has become a very successful, not-for-profit organization. It has gained support and become the standard for land-management agencies and corporate partners throughout the United States and other countries. Today the efforts of the

**Figure 11.3**   Principles of the Leave No Trace Center for Outdoor Ethics

## Plan Ahead and Prepare

- Know the regulations and special concerns for the area you'll visit.
- Prepare for extreme weather, hazards, and emergencies.
- Schedule your trip to avoid times of high use.
- Visit in small groups when possible. Consider splitting larger groups into smaller groups.
- Repackage food to minimize waste.
- Use a map and compass to eliminate the use of marking paint, rock cairns, or flagging.

## Travel and Camp on Durable Surfaces

- Durable surfaces include established trails and campsites, rock, gravel, dry grasses, or snow.
- Protect riparian areas by camping at least 200 feet (60 m) from lakes and streams.
- Good campsites are found, not made. Altering a site is not necessary.

*In popular areas:*

- Concentrate use on existing trails and campsites.
- Walk single-file in the middle of the trail, even when wet or muddy.
- Keep campsites small. Focus activity in areas where vegetation is absent.

*In pristine areas:*

- Disperse use to prevent the creation of campsites and trails.
- Avoid places where impacts are just beginning.

## Dispose of Waste Properly

- Pack it in, pack it out. Inspect your campsite and rest areas for trash or spilled foods. Pack out all trash, leftover food, and litter.
- Deposit solid human waste in catholes dug 6 to 8 inches (15-20 cm) deep at least 200 feet (60 m) from water, camp, and trails. Cover and disguise the cathole when finished.
- Pack out toilet paper and hygiene products.
- To wash yourself or your dishes, carry water 200 feet (60 m) away from streams or lakes and use small amounts of biodegradable soap. Scatter strained dishwater.

## Leave What You Find

- Preserve the past; examine, but do not touch, cultural or historic structures and artifacts.
- Leave rocks, plants, and other natural objects as you find them.
- Avoid introducing or transporting nonnative species.
- Do not build structures or furniture or dig trenches.

## Minimize Campfire Impacts

- Campfires can cause lasting impacts to the backcountry. Use a lightweight stove for cooking and enjoy a candle lantern for light.
- Where fires are permitted, use established fire rings, fire pans, or mound fires.
- Keep fires small. Only use sticks from the ground that can be broken by hand.
- Burn all wood and coals to ash, put out campfires completely, and scatter cool ashes.

## Respect Wildlife

- Observe wildlife from a distance. Do not follow or approach them.
- Never feed animals. Feeding wildlife damages their health, alters natural behaviors, and exposes them to predators and other dangers.

*(continued)*

**Figure 11.3**   *(continued)*

---

- Protect wildlife and your food by storing rations and trash securely.
- Control pets at all times, or leave them at home.
- Avoid wildlife during sensitive times, such as in winter or when mating, nesting, or raising their young.

**Be Considerate of Other Visitors**

- Respect other visitors; protect the quality of their experience.
- Be courteous. Yield to other users on the trail.
- Step to the downhill side of the trail when encountering pack stock.
- Take breaks and camp away from trails and other visitors.
- Let nature's sounds prevail. Avoid loud voices and noises.

---

center are proactive in educating users to apply the principles as an ethic that should be adopted—not rules to be followed.

# SUMMARY

Key players in the outdoor industry have always recognized their dependence on the outdoor resource; with this dependence comes a natural sense of responsibility to care for the wilderness environment. Outdoor programs can begin to make all operational procedures more sustainable, encourage participants to develop a personal sense of environmental stewardship, and contribute significantly to the symbiotic relationship between the human and the wilderness environment by working together as key players. Already there are programs in place, such as Leave No Trace, which is a minimum standard that outdoor program administrators should incorporate into any program. Collaborative efforts between individuals, providers, organizations, and government—with the providers of the outdoor industry playing a leading role among these key players—will ensure successful environmental stewardship of the current outdoor recreation resources for current use and future generations.

# Chapter 12

# Developing Policies, Procedures, and Guidelines for Outdoor Programs

*Mat Erpelding, MA, Curt Howell, MA, and Brien Sheedy, MA*

Outdoor program administrators often work within a department of a larger organization. This means administrators inherit sets of policies, procedures, and guidelines that they must follow to operate in consistency with the larger organization. At the same time, administrators must develop and write policies, procedures, and guidelines specific to their outdoor programs. Thus the ability to effectively develop policies, procedures, and guidelines depends on both the outdoor program administrator's detailed understanding of administrative practices and his or her overall responsibilities to the program and organization. As discussed in chapter 6, risk management is not limited to preventing and accommodating accidents that occur while in the field; rather, it is an overarching big-picture perspective on effectively avoiding and mitigating loss to enhance participant experiences and maintain a professional organization. Designing policies, procedures, and guidelines requires an ability to write clear, concise, and useful information for staff to use and follow while working for the program. This might range from procedures prescribing how to answer phones and engage customers, to guidelines on how to use a repair kit in the field. *Policies* represent the "rules" governing the organization and its employees. *Procedures* are the process by which a policy is implemented. Policies need to be relatively

consistent over time, but the procedures through which a policy is implemented may change based on technological advancements, development of new tools and resources, curricular developments, or risks associated with the activity that require a procedural shift. *Guidelines* are generally accepted practices or options written to aid and support staff in making decisions. They are sometimes referred to as SOPs (standard operating procedures) or AFPs (accepted field practices) and are not as rigid as policies. Guidelines allow staff the freedom to make appropriate judgment calls based on an immediate situation, but they must have sound justification for opting to act or proceed in opposition to the guidelines. Policies, procedures, and guidelines can generally be found by an employee in an organization's staff manual or handbook. Depending on the format of the manual, it may serve as a reference tool for trip leaders working in the field.

In this chapter we focus on developing effective policies, procedures, and guidelines for field practices, such as a trips program, challenge course, or special events. For our purposes here, three important sets of policies are discussed: administrative, incident prevention, and incident response. Consistent with one of the major themes of this text, assessment also serves a vital function in the development of an organization's policies, procedures,

175

and guidelines. Attention is given in this chapter to certain aspects of program assessment that facilitate the development of appropriate policies.

## CHARACTERISTICS OF QUALITY POLICY, PROCEDURE, AND GUIDELINE DOCUMENTS

In cases in which a policy does not require procedural directions, guidelines indicating best practices may be used to provide competent staff with the responsibility of enforcing a policy, but allowing the freedom to make procedural adjustments as needed. Appropriate policies rely on the ability of the outdoor program administrator to accurately determine the probable context of the policy application. As discussed in chapter 6, administrative risk management establishes context as a starting point for risk management, and this should remain consistent when considering policies. Depth, necessity, and design may vary based on location, emergency access, and accepted practices. The following are general considerations for an administrator when writing policies, procedures, and guidelines.

## Policy Clarity

Although outdoor programs must design unique protocols to match specific types of programming, there are some common characteristics that underlie their composition. First and perhaps foremost, policies and procedures should be stated as simply as possible to minimize interpretation errors. Here's an example:

**Policy**

- All participants and leaders must wear a seat belt while driving or riding in vehicles owned or operated by the organization.

**Procedure**

- Prior to starting the vehicle, the leader must explain that seatbelts are mandatory for everyone's safety.
- Perform a visual check to see if everyone is wearing a seat belt.
- Ask all participants to confirm that they will wear a seatbelt at all times when the vehicle is in motion.

As detailed in the example, policies, procedures, and guidelines need to minimize potential for

If a program includes a vehicle, then the program administrator needs to develop policies related to the use of the vehicle.

© Human Kinetics

misinterpretation. Each policy should be written as concisely as possible. An ambiguous policy creates opportunities for broad interpretations, some of them likely inaccurate. Policy clarity depends on the staff training and assessment model employed by the administrator. Policies need to be reviewed by all staff in a forum with opportunity for questions, especially in the context of field leadership. Merely supplying staff with a manual does not ensure that they understand the contents. Administrators are encouraged to check for understanding through question-and-answer sessions or even written tests if deemed necessary.

## Policy Consistency

Consistency is a key concept to keep in mind, especially for safety presentations and risk-prevention topics. The outdoor program administrator carefully weighs a policy to ensure that it remains a largely positive benefit to the organization. A common area of discussion is how much to document. Some administrators argue to keep things vague and minimize how much is printed to avoid unforeseeable policy violations that may put the organization at risk for litigation. Others argue to focus on what is in the best interest of participants. However, these decisions will be influenced largely by the size of your organization. Typically, the larger the company or organization, the greater the need for written policies, procedures, and guidelines to ensure consistency among staff members. Although instructor delivery methods may differ, there should be consistency on what is presented and the content within each topic. Thus important questions to ask are, Are all staff members conducting safety presentations and handling risk in a consistent fashion? and Will the policy address a majority of the contextual variations that leaders or guides will encounter in the field? If contextual variations might create inconsistent applications of the policy, it is best to write guidelines that can be applied in multiple situations.

Consider the discussion in chapter 7 indicating that once a program writes policies and incorporates those policies into a risk-management plan, failure to adhere to the policies may become evidence of negligence. Thus policies need to be both consistently and easily enforced.

## Ease of Access

To promote consistent use, policies and procedures should be easy to access and reference by staff in the event that a policy question occurs, be it in the office or at a trailhead. As with many other aspects of a quality risk-management approach, policies, procedures, and guidelines have positive and negative implications. Table 12.1 details the benefits and drawbacks of policies and procedures. Organizations that are large or that have many volunteer leaders and a less-skilled staff will find the need to rely more on staff manuals. Conversely, small organizations with just a few highly trained staff may not need comprehensive written manuals because critical information is being relayed verbally, staff members have appropriate experience and judgment to manage situations that arise, and the outdoor program administrator is regularly able to assess the staff.

In the office, a three-ring binder is very easy to open when considering a refund policy for a

**Table 12.1** Positives and Negatives of Policies and Procedures

| Positive outcomes | Negative outcomes |
| --- | --- |
| Clearly defines expectations | Possible misinterpretation |
| Consistent application by staff | Increased need for training |
| Establishes a minimum expectation | Enforcement problems |
| Provides appropriate flexibility | Legal concerns if policies are not followed |
| Legal defensibility | Decreased perception of staff flexibility |
| Higher program quality | Time consuming |

customer. However, weight, ease of access, usability, and contextual considerations need to be taken into account when designing field manuals that detail policies, procedures, and guidelines. In some cases, policies might be memorized, and in others a waterproof staff manual might be called for. Sometimes tools such as safety talk checklists (cheat sheets) are made on small laminated cards that leaders can stick in a PFD or pocket. Regardless of the method used, policies, procedures, and guidelines must be easily referenced or remembered when situations require a decision regarding a policy.

## Sustainability and Cost Effectiveness

Even well-written policies, procedures, and guidelines will need to be rewritten as the context for which they were written changes. However, a quality policy and procedure manual should remain generally consistent over time. In an office environment, a searchable document located online will save printing costs, support environmental considerations, and readily accommodate policy changes. However, in field-based situations, technology may not be as readily available, so traditional paper manuals are still commonly used. An effective staff manual might include the following information: the organization's mission, vision, and goals; incident-prevention policies, procedures, or guidelines; and an overarching incident-response plan. Thus the staff manual can serve as a regularly accessed tool for field staff personnel.

Staff should also be well versed in how to search, apply, and reference policies and procedures. Staff-training progressions must include administrative tasks such as learning outdoor program policies, procedures, and guidelines to ensure consistent application by staff.

## Responsiveness

Policies, procedures, and guidelines should respond to the needs of the staff and administration. Responsiveness refers to the time it takes to adapt, change, or update outdated or irrelevant policies within an organization. For example, an incident-response plan that has a specific calling procedure needs to be updated regularly with current assigned contacts

and their phone numbers. Many times, a policy is implemented but is only reviewed when it is needed. This "just in time" method is a poor administrative approach. Responsive reviews should occur regularly in all aspects of a program to identify areas for improvement before they are needed. Being proactive and regularly assessing and reviewing policies and procedures not only ensures accurate up-to-date information but also contributes to a culture of safety and professionalism.

## Accountability

Policies, procedures, and guidelines create a system of governance for staff members. Clearly written and concise policies coupled with appropriate staff trainings must be provided by management to ensure consistent application of policies, procedures, and guidelines. The consequences of inappropriate actions or inactions should be clearly expressed in a policy manual (e.g., ranging from minor to major: loss of employee propurchase privileges, loss of employee discounts, reduction of hours, demotion to a lower level of responsibility, suspension, and ultimately termination of employment or contract). An expression of clear, concise, and complete consequences is particularly important when enforcing policies and procedures that promote the safety and security of staff and participants.

In summary, policies, procedures, and guidelines are essential to effective management of an organization. Regardless of the context, whether administrative, incident prevention, or incident response, the general characteristics should include ease of access, cost effectiveness, responsiveness, and accountability to reach maximum effectiveness.

## CONSIDERATIONS SPECIFIC TO DEVELOPING POLICIES AND PROCEDURES

Policies and procedures are specific to each organization. Because of the variability in mission statements, program purpose, staff abilities, and course locations, writing policies and procedures is no easy task. Though variation exists among programs, there are common considerations essential to the development of program policies, procedures, and guidelines. Once program goals have been established, an administrator's work continues in developing comprehensive assessments of locations, equipment needs, and ultimately the participants who will be served in a particular program. Further, staff trainings must be developed along with program progressions for continual staff development as well as progressions for the various programs. As noted in chapter 1, the integration of outdoor, human, educational, and management skills is crucial to maintaining a balanced program; this integration helps define the policies needed to maintain a professional and well-managed program. A successful program continually evaluates the effective application of each of these skills, making changes as necessary (Nicolazzo, 2007). Statements such as, "Things are going pretty well, but how can we continue to improve?" are indicative of dynamic program cultures that emphasize continual growth and adaptation. This sort of administrative mindset often avoids complacency, thereby maintaining rich and forward-thinking programming. In the following sections we address general location, equipment, and participant assessments necessary for the development of policies and procedures for program activities. We also provide considerations for staff training and discussion on the nature and value of feedback to program growth. These are necessary assessments conducted prior to customizing policies and procedures for a program regardless of program type (e.g., challenge course, land-based, water-based, special events, etc.).

## Location Assessments

A thorough knowledge of the prospective locations an outdoor program administrator intends to use is key to organizing for successful programming. Location assessments might involve phone calls to land managers, guidebook consultation, discussions with other users of a location, online resources, and scouting trips. Of these, scouting trips are often the most informative for the development of accurate trip itineraries and risk-management plans, as well as for developing appropriate policies and procedures. However, the time and resources invested in scouting trips should be weighed against program objectives, current interest, and financial resources. If an organization is having a tough time finding participants for an Introduction to Rock Climbing program, then doing a reconnaissance trip to scout out some fabulous multipitch sport climbing at a "shot in the dark" activity location such as El Portrero Chico, Mexico, might not be the best use of program resources.

In general, programs often use only a select number of activity locations that have been designated appropriate for specific activities by the administration. As indicated, much time and expense can be invested on location assessments to gather pertinent information from which site-specific policies, procedures, and guidelines can be written. However, an intentional visit can provide a wealth of vital information that allows administrators to design quality programs and trips, increase effectiveness of risk management through accurate incident-prevention strategies, and write informed incident-response plans. Often administrators visit new locations themselves or send competent senior staff to lead scouting trips in an effort to broaden and invigorate the offerings of a program trip. Location assessments occur before, during, and after trips to develop a comprehensive and current understanding of the specific opportunities, challenges, and hazards of each location selected for a program. Creating and maintaining a venue guide for each location helps administrators keep record of these details. A *venue guide* is an organized compilation of data, such as the location features, potential activities, applicable maps, emergency action plans (EAPs), driving directions, routes to nearest hospitals, gas stations, local weather averages, and other pertinent information regarding a location that might be useful while planning or leading a trip. Figure 12.1 is a list of items that might be included in general location assessments.

## Equipment Assessments and Use Policies

Because of the need to provide appropriate and safe equipment for participants, the selection, care, and use of specialized equipment is critically important to an outdoor program. New technology has allowed manufacturers to develop sophisticated equipment that is both lighter and more reliable than previous generations of equipment. For an administrator,

---

**Figure 12.1** General Location Assessment

- Appropriateness for the intended activities and goals of the program
- Regulations and permitting (see chapter 10)
- Land manager contact information
- Frequency of use and high-impact seasons
- Hazard evaluation with respect to intended activities
- Evacuation options
- Driving directions (including to hospital)
- Water sources
- Local weather
- Camping and parking options
- Associated use fees
- Emergency contact information for search and rescue and police
- Recommended guidebooks
- Recommended maps
- Specific environmental impact considerations
- Specific technical skill considerations

---

purchasing decisions are typically based on the goals, needs, and resources of the program. New gear choices can be overwhelming to sift through because many of the new features of equipment do not reflect advances in technology and function but rather marketing hype to promote the sale of the product. Further, the addition of gender marketed items such as sleeping bags and backpacks designed specifically for women is helpful for increasing the comfort of participants, but administrators must now consider the costs associated with increasing inventory to provide this option. The issue of personal gear use during program activities should also be considered because it can represent a safety liability for both individual participants and the group as a whole. Administrators must decide what equipment can be provided by participants and what should be provided by the program. Personal items such as climbing shoes and sleeping bags are likely less of a safety issue than items such as climbing ropes, harnesses, and carabiners.

Additionally, administrators must regularly purchase equipment to replace damaged items, add to inventory, or replenish gear selected for sale. Developing policies regarding equipment inspection and reporting is necessary to ensure quality equipment remains in use and old or damaged equipment is removed from inventory. In choosing equipment for any program, administrators must consider which items the program will provide for effective facilitation of the intended activities. Networking with other programs can give an administrator valuable insight on available equipment options and which manufacturers are offering program-specific products.

Finally, equipment logs are useful for tracking inventory, repairs, and use. Having the purchase date and dates of repair documented is helpful when deciding to replace equipment. Program administrators are advised to check with their organization's legal counsel regarding the need and level at which to document equipment such as helmets, climbing ropes, harnesses, carabiners, and other items necessary to prevent serious injury or death. Figure 12.2 provides guidelines for developing policies and procedures for managing, maintaining, and replacing equipment.

## Accurate Pretrip Participant Assessment

Administrators and program leaders must assess program participants to ensure desired program

> ### Figure 12.2   Guidelines for Developing Policies and Procedures for Equipment
>
> - Identify necessary equipment to purchase and consider equipment that may be rented from other programs or outfitters.
> - Train staff on appropriate equipment use, care, maintenance, limitations, and life span. Always read and understand manufacturer recommendations.
> - Inspect equipment on a regular basis both pretrip by trip leaders and posttrip by equipment room staff. Note irregularities or changes in condition. Immediately remove anything with unusual signs of wear and tear or damage.
> - Use only UIAA- or CE-approved equipment for climbing and mountaineering, and in any situation when life relies directly on equipment.
> - Organize, label, and store equipment to prevent loss or damage.
> - Consider being consistent with type or style of equipment purchased to avoid confusion or accidental misuse by staff or participants.
> - Develop a culture that understands the need to inspect and report questionable equipment by providing easy access to damage report forms and examples of use.

outcomes are being met. For an accurate assessment, staff must first obtain a clear perspective on the interests of potential participants. If interest is lacking in certain areas, it is unwise to put much energy into creating programs for those areas. A fantastic whitewater kayaking instructor, all the latest gear, and flashy trip advertising does not mean that a whitewater kayaking trip will be successful. A program will not succeed when it fails to match the needs or desires of participants or does not effectively design policies, procedures, and guidelines to aid in the instructional and administrative process.

Assessing the current needs and abilities of participants is vital to the success of the overall program and each individual trip. To quote a cliché, forewarned is forearmed. An excellent way of making initial participant assessments is in the form of a pretrip meeting. Meeting prior to the activity allows the instruction staff to gather pertinent information about participants (e.g., fitness level, prior experience, food preferences, allergies, expectations). The information gathered provides the leadership with the particulars to design a trip that fits the specific group.

In many cases, attending pretrip meetings is made mandatory by program policy because these meetings serve as opportunities to address expectations from both the program's and participant's perspective. Certain standards may be set by the administration to ensure that each pretrip meeting includes the same elements. For example, a policy

may be written that each participant must sign a program assumption-of-risk waiver. The procedure for this may indicate that a staff member is to discuss the various types of risk associated with participation in the particular trip. A guideline for this might include that a staff draw a Venn diagram to highlight how risk increases when multiple factors combine such as poor weather, broken equipment, and negative attitudes. In short, pretrip meeting policies help ensure that critical information is not overlooked.

Assessing appropriate levels of difficulty or commitment for trips is also important. For instance, an eight-day Grand Canyon backpacking trip over spring break is a popular option among collegiate outdoor programs. However appealing the trip might sound, it is crucial that the difficulty of a trip match the capabilities of the participants. Administrators must ask themselves realistic questions about the feasibility of specific trips during the planning stages, and trip leaders must continue the assessment process throughout their interaction with participants. Is hiking 45 miles in five days realistic? How do we portray the challenges of this trip accurately? Participant assessments do not end at the pretrip but must also happen in the field and at a trip's conclusion. Ultimately, the responsibility of matching programs to participants lies with the program administration. See figure 12.3 for suggestions on assessing participants.

---

**Figure 12.3** Suggestions for Assessing Participants

- Design a universal comprehensive outline for pretrip meetings.
- Organize and execute thorough pretrip meetings highlighting trip intensity, hazards and risks, physical and mental requirements, and expectations of both participants and the program.
- Conduct regular check-ins with each participant to assess current level of enthusiasm, fatigue, and understanding.
- Ensure participants are properly hydrated and fed; this goes a long way toward preventing common ailments and preserving good expedition behavior.
- Use a trip evaluation form.

---

## Staff Training

Quality program staff might be viewed as the greatest resource a program can offer its customers. Staff

Geoff Harrison

Site-specific trainings are important for risk management and staff development.

members are the direct link between a program's mission and the individuals who participate in the program. With such a vital role, staff must understand their responsibilities and carry out their duties with diligence and care. Before leading others in the field, all field staff must obtain levels of competency in an activity and experience at the particular activity site or at venues that closely resemble the site (Petzoldt, 1974; Gookin and Leach, 2004; Nicolazzo, 2007). Minimum skill requirements for each activity must be clearly identified by the program and subsequently demonstrated by staff. In effect, this becomes program policy in the form of skill prerequisites for staff. All field staff trainings should concentrate on skill development and assessments of staff skills in the core areas of competency, as described in chapter 14. In creating a staff training process, Nicolazzo highlights the importance of ongoing training and mentoring coupled with developmentally supportive evaluations and feedback. He further suggests a need for supportive written material such as field manuals and program protocols that serve as accessible resources for ongoing staff development (Nicolazzo, 2007). Well-written policies, procedures, and guidelines complement staff trainings; the written material assists staff in recalling particular aspects of their training and in making responsible decisions.

Staff trainings should be designed to focus directly on an activity or an activity at a particular site. Site-specific trainings should target essential information about particular locations, such as hazard evaluation, incident prevention and response, teaching progressions, and group facilitation strategies. The nature of the activity and venue dictates the level of competency required by staff.

Another topic concerning staff training is the role of certifications within a program's risk-management model and subsequent policies and procedures. A major benefit of certification-based trainings is that they commonly require the learner to demonstrate competence via written and practical hands-on examinations. Moreover, certifications from nationally recognized organizations may have the added value of training and testing individuals to a standard recognized by a panel of experts. Certifications provided by external organizations such as American Canoe Association, Center for Outdoor Ethics, American Institute for Avalanche Research and Education, or the American Mountain Guides Association are recognized throughout the outdoor industry for maintaining high curricular and teaching standards and for delivering quality products and services. The Wilderness First Responder (WFR) certification has become an industry standard for outdoor leaders working in remote locations. Programs offering frontcountry trips often elect to train their staff in Wilderness First Aid (WFA) because of the proximity to urban emergency medical care. Determining specific certification expectations for staff is essential to developing policies and procedures manuals. In some programs, national certifications are not expected; site-specific trainings and internal competency measures are adequate. Other outdoor programs elect to use national certifications to augment internal and external training programs.

For example, an administrator who has completed a Leave No Trace Master Educator Course may have not only a deeper understanding of the application and teaching of environmental ethics but also be able to train staff members in the curriculum. By evaluating various strategies, philosophies, and techniques, administrators can decipher what may be in the best interest for their program. Inevitably, the decision to include professional training organizations in organizational policies and procedures is based on the program goals, internal staff competency, time constraints, and available human and fiscal resources. See figure 12.4 for recommendations on staff-training policies.

# Feedback

Feedback is essential to effective management, improvement, and advancement of outdoor programs. Many programs have simple policies in place requiring participant evaluations after a trip, but other considerations regarding feedback might improve the effectiveness of program components (e.g., staff trainings, incident prevention and response) and become standing policy. In the outdoor education paradigm, feedback is given for the purposes of improving performance and encouraging adaptive behaviors (Gookin and Leach, 2004). For outdoor leaders, feedback is a critical element of event processing and might assist in the development of judgment and competency (Petzoldt, 1974; Bandura, 1997). However, much of the current literature on feedback in outdoor education or outdoor leadership development has been vague in operationally defining the construct and, furthermore,

---

**Figure 12.4** Recommendations for Staff-Training Policies

- All staff must have learned and demonstrated a minimum level of competency based on each position (trip leader, assistant leader, logistics coordinator, rental staff, etc.).
- Staff must be assessed prior to advancing into a new position or technical skill area.
- Programs should use a variety of evaluative methods to assess staff skills, including participant evaluations, peer evaluations, and professional observation.
- Site-specific training is appropriate for training specific skills in specific areas and may be a required aspect of staff advancement.
- Supportive resources should be made easily accessible for field staff, including policies, procedures, and guideline manuals, course area guides, etc.
- Specific certification expectations may be a part of the policy choices made by administrators when training or advancing staff.

lacks empirical support relative to actual outdoor applications (Gookin and Leach, 2004; Drury et al., 2005; Nicolazzo, 2007). Although feedback is successfully integrated into many programs, further research is needed to clarify and support effective feedback strategies.

Before discussing the development of feedback policies we should take a closer look at the construct. For our purposes, *feedback* can be understood essentially as the information a person is confronted with during or after any experience wherein the self is directly or vicariously involved (Howell, 2009). The source of feedback could be the product of an event or particular behavior, the articulated perspective of another person on an event or behavior, or a by-product of self-reflection. Categorizing feedback into inherent and extrinsic sources provides a further distinction. Feedback inherent in an activity has been shown to be a catalyst for learning through self-regulatory processes (Zimmerman and Kitsantas, 1997). For example, a strong eddy line can provide immediate inherent feedback to a novice kayaker who is learning the technique of how to exit a river eddy. Extrinsic sources such as verbal instruction, modeling, and correction can support inherent feedback. If the novice kayaker is flipped by the current, the instructor, an extrinsic source, can verbally walk her through why she flipped and demonstrate the technique needed for success on the next attempt. Much attention in the literature has been given to extrinsic feedback sources such as instructors and peers and the potential effects on learning (Rosenshine and Stevens, 1986; Elliott and Dweck, 1988; Schunk, 1983; Bandura, 1997). Additional research may provide insight into how both inherent and external sources of feedback can be used by program administrators.

In general, feedback from program administrators has two related but separate approaches: (1) to reinforce successful actions or (2) to assist a learner in becoming successful, if difficulty or failure to meet a standard is experienced. Either approach should include information that stimulates a conscious critical review of a person's actions. This critical review is invaluable to meaningful learning because it allows one to relive or mentally reconstruct the actions or events and to consciously process the reasons for the result (Bandura, 1997; Narciss, 2004). If feedback is specific and includes information that details perceived causes, the recipient now has reinforcement for his own perceptions or new information with which he can evaluate its relation to his performance. Thus, the process is emphasized more than the performance. This emphasis on process encourages deeper understanding of the actions or strategies that lead to success. Also, focusing on the process discourages maladaptive behaviors, such as attributions to ability in the case of a failure or assuming competence after a single positive outcome (Weiner, 1986).

Some important factors increase the potential for feedback to be accepted and assessed by an individual. The provider must be viewed as credible and believed to have the welfare of the recipient in mind (Bandura, 1997). Here, efforts of healthy relationship development among program administrators and staff help facilitate the receptivity of feedback. Staff members are also more prone to valuing feedback if the one giving the feedback is seen as competent and offering information that helps the staff member in pursuit of her goals. The content must be something the individual has control over, such as a choice of strategy or equipment, attitude, or effort. Last, the more proximal the feedback to the event, the more likely the details will be clear for both the giver and receiver. See figure 12.5 for recommendations for giving feedback.

## Program Progressions

A successful outdoor program effectively integrates outdoor, human, educational, and management skills into all aspects of the program. Fundamentally, a program progression is an educationally oriented framework that refers to how individual components of a course, activity, skill, or set of skills are purposefully sequenced with regard to learning objectives (Nicolazzo, 2007). Practically, however, program progressions are the educational structures created within an organization to minimize risk, maximize skill development, and provide a positive experience. Progressions within each activity or training should be carefully designed to maximize development for staff and participants alike. Programs should have basic policies in place to review and examine course progressions on a regular basis; staff should be responsible for correctly and appropriately applying approved course progressions while in the field.

---

**Figure 12.5**  Recommendations for Giving Feedback

### Policy Recommendations

- Consider asking participants to fill out an evaluation after every trip.
- Consider implementing a staff or peer-to-peer evaluation process as part of the postcourse review.
- Consider staff retreats to bring the community together for feedback and planning sessions.
- Use feedback to reinforce, document, or alter staff behavior, trip designs, or other variations in program design.

### General Feedback Applications

- Encourage personal growth and leadership skills.
- Assist with learning *why* something happened the way it did.
- Maintain an open and honest program through mutual respect and humility.
- Develop and cultivate a community that values meaningful learning.
- Improve the program.

---

New outdoor skills are learned through well-designed learning progressions that include relating new information to prior knowledge and experience, modeling, practice, and feedback on performance accuracy. Attention to logical sequencing helps learners cognitively organize new information aiding retention and ease of learning. At the macro level, creating effective outdoor skill progressions requires administrators to be adept in educational theory and application. The nature of the majority of outdoor skills necessitates understanding of cognitive motor skill development and the implications of effective and ineffective modeling of desired behaviors.

Additionally, in various situations, administrators might encounter misconceptions held by staff or participants regarding outdoor skills. Research in constructivist theory suggests that people actively try to relate new information to what they already know (Schunk, 2008). Given that people are constantly processing and storing information into an active and creative mind, it is possible that some of that information will be inaccurate when processed, stored, and applied. Misconceptions arise in many ways but often manifest during communications in the form of misunderstandings caused by language barriers, incomplete information, failed demonstrations, poor modeling, or inaccurate perceptions. These misconceptions can lead to the creation of false beliefs and rationalizations of thought and action. One example is in teaching aspects of the Leave No Trace principles. Some people may believe that it is OK to disturb or even remove Native American artifacts from public lands; however, it is strictly prohibited by federal law. When encountering misconceptions, it is important to understand that they are often deeply rooted and might resist change.

This relates to policy creation because many policies are created with positive intentions but may be flawed in design because they are rooted in misconceptions, institutional precedence, or inaccurate data. An example includes a historically used but now outdated policy that requires a climber to tie a double-fisherman's knot above a rewoven figure-eight knot. This policy was common throughout the industry for years when climbers used a bowline knot to tie in. As the industry evolved, and the rewoven figure-eight knot became the standard knot for tying into a rope, the logic of the time inaccurately assumed that a rewoven figure-eight knot would, like a bowline, become loose and possibly untied.

Evidence now demonstrates that the double-fisherman "back-up" knot is unnecessary behind a properly tied rewoven figure-eight knot because it is, by design, a self-tightening knot. Now, even though literature written by international climbing organizations and manufacturers no longer advocates the use of the double-fisherman's knot, many organizations have continued the historic practice of tying "back-up knots." An understanding and prudent program administrator will continually and thoroughly investigate current industry practices when creating, reviewing, or adjusting policies and procedures.

As mentioned, program progressions are educational structures that guide an organization in executing effective risk management, offering positive skill-development experiences for participants. At times, administrators may require staff to develop course progressions and demonstrate that they meet the outcomes expressed by course marketing.

## Program and Policy Adaptations and Improvements

Recognizing the need for change may be harder than you think. Proactive administrators are those who continually seek ways in which to improve trips, be more effective with staff trainings, and meet the varying interests of participants. What's more, evaluation of the actual implementation of risk-management strategies and their effectiveness in specific contexts is of the utmost importance to developing a successful program. Supporting a culture of open dialogue among administrative staff, management, and field staff can facilitate regular evaluations of the various aspects of the program. Evaluations vary in formality and in depth of detail, from trip debriefings to external reviews by professional organizations. Nevertheless, it is critical that in-depth evaluations be regularly conducted to better understand the actuality of program elements, anticipate potential vulnerabilities, and maintain healthy momentum within the organization.

Programs evolve or programs dissolve. Over time, inevitable shifts occur in leadership, finances, philosophy, competency, clientele, and so on; these shifts affect the emphasis or overall structure of a program. Typically, administrators are keen to spot potential problems, but subtle shifts in participation levels or competencies of staff can be less noticeable, especially in large programs (Ajango, 2000). Recognizing current levels of staff competency might indicate a need to shift certain programming to more accurately align with current staff capabilities. Not offering a trip to a popular vertical cave because current caving staff have not demonstrated the educational skill proficiencies to teach others efficient ascending techniques is a tough but common type of decision. Many programs have high turnover rates for staff that can inhibit judgment development of junior staff caused by a lower level of field time, mentoring, and evaluation by administrators or senior staff. Moreover, changes in program administration also bring changes in expertise, subsequent training progressions, and supervision of field staff.

Along with staff assessments (see chapter 15), trip debriefs offer opportunities to find strengths and weaknesses within a program. Trip debriefings help administrators look critically at the status of the organization and its programs from the perspective of those leading in the field. Designing a procedure for debriefing trips can create opportunities for these assessments. The atmosphere created by the administration and internal relationships might dictate the candidness of feedback during these sessions. Loyalty to the program and mutual trust are important factors that must not be overlooked. Each of these components of program evaluation serve as a launch pad for determining the current status of programming. Overtime, near-misses and minor incidents can lead to a change in policy for curriculum, program progression, or group management. For example, a few near-misses while boiling water or a singular partial-thickness burn in the backcountry could be cause for the administrator to implement a curriculum policy change to prevent further burn-related incidents. A curriculum change notice to members of an outdoor program field staff could look something like this: (1) soft tissue injuries in camp and around the kitchen are common; (2) kitchen safety talks given by field staff to participants have been proven effective at other programs to reduce burns, cuts, and soft tissue injuries; (3) therefore, the following new policy has been instated:

### Policy

- A safety talk must be included the first time new participants use a stove, eat communal food, or stand near a fire.

**Procedures**

- All participants must be present.
- Content should be specific to the immediate topic (i.e., safe stove use, kitchen management, knife use, etc.).

**Guidelines: Kitchen Safety Talk Outline for Trip Leaders**

- Cover stove use and care (white gas or propane).
- Encourage use of dipper cups to avoid spilling large pots of water.
- Don't lift or pass hot pots or pans over body parts.
- Do not step over a stove that is lit.
- Do not sit when cooking; remain in an active position around stoves to be able to move in the event of a spill.
- Have people set cups and bowls down on a flat surface and then fill them with hot substances.
- Use thin metal spatulas and encourage cooks to cut cheese and other soft items with these "dull but effective" tools.
- Don't cut objects in hand. Use cutting boards (and always cut downward).
- Discourage whittling of wood.

# DEVELOPING ADMINISTRATIVE POLICIES AND PROCEDURES

In this text, administrative policy, procedures, and guidelines refer to the administrative practices of staff working in a facility such as an office or rental center. In short, administrative policies and procedures govern what happens in the office. Facilities such as climbing walls and challenge courses often represent a blend of administrative policies, field policies, incident-prevention policies, and incident-response policies. In general, well-written administrative policies contribute to the consistency of day-to-day operations carried out by staff members. Because program objectives drive the formulation of these policies, careful attention should be given to the means through which the objectives can be met. Also, concise clarity of language promotes

accurate understanding of the administration's intention. When drafting administrative policies, procedures, and guidelines, use the who, what, when, where, why, and how formula to promote thorough understanding among all staff.

Ranging from instruction manuals on how to use the computerized rental system to customer service expectations, administrative policies and procedures can be extensive because of the vast array of specialized duties expected of hourly staff. Many outdoor programs use hourly staff to aid with trip registrations, equipment rentals, special events, and customer relations. Because the hourly staff must know how to explain equipment to customers and answer trip questions, field staff trainings might be of benefit to them as well. If hourly staff cannot participate in field staff trainings, then, at a minimum, extensive office-based operational trainings should supplement and support the written administrative policies, procedures, and guidelines.

# DEVELOPING FIELD POLICIES AND PROCEDURES

Field policies are generally divided into two categories: *incident prevention* and *incident response.* Because of the variable nature of outdoor program trips, incident-prevention policies rely heavily on procedures in contexts in which the risk is too high to allow for individual interpretation to enforce a policy, and guidelines are used in contexts that will vary based on environmental conditions and staff experience. Curtis (2002) notes that staff competence levels create a balancing act for the outdoor program administrator. As staff competence increases and sound decision-making abilities are demonstrated by quality judgments, prescribed policies and procedures often decrease and, in many cases, morph into a series of effective guidelines. However, it is important to recognize that because staff competence varies, affecting decision-making capabilities, context-specific written policies without responsible trip design and staff training will not effectively address risk management. Figure 12.6 represents the relation of staff competence and the need for protocols. Prescribed policies and procedures are necessary in cases in which staff experience and judgment are low. As judgment increases, procedures may morph into guidelines.

As indicated in figure 12.6, some policies are essential to maintain program consistency, whereas the need for more procedures (versus guidelines) depends on staff competency. Incident-prevention and incident-response policies will vary in that incident-response policies are quite prescriptive, whereas incident prevention may be either procedural or guideline based, depending on context.

## Incident Prevention

It cannot be stressed enough that developing policies, procedures, and guidelines in conjunction with effective staff training is essential to preventing incidents in the field. Begin with creating policies for what documentation needs to be completed prior to leaving for a trip, and finish with strategies for how to keep the group safe in the field. Well-written policies coupled with a staff well informed and trained in the application of polices will help

reduce exposure to legal liability. Thus field policies, procedures, and guidelines should be based on due diligence, best practices, and training. For this reason alone, the policies, procedures, and guidelines should supplement ample staff training on incident prevention, and policies should not exceed what is necessary. When developing incident-prevention strategies, the three main policy areas to be considered are pretrip, trip, and posttrip.

## Pretrip Policies

Many organizations require all participants to attend a pretrip meeting for any trips offered by the program. Pretrip meetings generally cover the logistics, itinerary, equipment, risks, expectations, and relevant participant policies. Other organizations find other ways to deliver the information through printed literature or electronic media. Regardless of the way the information is provided, policies and procedures for what will be provided to participants should be established to maintain consistency of service.

Expectations from the leadership range from acceptable behaviors and attitudes to what equipment or personal items participants are required to supply for themselves. From the participant's point of view, expectations about the nature of the trip—location; level of physical demands; required personal equipment; transportation options; and type, quantity, and quality of meals—are often priorities. For trips in which the program supplies meals, food preferences may even be dictated by variables such as physical limitations from allergies, strong personal convictions such as vegetarianism, and religious beliefs. Finally, having knowledge of the interests, expectations, and capabilities of each participant allows the leader to better design and adapt a trip around the needs of the group. Clearly informing participants of the nature of the activities and dangers involved is the explicit responsibility of the program leadership, including administration, marketing, office staff, and trip staff.

Some pretrip meetings center risk discussions around the concept of *causative risk* (Paulcke and Dumler, 1973). Causative risk arises through a combination of uncontrollable and controllable elements that create an increase in potential for incidents, injury, or death. Each pretrip meeting informs participants that each trip includes uncontrollable

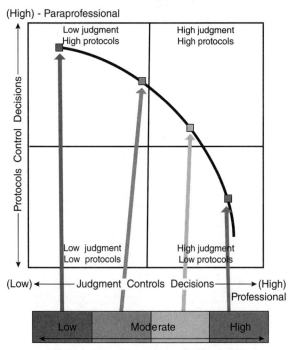

**Decision Making in the Field**

**Figure 12.6** Decision-making protocol.

© 1999, Rick Curtis, Outdoor Action Program, Princeton University. Adapted with permission.

factors or objective hazards such as moving water, weather, rock fall, wildlife, and terrain difficulty, just to name a few. In addition, there are factors over which each person is able to execute some level of control and are thus categorized as subjective hazards. Independently, these hazards simply exist or potentially exist. Regardless of particular form, if subjective and objective hazards are not effectively managed, the consequence is causative risk. Causative risk occurs when subjective hazards are inadequately managed or ignored or an increase in objective hazards occurs that exceed the ability of trip leaders to effectively manage. Unchecked, causative risks may lead to dangerous situations. Incidents or accidents do not just happen. Figure 12.7 provides an example of policies and procedures associated with pretrip meetings, which should include discussion of associated risks.

## Trip Policies and Procedures

Trip policies, procedures, and guidelines can be divided into frontcountry and backcountry

---

**Figure 12.7** Pretrip Meeting Policies

### Policy
- All trips must have a pretrip meeting; participants must attend, and trip leaders facilitate it.

### Policy
- All participants must sign an assumption-of-risk form and medical screening document at the pretrip meeting.

### Procedures
- Start with introductions, so leaders and participants learn each other's names.
- Cover in detail what participants can expect—itinerary, menu items, and transportation.
- Cover the equipment list and provide a written list for participants.
- Discuss outdoor program policies and procedures.
- Discuss creating a positive learning environment.
- Address appropriate language, behaviors, and what constitutes harassment.
- Discuss both potential objective hazards and subjective hazards and ways to mitigate them to avoid causative risk.
- Discuss prohibited items such as alcohol and recreational drugs and consequences of bringing them on the trip.
- Discuss risk and trip paperwork; assumption-of-risk and medical forms need to be signed by participants.

### Guidelines
- Rehearse the meeting so that the leadership team is organized and each leader has a role.
- Consider the meeting format ideas below.

### Introductions
- Consider using a name game or icebreaker.
- Consider asking for more information than just a name, such as why they came on the trip.

### Define what participants should expect.
- Consider providing a supplemental handout (in addition to registration paperwork) with as much detail as possible about the itinerary.

*(continued)*

**Figure 12.7** *(continued)*

- Define what equipment is provided and what equipment participants need to provide.
- Leaders should consider bringing everything on the list and laying it out for participants to see.
- The more information provided, the better the experience is for participants.
- Have a positive learning environment discussion. Get people to share how they like to be treated and types of behaviors they don't want to see in the group. Most organizations do a good job looking out for people's physical well-being, but attention also needs to be paid to ensuring emotional well-being by creating a positive, comfortable environment free from harassment of all forms.

**Draw the Causative Risk Model**

- Have the group assist in identifying both subjective and objective factors that could be encountered on the trip.

**Closure**

- Consider one more energizing activity to set the tone for the trip.
- Consider staying after the meeting to provide a forum for individual questions.

categories of programming. Frontcountry includes anything that happens to or from a backcountry trip or course, and might involve vehicle travel. Many parent organizations have policies and procedures already in place, and the outdoor program administrator may only need to make a few adaptations to ensure the outdoor program is in alignment with the larger entity. However, additional training for special topics such as vehicle loading and trailer loading and use might be needed. Backcountry includes anything that occurs while in the field. This includes policies for river management, backpacking, sea kayaking, caving, rock climbing, and more.

Trip policies, procedures, and guidelines need to provide a framework for staff to make decisions; they also must provide authorization for staff to use their judgment on the application of policies, procedures, and guidelines when appropriate. Figure 12.8 is a list of topics that an administrator might include in a policy manual for trip policies.

Designing trip policies and procedures is especially important because regional differences, program offerings, and staff competence vary dramatically across programs. Although some policies might be consistent, such as on campfires in relation to Leave No Trace principles, others might be completely different for a host of reasons. It is imperative that outdoor program administrators write original policies for the program being managed. This can

be accomplished by using all available resources, including policies, procedures, and guidelines from similar organizations, and then adapting the resources to fit the unique variables of the program.

## Posttrip Policies

Posttrip policies, procedures, and guidelines include aspects such as finishing participant evaluations, staff and peer evaluations, trip summary, submitting incident paperwork (patient SOAP notes, incident reporting forms, near-miss forms, etc.), equipment return and repairs, vehicle cleaning, returning a cash advance, possibly participating in a trip debrief, and other pertinent details regarding a trip's closure. As with pretrip policies, wrapping up a trip is likely to be very procedural in nature. This is especially true for vehicle management, equipment management, and cash advances. Any damages to equipment or a vehicle need to be reported immediately so that repairs can take place before the next time the equipment or vehicle is to be used. Especially in outdoor programs located in larger institutions, cash advances have specific policies and procedures, and rarely have extensive guidelines. Following is an example of a cash advance posttrip policy and procedure:

**Policy**

- The trip leader is responsible for accounting for all funds from a cash advance.

## Procedure

On returning from a trip, the following items must be returned on the next business day:

1. Cash-advance accounting form
2. Itemized receipts for all purchases made on the trip
3. Remaining funds from the cash advance

In summary, policies, procedures, and guidelines for incident prevention need to be written so that all staff are able and willing to follow them. This often means the administration should purposely seek staff involvement in writing or reviewing policy manuals to provide opportunities for questions, create buy-in, and make revisions as necessary. Well-written policy manuals emphasizing incident prevention can reduce the number of accidents, but because of inherent risk of outdoor activities, accidents will still occur. Thus a well-designed, rehearsed, and prepared incident-response plan needs to be a part of all outdoor program policy manuals.

## Incident Response

The amount of work that goes into preventing incidents in this field is astounding. Yet even a well-designed and managed program will occasionally have incidents occur. Incidents need to be managed appropriately from start to finish to ensure the most positive outcome possible. All the work that goes into establishing policies and procedures, training standards, and equipment maintenance and inspections is essential. However, creating a comprehensive incident-response plan is equally as important. An incident-response plan is commonly defined as a comprehensive set of policies and procedures enacted in the event of a serious injury or illness or fatality associated with a sponsored activity. However, each incident will vary based on the situation, injury, location of the group, and severity, so an incident-response plan needs to allow for flexibility within its procedural aspects. Thus an incident-response plan is the "map" for an organization's initial response to an emergency. Effective staff training, predetermined evacuation routes, contacts, and communication strategies are essential to an incident-response plan.

**Figure 12.8** List of Topics That an Administrator Might Include in a Policy Manual for Trip Policies

**Frontcountry**
- Alcohol and drug-use policy
- Driving policies
- Appropriate vehicle use
- Appropriate trailer use
- Groups in cities or towns
- Motel or urban camping (KOA)
- Harassment policy or PLE

**Backcountry**
- First aid
- Lost or separated
- Search and rescue
- Leave no trace
- Campsite selection
- Hygiene and sanitation
- Footwear use
- Blister prevention and feet care
- Lightning
- Food storage
- Water filtration or purification
- Equipment use
- Discipline-specific expectations
  - Climbing
  - Caving
  - Skiing
  - Rafting
  - Whitewater kayaking
  - Sea kayaking
  - Canoeing
  - Cooking and kitchen safety talk

## Provide Appropriate Treatment

The initial incident requires the trip leadership team to act quickly to provide any appropriate treatment required for the person or persons injured. Generally speaking, field treatment is limited to a combination of three options:

1. Remove the participant from the hazard.
2. Administer appropriate first aid.
3. Determine if an evacuation is necessary; facilitate if needed.

Providing appropriate treatment is the responsibility of the staff in the field; thus an outdoor program administrator should have a detailed assessment of staff training, abilities, and competency. Initiating an emergency evacuation for a sprained ankle, or remaining oblivious to the signs of heat exhaustion, are examples of mismanaged problems in the field. Appropriate wilderness medical training for staff is essential for effective field treatment. In essence, the administrator is responsible for sending appropriate staff into the field, and should not knowingly send incompetent staff into the field. Further, programs should have a medical director, and staff should be operating under protocols authorized by the medical director. Most wilderness medicine providers will help program administrators with developing protocol in alignment with the level of staff training (WFA, WFR, WEMT). An extremely useful, and descriptive SOAP (subjective, objective assessment plan) has been provided by the Wilderness Medicine Training Center (see figure 12.9). It is important to create a clear document that instructs staff on what to do and who they should contact in the event of an emergency incident.

## Communication Devices

Evacuation is one of the three treatment options available in the field. Cell phones, satellite phones, personal locating beacons, or two-way radios are usually carried to aid in the evacuation process. Participants might also expect that some form of communication in the field is available (if this is not the case, the issue needs to be discussed as a part of the incident-prevention plan). Creating a clear response plan for the use of cell phones is necessary. Cell phones are routed through towers, and depending on the location of the cell tower, 911 dispatch may be located in another state. Thus best practices might dictate using direct phone numbers for the emergency response teams most likely to respond (e.g., county sheriff's office). Each

Geoff Harrison

Staff practicing throw-bag rescues during a raft guide school.

trip location should have local emergency contact numbers included in the emergency response plan customized for that area.

## Evacuation Routes

Many short trips have straightforward evacuation routes because the vehicle is close, but on longer trips covering larger distances you might find that a trailhead to the north, south, east, or west is closer than the trip's origination point. Consequently, prior to going in the field, the administrator should work with field staff to predetermine extraction points throughout the trip's expected course. This will be an essential component of an effective emergency response if the evacuation takes place via a new extraction point.

## Determining Emergency Contacts and Responsibilities

To start, the outdoor program administrator must determine who will be contacted in the event of an emergency. The administrator must work with

# Patient SOAP Note

## Patient Information

LEAD RESCUER'S NAME

| PATIENT INFORMATION | | Name | | |
|---|---|---|---|---|
| Age | Weight | | Male | Female |

| Address | | Phone |
|---|---|---|
| | | Date |
| | | Time |
| Contact Person | | Phone |

**DESCRIBE MOI** ☐ Trauma ☐ Environmental ☐ Medical
If Trauma, tell a brief story that addresses speed, dispersal of KE, & location of impact.

**DESCRIBE WEATHER CONDITIONS**

Temp _____ ☐ Sun ☐ Partly Cloudy ☐ Overcast ☐ Wind ☐ Rain ☐ Snow

| PATIENT FOUND | INITIAL PX |
|---|---|
| ☐ Right Side ☐ Left Side | ☐ No Respirations ☐ No Pulse ☐ Vomiting |
| ☐ Front ☐ Back | ☐ Unstable Spine ☐ Severe Bleeding |
| ☐ Lying ☐ Sitting ☐ Standing | ☐ Blocked Airway ☐ V P U on arrival |

**INITIAL TREATMENT**

☐ Direct Pressure ☐ Pressure Dressing _____ ☐ Tourniquet _____
☐ Chest Compressions ☐ Rescue Breathing ☐ Abdominal Thrust ☐ Suction
☐ C-Collar ☐ Stabilize Spine ☐ Remove Wet Clothes ☐ Hypothermia Package
☐ Cool Pt ☐ Glucose ☐ Med _____ ☐ Shelter ☐ Evac 1 2

## Subjective Information = What the patient tells you

**SYMPTOMS** = Describe onset, cause, and severity (1-10) of chief complaints.

Time

**ALLERGIES** = Local or systemic, cause, severity and treatment.

**MEDICATIONS** = prescription, over-the-counter, herbal, homeopathic, & recreational.

| DRUG | REASON | DOSE | CURRENT |
|---|---|---|---|
| | | | Yes / No |
| | | | Yes / No |

Notes

**PAST RELEVANT MEDICAL HISTORY** = Relate to MOI

**LAST FOOD & FLUIDS** = Intake & Output

| H₂O | Calories | Electrolytes |
|---|---|---|
| Urine Color | Urine Output | Stool |

**EVENTS** = Patient's description of what happened.   Memory Loss Yes / No

## Objective Information = What you see

**PHYSICAL EXAM** = Look for discoloration, swelling, abnormal fluid loss, & deformity. Feel for tenderness, crepitus, & instability. Check ROM & CSM.

Time

**VITAL SIGNS** = Get a baseline, then record changes. Record normal VS if known.

| Time | Pulse | Resp | O₂ Sat | BP | Skin | Temp | AVPU |
|---|---|---|---|---|---|---|---|
| Normal | | | | | | | |
| | | | | | | | |
| | | | | | | | |
| | | | | | | | |
| | | | | | | | |
| | | | | | | | |
| | | | | | | | |
| | | | | | | | |

**FOCUSED SPINE ASSESSMENT**

| Time | Yes No | | Yes No | |
|---|---|---|---|---|
| | ☐ ☐ Reliable Patient | | ☐ ☐ | Squeeze 1st & Ring Finger |
| | ☐ ☐ Spine Pain | | ☐ ☐ | Press Down on Hand or Fingers |
| ☐ Pass | ☐ ☐ Spine Tenderness | | ☐ ☐ | Press Up on Foot or Big Toe |
| ☐ Fail | ☐ ☐ Shooting Pain | | ☐ ☐ | Press Down on Foot or Big Toe |
| | ☐ ☐ Distinguish between Pinprick & Light Touch on hands and feet | | | |

## Assessment = What you think is wrong

| POSSIBLE PX | TIME | CURRENT PX | ANTICIPATED PX |
|---|---|---|---|
| **Traumatic Px** | | | |
| Unstable Spine | | | |
| Concussion / ↑ ICP | | | |
| Trunk Injury | | | |
| Respiratory Distress | | | |
| Volume Shock | | | |
| Unstable Extremity Injury | | | |
| Stable Extremity Injury | | | |
| Wounds | | | |
| **Environmental Px** | | | |
| Dehydration / Low Sodium | | | |
| Cold / Hypothermia | | | |
| Heat Exhaustion / Stroke | | | |
| Frostbite / Burns | | | |
| Local / Systemic Toxin | | | |
| Local / Systemic Allergy | | | |
| Near Drowning | | | |
| Acute Mountain Sickness | | | |
| Lightning | | | |
| SCUBA / Free Diving | | | |
| **Medical Px** | | | |
| Circulatory System Px | | | |
| Respiratory System Px | | | |
| Nervous System Px | | | |
| Endocrine System Px | | | |
| Gastrointestinal System Px | | | |
| Genitourinary System Px | | | |
| Ear Px | | | |
| Eye Px | | | |
| Tooth & Gum Px | | | |
| Skin Px | | | |
| Infectious Disease | | | |

**ADDITIONAL PATIENT NOTES**

## Plan = What you are going to do

| FIELD TREATMENT | MONITOR |
|---|---|
| Time | |

**EVACUATION PLAN**

| Time | Level | Type |
|---|---|---|
| | 1 2 3 4 | ☐ None ☐ Self ☐ Assist ☐ Carry ☐ Litter ☐ Vehicle |
| | 1 2 3 4 | ☐ None ☐ Self ☐ Assist ☐ Carry ☐ Litter ☐ Vehicle |
| | 1 2 3 4 | ☐ None ☐ Self ☐ Assist ☐ Carry ☐ Litter ☐ Vehicle |

## Additional Information

| RESCUER 1 Name | | Age | |
|---|---|---|---|
| E-mail | | Male | Female |
| Address | Phone | | |
| | Cell | | |
| | Organization | | |

| RESCUER 2 Name | | Age | |
|---|---|---|---|
| E-mail | | Male | Female |
| Address | Phone | | |
| | Cell | | |
| | Organization | | |

| WITNESS 1 Name | | Age | |
|---|---|---|---|
| E-mail | | Male | Female |
| Address | Phone | | |
| | Cell | | |
| | Relationship | | |

| WITNESS 2 Name | | Age | |
|---|---|---|---|
| E-mail | | Male | Female |
| Address | Phone | | |
| | Cell | | |
| | Relationship | | |

| WITNESS 3 Name | | Age | |
|---|---|---|---|
| E-mail | | Male | Female |
| Address | Phone | | |
| | Cell | | |
| | Relationship | | |

**EMERGENCY CALL LOG**

| Time | Number | Person/Organization |
|---|---|---|
| | | |

**Figure 12.9** Wilderness Medicine Training Center SOAP note.

Courtesy of the Wilderness Medicine Training Center.

those people in the organization, whether military, college, parks and recreation, or otherwise, to determine who the necessary people are in the emergency contact list. Additionally, determining an incident commander who is responsible for assessing the incident, coordinating the parties involved in the emergency, and disseminating information to relevant stakeholders is necessary. In many cases, the incident commander might change based on who is currently available or who is best suited to manage the particular circumstances. Thus effectively training anyone who is expected to act as an incident commander in the event of an emergency is essential to efficient and careful execution according to organizational policies.

Many organizations use existing management structures to create an incident-response plan. This might work if the incident-response plan is clear to all members. Often, outdoor programs will unknowingly operate in a vacuum and implement incident-response plans without educating, training, or regularly reviewing and updating the plan with all relevant members of the response plan. Figure 12.10 shows a common emergency response diagram indicating the director of a university ll relevant members of the response plan. Figure 12.10 shows a common emergency response diagram indicating the director of a university recreation department as the center of operations. This type of hierarchical chain may not be the most effective, and many times, is not what is used in dedicated outdoor programs, such as NOLS or smaller nonprofits. However, outdoor program administrators working in large institutional organizations need to effectively educate superiors on the importance of this response plan.

As shown in figure 12.10, a number of roles must be established to maintain an organized and coordinated approach to managing an emergency. Generally, the outdoor program administrator is the

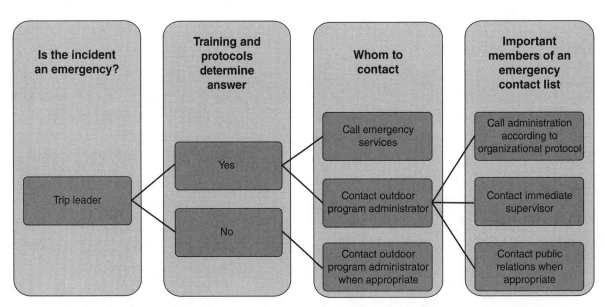

**Figure 12.10**  A common emergency response diagram of a university outdoor program.

person responsible for coordinating all field-related efforts. This is especially true in large organizations because the administrator may be the only person who is extensively familiar with the exact trip location, itinerary, and evacuation plans. In other organizations solely devoted to outdoor education, the administrator position is commonly referred to as a field coordinator. The field coordinator is responsible for coordinating rescue efforts and making personnel decisions with regard to sending additional staff into the field to support the trip after the incident.

It is often essential to have another person responsible for gathering reports, statements, and field documentation from those involved in the situation. Generally, it is best to assign a person to this role who is able to solely focus on this responsibility. A documentation coordinator should have a detailed understanding of what to collect and how to collect the information. Figure 12.11 includes a list of important information that needs to be collected during the process of managing the emergency. This person may or may not be an outdoor professional.

## Postincident Debrief

The impact of a serious incident on the victim, other participants, and both field and organizational staff can be severe. The organization should provide ample assistance for each member of the group to ensure mental emotional security. A *critical incident stress debriefing* (CISD) should occur 24 to 72 hours after an incident; this debriefing should include anyone involved in the incident. CISDs are designed to help with initial processing of a stressful event, such as a severe injury or death, and might involve a professional counselor. But initial CISDs are often not enough, and outdoor programs should have a plan for critical incident counselors to be available for participants for at least several days after the incident.

---

**Figure 12.11    Important Information to Be Collected While Managing an Emergency**

- Name of the person(s) involved in the incident
- Names of the persons on the trip but not involved in the incident
- Subjective and objective information as detailed on the SOAP note
- Detailed assessment and treatment plan as detailed on the SOAP of the patient
- Trip leader's description of the incident
- Assistant leader's description of the incident
- Witnesses' or other participants' descriptions of the incident
- Details of specific requests from field staff for support
- Evacuation techniques and route
- UTM coordinates
- Check-in times between incident coordinator (outdoor program administrator) and field staff

---

## COMMUNICATING WITH THE MEDIA

For serious incidents, the media will expect information about the circumstances, decisions, and staff involved to be provided by the organization very quickly. Using an existing public relations department for all contact with the media is an excellent option. Encourage all members of the incident-response team to defer questions to those responsible for communicating with the media. During an incident, the most important focus is on the injured person's care and rescue. The following is a list of dos and don'ts when communicating with the media.

### Dos

- Through press releases and interviews, provide the media with as much factual information as possible.
- Address the media in a straightforward manner, addressing only the facts of the situation.
- Prepare a script and press-release prior to engaging in an interview.
- Prepare information about the organization, its history, it operations, and its mission prior to meeting with the press.
- Express that an accident has occurred, and that emergency protocols have been enacted.
- Explain why certain information cannot be released, such as notification of next of kin, legal considerations with an ongoing investigation, safety of injured patients, and respect for those involved.
- Provide factual information such as where, what, and when something happened.
- Express concern for the injured party, the family, and the participants still involved. Indicate if the program director or organization representative is involved in meeting with those involved.

### Don'ts

- Do not deny the press an opportunity to ask questions.
- Do not engage in speculation about why an incident has occurred.
- Do not give names of injured parties until next of kin have been notified.
- Do not provide information pertinent to an ongoing criminal or civil investigation.

## SUMMARY

Proper planning and practice prevents incidents. Developing policies, procedures, and guidelines is an essential step to developing a professional outdoor program that provides enjoyable experiences to participants. It is essential that policies, procedures, and guidelines be used in conjunction with staff hiring, minimum training standards (e.g., required certifications), and assessment methods (see chapter 15). However, even the most effective incident-prevention plan cannot always prevent an accident. Risk can be managed and mitigated but not entirely removed. A detailed incident-response plan must be in place to ensure that the injured party is cared for, that staff maintain a controlled environment, that participants are supported through the experience, and that the program is able to effectively manage the incident. Overall, developing policies, procedures, and guidelines is time consuming but essential to effective outdoor program administration.

# PART III

# Staffing Considerations

# Chapter 13

# Staff Recruitment and Supervision

*Jeff Turner, PhD, and Leigh Jackson-Magennis, MEd*

In this chapter we outline many of the common human resource tasks undertaken by the outdoor program administrator. Human resource management includes those practices that attempt to maximize organizational productivity through employee commitment, satisfaction, and competence. Human resource management is especially important in industries that provide services because, in essence, the staff *is* the product.

This chapter focuses on tasks related to staff recruitment and supervision. The information in this chapter is written with the assumption that the outdoor program is part of a larger organization (be it part of a university, military service, or municipality) that has a dedicated human resources department. Many tasks commonly covered by the human resource department (such as benefits management and payroll) are not covered in this chapter. Outdoor program administrators are highly encouraged to work closely with their human resource departments to ensure that their work falls within state-specific laws and institutional policies. Those outdoor program administrators responsible for all aspects of human resources are encouraged to consult with or outsource tasks to human resource or employment law specialists.

The focus of this chapter is on three stages of human resource tasks, discussed in three separate sections. The first section describes human resource planning tasks conducted on a program level that create a structure for staff to work within. These tasks include the determination of staffing needs, the design of specific jobs, the differentiation between types of employees, the development of an organizational structure, and the development of job descriptions. In the second section we discuss tasks related to selecting staff for particular positions, including the process of recruiting and interviewing candidates, and the hiring of new employees and orientating them to their new positions. The third and final section describes tasks related to ongoing staff supervision and includes an overview of supervision roles, employee satisfaction, organizational justice, personnel policy, reward-discipline systems, and procedures for staff leaving their positions. Later chapters in the book cover training (chapter 14) and assessment (chapter 15) more in depth.

## HUMAN RESOURCE PLANNING

The following section describes tasks related to the initial planning and development of staff structure. This planning includes analyzing staffing needs and designing work functions. It also includes the structuring of organizational hierarchies and the development of job descriptions.

## Personnel Planning: Determining Staffing Needs

The first step in developing, expanding, or restructuring an organization is to have a clear understanding of what the current and projected staffing and managerial needs are for the program. Personnel planning should focus not only on the present but look to the future as well. *Personnel forecasting* refers to the long-term planning for changes in staffing needs caused by the expansion or contraction of an organization's operations as well as planning for the replacement of current employees when they leave their current jobs. Outdoor programs often experience high turnover in part-time, seasonal, and volunteer staff. Staff in military programs may be lost because of reassignment to new posts, whereas staff in college programs often relocate following graduation.

Personnel planning should be based primarily on four factors: the organization's mission (grounded in the mission of the larger organization), its program delivery model (as described in chapter 3), budget, and types of services (e.g., trips, rentals, etc.) that the organization does and expects to offer.

The missions of outdoor programs vary quite dramatically depending on the overarching goals and objectives of the organization. Some programs simply provide basic outdoor experiences to clients, whereas others provide significant instruction or skill-development opportunities for clients. Others yet have a significant focus on providing leadership opportunities for developing professionals. An organization's mission should be congruent with its program delivery model. Club and Common Adventure models typically suggest that dedicated professional staff members only serve as advisors, whereas other delivery models require significantly higher levels of staffing and administrative oversight. Outdoor program administrators should routinely ask themselves if their current staffing plans best meet the delivery model that guides their program in fulfilling its organizational mission. Regular programmatic self-assessments identify areas of need and yield opportunities for modifying staffing procedures.

Budgetary constraints provide clear guidelines to the types and amount of staffing available to operate outdoor programs. Staffing plans should be in line with projected expense and revenue budgets as established in annual business plans. Similarly, the types of services offered by each program should be reflected in the process that guides staffing decisions. Facility-based services such as equipment rentals and climbing walls often dictate regular part-time work for front-line

staff. Instructional, tripping, and challenge course programs, on the other hand, often require a more irregular workforce. Higher-risk and longer-term activities generally require more skilled employees because of higher standard-of-care expectations. Often these staffing needs cannot be met through a part-time or temporary workforce.

## Job Analysis: Creating a Relevant Position

Job design is a key human resource management task. There is much more to job design than writing a job description or cobbling together a list of responsibilities. Job design is a critical human resource task for administrators because well-designed jobs are much easier to recruit and retain staff for. Job design often begins with a job analysis.

A *job analysis* begins with listing all the tasks that an organization would expect an employee to complete within his or her scope of responsibility. These tasks can best be captured by interviewing or observing employees in similar positions. Major task areas should first be defined for the position; then specific tasks under each area are more fully detailed. The tasks should include all responsibilities the employee might have.

For example, a climbing wall staff might need to be competent in the following broad task areas:

1. Provide excellent customer service and supervision to wall customers.
2. Provide customers in the wall area with a basic rock-climbing experience.
3. Manage climbing wall equipment and facilities.

After the broad task areas have been defined, specific tasks under each area should be detailed. For a climbing wall staff, the three task areas might be expanded to include the following tasks:

1. Provide excellent customer service and supervision to wall customers.
   a. Welcome customers to the climbing wall.
   b. Manage transactions for climbing wall fees.
   c. Review waivers and climbing wall policies with customers.
   d. Supervise nonstaff belayers and spotters.

2. Provide customers in the wall area with a basic rock-climbing experience.

   a. Discuss basic movement on rock strategies and climbing safety systems.

   b. Properly fit helmet and harness to customer.

   c. Provide a belay for climbers.

3. Manage climbing wall equipment and facilities.

   a. Inspect climbing wall equipment according to inspection schedule.

   b. Set up and take down the climbing wall at opening and closing.

   c. Assist with route-setting duties.

   d. Maintain a clean climbing wall area.

The tasks can be further specified at additional sublevels if necessary to fully delineate responsibilities of the position. After tasks have been detailed, the outdoor, human, and educational competencies necessary for each task should be listed. These competencies should include the knowledge, skills, and attitudes necessary to complete each task. For example, the outdoor skill set for the route-setting task just mentioned might include the following:

## Knowledge

1. Staff should understand the Yosemite decimal system and be able to approximate the difficulty of a specific route using the system.

2. Staff should know basic movement on rock techniques and how to sequence holds for specific techniques.

## Skill

1. Staff should be able to comfortably climb at the level of route they are setting.

2. Staff should be competent at rope ascending and descending techniques to access the entire wall.

## Attitude

1. Staff should be committed to setting routes designed to maximize the customer's experience.

2. Staff should exhibit high levels of craftsmanship in setting new routes.

The process of determining all the outdoor, human, and educational skills necessary for a particular job can be rather lengthy. But this task is necessary for the design of effective staff recruitment, selection, training, and assessment systems.

The basic taxonomy that Bloom proposed has been revised over time. Anderson and Krathwohl (2001) provide a more recent overview of this area. Additionally, many websites include an overview of the taxonomy for each domain and lists of verbs that can be used in a task analysis that reflect each level of competence.

---

### USING EDUCATIONAL TAXONOMIES IN TASK ANALYSIS

The use of knowledge, skill, and attitude competencies is most common in task analysis in human resource management. In education, the terms "cognitive," "psychomotor," and "affective" indicate the three learning domains associated with these competencies. Educators commonly use a taxonomy first proposed by Bloom (1956) to differentiate levels of learning across the three domains. Though focused on educational achievement, the levels may also serve as guides for developing the most effective task analyses.

For example, different climbing wall employees might need different levels of knowledge about climbing wall construction. In the cognitive domain, Bloom proposed six levels: (rote) knowledge, comprehension, application, analysis, synthesis, and evaluation.

A climbing wall staff member might need to have rote knowledge of how climbing walls are constructed, but a climbing wall manager might need to have evaluation level ability to inspect a climbing wall or to be able to choose between multiple climbing wall companies to build a new course.

## Employment Status

The job design should also include the type(s) of employee classification that will fill the position. Employees will have one of the following employment statuses as they relate to work expectations and benefits—although many positions can be filled by individuals from more than one of these classifications. The following sections describe the role of each status and the benefits of working with each type of employee.

### Full-Time

Full-time employees are the core of any organization's workforce. They are the long-term professionals who receive higher levels of pay (whether salary or hourly wages) as well as benefits in return for their greater commitment to and responsibility for the organization. Full-time employees are necessary when performance expectations and required skill levels are high. Full-time staff members often serve in managerial roles in the organization or have work productivity expectations that are crucial to the organization.

### Part-Time and Temporary

Part-time and temporary serve as catch-all categories for a variety of staffing needs and can vary from full-time employees working for a predetermined duration of time to part-time employees working fewer than 40 hours for an undetermined, extended period of time. Temporary (also called seasonal) employees work for a predetermined period of time and can work either a full-time or part-time schedule for the duration of their employment. Temporary and part-time employees usually receive few, if any, benefits outside of their hourly wage and generally have a narrower scope of responsibility and lower levels of training and experience than full-time permanent employees have.

Many organizations use a large staff of part-time employees in lieu of a few full-time staff members. Part-time employees are useful for completing regular operational functions and often work both short duration and irregular work shifts. Outdoor programs commonly use part-time employees to fill positions in office support, water-front staff, rental center staff, climbing wall attendants, and trip leaders. Outdoor programs often use temporary employees to fill staffing needs during short periods of increased workloads, such as a busy programming or rentals season. Hiring an employee under temporary status is also an excellent option for filling a short-term vacancy caused by the loss of a full-time employee. Temporary employees can be hired to serve in place of an

When a new staff member gives a river safety talk, an administrator should assess the content and delivery.

Geoff Harrison

> ### OUTDOOR PROGRAM ADMINISTRATOR AND THE TRADITIONAL WORK WEEK
>
> The inherently varied roles and responsibilities of outdoor program administrators require them to work in many capacities and work environments; consequently, they must maintain positive channels of communication with supervisors to ensure they are accurately recognized and rewarded for the work they accomplish on behalf of the organization.
>
> The Fair Labor Standards Act (FLSA), first enacted in 1938, includes minimum wage, overtime pay, and child labor protections for workers in the United States. Currently, workers covered by the FLSA are entitled to the minimum wage and overtime pay at a rate of not less than one and one-half times their regular rate of pay after 40 hours of work in a work week. The protections established by the FLSA may or may not apply to recreation professionals because the FLSA has always included exemptions for executives and administrative professionals, outside sales workers, and employees of seasonal recreation and amusement establishments (United States Department of Labor, n.d.).
>
> Many for-profit, nonprofit, and government organizations hire employees under an exempt employee status so that they are not held to the overtime pay regulations established by the FLSA. Exempt employees receive a predetermined annual salary rather than an hourly wage. The practice of hiring staff under the exempt employee status is done as a fiscal management tool because it helps to protect an approved and allocated budget from excessive overtime charges. In general, exempt employees are expected to work as many hours as necessary to accomplish the organization's desired outcomes. Thus work in excess of 40 hours is not financially rewarded.
>
> However, outdoor program administrators are regularly required to work more than 40 hours because the inherent nature of their work often requires them to be in the field for multiple days teaching and training staff and participants. As such, it is critically important for outdoor program administrators to work with their supervisors to create a work–nonwork balance that honors both the fiscal limitations of the program and the lifestyle needs of the administrator. Administrators need to collaboratively work with supervisors to develop a flex-time program. Flex time allows salaried professionals to accrue a preapproved and reasonably proportionate amount of time off to compensate for the time they work in the field. Formulas for flex-time programs vary across organizations, but work in the field requires, at a minimum, 12-hour days, and the leader is generally working the entire time (no breaks). Given that most professional positions are based on a 40-hour work week, a frank discussion should take place between administrators and supervisors to find an equitable arrangement.

employee who is out on medical leave or when an organization is in the process of recruiting applicants to fill a vacant position. Temporary workers are also used to supplement regular employees during periodic busy seasons, such as camp positions in the summer and ski resort positions in the winter.

## Independent Contractors

Often called consultants, subcontractors, or third-party vendors, independent contractors are hired to provide services to a program from outside the resources of the general organizational structure. In a process commonly known as outsourcing, these employees provide services that the organization cannot do on its own. These services often take the form of short-term, irregular, but highly specialized, work. Because independent contractors do not receive benefits there are special requirements for issues such as income taxes and worker's compensation insurance that differ substantially for them compared to regular workers.

204 Turner and Jackson-Magennis

## Volunteers

Volunteers vary in their level of involvement within any organization. We need to distinguish between someone who does *voluntary* work with no responsibility and someone who fills a *volunteer* position in which there are clearly defined responsibilities. Our discussion will focus on the supervision of the latter, although it is also important to check with a human resource specialist to understand the implications of accepting employees for short-term, voluntary work.

Regulations for volunteer employees vary from state to state, but volunteers should be viewed as the unpaid "employees" of an organization because they require a similar level of human resource management as other types of workers. Volunteers can serve in a role that is similar to an employee of the organization or to an independent contractor. Whether a staff is operating in a paid or unpaid role, emphasis should always be placed on the job's requirements and responsibilities. Thus volunteers should go through a similar selection and hiring process as paid employees do. When managing a volunteer workforce, supervisors should always reserve the right to conduct performance appraisals on volunteers and to "fire" them if they are performing in a manner unsuitable for the role they are serving.

Many organizations use memorandums of understanding (MOUs) in lieu of an employment contract to create a formal agreement between a volunteer and the organization. These MOUs often stipulate the work that volunteers will do, the nonmonetary benefits that they are eligible for (for instance whether or not they are eligible for worker's compensation if injured), and provide a clear explanation of their status as a member of the organization.

Volunteers offer organizations many benefits as well as challenges. They are often passionate about their work, as evidenced by their willingness to work unpaid. They often, however, receive nonmonetary rewards in the form of training and discounts to program services in addition to the general work experience they receive. Volunteers often allow organizations to offer programs or services they wouldn't normally be able to afford to offer.

One of the challenges of working with volunteers is they often will have limited hours to commit to a position. Another is that they may confuse *volunteering* with *voluntary* and agree to do only the aspects of the job that they find enjoyable (and *when* they find them enjoyable). They might be unwilling to commit to regular work and mandatory training. Volunteers unwilling to accept all the responsibilities of a position should be steered toward jobs with a scope of responsibilities they are willing to accept.

## Internships

Many outdoor programs offer formal or informal internship opportunities for students or new professionals. Internship positions are usually offered either on a volunteer basis or a paid temporary position and share the benefits and negatives of both types of positions. Supervisors should be aware of the additional supervision that interns often require as well as the academic requirements that are part of many formal internship experiences.

# Organizational Structure

Following the development of job designs, outdoor program administrators should review the organizational structure of their programs to examine how each position in the organization fits with the others. Organization structure is usually depicted in the form of an organizational chart (see figure 13.1). Organizational charts indicate the relative rank of positions and the lines of supervision of employees.

Two related concepts, unity of command and span of control, should guide the development of organizational structure. *Unity of command* refers to the basic principle that each employee should have only one supervisor from whom they receive directions. This principle helps to minimize times in which employees receive conflicting directions on which tasks they should complete and how they should complete them. This structure also provides clear directions for employees about whom they should seek out if they have questions or concerns about their job.

*Span of control* focuses on the number of employees that a supervisor can effectively coordinate. Relatively low numbers of employees per supervisor leads to a very tall organizational structure with significant numbers and levels of middle management (see figure 13.1). Higher numbers of employees per supervisor leads to a flat structure with significantly fewer levels of supervision and fewer supervisors at each level. The actual number

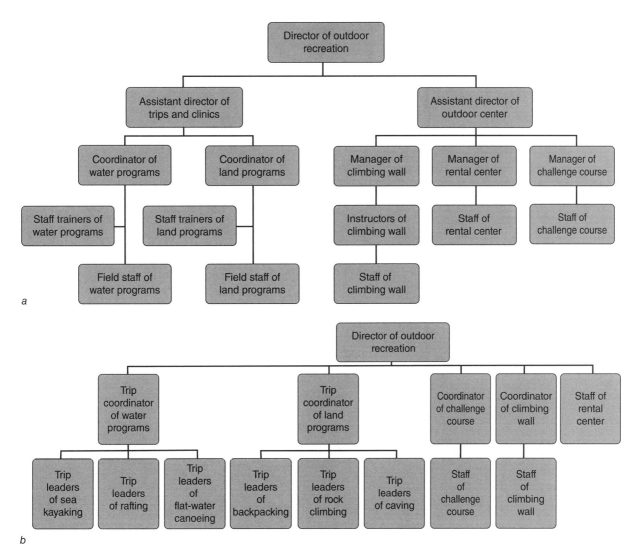

**Figure 13.1** Examples of organizational charts. *(a)* A tall organizational chart with five levels of organization and *(b)* a flat organizational chart with three levels of organization.

of employees that any supervisor can effectively oversee is based on several criteria. First, managers can supervise larger numbers of employees if the employees possess a high degree of competence in their areas of responsibility and require a low level of direct supervision in order to execute their positional tasks. Second, managers can supervise more employees if communication flows easily between employees and the manager. Third, managers can supervise more employees if the employee's jobs are similar. An outdoor program administrator might be able to supervise a large volume of staff if all staff members complete a similar set of functions and responsibilities. It is difficult for an outdoor program administrator to be effective in manag-

ing a large staff that functions in different areas of the operation because of the challenges associated with differentiating tasks and responsibilities for the staff members.

## Job Descriptions

Once a job has been conceptualized and designed in a way to meet the needs of the organization, the process culminates with the development of the job's description. A job description at a minimum should include an overview of the position, job duties, qualifications, and benefits.

The overview of the job description often includes the title of the position, a general description of the position, the type of position (full- or part-time, permanent or seasonal), the location of the position in the organizational structure, and whom the employee reports to or oversees.

The job duties section details the type of work the employee will complete. Each required task should be listed separately and be grouped with similar tasks. Employees in smaller organizations often fill multiple roles, but it is important to be as detailed as possible with all the tasks the employee might be asked to do. More detailed job descriptions often indicate the amount of time the employee will spend on each responsibility. The duties section should also clearly indicate when the employee will be completing their job responsibilities. Outdoor programs often require employees to work evenings and weekends as part of their job duties, and field staff are often responsible for clients on a 24-hour-a-day basis. Clear expectations about these requirements are best set by including them in the job description.

The qualification section of the job description lists all the minimum requirements for employees hired into the position. This section should specify which qualifications are required and which are simply preferred. Each qualification should be tied directly to one or more of the position's responsibilities.

Common qualifications include a minimum age, educational background, work experience, professional training or certifications, functional abilities, and required skill sets. Age requirements are often determined external to the program (e.g., a minimum age set by the organization's insurance to be able to drive a program vehicle). Education requirements should list the level of the degree (e.g., high school, bachelor's, master's, etc.) and area of study (e.g., a major in outdoor recreation or education or related fields, or any major). If previous work experience is required, the type and duration of the experience should be specified (e.g., minimum 100 days of backcountry trip leadership). Professional certifications might include medical certifications (e.g., CPR, first aid, wilderness first responder), licenses (from driver's licenses to state licensure for mental health providers or even Coast Guard licenses for sailing programs). If the credential is a local credential (e.g., a specific state's driver's license) the requirement is often listed as "the ability

to obtain a driver's license in the state of . . ." The functional abilities listed should include all physical, mental, and social skills that the employee will need to possess to complete the required tasks. These might include skills such as "the ability to carry up to 50 pounds over uneven terrain" for backpacking trip leaders, or "the ability to work in confined spaces" for caving trip leaders. Mental and social skills, such as the ability to interact with clients or to read and follow written directions, might also be included. The qualifications should also detail the human, educational, outdoor, and management skill sets required.

The final section of the job description should include the benefits employees will receive for their efforts. This might include wage information, medical insurance, vacation, or retirement plan information. Don't overlook smaller benefits such as access to professional purchase programs, free or subsidized trainings or certifications, or other perks that might also be made available to employees.

## STAFF SELECTION

This second section describes tasks related to selecting staff for specific positions, including recruiting and interviewing candidates. This section also covers hiring and orientating employees to their new positions.

## Recruitment of Applicants

Effectively selecting new staff members is predicated on having a sufficient pool of qualified applicants. Administrators use multiple forms of recruitment to develop the applicant pool for a specific job search. Such applicants can be gathered either from within or outside the organization.

Internal forms of recruitment include rehiring former employees, promoting or transferring current employees, and receiving referrals from current employees. External forms of recruitment include advertising (through radio, newspaper, e-mail list serves, the Internet, or other media outlets), employment and career counseling agencies, recruiting fairs or open houses, and recruiting services. Online job postings can reach a wide audience at relatively minimal cost. See figure 13.2 for a list of popular online outdoor job websites that provide job-posting

---

**Figure 13.2** List of Current Online Outdoor Job Sites

- www.bluefishjobs.com
- www.coolworks.com
- www.ecojobs.com/index.php
- http://jobsclearinghouse.aee.org
- www.mysummercamps.com/jobs
- www.outdoored.com/jobs/oe/default.aspx
- www.outdoorindustry.org/careercenter.html
- www.nrpa.org/careercenter

---

services. Some of these websites also provide job seekers a place to post resumes for outdoor program administrators to review and consider.

Internal recruitment is often faster and less expensive than external recruitment, but it is often not sufficient to meet all recruitment needs. External methods provide candidates from outside the organization who can bring in new and diverse perspectives that can benefit the organization. External recruitment efforts are often necessary for jobs with specialized skill and knowledge requirements. Outdoor program administrators might also take advantage of informal means of recruitment. Informal sources include participants of the organization's programs, local outfitters and guide services, recreation clubs and organizations, and participants of competitive events (e.g., climbing competitions).

Recruitment materials should provide potential applicants with a full written job description, information about the organization, and details on the application process. The job postings should simultaneously entice potential candidates to apply and aid unqualified candidates to self-select and not apply for the available position.

All candidates should complete a formal written application and provide any necessary supporting documentation—a resume, professional references, field leadership log, evidence of training and certifications. Not every applicant will meet the minimum requirements for the job. Candidates who have completed the required application documents and who meet the minimum requirements should be considered part of the official candidate pool and be eligible for interview consideration. Candidates who fail to meet minimum requirements can be counseled into applying for other jobs within the organization that better fit their qualifications.

## Interviewing Candidates

Interviewing candidates is the next step in employee selection. In the interviewing process you are concerned with finding a strong match between applicant and job. To this end, be mindful that interviews are a two-way street; applicants are interviewing the organization just as the organization is interviewing them. An effective interview should certainly determine whether the candidate is qualified for a position, but it should also serve to sell the organization and position to the candidate. The interview should give the candidate an accurate understanding of what the job entails and what benefits they will receive from working for the organization. Ultimately, the interview process is a two-way assessment that allows both parties an opportunity to assess the viability and sustainability of the relationship they aspire to create.

To determine which candidates are the best fit for a given position, interviews may take many forms. In addition to formal, oral interviews, the process might include employment tests and background checks. The order in which these are conducted may vary based on the position being filled. Some interview processes might start with a brief phone interview followed by an in-depth face-to-face interview. The sequence for interviews should be determined in advance and should be the same for all applicants for the same position. If several candidates are eligible for participating in the interview process, the candidates should be ranked, with only the top candidates advancing to the interview process. At any point during a search, administrators may elect to go back to the applicant pool and reconsider lower-ranked candidates. As a professional courtesy, candidates should be notified when they are no longer being considered for a position.

## Tests

Employment tests can take many forms, from written personality or knowledge tests to technical skill testing to work simulations. Climbing wall staff might need to show that they can effectively belay a climber. Challenge course facilitators might be asked to facilitate an activity for a hypothetical group. The key to remember with all testing is that the content of the test must be directly related to the job requirements and responsibilities.

## Formal Interviews

Interviews occur in many formats. Candidates can be interviewed individually or as part of a group. Individual interviews provide a greater depth of information about each candidate but also take a lot of time. Group interviews allow candidates to interact with each other and are often used early in an interview process or for searches in which several similar positions are being filled. Interviews can be done either by one individual or a panel of interviewers. More than one interviewer can provide a greater range of candidate assessment and often present more objective findings than an individual because of the risk of personal bias. Interviewers can represent several constituencies of stakeholders. For example, an interview for a supervisor candidate might include the position's subordinates, peers, supervisor, and, in some cases, clients.

Most interviews should follow a similar format. Interviewers should begin by establishing a level of rapport with the candidate and framing the length and content of the interview. This might help set the candidate at ease and thus allow for an accurate assessment of the candidate's human, outdoor, and educational skill sets. The interviewer then proceeds to ask the candidate a series of questions. The style for delivering the questions can range from being unstructured with no predetermined process or order of questions to a tightly structured interview with a firmly established list of questions. In either

unstructured or highly structured interviews, the interviewer(s) can use a scoring guide, but some organizations prefer to rely on notes. Following the questions-and-answers period, the lead interviewer formally wraps up the interview by allowing the candidate to ask any questions, and then provides an overview of the next step in the interview process. It is recommended that all parties participating in the interview process formally assess the candidates as soon as possible to ensure their memory remains accurate.

The quality of the questions asked during the interview is the most significant factor in how well the interviewer(s) is able to assess the candidates. Questions generally fall into one of the following categories. First, the interviewer can ask questions that relate to the candidate's qualifications, including education, training, previous work experience, and competency across the core skill sets of human, education, outdoor, and management skills. Second, the interviewer can ask questions that assess how much candidates know about the position and why they have applied for it. Third, the interviewer can ask questions that address how the candidate would complete the job duties of the position. These questions might address how the candidate has handled pertinent situations in the past or introduce hypothetical situations. The STAR method described on page 210 shows one format for organizing interview questions. Table 13.1 lists acceptable and unacceptable interview questions.

It is important to recognize that the types of questions asked during an interview can either expose or protect an organization from an employment discrimination case. Employers should not ask personal questions of candidates regarding matters such as age, marital status, religious background, hobbies, or other areas that have no bearing on how well the candidate would be able to perform the duties of the position. Information gathered during personal questions can lead to bias that might be construed as illegal discrimination.

## Background Checks

An interview sometimes includes a background check. Background checks can be as simple as talking to professional references to confirm previous work experience (figure 13.3 shows sample questions) or as complex as checking criminal, driving,

**Table 13.1** Interview Questions

| Topic | Unacceptable questions | Acceptable questions |
|---|---|---|
| Reliability or attendance | • Do you have any children? How many?<br>• Are you pregnant?<br>• Are you married? | • What hours and days can you work?<br>• Are there specific times that you cannot work?<br>• Do you have responsibilities other than work that will interfere with a specific job requirement, such as traveling? |
| Citizenship or national origin | • What is your national origin?<br>• Where are your parents from? | Are you legally eligible for employment in the United States? |
| For reference checking | What is your maiden name? What is your father's surname? | Have you ever worked under a different name? |
| Arrests and convictions | Have you ever been arrested? | Have you ever been convicted of a crime? If so, when, where, and what was the disposition of the case? |
| Disabilities | Do you have any physical or mental disabilities? | Can you perform the duties of the job you are applying for? |
| Date of birth | When were you born? | If hired, can you furnish proof that you are over age 18? |
| Personal finances | • Do you own your home?<br>• Have you ever declared bankruptcy? | None |
| Organization membership | Are you a member of any social clubs, societies, or lodges? | Inquiry into applicant's membership in organizations that are considered relevant to his or her ability to perform the job. |
| Military record | What type of discharge did you receive? | What type of education, training, or work experience did you receive while in the military? |
| Language | • What is your native language?<br>• How did you acquire the ability to read, write, or speak a foreign language? | Inquiry into languages applicant speaks and writes fluently only if the job requires the ability to converse in an additional language. |
| Worker's compensation | • Have you ever filed a worker's compensation claim?<br>• Have you had any prior work-related injuries? | None |
| Race or color | Inquiries regarding the applicant's complexion or color of skin. | None |
| Marital status | Do you wish to be addressed as Mrs., Miss, or Ms.? | None |
| Address | • How long have you lived at your current address?<br>• Do you own or rent your home? | None |
| Education | When did you graduate from high school or college? | Do you have a high school or GED or college degree (if having such degree is part of the job's requirements)? |
| Personal | • How tall are you?<br>• How much do you weigh? | Only permissible if related to a bona fide occupational qualification. |

## THE STAR METHOD OF INTERVIEWING

The STAR format is popular for behavioral interviewing. Interviewers ask open-ended questions about the candidate's previous experiences. The candidate then responds with a brief description of a specific **s**ituation, the **t**asks to be completed or goals to be accomplished in that situation, the candidate's **a**ctions that helped to achieve the outcome, and the ultimate **r**esults of the situation. Using the STAR format allows interviewers to gauge not only how candidates respond in similar situations but also the thought process that led them to make the decisions they did.

The following examples of behavioral interview questions may be answered using the STAR method:

- Describe a situation in which you provided excellent customer service to a customer.
- Can you tell me about a time when you had a disagreement with a fellow employee and how you handled the conflict?
- Give me an example of a time in which a project you were in charge of did not go as well as you had hoped it would.
- Can you tell me about the most important project that you worked on at your last job?

and financial records and requiring drug testing. Background checks normally occur relatively late in the interview process. They are often conducted following a conditional offer of employment but prior to a final offer. Employers will often have candidates sign a statement authorizing the use of such records. Federal law dictates that candidates should have access to specific types of background

information if the information caused a company to rescind an offer of employment.

## Hiring

Following the interview process, the remaining candidates should be ranked according to who is most qualified for the position. The ranking process

---

**Figure 13.3** Sample Questions for a Background Check

- What was the working relationship between you and this individual? How long have you known the applicant?
- Can you describe her primary duties while working with you?
- To your knowledge, why did this person leave the position or company?
- Did you evaluate this person's performance? Can you speak to her strengths and developmental needs?
- How would you describe the relationship between this individual and her supervisor, her coworkers, and her subordinates (if applicable)? If I spoke to those employees, how do you think they would describe her management style?
- How do you feel that this individual would do in this role? (Briefly describe position.)
- Would you rehire this person if the opportunity arose?
- Is there anything I haven't asked that you would like to share regarding this candidate?

should clearly be based on the job description, and the administrator should be able to justify the rank of all candidates based on these criteria. A final determination of the candidate or candidates who will receive a job offer is normally made, which often must be approved by, human resources or an equal employment opportunity officer prior to a formal offer being made. Generally, a conditional offer is made and, if the job is accepted by the candidate, this is followed by a permanent job offer in the form of a work contract pending completion of final steps such as drug tests, physicals, and background checks.

If at any point in the search process it is deemed that no current candidates are qualified for the position, the job is often reposted and new recruitment efforts are made. Administrators often have the option of appointing a temporary employee to the position while the search resumes.

## Staff Orientation

Following the hiring decision, employees usually go through some form of orientation, which is distinct from training. Training is specific to a position's job duties, whereas orientation is general for all employees of a program regardless of their responsibilities. See chapter 14 for in-depth information on training.

Orientations are designed to help employees understand and work within the organizational culture to meet workplace expectations. Common topics of orientation include worker safety topics (such as worker's compensation process and sexual harassment prevention), supervision topics (such as performance appraisal and filing grievances), and payroll and benefits topics (such as tax and insurance information).

# STAFF SUPERVISION

In this third and final section we describe tasks related to ongoing staff supervision, including an overview of supervision roles, employee productivity and satisfaction, organizational justice, personnel policy, staff assessment and reward-discipline systems, and procedures for staff leaving their positions.

## Supervision Roles

The outdoor program administrator fills many roles in supervising staff. Silsbee (2004) provides a useful

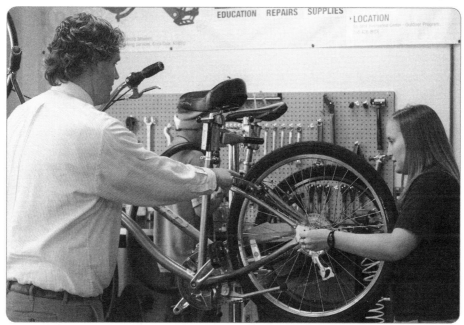

An administrator identifies an order of operations error and takes the opportunity to seize a teachable moment with a new staff member.

model describing seven roles that can provide an effective model for outdoor program administrators in supervising employees.

The role of the *master* is the most central and guides the work of the other six voices. The master is the home base that the outdoor program administrator returns to and works from. The master role is supported by the administrator's ability to actively engage with the employee and build a relationship built on compassion and respect. In this role, administrators must be aware of their own thoughts and behaviors, assess their staff, and use their assessment to select the correct role to guide their work in any given situation.

The role of the *partner* allows outdoor program administrators to establish a structure for how they will supervise their employees. The partner makes clear the roles and responsibilities for the administrator and the employee and continues to refine the relationship so that it supports the work of the employee as effectively as possible. The needs of staff change over time as their skill sets and tasks change, and the relationship between administrator and staff should change as well.

The role of the *investigator* allows the outdoor program administrator to help employees find answers to problems they are having with completing their tasks as effectively as possible. In the investigator role, the administrator asks staff members questions that require them to reflect on and assess their current situations. After thorough reflection, the administrator then helps employees to define a set of goals to work toward and to develop a critical path of action to achieve those goals.

The outdoor program administrator takes on the role of the *reflector* when he gives feedback to employees. Administrators who can provide employees with direct, timely, and accurate feedback can informally address issues that affect performance. The most effective feedback given by the reflector focuses on the employee's strengths, not on weaknesses. Similarly, administrators may support self-reflection from employees so they can continue their own development.

The outdoor program administrator may also take on the role of the *teacher* when he provides a staff member with expertise or challenges an employee's thinking process. When providing guidance, administrators (in the role of teacher) should always offer sufficient information relevant to the situation but not provide *all* the information they have in the relevant area. This promotes critical thinking among employees. Another way to promote critical thinking is to challenge assumptions held by staff and encourage them to seek win-win scenarios.

The *guide* role of the outdoor program administrator is grounded in encouraging and supporting actions by staff members. The administrator may offer guidance on what to do or may simply help the employee develop a set of alternatives to select from. In the role of guide, the administrator provides motivation for staff to act and direction to guide that action.

The *contractor*, the final role taken on by the outdoor program administrator, supports the other supervisory functions. The contractor holds employees accountable for the work they have done and the goals they have set. As a contractor, the administrator follows up with staff on the goals they've set and supports employees as they work toward attaining the goals.

Ultimately, effective supervision requires interactions that work across and integrate each of Silsbee's seven roles. With effective supervision over time, employees often begin to self-supervise and thus support their own work and development. This process allows for continued employee development and for the advancement of field staff. It also allows the outdoor program administrator to focus more on novice staff and provide greater support for their work.

## Employee Productivity and Satisfaction

At its best, staff supervision seeks to create a balance between company productivity and employee satisfaction. Although the importance of productivity cannot be downplayed, employee satisfaction is also critical to the overall health of an organization. Effective supervision improves satisfaction, which keeps employees productive and minimizes employee turnover.

There is a rather common myth that employees are most satisfied by a challenging job—that employees attempt to find work that maximizes their abilities and provides opportunities for growth and advancement. This is, unfortunately, not true. People do not always seek jobs for intrinsically motivated reasons. Some seek a position simply for the financial compensation or for the status they receive for having a particular job. Others look for work that requires little physical or intellectual engagement. The outdoor program administrator's responsibility is to supervise jobs in a way that enhances productivity regardless of the employee's motivation.

Administrators should especially consider the related areas of task identity and task significance, because they directly influence employee motivation. *Task identity* refers to the degree in which the employee is responsible for completed projects (or products) or recognizable parts of projects (or products). The higher the task identity, the more the employee relates to the project, and the more the success of the project is tied back to the employee. Projects that involve many people and that have little to distinguish the input of the various members have little task identity. *Task significance* refers to the overall importance of the project being completed. Employees who work on projects with little overall impact on the organization's efforts will have relatively low task significance. Overall, the more administrators can increase both task identity and task significance, the more motivated employees will be to be productive.

Additionally, administrators may use the related techniques of job enlargement, job enrichment, and job rotation because they serve to increase the overall effectiveness of an organization's employees by improving motivation. These processes minimize the boredom that often comes with repeating the same job tasks repeatedly. Job enlargement and job enrichment are similar in that each provides employees a greater number of duties. *Job enlargement* is a process through which an employee is given a greater breadth or variety of job duties of similar importance. For instance, backpacking trip leaders might be encouraged to become paddling trip leaders. *Job enrichment* is a process through which an employee is given a greater depth of job duties of increasing importance. In this case, backpacking trip leaders might be encouraged to become staff trainers or program coordinators. *Job rotation* is similar, but instead of additional duties being given to an employee, certain duties are exchanged for

others for a short time. In job rotation, an employee might spend a set period of time working with various program areas to become more familiar with each area. This technique is particularly useful for new managers or managers in training because they learn about each of the organization's operational areas. In the case of all three techniques, staff members are challenged with additional duties beyond what they traditionally have. These techniques make for continued professional development as employees gain competencies in their new areas of responsibilities. Such development is beneficial because employees are then better able to fill organizational needs as employees leave the organization or move to new positions.

## Organizational Justice

Organizational justice is a concept that addresses how ethically employees are treated within an organization. *Organizational justice* refers to establishing an environment in which an employee (or potential employees) has equitable access to their share of the organization's resources and benefits.

Equitable access to jobs within a company ensures that an employee has access to the most qualified applicants. Nepotism—the practice of hiring family or friends regardless of their qualification—discourages other, more qualified candidates from applying. Equitable access to benefits received by employees also encourages the greatest productivity. If employees see that a favored employee receives an undue share of resources or benefits, they will be less productive because they have less motivation to be productive. Similarly, the person who receives the undue resources might have no motivation to perform at her highest potential.

Organizational justice has a long legal basis. Several federal and state laws, executive orders, and judicial precedents have established a legal foundation that bars discrimination against employees. The Civil Rights Act of 1964 forbids discrimination based on race, color, religion, sex, or nationality and established the Equal Employment Opportunity Commission. Later acts and rulings barred discrimination based on age, disability, veteran status, and pregnancy. The Americans With Disabilities Act of 1990 increased the requirements for employers to make "reasonable accommodations" for disabled employees.

Outdoor program administrators committed to organizational justice should work closely with their organization's human resource professional responsible for managing equal employment opportunities. These specialists understand local and state laws and can help the administrator supervise staff in a way that meets all requirements. Administrators should also ensure that all job requirements and job testing are clearly related to job success.

Ultimately, in the event of a discrimination claim, it is the organization's responsibility to prove that discrimination did not occur, not the responsibility of the victim to prove that it did. Also, victims of discrimination need not prove that violations were intentional. As an administrator, it is not enough to be nondiscriminatory. You must actively attempt to create a culture of organizational justice.

## Personnel Policy

Practically all organizations have some form of personnel policies. Some organizations have formal written policies, and others rely simply on previous precedents or informal arrangements. Outdoor programs that operate under the umbrella of a larger organization should be aware of the need to support and implement the broader organization's human resource policies. Occasionally, unique service areas within a larger organization are granted the authority to develop their own specific personnel policies as long as they remain in alignment with the larger organization's policies.

Personnel policies have two primary purposes. First, they serve employees by creating a work environment in which employees know what is expected of them and in which everyone is treated fairly. Second, they serve administrators by being a guide for making decisions about common personnel issues, allowing for rapid decisions consistent across the organization. Development and implementation of personnel policies are evidence of dedication to organizational justice. "They may not stop grievances or court actions, but it is certain proof of your attempt to be in compliance with local, state, and federal rules and regulations" (Bannon, 1999, p. 185).

When developing and implementing a personnel policy, consider the following:

1. When developing the initial policy draft, gather information from a human resource specialist or employment lawyer to make sure the policy is in compliance with federal, state, and local laws. Have an expert review the final draft before implementing it.

2. Have all supervisors (facility managers, head trip leaders, etc.) review the policy and provide suggestions. Because they will be responsible for implementing the policy, make sure they understand it thoroughly and are willing to follow its guidelines. If they are not, the policy likely needs further revision.

3. Gather as much input from employees as possible. Employees' support of the policy will increase when they are offered a hand in creating it. They are also likely to bring up perspectives and issues to consider including in the policy that might not have been previously identified.

4. Review personnel policies regularly (see figure 13.4 for possible topics to address in a personnel policy). As programs and employees evolve over time, personnel policies need to be adapted as well. For instance, a policy related to the use of cell phones and text messaging while at work would have been unheard of 10 years ago.

5. Ensure that all employees understand personnel policies relevant to them. They should be reviewed as part of an employee's orientation, and updates to policies should be thoroughly described to all current employees as they come into practice. Employees should also have access to policy documents so they can answer any questions they may have.

## Staff Assessment

Staff assessment is a key responsibility for outdoor program administrators. Employees need feedback on their performance and to know what they need to do to be better at meeting their workplace expectations. Assessment should be done formally on a regular basis in a process known as performance appraisal. See chapter 15 for in-depth information on staff assessment as it applies to outdoor program

---

**Figure 13.4**   Possible Topics to Address in a Personnel Policy

- Work periods, including scheduling, breaks and lunches, and evening, weekend, and holiday work, as well as absenteeism
- Leave from work for military service, professional-development activities, family or sick leave, and vacations
- Orientation procedures and probationary periods for new employees
- Requirements for personal information, such as background checks, medical physicals, or drug tests
- Safety regulations, such as use of protective equipment and access to material safety data sheets
- Security procedures for access to facilities and confidential information
- Employee behavioral expectations beyond basic job requirements, such as employee dress and appearance, physical and mental readiness (e.g., rested and sober), or doing personal work, checking e-mail, or checking phone or text messages during work hours
- The timing and process for performance appraisals and possible outcomes for positive or negative results
- Warning and discipline procedures for when policies are broken, as well as employee grievance processes
- Procedures for leaving a position through advancement or promotion to a new position, retirement, termination, and other reasons

---

staff. In the following section we describe ways to recognize employees for superior performance and to discipline employees for substandard performance.

## Employee Recognition

Employees that consistently perform at an excellent level should be recognized for their outstanding performance. Recognition programs build employee morale and promote connections between the employee's work and the overall success of the organization. Such recognition leads to retention of high-quality staff while providing motivation for lower performing staff. Recognition is especially important for jobs that have relatively low levels of financial reward and so is crucial for volunteers.

Recognition can take many forms. It can be as simple as a pat on the back or an announcement to all staff at a meeting or via e-mail. Annual awards given to "staff members of the year," or even small incentives such as apparel, meals, or event tickets, also work well to maintain morale.

## Employee Discipline

Disciplining employees is one of the hardest aspects of the outdoor program administrator's job. To avoid confrontation, many administrators will simply look the other way when employees break company policy or underperform. This practice undermines the credibility of the supervisor and only serves to encourage other staff to act similarly. Discipline establishes clear expectations and boundaries for work performance and provides employees with guidelines for where they need to improve. In some cases, employees might simply be unaware of the problem, and discipline helps them improve in meeting professional behaviors and expectations. Disciplinary actions across time can indicate a consistent problem and might serve as the basis for dismissal of the employee.

Discipline should be consistent for all employees and should follow guidelines established in personnel policy. As with recognition, discipline can be informal, such as simply correcting an employee's work, or formal, in the form of documented disciplinary action. Disciplinary actions include verbal or written reprimands, suspensions from work, loss of rank or employee privileges, and, ultimately, dismissal.

## Discussing Personnel Decisions

Being able to deliver personnel decisions effectively, be they positive or negative, is a key skill for the outdoor program administrator. Personnel decisions should be grounded in objective performance standards or behaviors and should treat all employees equitably. Administrators may use information from performance appraisals or results of recognition or disciplinary actions or reference specific personnel policies as a basis for their decision. Administrators may also consult with their supervisor to make sure that he or she supports the decision and with their human resources specialist to ensure they fully understand the process used by their organization for cases resulting in either discipline or dismissal.

Carefully plan how to deliver the decision to the employee, because such decisions can adversely affect the morale of other staff members. Consider delivering the message early in the week, not just before the weekend or on holidays or special events. Deliver the decision in a private place, away from the employee's peers. Present the information with a colleague present to serve as a witness to the process. Clearly present the rationale for the decision, and provide the employee with time to ask questions. If your organization's personnel policy allows for it, discuss options for the employee to challenge the findings or to file a grievance.

## Staff Exit

Employees leave organizations for many reasons, but some of the most common include pending lifestyle changes, new career opportunities, job dissatisfaction, and poor performance. When an employer determines that an employee is no longer qualified or suitable for the position, they must be removed from the position. This section details the process of dismissing employees and describes the role of an exit interview for staff members who electively leave an organization.

## Dismissing Employees

The decision to dismiss an employee is often difficult to make. There are four rationales for dismissing an employee: "unsatisfactory perfor-

mance, misconduct, lack of qualifications for the job, changed requirements of (or elimination of) the job" (Dessler, 2005, p. 538). Employees may be dismissed for unsatisfactory performance if they display a persistent and documented inability to meet performance standards. Misconduct exists when employees violate organizational rules and policies. Employment issues involving a lack of qualifications can occur when employees are unable to complete required tasks despite an organization's efforts to train the employee to the required performance level. Changed job requirements are indicated when a job position is no longer necessary (such as in layoffs) or when a job's responsibilities change dramatically enough that the employee can no longer do the job.

## The Exit Interview

Exit interviews are conducted to help an organization understand why an employee is leaving the organization (if they were not dismissed) and to try to learn from the employee's experience how they might improve the employee's job in the future. Common information collected in the exit interview includes information pertaining to how they would rate their supervisor, how well their actual work matched their job description, and suggestions they would offer to improve their job for future employees. Exit interviews are often conducted by someone other than the employee's supervisor (often a human resource specialist). The information gathered from exit interviews helps alert administrators to trends in job design or organizational structure that may be corrected and can provide useful details on the effectiveness of supervisors.

## Giving References

After employees leave a program, they will remain linked with the organization as a previous employee. Administrators are often asked to provide references for these individuals. State laws and organizational policy differ on what information may be provided to others. In some cases, previous employers may simply be able to confirm that the individual worked for the organization in a specific position during a specific time period. Sometimes, organizational policies allow employers to indicate whether the individual is eligible to be rehired. In many states, though, laws protect employers who provide objective information about previous employees.

Providing proper references helps to avoid negligent hiring claims. The goal of a reference is to provide information to another potential employer that ensures the applicant is qualified for the new job. The following steps help protect those giving references.

1. Get the written consent of an individual for whom the reference is sought.
2. Request that any questions be sent in writing, and prepare a factual written response.
3. Respond to questions that are permissible under law or organizational policy.
4. Respond with factual information based on the employee's documented job performance. Avoid offering opinions, or elaborating on points beyond what is specifically requested.

## SUMMARY

Human resource management is one of the primary tasks of any outdoor program administrator. It can be viewed as the connected tasks of planning and designing jobs, selecting individuals for positions, and supervising employees. We have emphasized the importance of thoroughness at each stage of the process. Time invested in the planning stage will pay dividends in the quality of staff selected. Higher quality staff leads to greater productivity and fewer problems in supervising staff.

The examples provided in this chapter and resources adapted from other agencies should be reviewed critically and adapted as necessary, because the needs of two organizations are rarely the same. Additionally, institutional policy and state laws vary substantially, so the outdoor program administrator should always consult a human resource specialist to make sure that the general information provided in this chapter is appropriate for a specific context. Similarly, administrators should coordinate closely with human resources specialists to ensure that general human resources forms and processes are adapted for the specialized context of outdoor programs and services.

The following two chapters detail the human resource tasks of staff training and assessment. These chapters build on the basic human resource concepts developed in this chapter and provide a foundation to guide the outdoor program administrator in decisions related to staff management.

# Chapter 14

# Staff Training

*Bruce Saxman, MA, and Tom Stuessy, PhD*

There are many avenues outdoor program administrators can take to train staff. Serving as a critical function of program administration, staff trainings achieve a variety of outcomes and are the backbone of many high-quality programs. Effective staff-training programs are influenced by several factors: employee competence in each specific discipline (climbing, rental operations, kayaking), existence of effective mentoring for inexperienced employees, meeting client requests for programming, availability of resources, geographic location, and fiscal accountability; all combined, these factors provide a significant challenge for outdoor program administrators when designing and assessing staff-training programs. In this chapter we outline how to establish goals when designing effective staff-training programs, share techniques for delivery and assessment, and detail how to employ ongoing staff development and mentoring systems.

Every outdoor program is unique relative to its mission, location, programming, management structure, and available expertise among staff. The nature of staff training requires careful consideration among a seemingly endless list of considerations. An outdoor program administrator can establish a professional tone and communicate a program's subtle nuances and cultural ethos during training. From a programmatic perspective, a clear and progressive staff training design will result in confident and competent staff. Realizing the most potential from staff training requires administrators to continue to explore fresh opportunities.

## NEEDS ASSESSMENT

Even the most seasoned program administrators can learn more about their program and enhance their training systems. Prior to developing a training model, a needs assessment focused on training may shed light on new opportunities to promote program growth. Needs assessments provide both a systematic exploration of how efficiently a program operates and an opportunity to identify potential areas for development. Particular to staff training and relevant to all areas of programming, needs assessments are often divided into phases, each providing a unique lens through which to view training goals and outcomes.

Phases of a standard needs assessment often include the following:

- *Organizational review.* In this phase, time is taken to review the organization's mission, vision, and training goals and outcomes in concert with documentation regarding organizational effectiveness. In other words, is the organization doing what it is expected to do? Are the goals being achieved on an ongoing basis among all programming areas? Accurate and efficient documentation systems are a great way to answer this question.

- *Discipline-specific review.* In this phase, the review focuses on specific areas within the program such as the climbing wall, rental center, or kayaking program. The reviewers identify specific issues and the related influences within the program. This phase promotes a clear understanding of specific program disciplines, which allows administrators to thoroughly address areas of deficit, promote positive aspects of a program, and develop concise training outcomes.

- *Determining resource availability.* Many times, this phase will determine which type of training is needed (initial standardized training, discipline-specific training, or staff retreat) and whether internal or external assistance is required to meet the training outcomes. In this case, resources determining internal versus external trainings include administrator competency, administrative workload, and financial resources.

- *Establishing a course of action.* This phase includes the intentional design and implementation of a programmatic training progression. For a comprehensive explanation of needs assessment, refer to chapter 6.

After needs have been identified, administrators can begin the process of establishing or revising training goals and placing them into a training progression.

## STAFF-TRAINING PROGRESSION

For the administrator, an effective training progression that uses training and mentoring is essential to an agency's overall staff development plan. Purposeful training programs bring staff into an organization, develop effective employees, and provide consistency of experience and institutional knowledge. For the employee, a training progression provides a clear path for professional development and advancement and supports competency in the delivery of products and services. Further, a clear progression increases integration among core skill sets (human, educational, outdoor) through concurrent training. Staff-training programs should include the following components: initial training or orientation, regular assessment, formal mentoring, discipline-specific training (rental staff, kayak instructor, cave leader), and ongoing evaluation (see figure 14.1). Beyond the initial staff orientation, the order of these components will vary based on the

design of the outdoor program. A program's staff-training curriculum should directly reflect the core mission and values of the agency.

Staff trainings should be mixed with a combination of personal experience, discipline-specific training and certifications, staff meetings and interactions, and mentoring opportunities. How these factors combine varies widely across programs. There are no best-prescribed formulas or methods for a staff-training progression. The appropriate level of training, certifications, and experience required for staff will be influenced by the current level of skill in the organization's staff pool, site-specific hazards of selected programming areas, and overall budget limitations.

## Initial Standardized Training

New staff members are typically introduced into a program through initial standardized training. Initial trainings are often offered internally because

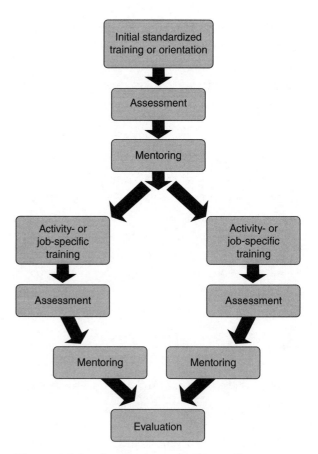

**Figure 14.1** Outdoor recreation staff-training progression.

they can be customized to fit program needs, staff abilities, and environments used by the program. An initial training has several purposes as it serves to be; an extended interview for administrators to learn about new staff; a welcome and orientation to the mission and philosophy of the organization; opportunity to introduce the program's manual, forms, policies, standard operating procedures, and program processes; and other supporting materials. Many organizations organize initial training programs that are focused on skill development and assessment in specific skill areas (outdoor, human, and educational). Similarly, many organizations hire new staff in cohort groups of 8 to 12 members.

Initial standardized trainings should bring all staff competence up to an expected minimum skill level. Prerequisites and qualifications vary greatly depending on program mission, philosophy, environments, and activities. It is important for the administrator to recognize that ideal qualifications for staff often emerge as the program develops. In broad spectrum programs (programs offering many different types of activities including rafting, climbing, caving, mountain biking, etc.), it is important to design an initial standardized training that assesses basic outdoor skills, educational skills, and human skills. A cross-discipline activity such as a backpacking trip often serves as an acceptable platform for an initial training.

For the program administrator, the initial standardized training is a time to introduce staff to the entire training progression, including mentoring and assessment. At the outset of their employment, it is important to work with new staff to ensure a shared vision of program goals, develop a path of personal development, connect with coworkers, and make contributions to the program.

## Discipline-Specific Trainings

Depending on the needs of the program, discipline-specific trainings are offered throughout the course of a year to ensure proper staffing, customer service, or educational outcomes. Discipline-specific trainings are the next step in the process of staff development after they have completed an initial standardized training. The types of discipline-specific trainings vary based on program needs,

current staff competency, and the time of the year they are offered.

For example, organizations aspiring to build a new mountain biking program will likely not require master mechanic certification among staff. Instead, basic mechanical acumen will serve well enough for repairs required after easy cross-country riding and basic bike repair clinics. Discipline-specific staff training relative to riding and mechanical skills will expand as the riding program grows and staff become more competent. Program administrators are well served if the levels of required expertise to operate a program and the opportunities provided staff for training and mentoring are in alignment.

Discipline-specific trainings often include internal trainings that support an area of the program. Internal discipline-specific trainings commonly include the following: rental center attendant, climbing wall attendant, anchor building, backpacking leader, Dutch oven cooking, raft guide school, or basic ski tuning. Additionally, discipline-specific trainings are associated with external certifications, including climbing wall instructor, canoe instructor, wilderness first responders, and swift water rescue technicians.

## Staff Retreats

Focusing on human skills, primarily interpersonal staff relationships, staff retreats enhance the culture of the program. Retreats may use discipline-specific skills such as rafting or climbing, but staff are not assessed on these skills during the retreat. Rather, retreats serve as an opportunity for staff to spend time together in a fun environment while focusing on the desired goals and outcomes of the program. Retreats may be used for the following: introduce new staff to existing staff members and formalize the mentoring relationship, develop a deeper knowledge of policies and procedures, take opportunities to review the previous season and prepare for the upcoming training, and introduce staff to discipline-specific skills (e.g., kayaking, rafting, caving) without specific instruction beyond what is necessary for group safety. This is generally considered an internal training, and may be led by experienced staff instead of the administrator.

# MENTORING

Mentoring should be integrated into every program. For the purposes of this chapter, mentoring is considered a relationship which raises the protégé's sense of competence, clarity of identity and professional effectiveness, and includes role modeling, acceptance and confirmation, counseling and friendship (Neyer and Yelinek, 2007). Essentially, a more-experienced member of an organization maintains a relationship with a less-experienced, often new member to the organization and provides information, support, and guidance to enhance the less-experienced member's chances of success in the organization (Campbell and Campbell, 2000). For example, the Fort Carson Military, Morale and Welfare program in Colorado Springs, Colorado, will mentor new staff for six or more months. Each new hire is paired with an experienced staff member and shown the nuances among all areas of the program ranging from administrative responsibilities to standard operating procedures for multiple field programs. During this process, feedback is intense, and subsequent improved staff performance is expected. After six months, an assessment is provided and informed by six or more months of evaluations of each staff mentor. Many programs, such as those in higher education, are established to develop leadership skills and are as much about a maturation process as they are about leadership training; therefore, ongoing assessment is highly integrated into the staff development process.

The mentoring relationship provides benefits for both experienced and inexperienced staff members alike, particularly through developing human skills, and is crucial to establishing a culture of peer respect and role modeling for others within a program. Mentoring should be shared by all staff and should occur at all levels based on training and experience. Becoming a mentor or being mentored may even be part of a training plan developed during an evaluation.

Opportunities exist on a daily basis for mentoring to be purposefully structured within a program. Key mentoring staff should be identified and assigned mentoring duties on an individual basis based on their goals and previous experience and training. Further, staff members providing mentorship should understand their role and limitations as mentors on the program's behalf before working with a protégé. In addition, administrators might consider meeting with seasoned staff and establishing mentoring goals prior to staff field experiences. For example, on a staff mountain bike ride, seasoned staff could simply ensure that qualified junior staff members know easy or difficult and long or short routes well. To ensure goals were met, junior staff should attempt to recall trail names, identify locations on a map during rides, or make estimations of how long they think routes will take to complete. If these conversations are followed by orientation to standard operating procedures and appropriate medical, risk-management, and skills training, the new staff members will quickly be acclimated and ready to assist on program rides. The primary point is that mentoring can be either subtle or fairly overt, but administrators should take every opportunity to mentor their staff. Figure 14.2

---

**Figure 14.2**   Mentoring Roles

**Assistant instructor to participants**
- Actively coach participants.
- Focus on teaching technical, rescue, medical, and equipment skills.
- Establish and maintain a real connection with each participant.

**Instructor to assistant instructor**
- Actively coach participants and the assistant instructor.
- Use operational language with the assistant instructor and staff; use lay language with participants.
- Give written and oral feedback on the assistant instructor's technical, rescue, medical, and equipment skills and teaching.

- Review the assistant instructor's site management after each activity, focusing on hazard assessment and related student and instructor positioning.
- Discuss, demonstrate, design, and manage course activities, focusing on accurate assessments, prioritizing safety before educational outcomes, activity progressions, and activity framing and closure.
- Discuss and use basic outdoor education and structural strategies during the course.

**Administrator to instructional staff**

- Actively coach participants and instructional staff.
- Use operational language with staff and lay language with participants.
- Check in and review course structure on a regular basis.
- Help lead instructor design and manage the assistant instructor's experience.
- Schedule formal check-in times, especially during assessment periods.
- Schedule site-management support and assessment at high-risk sites.
- Give ongoing written and oral feedback on staff's design and management decisions appropriate to their roles.
- Manage and evaluate the course.

© Wilderness Medicine Training Center. Used with permission of Paul Nicolazzo.

shows mentoring roles instructors might have at different levels of development.

Taking a few minutes before a program to check in with a new staff member to determine their goals and experience and establish responsibilities can make for a smooth and effective mentoring experience.

The list shown in figure 14.2 was created specifically for university outdoor programming. However, portions of each level of mentorship can be seen in both Anchorage's and Tempe's approach to staff training (see p. 224). The form, timing, and thoroughness of feedback are critical to program success, staff satisfaction, and participant outcomes. Taking the time to understand the mechanisms used in mentoring staff is a worthwhile investment for all administrators.

## STAFF-TRAINING ASSESSMENT

Assessment and evaluation of staff training can be a daunting and complex task because it must occur over three distinct areas: outdoor or discipline-specific skills, human skills, and educational skills. The level of integration represents a staff member's overall leadership effectiveness. An accurate assessment is an essential part of determining a new staff member's success during training. Although

the terms "assessment" and "evaluation" are often used interchangeably, in the context of program administration they are often different. *Assessment* refers to the process of gathering information on staff or students through observation. *Evaluation* serves as a judgment on staff and student ability. Thorough assessment and evaluation systems incorporate avenues for clear and immediate feedback, communication, response, and mentorship. Feedback based on assessment is best constructed and delivered in an atmosphere built on mutual trust and respect among staff and directors. Further, it is critically important that training has provided time for staff to thoroughly understand the functions of the program. This understanding among staff will translate into a solid platform for feedback to be used later during training or feedback.

As discussed in chapter 15, ensuring objectivity is paramount to effective assessment and evaluation. To accomplish objectivity, outdoor program administrators would be well served to keep program standards and mission in mind when making assessments. Performance expectations and paths to promotion should be clearly articulated to staff through staff manuals, meetings, and written evaluations. Administrators are encouraged to develop these systems for office staff, field staff, and even equipment staff. Often the most potent assessment structures for staff are those systems wherein staff

## MENTORING

Mentoring strategies may vary dramatically depending on competencies required, resources available, and types of programs. Further, mentoring in outdoor programs regularly happens on multiple levels. For example, administration may mentor senior program directors who subsequently mentor front-line program staff. Two examples of the levels of mentoring are described here. The first is from the Anchorage Park Foundation and provides a great example of youth mentorship. The second example is from the City of Tempe, Arizona, and illustrates a common full-time staff-mentoring model. Mentoring for collegiate programming differs significantly from municipal services.

### Anchorage City Park and Recreation Department

The Anchorage City Park and Recreation Department developed a progressive approach to mentoring young staff through city youth programming. Partnering with the Anchorage Park Foundation and the National Wildlife Federation, the city has devised a system of mentorship that provides opportunities for young people to work within the park system in conservation or recreation programs. During each season, the youth workers have access to parks and recreation professional mentors who share feedback and help direct projects. Established in 2007, the program works with over 75 Anchorage youth in the work program. The project serves multiple functions for the city of Anchorage, including general programming, professional mentoring for youth, and inspiring young people to pursue careers in recreation.

### Tempe City Park and Recreation Department

The Tempe City Park and Recreation Department in Tempe, Arizona, like many other parks and recreation programs, takes a more general approach to training. After orientation, new staff members are typically paired with a seasoned staff member and work through job functions under direct supervision. This allows for immediate and clear feedback before working programs alone. In addition to job shadowing, Tempe recreation staff are required to attend a monthly meeting with staff mentors to review performance and important upcoming agenda items. Mentors in turn report back to senior directors, and staff members are slowly integrated into working programs on their own.

develops their own feedback with guidance from an administrator and more-experienced peers.

## MECHANISMS FOR TRAINING ASSESSMENT AND EVALUATION OF STAFF

Assessment and evaluation during training must be designed to provide timely, effective, and efficient feedback and occur in a way that provides educational opportunities for the individual and the group. The following mechanisms can be scheduled into staff training, or happen spontaneously to capitalize on a teachable moment.

>> **Check-ins.** Instructor and staff in-program check-ins are a way for instructors to provide quick on-the-fly assessments to staff managing a program. These check-ins should be short and deliver direct information that can be immediately implemented. They should be used judiciously and only for safety or educational delivery reasons because they can disrupt the flow of a program if used too frequently. Similarly, an effective coleadership dynamic can be undermined if one instructor feels the need to interject too often because it may appear to be a micromanagement condition that implies that the other staff members are not ready to run the program.

>> **In-program scheduled meetings.** On multiday programs, staff and students may schedule a

regular meeting. Often these meetings serve to process the day's events or the program to that point. It is also a time to deliver assessments to participants. These can be either staff-to-student assessments or instructor to staff. Feedback looping is one method for delivery at these meetings.

>> **Feedback looping.** Feedback looping is an opportunity for staff to critically assess themselves and others (see figure 14.3). To begin, the staff being assessed takes time to assess themselves in the core skill set (outdoor, human, and educational skills) in private. Back in a large group, or with an administrator, staff articulate performance contained in the core skill sets. For new staff, it helps if this is done in a checklist format with the subsets of each core skill set clearly articulated. Given that administrators should intervene for education and safety only, peers and administrators should not repeat accurate statements made by the staff being evaluated because these accurate assessments indicate an understanding of what actually has taken place among educational, human, and outdoor skills. Administrators and peers comment only when the staff being evaluated is finished with a self-assessment.

During the staff's self-evaluation, administrators should refer frequently to notes made during the training exercise. It should be an instructor

Feedback looping allows staff to critically assess themselves and others.

priority to remain in an engaged emotional state and optimal physical location to make accurate observations during staff performance. These observations should be referred to during the staff self-evaluations employed in feedback looping. Once a

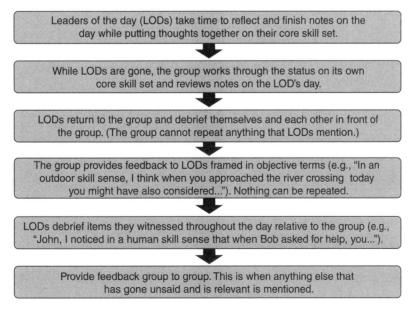

**Figure 14.3** Feedback looping.

student is finished with an evaluation, administrators and peers may include items not mentioned by the staff being assessed. The level of discrepancy between what that staff included and what peers and administrators feel obligated to include is a telling assessment piece for administrators considering promoting staff.

Feedback looping requires performance from all involved, including staff not being evaluated. Initially, the system encourages the primary staff to accurately self-assess. However, the rest of the staff is simultaneously paying close attention to the core skill set and seeking avenues to provide feedback. Given that accurate items cannot be repeated, the feedback grows more specific and articulate. Further, the system encourages students to objectively provide feedback to a peer. How often have administrators had great feedback lost because of poor delivery? It is critical that the "nothing repeated" rule be followed. If not, the debrief may be drawn out past its period of optimal effectiveness.

**» Postprogram meeting.** At the conclusion of a program, having staff meet to process the event is an important developmental step and becomes a way to track progress for your staff. Ideally, this meeting would occur immediately after the program to ensure recall of detailed feedback points. A delay can cause feedback details to be forgotten and important learning opportunities to be missed. Because this is a method to track staff development and performance, a tracking device is recommended, such as a peer leader evaluation form or a performance rubric. For example, apprentice instructors on Wilderness Education Association courses are required to complete an Instructor–Instructor Apprentice evaluation form that assesses the individual's knowledge of the WEA curriculum as well as his or her knowledge of WEA philosophy. Once completed, this evaluation form is discussed among instructors and the apprentice and becomes part of the apprentice's instructor file.

# STAFF-TRAINING DESIGNS: INTEGRATED TRAINING MODEL

The core skill sets described in chapter 1 provide a platform from which outdoor program admin-

istrators can identify training and mentoring opportunities. Outdoor program administrators are encouraged to develop training strategies that highlight each core concept as they relate to the unique culture and services offered by respective military, municipal, and college programs. What follows are three initiatives that administrators can employ to integrate core skill competencies into staff training. According to Nicolazzo (2007), the anatomy of an activity can be broken down into three elements: framing, activity, and closure. *Framing* is common in any form of teaching whereby basic information, safety considerations, and desired outcomes are framed at the beginning of an activity. *Activity* could be an entire 10-day trip or a 15-minute microlesson on flora. *Closure* may include a check for understanding, a simple "good job," or an extensive debrief. The following initiatives contain activity anatomy and assist administrators in the delivery of the initiatives.

## Initiative I: Competency (Human Skills)

### Framing

The perception of competence is necessary for all individuals operating in a leadership capacity. Human skills, as presented in chapter 1, are defined as one's ability to accurately self-assess and recognize inaccurate self-assessment in another. This activity will assist administrators and staff in understanding how to design and manage activities safely and effectively.

### Activity

1. Do this activity after staff members have chosen a teaching topic to be delivered as part of training. Once outdoor and human skills have been redefined and are understood, ask each staff member to make a self-assessment using the following scale.
    a. Rate your outdoor skills on a scale from 1 to 5.
    b. Rate your educational skills on a scale from 1 to 5.
2. Put the self-assessment aside and engage the group in a discussion surrounding the levels of competence. (See figure 1.4, p. 8.)
3. After confirming a conceptual understanding of the model, administrators might consider

setting up a hypothetical situation in which students are asked to gauge the level of competence they would expect from an outdoor leader if they were a participant. Administrators should encourage students to articulate why they would want a particular level of competence as an avenue for an administrator to hear student thought processes relative to competence. Further, this discussion may provide more time to ensure the core skill set is understood among staff. For example, as suggestions come forth, administrators may simply categorize responses on a whiteboard in three distinct lists, each a core skill set.

4. Once the discussion is drawing to a close, instructors should illustrate the levels of competency and fix any lingering misconceptions.

5. At this point have staff return to their original self-assessment and number the five levels of competence from unconsciously incompetent (1) to subconsciously competent (5). The discrepancy between how they rated themselves and what they expect from instructors as a participant is a clear signal to staff regarding how much work may need to be done for a skill set prior to designing and delivering topics to agency or program clientele.

## Closure

Instructors may choose to definitively close this initiative or to invite an ongoing dialogue with staff regarding levels of competence as it relates to self-assessment. Administrators are also encouraged to reiterate that as self-assessment becomes more accurate, the remaining parts of the core skill set are more easily integrated, and subsequently programs become more effective at all levels.

## Initiative II: Outdoor Skills (Discipline-Specific Kayaking Skills)

### Framing

Many programs offer specialized activities like river kayaking. This activity requires administrators to train beyond the basics of paddling technique and equipment. Additional items are hydrology, rescue, and trailer driving skills. This initiative will use an outdoor skill, setting up and using a z-drag, to highlight integration of the three core competencies.

## Activity

Once the activity has been thoroughly framed for staff and the site has been well set up relative to risk management, administrators can begin with an onshore demonstration of a z-drag while highlighting the components of the system, inherent hazards of boat recovery, and limitations. Further, the steps of boat recovery should be discussed, each step being fully analyzed. Once students have demonstrated they can swim well in current, rescue vest and throw bag use has been mastered, a boat pinning scenario may be considered. Once safety is in place, students can run the scenario recovering the pinned boat.

Once completed, staff may be encouraged to take 10 minutes to recall the process relative to the chronology of the recovery, communication issues, where and when particular people assisted, and time lapsed. After this reflection, the staff should compare notes in an open discussion to identify where gaps in awareness existed during the recovery.

## Closure

Closure of this initiative is twofold. Specific to pinned boat recovery, students should recap gaps in awareness and describe the correct steps in pinned boat recovery. This type of initiative is also a great avenue to illustrate integrated skill sets by asking staff to analyze the staff trainer's ability to set up and manage the scenario.

## Initiative III: Educational Skills

At many programs, new leaders often prepare presentations during staff trainings. At Green Mountain College, students are encouraged to approach their teaching opportunities as events to be managed that are clearly integrated into a training progression, not an isolated presentation. Giving a presentation implies that there is an instructor and listeners. An event, on the other hand, implies action, outcomes, and intense learning as a result of a well-structured experience.

### Framing

Before leaders can manage events during staff training, a thorough assessment of participant, outdoor, human, and instructor educational skills must be made. By doing so, leaders will have the best opportunity to deliver an event that will ensure two important pieces of information: First, a well-delivered lesson will be the best representation of a student-integrated skill set for an administrator to witness during training. Second, the event will likely be effective beyond a leader-teaching assessment in that it will add information to the training.

For this initiative an instructor matrix (Stuessy, 2010) is used to identify exactly what skills the instructor needs to be effective regarding the desired learning outcomes in addition to the skills assumed among a staff's peers taking part in the event.

### Activity

The instructor matrix is a tool to encourage staff to make accurate self-assessments in concert with understanding where participants are starting relative to the new skill being taught. Table 14.1 is an example of a matrix dedicated to the skill of lighting a MSR Whisperlite stove; the matrix illustrates the human, outdoor, and educational skills required of staff and participants before beginning a lesson.

### Closure

It is clear to see in table 14.1 the skills required of student and instructor before engaging in a lesson in which students learn to safely light a stove. This example is extremely simple. The instructor matrix grows exponentially as the complexity of the lesson increases. Take time to consider the required skills among students and instructors in an avalanche safety lesson or in building artificial climbing anchor systems.

## ACTIVITY-SPECIFIC TRAINING

As staff progress through an agency's training progression, they must move past basic skills and continue to develop competency in the activities they are teaching or leading. Program safety is increased by having knowledgeable, competent staff working on programs; this may also be seen as a job benefit for recruiting and retaining staff. Depending on the activity and training goals, components of an activity-specific training could include technique training, coaching and student assessment skills, rescue skills, or equipment repair and modification. Internal and externally sourced trainings and certification courses all offer opportunities to outdoor program administrators for increasing training in the activities offered by an agency. When deciding how to design and structure a training program, outdoor program administrators should consider needed staff experience as well as the cost and benefits associated with their chosen training platform.

## Personal and Vocational Experience as It Relates to Staff Training

Experience is a key determinant to activity-specific training because it serves as the foundation from which subsequent trainings are built. Individuals need appropriate experience before a training course, unless it is entry level or the course will provide all the training to meet the administrator's needs. For example, a wilderness first-responder course often has no prerequisites because most training companies provide students with pre-study materials before the course and the instructor-led portion is designed to cover all training topics and activities required to meet the certification standard. Often if a student does not meet the prerequisites

**Table 14.1   Participant and Staff Skill Sets: Lighting a Backcountry Stove**

| | Human | Outdoor | Education |
|---|---|---|---|
| Participant | • Patience<br>• Functional in a group<br>• Open to learning | Knows how to set up stove correctly | X |
| Staff | • Has assessed student readiness for lesson<br>• Has developed effective instructor relationship with student | • Has established clear boundaries<br>• Has mastery of lighting a stove<br>• Has mastery of stove repair | • Has designed a well-structured learning experience<br>• Has placed lesson correctly within course progression |

Bruce Saxman

Activity-specific training should include rescue skills training such as in activities where there are risks of avalanche.

for a course, it will require inordinate instructor resources to manage that individual, and they will not be able to understand the total value of the information being presented and how it can be applied. For instance, during a kayak extraction exercise a beginner paddler will not have the number of experiences to draw on that a more advanced paddler will have. The beginners might think that they are learning a cool trick, whereas the more-experienced paddlers may be considering how they could have handled a previous situation better.

## Costs and Benefits of Internal Versus Contracted Trainings

Outdoor program administrators have the option of providing staff-training opportunities that are offered internally, externally, or in a combined format. While many outdoor program administrators may initially consider internal training to be a cheaper option, contract trainers can often provide a needed acceleration in staff development, competency in a skill set not readily available within the program, or an opportunity for staff to learn from other professionals. The high cost up front might save time in the future as well as provide a more competent staff. As staff members train at a higher

level, they become adept at training and mentoring new staff. The overall competency of staff increases, leading to safer and increasingly well-run programs.

## Internally Sourced Training

Internally sourced trainings can be similar to initial standardized training, but it is used to increase staff competency and establish program norms in other instructor skill sets, such as rock climbing, whitewater rafting, or environmental education. Some benefits and goals are the same, such as reviewing and reinforcing policies and operating procedures and familiarizing staff with program equipment and resources. Internally sourced trainings depend heavily on the administrator or trainer's own instructional abilities. As mentioned in chapter 1, care should be taken to ensure that the program administrator has the competency to manage the programs being offered. He or she should have strong field experience in the activities being managed. For example, if the administrator knows very little about developing whitewater kayaking instructors, he or she may not have the experience to safely manage that aspect of the program, and it would be appropriate to consider an external source for the training.

# Externally Sourced Staff Training

Some programs offer many distinctly different activities, all of which require trained staff. This can be a lot of training for an outdoor program administrator to manage. Having training requirements and progressions clearly defined and regularly scheduled are necessary for maintaining a sustainable training system.

Administrators frequently develop close relationships with staff because of time spent in the field together, intense work in a stressful environment, and the camaraderie that comes from an active life in the outdoors. Most of the time, strong relationships between staff and supervisors enhance the program's effectiveness. However, these relationships can cause a training bias in which the administrator might temper feedback to the point of reduced or minimal effectiveness; in other cases, the staff member's ability to hear and receive feedback might be reduced because of familiarity with the administrator. Training bias can affect even the most objective staff members and administrators.

For these reasons, externally sourced staff training is a valuable method to get unbiased assessment of staff from an outside source and to relieve time and work pressure from administrators. There may be consensus among outdoor professionals on broad-based concepts, but there are few industry standards or specific methods for most activities managed and offered by outdoor programs. Thus it is important when seeking outsourced trainers to find an individual or agency that shares similar philosophy, mission, and methods to your own to maintain alignment among staff and the program. Identical methodology will result in minimal growth, whereas radically different methodology can cause confusion and misalignment among staff and administrators. Feedback received by staff from outsourced training should reinforce internal training while providing a fresh perspective via assessment of the staff's competency from an unbiased third-party assessor.

Outsourced training might also be useful in introducing new ideas and energy into a program. If training is done entirely in house, it might prevent new ideas or techniques from infusing into the program, result in outdated methodology, and contribute to the dilution of training. For example, a ropes course director might choose to outsource program training despite having the competency to do it in house so that course facilitators learn new activities or different facilitation techniques. Further, outsourced training provides opportunities for staff to create professional contacts beyond the scope of MWR, park and recreation organizations, or university communities.

## Certification

It might be tempting to rely on certifications as a primary training opportunity for staff. However, without being able to integrate those certifications into a program's training curriculum and philosophy, an important link is missing. Certifications are useless without experience to go with them and ongoing training to keep them up. As mentioned in chapter 1, there is a wide variance in content among providers of professional trainings. Certification courses should have clear standards that staff must meet. Standards should match or complement the training standards within a program or agency. A certification remit defines the parameters in which staff may operate. These parameters might include environments, weather conditions, supervisory level, and numbers of students. For instance an American Red Cross certified shallow-water attendant is authorized to lifeguard only in water less than 4 feet (1.2 m) deep. It would be inappropriate and dangerous to have this lifeguard monitor a pool with a 12-foot (3.6 m) deep end. Further, certifications are only as valuable as the organization doing the certifying. Research potential providers to make sure they are instructing at the most progressive and effective level and that they will complement your program's internal trainings. The St. Michaels College wilderness program is an example of certifications being used within a training progression.

## Accreditation

Beyond certification and training, administrators may choose to embark on an accreditation process. Accreditation is a comprehensive agency-wide assessment through which staffing, mission (or vision), resources, facilities, training, and fiscal planning are assessed by external review teams.

## SAINT MICHAELS WILDERNESS PROGRAM

St. Michaels College in Colchester, Vermont, requires a combination of internal training, vocational experience, and nationally recognized certification. They require their coastal kayak instructors to be trained and certified as American Canoe Association Level 3 Coastal Kayak Instructors or British Canoe Union (BCU) Level 2 Coaches. The program director, various professional staff, and alumni initially train students within the program, culminating in an ACA Instructor Development Workshop (IDW) or BCU Level 2 Coach Training. Upon completion of the IDW or coach training, students work in an apprentice capacity with student and professional staff, continue to develop personal skills, and build a log book for three months to a year. After instructor candidates complete their apprenticeship and log book, they are then eligible to take an ACA Instructor Certification Exam or BCU Coach Assessment with another ACA instructor trainer or BCU assessor not affiliated with the college.

The following sections identify three accreditation systems and their likely applications.

## National Recreation and Park Association (NRPA)

Municipal and collegiate recreation programs have an opportunity to become accredited by the National Recreation and Park Association (NRPA). Accreditation through the NRPA requires a comprehensive review and assessment of all aspects of an agency's operations, administration, staff, programming, and facilities. Describing this entire process is beyond the scope of this chapter, but the NRPA accreditation process includes items relative to staff hiring and training. For example, the hiring process requests that administrators articulate the staff-recruitment process, diversity policy, background checks, and benefits plan. The accreditation system also issues criteria for mentorship, supervision, disciplinary actions, and promotion. The NRPA accreditation process offers organizations an opportunity to both self-assess and externally assess overall program effectiveness. For more information on this opportunity, visit www.nrpa.org.

## Association for Experiential Education (AEE)

The Association for Experiential Education (AEE) has been accrediting adventure programs since 1994. The AEE's accreditation process was the first of its kind to focus on organizations offering experiential education programs and activities. The AEE is committed to identifying best practices and setting standards for risk management and safety in the field of experiential education. The goal of AEE is to ensure that accredited programs meet or exceed industry standards and demonstrate a commitment to continuously improve. Organizations seeking to obtain accreditation make a conscious commitment to continued excellence and improvement by allowing their programs and services to be externally assessed by an objective review process.

The AEE accreditation system is divided into the following primary areas:

- Philosophical, educational, and ethical principles
- Program governance
- Program operations, management, and oversight
- Technical activities—land, water, and miscellaneous

For more information on the Association for Experiential Education, visit www.aee.org.

## Wilderness Education Association (WEA)

New to accreditation, the Wilderness Education Association (WEA) is leading the way among accreditation models that engage the entire agency and academic program, including the agency, senior staff and faculty, and junior staff and students. WEA accreditation encourages all levels of a program to actively develop professionally and establish a connection with the greater outdoor leadership industry. Programs have the opportunity to become accredited at four distinct levels:

- Steward accreditation
- Outdoor leader accreditation
- Steward instructor accreditation
- Outdoor leader instructor accreditation

To obtain affiliation status, programs are required to develop a self-study, which is subsequently reviewed by a team of professionals. The self-study highlights important aspects of an agency's operations, including the following:

- Program and instructor characteristics
- Mission, vision, objectives, and goals
- Instructor evaluation
- Students
- Instructional resources
- Risk management
- Ethical conduct

Once accreditation is achieved, WEA affiliates can certify staff and students as outdoor leaders. Each student or staff member must fulfill prescribed standards in each of the following categories before achieving certified outdoor leader status.

- Outdoor living incorporates the outdoor skills essential to individual and group sustainability in the backcountry.
- Planning and logistics incorporate the knowledge, skills, and ability to design, implement, and prepare outdoor expedition trips at least seven days in duration.
- Risk management is a structured approach to managing actual, emotional, and perceived risk through risk assessment, use of management and instructional resources, and development and execution of emergency protocols.
- Leadership develops the ability to accurately self-assess as well as essential skills concerning or involving relationships among people. It involves the ability to effectively implement a decision.
- Environmental integration encompasses the concepts that embody ecological and cultural literacy along with cooperative planning and management skills required to ensure preservation of resources through personal connections for past, present, and future generations.
- Education is the ability to know and implement theories and practices of teaching processing and transference.

Bruce Saxman

To achieve certified outdoor leader status, a staff member must fulfill prescribed standards in six categories, one of which is leadership.

## STAFF APPRAISAL

At the completion of a training cycle, an appraisal should be performed for each staff member. This appraisal should contain three parts: a review of evaluations, an objective analysis of the staff member's current skills, and the formation or maintenance of a development plan for that staff member. See chapter 15 for more information regarding staff assessment, including appraisal.

## SUMMARY

A thorough needs assessment, rigorous hiring practices, and established training standards will set the bar for staff qualifications. Adopting an integrated approach to training with an effective training progression that includes initial standardized training, mentoring, assessment, and activity-specific training provides a clear path for administrators and staff alike. Each should be viewed as an interconnected piece equally important as the next.

Many outdoor program administrators report that staff training is among the most rewarding aspects of a professional life, and for good reason. It is gratifying to see time spent educating and mentoring staff pay off through witnessing staff perform at a high level. Effectively trained staff can reduce time and work pressure on the administrator by increasing program offerings with less direct supervision. Stress is also reduced on administrators for programs in the field because they know staff members are prepared to teach participants and manage the environmental and program risks associated with the activity.

# Chapter 15

# Staff Assessment

*Jenny Kafsky, PhD, and Mark Wagstaff, EdD*

Staff assessment is a key function of an outdoor program administrator. The ability for a program to reach its organizational mission and goals depends on the contributions of the individuals that comprise that organization. Work toward a strong and effective staff-assessment program that helps guide individual contributions is a sound investment in the professional growth of individual staff members and ultimately the program's success. In this chapter we present the key tools and resources to help develop a strong and effective staff-assessment system.

This chapter highlights the twofold purpose of staff assessment, providing a clear motivation for investing in the development of a strong and effective assessment system. We identify key elements that when present in the work environment create a setting conducive to self-reflection, feedback, and assessment. The criteria by which an administrator may evaluate performance is introduced, providing a selection of resources that may guide the identification of sound criteria specific to the program and position responsibilities. We provide guidance to outdoor program administrators in the development of effective evaluation tools, specifically checklists and rubrics. A selection of examples is provided to assist administrators in creating tools pertinent to the roles and responsibilities of their staff. It furthermore identifies the importance of documentation of data and provides ideas that when incorporated help make these tools useful and accurate. Finally, with the criteria, tools, and support information in hand, the outdoor program administrator is guided in creating an ongoing system for the assessment

of staff that will lead to quality feedback and result in the utmost personal, professional, and program benefits.

## THE BASICS AND PURPOSE OF STAFF ASSESSMENT

An effective staff evaluation system forms the foundation for a productive, functional, and satisfying work environment. Outdoor program administrators that create an effective process for giving and receiving employee feedback are setting the organization and its employees up for success. In the world of outdoor program administration, giving and receiving feedback has become a norm at all levels within the profession. Whether it's soliciting participant feedback during a backpacking trip or inviting staff feedback after a challenge course experience, outdoor program administrators know the value of reflection as an integral part of a learning experience. Evaluating staff should be no different. Staff-evaluation systems must be viewed as an opportunity to improve program services and assist in the employee's growth and development. The administrator that implements an effective staff-evaluation system based on sound criteria tends to be a successful leader. Successful administrators meet organizational goals and foster a healthy work environment conducive to employee growth and satisfaction. Let's look closer at the purpose of staff evaluation to understand the values and benefits.

The driving forces behind staff assessment can be summarized in two broad categories.

Assessment in an outdoor programming context should be guided by: (1) a larger set of goals and (2) the intent to foster staff development. First, a quality staff-assessment system is driven by a larger set of goals. Larger goals originate from numerous sources, such as organizational goals and mission, departmental goals, or program goals. It is up to the outdoor program administrator to determine priorities and what should drive the staff-assessment process. For our purposes in this chapter, we will use the term "program goals" as the generic term for a larger set of guiding goals.

In the outdoor profession, administrators take great pride in offering quality outdoor programs. Common factors that signify the pursuit of program quality are to strive for participant satisfaction, properly manage risks, foster environmental stewardship, meet educational outcomes, and provide a memorable leisure experience, just to name a few possibilities. More than likely, larger program goals will reflect these and other desired outcomes. Staff assessment systems must be designed with these larger goals in mind. As we all know, employees play a critical role in actualizing or carrying out the larger goals. To this end, an effective evaluation system must be in place to guide staff members. An effective system allows all involved to accomplish program goals through desired staff performance. It is also important to mention at this point that an effective evaluation system is a two-way process. Not only the employee receives feedback; the employee also has the opportunity to provide supervisors with feedback. This two-way process reflects an effective and efficient way to accomplish larger goals.

Second, the desire to foster staff growth and development should be a primary focus when implementing an effective staff-evaluation system. In this profession, most administrators have a duty to promote personal and professional development. Many employ students, interns, and entry-level staff. These employees gain valuable work experience. Effective staff evaluation systems foster personal and professional growth by assessing performance. Constructive feedback creates an environment for change. Intentional constructive feedback provides insight into issues such as skill development, behavioral patterns, or attitude adjustment to improve employee performance. This growth opportunity nurtures positive change that will benefit the indi-

vidual far into his or her working future. It should be mentioned that the same holds true for full-time professionals employed by the program. However, full-time professionals' developmental needs are different from the part-time student's or intern's. For example, professionals might desire experience with specific skill sets such as supervisory experience or budget management to foster upward mobility. Whether a full-time or a student worker, we all grow and improve when we receive effective feedback.

# AN EFFECTIVE ENVIRONMENT FOR ASSESSMENT

Before we begin a discussion of the details, we will discuss the groundwork necessary for preparing an organization for a successful evaluation system. The outdoor program administrator must work to create an environment conducive to effective assessment. Building a strong community based on trust, respect, open and honest communication, challenge, and reflection is a foundation of outdoor recreation and education programming. Creating this community within our staff is a valuable piece to developing an effective staff-assessment process. There are additional elements of a successful process worth further consideration. These include keeping a future outlook and respect for the employee at the core, engaging staff participation in the staff-assessment process, and fostering reflection.

## Mutual Respect

Mutual respect is fundamental to an effective staff-assessment system. Administrators who have a clear respect for their employees are more willing to invest their time sufficiently to develop their staff. Employees who feel respected will be more likely to have faith in and fully engage in the system. They are more likely to take goal setting and achievement more seriously and be more willing to share honest feedback within the organization. If an administrator maintains this respect for employees as the heart of any action, whether delivering praise or constructive criticism, trust and communication is enhanced. The result is a greater likelihood of success in the development of employees and the achievement of program goals.

## Future Outlook

A successful staff-assessment program has an outlook oriented toward the future and one that focuses on goal achievement. All actions are taken with the aim of positively influencing the future. In a future-oriented system, we examine past behavior from the developmental perspective of learning from both successes and failures. We address counterproductive behavior with the added step of helping to develop strategies to keep an employee on target for achieving his or her goals. Overall, this creates a motivating and supportive environment, and one that may more successfully foster accountability.

## Employee Participation

Administrators can integrate employee participation in a staff-assessment system in several key ways. The first is in the development of tools used within the system itself. Evaluation tools become more valuable, useful, and fair when administrators and employees collaborate to develop employment standards, assessment criteria, and assessment tools. Involvement in this context also helps to more clearly communicate clear performance standards. With this collaborative experience, employees and administrators are better prepared to work together to set and chart progress toward individual performance goals. Employee involvement in setting these individual performance goals is essential, and is yet another way that they may work cooperatively with their program administrators. There are also obvious benefits to employee self-reflection on goal achievement and performance. Employee self-evaluation helps to engage employees and contributes to more open and honest feedback within the assessment system. This helps prepare employees for meaningful involvement in the performance appraisal meeting, enhancing their ability to give and receive honest feedback.

As there are many ways from which an administrator may choose to involve employees in the staff-assessment system, there are also many benefits to doing so. The foremost benefit is that with meaningful participation from employees, the system inherently becomes more valuable within the organization. There is a stronger belief in the system by both employee and administrator, and

with important associated benefits. A meta-analysis provided evidence that performance appraisal system participation was strongly associated with appraisal satisfaction and acceptance (Cawley, Keeping, and Levy, 1998). The literature cites that satisfaction with appraisal feedback is positively related to organizational commitment, commitment toward and satisfaction with their administrator, and overall job satisfaction (Jawahar, 2006). Involvement of the employee in the process results in many positive outcomes for the individual and the program and will likely be well worth the effort.

## Fostering Self-Reflection

Program managers can enhance the value of individual participation, and thus enhance the overall effectiveness of a staff-assessment program, when the individual's ability to accurately reflect on and express his or her abilities is fostered. There are many useful tools program managers can use to help develop an employee's ability for self-reflection. SWOT analysis and 360-degree feedback are two such tools. These tools help individuals become more fully aware of their strengths and weaknesses, and help them more effectively build a plan for development.

SWOT analysis is a strategic planning tool commonly used by businesses to assess the organization as a whole, but can also be a useful tool for an individual. In a SWOT analysis, an individual uses a simple matrix to consider and objectively identify strengths, weaknesses, opportunities, and threats (Hill and Jones, 2004). Table 15.1 provides a template for individuals to reflect on their attributes and on the external conditions that may either help or hinder them in accomplishing their goals. The individual is encouraged to consider these items and then move forward toward a plan for personal development. This analysis is an ideal tool to help provide balance in self-assessment—enhancing strengths with attention to refining or working with weaknesses.

In 360-degree feedback, or multisource feedback, individual employees receive feedback from multiple sources with firsthand knowledge of their performance (Maylett and Riboldi, 2007). These sources commonly include supervisors, the employees themselves, peers, team members, and

**Table 15.1** SWOT Analysis Worksheet

| Strengths | Weaknesses |
|---|---|
| What do you do well?<br>What unique resources can you draw on?<br>What do others see as your strengths? | What could you improve?<br>Where do you have fewer resources than others?<br>What are others likely to see as weaknesses? |
| | |
| **Opportunities** | **Threats** |
| What opportunities are open to you?<br>What trends could you take advantage of?<br>How can you turn your strengths into opportunities? | What threats could harm you?<br>What is your competition doing?<br>What threats do your weaknesses expose you to? |
| | |

subordinates of the individuals being rated, but may also include clients, customers, and students. The premise of 360-degree feedback is that by connecting all of these different perspectives, a more complete view of an individual's strengths and weaknesses is constructed. There are a variety of 360-degree professional software packages available on the market, ranging from companies that offer tool development to full-service providers. Outdoor program administrators can draw on the philosophy and structure of 360-degree feedback and use their own tools to seek feedback from multiple sources such as supervisors, peers, and clients.

This kind of feedback was originally intended as a human resource development tool—that is, a tool for the development of individual staff members. But 360-degree feedback is also used by organizations as an administrative performance evaluation tool. There is some concern over the practice, or even of the practice of sharing the 360-degree feedback with the individual's superior (Eichinger and Lombardo, 2003). Those critical of the practice cite concern for the quality of the feedback by peers when the feedback is linked to an official performance review, particularly when related to raises or promotions

(Mondy and Mondy, 2010). Others believe that the individual being reviewed might feel that the feedback is too sensitive for a superior to view. Overall, the best use of a 360-degree feedback system is for developmental purposes, helping an individual gather data on observable skills from the perspectives of multiple sources, potentially gaining insight into hidden strengths that can be maximized or exposing blind spots for weaknesses that can lead to performance refinement. In the outdoor recreation field, with relationships and development as central values, this feedback from multiple sources may be used by administrators to help coach employees in building personal-development plans. Figure 15.1 is a partial example of a tool developed by an organization to help employees of an adventure program gain self-awareness by blending self-evaluation, coinstructor feedback, and supervisor feedback. The administrator may further determine that at significant points in the staff-assessment cycle that the staff member might benefit from feedback generated from peers, students, and clients or customers and incorporate a process to gather such information into the assessment plan.

**Figure 15.1**   Portion of a Multiple Source Evaluation Form

## Adventure employee evaluation—feedback or performance form

|                      | Preseason | Mid | Final |
|----------------------|-----------|-----|-------|
| **A. Self-evaluation** | ❑ | ❑ | ❑ |
| **Coinstructor**     | ❑ | ❑ | ❑ |
| **Supervisor**       | ❑ | ❑ | ❑ |

**B. Employee being evaluated**

Name: _____

Job title represented: _____

**C. Review or feedback**

Coinstructor name: _____

Supervisor name: _____

### Process

**Preseason:** Employee should self-evaluate, share, and strategize with a coinstructor and give to the supervisor for review and file.

**Mid or after session I:** Employee and coinstructor should complete an evaluation of each other as well as themselves, share, and strategize and give both forms to the supervisor for review and comment. The supervisor should add comments to the employee's self-evaluation and, following the employee review and comments, should file it.

**Final:** Repeat instructions for midseason instructions.

### Instructions

Circle the place along the continuum that best describes the employee being evaluated. Comment to support your appraisal as needed. Please note that a rating at midrange should be considered perfectly acceptable and above midrange is reserved for exceptional employees.

### Quality Service

| Participant interactive skills | Irritates, ignores, and discounts the participant. Displays a belligerent attitude toward participant. | Sporadic at meeting participants' needs. Sometimes gets hooked by frustration. Reluctant to meet participant requests. | Displays an active awareness and concern for meeting participants' needs. Portrays professional image and attitude. | Regularly exceeds the participants' expectations. Goes "the extra mile." | Effectively handles highly sensitive issues with participants. Helps others do the same. Finds the positive in pursuing difficult requests. |
|---|---|---|---|---|---|

Employee comments: _____

_____

_____

Employee goals: _____

_____

_____

*(continued)*

**Figure 15.1** *(continued)*

Coinstructor or supervisor comments (circle one): _____
_____
_____

**Acknowledgment of review**

_____          _____
       **Signature of individual evaluated**                    **Date**

_____          _____
       **Coinstructor signature**                              **Date**

_____          _____
       **Supervisor signature**                                **Date**

Adapted with permission from the City of Raleigh Parks and Recreation Department.

# ASSESSMENT CRITERIA

The basis for a quality staff evaluation system rests on the evaluation criteria used to structure the process. Evaluation criteria make up the attributes on which performance is assessed. There are numerous factors on which to base evaluation criteria. Do administrators focus evaluations to assess customer service skills, administrative skills, employee attitudes, technical skills, or leadership skills? This question must not be taken lightly. Effective evaluations that fulfill program purpose and promote staff development are based on well-defined criteria. In the outdoor profession, criteria are assessed on multiple levels. For example, employees in the outdoor field may be assessed on human, educational, and outdoor skills. Outdoor proficiency could mean displaying the skill set needed to be a competent lead climber. Human skills might include the ability to manage a group on a two-day outing. Educational skills might include an employee's ability to teach and disseminate information. Later in this chapter you can view examples of specific criteria when learning about various methods or tools for assessment. At this point it is more important to understand the origin or sources for sound evaluation criteria. The following sections outline potential sources for assessment criteria.

# Program Goals and Objectives

As discussed earlier, evaluation systems should be based on the larger organizational program goals and objectives. Evaluation tools should reflect these goals in the context of employee performance. If an organization's goal is to provide quality customer service, the evaluation tool should include criteria that reflect this. For example, an employee could be assessed on ability to communicate effectively with customers, professional demeanor when serving customers, and overall respect and patience when working with customers. Quality customer service might also include administrative functions such as managing program paperwork in a timely manner. An organization with well-articulated goals and corresponding objectives provide a rich source for assessment criteria.

# Job Descriptions

An employee's job description is another potential source for assessment criteria. Most well-written job descriptions clearly define duties and behavioral standards. These duties and standards translate easily into assessment criteria. Most of the time, job descriptions are in line with overall program goals and objectives. However, job descriptions provide more detail for specific positions within the organization. If the job description states that this position is responsible for implementing an equipment inventory system, then evaluation criteria can be pulled from this section to assess the individual's ability to implement the system. Job descriptions may also be written to describe ideal behavior and attitudes. If an employee is expected to be a motivated worker that consistently takes initiative, these expectations can be transposed to an evaluation tool that reflects level of performance in these areas. With a little time and effort, outdoor program administrators can create or improve evaluation tools based on a well-written job description.

## Employee Goals

In some cases, assessment criteria are based on employee-generated goals. It is not uncommon for a supervisor and employee to collaborate in the creation of an employee performance plan. The employee and supervisor generate a specific list of goals or accomplishments to be completed in a specified amount of time, such as an annual performance plan. These intended goals or accomplishments are then evaluated at the end of the specified time period. This is an excellent way to empower employees by introducing a mechanism for self-direction and motivation. Staff-evaluation criteria are designed around these self-generated goals.

## Professional Standards

Especially in the outdoor profession, staff-assessment criteria can be found within a multitude of professional standards. For example, rock-climbing staff might be expected to adhere to the standards set forth by the American Mountain Guides Association. Paddling staff might be expected to teach according to the curriculum of the American Canoeing Association. Challenge course staff members are held to the facilitation standards of the Association for Challenge Course Technology. Some outdoor programs are required to follow state licensing guidelines for their trip leaders and guides. Some professional associations, such as the National Recreation and Parks Association, have created a professional code of ethics for their members. Outdoor program administrators may have the option

to integrate these ethics into expected performance criteria. Finally, another important source must be considered when integrating standards into an assessment system. All outdoor programs establish standard operating procedures through program manuals and staff policies. Assessment criteria can be generated from this important body of information for desired staff performance.

# ASSESSMENT TOOLS

Now that we have identified the resources by which an administrator can develop assessment criteria, we will begin a discussion of effective performance-evaluation tools. In the following section, the design and use of checklists and rubrics as performance-assessment tools are covered in detail.

## Checklist Assessments

Checklists are popular tools for outdoor program administrators. Checklist assessments are simple to design and implement as performance-evaluation tools. To create an understandable foundation for this discussion, see the skills checklist example (table 15.2) used to assess rafting trip leaders (Pelchat and Kinziger, 2009). This is a classic checklist design that highlights the necessary technical skills to become a whitewater rafting trip leader. In this case, the administrator, with many years of rafting experience, sat down and created a list of essential technical skills that trip leaders must demonstrate. The administrator schedules a preseason training session during which staff participate in a number of training trips. On the last training trip, the outdoor program administrator and other qualified leaders assess each of these skills for all the new trainees. If a trainee demonstrates minimal competency, the trainer checks off the skill. Notice in the second column of the checklist there is a box to mark if the skill is completed. This process is straight forward and simple from an administrative standpoint because it is basically a pass or fail concept. The trainee either demonstrates or does not demonstrate the skill.

Looking at this system critically, you might feel something is missing. And you would be correct. Where is the quality rating for the observed performance? In other words, how well or at what

**Table 15.2**   Whitewater Rafting Skills Checklist

| | Completed |
|---|---|
| **Equipment and use** | |
| Knowledgeable of proper equipment identification | |
| Proper equipment application and raft rigging | |
| Ability to properly maintain equipment | |
| **Safety considerations** | |
| Capable of creating a pretrip safety plan | |
| Proficient at executing a thorough safety briefing | |
| Ability to demonstrate each paddle command | |
| Ability to demonstrate signaling commands | |
| **Transporting a raft** | |
| Proficient at transporting a raft from vehicle to the water's edge | |
| **Preparing to paddle** | |
| Proficient at executing a thorough paddle captain briefing | |
| Ability to evaluate crafts for water readiness | |
| **Maneuvering an oar rig** | |
| Ability to execute the following strokes: | |
| • Back rowing while tracking in a straight line | |
| • Portegee | |
| • Left turn | |
| • Right turn | |
| Proficient at ferrying a raft across the river | |
| Able to enter an eddy | |
| Capable of exiting an eddy | |
| **Maneuvering a paddle raft** | |
| Ability to execute the following strokes: | |
| • Forward | |
| • Back | |
| • High and low brace | |
| • Draw | |
| • Rudder | |
| Capable of tracking forward in a straight line using the crew | |
| Proficient at turning the boat right using the crew | |
| Proficient at turning the boat left using the crew | |

| | Completed |
|---|---|
| **Basic rescue** | |
| Ability to deploy a throw bag twice in 20 seconds | |
| Ability to right a flipped raft in 20 seconds | |
| Proficient at assisting swimmers back into the raft | |
| **Advanced rescue** | |
| Proficient at setting up a foot entrapment rescue | |
| Competent at setting put a mechanical advantage system to unpin a raft | |
| **Leave No Trace considerations** | |
| Knowledgeable of setting up a minimum impact camp environment | |
| Proficient at dealing with the health and sanitation of human waste disposal | |
| Competent at fire pan use and fire waste removal | |

Adapted, by permission, from C.R. Pelchat and M.L. Kinziger, 2009, Rafting. In *Technical skills for adventure programming: A curriculum guide*, edited by M. Wagstaff and A. Attarian (Champaign, IL: Human Kinetics), 620.

level did the trainee demonstrate the skill? Was the demonstration excellent or below average? This concern can be easily addressed by adding a Likert scale to the evaluation, such as the following scale: 5 = outstanding performance, 4 = good performance, 3 = fair performance, 2 = needs significant improvement, 1 = demonstrated no grasp of the skill. The Likert scale adds a descriptive measurement or scoring mechanism to the process. Other questions surface in this discussion when integrating more descriptive measurements. What are these descriptors based on? What constitutes outstanding performance? Scores could be based on measurement criteria found in standards of the American Canoeing Association's rafting curriculum. Or the performance criteria might be described in a staff manual. If curricula and standards are already in place, the checklist assessment is a more valid and effective tool. Using a checklist without clearly defined criteria becomes a subjective process driven entirely by the evaluator's judgment and potential biases. However, this is not always a problem. It depends on what is being assessed. There are some instances in which an evaluator's judgment is enough. For example, a program manager might simply need to know that staff members can complete specific tasks such as check in, clean, inventory, and check out equipment in a rental shop. Once these skills are demonstrated during

a probationary period, regardless of quality, it is enough to obtain an entry-level position, with more training and extensive evaluation to come later. For a final checklist example, see the basic camping skills checklist (figure 15.2) used to train outdoor leaders. This is a basic checklist of essential camping skills used for self-assessment and instructor assessment on a 28-day outdoor leadership course. This checklist is one small part of a larger assessment system for training outdoor leaders.

We hope you are now clear on the benefits and limitations of a checklist assessment system. If used correctly and in proper contexts, checklists are useful evaluation tools. Based on the discussion, it is probably apparent that a more powerful tool is needed when the quality or level of performance must be assessed and documented. The next section describing rubric evaluations addresses this issue and adds another assessment option to outdoor program administrators.

## Rubric Assessments

This section is devoted to the design and use of rubrics as assessment tools. Rubrics provide a powerful way to evaluate staff performance or competencies on a number of levels. Rubrics differ from simple checklists because the design includes specific performance criteria or desired outcomes

**Figure 15.2**   Basic Camping Skills Checklist

Journal checklist                                    Name: _____

On a daily basis, record the skills you have used that day; *denotes that instructor must initial at least one day.

| Day of week | T | W | TR | F | SA | SU | M | T | W | TR | F | SA | SU | M | T | W | TR | F | SA | SU | M | T | W | TR | F | SA | SU | M | T |
|---|---|---|---|---|---|---|---|---|---|---|---|---|---|---|---|---|---|---|---|---|---|---|---|---|---|---|---|---|---|
| Day of course | 1 | 2 | 3 | 4 | 5 | 6 | 7 | 8 | 9 | 10 | 11 | 12 | 13 | 14 | 15 | 16 | 17 | 18 | 19 | 20 | 21 | 22 | 23 | 24 | 25 | 26 | 27 | 28 | 29 |
| Bath | | | | | | | | | | | | | | | | | | | | | | | | | | | | | |
| Baked* | | | | | | | | | | | | | | | | | | | | | | | | | | | | | |
| Home-made dessert* | | | | | | | | | | | | | | | | | | | | | | | | | | | | | |
| Cooked break-fast* | | | | | | | | | | | | | | | | | | | | | | | | | | | | | |
| Cooked dinner* | | | | | | | | | | | | | | | | | | | | | | | | | | | | | |
| Paceset-ter | | | | | | | | | | | | | | | | | | | | | | | | | | | | | |
| Leader of day | | | | | | | | | | | | | | | | | | | | | | | | | | | | | |
| Logger | | | | | | | | | | | | | | | | | | | | | | | | | | | | | |
| Scout | | | | | | | | | | | | | | | | | | | | | | | | | | | | | |
| Operated stove* | | | | | | | | | | | | | | | | | | | | | | | | | | | | | |
| Sweep | | | | | | | | | | | | | | | | | | | | | | | | | | | | | |
| Taught lesson | | | | | | | | | | | | | | | | | | | | | | | | | | | | | |
| Pitched group fly* | | | | | | | | | | | | | | | | | | | | | | | | | | | | | |
| Natural history tip* | | | | | | | | | | | | | | | | | | | | | | | | | | | | | |
| 4 Camp knots* | | | | | | | | | | | | | | | | | | | | | | | | | | | | | |
| Food hanging | | | | | | | | | | | | | | | | | | | | | | | | | | | | | |

that serve as the basis for measurement. The design uses a matrix format that includes defined levels of quality to assess performance criteria. Most administrators find rubric evaluations extremely effective if the rubric is well designed and used in an appropriate context. A significant amount of literature exists for administrators that wish to use this effective tool (Andrade, 2005; Boston, 2002; Lund, 1999; Goodrich, 1997).

To begin to understand rubrics as evaluation tools, look at figures 15.3 and 15.4. Figure 15.3 illustrates a conventional checklist combined with a scoring mechanism used by a university outdoor program administrator to assess front-office student workers. Front-office workers are expected to provide basic program information, register customers for trips, and accomplish simple administrative tasks. The design of this checklist format allows the supervisor to assign a quality rating (excellent, good, fair, or poor) to each of the evaluation points. This form provides 10 items or performance expectations the supervisor has for front-office workers.

**Figure 15.3**   Front-Office Employee Evaluation Form

Name: _____ Date: _____ Evaluation period: _____
(Designate with X the type of evaluation) Supervisor's evaluation: _____ Self-assessment: _____

| Expectations | Excellent | Good | Fair | Poor |
|---|---|---|---|---|
| Performs neat and accurate work. | | | | |
| Is consistently on time for shifts worked and for staff meetings. | | | | |
| Ensures shifts are filled if unable to work. | | | | |
| Exhibits appropriate work ethic during each shift. | | | | |
| Engages in professional relationships with coworkers. | | | | |
| Self-motivated and takes initiative. | | | | |
| Is knowledgeable of department's programs and services. | | | | |
| Exercises judgment and problem-solving skills. | | | | |
| Provides quality customer service. | | | | |
| Consistently follows office procedures. | | | | |

Turn over for additional comments.

General comments: _____

_____

_____

_____

Although this tool is simple and easy to use, a more effective way exists to evaluate and clarify the expectations for the front-office position.

Figure 15.4 shows a rubric designed from the same 10 expectations used in figure 15.3. The 10 expectations are modified and clarified into 11 specific performance criteria or desired outcomes.

The desired outcomes are then qualified using three levels: exceeds expectations, meets expectations, and does not meet expectations. Qualifying the outcomes with detailed descriptions promotes a number of benefits. First, employees have a clear and concise understanding of supervisor expectations for each outcome. Second, the supervisor has the option to integrate specific expectations into the rubric based on factors found within the specific working environment. For example, worksite-specific issues such as completing homework while working, balancing peer or coworker relationships, and mastering a computer-based registration program all represent issues in this specific work environment. Finally, employees have a clear ideal to strive toward to exceed expectations, thereby promoting feelings of success and pride.

---

**Figure 15.4** Front-Office Employee Evaluation Rubric Form

Name: _____ Date: _____ Evaluation period: _____

(Designate with X the type of evaluation) Supervisor's evaluation: _____ Self-assessment: _____

Peer assessment: _____

| Criteria | Exceeds expectations | Meets expectations | Does not meet expectations |
|---|---|---|---|
| **Quality of work** | Consistently neat and thorough with office paperwork and forms. Completes all tasks in timely manner. Others never have to follow behind to adjust paperwork inaccuracies. Demonstrates high level of skill in all office tasks. Consistently communicates all issues and concerns to trip leaders; trip leaders have learned to depend and trust thoroughness. | Work is reasonably neat and thorough. Forms and paperwork completed on time. Rarely needs assistance to complete paperwork. Is able to self-correct and catch inaccuracies. Is constantly working toward developing skills in all areas needed to perform office functions. Works well with trip leaders to prepare trip participants. | Work is not completed on time. Others must follow up to complete tasks. Lack of attention to detail. Work lacks neatness and contains inaccuracies. Does not demonstrate desire to improve quality of work or to develop necessary skills. |
| **Attendance** | Always ready to work before shift starts. Takes breaks only when appropriate. Always ensures front area is covered. Finds replacements for shifts far in advance and always follows procedure to ensure shifts are covered. Makes staff meetings on time and is highly productive during meetings. | Shows up to work on time. Covers front desk adequately; rarely leaves front area unattended. Covers shifts appropriately when not able to work. Makes staff meetings on time. Informs supervisor in advance when meetings cannot be attended. | Has issues showing up on time for shifts. Does not adequately cover shifts. Does not act in advance to cover shifts when unable to work. Does not consistently make staff meetings. Does not always ensure front desk is covered. |
| **Work ethic** | Consistently maintains organized work area by keeping all paperwork and items in their respective places. Is never idle. Always searching for ways to improve office area and process. Always considerate of others and serves as a role model with work habits. Safety is always a priority. Engages in homework only when appropriate. | Spends majority of shift taking care of work tasks. Only engages in personal homework when office tasks are complete. Maintains a neat organized work space. Is conscious of safety issues. Shows consideration of others. Will always complete tasks when asked. | Demonstrates lack of desire to complete work duties. Spends inappropriate amount of time completing homework while on shift. Work area is not always neat or organized. Has to be reminded of safety issues. At times not considerate of others. |

| Criteria | Exceeds expectations | Meets expectations | Does not meet expectations |
|---|---|---|---|
| **Relationship with coworkers** | Maintains healthy, professional relationships with coworkers. Coworker relationships never interfere with customer service or office tasks. Conversations are always appropriate. Serves as a leader and positive role model for coworkers. | Engages in appropriate coworker relationships—appropriate language and no horse play. Maintains professional demeanor. Monitors appropriate conversations. Ensures that customer service is a priority over coworker relationships. | Engages in inappropriate coworker relationships, such as inappropriate conversations. Spends more time socializing as opposed to completing office duties. Tends to let peer relationships interfere with customer service. |
| **Initiative** | Consistently exhibits self-motivation. Resourceful and self-reliant. Does not require direction from supervisor or other senior office staff. Readily identifies tasks and completes them to keep the front office running smoothly. Always demonstrates positive attitude when at work. | Performance does not require supervisor to monitor quality or motivate while on the job. Understands office tasks and readily completes duties without reminders. Demonstrates positive attitude and demonstrates a genuine desire to do good work. | Supervisor must remind and motivate during shifts. Tends to demonstrate a noncaring attitude. Rarely completes additional or extra tasks. Must be asked to do things. |
| **Knowledge** | Expert on all office procedures. Highly knowledgeable of procedures to register program participants. Intimately knows all facets of outdoor program services as well as the larger department of campus recreation. | Familiar with all operations and programs associates with the outdoor program. Willingness to learn new information and to stay informed. Has solid grasp of program registration procedures. | Not knowledgeable of outdoor program services. Does not consistently register participants properly. Does not show desire to learn new information or procedures. Must rely on others for information. |
| **Judgment and problem solving** | Demonstrates excellent decision-making abilities. Able to solve problems without supervisor's support. Ability to prevent problems by critically analyzing all issues. Has ability to quickly learn from experience and easily applies all information provided at staff trainings and meetings. When problems occur, quickly able to problem-solve. | Demonstrates basic ability to problem-solve. Addresses problems as soon as they occur. Does good job of keeping supervisor informed of all issues. Not afraid to ask questions, and actively seeks way to improve ability to deal with issues. | Does not actively problem-solve. Leaves issues and problems for others to deal with. Does not consistently inform supervisor of issues. Avoids challenges and tough situations. Relies on others to alleviate or reconcile problems. |
| **Customer service** | Quickly and efficiently meets the needs of all customers. Able to effectively register trip participants so they are fully informed of the process. Very patient when serving first time customers and able to educate them effectively concerning outdoor recreation services. Customers consistently respond in a positive manner to service provided. | Demonstrates a customer service ethic—the customer comes first. Effectively serves customers. Adequately prepares trip participants for pretrip meeting. Demonstrates patience when serving customers. Represents department of outdoor recreation as a professional. | Tends to be more self-centered as opposed to customer centered. Does not adequately brief or inform trip participants. Tends to lose patience with customer or show disinterest. Not quick to address the needs to customers. |

*(continued)*

**Figure 15.4** *(continued)*

| Criteria | Exceeds expectations | Meets expectations | Does not meet expectations |
|---|---|---|---|
| **Administrative ability** | Never makes mistakes or errors concerning the collection and accounting of fees. All forms are completed with accuracy and filed appropriately. Consistently informs supervisors of problems or issues. Able to forecast office needs and requests supplies, forms, and other office items in a timely manner. Actively assists in improving office procedures. Balances cash register with no errors after each shift. Never has to rely on business manager to balance shift transactions. Very comfortable with computer program registration system—able to teach others. | Rarely makes mistakes concerning paperwork and record keeping. If mistake is made, has ability to identify mistake and rectify appropriately. Consistently follows all office procedures. Able to identify problems and issues and communicates with supervisor. Able to balance cash register after shift. Quick to receive assistance from business manager if fail to balance. Able to competently use computer registration system. | Consistently makes mistakes. Does not always follow proper procedure. Others must adjust forms and paperwork resulting from lack of attention to detail. Unable to catch own mistakes. Consistently fails to balance transactions at the end of a shift. Continues to struggle with computer-based program registration system—requires assistance to process registrations. |

Turn over for additional comments.

General comments: _____

_____

_____

Strengths: Describe the student's outstanding abilities.

_____

_____

_____

_____

Suggestions for improvement: Describe the areas in which the student needs the greatest improvement.

_____

_____

_____

This approach provides the necessary information for employee growth and development. Notice that figures 15.3 and 15.4 can either be completed by the administrator or completed as a self-evaluation. The rubric design provides a much more meaningful way to self-evaluate because the carefully articulated quality levels do not leave as much room for open interpretation. Employees can self-evaluate with more accuracy, which will promote a quality conversation when reviewing the results with the supervisor.

## Rubric Design

If enough time and energy are allocated, designing rubrics does not have to be difficult. Those in the position of evaluating staff must take the time to develop sound evaluation or performance criteria and then must dedicate substantial thought to articulating the levels or gradations of quality. Figure 15.4 represents a typical format. The first column lists performance criteria. The following three columns describe the levels of quality: exceeds expectations, meets expectations, and does not meet expectations. In some cases, agencies mandate a more quantitative approach to evaluation. This is not necessarily a limitation for a good rubric. Quality levels could be assigned a numeric rating. Once numeric ratings are assigned, the instrument is known as a scoring rubric. To clarify this point, see table 15.3 to view a portion of a larger rubric designed to assess challenge course facilitator skills (Wagstaff and Quinn, 2007). Table 15.3 highlights the portion that assesses knot tying. Note that the three quality levels—target, acceptable, and unacceptable—are assigned numeric ratings of 1, 2, and 3, respectively. To pass or display competency, a score of 2 or higher in each competency area must be achieved. Determining the numeric passing point varies depending on the situational context. Sometimes, standards exist that dictate minimal competencies. Or, organizational policies determine competencies. In other cases, the minimum may fall on the expertise and judgment of administrators and trainers.

More information concerning the development of quality ratings will be helpful at this point. Avoid using descriptor words such as "good," "poor," and "excellent" when writing quality ratings. For example, stating that "displays good organizational skills" does not really provide an ample description for the expectation. Instead, a more appropriate description might be "consistently maintains the front desk area in a neat and organized fashion." This provides the employee a very clear expectation of what is meant by good organizational skills in this context.

Note that the two rubric examples shared thus far provide only three gradations or three quality levels. Well-designed rubrics might list four or five gradation levels. Teachers typically design assignment rubrics to reflect five gradation levels of A, B, C, D, and F. This makes perfect sense in the context of the academic evaluation system. Another important item to note is the competency breakdown found in the knot-tying rubric (table 15.3). The evaluators are assessing the physical ability to tie a knot (skill). They are also assessing the body of knowledge associated with knot tying (knowledge). Finally, they are also assessing the habits, beliefs, and attitudes associated with performing the skill (disposition). This breakdown demonstrates another way to develop performance criterion.

## Analytic Versus Holistic Rubrics

Another point worthy of discussion involves the complexity of the rubric. The literature distinguishes between analytic and holistic rubrics (Moskal, 2000). The rubric found in figure 15.4 provides an example of a holistically developed rubric, whereas analytic rubrics break down performance criteria in much more detail. For example, see figure 15.4 and view the final outcome category of administrative ability. Notice that a number of factors are listed or lumped within the quality ratings. The employee is expected to be competent with the computer registration system, competently use the cash register, and properly manage the associated paperwork. In an analytic rubric, the three distinct skills would be listed as separate evaluation criteria, and quality ratings would be developed for each. The advantage of this design allows the employee and administrator to evaluate each specific skill associated with the job. In a holistic design, specific feedback can be lost or overlooked when things are lumped together unless the evaluator takes time to document and explain the specifics during the evaluation process. However, breaking down all necessary skills might be too cumbersome and promote the creation of lengthy evaluation tools that are overwhelming to all involved. It is up to administrator judgment and the evaluation context when deciding whether to create an analytical or holistic rubric design.

In summary, rubric evaluation tools tend to be extremely effective when the outdoor program administrator wishes to provide a clear picture of expectations, when he or she wishes to create a mechanism for employee growth and development,

**Table 15.3** Knot Rubric Excerpt

**Challenge Course Technical Skills Assessment Tool**

| Technical skill competencies to be assessed | Target (1) Targeted performance is evidenced by . . . | Acceptable (2) Acceptable performance is evidenced by . . . | Unacceptable (3) Unacceptable performance is evidenced by . . . | Comments |
|---|---|---|---|---|
| **General knot tying** *Skill* | having every knot attempted in perfect form, each knot is dressed properly, all loops and bights are of the proper size and dimension, and every knot is correctly tied off when necessary. The knot is tied with ease, confidence, and little effort. | knots that are basically tied correctly but are not of perfect form (e.g., the dressing or tie off knot is not performed properly). The prototype is resembled but is not identical. | looseness within the knot. Rope is not oriented to itself correctly, loops are grossly undersized or oversized, or the knot does not resemble the prototype. There is an obvious struggle, in untying and retying, to remember the correct sequence for tying the particular knot. | Score _____ |
| **General knot tying** *Knowledge* | an ability to tie knots with more than one procedure. An ability to match the appropriate knot to the needed function. An ability to glance at a knot and know immediately if something is wrong. | an ability to recognize knots that are incorrect but inability to correct them without starting completely over. Facilitators are aware of only a few knots for the activity they are practicing. | inability to recognize incorrectly tied knots; consistent misapplication of knots and lack of awareness of potential hazards caused by poor or incorrectly tied knots. | Score _____ |
| **General knot tying** *Disposition* | appreciation for the reasons why knots must be tied correctly, each and every time. Facilitator makes the effort to ensure that knots are correct before being put into use. | a readiness to tie knots consistently but sometimes accepts knots that are not precise or complete. | not caring if knots are properly tied or finished. Facilitator rushes or rarely double-checks work. | Score _____ |

and when the purpose is to create an objective evaluation in which specific language is needed to describe desired performance. Rubric design does not have to be difficult. Outdoor program administrators must have a clear vision of evaluation criteria and take the time to develop quality ratings that describe performance criteria in detail. When developing a rubric, do not hesitate to use the assistance of peer professionals for feedback and reviews of instruments under construction. Outdoor program administrators will discover a distinct shift in employee performance if appropriate tools are used within the overall staff-assessment process.

# AN EFFECTIVE ASSESSMENT SYSTEM

To this point we have discussed the various sources of assessment criteria, examples of effective assessment tools, and the types of data points an administrator might use to more accurately and fairly assess employees. We will now take a look at steps common to productive staff-assessment systems. The effective assessment system begins with setting goals and standards for performance. The supervisor observes and documents employee performance relative to performance standards and goals, and concurrently provides ongoing feedback that shares those observations. Finally, formal assessment meetings held at least midway and at the conclusion of every assessment cycle help track goal progress and individual performance plans. These steps will be presented in greater detail in the section that follows.

## Goal and Standard Setting

An organization with well-articulated goals and objectives creates a starting point for establishing individualized employee goals. Setting performance goals and discussing criteria for assessment is the first step of the assessment cycle and should be done in a collaborative manner with the employee. This process can be as simple as asking the part-time student employee to identify simple goals to work toward. These goals can be based on the criteria on which they will be assessed or on the feedback from a self-reflection tool or a previous performance review. Or the process might be as complex as a formal goal-setting process with an assistant director of a program targeting objectives and identifying potential resources. The depth in which an individual performance plan is addressed and developed is parallel to the context of the position responsibilities and tenure of the employee. Whether simple or complex, whenever goals are set and managed by employees, there is much more motivation toward achievement and a wider breadth of accomplishment. The direction and goals of an organization must be met by the individual staff members that comprise that organization; thus the program benefits when we as administrators invest the time to develop and nurture the performance goals of the individual.

## Supporting Data

A challenging issue faced by all administrators relates to effectively obtaining specific and observable data needed to complete any type of staff-assessment tool. There are several points of information an administrator can use to help track performance and determine the degree to which a staff member is meeting the established assessment criteria and performance goals delineated on staff evaluations. These resources help outdoor program administrators assess employees fairly and accurately and keep them aligned for goal achievement. This supporting data may include information generated by the employee or supervisor, or even by others who can provide wisdom into the employee's performance. This supporting data can be found through use of the tools and processes discussed so far. It is important to note that this supporting data may be either objective and subjective nature, and that both are important when building an accurate and holistic assessment of staff performance.

## Objective Information

Information that aids the administrator in understanding employee performance may be objective or quantitative in nature. Objective information relates facts not influenced by opinions. Examples of objective data in the outdoor field include budget reports, attendance records, time records, trip plans and reports, training records, and samples of employee work. Objective information proves to be more helpful to interpreting when the criteria for the assessment of performance are set.

## Subjective Information

Subjective (or qualitative) information is also important to fully assess performance. One of the most important pieces of employee assessment rests in the outside recreation administrator's direct observation of performance. The administrator may create tools such as checklists and rubrics to help track performance throughout the assessment period. He or she may develop an acknowledgment system or use a performance log to acknowledge and record noteworthy events that give insight into the quality of performance. Qualitative evidence often provides the context in which to understand the objective information. For example, an equipment manager might be impeccable when it comes to balancing the gear budget, but she might not allocate funds sufficiently to provide field staff with the appropriate equipment. Qualitative information also provides insight into performance items not able to be ascertained purely by objective information. For instance, to measure the effectiveness of a field instructor, we need to understand his ability to relate to participants in the field. Evidence of this ability may be found in participant course evaluations or in reviewing compliments and complaints. Asking for opinions from key individuals as points of information about the individual's performance is reasonable, and if used in the context of the big picture might minimize the potential for bias in the assessment. Feedback processes that are multifaceted, such as in a SWOT analysis, and that incorporate multiple sources, such as in 360-degree feedback, help in building an accurate and holistic understanding of performance.

## Data Management

Whether qualitative or quantitative in nature, all of this gathered information is essential for the administrator to consider before drawing conclusions about employee performance. This can mean managing a great deal of information, or data, for each employee. The key to using the data effectively is to establish a consistent and regular system for collecting and managing data interpretation. Later in the chapter, we will discuss a technique to simplify the management of data through the use of employee performance files.

## Ongoing Observation and Feedback

To chart our progress toward meeting goals at an individual or program level, we must be actively involved in reflection and in giving and receiving feedback. In the outdoor field, feedback occurs frequently because it is embedded in our philosophy and practices. The more frequently the conversation about performance is opened, the more easily challenges can be addressed and successes be maximized. This is accomplished by providing ongoing feedback throughout the staff-assessment cycle. The administrator may exchange this ongoing feedback in a conversation or in written form or both. Sharing positive and negative observations as they arise helps nurture positive performance and encourages employees to stay on track. A responsible and effective supervisor delivers and asks for feedback in a timely manner. An administrator would be considered irresponsible if after a year of watching and documenting a counterproductive behavior communicates the observation for the first time in an end-of-year written job appraisal.

Mark Wagstaff

An outdoor program administrator gives an employee constructive feedback on rappelling procedures during trip leader training for caving.

A supervisor who fails to notice the outstanding efforts of employees may negatively affect employee motivation. Addressing issues as they arise throughout the assessment cycle allows for more time in the formal assessment meetings to be goal oriented and focused on exploring new opportunities for development. Frequent feedback demonstrates an interest and investment in the development of the employee and thus nurtures the working relationship.

## Ongoing Documentation

An outdoor program administrator has many tools accessible to document ongoing feedback. To keep track of these tools use a checklist (figure 15.5).

He or she might send a memo of appreciation for exceptional accomplishment or to attempt to motivate an employee to redirect and improve performance. It might also be necessary to document employee involvement through an incident report, or to create a memo that documents a disciplinary action. Programs can have a system in place, or can create a system, to help recognize significant events. Regardless of the method, documentation increases the effectiveness of a staff-assessment system by serving as a resource to record data that can help administrators assess a staff member fairly and accurately. Gathering and using this information prevents staff appraisal pitfalls such as focusing on specific incidents or relying on memory as we

---

**Figure 15.5** Personnel File Checklist

### Employee Information

- Name
- Date hired
- Positions held
- Employee contact information

### Hiring Record

- Record of contacts with applicant
- Application
- Reference forms
- Reference follow-up documentation
- Background check documentation
- Interview documentation

### Certification Record

- Certifications
- Expiration dates
- Copies of certifications

### Training Record

- Trainings completed: preservice, in-service, professional development
- Dates or times and brief narrative content of trainings

### Performance Log

- Performance log sheet
- Supporting documentation related to job performance

### Performance Assessments

engage in the process of staff evaluation. Documentation helps us focus on the bigger picture of employee performance over the entire assessment period. It provides concrete information to aid in the delivery of feedback, and helps justify administrative actions in the face of a challenge on fairness or legality. Clearly, documentation is a critical aspect of staff assessment, so it is important to develop a consistent system for its management. Management of documentation can be accomplished by using employee performance files and logs.

A performance file should be kept on each employee, starting at the date of hire or as soon as possible thereafter. This file contains documentation of key data relative to performance. The file should begin with a checklist (figure 15.5) that identifies the supporting documents contained in the file. The key element of the performance file is the performance log, which serves as a chronicle of any documentation, actions, or significant events that relate to the employee (figure 15.6). The log helps to convey the comprehensive outlook of the employee's performance. Notes recorded in the log should be simple and concise. You might include observations of work, including attendance, timeliness, and work progress. The log is focused on objective facts, not opinions. An administrator may choose to include impressions of the employee's quality of work when these impressions are supported by facts or documentation. Noteworthy accomplishments, successes, and setbacks should be referenced in the journal. Any feedback given, including notes or discussions of recognition or redirection, should be recorded in the log with copies of that feedback cross-referenced and saved in the file. The log also serves as a location to record evidence of the employee's and organization's commitment to development, such as training opportunities completed or offered or overtime worked or offered.

Using and regularly updating performance logs has many benefits. Doing so helps keep you more closely attuned to your staff, improving your ability to help them succeed in meeting goals and responsibilities. The logs provide a wealth of material for staff appraisal, greatly facilitating interim and annual performance meetings. They also help provide objectivity and support in the face of difficult staffing decisions that outdoor program administrators often face. Organized and consistent documentation also aids in protection in the event of a lawsuit.

## Formal Appraisal Meetings

In addition to sharing feedback on an ongoing basis, formal performance assessment meetings should also be scheduled with each employee. Minimally, formal performance assessments consist of one interim meeting and culminate with an annual appraisal meeting at the conclusion of the assessment cycle (DelPo, 2005). Usually, the assessment cycle is a year-long period, but the duration from goal setting to final assessment may be shorter to match duration of time that an employee is contracted. Interim meetings may be scheduled more often and at irregular intervals in harmony with the operation cycle of the program or responsibilities of the position. For instance, performance feedback might be exchanged with a field instructor in multiple interim sessions at the end of every expedition, with one annual formal performance assessment. An interim performance assessment of a seasonal equipment manager may be scheduled midway through the summer, with an annual meeting at the conclusion of the busy trip season. The outdoor program administrator best determines the frequency and timing of formal assessments with consideration of the program's cycle of operation and the employee's performance plan.

The performance and job satisfaction of new employees can be enhanced when an interim appraisal is conducted early after a period of initial work. This appraisal might be scheduled after the first month of employment, or after the first significant job assignment, or at the conclusion of a training period. Early performance appraisal provides an opportunity to establish rapport with employees and to help them buy into the program's philosophy and system of assessment. Early discussions of performance also help employees set goals for development and address potential concerns. Note that a discussion of performance assessment should also occur at significant transitions in employment—after a promotion or transfer into another area of the program, for example.

**Figure 15.6** Staff Member Performance Log

Staff member: _____ Position title: _____ Date hired: _____

Record the job-related significant events that take place during the employee's term of service. Provide objective details (not opinions) that build a narrative of the job related event and the follow-up actions of the supervisor. This can include positive and constructive feedback delivered in oral and written forms and either formal or informal in nature. Performance reviews and goal-setting sessions should be included. This record helps to provide documentation that when reviewed can provide insight to aid in the growth of the employee, guide disciplinary actions, and build rationale for the allocation of resources and interventions to enhance employee performance. Attach any supporting documentation with date of corresponding entry on the top right corner.

| Date | Event narrative (people, event, place, date, time, action taken) | Nature of action or follow-up | Source name |
|---|---|---|---|
| 4/26 | Kim is hired as a climbing staff member for the outdoor program for 2012-2013. | Employee file is created with documentation and performance log. Staff training dates are confirmed for the fall. | Sarah Stone, program director |
| 8/27-9/4 | During the staff-training week, Kim related positively with the returning staff and actively participated in the training activities. | Preservice training | Sarah Stone, program director |
| 9/21 | Today Kim volunteered to serve as an assistant leader for the afternoon bouldering trip to cover for a staff member that called in sick. I thanked Kim for her flexibility and dedication to the program. | Verbal acknowledgement of extra effort | Michael Rivers, supervisor |
| 10/20 | Kim arrived at 9:00 today, 30 minutes late for her shift at the climbing wall. My phone call woke her, and she arrived within 15 minutes. I spoke with her when she arrived. She reported that the electricity was out at her home, and she did not have an alarm. I spoke with her to remind her of the importance of arriving at work on time, if not early. | Oral reminder | Chris Sage, wall manager |
| 2/3 | Kim volunteered to stay late to work on the climbing routes for the upcoming competition. | Verbal and written acknowledgement | Chris Sage, wall manager |

## Interim Appraisal Meetings

The purpose of the interim meeting is to check progress toward job requirements and goals, and also to ascertain whether requirements and goals are appropriate and realistic or need to be adjusted. At this meeting, administrators can acknowledge discovered talents and identify opportunities for their use. This is also a time to identify and employ untapped resources that might help achieve the goals. Most of all, the interim appraisal meeting is an ideal time to encourage efforts and invest in the relationship with the employee.

## Year-End Appraisal Meetings

The year-end appraisal is the more formal of the appraisal meetings, marking the culmination of a year's worth of ongoing feedback and documentation. It is during this meeting that the written evaluation is used, ideally by both the administrator and the employee. The structure for the session may begin with an exchange of feedback focused on the written evaluation and on progress toward the individual performance plan. It is likely that disagreement will arise in the discussion. Open discussion of any disagreements and sharing rationale that led to each person's viewpoint can help correct any misconceptions, developing self-awareness. Another essential part of the year-end appraisal meeting is to develop an individual performance plan for the upcoming year. Together, you review job responsibilities and launch a new set of goals for performance, setting a new assessment cycle under way.

## Preparation for Appraisal Meetings

Be it an interim or year-end appraisal, the key to a successful meeting is preparation. An outdoor program administrator can prepare for appraisal meetings in several ways. Before drawing any conclusions on an assessment tool, the effective administrator assembles and reviews documentation relative to employee performance. When offering positive or constructive feedback, the administrator does so equipped with examples of what is being done right and what could be done better. He or she takes steps to conduct the meeting with confidentiality and to be certain that adequate time and undivided attention have been allotted for the meeting. Armed with ideas and resources for available training and development opportunities for the employee, the administrator can demonstrate a genuine interest in the employee's development. Most important, the administrator works throughout the assessment cycle on ongoing feedback and documentation and to create an environment conducive to assessment.

## SUMMARY

Assessing staff performance is an essential administrative function. An effective staff evaluation system fosters the health and growth of an organization. Staff performance is directly related to accomplishing larger goals, such as an organization's mission and program objectives. A quality evaluation process provides workers with a realistic view of their performance related to the expectations associated with their position. Employees that receive quality feedback tend to be more satisfied at work. Quality feedback promotes personal and professional growth, which is a major source of motivation and satisfaction.

One of the first agenda items an administrator must consider is the overall assessment environment. Is the overall environment conducive to an effective staff-assessment process? The administrator must assess to ensure the work environment is a functional community based on trust, respect, and open and honest communication. In addition, the process improves when it is future oriented and when respect for the employee is at the core. This fosters much deeper and more meaningful self-reflection. Using the SWOT analysis provides the means for carrying out meaningful self-reflection. Finally, administrators who incorporate multisourced feedback analyses ensure that employees receive realistic and meaningful feedback to help reinforce or clarify perceptions of self.

Another factor for ensuring an effective evaluation process focuses on developing sound evaluation criteria. Program goals, job descriptions, policy manuals, and professional standards all serve as sources to create sound evaluation criteria. Evaluation criteria are used to develop appropriate qualitative and quantitative assessment tools. In this chapter, checklists and rubrics are described as two suggested methods for outdoor program administrators to use to evaluate staff. But these tools are useless if administrators do not collect and document the data needed to accurately complete these tools. The ultimate goal of the administrator is to create an effective staff-assessment system. One of the first steps is to include the staff member in a goal-setting process. A portion of the assessment should be based on individual goals. Staff members with concrete goals tend to be more motivated and productive. Regular feedback, consistent appraisal meetings, and performance logs all serve as techniques to collect and document performance. Outdoor program administrators who do not use data-collection and documentation techniques and rely only on a year-end review tend to be ineffective. Administrators who create effective systems will ultimately maximize the benefits of a quality staff-assessment system.

# Facilities and Programs

# Chapter 16

# Rental Operations

*Rob Jones, MS*

Unlike a trip program, which uses a variety of locations for the delivery of services, a rental operation is conducted from a physical brick and mortar location. Rental operations are generally the central location for all of a program's business tasks and often include the following functions: administration, trip and activity planning, rental services, bike repair, trip registrations, trip logistics, and customer service via web, phone, and in person. Another common feature of a rental operation is that outdoor program administrators' offices are usually housed in the same physical space. A well-managed rental operation can serve as headquarters for the success of an organization's entire set of programs.

Though the largest component of an organization's total program offering, the rental operation's significance is often overlooked because it does not offer the glitz and glamour customers and staff associate with trip programs. Contrary to common perceptions, effectively managed rental center operations represent the backbone of an entire program. A comprehensive rental operation provides customers with access to outdoor recreational equipment that can be used for personal adventuring or activities facilitated by an outdoor program. Rental centers also attract new participants to trips programs, generate income for use throughout the outdoor program, and promote outdoor activities by providing quality equipment for use in trips and educational programs. In short, a rental operation should be seen as the foundation on which the rest of the program is built.

Interacting with customers, training staff, forecasting budgets, and promoting products and services all require an outdoor program administrator to be able to effectively use the four core skills sets—human, outdoor, education, and management—in one location. This chapter is broken into three sections to enhance the outdoor program administrator's ability to effectively operate and support the rental program. These three sections are planning, purchasing, and operations.

## PLANNING

An organization's vision and mission serve as the anchor for the development of goals and objectives for a rental operation. Who is served, how they are served, and at what level of compensation they will pay for products and services all need to be detailed in a rental operations plan developed by the organization. In general, most rental operations offered by university, municipal, and MWR programs are intended to function as a source point for revenue generation. Depending on the rental operations plan of the organization, these businesses might function on a subsidized, break-even, or profit-driven model. Regardless of the desired financial outcome, all rental operations should have a plan for operating developed specifically to meet the needs of the organization. A failure to plan and prepare often leads an organization financially astray. This section focuses on the steps an outdoor program administrator needs to take to expand an existing rental program or to begin a new rental operation.

## Performing a Needs Assessment for a Rental Operation

Whether you choose to survey the students, faculty, and staff at your institution; community members served by your organization; military and civilian personnel serving at your base; or professionals operating existing programs in the area, outdoor program administrators need to get good data from their customer base.

A customer-focused assessment is necessary to answer these questions:

- Is the market year-round or seasonal?
- What services would provide the greatest customer demand?
- How often will customers use the offered services?
- What type of equipment would get used most frequently?
- How much will customers pay for the offered services?

An internal needs assessment is necessary to answer these questions:

- What financial resources are available to be invested in the development of an equipment inventory?
- From what type of equipment can I expect to get the most return on investment?
- Can equipment used in the rental operation serve a dual function and be available to an organization for trips and outings?

Whether you are looking to add a new type of equipment to an existing program or start a rental operation from the ground up, these questions and others specific to an organization's needs must be answered as part of a needs assessment.

## Rental Operations Plan

If the needs assessment results support the development of a rental operation, then the outdoor program administrator can use the collected data to begin developing an operational plan to guide business development. The rental operations plan (ROP) should include the type of equipment to add, the pricing structure, the target rental constituencies, and the revenue expected to be generated over time from the equipment.

A common strategy for a new organization is to purchase equipment that can be used for multiple functions, including rental, instruction, and trips.

### AMERICANS WITH DISABILITIES ACT AND ACCESSIBILITY ISSUES

Outdoor programs should offer inclusive services to all members of their customer base. Many pieces of equipment are available directly from manufacturers with no modifications, but if you modify a piece of gear to make its use accessible, you may be placing your program at risk for product liability. So be sure to work with your organization's office of risk management and legal council before modifying any piece of equipment.

Outdoor recreation administrators should work with their organization's office of disability services or local disability resources to determine if there is a need for adapted equipment in the program. There might be other agencies within your community who provide accessible equipment and the staffing and personnel to assist customers in proper fitting and adjusting of this equipment. Equipment designed to be used by individuals with disabilities can be very expensive and often requires a great deal of training in proper use, maintenance, and fitting. The goal is to create an inclusive environment that attracts all people out to experience the places we love.

If camping and backpacking instructional and trip programs are intended to be offered, then the rental operation should include tents, sleeping bags, sleeping pads, backpacks, and stoves. Beyond basic equipment, there might be a demand for additional camping accessories such as lanterns, headlamps, coolers, cook kits, camp chairs, water-storage containers, water filters, and more. If there is a local climbing area in the region, there may be a customer need for rock shoes and helmets. Rental operations located in four-season climates might consider offering products such as winter sleeping bags, snowshoes, cross-country skis, and alpine equipment like snowboards and skis. All equipment purchased for a rental operation should reflect items identified by the needs assessment and supported by knowledge of local outdoor activities.

# Rental Center Budgeting

The budget format and process for a rental operation is defined by the organization supporting it. For example, a municipal parks and recreation program will likely use different processes and procedures for budgeting than those used by either a MWR or university program. Budget formats are as diverse as programs are. With this in mind, there are generalities that exist in some form or fashion in all programs. Thus the following sections will highlight common components and considerations for a rental operations budget. Although purchasing is covered briefly in this section, most of the material presented pertains more to the general operations of a rental program. Specific details about purchasing will come later in the chapter.

## Staff Planning

Personnel expenses reflect one of the greatest expenses of a rental operation, so the outdoor program administrator must accurately forecast costs related to staffing the rental operation.

An easy method for determining a staffing budget begins with calculating the total number of hours the program will be open during the fiscal year. Next, determine busy times and staff needs during those times. Calculate the total number of staff hours you will need. Next, multiply the number of staff hours times the average hourly rate of compensation, and you will have an estimate of your annual staff budget. You can hedge unknown needs by adding a predetermined percent to your base number. This allows for a program to increase its volume of staffing to meet unexpected demands on labor.

Another substantial expense is the cost of benefits for your employees. Benefits can cost as much as 50 percent of the base salary for full-time employees, so you must include the cost of all benefits as part of an accurate salary forecast.

## Determining Pricing Structure

Each piece of rental equipment has an expected lifespan that relates to the expected use and inherent durability of the product. This piece of data should be considered in the organization's ROP because it will help establish a timeline for equipment serviceability and disposal. If the ROP dictates that an organization operates on a four-year life cycle for equipment, then the pricing of the rental gear needs to ensure that the purchase price plus a preestablished rate of profit is gained by renting the equipment over the four-year period. Rental prices are influenced by the mission and goals of the organization. An example of a two-fold mission-driven rental formula would be that the program needs to both self-generate revenue and provide the lowest rental rates for the organization's predetermined customer base (military personnel and families, members of a municipality, members of a campus community, and so on) with rates potentially being increased for groups outside the primary base of service. Unfortunately, multipronged directives can be at conflict with each other. A rental operation may easily establish rates that allow it to pay the bills, but those rates may be too high for customers who desire to rent the equipment. Many rental operations create a variable rate structure that accommodates all user groups (core customer base and peripheral customers). Establishing variable rate structures requires more time and planning on the part of the outdoor program administrator, but it can create a system in which current core members of the institution's community receive the best possible prices and peripheral members can pay a bit more for the services provided. Thereby one user group partially subsidizes the costs of another.

The expected days and hours for operation directly influence the rental rate structure. If a program is open seven days a week, it might be reasonable to set a one-day rental rate and charge that rate for each day the equipment is out. If your program is open only Monday through Friday, a daily rate will not work for a customer who seeks to use equipment for just one weekend day. Many operations who do not have weekend hours elect to create a multi-tiered rate structure that allows for both a one-day rate and a two-to-three-day or weekend rate. For most programs, weekends are the period of predominant use, so establishing a weekend rate is common. Because most equipment rentals will go out on Friday and return on Monday, a weekend rate can be priced slightly less than two times the one-day rate. This discount is perceived as a good deal by customers and creates a net personnel savings for the operation if it elects not to be open on weekends. The proximity of recreation opportunities to the rental operation is also an influencing factor when developing pricing structures. To raft on the Payette River in Idaho, renters choosing to pick up a whitewater raft from Boise State University can reasonably pick up a raft, drive 45 minutes to the river, raft, and get the boat back in a one-day period. However, a customer using the MWR program in Mountain Home, Idaho, might not be able to pick up a raft, drive 120 minutes to the river, raft, and get the boat back in one day. Table 16.1 shows three pricing options for a sleeping bag rented by a customer for one to seven days.

Finally, it might be easier to count the number of days an item is out by actually counting the nights the equipment is away from the program. This way, if a customer wants to take an item on Monday and return it Thursday, it is out three nights and the standard 2-3 day or weekend rate can apply. Rental

price structures and the formulas by which they are applied are as varied and unique as programs are. Ultimately, the rates charged by a program should be mission driven and in alignment with the current operating plan.

## Assigning Depreciation Values

Equipment purchases are commonly viewed as a multiyear expense, with the equipment losing part of its initial value each year it is placed in service. Organizations need to determine a lifespan for each product they offer to customers to establish a rate of depreciation for each piece or equipment. Depreciation in this context reflects the value of each piece of equipment at a particular point during its lifespan. How an organization decides to depreciate equipment depends on how often it chooses to purchase new equipment. Equipment kept in the rental fleet until it is paid off and then sold does not allow the equipment to generate any profits. If equipment is purchased and remains in service past the break-even point, it will begin to return a net profit back to the organization as long as it remains serviceable and desirable to the client.

Depreciating at 25 percent per year is appropriate if a program does not have a mechanism to make revenue on the equipment nor intend to sell the equipment when retired. However, if equipment is intended to both generate rental revenue and be sold when it is retired, the administrator might elect to depreciate the equipment at a lesser percentage because rental revenue and the future sale of the equipment will offset the cost to replace the equipment. An example of a depreciation schedule for a piece of equipment with a four-year product lifespan

**Table 16.1** Three Pricing Structures of a Sleeping Bag Rented for Seven Days

| Sleeping bag | 1-day rate | 2- to 3-day rate | Additional day | 7-day rental |
|---|---|---|---|---|
| Option 1[a] | $4.00 | $6.00 | $1.00 | $13.00 |
| **Sleeping bag** | **1-day rate** | **+ 1-day rate** | **Additional day** | **7-day rental** |
| Option 2[b] | $7.00 | $2.00 | NA | $19.00 |
| **Sleeping bag** | **1-day rate** | **+ 1-day rate** | **Additional day** | **7-day rental** |
| Option 3[c] | $6.00 | NA | NA | $42.00 |

[a]Option 1 uses a discounted 2- to 3-day rate + a discounted additional day rate for days 4-7.

[b]Option 2 uses a day rate + a discounted daily rate for days 2-7.

[c]Option 3 uses only a day rate structure for days 1-7.

**Table 16.2** Depreciation Based on a Four-Year Lifespan[a]

| Item | Purchase price = replacement cost in year 1 | Replacement cost 2nd year of use | Replacement cost 3rd year of use | Replacement cost 4th year of use | Price of item when sold at the end of year 4 |
|---|---|---|---|---|---|
| Tent | $100.00 | $88.00 | $77.00 | $68.00 | $60.00 |

[a]Factored at a depreciation rate of 12% per year.

is shown in table 16.2. Using this system, if a tent is lost when it is three years old, the customer would be charged a replacement cost less than 36 percent for depreciation. Between the 64 percent of replacement cost collected and the income generated over the past three years of rentals, the program should have generated a positive net income for that item. When finally retired after the fourth year of use, the program would sell the equipment and use the proceeds to reinvest in new equipment.

For support items such as canoe paddles, PFDs, or sleeping pads, a program might choose not to depreciate these items because, unless they are damaged, the equipment will last for many years, generate minor income on an individual rental basis, and support the overall rental of another higher-priced item such as a canoe. In this case, if a customer loses a canoe paddle, the replacement cost charged would be the actual replacement cost.

## Sales Tax

State, county, and local governments will all influence the amount of sales tax that will need to be collected on each transaction. Most organizations have accounting personnel that will be able to help identify which items to collect sales tax on and at what rate. Depending on your state, you might be required to charge tax on a rental item, but not on a late fee or service, such as a ski wax. An error in the calculation of sales tax could represent a significant liability for a program, so ensure that the rate charged for each item is accurate.

## PURCHASING

Expending money from a budget that ultimately needs to generate revenue is not to be taken lightly. If an appropriate needs assessment, ROP, and pricing structure are in place, taking the next step to make purchases for the program should be fairly straightforward. However, many programs have limited annual budgets for purchasing equipment. Whether your program spends $3,000.00 or $50,000.00 per year on equipment, equipment purchasing must be a purposeful process because poor choices negatively affect future performance. Immediate expenditures need to maximize future revenue generation. Effective outdoor program administrators increase the purchasing power of their rental equipment budget by developing and maintaining relationships with vendors and manufacturers and by taking advantage of available purchasing terms and discounts.

## Manufacture Direct or Wholesale Purchasing

Whenever possible, outdoor recreation administrators should purchase directly from manufacturers or wholesale distributors rather than from local retailers. Purchasing directly from the manufacturer removes the middle man and saves your program money. Retail stores commonly mark up a product 30 to 50 percent above their purchase price from the manufacturer. Obviously, buying direct saves your program this 30 to 50 percent.

A proven purchasing strategy is to build and replace a fleet of equipment slowly over a four-year plan. This allows for annual buying and retiring of equipment. For example, build a fleet of tents by purchasing one-fourth of your fleet each year for four years. Then begin retiring the first tents purchased after four years of income generation. This purchasing strategy allows for a couple of things: first, you don't get hit with huge expenses to purchase or replace a full line of equipment at one time; second, you always have new equipment on hand to meet the needs of your customers. Employing this strategy also allows you to budget for a known expense each year and helps predict rental income growth and future purchasing needs as demand increases in lieu of large cash outlays for products before substantial demands exist.

To manage wear and tear on equipment, the outdoor recreation administrator must rotate equipment so that the last piece of equipment purchased is always the first piece of equipment sent out. Last in and first out (LIFO) is an effective means of distributing the use on a fleet of equipment so that the concentration of use is always on the newest equipment (see table 16.3).

Two things occur when a program employs a LIFO strategy to issue equipment: the rental customer always gets the newest equipment, and the highest concentration of use is applied to the newest equipment rather than to older products. This method helps distribute use on the equipment at a diminishing volume over the life of the product. By adhering to this philosophy, use is spread out uniformly across the entire fleet of equipment. Consciously balancing the wear and tear on rental equipment financially helps a program when it decides to retire and sell a four-year-old item. Items sold at a used equipment sale fetch a higher price because there is still plenty of life left in the product. The income from the sale is then returned to the program to reduce the investment associated with purchasing new equipment.

## Volume Purchases

Outdoor program administrators who adhere to their ROP will strategically time the purchase of items so that they can take advantage of discounts supplied by manufacturers for both volume and timing. For example, bulk equipment can be purchased in the fall for the next summer season. By ordering early, the outdoor program administrator can take advantage of possible end-of-season sales offered by distributors and manufacturers. The cost savings of ordering a large quantity of equipment early is significant. These savings can then be redirected toward other areas of need within the program.

A less conventional option is to see if there are other programs nearby and contact them to see what their plans and needs are for purchasing equipment. You can often increase the volume of your purchase if other programs in your area are also planning to purchase the same equipment. This requires coordination, flexibility, and preplanning, but it is worth a few phone calls to reap significant savings.

## Preseason Orders

An ROP can help an administrator plan ahead and take advantage of preseason purchasing discounts offered by manufacturers. Most manufacturers offer deep discounts for preseason purchases, and many also offer payment dating that allows for payment after the item has begun to generate revenue. For example, an outdoor recreation program might order ski equipment in February 2011. The equipment is shipped to the program in October 2011, but the payment for the equipment is not due until March 2012. Using this preseason order system, the program gets to accumulate a full winter of rental income before the bills are due. This type of buying system has significant advantages for program managers, but it necessitates that the rental manager plan ahead to ensure maximum savings (see table 16.4).

## In-Season Orders

Overproduction is a costly mistake for manufacturers because they will have more product than

**Table 16.3** LIFO Four-Year Equipment Rotation Schedule Maximizing Use on Newest Equipment

| Equipment type | Year purchased | 2nd year use | 3rd year use | 4th year use | Equipment to be sold |
|---|---|---|---|---|---|
| Snowboard | 2012 | 2013 | 2014 | 2015 | 2016 |
| Snowboard | 2013 | 2014 | 2015 | 2016 | 2017 |
| Snowboard | 2014 | 2015 | 2016 | 2017 | 2018 |
| Snowboard | 2015 | 2016 | 2017 | 2018 | 2019 |
| Snowboard | 2016 | 2017 | 2018 | 2019 | 2020 |

**Table 16.4**  Example of Preseason and Volume Purchasing Discounts

| Item | Retail | Wholesale quantity 1-4[a] | Wholesale quantity 5-9[b] | Wholesale quantity 10+[c] | Preseason discount[d] |
|---|---|---|---|---|---|
| 2-P Inflatable kayak | $1400.00 | $1120.00 | $1077.00 | $1037.00 | $943.00 |
| PFD | $85.00 | $68.00 | $65.00 | $63.00 | $57.00 |

Note: Quantity discount varies based on units. Terms = net/60.

[a]1-4 = 25% off manufacturer's suggested retail.

[b] 5-9 = 30% off manufacturer's suggested retail.

[c] 10 + = 35% off manufacturer's suggested retail.

[d]Preseason discount = 10% off of 10+ pricing. Terms = net/180.

buyers. To protect themselves, manufacturers will use preseason orders to judge how much equipment they will need to make for a particular season. Beyond the volume of preseason orders, a manufacturer might elect to produce a small percentage of product over the amount of preseason orders to accommodate vendors that need to make additional in-season orders. As such, many manufacturers will have a small volume of products available to purchase throughout the season. However, the cost of in-season items is higher than if you purchase preseason or postseason through equipment closeouts. Try to limit in-season purchases, if possible, because the lack of equipment availability and the additional cost associated with the order reduces cash flow that can be directed toward other areas of the program.

## Postseason Closeout Purchases

Regularly check with your vendors to see what items are available through closeout deals. For summer equipment, the closeout period is usually fall or early winter. For winter equipment, the closeout period is typically early spring. Each vendor has different needs when it comes to clearing items from their warehouse, so contact vendors early to learn the details of their closeout plans. Often manufacturers make closeout deals available exclusively to members of associations such as AORE, AEE, WEA, and AMGA. The membership benefits such as having access to exclusive closeout deals often outweighs the cost of the membership in an association or trade organization.

Purchasing equipment through closeout sales can save money, but it does have drawbacks. One

drawback is that you might not have access to the same item your program currently uses. As you can imagine, it is easier to maintain a fleet of cars from the same manufacturer rather than to have a mixed vehicle fleet. Maintenance practices and parts vary on a mixed fleet. Thus it is beneficial to keep, for example, all your tents the same. However, the tent you use might not be available through closeout. Another potential problem is that you might need repair items for a specific type of tent that is no longer available once the product is no longer produced by the manufacturer.

## Requests for Bids

Most government entities such as universities, parks, and recreation programs and military MWR (morale, welfare, and recreation) programs require bids to be gathered from multiple vendors for large purchases. The rules for bidding processes vary, but many of the general principles are similar enough to provide common lessons.

Once you have identified the need to make a purchase that exceeds the predetermined purchasing limit of your institution, you need to identify a number of manufacturers who make the equipment needed to purchase. To ensure competitive bidding, be sure to develop general specifications for the equipment you plan to purchase. Outline your needs, paying particular attention to durability issues, size and weight requirements, and intended use of the equipment. The specification step is a crucial piece of the bidding process, so it is critical that you work with your purchasing office before beginning the process. During this step in the bidding process, remember that you might be the only professional in your organization with prior tangible experience with the type, quality, and usability of the equipment that you desire. Often you can make this process easier by meeting in person with your purchasing officer to review your equipment specifications, providing the purchasing office with wholesale price lists and catalogs from the various vendors you have identified. The time spent upfront with a purchasing officer helps to ensure that in the end you receive the equipment that you want rather than an inferior product.

Some institutions allow you as the expert in the department to place an order with a specific vendor even if their prices are above what could be found by another provider. This is often called sole-source or single-source purchasing. Sole-source purchasing can occur if there are overriding factors such as compatibility with existing equipment, higher durability, better warranties, or existing training and repair knowledge that will need to be relearned if a new vendor began to supply the equipment.

## Managing Equipment Provider Relationships

As in all relationships, honesty and open communication can lead to successful long-term alliances. It is the job of the outdoor program administrator to nurture and maintain each vendor relationship. The amount of time spent maintaining a relationship will often be based on the volume of equipment purchased, the length of your relationship with them, and frequency of prior communication. Relationships with vendors should be guarded because they equate to the purchasing power of an organization. If a relationship sours, it might cost your organization more to purchase from another vendor. Thus many organizations elect to limit the number of people who serve as contacts with vendors. These individuals will place orders, request information, deal with warranty issues, and so on. The familiarity with the organization and equipment possessed by these individuals helps to ensure a manufacturer that the equipment being purchased will be used in the rental center or in the trips and outings program and not made available to club members looking to save money by purchasing wholesale instead of buying their equipment from retail shops.

## Retail Purchasing

This option should be reserved only for those items that you absolutely must have right now, and in quantities small enough that your budget can withstand the higher price. Retail purchases generally cost an organization 30 to 50 percent more than ordering direct. With proper planning, these types of purchases are rare, and usually constitute small repair items or replacement items that cannot be lived without until an order can be filled by a manufacturer or distributor.

An example of a small retail purchase is the need to replace a bike helmet lost by a customer that is needed immediately for a bike rental reservation that has already been made. If it costs the program $30 to purchase a helmet at the local retail shop, but the rental income generated for the bike rental is $50, it is well worth the cost of the helmet at the retail level. The additional cost of purchasing the helmet at retail will be recouped in the long term by providing quality service to the next customer who has prepaid the bike's rental fee.

# RENTAL CENTER OPERATIONS

Once equipment has been purchased and is on the shelves, it becomes time to serve customers. Rental operations are generally seasonal in nature, with boom and bust cycles based on what the weather is doing on any particular weekend. A year of poor snowfall and warm temperatures will affect winter rental sales, and a big water year might scare people away from renting rafts. Although in any given year weather might affect revenue performance, outdoor program administrators need to develop an operating plan that addresses methods for staffing, training, inventory management, equipment maintenance, depreciation, and replacement.

## Staffing a Rental Operation

All rental operations, regardless of location and organizational structure, have in common the need to provide a knowledgeable, courteous, and approachable staff—they are the gate keepers to a positive customer experience. Providing quality

Geoff Harrison

Outdoor program staff participate in a vendor-sponsored mountain bike clinic to learn how to use the equipment.

equipment and accurate information will help the customer have a good trip, learn new skills, and gain an appreciation for the activity. This will encourage them to return and rent the same equipment again or try other equipment and activities. Providing the best customer service possible is the goal of each interaction.

The staffing requirements of each rental operation depend on the regional accessibility of the outdoor environments in which people want to get out into. If you have a local ski hill nearby, customers might want to get out for a half-day ski after a midweek class or for a postwork miniadventure. However, if getting out to play means a weekend at a minimum, you might not need a large staff on Tuesdays, Wednesdays, or Thursdays, but you will certainly need to have staff on hand on Fridays to check out the equipment and on Mondays to check it back in. Tuesdays, Wednesdays, and Thursdays could then be used as cleaning and maintenance days, along with getting equipment ready for the upcoming weekend.

## Staff Training

Each program has its own requirements for employees. Some programs require staff who can work in multiple areas of the business unit. In a multiuse facility on a military base or at a municipal recreation center, this may require staff who are competent to rent and maintain equipment, staff the front desk of the recreation center, lead an educational outing, and reset a treadmill that has had an electronic glitch. Regardless of the extent of the duties required, making certain that the staff know how each piece of equipment works is essential to a successful rental operation.

Staff trainings should focus on human, educational, and outdoor skill sets to ensure that staff are capable of seamlessly moving from an equipment maintenance function to interacting effectively with coworkers to educating a customer on how to use a particular piece of equipment. Customers often have a desire to try a new activity, and a properly trained staff member can help select the right equipment, make sure it fits correctly, and explain the proper use of and care for the equipment. Armed with proper knowledge, a well-trained staff member helps to ensure the customer has a good experience. Ultimately, a good experience means the customer is more likely to be a return user and that the equipment is returned in a condition that allows for a quick turnaround for the next user.

Perhaps the best type of training for many of your student staff is found on the job. Staff can learn how equipment is set up, checked in and out, and repaired by working closely with a current senior staff member. Get your students out on field days to learn how to use equipment through hands-on practice in the field. Staff members should be encouraged to try on equipment such as ski boots or backpacks so they know how it fits and how heavy it is. The best possible training for a student is to have experience using the equipment. They can speak to customers with firsthand knowledge and know how to present information a user needs to have a successful trip.

## Certifications

With the exception of downhill or alpine ski binding settings and adjustments there are no other current certifications required to rent human-powered outdoor equipment. However, if your program rents skis and snowboards, you might want to have employees attend a ski maintenance workshop. Often sponsored by the local ski resorts, these workshops range in topics from basic tuning to advanced base and edge repairs. If your program rents bicycles, you might have employees attend a basic or advanced bike maintenance workshop and receive a certificate of completion. Both ski and bike workshops can easily be found through an Internet search for "bike maintenance workshop" or "ski and snowboard maintenance workshop." The cost for the workshops can be paid either by the program as staff development or out of pocket by the employee. Either way, having the knowledge to maintain and repair these high-end rental items can support the overall mission of your program and provide a high-quality experience for the customer.

## Staff Compensation

The hourly rate an employee receives for working in the rental operation might be just the beginning of their compensation package. Many programs offer employees discounted equipment purchasing through their suppliers. These "pro-deals" allow employees to purchase equipment at deeply discounted prices, and enables them to gain experience using the same equipment in the rental program. Manufacturers often protect their retail clients by strictly controlling who has access to these deals, and it is incumbent on the outdoor program administrator to ensure the manufacturer's rules are followed. Sometimes these deals are also available to members of associations, such as the Association of Outdoor Recreation and Education (AORE).

Employee use of rental equipment is a common industry practice. Many outdoor program administrators offer this benefit to employees because they feel that familiarity with the equipment helps staff serve customers more effectively. Each program needs to establish policies and procedures that define the terms and conditions for employee use of program equipment to ensure that equipment is available on the shelves for customers and not abused by staff.

## Rental Center Inventory Management

Maintaining accurate inventory records is vitally important to the overall success of a rental operation. Because most programs' budgets don't allow for special equipment designated for "trip use only," the same equipment used by trips programs is often rented to the general student population to generate the income to run the overall program. Equipment used for a variety of programs (rentals, trips, and training) runs the risk of being already booked, misplaced, damaged, or inadvertently taken by participants or staff. Proper inventory management helps keep equipment in stock, repaired, and ready to rent to customers.

One of the easiest ways to begin an inventory-management system is to create a spreadsheet for each type of equipment in inventory as the equipment is received. A typical spreadsheet includes an inventory number and description, including size, purchase cost, and date of purchase. This method of inventory management can be easily added to as additional items are purchased. By keeping items listed in inventory by purchase date, an outdoor program administrator knows which equipment to retire at the end of its prescribed life cycle.

Keeping track of equipment throughout its season of use is easy if storage shelves are designed so that each item has its own space complete with an ID label. To inventory a rack of tents, for example, all you have to do is look at the rack and see which spaces are empty. Cross-check the empty spaces with the equipment that is checked out, and you have easily accounted for those items. This type of shelving system works well with items such as tents, ski or snowboard boots, river bags, and more (see figure 16.1).

Some equipment comes from the manufacturer with a built-in inventory number. For skis or snowboards, an easy inventory system is to use the size and the last four digits of the serial number to identify the item. For a 165-cm ski with a serial number of 07-23M-6598, the simple inventory code is 165-6598. This number is cross referenced on the inventory spread sheet with the full serial number, but when the ski is checked out only the 165-6598 need be noted on the rental contract (see table 16.5).

Although keeping track of all equipment is ultimately the outdoor program administrator's responsibility, it might not make sense to create an inventory number for each and every item in stock, such as individual canoe paddles or foam sleeping pads. For example, a program might have 400 canoe paddles, and it might not be necessary to know exactly which 3 paddles were given to which

**Figure 16.1**  Example of ski and boot storage.

customer as long as all 3 checked out are checked back in. Items like this are regularly lost by customers, so just be sure to do an inventory preseason, midseason, and post season to see where you stand and how many need to be replaced.

**Table 16.5**  Example of Ski Inventory

| Outdoor recreation inventory | | Telemark skis | | October 10 | |
|---|---|---|---|---|---|
| Description | Serial number | Cost | Purchased | ID number | Size |
| Rossignol Powderbird | 160-6-198205 | $325.00 | Nov. 2007 | 160-8205 | 160 cm |
| Rossignol Powderbird | 160-6-198240 | $325.00 | Nov. 2007 | 160-8240 | 160 cm |
| Rossignol Powderbird | 160-6-198370 | $360.00 | Nov. 2008 | 160-8370 | 160 cm |
| Rossignol Powderbird | 168-6-145564 | $325.00 | Nov. 2007 | 168-5564 | 168 cm |
| Rossignol Powderbird | 168-6-145169 | $360.00 | Nov. 2008 | 168-5169 | 168 cm |

*(continued)*

**Table 16.5**   *(continued)*

| Outdoor recreation inventory | | Telemark skis | | October 10 | |
| --- | --- | --- | --- | --- | --- |
| Description | Serial number | Cost | Purchased | ID number | Size |
| Rossignol Powderbird | 168-6-148368 | $360.00 | Nov. 2008 | 168-8368 | 168 cm |
| Rossignol Powderbird | 176-6-143342 | $325.00 | Nov. 2007 | 176-3342 | 176 cm |
| Rossignol Powderbird | 176-6-149152 | $325.00 | Nov. 2007 | 176-9152 | 176 cm |
| Rossignol Powderbird | 176-267827 | $360.00 | Nov. 2008 | 176-7827 | 176 cm |
| Rossignol Powderbird | 176-267827 | $360.00 | Nov. 2008 | 176-7831 | 176 cm |
| Rossignol Powderbird | 181-198131 | $325.00 | Nov. 2007 | 181-8131 | 181 cm |
| Rossignol Powderbird | 181-198142 | $360.00 | Nov. 2008 | 181-8142 | 181 cm |
| Rossignol Powderbird | 181-198143 | $360.00 | Nov. 2008 | 181-8143 | 181 cm |

Inventory management is a critical function of a rental operation because each misplaced piece of equipment represents an expense to the organization. Formal inventories should be done regularly to supplement daily inspections done by rental operations staff.

## Technology in Rental Programs

A good rental system should be able to assist with inventory tracking, maintain a customer database, and keep track of revenue and expenses associated with the operation of the program. Collecting revenue data by day, month, and year allows outdoor program administrators to spot trends in use patterns and to determine easily when particular items are paid for and how much profit they are generating (see table 16.6). It is also important to collect data on the number of customers served each day because this allows administrators to spot trends in user demands and to staff.

Although there are currently no complete "do everything" computer-rental systems available, there are products and systems available such as RentMaster, a stand-alone rental system, or CSI and RecTrac, which have rental modules as part of the overall facility management software. Because each rental operation has different accounting, inventory management, and equipment issuance needs, it can be difficult to use an out-of-the-box application that cannot be customized. Some programs have written their own rental software using common applications like Microsoft Access or Excel. This approach allows for customization but requires administrators to have excellent technology knowledge and skills. Although these systems can work, the limitation is that precautions must be taken to ensure continued support after those who wrote the program are no longer working with the institution. Because programs like RentMaster are relatively new, many programs rely on paper rental contracts and spreadsheet systems to perform these basic functions. Unfortunately, paper rental contracts don't allow for a customer database without an employee manually entering information into some stand-alone database software.

## Rental Agreements and Policies

The gathering of accurate customer information and the documentation of expected equipment use are critical risk-management steps that must be part

**Table 16.6** Revenue Data for Two-Week Time Period

| Date | Rafts | Duckies | Kayaks | Canoes | Wetsuit | Dry bags | PFDs |
|---|---|---|---|---|---|---|---|
| Jul 10 | | | | | | | |
| 15th | | | | | | | |
| 16th | $ 105.00 | $ 397.00 | | $ 60.00 | | | $ 48.00 |
| 17th | $ 200.00 | $ 118.00 | $ 14.43 | | | | $ 180.00 |
| 18th | $ 510.73 | $ 92.00 | $ 34.00 | | | $ 6.00 | $ 96.00 |
| 19th | $ 179.61 | | | $ 60.00 | | | |
| 20th | $ 165.00 | $ 108.00 | $ 40.00 | $ 30.00 | | | $ 12.00 |
| 21st | | | | | | | |
| 22nd | | | | | | | |
| 23rd | $ 100.00 | $ 100.00 | | $ 255.00 | $ 48.00 | | |
| 24th | | | | | | | |
| 25th | $ 620.00 | $ 542.00 | $ 40.00 | $ 70.00 | $ 18.00 | $ 11.50 | $ 80.00 |
| 26th | $ 570.00 | $ 92.00 | | | | | $ 16.00 |
| 27th | $ 300.00 | $ 164.00 | $ 120.00 | | $ 22.00 | | |
| 28th | | | | | | | |
| 29th | | | | | | | |
| 30th | $ 430.00 | $ 69.00 | $ 120.00 | $ 150.00 | | | |
| 31st | | $ 770.00 | $ 40.00 | | | | $ 6.00 |
| **Period total** | | | | | | | |
| 2010 | $3,180.34 | $ 2,452.00 | $ 408.43 | $ 625.00 | $ 88.00 | $ 17.50 | $438.00 |

of every rental transaction. All rental agreements should include customer contact information such as ID number, address, phone numbers and e-mail address, pick-up and return dates, a list of specific items rented, a late-return clause, a release clause, a damage or loss clause, a theft clause, and a waiver of product liability. Because this document is a legal document, it should be written with the assistance and support of your organization's office of legal counsel.

When customers rent equipment they are responsible for returning it on time and in a condition so it is ready to go out to another user. Sometimes this does not occur, so it is necessary for the outdoor program administrators to have policies in place to deal with late, lost, damaged, or dirty equipment.

## Late Policies

Similar to an airport rental car service, customers of rental operations make reservations for equipment

with the expectation that it will be available when they need it. Like a traveler who finds out that they don't have a car because it was not returned on time, a customer trying to pick up rental equipment that is not there might experience a ruined vacation. Rental contracts must stipulate the responsibilities of the customer and the liability of the organization. Late fees are commonly applied to customer accounts for equipment not returned on time. Depending on the organization, these fees can range from a predetermined percentage to an hourly rate to a full-day charge with penalties. The outdoor program administrator must train staff to be consistent in charging these fees because they generate income for the program, and it is not fair that one customer is charged a late fee and another is not.

## Damage or Cleaning Policies

When a customer returns a piece of equipment, it needs to be in a condition that will allow it to be rented to the next customer. A program might ask customers returning a dirty piece of equipment to clean it so that it is ready for the next customer. It is fairly easy, for example, to hand someone a roll of paper towels and some cleaning supplies to clean a dirty camp stove. This allows the customer to take responsibility for cleaning up his own mess and ensuring the equipment is ready to go for the next user. Sometimes it is necessary to charge a fee for equipment returned dirty or in nonrentable condition. Administrators can set these fees based on the process required to return the item to a rentable condition. If you have an in-house washer and dryer, a $5 fee for a dirty sleeping bag might be adequate. However, if you have to drive into town to use a commercial washer at a laundry mat, a $15 or higher fee might be required to offset the time and labor it took to get the equipment back to a rentable state. Programs need to have adequate space to hang wet tents or sleeping bags to dry before they are put away. Storing equipment dry will prevent mold and mildew from permanently damaging the equipment. Space allocations vary greatly from program to program, which can make performing proper maintenance, cleaning, and storage space of equipment a bit problematic. Rental or purchase of stand-alone metal storage containers is an inexpensive option when compared with the cost of constructing a new storage space.

For items that are easily damaged or lost—tent stakes, lantern globes, canoe paddles—administrators can create a price menu. Make sure the charge to the customer covers the cost of replacing the item (including purchase, shipping, and administrative time), and have replacement or repair parts on hand so that the equipment can be repaired and ready for the next customer. It is impossible to generate revenue from a tent that can't be rented because a pole is broken or if there are not enough stakes to include in the rental.

Occasionally it is up to the administrator to decide if damage to an item is normal wear and tear or abuse. For example, a tent zipper slider will eventually wear out and fail, and customers should not be charged for this repair. But if a customer sets the tent up near a campfire and returns it with 15 small burn holes on the rain fly, he is obligated to pay for at least the depreciation of the equipment and the time and materials needed to repair the rain fly. Some organizations would require him to pay the entire cost of the tent.

## Check-Out and Check-In Policies

Outdoor program administrators must train staff to be thorough in both the check-out and check-in process of rental equipment. By completing a thorough check-out of equipment with the customer, staff gives the customer the opportunity to see that the equipment is in good working condition and to learn how to set it up and properly use it. For instance, staff should demonstrate how to set up a tent or prime or to light a stove or lantern. With inflatable boats, the boat should be inflated for the customer to inspect before deflating it again and loading it into the car. This allows the customer to see that the boat indeed holds air.

Upon return, the staff member should thoroughly inspect the equipment for any problems. For example, they should open tents and inspect poles, stakes, fly, and tent body in the presence of the customer who is returning it. They should check all zipper sliders and guy out lines to make sure they are in place and fully functional. Any programs renting inflatable boats should require customers to inflate the boats on check-in and to display support equipment included with the rental. This process allows all equipment to be inspected.

If these check-out and check-in policies are written and agreed on as part of the rental process, most customers are more than willing to do their part to help go over the equipment on both check-out and check-in.

## Equipment Repair, Maintenance, and Replacement

Whenever possible, equipment repair should be performed in house to minimize expense and reduce the amount of time the equipment is out of service. Offsite repairs often prove to be a disservice to all parties involved because of the excessive time and cost associated. Everyone suffers when a tent is sent back to the manufacturer for a broken pole when it could easily be repaired by the program staff and sent right back out with the next customer. To this end, programs should maintain a good selection of repair

Geoff Harrison

Staff regularly maintain equipment to ensure that it is ready to go for the next rental customer.

parts and equipment. Spare buckles, lantern globes, mantles or bulbs, stove parts, raft valves, and patching materials should all be kept in stock. A supply of nylon repair tape and adhesives for outdoor fabrics allow for in-house patches on tents or sleeping bags. When a program purchases a new line of tents, it is wise to budget in and purchase one complete pole set for each model of tent purchased. This way when a pole breaks, a replacement can be pulled from spare inventory; damaged poles can be used for replacement parts as further repairs are needed.

If your program rents alpine ski equipment, it is important to clean, inspect, and maintain the skis so that they will pass the safety test required by the equipment manufacturer. Most alpine bindings are indemnified by the manufacturer only if the shop is performing, and documenting, required maintenance and testing.

Programs might find that they must use chemical solvents such as ski base cleaners or adhesive removers for some equipment repairs. If your program is using these materials, it is imperative that all Environmental Protection Agency (EPA) guidelines on storage, use, ventilation, and document management are followed. Often these chemicals are necessary for maintaining equipment, so the administrator is responsible for providing proper training and safety equipment to protect staff and the environment. When possible, nontoxic alterna-

tives should be used. Last, administrators must plan to replace equipment while there is still enough life left to generate good revenue at a used equipment sale or gear swap.

## Retiring Equipment

One of the most effective ways to retire equipment is to hold a used equipment sale or gear swap at least once a year. These events draw people to your program, generate traffic and income, and allow you to show off the other services you offer to people who might stop by only for the sale. It is important to retire equipment while it still has a high perceived value. Try to set the sales price at or near the projected depreciation value. This will vary from product to product, but take into consideration how old the equipment is and how much life is left. The final sales price combined with the multiyear rental revenue the equipment has generated should be adequate to replace the equipment.

Some institutions might require that used equipment be retired through the "surplus or salvage" office. This can be problematic because the surplus staff will not know the history or use information for the outdoor equipment to be sold. Whenever possible, outdoor program administrators should find a way to hold the sales themselves. When a customer has questions about equipment being sold, the outdoor program staff are best qualified to answer the questions and are more likely to ensure the equipment is sold at a fair price. It is, then, in the best interest of the outdoor program for the administrator to meet with those responsible for surplus sales to design a way for the program to host a self-managed used equipment sale. If required, once the sale is over, the outdoor program could transfer a small portion of the revenue and the retirement paperwork to the surplus office. This way, the surplus office can properly account for the program assets and generate some revenue to help cover expenses without having to display, store, and sell the equipment.

If your facility has space to support a large equipment sale, the community might be encouraged to be part of a community gear swap in which customers bring items to be sold on consignment. Your organization could charge a fee to display the equipment for sale by the customer. This fee could be a flat $2 to $5 per item or a percentage of the sale amount. These events draw larger crowds to your program, increase the amount of equipment available, allow customers to retire their equipment as they upgrade to newer items, and provide increased revenue for your program.

# Special Program Operational Concerns

Most outdoor programs are nested within a larger organization such as a municipality, university, or military base. Policies and procedures are often developed by the parent organization that are intended to serve the broader needs of the organization and at times might not seem reasonable for some preferred practices of an outdoor program administrator. Similarly, on a larger scale, an outdoor program might be bound to operate under regulations established by a state or federal entity. Administrators must stay abreast of changing regulations, policies, and procedures to ensure their program is operating in compliance with organizational protocol. In the following section we highlight a few nuances of rental operations that do not fit cleanly into previous sections of this chapter.

## Livery Operations

Many states require programs that rent boats to conform with state regulations pertaining to livery operations. Such regulations might include clearly marking equipment with the program name, providing specific safety equipment or documentation, or paying a registration fee for each boat. Before any program begins the process of renting boats, it is wise for the outdoor program administrator to contact the state office to see what is required to initiate such a program. The state agency that manages boat livery operations is often within the state parks or wildlife management office.

## Equipment Storage Options

The type of storage systems used by any given program is determined by its unique operational needs. Factors include amount and type of equipment, floor space available within the shop, budget limitations, and so on. Similar to other industries, equipment must be stored in a manner that makes it both accessible and protected from damage. An example of an accessible and protected storage system for sleeping bags is to hang the bags from a rack rather than storing them on a shelf. A hanging system makes it easy to identify available equipment and protects the bags from losing their insulating properties. Shelving and mobile carts serve as effective storage locations for items such as tents, helmets, and ski boots. To adequately store all rental equipment in an accessible and protected manner, many programs elect to use wheeled carts so that seasonal equipment can easily be moved out of storage as needed.

## Resource Library and Centers

Many programs benefit from dedicating a small space for helping customers plan their own trips and activities. Resource libraries and trip-planning centers can help immeasurably in building a sense of community within your outdoor program. All that is really needed is a bookcase, a file cabinet, and a small table with chairs. Have regional or popular guidebooks and maps available for customers to use in their planning. It is not necessary to check out books or maps, as they often are damaged being stuffed into a pack. One alternative is to allow customers to photocopy select pages for a small fee. Another means of providing a service and generating some revenue is to have a dedicated computer loaded with map software and a color printer with easy access. This allows the ability to print and sell maps to customers. The computer allows customers to check weather reports, avalanche conditions, or river flows. Finally, have how-to or introductory DVDs for rent. If someone gets excited about a kayaking video, they might want to take a class and eventually rent a kayak. Resource libraries and trip-planning centers often serve as loss-leaders that help generate revenue in other areas of your program.

## Retail Outlets

Many programs are in a position to generate additional revenue by maintaining a small retail section. Items for sale might include sunblock, insect repellent, water bottles, mugs, utensils, goggles, gloves, and hats. Prices are set to make enough profit to maintain the retail service. Do not try to compete with local outdoor shops, because many states prohibit public institutions from competing with local small businesses. You should carry only items that a participant is likely to forget and need. By referring customers to local shops when they need supplies, you build good relations with the shops and provide a service to your customers.

Private institutions might not have the prohibitions against competing with local businesses. In this situation, building a comprehensive retail operation can help generate income for the program, but this comes with many other headaches, including the need to spend somewhat limited resources on purchasing stock for resale and not having the resources you need to run the rental and trips program if too much money is tied up in unsold retail items. Administrators at small programs should think long and hard about establishing a retail shop. It might be better to negotiate with a local shop to provide a small discount to participants in your program rather than building the retail program in your facility.

## Risk Issues

According to some recreational lawyers, programs do themselves a major disservice by putting themselves in the position of evaluating a customer's skill level when deciding to rent equipment. If a shop determines one customer is skilled enough to rent a kayak but another is not, and the renter or someone in their party is injured, the program might find itself liable because it determined the individual was competent to use the equipment. A better process is to make any equipment available to whoever wants to rent it, provide copies of manufacturer's instructions, and get signatures on *all* rental

Bike shop retail operations help support educational programs and services.

Geoff Harrison

and release forms required by your organization. If customers understand that they are choosing to rent the equipment, and that they alone are responsible for the skill and knowledge necessary to safely use the equipment, there is little difference in renting a pair of snowshoes or renting an avalanche beacon.

For some equipment, such as boats and bikes, it is a good idea to provide safety equipment as part of a rental package rather than offering the safety equipment as an add-on at an extra cost. For example, programs should include a helmet with a bike package or a PFD with a canoe, at no additional charge. This way a customer won't decline to take the safety items because they cost extra.

For electronic items such as avalanche beacons and caving headlamps, there are two schools of thought regarding batteries to power the items. One school of thought recommends that you include batteries and make sure that they are either new or have 80 percent or more power at the time of check-out. The other recommends that programs provide batteries for the test of the item at check-out but require customers to provide their own batteries for using the product. There are pros and cons to each of these methods. The first allows the customer to leave the shop ready to go but might increase the liability on the shop. The second could limit the liability of the shop but requires the customer to purchase batteries they may not use again. In any case, when renting such items it is a good idea to include a copy of the manufacturer's instructions and to strongly suggest that customers read the instructions and practice with the equipment in a safe place before going out into the field.

For some equipment it is important to have rental agreements to cover liability issues. For example, alpine ski bindings are usually indemnified by the manufacturer provided the rental agency follows procedures set forth in a manufacturer's agreement. Such agreements might require certification of staff in proper adjusting procedures along with certain maintenance and testing of equipment throughout the season of use. Often these agreements also require that a program keep thorough records on maintenance and testing. Although these steps are time consuming and require an investment in testing equipment and maintenance, the income generated can be significant for many programs.

## SUMMARY

A well-organized and properly managed rental operation provides an outdoor program with resources to help meet the recreational or educational goals of the program. The rental component can generate interest and income, provide equipment to enhance educational or recreational trips, and draw new customers to your organization.

Employees of a rental operation have the opportunity to actively develop their human, educational, and outdoor skills. These skills include the ability to provide outstanding customer service, organize equipment, and use expanded knowledge about maintenance and repair of program equipment. These skills readily transfer to other vocational opportunities. In short, a rental center is a vital, integral component of most outdoor recreation programs.

# Chapter 17

# Indoor Climbing Walls

*John Bicknell, MA, and Guy deBrun, MS*

Indoor climbing walls have become a standard offering in many outdoor programs. A broad spectrum of organizations, including YMCAs, municipal park and recreation programs, camps, primary and secondary schools, universities, private businesses, and the military all manage indoor climbing walls, and over four million people a year in the United States climb on them (Outdoor Foundation, 2010). For many, if not most, climbers today, their first introduction to climbing as a sport is on an indoor wall, and many climb only indoors. Because of the modern proliferation of indoor climbing walls, the management of indoor climbing walls increasingly has been added to the job descriptions for many outdoor recreation professionals, and artificial walls provide a superb medium for teaching the essentials of climbing. In this chapter we will introduce the fundamentals of climbing wall operations and management, dealing in particular with risk management. Stiehl and Ramsey's *Climbing Walls* (2005) looks at climbing wall management in depth and is a good general reference.

## HISTORY OF ARTIFICIAL CLIMBING WALLS

The first climbing wall built in the twentieth-century included iron rungs for holds and was located in Milan in the 1920s (Thomas, 1988). The first climbing wall in the United States was Schurman Rock, which was built in 1939 by the Works Project Administration for the William G. Long Camp near Seattle, Washington (Smutek, 1974). This wall was constructed of natural stone. The sport of indoor rock climbing as we know it had its genesis at Leeds University in 1964. The wall there was built by Don Robinson, a lecturer in the physical education department. The University of Washington, Evergreen State College, and Hampshire College installed artificial climbing walls in the early 1970s. In 1987, Vertical World in Seattle became America's first commercial indoor climbing gym. Note that all these early walls were built in cool and rainy climates. The original purpose of climbing walls was to provide training and diversion for climbers through the winter off-season, when rock climbing outdoors was impractical or unpleasant.

Today there are more than 10,000 private and public artificial climbing walls in North America. Exact numbers are impossible to obtain, so this estimate was derived from contacting four of the leading manufacturers (who together have built more than 7,000 walls) and making a conservative extrapolation (personal communications with leading manufacturers Entre Prises, Nicros, Rockwerx, and Eldorado Wall Company, 2008). From 2006 to 2010, the number of Americans aged six years and older who have participated in sport climbing, indoor climbing, or bouldering has hovered steadily in the mid to high 400,000s (Outdoor Foundation, 2011). Although this statistic does not isolate indoor climbing participation, anecdotal evidence suggests that a very high percentage of these climbers use artificial climbing walls. Specialized public and private climbing gyms remain popular, but manufacturers are increasingly building walls for cruise ships, amusement parks, swimming pools, and a host of other markets. Artificial climbing walls now serve many purposes, ranging from climbing training to fitness, competition, entertainment, and amusement. Climbing walls are perhaps a one-time adventure for those visiting amusement parks, another ride to experience. The majority of climbing gym members likely see climbing gyms primarily as alternative health clubs where they can enjoy fitness benefits within an appealing social atmosphere. Though originally created for serious climbers, users of artificial climbing walls today represent a broad-based demographic that transcends ages, interests, and levels of fitness.

The first organization to form a professional group dedicated solely to indoor climbing facilities in the United States was the Climbing Wall Industry Group (CWIG), a subgroup of the Outdoor Recreation Coalition of America (ORCA). In 1993, CWIG created draft standards for climbing wall engineering and design. Prior to this, every wall builder was essentially building climbing wall structures in a vacuum, and wall users had no real way of evaluating the structural reliability of the structures they were climbing. The 1993 standards proved highly influential and successful; they still remain the basis for engineering standards when building climbing wall systems in the United States today. Despite the success of the standards and the obvious need they addressed, CWIG disbanded after ORCA became the Outdoor Industry Association and shifted the organizational emphasis to the manufacturing and distribution of outdoor goods.

In 2003, the Climbing Wall Association (CWA) incorporated as a trade association, filling the void formed by the dissolution of CWIG. The CWA formed with the mission of promoting industry self-regulation regarding industry practices and engineering standards. The CWA has been working to update the 1993 CWIG engineering standards, but industry consensus has been difficult to achieve. In the absence of widely accepted industry standards in the United States, many wall manufacturers now refer to more recent European standards, which have been in place with some updates since 1998 (EN 12572:1998). Again recognizing a need, the CWA has also published standards for industry practices. "The Industry Practices are intended to assist . . . climbing wall facilities in defining, understanding, and implementing a set of responsible management, operational, training, and climbing practices" (CWA, 2007). Formal training courses for

climbing wall instructors are also gaining momentum within the outdoor industry. The Association of Canadian Mountain Guides (ACMG) began running certification courses for climbing gym instructors in 2003, and several European countries are running similar programs. Currently the American Mountain Guides Association (AMGA), the Professional Climbing Instructors Association (PCIA), and the Climbing Wall Association (CWA) offer these trainings and certifications in the United States.

## CLIMBING WALL FACILITIES AND CONSTRUCTION

Climbing walls are a unique environment that must be understood before one can address sound operational procedures and risk management. Almost all climbing gyms have areas for top rope climbing and bouldering. Many gyms include areas for lead climbing (figure 17.1). Other features are less common—rappel towers, walls high enough to allow multipitch climbing, artificial ice and mixed climbing areas, and ropes and challenge course elements. Most gyms offer classes to train people specifically for these activities within their facility, and many also offer training to prepare climbers to climb outside. Many gyms have areas devoted specifically to climbing instruction. Similar to commercial health clubs, many climbing gyms have areas devoted to cardiovascular, resistance, and flexibility training to supplement the climbers' full spectrum of training opportunities.

In the 25 years since the first commercial gym opened in the United States, wall design and construction has evolved considerably. Walls have been constructed from materials including concrete, fiberglass, wood, and steel. Present wall costs run close to $100 per square foot, and there are now industry standards for engineering and design. Some organizations still build their own walls, but the professionalization of the industry means that few others but commercial wall manufacturers have the necessary expertise to build climbing walls successfully. Some of the leading wall manufacturers in the United States include Entre Prises, Eldorado Climbing Walls, Nicros, and Rockwerx.

The construction process from design to completion generally requires several years and considerable start-up costs. Many public institutions appoint

**Figure 17.1** This large commercial gym has areas devoted to bouldering, top rope, and lead areas. The upstairs mezzanine area is devoted primarily to kids and core skills programming.

a building committee to work with a facilities or planning department. In general, proposals are developed, funds procured, and bids are requested from the leading manufacturers. The process begins with the development of a business plan that is tied to the mission and goals of the program. Unless the purpose of the wall and the needs of the wall user are established in advance, good choices relating to design are difficult to make. This will be illustrated in the next sections.

## Construction Types

Commercial wall manufacturers offer several types of artificial climbing walls. Most walls are housed within a larger indoor structure, either preexisting (grain silos, racquetball courts, and old warehouses have frequently been used) or in a new structure built expressly for the climbing wall. Some climbing walls are free-standing structures that can be walked around, whereas others wrap around the interior perimeter walls of the building. The most common type of artificial climbing wall is a composite construction consisting of a textured surface overlying a plywood frame that is attached to a weight- and force-bearing steel frame (figure 17.2). Once the wall is built, climbing holds are attached

**Figure 17.2** Composite style wall under construction. Note the plywood sheets being attached to the steel superstructure. Later, texture will be applied to increase the attractiveness and resemblance to actual rock.

to the plywood frame, and protection anchors and belay anchors for top-roping are attached directly to the steel frame. Composite construction is very versatile and functional; it is designed to allow for climbing routes to be created and changed easily over time. Most companies also offer climbing walls that closely resemble real rock (figure 17.3). These are generally molded or precast surfaces that are sometimes designed to resemble specific climbing areas.

Among these alternatives, the correct surface and design choice depends entirely on the program purpose and desired service demographic. For example, outdoor retail stores like REI often choose to install free-standing pinnacles resembling real rock. They want a wall that is visually impressive and beautiful that will inspire store customers to want to climb (and buy climbing gear). The molded forms they choose are difficult to change climbing routes on, but because REI customers do not return daily to climb this is not an important consideration. By contrast, The Foundry in Sheffield, England, is one of the original commercial climbing gyms. Catering mostly to passionate and experienced climbers, the climbing walls are designed to maximize training for climbing. The Foundry installed composite walls in such a way that climbing routes are not permanent; in fact, new routes can be created daily. This is necessary to avoid monotony for climbers who climb in the facility several times a week.

## Surface Types

When considering a climbing wall, an outdoor program administrator has several choices of surface type. If budget is a concern, then an additional surface material can be forgone and the plywood frame and sheeting used as the primary surface. This leaves a flat surface that can be painted with a little sand added to the paint to allow for some friction. Flat-panel plywood walls lack the visual appeal of textured concrete and synthetic modular surfaces. However, from a functional climbing perspective, a plethora of modular holds can be placed because the entire surface is flat. The featureless surface leads to infinite route-setting possibilities through the use of modular hand and foot holds. To continue the previous example, the Foundry has several plywood walls, not visually impressive but offering solid training potential. A textured surface is most common today. Most of the leading manufacturers have their own proprietary mixture, which can be described as a stronger, more durable form of stucco or grout applied over the interior framing. This type of surface offers better friction than paint over plywood. The texture itself is often

John Bicknell

**Figure 17.3**  Side-by-side example of simulated rock texturing (this version closely resembles limestone) and composite style walls.

painted or stained to resemble natural rock and usually has a few features sculpted out of the texture to provide relief and mimic real rock features such as pockets or pinches. This surface type offers the same route-setting advantages of plywood in a more attractive package. Some "real rock" frameworks are created from synthetic concrete, which forms its own surface, needing no additional covering; others have a surface texture added over the mold, the texture similar to those used over composite frameworks. These "real rock" forms are perhaps the most aesthetic; Rockwerx refers to its product as a "climbable work of art" (www.rockwerxclimbing.com/index.xml). They are also the most expensive. Modular climbing holds can often be attached to the molds, but the highly featured and varied surfaces of these walls limit flexibility in hold placement and make creative route-setting difficult. Many public climbing gyms offer their members a combination of wall surface types and textures—some areas of "real rock," some areas of textured composite, and perhaps some areas of painted and sanded plywood. The demographic attending climbing gyms is varied (kids, one-time visitors, core members who climb several times a week), and their choice of wall types and surfaces is correspondingly varied.

## Angles and Features

Another consideration for administrators is how to best choose the angles at which walls are built and which, if any, features should be included. Once again, these choices should be made with the intended demographic in mind. Most climbing walls include varied terrain to appeal to a wide diversity of climbers. Facilities catering to experienced climbers should include a healthy amount of steep and overhanging terrain, whereas those interested in attracting novice youth and adult climbers should favor less than vertical and vertical terrain. Experienced climbers generally prefer higher walls for more continuous training, whereas newer and younger climbers are less intimidated by shorter walls (less than 30 feet [9.1 m] high). Possible wall features include cracks, Tufas, and rappel platforms. Cracks are helpful to teach climbers crack-climbing technique in preparation for outdoor climbing. However, cracks cannot be changed and thus limit the total amount of space available for route-setting. Cracks are not recommended for small facilities

for this reason. Rappel platforms are excellent if program goals include teaching rappelling. The disadvantage of rappel platforms is that, depending on their location, they may reduce the total climbable surface area. Tufas are interesting features to climb, but they are costly to construct and have a limited appeal to most climbers.

## Indoor Climbing Holds

The first indoor climbing holds were real rocks glued and later bolted to the surface. The next generation of holds was fashioned from wood. The vast majority of today's holds are fashioned from polyurethane. Interestingly a new generation of both wood and real rock holds have made it back into today's route-setters' arsenal. Many manufacturers now make climbing holds; it is best to buy from several of these to add variety to your selection. Holds are attached via t-nuts to the surface material of the climbing wall. The t-nut is installed into the backside of the climbing wall surface material and is left in place unless it becomes damaged. A bolt is then inserted through the climbing hold and attached from the front side of the climbing surface to the t-nut with an Allen wrench. Composite walls are designed to allow easy access to the back of the wall, which allows damaged t-nuts to be replaced (stripped t-nuts are a common occurrence on climbing walls because of the forces applied by climbers to the holds and poor route-setting practices). Climbing wall design is the primary factor in whether or not there is easy access to the rear of the structure for routine wall maintenance. Some molded real rock forms are designed to be installed directly to the building's existing walls, which can make it harder to access them from behind to replace t-nuts. This is another reason why composite walls are preferred from a route-setting perspective.

## Indoor Climbing Anchors

Protection anchors are attached directly to the steel frame. The two most common top anchors are a welded belay bar or equalized bolts and chains (figure 17.4). All indoor anchors must meet UIAA (Union Internationale Des Associations D'Alpinisme) climbing standards for real rock anchors. Consistent with UIAA Standards, belay anchors should withstand vertical forces to 50 kN

John Bicknell

**Figure 17.4** Example of top anchors—belay bar and chains. A top rope has been wrapped once around the belay bar (this increases friction and lowers the forces the belayer must hold). A top rope could also be clipped through two chains, or a lead climber would clip the rope through two chains prior to lowering.

(11,000 lbs) (European Committee for Standardization, 1998). In every case, anchors are attached to the underlying structural framework. Most facilities also have floor anchors for belayers; these are used mostly by beginning climbers and in cases where the belayer is substantially lighter than the climber.

## Flooring

After the walls are finished, flooring is installed. Almost all North American climbing facilities have an impact-attenuating surface (padding) installed in all climbing areas. This padding is often made of a composite flooring system comprised of a bottom layer of open-cell foam and a top layer of closed-cell foam with a carpet bonded to the top layer. Another popular choice is shredded rubber mixed with an epoxy that bonds the rubber pieces together, forming a floor several inches (about 12 cm) thick. Various other systems including pea gravel, gymnastics pads, and loose shredded rubber are used. It is very common to augment bouldering areas with "crash pads" over the primary floor. These movable pads are often made up of a combination of open- and closed-cell foam surrounded by a layer of tough nylon. One example of a popular pad manufacturer is Asana Climbing. Asana makes fully integrated pads, which help minimize the risk of a fall resulting

in a twisted ankle from hitting the edge of a dragged bouldering pad. Most gym operators believe good flooring is a crucial risk-management element in wall operations; however, there is little research available on the effectiveness of the various flooring systems. Additional climbing wall equipment will be addressed in the facilities management section.

## CLIMBING WALL ACTIVITIES

The facilities section began with an overview of features and activities found in climbing gyms. In this section, only the most universal activities are reviewed in detail—top rope climbing, bouldering, and lead climbing. Rappelling, ice climbing, multipitch climbing, ropes courses, and challenge courses—all of these activities (and many others) can be found in public climbing facilities. Because relatively few facilities offer these features, they will not be reviewed here.

## Bouldering

Bouldering is a type of climbing in which the climber climbs near to the ground without a rope (figure 17.5). Industry standards set no absolute height limits for bouldering, but most facilities set a maximum height between 12 and 14 feet (~3.7-

John Bicknell

**Figure 17.5**   Climber and a spotter in the bouldering cave.

4.3 m), though some facilities allow bouldering to 20 feet (~6.1 m). Many facilities have dedicated bouldering areas; others simply allow unroped climbing to a specific height on the main walls. An old climber's adage is that every bouldering fall is a ground fall. As such, bouldering injuries are fairly common, particularly extremity injuries. Many gyms supplement their standard flooring with movable bouldering pads. These pads definitely soften landings, but unfortunately the pads themselves are associated with injuries. Often, when a falling climber lands feet first near the pad's edge and rolls off the edge onto the floor below, fractures of the bones of the lower leg and sprained ankles occur.

## Top Rope Climbing

Partnered top rope climbing can be defined as climbing that occurs with the rope running from the climber to a fixed anchor and a belayer (figure 17.6).

John Bicknell

**Figure 17.6**   Partner top-roping. The rope goes from the belayer over a belay bar and down to the climber. The rope is always snug on the climber, limiting fall distance and forces.

Gyms commonly use a "sling shot" system in which the rope runs from the climber through a top anchor and back to a belayer stationed on the ground. Done properly, with an attentive belayer who keeps the rope snug on the climber, falls generate roughly body weight forces, and the climber falls only a short distance due to rope stretch. Gyms also can support climbers who don't have a belay partner by providing an auto-belay system that allows a climber to ascend solo while still on a top rope system. In this case the auto-belay system is fixed at the top of the structure to the structural frame, and the auto belay automatically catches and lowers a falling climber (figure 17.7). Top rope walls differ hugely in maximum height within the same gym and from gym to gym across the country, from less than 20 feet (6 m) to higher than 80 feet (24 m). Most gyms have walls in the 30- to 40-foot (9-12 m) range. Some walls are devoted only to top-roping; others allow bouldering, top-roping,

John Bicknell

**Figure 17.7**   Auto-belay top-roping. The cable runs from the climber into the auto-belay device and is always snug on the climber. When the climber falls or decides to lower, the mechanism lowers him or her slowly back to the ground. No partner is required.

and leading all on the same wall. Other than minor scrapes and bruises, injuries from top-roping are extremely uncommon because of the low forces and short falls. Given the height of top rope walls, if belay system failure does occur due either to human error or (very rarely) equipment malfunction, the potential for catastrophic injury or death does exist.

## Lead Climbing

Lead climbing involves a climber clipping the rope progressively through pieces of intermediate protection as he or she climbs (figure 17.8). This protection is made up of bolts drilled through the surface of the climbing wall and attached to the main load-bearing structure of the wall. These individual anchor points should hold 20 kN (4,400 lbs) vertical forces (European Committee for Standardization, 1998). A quickdraw is attached to the bolt, and the climber clips the rope to the quickdraw. At the top of the climb, the standard practice is for the climber to clip the rope through two draws or chains and be lowered by the belayer back to the ground. Lead falls generate larger forces than top rope falls, and the lead climber falls longer distances (twice the distance back to the highest protection point plus rope stretch). As such, lead-climbing accidents are more common than top rope accidents, and the consequences are often more severe.

## Climbing Wall Activities and Accident Rates

Risks are often calculated from a matrix of probability and consequence. In other words, how likely is an accident to occur, and how bad is it likely to be? Looked at in this way, bouldering injuries are by far the most common in gyms; sprains, strains, and even fractures occur in bouldering. Lead climbing shares with top rope climbing the potential for falling 30+ feet (9+ m) to the surface, and because the forces are greater and the chance for human error greater, these accidents occur more often in lead climbing than in top rope climbing. There are fewer lead-climbing injuries than bouldering injuries, but the chance for catastrophic injury or death is greater. Indoor climbing is in its infancy in terms of any systematic attempt to compile accident statistics throughout the industry. Relative to the approximately seven million users per year,

**Figure 17.8** Lead climbing. The leader clips the rope progressively through pieces of protection as she climbs. Here the leader is about to clip the rope to a quickdraw attached to a bolt.

climbing in the United States is a safe sport. Deaths occur but are very rare, with approximately one a year being reported in the United States. Serious injuries involving hospital visits are slightly more common; a recent small study suggested a rate of about one per year per facility (deBrun and Turner, 2008). These injury rates are low compared to most forms of athletics and outdoor adventure activities.

# CLIMBING WALL MANAGEMENT

Once a wall is constructed, the focus shifts toward the management of the wall. This is a wide topic covering more areas than can be reviewed here, including administrative and business practices, human resource management, and climbing and facility operations. These areas in turn cover topics such as gym cleaning and maintenance, equipment maintenance and inspection, hiring and firing practices and employee records, insurance needs, and legal and regulatory obligations. A broader overview of these topics can be found in *Climbing Walls* (Stiehl

and Ramsey, 2005). Our primary focus here will be on climbing wall programming and climbing wall operations viewed from a risk-management perspective.

# Climbing Wall Programming

Indoor climbing programs can be categorized as follows: open climbing, core skills courses (including top rope belay instruction and testing, movement technique instruction, bouldering instruction, lead-climbing instruction, and advanced skills instruction), group climbing programs, and team-building programs. Open climbing makes up the majority of programming and is comprised of participants using the facility at their leisure while facility staff monitor for safety and policy compliance. Before individuals can begin open climbing, they must usually pass specific skills assessments required by the facility.

## Core Skills Programming

Depending on the facility, basic climbing skills may be taught at an indoor facility to maintain safety at the climbing wall, but also to prepare students to climb outside. Commonly, top rope belay instruction and testing consists of teaching participants how to belay and then evaluating their belay skills through a competency assessment. It is an industry standard that all individuals pass a belay test before belaying without direct staff supervision in the facility. Lead climbing varies from facility to facility; therefore, instruction is specific for how to safely lead indoor climbing routes at a given facility. It generally includes instruction in belaying a leader and the mechanics of properly clipping bolts and lowering from top anchors. As with top rope climbing, passing a lead skills test is generally required prior to lead climbing during open climbing programs. Climbing movement instruction involves staff teaching participants the principles and techniques of moving over rock—or in this case modular plastic handholds. Movement is often best taught through bouldering activities, but movement instruction can also be included while top rope and lead climbing.

The gym often serves as the classroom to teach skills that are applied outside while rock climbing. Many gyms offer programming addressing a range of advanced climbing topics—rappelling, multipitch climbing, rock rescue, anchor construction, and aid climbing. Usually, there is not much application for these skills in the indoor environment. Finally, if the climbing wall is used to prepare participants to go outside, consider including an environmental impact section in the teaching process. The climbing wall is a great location to discuss the impacts climbers have on the environment, from chalk to soil compaction.

## Custom Group Programs

Custom group programs include birthday parties, youth groups, corporate outings, and the like. The emphasis is on providing a fun climbing experience and generally includes only enough instruction to provide a safe experience. Some facilities offer team-building programs at their climbing facility. These programs are designed to increase trust and communication, among other things, and are similar to programs usually associated with challenge courses.

# Climbing Wall Operations and Risk Management

Risk management is the single most important job responsibility for any outdoor program administrator professional. According to Hansen-Stamp (1999), risk management is the design and implementation of plans, procedures, guidelines and policies to eliminate, minimize, or manage exposure to loss while pursuing reasonable programmatic or organizational outcomes. Sometimes lost in formal definitions of risk management is the assumption that these policies are carried out while still pursuing reasonable programmatic goals—for our purposes, it is not merely about keeping everyone risk-free—it is about minimizing risks and working with them while operating an indoor climbing program. Risk management can be divided into two parts: incident prevention and incident response. Both are important, both are necessary, but the greatest benefits come from a strong focus on incident prevention.

## Incident Prevention

The goal in any risk-management plan is to create a continuous feedback loop so that potential risks are addressed in program design, dealt with in program delivery, and debriefed and analyzed postprogram. Classic tools for climbing wall risk management include participant orientation, risk-management documentation, effective customer and staff education, staff training, client testing, database management, equipment maintenance, and facility management. More than this, quality incident prevention involves thoughtful program planning with clear goals and carefully developed curricula. During program delivery, careful student assessment and well-trained staff with solid judgment and decision-making skills help greatly to lessen the rate of incidents. Unfortunately, incidents still happen even in the best programs. When accidents occur, they must be analyzed and policies and programs updated to incorporate the findings; improvements to practices can always be made. Good incident prevention processes are the first step in providing superb customer service and a superior customer experience.

**Participant Orientation**   There are many field risk-management concepts that apply to climbing facility operations. The first is the general participant orientation. All new participants to a climbing facility should receive an orientation that includes a facility tour, an explanation of policies and procedures, and an explanation of the risks of indoor rock climbing. Some facilities do this via a personal guided tour and a talk with a staff member. Another way to accomplish this is by creating an audiovisual orientation and requiring all new participants to watch it before they use the facility. The ideal approach may involve a combination of both—incorporating the human element and responsiveness of the personal tour with the consistency of an audiovisual program viewed by every facility user.

**Risk-Management Documents**   Another aspect of general risk management involves the use of documents that reduce legal liability. All participants at a climbing facility should sign a waiver and assumption-of-risk document prior to engaging in any training or climbing. Medical history documents may be necessary as well. These documents transfer risk from the facility and its insurer to the participant; they are a tool for lessening the consequences of the incident (at least for the facility) as opposed to a tool for incident prevention. These documents should be completed and signed as part of the client orientation. It is a key legal concept that participants cannot waive risks that they do not understand. The client orientation serves as a tool to create an awareness of the risks associated with climbing. Only once that awareness has been created can a participant waive those risks in a way that is legally binding.

It is worth noting that the laws detailing how these documents may be written (and even if they may be used at all) vary from state to state. There is no standard practice on how often or at what recurring intervals participants should sign waivers. It is prudent to consult both your insurance company and a lawyer in your state when developing these documents. More information on this topic can be found in chapter 7.

**Participant Education and Testing**   In addition to the general participant orientation, every climbing wall activity has its own unique features, and participants should receive some instruction in these prior to engaging in the activity. Specific orientations should be developed for bouldering, partner top-roping, auto-belay top-roping, and lead climbing. Lesson plans should be designed for each skill set, and staff should receive training in coaching climbing movement and in general teaching and presentation skills. The goal is program-wide consistency regarding how climbing skills are taught and how participant tests are conducted.

Prior to unsupervised bouldering, the participant should be informed of inherent risks and ways of reducing those risks (good falling techniques and proper use of spotting, for example). The advantages and disadvantages of the flooring and pads should also be discussed. Facility rules for bouldering should be reviewed during climber orientations and prominently posted in the bouldering area.

Top rope and lead climbing have their own sets of concerns for incident prevention. Consistency in belay instruction and testing is crucial because it reduces the chance for errors during open climbing, which is when the majority of climbing wall incidents occur. Solid testing procedures have advantages that go beyond incident prevention. For example, the social atmosphere improves when facility users trust one another to belay, knowing that each participant has passed the same skills test. The outdoor program administrator must also decide what types of belay devices will be allowed and what belay techniques will be acceptable. Presently, rules vary from facility to facility around the country. To give one particularly arbitrary example, some gyms require all belays to be from a Petzl Gri-Gris, whereas, other gyms forbid the use of Gri-Gris. A less arbitrary approach would be simply to require that all climbing equipment be UIAA approved and used in accordance with the manufacturer's instructions. All belays must meet essential criteria (CWA, 2007):

- Proper configuration and use of belay device according to manufacturer's instructions
- Ability to properly feed rope through device
- Maintaining a brake hand on the rope at all times
- Ability to brake at all times
- Ability to demonstrate an appropriate behavioral reaction to a fall (i.e., the belayer must reflexively react to break a fall—even if surprised, stressed, fearful, etc.)

We include this checklist here because it is an example of criteria based on fundamental skills as opposed to a specific technique that must be followed exactly; it is both more general and reflects a higher level of conceptual understanding. More than one belay technique meets the criteria. Whatever protocols are chosen for a facility, staff must be trained accordingly. The facility manager or upper-level staff should periodically audit staff while they are teaching to check for quality and consistency. The theme here is that consistency in participant education helps prevent incidents.

Many of the risk-management concerns for lead-climbing instruction were addressed in the belay instruction and testing section. A good review of indoor lead-climbing risks can be found in the ACMG publication, *Climbing Gym Instructor Program Technical Manual* (Spear, 2003). When testing a lead climber's skill competency, it is a good idea for the leader to complete a "mock lead" prior to a live lead. A mock lead is simply a lead climb performed with the added security of a top rope belay. This allows staff to evaluate the climber's climbing ability and understanding of the mechanics of leading, such as proper clipping and lowering, in a reduced risk environment.

Bouldering, top rope, and lead-climbing programs all involve climbing movement and technique. Part of participant education in movement technique is education in injury prevention. Participants should learn about the nature of overuse injuries and how to avoid them. Participants should learn warm-up and stretching techniques. Staff should receive instruction in coaching movement.

Managing risks for groups and team-building programs mostly requires effective supervision ratios and techniques that were previously discussed. If participants will be allowed to belay, then the use of a backup should be employed. It is important to ensure that all participants have signed the appropriate risk-management paperwork.

Primary incident prevention concerns during open climbing involve improper equipment use and mistakes in belaying. The education and testing procedures already discussed will mitigate these, but good facility supervision remains critical. Staff must have sharp error-detection skills and the confidence to appropriately remedy observed errors. Many of your baseline staff may be younger and new to the sport and may lack the confidence to confront participants for error correction. Customer-service training in assertiveness can be very helpful for staff at a climbing facility. Uncorrected errors can be both self-perpetuating and contagious; other facility users observe unsafe techniques and might imitate what they observe without recognizing the dangers. An incident cycle is created until appropriate supervision and error correction is achieved.

**Staff Training**  As should be clear from the previous section, staff selection and training is a key component of a well thought-out risk-management plan. Staff must be knowledgeable in technical climbing skills, instructional skills, job administrative requirements, and customer service. Staff must be entirely conscious of facility plans for incident prevention and incident response. They must consider these risk-management elements the foremost components of their jobs. Achieving this is not easy, and curricula for staff training will necessarily vary from facility to facility. Table 17.1 presents a detailed template for a suggested staff-training curriculum.

The climbing wall manager should document staff training for each employee. This documentation should include the topics covered, date of the training, and the person who conducted the training.

**Facility and Equipment Management**  Facility management is another element of quality incident prevention. Some of this seems straightforward and obvious—all climbing gear and equipment should be inspected periodically, personal climbing gear brought to the facility should be visually inspected, the inspections documented and appropriate steps taken. Ropes age quickly at a busy climbing facility; retirement needs to be determined by physical inspection, which needs to be done on a routine basis. Other gear (quickdraws, rental harnesses and shoes, carabiners and belay devices, chains, anchors, etc.) is much more durable but still needs periodic inspection. Cleaning of rental shoes and helmets is another consideration, because hygiene in a facility is also an extremely important aspect of incident prevention. Climbing holds often spin because of stripped t-nuts and occasionally break because of high loads and materials fatigue. Identifying these holds and replacing them prior to their breaking or spinning reduces the chance of injury to participants from unplanned falls or falling holds. The route-setting program itself has high potential risks because route setters work from ladders and self-belay from ropes to establish climbing routes. Establish training and risk protocols for all route setters. Route-setting is a key element of good incident prevention; a poorly planned route can lead to injury. Set routes such that technically difficult moves are located in safer areas, where falls will be less hazardous to the climber, belayer, and other gym users. Good route-setting also minimizes overuse injuries (e.g., routes that emphasize open hand grips as opposed to crimps, and fluid, controlled moves as opposed to high-force dynamic moves).

**Facility Supervision**  Facility supervision is an important component of a risk-management plan, crucial to both incident prevention and effective incident response. When considering appropriate facility supervision, the ideal ratio between staff and participant depends on several factors: age and skill of the participants, content of the instruction, age and maturity of the staff, and length of instruction. When considering supervision ratios for group programs, it is useful to group participants into rope teams. A rope team consists of, at minimum, a climber and belayer and may include a backup belayer, a rope organizer, and an "encourager." The encourager points out holds and gives general sup-

**Table 17.1**   Suggested Climbing Wall Staff Training Components

| Technical skills | Instructional skills | Administrative components | Customer service skills | Safety skills |
|---|---|---|---|---|
| Belaying<br>• Tube and auto-blocking (pros and cons)<br>• Parallel vs. non-parallel (pros and cons)<br>• Using ground anchors (pros and cons)<br>• Belaying off of ground anchors | Preparing lessons | Participant orientations | Assertiveness and policy enforcement | CPR and AED |
| Knots<br>• Overhand<br>• Overhand on a bite<br>• Figure 8 follow-through<br>• Two-loop figure 8 on a bite | Presenting skills | Policies procedures | Creating a welcoming environment | Facility monitoring and error detection |
| Equipment use<br>• Types of harness<br>• Fitting harness<br>• Carabiners<br>• Helmets | Teaching belaying<br>• Lead and top rope<br>• Spotting | | | Equipment inspection<br>• Ropes<br>• Helmets<br>• Carabiners |
| Route setting | Conducting belay skills tests | | | Emergency action plans |
| Spotting | Teaching and coaching movement skills | | | |
| Adaptive skills | Group management | | | |

port to the climber. Organizing rope teams into these five positions is useful in managing large groups—it gives everyone something to do (see table 17.2).

Even during open climbing, some level of facility supervision is needed. It is not industry practice to allow climbing during hours when no staff are on hand. Even when staff are present, it is sometimes questionable how effectively they can supervise facility users. In a well-designed climbing gym, someone at the front desk should be able to see all or most of the climbing areas. If this is not pos-sible, or if the gym is busy, it might be necessary to have additional staff present on the floor at all times. Knowing when it is necessary to intervene and when intervention can be delayed and handled less obtrusively is a key and subtle issue in staff training. Finally, in multiuse facilities such as recreation centers, when the facility is closed it should be clearly signed, and the climbing area should be secured. This includes raising ropes and roping off the area. Facility employees should monitor to make sure that unauthorized use is not occurring.

**Table 17.2**  Factors Adjusting Rope Team Supervision Ratios

| Can supervise more rope teams | Can supervise fewer rope teams |
|---|---|
| • Participants are older.<br>• Participants are skilled belayers.<br>• Participant are using autoblocking belay devices.<br>• Instructor is experienced. | • Participants are younger.<br>• Participants are new belayers.<br>• Participants are using nonautoblocking belay devices.<br>• Instructor is inexperienced. |

It is easy to think only of the physical risks of climbing when designing risk-management plans for climbing facilities. This neglects the truth that both social and psychological risk also exist. Creating a desirable atmosphere in a climbing facility is crucial. In customer surveys, climbing gym members often talk of how much they value clean gyms, nonoffensive and enjoyable music, and some guidelines for dress and language on the part of members and staff. When these are neglected, members begin to feel uncomfortable or even harassed.

**Database Management**  To be effective, all of the risk-management techniques described here and chosen by your facility must be recorded in some form of database. A waiver and assumption-of-risk document should be kept on file for each participant who uses your facility. Belay and lead tests should be kept on file to verify a participant's skill competency. Equipment records must be kept and inspections documented. User data and membership information can be tracked either via a variety of commercially developed database applications or through systems that are created in house by the climbing gym operators. Because database systems change continually, what matters most is that the selected style program has an effective means of documenting its participants and procedures and tracking the documents.

## Incident Response

Good risk management is primarily incident prevention and planning, but some thought should also be given to emergency response protocols. Even the most effectively managed gyms eventually have a serious incident. Be it a physical injury,

interpersonal conflict, or both, the second part of a good risk-management plan is incident-response. As a last resort, a well-designed incident-response plan creates understanding and organization if the worst happens. This plan should be familiar to all staff and regularly reviewed. It should be prominently posted, not lost in a file cabinet. This plan must take into account the level of medical training required of employees. It must establish the emergency procedures to follow in case of serious accidents or sudden illnesses—for example, at what point the police or an ambulance will be summoned. It establishes protocols for anticipated rescues—for example, how to bring down a climber stuck midway up a wall. It clarifies what emergency equipment will be on hand and where it will be stored. The exact needs and protocols for rescues and incident response will vary from facility to facility but must be addressed regularly through hands-on staff-training opportunities.

## SUMMARY

Indoor climbing walls are an accepted part of the modern sports world. There are now thousands of walls across the United States and millions of users per year. What began as a training tool for "real climbing" is now for many participants a sport in its own right. For many, climbing is a lifetime sport that is tremendously enjoyable while providing great long-term health benefits. Injuries and accidents do occur, but not often, and almost always as a result of participant error. Good facility designs and thoughtful risk-management plans coupled with ongoing proactive staff and participant training can dramatically reduce the rate of accidents in a climbing facility.

# Chapter 18

# Challenge Course Management

*Christina Carter Thompson, MS, and Adam Bondeson, BA*

Managing a challenge program may be an essential aspect of the outdoor program administrator's job description. A well-managed challenge course provides the outdoor program administrator with opportunities to provide programs to groups and participants who might not be interested in specific outdoor adventure programs. Additionally, knowledgeable and trained staff is able to customize programs to meet the needs of the client while minimizing actual risk exposure to the organization and participants. In this chapter we provide a brief history of the challenge industry, information on relevant theories pertaining to challenge course purpose, and describe the different types of courses and their common uses. We also make recommendations and provide background information on course design, vendor selection, and equipment resources. Finally, the chapter provides administrative guidelines related to risk management, staff training, organizational support, and budget planning associated with challenge course management.

Challenge programs are an incredible tool for working with groups as well as fostering individual growth. Programs are custom designed to meet almost any group's goals and objectives. However, because of the implicit differences between outdoor recreation and challenge course facilitation, outdoor program administrators must have a thorough understanding of specific terms, philosophical underpinnings, and unique facility differences in order to manage these programs effectively.

## CHALLENGE TERMS

*Challenge programs* provide experiential learning or recreational opportunities using games, initiatives, and elements to reach desired outcomes with portable props or permanently installed structures. *Challenge courses* are a series of elements installed on trees, poles, or other structures. *Elements* are activities or challenges installed on high or low challenge courses. *Games,* or icebreakers, are activities used throughout a challenge program to help groups and individuals relax and refocus or begin to form into a team; these activities generally use minimal props. *Initiatives* are activities that have a desired outcome; these activities may or may not use portable props, and may require group members to brainstorm solutions, challenge ideas, communicate differences, and implement plans to solve the task. Often, challenge programs emphasize or combine recreation with educational and transferable skills. In the case of challenge courses with permanent elements, groups come to the site for programming. In the case of initiatives and games, facilitators (staff) might travel to virtually any site to conduct a portable challenge program for an interested group.

Challenge courses vary from site to site and include both belayed and spotted elements. Climbing towers, power poles, and flying squirrels are but three of the possible high elements on a course. Whale watch, nitro crossing, tension traverse, swinging log, and giant's thumb are among possible elements on a low course. These elements make for a complex management responsibility for an outdoor program administrator. Regardless of location, construction design or managing organization, challenge courses have commonalities that center on human development. Historically, challenge programs have been fundamentally related to outdoor recreation in that much of the history and many of the theories spawn from outdoor recreation programs.

## HISTORY

Challenge courses, also known as ropes courses, have been around in different forms for over 70 years. As a part of many military training programs, ropes courses focused more on the physical challenges than on any concurrent personal development gained through the experience. Meanwhile, character education was occurring as part of the many outdoor education programs. As participation in programs such as Outward Bound and the National Outdoor Leadership School (NOLS) increased, experiential education theory and its applications increased as well. Experiential education practitioners began to demonstrate that challenging experiences could add to the lives of those participating, and that the location did not necessarily need to be the wilderness.

Consequently, in the 1960s and '70s the first "formal" ropes course companies burst onto the scene. Building off of the work of Kurt Hahn, early challenge course leaders such as Karl Rohnke and Jerry Pieh began to formally advance the industry. Project Adventure, an early leader in the industry, received federal funding in 1974 through the National Diffusion Network to establish and expand its efforts to over 400 schools across the United States.

As the challenge industry matured, several professional organizations were established. Today, the Association of Experiential Education (AEE) is a nonprofit, professional membership association dedicated to experiential education and the students, educators, and practitioners who subscribe to its philosophy (www.aee.org). In the late 1980s, a group of course installers and program trainers formed the Association for Challenge Course Technology. ACCT is a not-for-profit trade organization serving challenge course professionals all over the world. The purpose of the ACCT is to promote the use of challenge courses and to set minimum standards for challenge course installation, operation, certification, and inspection. Originally founded by vendors, ACCT membership has expanded to include challenge program administrators, facilitators, installers, and trainers. Its membership builds nearly 75 percent of the new challenge courses in the United States each year (Association for Challenge Course Technology, 2008). The ACCT has been setting challenge course standards since 1994 and is now accredited by the American National Standards Institute (ANSI) as a standards developer (Association for Challenge Course Technology, 2008).

Established in 2003, the Professional Ropes Course Association is a privately held association that represents vendors, installers, facilitators, administrators, and trainers. The association is comprised of a board of directors, peer-reviewed vendors, challenge program organizations, and individual members. The PRCA functions as a nonprofit association without federal recognition and is accredited by the American National Standards Institute (ANSI) as a standards developer (Professional Ropes Course Association, 2011). Together, the AEE, ACCT, and more recently the PRCA have established the challenge course industry as a growing and accepted profession. For more information about the history of outdoor recreation and education refer to chapter 2.

Today it is estimated that over 15,000 challenge course programs exist in the United States (Attarian, 2001). This is an impressive amount of growth from a programming model that is an extension of the outdoor recreation field. This growth has expanded the outdoor recreation industry dramatically, and has helped bring experiential education and adventure programming to populations less likely to participate in wilderness excursions.

## CHALLENGE COURSE PROGRAM DESIGN AND OUTCOMES

According to Martin et al. (2006) challenge programs commonly have three possible general outcome orientations: recreational outcomes, educational outcomes, and therapeutic outcomes. It is common to combine these outcomes into a single program as specific program needs are worked out with the client. Additionally, the three general outcomes vary in complexity and facilitator requirements.

>> **Recreational outcomes.** According to Siedentop (2008), people participate in recreational activities by choice and use their leisure time to do so. In other words, recreational outcomes should be fun and provide opportunities for socialization and informal community interaction. Additionally, challenge programs have a level of perceived risk that allows participants to feel an adrenaline rush or thrill when participating in programs. According to Martin and colleagues, therapeutic and educational outcomes may come from a recreational challenge program, but it is the responsibility of the participant to come to those conclusions (2006). Additionally, facilitators are there to provide risk management and basic instruction but not necessarily to facilitate goals such as leadership, team cohesiveness, or problem solving.

>> **Educational outcomes.** Although they are often enjoyable, and thus recreational, educational challenge programs have specific and measureable learning outcomes tied to them. In general, the content of the learning outcomes centers on human skills, including improved communication, self-reflection, self awareness, and group development. Administrators need to ensure that facilitators and clients have an opportunity to meet and develop programs that will address educational outcomes. Using educational theory (described later) and facilitation techniques listed in figure 18.2 (p. 297), facilitators guide groups and participants toward a set of educational outcomes using direct experience and metaphorical connections.

>> **Therapeutic outcomes.** According to Martin et al. (2006), challenge programs with therapeutic outcomes are often based on a model associated with counseling or therapy. If a program is truly a therapeutic model, licensed counselors, psychologists, or other mental health professionals are involved in establishing outcomes, facilitating the program, and providing support to participants.

Outcomes associated with therapeutic challenge courses include healthier coping mechanisms, appropriate behavioral reactions to conflict, substance abuse abatement, and posttraumatic stress disorder improvements.

# PRIMARY INFLUENCES ON CHALLENGE PROGRAMMING

The literature includes extensive support for challenge programming as it relates to psychology, sociology, education, and leadership theories. Consequently, this section is designed to provide a brief overview as an aid to outdoor recreation program administrators. A basic understanding of theory and background will help the administrator further understand the process and design and run an effective program.

## Experiential Education and Learning Theory

The Association for Experiential Education defines *experiential education* as " a process through which a learner constructs knowledge, skills, and values from direct experience" (Association for Experiential Education, n.d.). John Dewey, an influential thinker in the foundations of experiential and progressive education, states that an experience is only truly educative if it leads to a new level of thinking or experience (Dewey, 1938). Growth through learning never stops; it only builds on prior learning and experience. Learning from one experience becomes necessary for the next experience. In this model, learning is growth, and the learning can involve any number of areas, including physical, mental, social, and, with some groups, even spiritual. The experiential learning cycle is a way to understand and guide maximum learning from challenge experiences. During an experiential learning activity, participants can develop ownership of the experience because they are responsible for accomplishing or solving the presented challenges. Figure 18.1 provides a diagram for the experiential learning cycle.

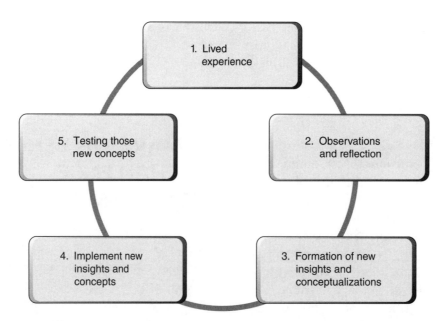

**Figure 18.1**    This figure is a simplified version of the common experiential learning cycle as theorized by D. Kolb.

Reprinted, by permission, from K. Gilbertson, T. Bates, T. McLaughlin, and A. Ewert, 2006, *Outdoor education: Methods and strategies* (Champaign, IL: Human Kinetics), 30. Adapted from D.A. Kolb, 1984, *Experiential learning* (Englewood Cliffs, NJ: Prentice-Hall).

## Theory of Challenge and Support

Moving beyond experiential learning theory, Neville Sanford wrote that challenging experiences produce moderate discomfort (growth zones) which when appropriately managed create potential for personal improvement (Sanford, 1966). Challenge course programs attempt to address this potential growth by building adequate support within the group and by providing challenging experiences during the program.

As such, the course facilitator may take a proactive role in the learning process. However, it is incumbent on the facilitator to avoid becoming too involved in the process. Figure 18.2 describes several important components of the challenge experience that is provided and structured by the facilitator.

## CHALLENGE COURSE FACILITIES

The general outcomes and theoretical framework associated with challenge programs are constant, but the types of facilities installed and used vary based on many variables. Challenge courses activities range in size from portable activities to large structures stretching several stories into the air and occupying large footprints of land.

As stated previously, challenge course programming involves generally one of three types of activities: portable activities, low-challenge course elements, and high-challenge course elements. The activities are listed in a common order of progression. It is important to understand that a likely progression of activities is developed with the group outcomes in mind. There is a great deal of variety in how activities are facilitated. Many times, a low-challenge course experience includes portable activities, and a high-challenge course experience includes low-challenge course activities as well as portable activities. Each course has its own benefit and value based on the situation, location, program goals, and available facility.

## Portable Challenge Programs

Portable challenge programs (also called team initiatives) include activities that use props such as bandanas, ropes, beach balls, or portable platforms (see figure 18.3). Portable challenge programs allow organizations to facilitate at virtually any site, and

> ### Figure 18.2  Traditional Facilitation Terms and Techniques
>
> *Processing the experience:* The cycle begins with a direct experience, in this case on the challenge course. The importance of sequencing these experiences is discussed later. The facilitator frames an activity to ensure participant understanding.
>
> *Framing* refers to how a facilitator introduces an experience. A variety of approaches can be used, but at least three components need to be addressed during the framing process: desired outcomes, safety concerns, and the rules or requisite boundaries required from the group to complete the challenge. Once participants are clear on the challenge presented and the criteria for success, the facilitator moves to managing the activity.
>
> *Activity management* refers to the role of the facilitator during challenge activity. The facilitator is responsible for managing the safety of the group but should remain separate from the group's challenge. If the facilitator is too involved, participants will start to look to him or her for answers. The facilitator should watch behaviors, listen to participants' comments, and take notes on the group's progress. By taking notes, the facilitator can design effective questions to stimulate relevant discussion during the processing phase.
>
> *Debriefing* or *group processing* occurs between activities and provides a forum for discussion and reflection. The end of the activity is a subjective term representing the time when the group is together and speaking about past events or occurrences. Ultimately, the facilitator refrains from making statements to participants except to provoke discussion. In this way, participants are not dependant on the facilitator for answers. Through questions and discussion, participants begin to take ownership of the experience. After the group has an experience, they may or may not have been "successful", or they may disagree about the level of success. The individuals begin to naturally reflect on the experience both during the challenge and after the challenge is completed. Individuals may examine how they could have done better, the role they played in the group, or how they interacted with the group.
>
> *Reflection* is the process whereby individuals consider past experiences in search of value and improvement. This is an ongoing process for all people. Reflection can be free form or guided. Challenge courses generally provide structured reflection and discussion during the processing phase. Processing is not limited to asking questions; it can be accomplished through, art, skits, activities, and many other forms of expression. The art of processing a group within a challenge course experience is far too complex and detailed for further detail and requires significant time and effort to master. Participants and groups eventually begin to "self-process" experiences, which indicates that the group is beginning to take ownership of the experience, which potentially leads to the final state of processing, which is transference.

may be used prior to the group's visit to a permanent high or low course. The benefit of portable activities is that they can be used almost anywhere and offer an alternative to meet client expectations and goals. Portable activities can be very inexpensive and will expand the scope and value of a program. Commonly, portable activities are used in conjunction with more complex challenge programs that use permanent high or low elements. Because of their versatility and variability, an effective facilitator is able to use portable activities to enhance the outcomes of a program. Thus many facilitators use portable activities regularly to illustrate key points or learning outcomes.

Educators often use portable initiatives to engage students through active learning versus traditional note-taking sessions. Many outdoor programs use portable activities as a way to create a sense of community for students prior to and during trips by adding games or initiatives to help them learn about and become more comfortable with each other. Additional reasons for using a portable course include the following:

- Fixed course is too expensive.

- Time allowed does not provide for use of low or high elements.

- The group has asked the organization to facilitate at their site.

- Only a few activities are needed to illustrate points and help a group move forward on tasks.

Portable activities can also serve as assessment tools when groups are progressing through an educational sequence. When a group arrives, information is often limited to registration forms and portable challenges to help build a more comprehensive picture of how individuals will interact within the group. An assessment allows facilitators to amend and calibrate the program's sequence prior to moving participants to permanent elements on a low or high course.

## Low-Element Challenge Courses

Low-element challenge courses are usually permanent structures, either as a stand-alone facility or proximal to a high-element challenge course. Low-course construction may include existing trees, utility poles installed in the ground, aircraft cables, or other building materials permanently placed to create an element. Names of common elements include wild woozy, whale watch, wall, nitro crossing, portal, balance log, and the classic spider web (see figure 18.4).

Low elements often require more resources to build and maintain, such as accessibility, land or space, and teaching tools or props. Low courses installed on trees, poles, or freestanding structures

need active maintenance and inspection. There are aesthetic benefits to using existing trees for construction, but treated poles offer significant benefit for durability and longevity. Depending on course design and space available, elements may be spread out over many acres or placed close together. Generally, although regulations vary, installing low ropes courses does not require building permits because they are considered to be recreational equipment (similar to playgrounds).

Low elements may take place off the ground, not high enough to require belay systems, but they often require safety precautions. Effective spotting skills are essential to many low elements to manage risk and to engage the group in the task. As a result of the increased risk associated with low-element challenge courses, additional training for facilitators might be warranted. A 20-hour facilitator training course taught by a qualified trainer can provide a good base for effective programming (Association for Challenge Course Technology, 2008).

Low course elements may be used to assess participants and to determine if they are ready to move to a high-element challenge course. Adequate funds and time must be allocated, both when new facilitators are hired and on a continuing basis to reduce risks on the course and to deliver effective programs. A well-managed low-element challenge course will support a high-element challenge course.

## High-Element Challenge Courses

High-element challenge courses often reflect low elements but are constructed higher off the ground and use a belay system to help limit risk. Depending on how the facilitator chooses to use them, portable programs, low elements, and high elements can all be employed to address any and all of the desired program outcomes. High elements tend to focus on the individual rather than the group because only a couple of participants can be off the ground at the same time. While one or two people climb, remaining group members may provide verbal support, ongoing communication, or safety by belaying. Using perceived risks, high elements provide an opportunity for the participant to accept a personal challenge.

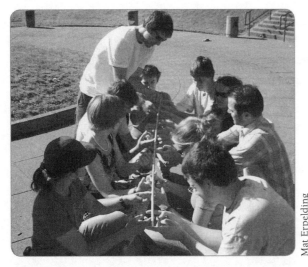

Mat Erpelding

**Figure 18.3** Using a tent pole, the group tries to lift the pole using their index fingers. To be successful, all fingers must stay in contact with the pole as the group lifts it.

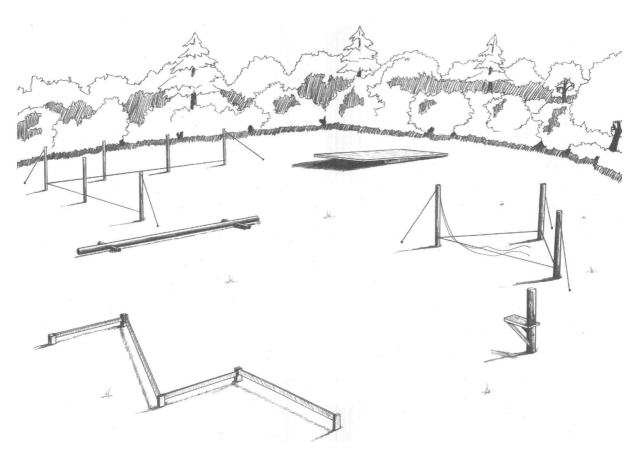

**Figure 18.4**   This is an example layout for a low course. This image includes low elements such as the wild woozy, whale watch, triangle traverse, trust platform, cable walk, and balance log.

Courtesy of Signature Research Inc.

High-challenge courses require extensive resources for construction, including appropriate site selection (indoors or out), poles, trees, and other structures (figure 18.5). To minimize risk to participants and employees, installers must be vigilant when reviewing the design specs and constructing the course. A variety of high elements exist, including the power pole, high balance beam, flying squirrel, Burma bridge, and beam crossing. Although different elements represent possible activities available on a course, high-element challenge courses are characterized by the type of system used as a belay. A variety of belay systems are available on challenge courses, including dynamic belays, static belays, continuous belays, M belays, and auto-belay systems.

## Dynamic Belay

This system uses a top anchor, usually with a belayer on the ground while the participant climbs or

**Figure 18.5**   High-challenge courses require extensive resources for construction and include elements such as the beam bridge crossing, shown here.

traverses an element. This most resembles a "sling-shot belay," as seen in many indoor and outdoor climbing programs. A participant can be lowered at any moment if needed. Sometimes a dynamic belay is used on several elements that are strung together in a row, with a single belay cable overhead. The belay could be off of a harness, on a facilitator or a participant, or through a "Just Rite Descender," which is a post with holes drilled through it (figure 18.6).

## Static Belay

This system uses an individual sling or tether that connects a participant to an overhead cable or track. Participants move from element to element using their tethers, sometimes called crab claws, lobster claws, or bunny ears as a belay. Participants transfer the tethers from one element to another as they progress through the course. The tethers

**Figure 18.6**  A Just Rite Descender. Notice the holes in the pole allow the rope to move through it, and the bends create friction. The friction of the rope bending through the pole coupled with belayers managing the rope creates a safe belay system for participants.

generally have two arms, so that one side is always connected to an anchor point, cable, or otherwise. If a participant reaches a point at which she cannot continue for any reason, a separate system may be needed to belay her to the ground. This rescue takes a higher level of training by staff to accomplish. Static courses generally require a higher staff-to-participant ratio, often as high as 1:6.

## Continuous Belay

In a continuous belay, participants use tethers to aid in the experience, but an overhead cable or rail extends over many elements in a row to minimize the number of transfers needed to complete the elements. Continuous belay systems are similar to a static system, except tethers do not need to be switched from one anchor to another. The connection to the overhead anchor slides with the participant as he traverses the element and is not unclipped by either the participant or facilitator until they have reached a safe transition point. This system is usually quicker and can accommodate many participants at a time. A continuous belay is a good choice for programs that are purely recreational or high volume because it increases the number of participants who can move through the course per day.

## M Belay

Although often lumped together, two separate systems fall into this category. For traversing elements, a rope runs from an anchor point above the element, to the ground, back up and through another anchor point on the far tree or pole and then through another anchor at the base of the pole or tree. The overhead rope makes most of the letter M—hence the name. A tether is hooked from the participant's harness to the rope. As the participant climbs, belayers on the ground pull the rope through the lower anchor; this reduces the angle of the middle portion of the M until it is almost straight across. When a participant falls or is lowered, she slides toward the middle of the rope and the lowest point in the system. This system often has several participants on the rope, as a participant belay, with three or four participants on each rope. The two or three anchor points that the rope runs through add friction to the system as a belay device does for a dynamic belay.

## Auto Belay

Currently there are two types of auto-belay systems. One system uses a cable that goes from the climber through a series of pulleys connected to a hydraulic ram. As the participant climbs, the ram contracts and the cable holds tension on the participant. When the participant lets go or falls, the ram expands and the climber is lowered slowly to the ground. The other system uses an enclosed spool about the size of a briefcase. This type of system uses a spring to pull cable or webbing up and a centrifugal break to slow the descent. Both systems need to be regularly serviced by either the manufacturer or a qualified vendor. Auto belays can work well for either a tower or climbing wall element when a high volume of participants is the goal.

The benefit to using a high-challenge course is the time and attention being placed on an individual participant. However, high-element challenge courses are more complicated to manage because of the belay systems involved, the time spent on individuals, group management, and level of facilitation skills required to provide a meaningful experience.

High-element challenge courses require attention to details with regards to facilities, training, and operations. Training and inspection should occur annually to allow for consistent maintenance and help manage the inherent risks associated with a challenge course. Trainings should be specific to the type of course and program mission. An accepted practice for new high-element challenge course facilitators is a 40-hour training course focused on facilitation, belay, risk management, group management, and other technical skills.

## Towers

Although towers are considered high-element courses, they deserve a separate mention because of their unique design and use. Towers might have climbing and rappel faces as well as multiple vertical elements (see figure 18.7). Tower designs have evolved considerably from the original military style rappel tower. Towers can have a multitude of elements and are a good choice when space is very limited.

## Zip Lines and Canopy Tours

Although zip lines have been a part of challenge courses for a long time, they have recently grown in popularity as a stand-alone activity or in a series, often called a canopy tour. Building on the popularity of canopy tours in places such as Costa Rica and other vacation destinations, companies have begun to build them in the United States. As of this writing, an estimated 150+ canopy tours exist in the United States. A zip line or canopy tour is a series of zip lines or bridges that a participant can travel across. Zip lines range in length from about 150 feet (~45 m) long up to about 1.5 miles (2.4 km) of continuous cable. Generally a participant rides across a zip line cable to a platform where he is transferred to another zip line. Although zip lines can be used to accomplish the three general challenge course outcomes (recreational, educational, therapeutic), some tours add a fourth outcome called ecoeducational. Zip lines use static belays to keep participants connected to the zip cables, platforms, and associated elements.

# DESIGNING AND CHOOSING A COURSE

When considering a challenge course design, many factors influence the decision, including potential

**Figure 18.7**  Challenge tower.

Photo of the Alpine Tower at YMCA Blue Ridge Assembly, Black Mountain, NC, by Julia B. Parker. Used with permission.

clientele, available space, financial resources, general course outcomes (recreational, educational, therapeutic), and staffing options. Outdoor recreation administrators involved in the design process should establish a detailed understanding of the participants who will be using the challenge course. All challenge courses should be built to meet the ACCT or PRCA installation standards. These standards have been created with input from all aspects of the challenge course field and serve as a baseline for creative design and long-term installation. The standards take into account manufacturer's recommendations, engineering designs, and end-user input. Anyone who builds a challenge course should be familiar with industry standards and applicable building codes. Many areas have no building codes or regulations that relate to the average challenge course, so the ACCT or PRCA standards should be used as the baseline for any design or installation. A detailed needs assessment is an essential step in the process. Additional information on needs assessments can be found in chapter 6.

## Anticipated Clientele

The driving force behind establishing a challenge course should be the development of a core mission used to guide the challenge program as it works with and expands its clientele. Additionally, determining if the course will be recreational, educational, therapeutic, or a combination will help the administrator determine who will likely use

the course. Figure 18.8 includes a list of essential questions to help administrators assess potential clientele.

## Staffing

To effectively budget for wages and staff-training fees, the outdoor program administrator needs to develop job descriptions and responsibilities prior to installing the challenge course. Staffing needs will vary depending on the course design. Staff-to-participant ratios will vary dramatically depending on the complexity of a challenge course and the level of risk management needed to ensure safety. Additionally, training levels will vary based on the type of challenge course being installed. Generally, high courses require 40 hours of training, and low courses require 20 hours, but these amounts may vary depending on course design, desired learning outcomes, and demographic of expected participants. Facilitators must be adequately trained and understand the needs of the clients. Ultimately, a small course with well-trained staff might be far more effective and financially viable than a large course with untrained or mismanaged staff.

## Location and Space Considerations

An administrator must be visionary and consider long-term implications when building a course. Prior to and during the design process, the admin-

**Figure 18.8**  Examples of Questions for Determining Clientele

1. Who will the course serve: youth, adults, people with disabilities, clubs, student groups, or in conjunction with other outdoor programming?
2. What is the purpose of the course: recreation, leadership development, team building, professional training, or a community resource?
3. Do the target groups have the resources for the programming?
4. How much space is available, and what is the participant capacity?
5. How will ongoing costs of training and inspection be accounted for?
6. What is the starting budget for installation, training, and marketing costs?
7. What other courses are in the area, and whom do they serve?
8. What age groups will your course serve: youth, adults, or a mix?
9. How long will participants be at the course (1 hour, 3 hours, 2 days)?

istrator should consider the amount of space available for the challenge course. It is also important to consider whether the area allotted for the course is appropriate for the desired general outcomes. For example, is it possible to frame, participate, and debrief elements without dealing with environmental or social distractions? The distractions caused by a challenge course located adjacent to a busy set of train tracks or a retreat center's dining hall could make it challenging for participants to be fully immersed in the experience.

Additionally, the administrator should consider if there is enough room to later expand the course or build the course in stages. If the course is servicing large groups or is financially successful, expanding may be an option, especially if it was considered during the original planning phase. A good installer or designer will think into the future as the initial design is conceived, but the administrator ultimately drives the process.

Where is the course being installed? Different regions require different materials and designs because of environmental conditions such as humidity levels, tree size, temperature extremes, and precipitation levels. Regions of the country also determine the number of days that environmental conditions will allow the course to be used. This directly affects the financial implications for the course, both during the planning phase and once the course is in operation.

## Developing a Strategic Plan

The strategic plan (as discussed in chapter 6) should establish a three- to five-year growth forecast for the course. This forecast should include operational considerations and course improvements needed after construction is finished. Location, space considerations, available clientele, and staffing options should be combined to create a detailed prediction of future growth. A detailed strategic plan smoothly guides the outdoor program administrator through the financial-planning phases, bidding process, and building process, and into the operational phase.

## Financial

An administrator must develop a financial model that balances the costs of operation with the avail-

able market of clients. Estimating the operational expenses of the course is essential to challenge-course administration. Information on financial management can be found in chapter 8, but a few issues specific to challenge-course operations need to be addressed here. Will this course need to generate revenue? If so, how much? How will the pricing structure be set up? Many courses use a tiered pricing model to account for the different types of groups that use challenge courses. For example, not-for-profit programs might pay one price, whereas corporate or for-profit organizations might pay a higher price.

Determining a realistic growth forecast is critical to establishing reasonable revenue goals. A full cost analysis is necessary to effectively determine how much building a course will cost and how long it will take before that capital expenditure is paid off. Following are some of the financial considerations necessary to plan and purchase a course:

- Initial development or site visit
- Additional insurance costs (if any)
- Installation of course elements
- Program gear
- Initial training
- Ongoing costs
- Annual inspection
- Annual training

Annual expenses such as inspection, maintenance, training, and equipment depreciation have significant financial implications and should be considered during the development stage. Often organizations will make large financial commitments for an attractive structure but fail to budget for ongoing training and staff development. Administrators who develop an appropriate budget for ongoing operation provide higher quality programs, build more sustainable programs, and in the long run can increase revenue production.

## Final Considerations

The planning process needs to be intentional and well thought out. Hiring a challenge course installer or an independent consultant may help complete a feasibility study. Although this is a viable option, the process must be driven by the organization that will run the course. The installer or consultant might be able to express ideas and concerns regarding specific elements or challenges to ensure that the finished product meets the organization's needs. Although there is flexibility in many designs, it is necessary to decide on a design that is in alignment with the mission of the organization and serves the programming vision.

Challenge courses are often conceived or designed based on the personal history of an administrator. Remember that there are many types of courses; just because one design worked well at another site does not mean it will fit the needs of a current site. The past experience of an administrator can be a great asset, but the needs of the current site should be the main consideration used to guide the development process.

## BIDDING PROCESS

The price of challenge course facilities varies based on design, construction techniques, and site limitations. The outdoor program administrator will need to start by contacting potential vendors prior to beginning the bidding process. A good vendor will work with a client to determine how they want to use the course, potential clientele, and seasonal limitations, if any. If the administrator has adequately prepared the desired course specifications, the bid process should ensure the best value for the course.

There are generally two types of bids an administrator can pursue: a turnkey installation or a facilitated bid. A *turnkey bid* is when the chosen vendor provides all the services, labor, and materials, and in some cases even the staff training. A *facilitated bid* is when the contracted vendor sends one or two employees to serve as foremen and to coordinate volunteer or paid staff while building is occurring at the site. A facilitated bid, and the consequential build, is less expensive because it decreases labor expenses, while providing the expertise and support from a vendor. A facilitated bid can serve as a great partnership between the owner and builder because the process can serve as a learning experience for the staff that will eventually facilitate on the course. Table 18.1 shows the strengths and weaknesses of each bid process.

The bid process is generally the same whether the challenge course is new construction, a renovation and repairs project, or an inspection. Figure 18.9 includes several considerations when choosing a vendor for services.

## BUILDING PROCESS

Ushering a challenge course from the design phase to a finished product is a huge undertaking. It may be one of the largest financial projects that an administrator ever manages. Once the bidding process is complete and a contract has been signed with the vendor, the next step is construction of the site. A quality contract lays out the basic legal liabilities between parties as well as what each party is responsible for during the construction process. If a challenge administrator chooses to do training in-house, the vendor should ask for a release of liability once the course has been completed.

If a turnkey bid was accepted, the vendor is responsible for most of the construction process. A few expectations will still remain with the contracting party, including securing building permits (if necessary), locating where utilities are buried under the site, and ensuring electricity is available for the vendor. It is helpful to have a storage area ready for the vendor because they will often ship materials in advance of the project. Finally, once the vendor is onsite, it is best to have a single point of contact available to work with them as the course is being built. This limits confusion and streamlines the process.

If a site chooses a facilitated approach to installation, then the site is responsible to organize the staff or volunteers that are working with the vendor. A facilitated approach provides an opportunity for staff to help with the installation and gain a greater knowledge of how and why a course works. However, there is a commitment required by the site to provide the labor agreed on. Some vendors will not use a facilitated approach based on poor follow-through by clients in the past. If you take this route, your volunteers must be well coordinated, insured, and show up on time, or the job may be delayed or not meet its budget.

## THE CHALLENGE COURSE ADMINISTRATOR

Once a course has been built, the administrator's scope of duties shifts from deciding what to build to

**Table 18.1** Strengths and Weaknesses of Each Bid Process

|  | Turn-Key Approach | Facilitated Approach |
|---|---|---|
| Pros | • Quickly gets a project done.<br>• Less complicated in terms of scheduling. The project can be wholly turned over to an outside vendor. | • Usually less expensive because of less labor and travel costs on the part of the vendor.<br>• The installation process can be used as a learning tool for those who will staff the course.<br>• The site has more involvement with the process, and those staff that help have a higher level of buy-in to the process. |
| Cons | • Typically more expensive than option two.<br>• Less involvement from the site.<br>• Fewer learning opportunities for current and potential staff. | • Not all sites will allow students or staff to work or volunteer in this manner. It is *important* to check with risk management before taking this approach.<br>• The site is responsible to provide certain things, such as labor and materials to make the job happen. This can take extra time on the part of the site. |

deciding how to manage the facility. When taking over an existing course, administrators must assess current operations to determine if any changes need to occur in managing the facility. Administrative management revolves around risk, which has two important and distinct categories. *Incident prevention* minimizes risk and ensures positive participant experience; whereas *incident response*

accepts inherent risk and details how to handle an accident or incident. Challenge courses can be both emotionally and physically demanding experiences for participants; thus administrators need to have an understanding of the theories behind challenge course facilitation to effectively manage a course. Gaining a detailed understanding of staff training, equipment management, continued course

---

**Figure 18.9   Several Considerations When Choosing a Vendor for Services**

- Is the vendor accredited by either the ACCT or PRCA? This helps ensure the vendor is meeting the standards they claim to meet. Be sure to look into the process before choosing which accreditation you prefer—each organization does it differently.
- Is the vendor properly insured? Some smaller companies are run by the principle and thus are not required by law to carry workman's compensation insurance. Workers' comp is often a requirement of larger institutions.
- Does the vendor have demonstrated experience with the type of course that you need? If you are looking for a static course, then choosing a vendor with experience in that style is of course important.
- Does the vendor have experience in your part of the country? This can make a small or sometimes a great difference. There can be variations of installation and design techniques based on region as well as climate, soil conditions, altitude, culture, and other factors.
- Does the vendor have a good reputation in the field? Although this is a subjective area, it is good to check references and even to go and visit other sites installed by the vendor, if possible.
- Is the vendor in good standing with the Secretary of State where they are located?

maintenance and inspections, and essential documentation significantly improve the administrator's ability to perform and allows for the staff to serve participants more successfully. Following are some of the general responsibilities of the challenge course administrator:

- Hiring, training, and evaluating staff
- Marketing the program and preparing for participants' needs
- Maintaining and tracking course and equipment
- Raising income for the course via programs or grants
- Holding the vision of the program and keeping it on mission

# Program Design

To consistently deliver high-quality programs, administrators must understand the diverse philosophies of program design and delivery. During this stage of program development, administrators may serve as the primary activity programmer, so they must take into consideration their customers' or clients' desired outcomes for the activity, be they recreational, therapeutic, or educational in nature.

In the case of challenge programming, the program design is most relevant when addressing an individual program contracted by clients. In this section we focus on the following points: accurate assessment of the client's needs, establishing clear goals and outcomes, accurate staff assessments, developing a logical activity progression, and ongoing communications among all parties.

## Know Participants' Needs and Establish Clear Desired Outcomes

When working with the group's contact, clear goals for the day need to be established early in the design process. An accurate assessment of the participants' desired outcomes is essential to creating a quality program. Challenge course programs, and the hired facilitators, should provide the best possible program for each group. Gather as much information about the group as possible, including their goals, objectives, and desired outcomes. This includes key terminology unfamiliar to the facilitators, but that

is essential to the group. Also, find out if any of the participants speak a different language. Obviously, staff members who are able to speak the language of the group, and who understand the group's specific discipline terminology, can increase the level of transferability to the group's regular setting. This is often done through first-hand conversations with the group contact. It can also be accomplished through carefully prepared surveys of the group members. Technology enables this to happen on paper as well as online. Survey tools are available on the Internet; participants can complete them online, and they can be used to collect, compile, and analyze data.

Language issues are very important; also important is not to assume that you can understand a group's dynamics based on an interview. New staff can make the error of assuming that they understand a group, which can be problematic in the delivery of the program. Facilitators must always remember that they are visitors to the group they are hired to work with. They are hired to provide an experience and provide tools in working with the group, but not to become group members. If the program occurs during a retreat, class, or outing, find out what they did before and what they will do after. Find out what the group contact expects from you on the day of the activity. What are the goals and objectives of the group? This can be done in person, over the phone, or via e-mail. The more information an outdoor program administrator can provide to facilitators about the client, the better. Sometimes it is appropriate to gather information on each individual within the group (e.g., when the group is working on conflict resolution or in a therapeutic setting).

## Accurate Staff Assessment

Knowing the strengths and weaknesses of each individual staff member is essential to planning a group program. This includes choosing who will work with a specific group along with who will be the lead facilitator. There are many forms of assessment, both self and organizational, that can be used to identify each facilitator's strengths and areas of improvement. If staff are new or are providing programming to a new type of group, they will require more planning time with an administrator. It is often easiest to gather all staff for a designated program together for a planning meeting. When this is not an option (because of time, space, or travel concerns), written communication is best. Developing a program-planning document is another task that allows facilitators to build a program, once necessary information has been gathered. This document should be approved (or modified) by the administrator.

If an administrator effectively pairs the skill sets of the assigned facilitators with the unique needs of the clients, a quality custom challenge program can be developed. Having staff that is well-prepared is the first step in offering a proactive, rather than a reactive, program. It is important to emphasize the philosophy of personal choice; if participants feel forced to be at an event, or that they will be forced to do certain activities, this can start a program off on a sour note. Forced activities can also negate an individual's freedom to engage in the group process. Active dialogue with your staff is a key to reducing human errors during the program.

## Develop a Logical Challenge Progression

Risk is an intrinsic part of any outdoor program, recreational or otherwise. By informing participants of the risk involved, a program reduces its liability and adds to the educational value of the activity. Participants are more likely to commit to an activity if they know exactly what will be involved. Developing a sound program progression is an essential incident-prevention tool. The administrator must have confidence that the staff is able to effectively develop the program as determined by the group's needs. Figure 18.10 is an example of a challenge course; progression of the course could include all elements shown or use of select elements based on group's time, goals, and skills.

At a minimum, staff must develop an understanding of core challenge principles early in their career as challenge course facilitators. For example, challenge is about individual choice. Participants choose how involved they will be throughout the course. Additionally, a "full value contract" (FVC) can serve as an outline that participants and facilitators agree on as a guide for acceptable behavioral conditions. Many times, each FVC is individually created based on the group; it often concerns effective and constructive communication

and physical and emotional safety considerations. In fact, the full value contract is developed early to maximize mutual respect and create nonnegotiable boundaries.

Sequencing activities also helps participants to acclimatize to risk and aids them in making appropriate choices for their participation. *Spotting*—that is, providing support to someone engaging in an activity in which she could lose balance, fall, or be hurt—is an essential skill that needs to be sequenced before any activity that might require it. Spotting participants is essential from a risk-management perspective. Good spotting consists of protecting the head and neck of a falling person. Spotting becomes more important as participants move to the more physical activities of the low-challenge course. Finally, it is important to consider the type of group participating and issues surrounding physical boundaries, body image issues, or past trauma. Physical contact during a challenge course program can pose an emotional risk that must be considered.

## Establish Clear Communication Lines

In the administrator's case, good communication starts with the interaction between the administrative office and the facilitating staff. Information that needs to be provided to staff includes the following:

- Group name
- Goals and objectives
- Time frames for program
- Gender breakdown
- Age range
- Affiliation of group (do they know one another?)
- Pertinent religious or cultural information (e.g., group taboos)
- Overview of activities

In addition to providing this information, it might be necessary to hold a planning session to help staff establish the following: Who will do the welcome? How will the groups be split up to complete the course? What elements will each staff be doing (if they need to share elements)? Who is providing the closing activity (if the group is doing

---

**Figure 18.10**   Example Challenge Course

## Tall Trees Adventure and Challenge Center

**Date:** 9/20/2011

**Location:** Challenge course                           **Times:** 9 a.m. to 5 p.m.

**Activities:** Portables, Lows, Highs                   **Number of attendees:** 36

**Group name:** The Team Group

**Contact:** T.R. Walker

**Contact phone:** 555-616-5555

**Client's stated goal for program:** Build upon lessons and concepts from last year's retreat. "We want them to focus on getting the members to trust each other and work together as a community. Learn that we need each other to succeed. If one of us fails, we *all* fail. We also want participants to have fun and bond with each other."

**Desired outcome:** Participants develop awareness of need to take care of themselves, each other, and the organization.

**Goals or concepts:** Client states: "There seems to be a disconnect between what we say we stand for and what our actions are showing." We would like facilitators to link the concept of "It is not what I say, but what I do" to activities with trust being a central theme.

**Staff:** 3 staff (12:1 ratio)

### Proposed Itinerary

**Welcome and overview:** Full Value Contract and Challenge by Choice Philosophy

**Warm-up activities:** Instructor choice

**Energizers:** Elbow Tag and Pirate Ship (use to break group into smaller subgroups)

| | | | |
|---|---|---|---|
| **Portables:** | Mind Field | Calculator | Warp Speed Build-Up |
| **Spotting sequence:** | All Aboard | TP Shuffle 1 | TP Shuffle 2 |
| **Lows:** | Tension Traverse | Spider Web 1 | Nitro Crossing |
| | Whale Watch | Criss-Cross | 3D Web |
| | Mohawk Walk | Web We Weave | Log Jam |
| **Low to high transition:** Team Wall | | | |
| **Highs:** | Climbing Wall | Zip Lines | |

**All group wrap-up**

---

one together)? Additionally, staff might need to offer a follow-up assessment to the group, so make sure they have the tools they need to complete the assessment, and establish who is collecting the forms.

Staff should strive to provide an open forum for participants. During the warm-up stage (which should include some sort of stretching), the facilitator should be looking for and asking about any physical limitations among participants (past injuries, limited range of motion, allergies, and so on). While discussing the day's overview, tell participants to see a facilitator if they have any personal past histories or injuries that might be important for staff to know about. Ask participants if they are out of their comfort zone. Some might be out of their comfort zone just because of the unfamiliar location or because they are working with people they don't know well. Emphasize support, communication, and the desired outcomes of the day to those who are uncomfortable with the new environment.

## Documentation

Documentation is an extensive subject, including policies and procedures, assumption-of-risk forms, staff files, and inspection reports. When available, the outdoor program administrator should work with the organization's risk manager (RM) to determine what needs to be documented and what does not. Some programs have an entire department that looks at risk management for the entire institution; other programs rely on the challenge course manager to do this. Additionally, documentation requirements vary from state to state, requiring the administrator to consider seeking legal advice.

In terms of working with participants, the administrator needs to ensure that the group contact person is provided and that this person supplies all necessary information to the group members to prepare them for the day. Figure 18.11 is an example of a "what to wear and how to prepare" document.

Most challenge course operators require waivers or health statements to be collected prior to their participants coming to the challenge course for a program. These legal forms and documents should be distributed to participants early in the contracting process to ensure that they have time to complete them and get them back. These legal forms and documents collect personal information about participants, so they should be stored in a secure location. The duration for storing legal forms and documents varies from state to state; check with the legal counsel at your organization.

## Staff Training

It cannot be emphasized enough that staff members need to be trained, be evaluated, be given feedback

---

**Figure 18.11**   Example of a What to Wear and How to Prepare Document

### Tall Trees Adventure and Challenge Center

### Recommended Clothing and Equipment Checklist

Planning ahead for your general needs when preparing for your team-building challenge-course experience can make the outing much more comfortable. Your advanced preparation will give you the ability to adjust and deal with different weather extremes like rain, sun, cold, heat, and so on. You could turn a miserable situation into a fun, enjoyable one. Prepare for the worst and then hope for the best!

### Recommended Summer Clothing Checklist

- ❑ T-shirts, long-sleeved and short-sleeved; SPF shirts are great!
- ❑ Socks
- ❑ Shorts (make sure they are midthigh length)
- ❑ Sunscreen
- ❑ Lightweight long pants
- ❑ Refillable bottle
- ❑ Sun hat with brim
- ❑ Appropriate footgear (tennis shoes with closed toe and backs)
- ❑ Raingear

### Recommended Equipment Checklist

- ❑ Bandana
- ❑ Insect repellant
- ❑ Personal first-aid kit
- ❑ Chapstick
- ❑ Sunglasses (with keeper strap)

*Additionally, you may be interested in bringing a digital camera, journal, and pen.*

to, and take part in an annual training plan. If your organization does not have a qualified trainer on staff it might be necessary to hire an outsider to train staff and assess their skill set. Although there are common similarities, training is very site specific based on the type of challenge course, elements available, and general outcomes. It is also important to know what OSHA guidelines apply to your staff when they are working on a challenge course. There are general regulations that cover any employee working at height. An administrator should be aware of what they are and how they are applied to participants or employees. Challenge course trainings can range from a 2-hour workshop to 60+ hours of training for certification. Training should be specific to facilitation skills, challenge-course management, portable elements, low elements, high elements, and rescue procedures.

Many challenge courses require individualized training regardless of previous experience to help facilitators learn the course policies and procedures. Development of annual training, professional-development plans, and staff-exchange programs with other challenge courses contribute to a well-rounded and highly skilled staff. The ACCT and the PRCA have recommended guidelines regarding training levels for facilitators and course management. Many vendor companies specialize in challenge course trainings. Administrators should review all options regarding certification, training, and their personal experience when conducting training.

Although training methods vary, one universal finding regarding risk management is that proper documentation of all training and certifications, whether in house (done by current staff or administration) or through another vendor, is extremely important. In a worst-case accident scenario, an administrator will be asked to provide written documentation on training and procedures for everyone involved. It is also essential to document additional training and certification that might be auxiliary to challenge course operations. Examples include level of first-aid training, rock-climbing training, or facilitator skills education. Documentation of the course training, dates, times, and members is essential. One recommended software program that will track all course certification, and let you know when certifications are expiring, is Know the Ropes (www.knowtheropes.net).

Staff training is an ongoing process. Mentoring and shadowing are beneficial to staff development and program enhancement. Shadowing allows for newer, less-experienced staff to watch and listen to more-experienced staff as they navigate through program design, implementation, and problem solving. Recognizing that facilitation styles vary as much as challenge courses do, it can be beneficial for newer staff to rotate shadowing time among various lead and return staff. After the initial training is complete, placing staff in mentor-mentee roles allows for both parties to continue sharing in the development process. The postprogram evaluation meeting is a great time to use self-assessment and peer feedback to allow facilitators and program administrator to make improvements for future events.

## Equipment Management

The equipment used at a challenge course is subject to both environmental factors and use practices that can degrade its strength and structural integrity. Ropes, cables, carabiners, and other equipment are all subject to damage from regular use and user neglect. To reduce potential risk to clients, administrators of challenge courses must develop methods and practices for managing the issuance of equipment, tracking equipment usage, and maintenance of equipment.

Equipment management methods and practices will vary among types of courses (portable, low, or high) a program has to offer. Daily, monthly, and annual inspections of equipment to identify necessary equipment maintenance and retirement are necessary administrative tasks to ensure for a safe challenge course experience for participants. Currently, the only known web-based challenge course-tracking program is Know the Ropes (www.knowtheropes.net). This is a comprehensive tool for administrators to use for tracking group information, program details, training, staffing, equipment inventory and retirement, and finances.

## Course Maintenance and Inspection

The outdoor program administrator should inspect the course each time it is used; a tracking sheet should be filled out after each inspection to ensure minor repairs or element closures occur. The daily inspection must be augmented by a yearly inspection by an outside vendor, as defined by the ACCT or PRCA, or based on the recommendations of the installer of the course. ACCT and PRCA standards vary and are subject to change, requiring an administrator to stay connected with the most current recommendations. The yearly inspection should be done by a qualified and insured challenge course professional.

# ORGANIZATIONAL SUPPORT AND RESOURCES

Although challenge programming is a relatively small (but growing) profession, there are many support agencies and networks out there for administrators and providers. Many local regions have support networks via list serves or local meetings. Texas offers TERA (Texas Experiential Resources Association, Inc., www.txtera.org), and many other states have similar networks. Many conferences and training opportunities are available through organizations (see list at the end of this section). ACCT and PRCA provide a list of accredited vendor members who are recognized by their standards as challenge course–building and training companies.

There are also many resources available for learning group initiatives and portable activities. At your library or bookstore, search on a computer for "experiential education" to locate a great number of resources. Challenge-course builders and training companies also offer trainings on these activities, and many universities offer "play days," when they invite visitors to share ideas and variations to common team initiatives. This is a great way to learn new and different portable activities.

## Resources

**» ACCT: Association of Challenge Course Technology.** This association establishes and promotes the standard of care and measure of excellence that defines professional practice and effective challenge course programs. ACCT develops, refines, and publishes standards for installing, maintaining, and managing challenge courses, provides forums

for education and professional development, and advocates for the challenge-course industry internationally. www.acctinfo.org

**» AEE: Association of Experiential Education.** The mission of this association is to develop and promote experiential education. AEE is committed to supporting professional development, theoretical advancement, and the evaluation of experiential education worldwide. www.aee.org

**» AORE: Association of Outdoor Recreation and Education.** The AORE mission is to provide opportunities for professionals and students in the field of outdoor recreation and education to exchange information, promote the preservation and conservation of the natural environment, and address issues common to college, university, community, military, and other not-for-profit outdoor recreation and education programs. www.aore.org

**» PRCA: Professional Ropes Course Association.** The PRCA promotes, enhances, supports, and contributes to the ropes course industry worldwide. This is accomplished by the development of industry standards for ropes challenge courses and canopy tours and zip line tours. Standards include installation, inspection, operation, training, and certification standards. The PRCA also provides ongoing development of operational, construction, inspection, accredited vendor reviews, and training standards for the ropes challenge course industry. www.prcainfo.org

# SUMMARY

The administration of challenge courses can be viewed merely as a variation on traditional outdoor recreation activities. However, challenge courses represent a unique facet of programming that allows facilitators to design and modify activities to accommodate the desired outcomes of the contracting client via customized experiential learning. Challenge courses are often used in partnership with and to enhance outdoor recreation or education, improving participants' overall experience and extending their learning beyond the activity. Serving as an administrator of a challenge course can be one of your most rewarding experiences, allowing you to witness amazing growth and development of participants and staff.

# Chapter 19

# Land-Based Programming

*Curt Howell, MA*

In childhood we are drawn out of doors by an irresistible call to explore. Perhaps it is our natural curiosity or need for excitement and wonder that allows nature to envelop us. Growing older doesn't mean these experiences as children should be forgotten. The magic remains the same, but the way in which we encounter it may be different. Hiking up the Sulphide glacier on Mt. Shuksan in Washington, rappelling by headlamp into the underground labyrinths of the desert southwest, or climbing on finger pockets in the Red River Gorge all provide an encounter with the wonder, beauty, and challenges of nature. Outdoor program administrators share a great privilege in introducing others to these wild places.

In this chapter we will explore essential design components of the major land-based activities that outdoor programs typically include in their programming. Throughout the chapter, consideration is given regarding how to successfully plan, organize, and manage these activities according to the most current professional and educational practices. In addition, this chapter is designed to work in concert with chapter 12 (on policies and procedures) in an effort to include attributes of individual land-based activities that an administrator may consider when developing policies, procedures, or guidelines for a program. However, the goal here is to provide the outdoor program administrator with a reference tool for effectively organizing and managing a land program, not to list specific policies. Although

critically important to successful administration, a comprehensive discussion regarding risk-management protocols, skills and techniques, and specialized equipment necessary for the accurate execution of each activity is beyond the scope of this chapter. Moreover, it is understood that each outdoor program that incorporates the land-based activities discussed here will vary in their implementation of each activity according to the level of difficulty or challenge deemed appropriate for participants, investment of resources, and expertise of administration and staff. Thus through the lens of administration, commonalities between land activities are highlighted, learning progressions are considered, and basic programming assessments are discussed. Essentially, the following sections aim to facilitate critical assessments of land-based activities and illustrate a consistent approach to the concerns facing administrators so that they may develop well-designed protocols and critically managed programs. High levels of consistency within a program are largely the by-products of an adept administration. This often results in increasing program continuity and the reduction of potential weaknesses and frustrations. Recommendations for further information and supplemental resources are included when appropriate.

Often, the heart of an outdoor organization lies in the land-based programs that it offers its participants. Land programs can range from a two-hour map-and-compass or Dutch Oven workshop in a local park to a 30-day expedition through the Gates of the Arctic in Alaska. Regional geography often dictates the types and duration of trips and other land programs that are offered locally by an outdoor program; however, the sky is the limit on the diversity of programs available once a program commits to traveling to sites outside of its proximate area. Land-based programming encompasses a variety of human-powered activities. This chapter will focus on climbing, caving, backpacking, mountaineering, winter sports, and cycling. Regardless of the selected activities, outdoor program administrators must be able to competently assess the inherent logistical, educational, safety, and training needs for different outdoor activities and activity sites.

# INCIDENT PREVENTION AND INCIDENT RESPONSE

When designing and managing land programs, each type of activity includes benefits and risks for the outdoor program administrator. Many of these risks and appropriate management strategies are transferable across activities, although it is critical that risk be evaluated in its scope according to each context. For program administrators of land-based activities, hazard and risk assessments must be given special consideration. Incident prevention or response requires more than an ability to effectively implement the right skill at the right time. Undoubtedly, this cliché is most indicative of incident response, as a staff member acts purposefully to combine training, program protocol, and judgment into a plan of action. However, surrounding all incidents are complex factors such as the environment, available resources, training, administrative practices, and personal attributes that must be considered by the administration in the design and implementation of their organization's protocols and training (Nicolazzo, 2007).

Incident prevention is the nucleus of program design. Comprehensive assessments, thorough planning, and appropriate staff training are all components of incident prevention, which lead to successful programming. Central to the administrator's responsibility is designing land-based programs that appropriately balance the competencies of the field staff with the demands of the activity,

participants, and environment. Each activity presents unique elements for consideration during the design phase. The prudent administrator analyzes each element with the objective of creating staff training that emphasizes common elements such as hiking with a backpack, using a stove, or planning a menu in effort to link consistent incident prevention measures. Thus, this linking of incident prevention measures may enhance staff understanding in the transferability of approaches across most land activities, thereby creating a baseline of knowledge from which elements such as hiking with a backpack while wearing snowshoes or crampons can be added. Because there is often more than one effective incident-prevention strategy available, administrator must understand their needs and the administrative and educational requirements when selecting designs for intended activities.

*Incident response* refers to actions taken by program staff and administration in light of an emergency in which there is an immediate threat of injury or death. Program staff must receive training and instruction on the protocols that govern their actions in response to emergencies in the field. Likewise, administrators must be prepared when the call comes that there is an emergency in the field. Incident-response guidelines are addressed in chapter 12. However the administration chooses to create and implement incident-response strategies, it is imperative that field staff be able to refer to a protocol during an emergency. Emergencies create significant stress for all parties, which can lead to impaired judgment; a concrete reference tool for field incidents provides an element of objective clarity from which staff can formulate context-specific plans. Efficient and precise incident-response strategies can be included in a program's incident-response plan (see chapter 12) and carried with instructors in the field. An incident-response plan, also called an emergency action plan, is context specific and provides written protocols, procedures, and guidelines that assist field staff in implementing plans of action based on objective factors set by staff's assessments of the situation at hand (Gass, 1998). As discussed in chapter 12, well-managed risk in the field is an outcome of careful planning and purposeful integration of outdoor, human, educational, and management skills into the program learning and activity progressions for each land program offered by an organization. In this chapter, attention is given to incident prevention and incident response as important components of programming for each activity.

# COST ANALYSES

A major component of managing a land program is conducting accurate cost analyses to assess current and future financially viability. Calculating all associated costs for a particular trip, including staff wages, transportation, food cost, and equipment use, allows outdoor program administrators to judge whether a potential trip is within a predetermined range of expense. Programs responsible for generating a majority of their own income must look not only at each particular trip but also at cumulative income versus expense to ensure positive numbers at the end of the year. A cost analysis conducted prior to a trip also indicates a minimum amount

to charge per participant to cover expenses and, if applicable, make a predetermined level of profit (see table 19.1). Some programs operate with a set minimum number of participants for each trip, such as six or eight. Many others may have either the financial freedom to run small trips or have transportation options (e.g., minivans versus 15-passenger vans). Furthermore, these expense and income predictions must be compared to actual costs so that administrators have data with which to adapt according to each expense variable. A trip report, such as the one shown in table 19.2, detailing all associated costs, income, and trip statistics, should be completed after each trip and entered into a database to prepare the administrator for reporting upwardly to department managers or officers and downwardly to front-line staff. Analyzing this data regularly keeps administrators apprised of the trip program's financial status and adds one piece of the program evaluation puzzle.

**Table 19.1** Outdoor Program

| Trip expense report | | | | | Trip income report | | | |
|---|---|---|---|---|---|---|---|---|
| Trip name _____ | | | | | **Number of participants** | **Trip price** | **Income** | |
| Staff names _____ | | | | | | | $ — | |
| Trip dates _____ | | | | | | | $ — | |
| Number of staff or number of participants _____ | | | | | | | $ — | |
| Vehicle: daily charge (OP van $20 per day) | $ — | | | | Cancel income | | $ — | |
| Vehicle: mileage charge (OP van $.20 per mi) | $ — | | | | **Total income** | | $ — | |
| Gas cost (total gas receipts) | $ — | | | | | | | |
| Shuttle or other transportation fees | $ — | | | | **Income statement** | | | |
| Groceries (purchased in advance for trip) | $ — | | | | Total income | | $ — | |
| Groceries (purchased in field) | $ — | | | | Operating cost | | $ — | |
| Leader meals at restaurants (maximum allowed for meals is $26 per day) | $ — | | | | Subtotal | | $ — | |
| **Equipment charge** | | | | | If subtotal is positive, trip profit | | $ — | |
| Item | Quantity | Item cost | Total | | If subtotal is negative, trip loss | | $ — | |
| Tents | 0 | $10 | $ — | | | | | |
| Backpacks | 0 | $10 | $ — | | **Cash advance** | | | |
| Sleeping bags | 0 | $5 | $ — | | Total of travel advance | | $ — | |

*(continued)*

**Table 19.1** *(continued)*

| Trip expense report | | | | | Trip income report | |
|---|---|---|---|---|---|---|
| Ensolite pads | 0 | $2 | $ — | | Actual expenses in field | |
| Ice chest | 0 | $5 | $ — | | Camping or lodging | $ — |
| Outfitter stoves | 0 | $15 | $ — | | Meals | $ — |
| Backpacking stoves | 0 | $6 | $ — | | Shuttle | $ — |
| Lanterns | 0 | $8 | $ — | | Groceries in field | $ — |
| Canoes and kayaks | 0 | $25 | $ — | | Entrance fees | $ — |
| PFDs | 0 | $5 | $ — | | Miscellaneous | $ — |
| Harnesses | 0 | $3 | $ — | | Total of expenses | $ — |
| Climbing shoes | 0 | $3 | $ — | | **Balance of unused cash** | $ — |
| Rope | 0 | $10 | $ — | | | |
| **Total rental income** | | | $ — | | | |
| Camping or lodging fees | | | $ — | | | |
| Entrance fees | | | $ — | | | |
| Guide fees | | | $ — | | | |
| **Total fees** | | | $ — | | | |
| Field trip insurance ($.30 per person per day) | | | $ — | | | |
| **Total operating cost** | | | $ — | | | |

**Table 19.2**  Sample Trip Cost Analysis: Gila Wilderness Backpacking and Hot Springs

| | Quantity | Total amounts |
|---|---|---|
| Number of staff | | 2 |
| Number of participants | | 8 |
| Number of days of trip | | 5 |
| Number of meals per person | | 11 |
| Total mileage of trip | | 1,075 |
| **Internal trip expenses** | | |
| Vehicle charge—$20 per day | | $100 |
| Vehicle mileage charge—$.20 per mile | | $215 |
| Estimated fuel purchase ($3.50 per gallon) | | $295.63 |
| Shuttle fees | | $0 |
| Groceries ($2.70 per meal per person) | | $237.60 |

| | Quantity | Total amounts |
|---|---|---|
| Trip leader pay ($10 × 20 hrs) | | $400 |
| Leader meals—$20 per person per day, maximum | | $200 |
| **Equipment rental cost** | | |
| Tents—$10 | 4 | $40 |
| Sleeping bags—$5 | 10 | $50 |
| Sleeping pads—$1 | 10 | $10 |
| Backpacks—$8 | 10 | $80 |
| Coolers—$5 | 2 | $10 |
| Stoves—$9 | 1 | $9 |
| Lanterns—$8 | 1 | $8 |
| **Total rental cost** | | **$207** |
| **External trip expenses** | | |
| Lodging or campground fees | | $40 |
| Entry fees | | $0 |
| Guide fees | | $0 |
| Insurance cost ($.30 per person per day) | | $15 |
| Subtotal | | $1,710.23 |
| 10% reserve cost | | $171.02 |
| **Total trip expense** | | **$1,881.25** |
| **Cost per participant** | | **$235.16** |

In addition, trip cancellations, whether caused by lack of enrollment, weather conditions, or other factors can adversely affect not only staff morale and participant perceptions but the budget as well. Policies regarding trip cancellation should be in place to protect the program, as much as possible, from last-minute cancellations that could lead to a significant reduction in participants or income, thus jeopardizing the actualization of the trip. A policy could be written stating that if a person cancels at least five business days before a trip, a full refund is issued (minus a small processing fee). It is also common to offer a credit voucher for future use with the organization instead of providing a cash refund. This option works well for university programs—any refund can simply be applied to a student's university account.

# DETERMINING LEARNING OUTCOMES

As discussed in chapter 6, the types of programming conducted by an outdoor program are driven by the organization's mission statement, which serves as an identity marker and as a measure of success during all program evaluations. Each land-based activity should support the objectives of the organization. If the design of a particular trip doesn't match the mission, then closer evaluation is warranted to understand why. Sometimes, however, program goals change and new areas of emphasis emerge from new leadership, budget cuts, or departmental and divisional paradigm shifts. In these or other instances, the organization's mission may be adapted or recreated to continue providing guidance. In concert with an organization's mission, many programs must report learning outcomes to indicate the benefits of participation in land-based activities and program effectiveness. It is the province of the program to decide which appropriate learning outcomes are relevant to its mission and goals (CHEA, 2003). Learning outcomes for land programs can be categorized into the three skill sets—outdoor, human, or education—or may require selection from a predetermined list developed by the organization. As a derivative of the organization's mission, learning outcomes should be carefully selected and measured.

Administrators must ask themselves: Do the variety of activities and courses we provide to our participants accurately reflect our learning outcomes (Sullivan and Thomas, 2007)? In choosing learning outcomes, administrators must also decide what is realistic for participants or staff to come away with after a trip or training course. Learning outcomes for participants are often quite different than for staff. For instance, participants may take part in only a day or weekend trip, whereas staff may be involved for multiple years.

Whether a learning outcome is selecting appropriate equipment for a backpacking trip, effective communication between coleaders, or demonstrated competency for decision making in a leadership position, learning outcomes must be operationally defined and measured appropriately. Here are some examples of land-based learning outcomes (Ewell, 2001):

- Knowledge—LNT principles, anchoring systems, leadership styles
- Technical skills—belaying, cooking, decision making
- Affective—self-efficacy, ethics, respect for others

## RISK MANAGEMENT

Simon Priest, in his chapter describing the components of effective outdoor leadership, states "risk management refers to the collective actions that an outdoor leader or organization might take before, during, and after an outing in order to reduce the potential for an accident and in order to minimize the potential for injury or loss" (Ajango, 2000, p.

44). As Priest indicates, risk management strives for a reduction in accident potential. Administrators work toward this goal by incorporating skill training and wilderness medicine courses and scenarios into their programs, and by teaching or encouraging cognitive processing skills such as decision making, feedback processing, and judgment development.

As noted, many program components contribute to the ability of staff to manage risk appropriately. However, it is essential that the administration continually evaluates the actuality of the theories and risk management models that have been selected and used by the program. Regardless of the training and competence of staff, complex situations (which are the norm in outdoor recreation) require a staff member's choices "in the moment" to be recognized as one of the most significant variables to be evaluated by the administration. Often, the most informative measure of a program's risk-management strategy comes from trip debriefings, staff performance interviews, and observing programs in the field. In these instances, administrators can explore how well the strategies are understood and executed in specific situations, which provides insight into the effectiveness of the program's risk management. Because this chapter deals with land-based activities, it is important to refer to chapter 12 to develop policies and procedures specific to the technical skill areas being discussed in the sections that follow.

## BACKPACKING

Many land programs began with backpacking as the initial outdoor activity. Weekend excursions to weeklong, or even multiweek, expeditions are often popular activities in a land program. Backpacking provides opportunities for participants to learn many skills that are useful for a lifetime of outdoor experiences. Setting up a tent, packing and carrying a backpack, and backcountry cooking are just few of the skills commonly taught on backpacking trips. When designing a backpacking program, administrators should consider equipment needs and location regulations as well as terrain and local weather patterns. The following considerations and table 19.3 serve as a general overview of the essential components of a backpacking program.

**Table 19.3** Backpacking Assessment

| Backpacking site assessment | Equipment assessment |
|---|---|
| • Terrain appropriateness<br>• Trail difficulties<br>• Seasons of high use<br>• Difficulty of the routes<br>• Local weather patterns<br>• Water sources | • Backpack volume and fit for each participant<br>• Shelter type and size<br>• Types of backpacking stoves<br>• Water purification type |

# Backpacking Equipment

To offer backpacking programs, administrators must first decide on what equipment to purchase. Backpacks, sleeping bags, stoves, cookware, and tents are the norm. There are many options for program equipment, but careful consideration should be given to durability and ease of use. Manufacturers are often eager to answer questions regarding their products' designs, durability, and appropriateness for program use. Some manufacturers have products, such as expedition-size backpacks, that are designed uniquely for program use and not offered at retail stores or advertised online. With some manufacturers designing equipment specifically for outdoor programs, selecting the right gear for a program is becoming easier. Also, for programs with rental equipment, keeping the backpacking program's equipment separate may prolong its life and help you avoid running short on inventory for a trip.

# Location Assessments

Creating a backpacking program involves an enormous amount of research on the areas intended for use because each area offers its own set of challenges and opportunities. Building a library of maps and guidebooks is helpful for trip planning. Guidebooks and online resources can provide great information on trails, terrain, weather, and more. As for selecting backpacking locations, be familiar with each governing land-management agency for the regions you anticipate offering programs. The Bureau of Land Management, National Forest Service, and other public and private land agencies have particular guidelines regarding use by organized groups. Some places have general regulations on group size

and, frequently, permitted areas restrict group size and camping locations. Prior to a trip it is wise to contact the appropriate land-management agency to find out if there are any current area closures or fire restrictions that will affect intended group travel.

Assessing the terrain usually begins in the office with a map and guidebooks. Selecting appropriate trails may be simple and straight forward with these

© Human Kinetics

Selecting appropriate trails allows the outdoor program administrator to match the level of difficulty to the participant, which is important to the success of the trip.

resources and actual experience in the selected activity site. Matching the level of difficulty to the group is important to the success of a trip. For many backpacking trips, hiking on trail will offer participants plenty of challenges, such as uphill hiking, loose rock, river crossings, and extended distances. Off-trail travel is a great way to avoid crowds and experience more remote areas, but traveling off-trail requires a high level of competence among staff and participants. Managing a group off-trail can be daunting but very rewarding. Consider reserving off-trail travel to staff with higher levels of experience and familiarity with the location.

## Incident Prevention and Response for Backpacking Programs

Training staff on pack fitting, foot care, and proper hydration and nutrition are basic ways to help prevent common backpacking ailments. Other training topics include sanitation, river crossing, weather assessment, and campsite selection. Program policies and procedures should provide staff with necessary information for effective field management. An incident-response plan for a backpacking trip includes having a detailed itinerary with contingency plans and alternative campsites.

## CLIMBING

As is true of many sports, climbing continues to evolve. New developments in technology have been a catalyst for many of the changes in equipment, and new techniques have increased the range of possibilities for vertical pursuits. High-performance climbing shoes, leashless ice tools, skinnier ropes, and all-around lighter equipment amount to seemingly endless potential. Plus, new and previously unthinkable routes are sprouting up all over the world as climbers continue to push themselves toward bigger goals and accomplishments. Another trend within the climbing community is that many climbers tend to specialize in a particular aspect of climbing. Outdoor programs will benefit from recognizing the similarities and differences within the sport of climbing. A vibrant climbing program is one that has mastered the fundamentals and effec-

tively applies sound training and risk-management practices.

As a recreational activity, climbing can now be categorized in the following forms:

>> **Top rope climbing** is the term used to describe the arrangement of safety equipment in which an anchor at the top-most point of a route is established prior to climbing. The climbing rope runs through the anchor at the top of the route, connecting the climber and belayer. In top rope climbing, falls can be arrested with minimal distance traveled because the rope attached to the climber runs up to the anchor rather than trailing down to an anchor below, as in lead climbing.

>> **Sport climbing** is the term used for climbing with the use of safety equipment permanently secured (by the lead climber) to a rock wall (e.g., stainless steel expansion bolts drilled into the rock). Sport climbers clip their rope trailing beneath them into these permanent anchors as a means of avoiding serious injury in the event of a fall.

>> **Traditional climbing** is the term used for climbing with the use of safety equipment temporarily placed (by the lead climber) in naturally occurring rock features, such as cracks, as a means of avoiding serious injury in the event of a fall. Traditional climbers place and remove personal safety protection from the rock as they are climbing.

>> **Bouldering** is the term used for climbing without the safety of a rope at heights generally less than 20 feet (6 m).

>> **Ice climbing** is the term to describe the ascension of frozen waterfalls by climbers. When climbing ice, climbers place safety equipment (removable or fixed protection) into the ice or surrounding rock as a means of securing their safety during the climb. Ice routes may be climbed using top rope or lead-climbing arrangements.

Despite the many kinds of climbing, some foundational elements remain consistent among them. Whether a program is offering top rope or lead-climbing opportunities, a solid foundation in rope management, anchoring, communication, and movement are essential components of a climbing program. Resources such as John Long's *How to Rock Climb!*, the AMGA *Technical Handbook for Professional Mountain Guides*, the NOLS *Climbing Instructor Note-*

*book,* and the classic text *Mountaineering: The Freedom of the Hills* provide excellent insight into the nuances of climbing equipment, techniques, and instruction. However, be aware that some misconceptions have developed through inaccurate understanding regarding equipment use and various technical systems of climbing that are in conflict with manufacturer's recommendations or without empirical support. For example, it is not uncommon to find a belayer using a Petzl Gri Gri who believes that it is designed to be used as a hands-free device. On the contrary, the manufacturer clearly advises that a hand must always remain in control of the braking side of the rope. Fortunately, many manufacturing companies such as Petzl and Black Diamond are beginning to increase efforts in educating consumers on the performance, testing, and inspection of personal protective equipment as well as on climbing knots, hitches, and common technical systems. Many manufacturers have also begun to use their websites as resources for information regarding the appropriate use of their equipment. Following manufacturer recommendations is, at the least, prudent for the outdoor program administrator.

## Climbing Equipment

When selecting equipment for a climbing program, all personal protective equipment—helmets, ropes, carabiners, and so on—should have UIAA or CE endorsement. Manufacturer's recommendations should be followed in equipment application, inspection, and decisions regarding the discontinuation of use. By using available written resources and consulting manufacturers and professional climbing organizations, you can make informed decisions concerning the best equipment and techniques for the program. Equipment and the techniques associated for their appropriate use are often highly interwoven. For example, when teaching basic belaying to participants, there is a choice between *tube-style* and *assisted-braking* devices, or both; which device you choose to use affects equipment purchase and educational strategies. Greater adaptability is possible when administrators and staff alike hold a comprehensive understanding of the principles and applications underlying each component of the climbing system. See table 19.4 for an overview of climbing assessments.

## Top Rope Climbing

The majority of climbing programs include top rope climbing. Most programs are base-managed sites, and routes can be set either by access from the top of the cliff or by leading. For staff, route selection and setting the anchors are the primary concerns. Particular consideration should be given to the type of equipment and anchoring techniques selected for the site. All staff must be trained appropriately. For participants, indoor climbing instruction is easily transferable to outdoor top rope settings. However, highlighting the differences is as important as testing the competence of belayers and climbers prior to independent climbing. While managing the site, staff should be positioned to observe climbing teams and intervene when necessary.

**Table 19.4** Climbing Assessment

| Climbing site assessment | Equipment assessment |
|---|---|
| • Type of climbing (e.g., sport, top rope)<br>• Rock or ice fall or avalanche potential<br>• Level of difficulty and time for approach<br>• Accessibility to the top of the cliff for setting top rope anchors<br>• Quantity and difficulty levels of the routes<br>• Popularity of the area or specific routes<br>• Route finding<br>• Exposure | • Use of *UIAA* or *CE* approved climbing equipment<br>• Understand manufacturer recommendations for use and recommended lifespan<br>• Be consistent throughout the program<br>• Regular inspection of equipment prior to usage<br>• Consider designating lead-only ropes to avoid losing elasticity caused by lowering cycles during top-roping |

## Lead Climbing

Teaching lead climbing requires a level of climbing experience and training beyond that necessary for managing a top rope site. In selecting the venue and individual routes, many variables that are not as critical to a top rope site must be taken into account. For instance, if sport climbing, bolt placement, ground fall potential, and type of anchors are just a few of the items that need to be assessed. If teaching traditional climbing, gear placement should be well-rehearsed with both feet on the ground before leading. New lead climbers must learn and practice on routes well below their climbing ability so that they focus on the protection system rather than on the climbing.

Mock leading, for instance, is a great way for new leaders to develop skills and confidence while remaining under the protection of a top rope. This is one of the ways administrators can balance the increased risk of lead climbing with an additional risk-management technique. Like top-roping, transferring indoor leading skills outside has a distinct advantage. Participants with indoor leading experience have a knowledge base that an instructor can build on to enhance the learning experience. Addressing differences between indoor and outdoor leading should be a component of the curriculum.

## Multipitch

Programs that include multipitch climbing should have highly experienced or professionally certified instructors to oversee this aspect of the climbing program. The complex nature of the multipitch environment requires the use of complicated rope and equipment systems for ascension, lowering, and rescue. This increased complexity requires administrators to assess the feasibility of incorporating this aspect of climbing in their programs. The competence of climbing instructors, participants, and selecting suitable terrain are a few of the essential assessments necessary for progressing to this level of climbing. As with other climbing skills, much can be taught in a gym and transferred outside. For example, belaying the second from the anchor, belay transfers, rope management, and rappelling are all great options for teaching indoors prior to a trip. Regardless of the approach, a multipitch element builds on a well-developed top rope and lead program. Administrators without the expertise or resources to lead such trips may choose to work with another program or guide service.

## Bouldering

Developing a bouldering component allows for another popular aspect of climbing that enhances a land program. Bouldering has attractive qualities, including minimal equipment, intense movement, and the freedom to focus just on the art of climbing. However, bouldering brings unique risk-management considerations and techniques. The landing zones beneath boulder problems are often full of rocks and uneven terrain. Crash pads help mitigate these hazards by providing a surface that attempts to cover the rough terrain and absorb impact from a falling boulder. A common misconception that crash pads prevent injuries can lead to a false sense of security. The use of crash pads provides limited amounts of protection from injury and should not affect a decision on the bouldering height allowed. Similarly, the majority of climbing helmets are designed to protect against impact from above (CE EN 12492) and do not protect the lower portion of the back of the head as ski or bike helmets do. As not all boulderers land gracefully on their feet like cats, there is potential for stumbling or rolling back and hitting the back of the head on rocks or other objects. At times, depending on the orientation of the boulder, the torso may strike the ground before the feet. Falls from any height pose threat of injury, whether wearing a helmet or not. Instruction on appropriate spotting should be part of the program progression. Boulder problems should be evaluated for fall zones, top outs, and descent options.

## Ice Climbing

When winter comes, climbers turn their attention to ice. From the administration perspective, programming for waterfall ice climbing is similar to rock climbing. For example, because much of the systems and equipment are the same, transitioning to an ice program may be a logical extension for a program. However, a major difference in ice-climbing equipment versus rock climbing is the initial cost for the necessary tools. Purchasing a size run of plastic boots and several sets of crampons and ice tools is a major investment. Thus, depending

The curriculum for a climbing site-based training should cover those aspects of climbing that a program facilitates.

on program goals, it might be advantageous for a program to rent equipment and avoid the initial cost and storage. This is a good choice if ice climbing is not a major part of the program. Alternatively, including ice equipment in a rental program may help offset the cost and further develop interest and opportunities for the program. Furthermore, much of the risk management is the same for top-roping or leading on rock and ice. Land programs that run both rock and ice trips should implement similar risk-management principles to minimize confusion. Because the medium is constantly changing, it might be necessary to make more frequent site evaluations to ensure the appropriateness of a particular site. Consideration of a site must take into account avalanche danger. Staff must have training and experience in the winter environment to competently assess current conditions. When planning a trip, scouting more than one site will provide alternatives if the intended site has not formed or new snowfall has increased the avalanche potential.

## Incident Prevention and Incident Response for Climbing Sites

Incorporating a climbing site management strategy into your staff-training framework is a major part of introducing not only the skills training but the risk-management strategies needed to conduct the activity. The curriculum for a climbing site-based training should cover those aspects of climbing that a program facilitates. Core components are instruction on the fundamental aspects of personal protective equipment, rope management, anchoring, communication, and movement. Attention should also be given to terrain and participant assessments, hazard mitigation, and rescue techniques. Identification of pertinent risks is critical, and staff must be trained on how to properly manage all climbing sites that they will be responsible for operating. Once they have been observed by trainers (e.g., administration) and gained subsequent experience at a particular site, staff may be ready to apply their knowledge to other venues. Also included in a site-based training are the incident-response strategies or the incident-response plan created by the administration. This may include training on basic climbing rescue techniques and plans for reaching outside help if needed. The incident-response plan for a particular site should be discussed and available for staff to update and bring on each trip.

## CAVING PROGRAMS

Caving programs provide unique experiences in otherworldly environments. A sense of wonder and play accompany these trips into the underground chambers of the earth. Caves are formed through a variety of ways. *Solution caves* are formed by mildly acidic water that seeps through soluble rock, like limestone, causing the rock beneath the surface to dissolve. *Transverse caves* have horizontal shafts that often interconnect, leading to rooms and passageways. *Vertical caves* are similar, but the main feature is a vertical entrance or other chambers that often require hand-lines or even rappelling and ascending. Many caves combine vertical and transverse elements. Regardless of the type, caves vary in size, level of difficulty, and risks involved. Land programs incorporating caving trips must research the types of caves, permitting, and regulations regarding group size and other restrictions for the caves selected. Area grotto clubs and the land agencies governing access to the caves may serve as vital resources for selecting appropriate venues and developing program policies. Basic outdoor skills such as navigation using step-logs and knowing how to protect the caving environment are essential. Human and educational skills such as coaching participants through narrow crawlways and modeling safe travel are also important in caving. A valuable resource on caving is the National Speleological Society, an organization that strives to protect caves and educate others about conservation efforts for these natural resources.

## Caving Equipment

Outdoor program administrators should consider designating equipment for caving. Because caving typically involves a lot of crawling through dirt and mud, the equipment will need to withstand abuse. Large diameter ropes should be used for rappelling and hand-lines. Harnesses without gear loops are nice because they have less to catch on protrusions when working through tight openings. As with climbing equipment, all protection equipment (ropes, anchoring and attachment materials, and helmets) should have a UIAA or CE endorsement. Program equipment may also include headlamps, ascenders, and funnels for urinating into bottles. Most caving regulations stipulate that each participant wears a helmet, has at least three light sources while in the cave, wears gloves, and has clothing that covers all skin that might come in contact with the cave. A jumpsuit or overalls make for great caving outfits. Also, filtering dust masks are sometimes used in caves because of the high concentration of guano, soot, or dust. See table 19.5 for an overview of caving assessments.

## Incident Prevention and Response for Caving Programs

A site-based training for caving can give staff the tools to make sound decisions while leading a group. Other than the obvious darkness, some hazards found in caves are cave-ins and rock fall, speleothems (mineral deposits such as stalagmites), wildlife, and moisture. Cave-ins are rare in most well-traveled caves because land managers monitor for this possibility and typically close off a section, or the entire cave, if this potential exists. Some caves contain live formations that can be damaged by human contact either by breaking or through the oils on the skin. A general recommendation, which is often a requirement by land-management agencies, is that cavers wear clothing that covers all skin areas that might come in contact with the

**Table 19.5** Caving Assessment

| Caving site assessment | Equipment assessment |
|---|---|
| • Approach difficulty and time<br>• Cave regulations (e.g., group size, season, restrictions)<br>• Type and difficulty of the cave<br>• Air quality in cave<br>• Necessary equipment<br>• Known hazards (e.g., loose rock, flash flood potential, rattlesnakes) | • Use of *UIAA* or *CE* approved climbing equipment<br>• Headlamps should be durable and extra batteries and bulbs should go in the cave<br>• Use of low profile harnesses without gear loops to minimize snagging<br>• Use of appropriate back-ups while rappelling or ascending |

cave. It is also important to remember that caves are home to many species of wildlife, including snakes, salamanders, and bats. All cavers should take care not to disturb the inhabitants of the caves they visit. For instance, in caves with bat populations it is important to respect the winter hibernation and summer maternity seasons of bats in order to protect their natural cycles. Finally, the moisture that helps create the beautiful formations in some caves also causes travel to be slippery and even treacherous. Cautioning participants and modeling careful behavior helps to minimize incidents or injuries. When necessary, hand-lines may be used to provide security in places where it is slippery and a fall would damage a formation or result in an injury. Sometimes it is appropriate to belay participants through sections that pose significant risk.

In the event of an injury or emergency, your program's caving incident-response plan should be a guide for action. For minor incidents, participants might have appropriate training to manage the situation without compromising safety. A twisted ankle can be taped and the injured participant assisted out of the cave. However, an injury that warrants spinal immobilization elicits a much different response. Land managers issuing caving permits may have specific protocols regarding caving emergencies and trained rescue personnel. Program administrators should create their incident-response plan with consultation of the particular agencies that may be involved during an emergency.

# MOUNTAINEERING

From the perspective of the program administration, mountaineering is a combination or perhaps culmination of many skills developed through other land-based activities. Beyond the skills needed for backpacking, some venues or routes may call for learning only how to self-belay or self-arrest, but others might require advanced rock- and ice-climbing skills such as fixing rope lines or short-roping techniques. During a mountaineering adventure, leaders practice the art of anticipation, adaptation, and implementation of arguably all the tools in their arsenal of outdoor skills. Because the mountain environment often affords complex and unpredictable physiological and environmental conditions, administrators must carefully consider each

component involved in a mountaineering course, implementing rigorous staffing qualifications and supporting staff with written policies.

## Special Considerations

In designing a mountaineering element for a land program, administrators should consider how to build on the current skill foundation of the program staff. Sequencing the overall training progression of staff to advance toward a subsequent training in which previously learned skills are applied in a mountain context can assist in skill transfer. Skills in glacier travel, ice ax use, crevasse rescue, and snow pack evaluation can then be added more effectively. A "snow school" consisting of principle ice ax positions, self-arrest practice, crampon techniques, and glissading may often be the initial part of a mountaineering course progression. Ultimately, the terrain or route dictates the necessary techniques required to support successful risk management.

## Equipment Selection

Much of the required equipment for a mountaineering program may be inventory already in use for backpacking and rock-climbing programs. Administrators may be able to purchase items that they are able to use in multiple environments. For example, backpacks, tents, stoves, and sleeping bags used for backpacking courses are also appropriate for mountaineering. However, considerations such as exposure to high winds and colder temperatures should be taken into account if certain equipment items are selected for use across multiple course environments. In addition, there are many items that are more specific to the mountaineering environment. Crampons, pickets, snow stakes, just to name a few, are items that might not be used in other aspects of the program. Administrators must consider whether to provide participants with necessary safety equipment, such as crampons and mountain axes, rent these items, or require participants to provide their own. Appropriate footwear is also vital to preventing cold-related injuries and to crampon compatibility. Thus programs may choose to provide mountaineering boots and purchase an assortment of sizes. Program assessment and design should guide administrators in equipment acquisition decisions.

# Incident Prevention and Response for Mountaineering Programs

A major part of incident prevention is the proper sequencing of skills necessary for mountaineering. Groups encounter trouble when attempting to move too quickly through some of the basic skills training so that it is "out of the way." Accurate assessment of the current conditions is also key to preventing incidents. Risk management for mountaineering courses may begin several weeks or months beforehand through weather forecasts, snow pack evaluations (discussed later), and scouting trips. As I have mentioned, the complex nature, elevation, and often harsh conditions found in the mountain environment require not only high levels of competency of field staff but also flexibility and an ability to accurately assess and adapt to changing conditions. Altitude sickness, as well as changing snow pack and weather conditions, must be anticipated. Table 19.6 identifies assessment considerations for mountaineering programs. Weather assessment, snow pack analysis, and training and frequent practice in basic avalanche safety, including beacon, probe, and shovel use, is crucial. Staff must also be conscious of the need to continually monitor the terrain and weather. With the remoteness of the mountaineering environment comes the increase for independence of the group on outside help for emergencies. A reliance on technology such as satellite phones or personal locator beacons can lead to overconfidence and jeopardize a group's safety. It is imperative that all members of a group be capable of self-evacuation and be apprised of the incident-response plan prior to a trip.

# SKI PROGRAMS

Winter storms in the mountains bring a variety of programming options that can serve novice to expert participants. Common winter activities offered by outdoor programs include snowshoeing, cross-country skiing, alpine and telemark skiing, and snowboarding. These activities can occur at both commercial resorts and in the backcountry and be organized and facilitated by either outdoor programs or third-party providers.

## Frontcountry Ski Programs

Frontcountry ski programs typically occur at areas developed specifically for winter sports. Commercial ski resorts that offer lift-serviced skiing and snowboarding and developed Nordic trails for cross-country skiing and snowshoeing are the most common destinations for frontcountry ski programs. Commonly, these locations operate via a fee-for-service basis and provide easy access to the activity site, an infrastructure system that offers parking services, equipment rental facilities, instruction, bathrooms, and options for food service and lodging.

Many outdoor programs offer both day trips and multiday vacations to ski resorts because they can serve a wide variety of interests, activity types, and individual skills and abilities. A frontcountry program can be offered as an all-inclusive

**Table 19.6** Mountaineering Assessment

| Mountaineering site assessment | Equipment assessment |
|---|---|
| • Level of commitment and skill involved in selected climbs<br>• Avalanche potential, seasonal, and current condition of snow pack<br>• Possible retreat options and alternate routes<br>• Appropriate group size and ratio of staff to participant<br>• Belay systems required for particular routes | • Usage of *UIAA* or *CE* approved climbing equipment<br>• Understanding of manufacturer recommendations for use and lifespan<br>• Be consistent throughout the program<br>• Regular inspection of equipment prior to usage<br>• Headlamps should be durable and extra batteries and bulbs<br>• Shelter type and size<br>• Types of backpacking stoves<br>• Water purification type |

package in which a participant receives food, lodging, transportation, equipment, and lift tickets for the price of the program. Many resorts in Colorado, Wyoming, and California market multiday trips under the theme of a "college ski week," for which they try to attract the collegiate demographic by offering a fixed price vacation that includes a combination of discounted lift tickets, lodging, events, and parties. Resorts often contract with an outdoor program to facilitate marketing efforts on campus and then to serve as the single payer for the contract. The outdoor program then sells sports to students on their campus. Contractually, as the number of participants increase, the resort provides free skiing and lodging to the outdoor program staff that are facilitating the trip. One free spot for a leader per 15 to 20 paid participants is a common ratio. Outdoor programs can also offer resort-based trips on a pay-as-you-go basis in which the cost paid to the outdoor program is only for transportation, and the participant pays for the additional services they desire once they arrive at the resort.

## Ski Equipment

Frontcountry ski programs can serve as a feeder activity for an outdoor program's rental equipment service because participants commonly need to rent skis, snowboards, snowshoes, and clothing for the activities. Purchasing and coordination of equipment that can be used for rentals and programs can create a win-win situation for an outdoor program. See chapter 16 for equipment types, rental cost structures, and management practices for equipment rentals.

## Incident Prevention and Response for Frontcountry Ski Programs

The risk management of frontcountry ski programs can be very challenging for an outdoor program because of the limited amount of participant oversight available once the program begins. During transportation to and from the resort, participants are in direct contact with the trip leaders; however, once the group arrives at the resort, participants generally disburse throughout the resort in search of terrain that accommodates their skills and abilities. Communication among participants and leaders becomes very challenging once on the hill. Great

snow conditions, sunny days, and lot of smiles are the general expectations; however, minor injuries, equipment failures, lost skiers, and major accidents are all plausible incidents a frontcountry group leader might face. Systems for centralized communication should include a regular time for in-person meetings and a location to leave notes between trip leaders and participants in case of emergency.

Additionally, for programs that offer lodging options, leaders will rarely be in contact with participants because they will be able to come and go as they please from the resort and lodging facilities. Though prohibited on most outdoor programs and trips, the use of alcohol and drugs may be more of an issue on frontcountry programs and can lead to acts of poor judgment, physical violence, and sexual misconduct—all of which may negatively impact the public image of an outdoor program, cause legal recourse, and affect the lives of the participants on the trip. A pretrip meeting sets program expectations for acceptable conduct during the trip, but participants might choose to act inappropriately. In such a case, program administration must have protocols for dealing with inappropriate or illegal conduct. Consultation with an organization's risk-management office or judicial services can assist in developing appropriate policy.

An extended period of separation between participants and leaders is not common on traditional outdoor program trips; thus specific practices and procedures for trip leadership should be developed internally to manage frontcountry programs.

## Backcountry Ski Programs

The quest for fresh untracked snow continues to draw more and more recreation enthusiasts into the backcountry. Backcountry touring, be it by ski or snowshoe, offers travelers a quiet, solitary, and rare glimpse at the beauty of winter without the abundance of people using commercial ski resorts. To meet demands of enthusiasts, manufacturers have increased the design and production of backcountry equipment such as avalanche beacons, randonee and telemark skis, and snowshoes. Commercial guiding companies have also increased the availability of instruction services, guided trips, and backcountry lodging opportunities in huts, wall tents, and yurts. Natural and human-triggered avalanches are an inherent risk of winter backcountry travel. The increased interest in backcountry exploration has come at a price. During the winter of 2007-2008, 33 backcountry avalanche fatalities occurred in the United States, and many more close calls were reported by skiers, snowboarders, climbers, and snow mobile riders (FSNAC). The inherent risks associated with backcountry travel require outdoor program administrators to design programs that both create access and accurately manage the expectations of their participants.

## Programming Options

Winter backcountry travel can occur high in mountains or in a snow-covered lowland valley. Summer backpacking skills transfer easily over to lowland winter adventures. As such, many outdoor programs offer winter camping, snowshoeing, and cross-country skiing programs for novices. Others have begun to meet the technical skill demands for backcountry skiing and snowboarding by offering in-house instruction programs that teach participants in avalanche hazards evaluation, terrain assessments, weather, and group decision-making processes. Other programs have chosen to offer a limited selection of programs but elected to outsource instruction to commercial providers. To complement instruction programs, backcountry-specific equipment can often be rented at outdoor programs located in areas that offer proximal access to backcountry skiing and snowboarding opportunities.

## Incident Prevention and Response for Backcountry Ski and Snowboard Programs

Having participants get lost, hypothermic, frost bitten, sunburned, and injured are all concerns for winter backcountry travel; however, natural and human-triggered avalanches are the primary concern for outdoor program administrators. Risk management of ski and snowboard programs will start in the office during the design stages when the administrator is setting the outcomes for the trip and identifying locations for the program. Risk management will then occur fluidly throughout the trip by means of continual assessments of the snowpack, terrain, weather, and contributing human factors of the group and program leadership (Fredston and Fesler, 2001). Ultimately, an outdoor program administrator will decide whether he or she wants to offer a program with in-house resources or outsource to a commercial guide service. Either way, it is imperative that all members of the group be capable of operating an avalanche beacon, companion rescue, basic route finding, self-evacuation, and be knowledgeable of the incident-response plan prior to a backcountry ski trip.

# CYCLING

Recreational cycling has increased in popularity over the last few decades. In some locations, the number of people choosing cycling as an alternate to driving has also grown over the past decade. This is due, in part, to local bicycle advocacy groups and public initiatives targeted at making cities more bike friendly (League of American Bicyclists, 2010). For outdoor program administrators, there might be potential to create programming promoting cycling, educating cyclists on safe cycling and bicycle maintenance, and opportunities for road and mountain-biking experiences. The variety of aspects a cycling program offers will vary by their design, and design will depend on the resources available to the program administration. Programs with limited resources, such as funding to support a fleet of bicycles, might simply organize road bike outings or mountain bike rides on local trails. Other organizations might be able to support a bike rental program and operate a full-service bike maintenance shop.

Regardless of the resources or goals of a particular program, there are some common considerations that administers interested in implementing a cycling program should take into account (see table 19.7). The following suggestions serve as a starting point for investigation into the many aspects of managing a cycling program.

## Equipment Purchasing

Purchasing a fleet of either road or mountain bikes requires much research into the type of bike, the quality and durability of the frame and components, and the different sizes available. Program administrators may benefit from working with dealers to

Moreno Novello/fotolia.com

Organizing opportunities for mountain-biking experiences is one programming option for a cycling program.

understand the strengths and weaknesses of the plethora of options available in choosing the most appropriate bikes based on program goals. In selecting a product, ease of maintenance and adjustment to fit various body types are key. Other necessary equipment items might include helmets, air pumps, tools, and spare parts. Before investing in a fleet of either road or mountain bikes, the prudent admin-istrator will give significant consideration to the maintenance cost of both parts and labor.

## Staff Education

If staff will be leading rides, teaching maintenance clinics, or be responsible for in-field repairs, there are pertinent considerations to be made regarding

**Table 19.7** Cycling Assessment

| Cycling site assessment | Equipment assessment |
|---|---|
| <ul><li>Off-road biking</li><li>Difficulty and quality of trails</li><li>Technical ability requirements for participants</li><li>Availability of trail maps</li><li>Appropriate group size and ratio of staff to participant</li><li>On-road biking</li><li>Existing bike route options</li><li>Road surface</li><li>Traffic volume and lane and shoulder width</li><li>Possible staging options and alternate routes</li><li>Visibility and potential blind spots</li></ul> | <ul><li>Proper sizing of bike to participant</li><li>Proper cycling helmet and fit</li><li>Eye protection</li><li>Regular inspection of air pressure, brakes, chain rings, and components</li><li>Minor repair kit contents (e.g., patch kit, tire levels, air pump, chain tool)</li><li>Spare parts (e.g., wheel-set, chain)</li><li>Lighting for front and rear if ride will be on roadways in low light or after dark</li></ul> |

the wealth of knowledge required to competently manage a group of cyclists, either on road or off road, and to make adjustments or repairs. Simple maintenance such as flat prevention and repair may be readily taught and learned; however, derailleur adjustments, hydraulic brake adjustments, and wheel truing take specialized training and hours of practice for proficiency. Also, the level of competence required of staff leading a road ride or mountain-biking trip is another point of concern. Knowledge of proper bike fit and ability to instruct novice riders on the nuances of gear shifting, braking, body positioning, and cadence is vital to participants' learning and enjoyment. Staff must also be familiar with traffic laws regarding cyclists, which vary across states, and how to manage a group of riders in specific contexts. To be successful, administrators must recognize the complex nature of a cycling program, identify the aspects of cycling that their program can successfully manage, and train staff accordingly.

Many resources are available to program administrators to assist in the design and education of staff on the many aspects of cycling. Four nonprofit organizations that support cycling efforts are

- The League of American Bicyclists,
- Adventure Cycling Association,
- Bikes Belong, and
- The International Mountain Bike Association.

## Incident Prevention and Response

Preventing incidents in cycling programs is related to educational progression. For instructors who ride frequently and for whom the complexities of gear shifting and body positioning may be intuitive, it could be challenging to understand the perceptions of a novice or their difficulties in learning how to change gears. Learning progressions that account for variances in abilities and are conscious of a new rider's limited experience can assist in incident prevention by appropriately sequencing necessary skills. In mountain biking for example, staff can gauge a rider's level of competence in shifting gears by having him or her ride on flat terrain. Once a rider is comfortable on flat terrain, staff may coach the ride in body positioning and to anticipate when

to shift in preparation to climb or descend steeper terrain. A rider comfortable with moving her body in and out of the saddle on flat ground will more readily grasp the need to keep her weight back on steep downhill descents. This basic skill then becomes incorporated into the risk-management plan by design. Finally, as many program rides may not be supported by a motor vehicle, having the appropriate tools to change a tube or fix a derailleur problem can help prevent a long walk.

In responding to incidents that occur while cycling, there are considerations that may not pertain to other program activities and are worthy of mention. Road crashes, especially in groups and near or among traffic pose the greatest risk. Each member of the group must be conscious of what to do in the event of a crash on a roadway. Staff should respond quickly to move uninjured riders out of traffic to as safe a location as possible and attend to injured riders accordingly. High speeds can be a factor in cycling incidents, and risk of severe trauma may be present. Helmets are not required to be worn by cyclists in many states, but their use is strongly encouraged. In creating EAPs for road rides, cell phone use may be a major component because frontcountry policies may be in place. A plan for what to do if a group, or group member, becomes separated because of traffic signals or traffic should be included as well as plans for mechanical problems.

## SUMMARY

Overall, in-depth planning based on thorough assessments will assist the program administrator in creating a land program that provides rewarding experiences to its participants. Deciding on which activities to pursue and the level of resources to invest should flow from an understanding of a particular outdoor program's mission and vision. It is the outdoor program administrator's prerogative to ensure that each of the activities align with the program's values and goals. With patience and the right strategies, creating a land program can provide meaningful learning experiences and unique recreational opportunities. One particular aspect about land activities, such as backpacking, is that courses can be developed that allow people from nearly all walks of life to enjoy the outdoors.

In this chapter, attention was given to the risk management of each activity discussed. The integration of outdoor, human, educational, and management skills produces competent personnel capable of making informed and appropriate decisions while leading in the field. Administrators must carefully plan and implement suitable staff trainings to develop competent leaders for each activity. Site managements are only as effective as the initial planning and learning progressions developed. Furthermore, incident-response plans are necessary components that guide program staff through stressful situations. Thoughtful preparation is needed to ensure accurate preparation and use of incident-response plans.

Finally, a successful land program is one that continually evaluates the appropriateness and value of each element of the program. This includes cost analyses, staff trainings, program progressions, equipment, and location choices. Maintaining a healthy relationship among administration and program staff is vitally important in order to receive honest feedback about the program's status. Administrators have many responsibilities, but a genuine relationship with each staff member validates and reinforces all other aspects of programming.

# Chapter 20

# Water-Based Programming

*Chris Stec, BS, and Geoff Harrison, MS*

Coastal kayaking in the Great Lakes . . . sailing in the Florida Keys . . . diving in the California Kelp beds—these are the headliners, but even relatively common activities such as swimming on a hot day or rafting to an isolated campsite along a river remind us of the importance of water-based pleasures in our lives. Water is a vital aspect of life that constantly draws people to it. However, the design, delivery, and management of water-based programs require that outdoor program administrators be extremely knowledgeable about water-based activities and where they take place. In this chapter we focus on common aspects present in water programming, be it boating on, swimming in, or diving under the aquatic environment. Although the type of water venue will vary, program administrators should focus on consistent administrative practices by maintaining the generalities of water programming while effectively adapting to the subtle nuances presented by each activity. This chapter considers common human-powered water sports offered by outdoor recreation programs. Each section elaborates on generalities consistent among water sports and addresses differences each category of programming presents and associated management practices that should be considered for each activity.

Water-based program administration must, like water itself, be fluid and malleable in nature in order to effectively manage the complexity of the medium. This chapter intends to serve as a general resource for the design, development, and maintenance of water-based programs. However, the chapter is not designed to serve as a comprehensive content guide because actual administration, management, and institutional practices need to be designed for each activity type and programming venue offered by an organization.

To cover comprehensively the range of water-based programs would require a text unto itself. As we have only a chapter, we will limit our scope to activities offered in three common program venues: flat water, moving water (including whitewater), and open water. Generalities that transcend venue and activity type will be discussed with attention on the unique nuances of activities occurring in each venue type and suggested incident prevention and incident-response considerations. Recommendations for further information and supplemental resources are provided to guide administrators toward further research and study.

## INCIDENT PREVENTION AND INCIDENT RESPONSE: NEEDS ASSESSMENT

Water programming has its share of hazards, with drowning being obviously at the extreme. But, as defined earlier in the text, *incident prevention* covers a broad spectrum designed to minimize an organization's exposure to physical harm, emotional harm, and other negative experiences. Both incident prevention and incident response begin and end with the backbone components of effective administration—outdoor, human, educational, and management skills.

Courtesy of The U.S. Coast Guard.

Participants learn the fine art of effective communication and balance of power during a tandem whitewater canoeing program.

Overall, the guiding incident-prevention and incident-response principles described in chapter 19 (on land-based programs) also apply to water-based programs. That said, each program type, be it on land or water, requires an outdoor program administrator to accurately apply his or her organization's mission and values to the desired objectives for participant safety and learning. When considering the development of water-based programs, a needs assessment can serve as a useful administrative tool for ensuring that proposed programs are in alignment with and in support of the overall organization's mission, values, objectives, and resources.

When assessing whether to provide water-based programs, an outdoor program administrator should apply a holistic, 360-degree assessment approach that looks both forward and backward to ensure all sources of data are incorporated into the management and delivery of each activity.

Planning should not be limited to the technical details and logistics of getting a program up and running and then onto the water. Rather, planning should be all encompassing in nature and use resources such as participant and leader feedback, peer reviews of the program, interactions with land management, industry trends, and the abundance of resources provided by trade associations and government organizations. Remember that similar to how water constantly moves through the hydro-

logic cycle, the administrative aspects of planning and preparation should not become stagnant but remain fluid to fit the needs of the organization.

Incident prevention and incident response for water-based programs requires the performance of regular assessments focused on six categories: programmatic need, cost analysis, equipment, venue, participant, and staff. These areas of assessment serve as a basis for developing risk-management strategies for all water activities. When accurately and consistently applied, the data gathered from each assessment will aid administrators in developing risk-management practices for particular activity types and selected activity venues. These assessments will aid in developing effective incident-prevention strategies and serve as a platform of knowledge for implementing an incident response. See also the Web Resources for additional information.

## Programmatic Needs Assessments

When performing a programmatic needs assessment, regardless of program type, any activities offered by an organization should align with and directly support the organization's mission and strategic objectives. Following are critical questions to consider when designing a programmatic needs assessment:

- What type of activity is being offered?
- What are the mission, strategic goals, and objectives of the organization offering the activity?
- What are the demographics of the participants to take part in the activity?
- What are the human, educational, outdoor, and management skills possessed by administrative and activity staff responsible for the activity, and what skills will need to be added through a staff-development program?

## Cost Assessments

Administrators must do both global and activity-specific cost assessments to determine the feasibility of offering water-based programs. Some equipment (e.g., lifejackets, wetsuits) can be used for multiple activities, but most water-based equipment will be specific to the activity. Items such as whitewater rafts, canoes, sailboats, and scuba equipment will require large capital investments to secure and maintain. Costs associated with getting to and from the activity site will vary depending on the type of craft that needs to be transported and how far it will need to go to be used. When completing cost analyses for water-based programs, an outdoor program administrator should consider the following items:

- What is the direct cost to acquire equipment?
- What is the cost to maintain equipment?
- What is the expected return on investment as it relates to the expected lifespan of equipment?
- What costs are related to getting participants to activity sites?
- What are the fixed costs expected to be incurred because of cancelled programs?
- What are the costs associated with training, assessment, and maintenance of staff skill sets?

## WEB RESOURCES

American Canoe Association (ACA): canoeing, kayaking, rafting, stand-up paddleboarding, and rescue instruction—www.americancanoe.org

American Whitewater—www.americanwhitewater.org

American Whitewater International Scale of River Difficulty—www.americanwhitewater.org/content/Wiki/safety:start#vi._international_scale_of_river_difficulty

Americans with Disabilities Act—www.ada.gov

Beaufort Wind Force Scale—www.spc.noaa.gov/faq/tornado/beaufort.html

British Canoe Union (BCU)—www.bcuna.com

College Sailing.org—www.collegesailing.org

FEMA—www.fema.gov/areyouready/thunderstorms.shtm

National Association of State Boating Law Administrators (NASBLA)—www.nasbla.org

National Safe Boating Council—www.safeboatingcouncil.org

NAUI—www.naui.org

Paddle Canada—www.paddlingcanada.com

PADI—www.padi.com

Safety Code of American Whitewater—www.americanwhitewater.org/content/Wiki/do-op/id/safety:start

U.S. Coast Guard Boating Safety Division—www.uscgboating.org

U.S. Coast Guard: Navigation Rules—www.navcen.uscg.gov/?pageName=navRulesContent

US Sailing—www.ussailing.org

# Venue Selection Assessments

Beyond performing a programmatic needs assessment and a cost analysis for a particular type of water-based programming, the outdoor program administrator requires the ability to make an accurate venue assessment. This assessment begins in the office during the trip-planning portion of program design and then continues into the field through the duration of the program.

A primary tenet for natural water environments is that they are for all to enjoy, but for this to occur, the environment must be used appropriately by all users. As the number of boaters, (sail, human powered, and motorized) increases, so do limits of the environment. In a growing number of wilderness areas, commercial, and sometimes even private, entities are required to have appropriate permits to recreate on our nation's waterways. Geared primarily for nonpermitted areas, the National Association of State Boating Law Administrators (NASBLA) has developed a program to help administrators at all levels begin to effectively manage the burgeoning traffic on our nation's waterways. NASBLA's document "A Guide for Multiple Use Waterway Management" is a leading publication in the area of waterway management and a good reference for administrators who might find their kayaks crossing paths with fishing vessels or even container ships.

The optimal choice of water venue for a trip depends on several variables—type of boat, weather and water conditions, experience of the program leader, participants' comfort level, and the desired outcome. Whether you start with the logical sequence of calmer to more turbulent conditions, or if other assessments dictate that a venue has a certain wind speed, wave height, or rapid classification, the baseline for learning will involve different factors for different participants. For example, stretching participants' comfort zones is an accepted practice in conditions appropriate for failure, but you do not want an experience to leave anyone turned off to the benefits of water-based recreation.

The venue must be appropriate from both a safety and education perspective and support the desired learning outcomes for participants. Whenever a variable changes in the assessments, the venue must be examined to ensure that it is still appropriate for the scheduled type of program. Regardless of venue type (flat water, moving water, whitewater, open water) the following questions should be considered:

- What are the known prevailing and acute environmental conditions at the activity site?
- What are the shoreline and terrain considerations at the site?
- Are there other types of activities occurring at the site (e.g., motorized traffic)?
- Do land-management regulations apply to the activity or activity site?
- What are the nearest access and egress points at the activity site?
- Will any manmade structures (e.g., dams, irrigation equipment, bridge or pier pilings, military installations) affect activity instruction or cause a hazard to participants?

# Equipment

As mentioned, some water-based equipment—wetsuits, booties, splash jackets—can be used across programs. Still, administrators must routinely assess the appropriateness of all equipment to ensure it offers both optimal performance and maximum safety. To ensure performance and safety, consider the appropriateness of equipment for the type of activity, the venue, and the physical size and skill levels of participants. Fortunately, manufacturers develop equipment for all types of activities and sizes of participant. For example, whether paddlers are beginners or experts, large or small, paddling solo or in tandem, on a day trip or a multiday expedition, and whether they are paddling on open water, whitewater, moving water, or flat water, a canoe or kayak has been designed specifically for their desired adventure. Innovations in equipment type, fit, and comfort have dramatically increased the accessibility of water sports and should meet the needs of almost anyone wanting to participate.

Equipment such as sailboats, kayaks, canoes, rafts, surfboards, and scuba equipment all represent a significant fiscal investment and overall organizational commitment toward water-based programs. Thus all equipment purchases should be well vetted to ensure that the equipment selected fits the mission and the programming needs of the organization. Poorly selected equipment, or equipment purchased on a whim, might end up sitting on a shelf more often than it is used. Additionally, equipment should not be reprovisioned to fit a purpose outside of the manufacturer's intended use. For example, never choose to use lake canoes on a class III or IV stretch of whitewater. Here are some general considerations for purchasing water-based equipment:

- Where is the intended activity venue(s)?
- What is the demographic of intended users (size, shape, ability, etc.)?
- What is the expected durability of equipment selected?

- What materials are used in the construction of equipment?
- What warranties do the manufacturers of the equipment provide?
- What are the direct costs of the product and associated shipping costs?
- Have you solicited feedback from similar organizations offering similar programming?

A requisite piece of equipment used for nearly all water-based programs is the lifejacket, also called a personal flotation device (PFD) (see figure 20.1). The manufacture and intended use of the PFD is

**Figure 20.1**   Different types of lifejackets, or PFDs: *(a)* type I, *(b)* type II, *(c)* type III, *(d)* type IV, and *(e)* type V.

Photos courtesy of the National Safe Boating Council.

governed by the United States Coast Guard. The USCG recognizes five types of PFDs (types I through V), which are either inherently buoyant, inflatable, or a hybrid (foam and inflation). The USCG is responsible for specifying the required test methods and minimum performance criteria for manufacturers to meet in order to receive a production approval. The testing must be performed on the product by a Coast Guard Accepted Independent Laboratory (USCG, 2010).

PFDs operate on the concept of enhanced buoyancy. Most adults need only an extra 7 to 12 pounds of buoyancy to keep their heads above water. The additional buoyancy provided by a PFD is intended to assist the wearer in performing a self-rescue or remain floating until help arrives. The weight of the wearer is not the only factor that determines the type and buoyancy required to keep the wearer floating. Body fat, lung size, clothing, intended activity for use, and type of water all factor into the type of PFD that should be worn (USCG, 2010). Nearly 70 percent of all drowning incidents involving canoes, kayaks, or rafts might have been avoided if the victim had been wearing a lifejacket. Ultimately, the best type of PFD is one that fits, is comfortable, appropriate for the intended activity, and most important, one that is likely to be worn by the user.

## Participant Assessments

The participant assessment should be anchored in the mission of the organization. The participants you anticipate serving with water-based programs should expressly fit the demographic established by the organization's mission. If you are a municipal program that serves the greater community, you will need to ensure that the range of activities and activity offerings can accommodate participants of all ages, skills, and abilities. A university outdoor program may have a narrower demographic and focus on students ages 17 to 26 but also those with varying skills and abilities. Participant assessments occur on a macro level initially through the identification of the intended user groups' ages, skills, and abilities and programming expectations. On a micro level, field instructors are responsible for dif-

ferentiating instruction and activity progressions so programs meet the needs of each individual learner.

A philosophical question that may come out of a participant assessment is whether participants need to become proficient in a certain set of skills before progressing to the next set, or should instructors have a set amount of time to show participants a series of basic skills with the hopes they will continue to fine-tune them on their own. This question warrants active dialogue because the answers will significantly influence both program design and field-management practices.

Participant assessments also allow an organization to consider incorporating a progression of participant-centered human and educational skills into the delivery of a program because they are an important aspect of participants' all-around development in a water-based discipline. As we know best what we can teach, educational skills for participants should be addressed if time allows and if they are intended to be a component of the curriculum.

Assessments can also be used to remind leaders to be cognizant of the desired outcomes for participants when following a curricular path established by the organization. The ability to mesh organizational goals, program leaders' objectives, and participants' individual goals aids in accomplishing the overarching outcome of the course.

## Staff Assessments

Once you have completed an assessment of participants, the logical next step is to perform an accurate staff assessment. Because of the dynamic nature of water-based sites, it is critical for outdoor program administrators to employ staff who can accurately assess the baseline and changing physical and emotional abilities of trip participants. Throughout a water-based program, participants will experience, hunger, thirst, fatigue, fear, boredom, and periods of being overwhelmed. Instructors must assess the state of being of participants and adapt the course content to meet the learners' needs. Instructors should always determine participants' abilities or inabilities to swim, their comfort level in water, and their motivation to learn the activity

## ADA CONSIDERATIONS FOR WATER-BASED PROGRAMMING

Whether snorkeling to view the marine life of an underwater reef off the shores of Catalina Island or learning how to kayak in a swimming pool in Ohio, water is the ultimate equalizer. People of all abilities should be given the opportunity to experience aspects of water-based programming. Nonprofit, municipal, military, or university recreation programs are all well positioned to serve the adaptive needs of their community. There are well-established types of adaptive programming, including therapeutic horseback riding, wheelchair basketball, and skiing; however, there exists an opportunity to examine all programming types to identify ways to modify activities to accommodate users with physical or cognitive impairments, or both. Programs such as the nonprofit Wounded Warrior project have championed creating adaptive recreation opportunities for injured service men and women of this generation. Wounded Warrior has adapted the formats for many moving water and whitewater instruction programs to better meet the needs of their population.

Kayaking can be adapted to meet the needs of a wide range of participants.

Photo courtesy of The U.S. Coast Guard.

Title III, sec. 302 (2)(A)(i) of the Americans With Disabilities Act (ADA) requires that eligibility criteria be equally applied to *all* potential participants. You will be a step ahead when developing program outlines and curricula if you focus on the abilities of individuals rather than their disabilities. The purpose for baseline participant eligibility criteria is to establish whether all potential participants can perform an activity's basic functions. An example of essential eligibility criteria for an ocean surfing program might be that participants must be able to swim (any stroke) at least 100 yards without resting on the bottom of a pool. To ensure participant safety, when constructing your comprehensive essential eligibility criteria, consider incorporating terminology that pertains to a range of physical, visual, auditory, mental, and psychological abilities. Here is an example of essential eligibility criteria:

- Must be able to manage all personal care and mobility independently or with the assistance of an accompanying companion
- Must be able to get in and out of a canoe, kayak, raft, or sailboat independently or with the assistance of an accompanying companion
- Must have experience paddling a canoe, kayak, or raft safely on flat water
- Must have experience safely sailing a sailboat under calm conditions
- Must be able to execute a wet exit independently

*(continued)*

*(continued)*

- Must be able to reenter the canoe, kayak, raft, or sailboat following a deep-water capsize independently or with assistance of one other craft
- Must be able to breathe independently without medical devices to sustain breathing
- Must be able to hold head upright without neck or head support
- Must be able to maintain a closed mouth and lips while underwater
- Following instruction in a pool, must be able to independently turn from face down to face up and remain floating face up while wearing a properly fitted life-jacket
- Must be able to manage personal care independently or with the assistance of an accompanying companion (friend or family member)

Once you have developed a draft set of essential eligibility criteria, work with your institution's leadership, legal counsel, and any other pertinent party with expertise in this field to ensure that the language selected provides the needed information and does not discriminate against potential participants.

Ultimately, the information gathered from participant declarations will help an administrator better design or adapt a water-based program to meet the needs of individual learners. With prior knowledge, administrators and leaders can work to adapt equipment to better accommodate participant needs. Use of boat ramps, high-back canoe seats, modified paddle grips, and padded side-walls in canoes and kayaks are all reasonable and easy accommodations to be made for participants. The goal of inclusive programming is to do just that—include—rather than exclude individuals in regularly offered programming. With an open mind, some additional equipment, and specialized training, you can expand your program's offerings while broadening your base of participants. Think *ability* and *inclusive* and you will be well on your way to incorporating an adaptive component to you program.

at the start of a course. This information aids the instructor in developing lessons and activities that can be customized to individual learners.

Unlike in a land-based program, it can be extremely difficult to stop the action in a water-based environment. Thus one of the primary focuses of an outdoor program administrator should be to honestly and accurately assess the skill level and rescue abilities of his or her organization's staff. The quality of this assessment is extremely important and might have positive or negative implications on the organization. Failed assessments can create situations in which unqualified staff might one day decide to successfully "push ahead" with a group of canoeists and make a final lake crossing as waves are beginning to increase as winds strengthen, and then tragically transfer that successful experience to a larger open-water

crossing when several tandem sea kayakers are still having issues paddling in a straight line. The decision-making process that precipitates a leader's judgment to either wait for the weather to pass or select a better and safer alternative route is a critical component of incident prevention and should be a focal point of a staff-competency assessment.

Administrators should regularly complete field assessments of their staff to ensure that outdoor, human, and educational skill sets align with the needs of the organization. Regardless of the activity type, field staff should have a combination of personal, educational, and vocational experiences that allow them to be effective in each skill set. Effective staff will possess the ability to do the following:

- Operate in a manner that supports the mission of the organization

New staff participate in a field skill assessment for whitewater rafting.

- Maintain a high level of self-care and self-leadership
- Navigate in demanding situations on both land and water
- Perform search, rescue, and evacuation procedures for activity type and venue
- Predict micro and macro weather events that will affect activity
- Connect with participants on both a personal and professional level
- Create well-designed and supported teaching progressions
- Differentiate instruction to meet the needs of all learners

Field-based assessments provide an outdoor program administrator with insightful information that can be used to design custom staff trainings that elevate outdoor, human, and educational competency. Consistent and competent field staff enhance incident-prevention strategies and help ensure effective incident-response practices.

All staff in water-based programs should be assessed in three categories: leadership competency (outdoor, human, and educational skills), venue progressions, and equipment progressions.

## The Leader: Outdoor, Human, and Educational Skills Assessment

Administrators must have a clear understanding of the design for each water-based program to effectively consider staff to lead each program. Outdoor, human, and educational skills must be assessed in relation to each activity that staff will be responsible for delivering. When considering a leader's outdoor skills, the administrator should assess staff in three core areas.

- What is the highest level of skills they can effectively perform at an individual level?
- What set of skills can they consistently perform at a demonstration quality level for students?
- What is their ability to self-rescue *and* rescue participants in a wide range of circumstances? A leader must be skilled in many rescue methods under a variety of conditions, including multiple victims.

Beyond demonstrated outdoor skill competence, leaders should possess effective educational and human skills. Educational skills have been described as the ability to teach, coach, and present information to participants. Human skills involve creating a connection with participants by conversing, soliciting feedback, and making appropriate adjustments to meet participants' personal goals or expectations. Whether it is coaxing an individual on her first solo sail out of the harbor or resolving a conflict between partners in a tandem canoe, human skills are crucial for all program staff.

Another assessment for water-based program leaders is a review of their outdoor skills. Do they have a history of sailing all types of boats, or only one type of boat? Learning the hard way through several seasons of personal paddling a whitewater kayak is valuable, but formal education across disciplines is more valuable for program leaders. Participation in courses from a reputable training facility or national organization, along with any certifications, adds value to the resume of a potential program leader. Universally recognized certifications also add credibility to your organization. Recognized organizations that provide training and certification in water-based recreation are listed here:

- American Canoe Association—canoeing, kayaking, rafting, stand-up paddleboarding, and rescue instruction
- British Canoe Union—canoe and kayaking instruction
- Rescue 3 International—river rescue instruction
- US Sailing—sailboat instruction
- American Sailing Association—sailboat instruction
- PADI (Professional Association of Diving Instructors)—diving instruction
- NAUI (National Association of Underwater Instructors) —underwater instruction

Geoff Harrison

Leader demonstrating technical skill competence during a staff development workshop focused on whitewater kayaking.

## The Leader: Venue Progression Assessment

In an office or classroom, common sense is easily used. But when a young program leader gets to the water's edge and gazes out, good judgment can sometimes become as cloudy as the skies overhead. Once all the preparations have been made and the group is standing on shore, it takes clear and knowledgeable judgment to take the next step and sail or paddle off from the relative safety of the shore or dock. It is extremely important to have written policies in place documenting which venues, weather conditions, and water conditions are appropriate for the level of a specific program. It is also important to document the types of training your program leaders have received. Allowing for individual judgment is an important aspect of any program, but the safety of participants is the highest concern. If they are safe, then fun and learning can occur. This all begins with a clear and well-defined instructional progression for venues and weather and water conditions for all discipline-specific water-based programs.

From a canoeing program at a local county park lake, to sailing on Lake Superior, to a multiday sea kayak expedition in the Kenai Fjords National Park, the three Ws—wind, weather, and waves—will always affect water-based programs and should be considered when planning activities. The three Ws are interrelated because they create the significant forces that act on any craft while on a body of water. These forces of nature can be used to your advantage for a nice afternoon sail, or they may test your rescue skills when a sea kayak turns over in deep water a quarter-mile from shore. Bodies of water are not static in nature; rather, they are subject to quick changes in condition caused by micro and macro weather events. This being the case, all venues must be selected for their appropriateness to ensure that selected sites support an organization's mission, strategies, and goals and create an optimal learning environment for participants.

## The Leader: Equipment Progression Assessment

Demonstrating a maneuver in a high-performance laser sailboat, and then asking participants to mimic the same maneuver in a Sunfish might be enjoy-able for the program leader, but it will not lead to effective learning among participants. However, with safety in mind (e.g., better ability to maneuver, room to carry more equipment, etc.), a program leader might choose to use a different kind of boat from the boat participants use. If leaders do so, they are responsible for explaining the differences in performance and techniques of the two boats to participants.

Choosing the right type of instructor and participant boats to meet the organization's program goals is a first step. With an appropriate boat, participants can be placed in the right type of learning environment to enjoy their initial boating experience while developing a desire to learn more skills. As participants acquire more skills and knowledge, they might elect to try other types of equipment and stretches of water.

# WATER-BASED PROGRAMMING: FLAT WATER

*Flat water* describes a water venue that is generally calm in nature and that lacks current, appreciable waves, and "chop." Flat-water venues, ranging from inland lakes to non-tide-affected estuaries, are fantastic locations for outdoor skill development. Nonmoving water gives participants opportunities to learn and refine skills in a relatively known and controllable environment. These venues are great for introducing basic skills that quickly allow for autonomy in other venues with similar characteristics. Flat water is also a good location to introduce a foundation of outdoor skills that can later be transferred to moving-water and open-water environments. In the following section we look at programming opportunities for flat-water canoeing, kayaking, and sailing.

## Flat-Water Canoeing and Kayaking

Canoeing and kayaking can be enjoyed in a wide range of boats paddled either solo or tandem. The basic differences in canoes and kayaks is that you sit on a seat or kneel in a canoe and paddle with a single-blade paddle, whereas you sit lower down in a kayak, with legs out in front, and paddle with a double-blade paddle. Kayaks come with either an open cockpit or a cockpit designed for a spray skirt to reduce water entering the boat from spray and splash. Most canoes are open decked, but specialty covers can be placed over them to minimize the amount of water that enters the boat.

When choosing a fleet of canoes or kayaks for your lake paddlesports program, keep the following in mind:

- Length determines carrying capacity and hull speed.
- Longer boats generally track better, but shorter boats are generally easier to turn.
- Wider boats are usually more stable.
- Narrower boats are usually faster but less stable.
- Carrying capacity for equipment and supplies is ultimately determined by the size and displacement of the craft.
- Solo boats offer participants an opportunity to experience an individual learning experience.
- Tandem boats offer participants an opportunity to learn how to share power and communicate effectively.
- You will need to store your boat either lakeside or on a trailer so you can move it from one location to another.

When designing canoeing and kayaking programs for flat-water environments, instructors might find value in scheduling either classroom or dry-land sessions that cover paddlesports history, paddling theory, nomenclature, entering and exiting boats, associated paddling equipment, program logistics, and course objectives. When designing a program, consider having participants learn and practice their skills on a calm lake or pond. This will help participants be more confident and successful when they make a larger lake crossing, paddle in a tidal environment, or take an extended excursion. The essential skills for canoeing and kayaking on flat water fall into three general categories: strokes, maneuvers, and self- and assisted rescues. Overall program design should include instructional progressions that move participants through the three categories of content before they embark on large-water crossings.

Courtesy of Boise State University.

Student learning to roll a kayak.

## Flat-Water Sailing

From a programmatic prospective, sailing can encompass a wide spectrum of activities, from learning the basics in a Sunfish on a day with light wind to racing in the ICSA championships. Maybe you expect to deal with only one end of this spectrum in your programming, or maybe you anticipate building a program that progresses through the entire spectrum of sailing options. Either way, the plan is similar.

A wide range of choices exists when selecting a sailboat. We recommend looking past the glitz and glamour (and the price tag) to search for boats whose functionality and ease of use coincide with your program's objectives. Regular maintenance requirements, repair ability, and on-land transportation should all factor into which boat or boats you choose to sail. If your primary objective is to introduce participants to the art of sailing, use equipment that will facilitate that outcome.

For most participants, simpler is better—simple boats, simple techniques, simple and straightforward goals, and hence simple progressions. Additional skills can always be added over time, but the basics, including self-rescue, should always be learned first. Ask yourself what you want participants to walk away with at the end of each session. What crucial skills must they learn to sail on their own?

Venue plays an important role. Certain conditions must be present in order to sail, and sometimes these conditions increase the chance of mishap or capsize. Sometimes a fine line separates being in control from being on the edge. Consider how quickly changing weather conditions might affect participants and the craft they are currently sailing.

Factors to consider when planning a flat-water sailing program include the following:

- Type of boats
- Acceptable wind and wave conditions
- Prudent sailing area, including distance from shore
- Ratio of staff, chase boats, and lookouts to participants
- "Rules of the road" for interactions with other water users
- On-water communication devices

## Incident Prevention and Incident Response for Flat-Water Venues

Flat-water venues are excellent for participants to build core paddling skills and knowledge. These venues are also prime locations for new instructors to build instructional judgment and content delivery skills. Though these venues are often easier to teach at from a logistical standpoint, they can present many environmental hazards that require a strong base of human, outdoor, and educational skills from instructors. The following sections discuss areas of incident prevention that outdoor program administrators and field instructors should take into account and plan for accordingly when designing and delivering flat-water programs.

**» Rescue techniques.** Self-rescue and assisted rescue techniques must be introduced and regularly practiced in water-based environments to ensure staff and participants can effectively orchestrate a rescue in the incidence of an unforeseen "out of boat event." A common and potentially dangerous mistake is to use kayaks and canoes that do not have a bulkhead or some type of supplemental flotation. This error makes self-rescue and assisted rescues extremely difficult because the boats can completely fill with water during a capsize, which makes them extremely heavy and difficult to manage. Another common mistake is to teach self-rescue and assisted rescues with empty craft, and then to set out on an overnight or multiday trip with loaded boats. Participants must practice in an environment that matches the situations expected on the trip. Practicing with fully loaded boats, although more difficult, better prepares participants for what might occur on the water.

**» Navigation.** Navigating over stretches of open water on the Great Salt Lake in Utah, or through the mangrove islands of the Florida Everglades, requires basic map and compass skills. One of the keys to navigation in a canoe or kayak is to always be aware of your surroundings and your position relative to them. A prudent practice is to have instructors use waterproof map cases and a deck-mounted compass during water navigation. Because techniques for water navigation differ from those for land navigation, staff must be competent in both styles (because a water trip can easily become a land trip as a result of weather, equipment failure, or participant need).

**» Communication.** On-water communication begins prior to leaving shore. In a pretrip talk, determine your on-water group-management strategy. Establish maximum distances between boats and what to do if one boat travels too far ahead or too far off to the side. How do participants alert others of a capsize? What if inclement weather approaches rapidly? A loud whistle that works when wet is an important piece of equipment to bring along. Whistles should be issued one per boat, or even one per person. Depending on the venue, other items worth consideration are waterproof two-way radios and cell phones or satellite phones. For expedition programs operating on large flat-water venues such as the Great Lakes, an emergency position indicating radio beacon (EPIRB) is a tool to consider; once activated, the beacon sends out a distress signal that indicates the craft's exact location. The USCG has regulations regarding signaling devices that apply to some small craft, which might include signal mirror, flashlight, and emergency flairs.

**» Weather.** Wind, weather, and waves can all affect your trip. Canoes generally have a higher profile and will be more affected by wind. Waves breaking over the bow or stern of an open canoe can also be a cause for concern. Even in a kayak with a spray skirt, bad weather, strong winds, and large waves can present significant challenges. Sailboats, regardless of design, also fall victim to wind, weather, and waves. Thus outdoor program administrators must remain vigilant about changing weather patterns. Minor weather events can make for challenging learning conditions, and major weather events can create significant hazards to participants. Volumes have been written about lightning and severe weather, both on land and water. All thunderstorms are dangerous. Every thunderstorm produces lightning. In the United States, an average of 300 people are injured and 80 people killed each year by lightning. Although most lightning victims survive, people struck by lightning often report a variety of long-term debilitating symptoms. When developing lightning and severe weather protocols, keep in mind that your participants might not be able to land on some sections of shoreline. Instructors must be vigilant when planning open-water crossings when extreme weather patterns are expected. In the event of a developing thunderstorm, they must get participants off the water and to a sheltered area as quickly as possible. Have participants squat low to the ground on the balls of their feet, with head between their knees and hands over their ears. The goal is to provide the smallest target possible and to minimize contact with the ground (FEMA, 2010).

**» Sharing multiuse waterways with other boaters.** Finally, kayakers, canoeists, and sailors all share flat-water venues with other users. The waves created by a personal water craft or a large motorboat might create a temporary challenging paddling environment. Remember that in a multiuse environment all craft has a right to use the water. The USCG and the ACA both offer information pertaining to the rules of the waterways. Instructors and participants should know their rights and how to engage with other craft.

# WATER-BASED PROGRAMMING: MOVING-WATER AND WHITEWATER VENUES

The wide variety of rivers in the United States allows for a diverse mix of programming opportunities, whether you choose to kayak on a slow-moving blackwater river in Georgia, canoe through a canyon in the desert southwest, or whitewater raft in the mountains of Montana. Because rivers can be used for a diverse range of programming, outdoor program administrators must expect a wide range of other users traveling on a river. From ocean vessels coming into port on the Hudson River to a fly fisherman on the bank of the Trinity River, other users must be taken into account when programming activities for moving and whitewater venues. Once water begins to flow downstream, all aspects of a moving water or whitewater trip must be considered, including participants' goals and safety, the experiences of others, and respect for the environment.

The shape of a river bottom and shoreline combined with the volume of water flowing over it will dictate whether a stretch of water is considered moving water or whitewater. The International Scale of River Difficulty uses a class I through VI rating system to identify general river characteristics for each class of water and the equipment, experience, and rescue skills suggested for traveling it (see table 20.1). Recreation programs commonly use stretches of water that range from class I through IV with the frequency of program use dropping off as the difficulty increases.

Here we will consider stretches of water in classes I and II as moving water. In general, class I and II stretches of river present paddlers with a fast-moving water environment with small waves and wide, clear channels free from major obstructions. The risk to swimmers is minimal because water conditions allow self-rescue. River touring in canoes and kayaks is covered in the moving-water section of this chapter.

Whitewater reflects class III and IV river conditions. Class III whitewater venues offer moderate, irregular waves capable of swamping an open canoe. These features might be difficult to avoid, but injuries while swimming are rare, and self-

**Table 20.1** River Classification Scale

| Class I rapids | Fast-moving water with riffles and small waves. Few obstructions, all obvious and easily missed with little training. Risk to swimmers is slight; self-rescue is easy. |
|---|---|
| Class II rapids: novice | Straight-forward rapids with wide, clear channels that are evident without scouting. Occasional maneuvering required, but rocks and medium-sized waves are easily missed by trained paddlers. Swimmers are seldom injured, and group assistance, while helpful, is seldom needed. Rapids at the upper end of this class are designated class II+. |
| Class III rapids: intermediate | Rapids with moderate, irregular waves that might be difficult to avoid and which can swamp an open canoe. Complex maneuvers in fast current and good boat control in tight passages or around ledges are often required. Large waves or strainers might be present but are easily avoided. Strong eddies and powerful current effects can be found, particularly on large-volume rivers. Scouting is advisable for inexperienced parties. Injuries while swimming are rare; self-rescue is usually easy, but group assistance might be required to avoid long swims. Rapids at the lower or upper end of this class are designated class III– or class III+. |
| Class IV rapids: advanced | Intense, powerful, but predictable rapids requiring precise boat handling in turbulent water. Depending on the character of the river, it might feature large, unavoidable waves and holes or constricted passages demanding fast maneuvers under pressure. A fast, reliable eddy turn might be needed to initiate maneuvers, scout rapids, or rest. Rapids might require "must" moves above dangerous hazards. Scouting might be necessary the first time down. Risk of injury to swimmers is moderate to high, and water conditions can make self-rescue difficult. Group assistance for rescue is often essential but requires practiced skills. A strong Eskimo roll is highly recommended. Rapids at the lower or upper end of this class are designated class IV– or class IV+. |
| Class V rapids: expert | Extremely long, obstructed, or very violent rapids that expose a paddler to added risk. Drops might contain large, unavoidable waves and holes or steep, congested chutes with complex and demanding routes. Rapids might continue for long distances between pools, demanding a high level of fitness. What eddies exist might be small, turbulent, or difficult to reach. At the high end of the scale, several of these factors might be combined. Scouting is recommended but can be difficult. Swims are dangerous, and rescue is often difficult even for experts. A very reliable Eskimo roll, proper equipment, extensive experience, and practiced rescue skills are essential. Because of the large range of difficulty that exists beyond class IV, class V is an open-ended, multiple-level scale designated by class V.0, V.1, V.2, etc., with each level more difficult than the last. Example: increasing difficulty from class V.0 to class V.1 is a similar order of magnitude as increasing from class IV to class V. |
| Class VI rapids: extreme and exploratory rapids | These runs have almost never been attempted and often exemplify the extremes of difficulty, unpredictability, and danger. The consequences of errors are severe; rescue might be impossible. For teams of experts only, at favorable water levels, after close personal inspection, and taking all precautions. After a class VI rapids has been run many times, its rating may be changed to the appropriate subclass V rating. |

The complete Safety Code of American Whitewater can be found at www.americanwhitewater.org/content/Wiki/safety:start.

Courtesy of American Whitewater: www.americanwhitewater.org.

rescue is possible (although group assistance might be required to avoid long swims). Class IV whitewater offers demanding rapids; large, unavoidable waves; hydraulic features; and constricted passages that require fast, complex maneuvers, often done under pressure. The risk of injury to swimmers is moderate to high on class IV whitewater, and water conditions can make self-rescue difficult. Group assistance for rescue is often essential and requires practiced skills. Rafting, canoeing, and kayaking activities are covered in the whitewater section of this chapter.

Outdoor program administrators must understand the general characteristics and forces of water when they design programs for a moving-water or whitewater venue. River volume is measured in cubic feet per second (cfs). A cubic foot of water moving past a single point in one second is considered one cfs. Small creeks might move at a flow of 400 cfs, whereas a large river such as the Salmon River in Idaho might flow upward of 90,000 cfs during spring runoff. Unless you view a river in the same spot at various water levels, it can be hard to discern how many cfs are present because other factors (e.g., depth and width of river) come into play.

To create a visual image of cfs, an average bathtub contains four cubic feet of water. If a river was flowing at a rate of 1,200 cfs, then every second about 300 bathtubs' worth of water would be moving past a single point in the river. A cubic foot of water weighs about 8 pounds (3.6 kg), which means that a kayak, without flotation and a volume of 80 gallons (302 L), might weigh as much as 640 pounds (290 kg) when submerged. The weight of a boat combined with the speed of water flow can make recovery extremely difficult, or impossible.

The volume of cfs and gradient of the river create the speed at which the water flows. If a participant fell out of a raft into a 1-mile (1.6 km) per hour current, they would float approximately 88 feet (26.8 m) in a minute. A 4-mile (6.4 km) per-hour current will move the same participant 88 feet in only 15 seconds. Understanding the speed and force of moving water is important when designing water-based programs because the choices you make influence the safety of the learning environment.

Common hazards for moving and whitewater venues are strainers, rocks, overhanging tree limbs, and manmade obstructions such as bridge abutments and low head dams. When the speed and force of water hits an object, there is potential that either a boat or a participant could become pressed against the surface and trapped underwater. A serious and often fatal hazard is a foot entrapment, which can occur when a participant stands in the moving current of a river and accidentally wedges a foot between two rocks. This type of hazard can be avoided by training participants to use a safe-swimmer position that places them floating on their backs with their feet pointed downstream.

Once a program progresses to a river environment, a different set of instructional challenges and incident prevention and response issues arise. Both staff and participants develop and refine their basic paddle strokes and technique in flat-water environments (pools, lakes, etc.) and then progress toward moving-water and whitewater venues. Whether it's different instructional progressions, on and off water hazards, or rescue techniques, program staff must have additional training to be effective leaders. The speed and force of moving- and whitewater require specific training in swift-water rescue. Organizations such as the American Canoe Association

and Rescue 3 International are recognized and credible sources for this type of training.

# Moving Water: Canoeing and Kayaking

The term "touring" in the paddlesports realm encompasses a wide spectrum of activities that occur on moving water. Touring generally refers to paddling in either calm-moving water or a lake. Almost any kayak or canoe can be used for touring (as long as conditions remain benevolent), and an average outing lasts only a few hours. Some extend the touring moniker to overnight or multi-day journeys. Touring is generally done for scenic or wildlife viewing, photography, noncompetitive exercise, or simply to enjoy being out on the water. It also provides valuable skill-building experiences for participants who seek longer trips or more challenging venues.

Touring on moving water, be it for an afternoon or a multiday camping trip, allows participants to travel longer distances with more equipment on board. Touring craft are designed to be stable, easy to handle, and capable of carrying large volumes of equipment. Touring designs might be either short or long in length, and most kayaks designed for recreational touring have large cockpits that do not require spray skirts. Touring canoes and kayaks typically have longer water lines and reduced rocker in the ends to allow the boats to track toward their destination.

Moving water requires participants to further their essential skill development in three basic categories: strokes, maneuvers, and self- and assisted rescues. Strokes include not only propulsion and turning but also stationary strokes that can use the power of the water current to move the boat toward a desired location. Maneuvers include tighter turns, edging, leaning, peeling in and out of eddys, and ferrying back and forth across the current. Self-rescues likely include bow rescues and Eskimo rolls.

# Whitewater: Rafting, Kayaking, Canoeing

Whitewater canoes, kayaks, and rafts come in an ever-increasing range of sizes and styles to meet the paddling needs and desires of consumers.

Whitewater rafts and catarafts come in styles that accommodate both day trips and multiday expeditions. Modern rafts and catarafts are self-bailing in nature and commonly range from 9 to 20 feet (2.75-6 m) in length with each size trying to offer a balance of performance and payload. Whitewater kayaks and canoes are generally shorter than touring boats because they are designed to be highly maneuverable to paddle around river obstacles. Some hard-shell whitewater kayaks are designed with an open cockpit and are known as "sit on tops." Inflatable kayaks are another craft for whitewater paddling that allow for easy entrance and exit from the craft. Most whitewater kayaks are decked craft that use a spray skirt to keep water from entering the boat. Kayaks and canoe designs fall into one of three categories:

- General river running—easy to learn in, stable, and moderately maneuverable

- Play boats—high-performance, for playing in river features such as holes, waves, and eddy lines
- Creek boats—high-performance river-running boats that possess large volumes, room to carry overnight equipment inside the hull; highly maneuverable for complex river moves on hard whitewater

Some canoes are designed for river running rather than flat-water paddling. Kneeling in a canoe is useful in whitewater; knee pads work well to improve comfort and performance. Small air bags in the bow and stern are important additions because they displace space in the boat that would be filled by water coming over the sides of the canoe. Also, painters (lines attached to each end of the canoe) are a valuable, though overlooked, piece of equipment because they help manage and control a boat when needing to swim it to shore or line it down a bank.

Geoff Harrison

Students participating in a whitewater rafting adventure on the class IV canyon stretch of the South Fork of the Payette River in Idaho.

When choosing rafts, canoes, and kayaks, think size and functionality. The latest model might not be the best when it comes to teaching beginners how to roll a kayak, row a rapid, or catch an eddy. When choosing your fleet of rafts, canoes, and kayaks, ask these questions:

- Do you need boats with large carrying capacities, or are you desiring craft for day trips?
- Do you want longer craft that tracks in a straight line or shorter, more maneuverable craft?
- Do you want wider more stable craft or narrower faster craft?
- What are the pros and cons of selecting tandem, solo, or multipassenger craft?
- Will your fleet of boats accommodate a wide range of body sizes?

## Incident Prevention and Incident Response for Moving-Water Venues

Once a program progresses to a moving-water environment, a new set of challenges and management issues arise. Whether it's different rescue techniques, an awareness of new hazards, or a different participant skills progression, whitewater venues require high degrees of competency from staff and administration. As a result of the media and subsections of the paddlesports industry, some new participants to whitewater arrive with a common question: What is the class of that rapid?

It becomes almost a status symbol to have paddled a class III or class IV rapid. In the world of whitewater paddling—whether you are in a canoe with airbags, a high-volume creek kayak, or a 16-foot (4.9 m) paddle raft—on-site judgment should always outweigh a guidebook's classification of a rapid. Factors such as air temperature, water temperature, water level, debris, how a participant has been paddling earlier in the day, and physical and mental energy levels should all play roles in the decision of whether or not to run a rapid. The outdoor program administrator must understand that many participants desire to kayak a class III rapid, and he or she must weigh that desire against the skills the participants possess.

Hazards of moving water range from other paddlers to rocks, strainers, hydraulics, and other natural or manmade features that alter the flow of water. Compare Warwoman Creek Rapid on section III of the Chattooga River on the Georgia–South Carolina border to Hermit Rapid on the Colorado River in the Grand Canyon. The Chattooga River might have a few hundred cubic feet per second (cfs) flowing through it, whereas the Colorado River has over eight thousand! On average, the fifth wave in Hermit Rapid is close to 20 feet (6 m) from trough to crest—that's two stories! The total vertical gradient in Warwoman Creek Rapid might be only 6 or 7 feet (1.8-2.1 m) spread out over 30 feet (9.1 m) of horizontal river. Hermit Rapid offers huge waves with exploding crests, so if you flip and swim you will be in for a wild ride until you reach the calm water of the eddy below. If you flip and swim in Warwoman Rapid, the likelihood of you or your boat getting stuck on or wedged under a midstream rock poses a significant hazard, even though the water might not even be waist deep!

Effectively and efficiently turning a canoe or kayak becomes an important skill for participants in whitewater venues. In moving-water environments, sharper turns might be required to paddle between rocks or to avoid a downed tree.

Knowledge about a specific river, or section of river, is important in your initial program development. Here are questions that should be addressed about each section of river prior to floating off from the put-in:

- What are the obstacles or hazards downstream?
- Are there natural objects and hazards in the river channel (e.g., downed trees, strainers, boulders, rapids)?
- Are there manmade objects and hazards in the river channel (e.g., low head dams, military installations, bridge abutments)?
- What are the general weather patterns at the activity site?
- Are there other users to be aware of (e.g., motorized boat traffic, fishermen, other commercial or individual paddling groups)?
- Do you know of all potential put-ins and take-outs along the river, including hiking trails?

Geoff Harrison

Paddler kayaking on Canyon Creek in Washington, class IV.

- Is all necessary equipment (group gear and safety equipment) properly secured in boats?
- What is the worse incident that could happen to a group on the most remote portion of this river section? How prepared are instructional staff to deal with it?
- Has a float plan or trip plan been filed?
- What would professional emergency response time be to the activity venue?
- Do you have a regular review cycle and evaluation process for this program?

As a result of current boat designs, there is a tendency to inadvertently fast-track participant learning experiences. But it is always important to take time to provide participants with skill progressions and assessments skills appropriate to the stated outcomes of the your programs. Properly trained and regularly assessed staff are crucial to successful whitewater programs. Staff must know the general characteristics of the activity venues, venue hazards, optimal learning progressions for the venue, and, most important, the mission and desired program outcomes of their organization.

# WATER-BASED PROGRAMMING: OPEN WATER

When freshwater turns to brackish water or saltwater, a series of additional considerations arise for program administrators. Just the equipment maintenance procedures alone could fill an entire chapter—from maintaining scuba tanks and regulators to cleaning boat hulls and washing lifejackets. Whether participants are under sail, paddling a kayak, or diving under the water's surface, a program needs to account for the intricacies associated with operating in these venues. The marine environment holds vast opportunities for meeting program and participants' goals, but these must be approached with proper planning to ensure enjoyable experiences.

Instructors and participants must follow some basic rules when sailing, paddling, snorkeling, or diving out in the marine environment. Because of the vastness of the venue, additional rules apply regarding visual and auditory communication devices. Even if your human-powered craft might technically have the right of way in a marine environment, that shrimp trawler or speedboat might not see you or heed the regulation—and, unfortunately, size and speed will always win. Thus it is critical that buoys, markers, and signals are recognized and understood by all instructors and participants. When in doubt, always yield to a larger craft, because it is more difficult for it to change course than for you to maneuver and pass to the rear of the boat in your path.

The water surface conditions in a marine environment can change rapidly. Rip currents can form and dissipate; sets of waves can change in frequency or height as a result of fetch and wind speed. Tidal fluctuations must be considered in terms of timing, height, and current speed. Unlike in a river environment, where you can swim to shore or where a rapid might end in a calm pool, the waves and currents of the ocean continue relentlessly.

Seamanship is not learned only from books or in a classroom but from being regularly out on open water. Practical, hands-on experience can be one of the best teachers. That said, basic skills learned ahead of time will prepare participants for success better than simply sailing into the blue. Thus, to promote participants' learning and success, basic skills should be practiced repeatedly in a suitable environment before putting them to the test in an off-shore (or even near–shore) environment. It's one thing to capsize in a small, warm-water lake relatively close to shore; it is quite another if you're a half-mile from the nearest marshy area in a two-foot (.6 m) swell. As usual, keys to incident prevention are a solid knowledge base, proper preparation, skills that have been routinely practiced, and good on-site judgment.

## Snorkeling and Scuba Diving

From the rich aquatic life of the Dry Tortugas, 68 miles (109 km) from Key West, to the cold waters of Prince William Sound in Alaska, snorkeling and scuba diving are lifetime recreational activities that open up new worlds to be explored.

Marine open-water sites are most commonly used for snorkeling programs; however, they can be run from just about anywhere, including freshwater lakes, slow-moving rivers, coastal bays, and the open ocean. A participant's comfort in the water and ability to swim are key prerequisites that must be discerned. Even competent swimmers should wear a flotation aid such as a snorkel vest. Doing so allows more energy to be spent in enjoying the view rather than in maintaining buoyancy.

One significant wrinkle regarding scuba programs is that individuals must be certified to participate; however, becoming certified is not a huge hassle. Several major organizations in the United States offer scuba certification:

- PADI (Professional Association of Diving Instructors)
- NAUI (National Association of Underwater Instructor's)
- SSI (Scuba Schools International)
- YMCA Scuba (Young Men's Christian Association)

Incorporating a scuba-certification course into your yearly schedule, strategically followed by a series of trips to far and near diving destinations, allows for a logical progression for your program participants. When organizing your program, remember that many professional dive operators are concerned when students do their "check-out" dives only in the local quarry rather than gaining true diving experience via diving from a boat.

There are various equipment considerations in running a scuba program. Programmatic choices range from owning an arsenal of rental gear, wetsuits, booties, fins, masks, snorkels, weight belts, buoyancy compensators, regulators, oxygen tanks, and compressors to partnering with a local dive operator to supply the needed equipment. Many programs choose the latter option because it reduces the need for specialty equipment knowledge, front-end equipment investments, and long-term costs associated with maintaining equipment.

Both curriculum and instructional methods are established by the associations responsible for certifying students; thus administrators can spend their energy on marketing a slew of domestic and international programs. Each association offers several trainings for an administrator to pick from when designing programs for their participants. Courses range from resort courses to courses in advanced open-water diving and rescue diving.

# Open-Water Sailing

Marine sailing venues vary widely, from sailing in Long Beach Harbor, California, to cruising along the Gulf Coast, to blue-water sailing from the east coast of Florida to the Bahamas. Equipment maintenance concerns, prudent participant progressions, and the ability of staff to assess and manage the quickly changing conditions of the marine environment are some of the challenges of offering open-water sailing programs.

As in freshwater sailing, there are many boats and equipment choices in the marine environment. Saltwater environments require administrators to establish vigilant maintenance routines for all boats, trailers, and personal protection equipment. Equipment purchased for a sailing program should be designed specifically for the rigors of the environment. Both the financial cost and the knowledge required to maintain equipment should be considered when planning a purchase.

The intended learning outcomes for an open-water sailing program help determine the type of craft to choose. Instructional boats range from small, one-person craft, to laser sailboats, to four-person expedition boats such as the Drascombe longboat, to large keelboats built for overnight voyages. Each type of boat accommodates a different range of programming and requires staff to possess a corresponding set of outdoor skills appropriate for the activity and venue selected.

Sailing in an open-water environment requires instructors to have a complex array of outdoor skills complemented by experience and judgment. At a minimum, instructors must know how to teach and apply techniques and methods for

- sailing with nonworking equipment, such as a broken rudder, mast, or sail;
- effectively reading nautical charts and using celestial navigation, GPS devices, and long-range communication devices;
- anchoring under sail in both fair and foul weather;
- leaving a dock or mooring;
- managing a craft that becomes grounded;
- working on mechanical and nonmechanical equipment associated with the craft;

- controlling craft in all possible wind and sea conditions at selected locations;
- recovering participants and crew members who fall overboard;
- providing clear expectations and directions to crew members and participants; and
- surviving in a life raft when no land is in sight.

When designing and administering open-water sailing programs, several considerations should be made to reduce the potential for loss. Environmental conditions such as weather, waves, and currents; equipment failure; and staff competence can all affect the safety of participants. Proper program design and management must occur at all levels of the organization, including administration, logistics, and field staff. Practical, hands-on experience is very worthwhile, but basic skills learned in venues that support progressive instruction better prepare participants for sailing on their own.

# Open-Water Sea Kayaking

Whether it is an up-close encounter with orcas in the Pacific Northwest, manatee sightings in south Florida, or exploring the shoreline of Maine, coastal kayaking in the marine environment allows participants to experience the freedom of the open water—provided they have the skill and guidance to paddle there.

Instructing participants in open-water sea kayaking requires specialized equipment. Coastal kayaks must have secure hatches, preferably bow and stern bulkheads, spray skirts for cockpits, and grab lines. Length is important for traveling efficiently, and also dictates carrying capacity. Some kayaks designed for coastal use might have a rudder or dropdown skeg. The benefits of rudders and skegs are that they assist a paddler in controlling the kayak; a drawback is when one of the moving parts of a rudder or skeg breaks or jams. Paddling a kayak without the use of rudders and skegs is a skill worth practicing, just in case a "What if...?" scenario occurs. An abundance of safety and rescue equipment is on the market targeted directly at coastal kayakers. You do not need to purchase every gadget out there, but in preparing for an outing, ask yourself these questions, with your participants in mind:

- What do I need to communicate effectively with my immediate group?
- What do I need to communicate effectively with other boat traffic?
- What do I need to communicate with the Coast Guard or other rescue agency?
- In case of a capsize, what do I need to help me reenter my kayak and empty the water?
- What do I need to effectively navigate?
- Do I need special equipment for paddling in the early morning or late evening?

Whatever equipment you purchase for your program or provide to your program leaders or participants, remember that equipment is only as good as the training that goes along with it.

To increase the chances of a positive coastal kayaking experience for participants, their learning progression once again starts on shore, moves to a calm, protected body of water, and then progresses to a coastal environment. Devote ample time to teaching assisted rescues—not just instructor demonstrations but successful practice for each participant. Everyone involved should be adept in at least one technique to reenter a kayak, and preferably multiple techniques.

Being prepared for a significant change in weather or water conditions is mandatory in coastal kayaking program management. Researching tide, wind, and surface conditions are vital aspects of pretrip planning, but being able to discern changes while out on the water is equally important. This skill should be taught to all staff and participants, as well. Other aspects of sea kayaking worth mentioning involve the potential for surf-based launches or landings, hypo- and hyperthermia, and bottom topography (e.g., oyster bars, sharp rocky outcrops). Knowing how to deal with these conditions is important, and should be effectively conveyed to staff and participants.

## Open Water: Surfing and Bodyboarding

Surfing and bodyboarding are two near-shore activities that require very little equipment and stress a skill that most participants will already have: swimming. The transference of an existing kinesthetic skill set to a new venue helps reduce the amount of training participants must have before they can experience the activity. New knowledge and skills for surfing and bodyboarding participants includes information about the environmental aspects of the marine environment, body and board position for catching a wave, personal safety, and social norms for the sport.

Equipment required for surfing and bodyboarding includes a board, a wetsuit, and booties. Surfboards vary in construction from solid foam to foam interiors with an exterior coating of either epoxy or fiberglass. Bodyboards are typically foam with a plastic bottom side. Both kinds of board are usually used with a foot or wrist leash to keep the board from floating away after a wipeout or crash. Wetsuits are neoprene in construction and vary in thickness to keep users warm and comfortable. Booties are neoprene and used to protect the user's feet from hazards on the ocean floor.

## Incident Prevention and Incident Response for Open-Water Venues

When you are conducting water-based programs in open-water environments, several considerations can reduce the potential for injury or mishap. Environmental conditions such as weather, waves, and currents can all affect the safety of participants, as can staff competence. Depending on the type of boat and seamanship skills of participants, being ready for cold water immersion is important to prepare for ahead of time. Although cold water will not be a concern when sailing in Key Biscayne, Florida, in August, it certainly will be when sailing in Bellingham Bay, Washington, in any month. Maintaining body temperature is always a concern in water environments. Regardless of water temperature, the body will eventually cool down when immersed, so measures must be taken to avoid hypothermia.

The venues in which you sail, paddle, or dive all present their own set of challenges; a program administrator must always be mindful of preparing program leaders and participants for rapidly changing weather and water conditions. Theoretical discussions are helpful, but the trick is figuring out a way to practice preparations in a controlled environment.

In near-shore sailing, coastal kayaking, and off-shore diving, weather conditions significantly affect program preparation and decision making. Aspects to consider are tides, current speed, chop, wave height, distance from shore, distance from a safe harbor, other vessels, navigation skills, and dealing with marine life. Shark attacks are rare, but oyster cuts on feet are not. Scrapes and stings in the marine environment are often a direct result of inexperienced participants or poor instruction. Other hazards to be wary of are currents (both on the surface and at depth), and how current affects not only location relative to a boat or shore but also the level of energy required to maintain position. Written protocols and contingency plans are useful, but in hazardous conditions program leaders must be well practiced in making fast and accurate judgment calls as required.

When operating in the marine environment—whether sailing through a busy harbor or teaching students the basics of drift diving—significant discipline-specific training for program leaders is key. They need to know more than just the basic skills of the activity. A broad education on such topics as weather reading and emergency communication is extremely useful, if not essential. All staff should be familiar with the basics of the U.S. Coast Guard's "Rules of the Navigable Road."

# SUMMARY

Water-based activities require more than just the initial training. Continuing education is crucial to developing sound risk-management strategies and to increasing the success of your participants on and in the water. Whether the aim is to improve teaching an outdoor skill, define a human skill, or instill a mindset of judgment, outdoor program administrators should constantly strive to fine-tune their programs to get more people safely and responsibly enjoying the water.

A good mixture of classroom and on-water practice combined with well-thought-out learning progressions—including a healthy dose of respect for the hazards associated with each activity and location—will give program participants a solid base for future involvement with their chosen discipline.

Keep safety a constant topic of conversation. Play the "What if...?" game to give program participants something to think about during the drive to the local put-in or dock. For your own professional development and continuing education, stay abreast of the latest skills, techniques, and considerations in your discipline(s). Your continued competency in a kayak, on a sailboat, or underwater will instill confidence in your participants and staff.

# Chapter 21

# Special Events Programming

*Brent Anslinger, BS, and Amy Anslinger, BS*

Special events are critical to outdoor programs because they speak to broad audiences in an effort to expose individuals to available recreation opportunities in hopes they become participants. Ideally, this exposure, be it during a class aimed at skill development and knowledge acquisition or a visit to a developed outdoor recreation site, will invite participants into the broader outdoor culture.

Special events open up access to outdoor adventure culture and experiences to people hungry for the vibrancy that the outdoor industry creates. They bring attention to organizational programs that might go unnoticed or underappreciated, such as the organization itself or a special project of the organization. They help an outdoor program attract new audiences in ways a niche program or class might not accomplish. They create a vibrant, more visible outdoor community, which can become a driving force of the culture at large (Brumitt, 2005).

Special events also provide visibility for outdoor brands and retailers striving to build their business in the region and raise the profile of what, in some regions, is a hidden outdoor community. To engage new audiences with an outdoor program, and to energize core enthusiasts, the outdoor program administrator must provide a progression that has a consistent mix of outreach, attraction (such as special events), and many levels of engagement (e.g., classes and trips) from which to choose. This progression ultimately leads people toward a path of graduating into independent outdoor enthusiasts. Special events are central to keeping core enthusiasts engaged within the local outdoor scene well

into the future as they take ownership and pride in the outdoor culture being created (Brumitt, 2005). Outdoor culture is the community of people and entities that associate themselves with common interests through outdoor recreation; this includes supplemental components such as food and music that give this culture an identity that translates into an identifiable lifestyle.

Outdoor program administrators can be caught off guard by the complexity of event planning. Whether the event is a small-scale competition or a national conference, the logistics of many special events are similar. The details involved can be overwhelming for an unprepared administrator. Event details include, but are not limited to, defining the event; creating a timeline; determining location; applying for permits; creating or following policy and procedures, ranging from alcohol availability to accepting donations; managing staff; securing speakers and competitors; soliciting sponsorships; working with partners; creating a risk-management plan; marketing and promoting the event; arranging for awards and prizes; ensuring parking is adequate; maintaining a website; and arranging for equipment rentals. It is your job as outdoor program administrator to make sure that no detail, big or small, has been overlooked (Five Rivers MetroParks and Wright State University, 2011).

The success of the special event relies on the outdoor program administrator's ability to foresee complications. You must be organized and detail oriented to manage the many layers of the event. The veteran event planner is constantly drilling

Courtesy of Andy Williamson, Five Rivers MetroParks.

Introducing new people to the world of paddlesports at Paddle in the Park in Dayton, Ohio.

deeper into each layer of detail only to find more layers beneath, until the very last thank-you note has been sent and all postevent debriefing has occurred. All of this can be exciting, but also tiring and agonizing as each layer reveals yet another task to be accomplished. Your ability to capture, prioritize, and manage each task that turns up will pay off on event day.

For the new outdoor program administrator, special event planning can be an anxious time. A mistake or oversight in planning might be witnessed by hundreds of people, which could have negative consequences for your organization. On the other hand, a smooth, exciting event can advance your organization's reputation much faster than nearly any other method, in addition to showcasing your skill at coordinating a complex project with high public visibility. If you are willing to take a risk, you will often see the reward manifest itself in new opportunities through increased demand for programs and facilities. Ultimately, special events are the face of an outdoor program. A well-executed event can bring glory to a program and create a sense of pride in a community (Five Rivers MetroParks, 2011a). In this chapter we provide a foundation on which to build a dynamic special event.

## SPECIAL EVENT OPTIONS

Each event, though similar in logistics to other events, can have far-different particulars. Will the adventure race have a postrace party with live music, a cookout, and beer? Will the weekend outdoor exposition include a film festival and a 10K run or walk? Will the all-day music fest include a guest DJ, a duck race, and a 4H show? There is no one best mix to create a successful event—just a good idea, passion, desire, and an understanding of the market (Five Rivers MetroParks, 2011a). The discussion below is broken into two sections—the components of a festival and the components of a competition.

## Components of a Festival

The components of a festival may stand alone or be part of a competition in the form of a finish-line party, postrace music concert, or other festivity. Festivals can be effective for drawing together a wide range of demographics to one venue because they are often diverse in what they have to offer. An outdoor festival might bring together an assortment of people who are attending for different reasons, such as food, music, presentations, and equipment demos. A film festival is typically a popular draw, either unto itself or as part of a larger event.

## Film Festival

Hosting a film festival is a great way to infuse enthusiasm and knowledge into a local community. The films might share an outdoor sport or theme, or offer a variety of outdoor subjects to appeal to a broader range of viewers and promote a diversity of outdoor activities. Film festivals of any size can serve as fund-raisers through ticket sales or donations at the door.

If the film festival is part of a bigger event, it might be used as a kickoff to a weekend of outdoor activity, or to provide tranquil closure to an exhausting day of cycling or flat-water canoe racing. Your first step is to determine your goal, budget, and audience. After that, you can start planning a film festival that fits your established criteria. People traditionally pay an entrance fee to see a movie, so film festivals often serve as fund-raisers for outdoor programs.

Some traveling film festivals cost very little to bring to an event. For example, the National Paddling Film Festival Road Show costs only $200 for several hours of high adrenaline, thoughtful documentaries, and wild expeditions (Bluegrass Wildwater Association, 2011). Typically, the event staff will be shipped a box of DVDs a week before the event, along with limited marketing tools. This type of film festival is inexpensive enough to use as a supplement to another event, or it could be spun via marketing into a must-see event of its own.

If an organization has enough funds, or sponsors, a high-profile film festival can be brought to the community, such as the Banff Mountain Film Festival (www.banffcentre.ca/mountainfestival). These higher tier festivals cost a few thousand dollars and can be tough to schedule because of their busy calendar. But if you can get a festival like this to your venue, you will likely attract a large audience willing to drive a long distance. This kind of event brings with it a full package of marketing collateral for you to use, as well as a host of marketing done by the film festival owner. The exposure to your outdoor programs, though expensive, could be phenomenal.

A third option is to create an original film festival that caters to the needs of your organization. Boise State University's outdoor program designed and developed an independent film festival to generate funding for their student outdoor leadership development program. Between 2002 and 2009, Boise State's Sawtooth Mountain Film Festival received hundreds of film submissions that were juried by outdoor program staff. Top films were selected and mastered into an annual festival format that proved to meet three desired outcomes: the financial return on investment was maximized to help subsidize the cost of staff training, short films from aspiring directors were exposed to a large audience, and the local community was brought together for a weekend of viewing that highlighted "the spirit of adventure that is driving the cutting edge of adventure sports outdoor entertainment" (http://rec.boisestate.edu/sawtoothmountainfilmfest).

The net proceeds from the Sawtooth event were used to provide quarterly expedition-based leadership training opportunities for about 25 student candidates per year (Boise State University, 2010). Though a popular community event, the Sawtooth festival was ultimately retired because of the amount of administrative time consumed and associated expenses generated during the promotion and production of the event.

The following are questions to consider when organizing a film festival:

- Can you find or create a film festival that fits your program's goals and budget?
- What is the best facility to accommodate the anticipated audience?
- What are the contractual obligations and limitations of the chosen film festival?
- What fee (if any) will be charged of participants? Where will net profits go?
- Can you adjust the temperature of the facility?
- Is there ample seating, bathrooms, and enough parking for the expected attendance?
- What audiovisual equipment is necessary?
- Who will be your audiovisual support?
- What refreshments or meal options will the festival have?

## Expositions

Expositions are opportunities to showcase outdoor culture and experiences to the local community.

By bringing resources together from an organization's campus, city, or region, an outdoor program administrator can provide a format to provide resources to local and potential outdoor enthusiasts and promote a more cohesive local outdoor industry (Brumitt, 2005).

Expos may be product and experience based, bringing together outdoor manufacturers, outdoor retailers, and local sales representatives to showcase their wares, because gear is the one element that transcends all aspects of the outdoor market (Five Rivers MetroParks, 2011b). Expositions can also be resource based, drawing together local outdoor clubs, coalitions, nonprofits, and access-creating organizations, such as park districts and land managers. Or expositions can be a combination of product and resources, creating a venue in which guests can be inspired to join a local club or try an activity, and then turn around and learn about the gear necessary to fulfill their new-found dream (see figure 21.1). In combining product and resources, you provide a setting to recruit new enthusiasts into the outdoor adventure market while giving local enthusiasts opportunities to engage with manufacturers and the larger outdoor industry (The Five Rivers MetroParks and Wright State University, 2011).

National outdoor industry tours and advocacy groups can be a great way to add quality exhibitors to any line-up. These are generally road-based tours with limited flexibility in their schedule. The trick is to contact them early (one to two years ahead) and continue to follow up. The earlier the tour is contacted, the more likely they will be able to fit an event in their tour schedule (Backpacker Magazine, 2011).

Here is a suggested timeline for recruiting particular exhibits and tours:

- 1 to 2 years prior to the event for national tours and manufacturers
- 9 to 12 months prior for national organizations
- 6 months prior for local retailers
- 3 months prior for local clubs, organizations, and nonprofits
- 3 months prior, make follow-up phone calls
- Send follow-up information as soon as an exhibit or tour agrees to attend the event.

- Send out confirmations and final check-in information 3 weeks prior to the event.

## Gear Swaps

Expositions are one of the best venues for recruiting new people into the outdoor industry, but the perceived complexities and cost of gear is a huge hurdle in trying to truly engage new audiences. Gear swaps and consignment opportunities as part of an exposition can provide perfect opportunities for individuals newly interested in an activity or program to get the gear they need, be it a used backpack or a second-hand kayak. Swaps also allow experienced enthusiasts to pass along used gear in the efforts of hooking up a newbie, who, once hooked, might

**Figure 21.1** Print promotions set the tone and feel of the event, setting expectations for the quality and purpose of the event.

Courtesy of Wright State University and Five Rivers MetroParks, Dayton, Ohio.

later upgrade that same used gear and continue the cycle (Five Rivers MetroParks, 2011a).

The high price of new gear can be a deterrent for many people considering outdoor programs. They are not sure they will like the activity, so they are leery of making the investment in new equipment. This is why gear swaps and consignment opportunities are popular and beneficial in luring in new outdoor program participants. Gear swaps are win-win for outdoor program administrators because as buyers become potential program participants, sellers become investors in new gear that will encourage them to remain active in the outdoor market (Five Rivers MetroParks, 2011a).

## Music

Live music is a great match for festivals because it can create an ambiance and energy that transcends the festival itself. Music can be used as a featured part of a program, but with that decision comes increased cost in more areas than just the band itself. To find a band that has regional appeal, contact radio stations or concert venues that might aid in making connections.

Radio stations are sometimes willing to host and manage a music stage as an in-kind donation in exchange for the purchase of an advertising package. The stage, signage, viewing area, electric needs, and more can be increased significantly when committing to a large band presence—not to mention the influence of the sound on the rest of the festival, which could be good or bad. Be conscious of how invited exhibitors trying to interact with patrons might feel when placed in the vicinity of a sound system. Each aspect of a special event must blend with others to cause as few conflicts as possible (Five Rivers MetroParks, 2011b).

Live music that acts as a background to the main event is often a good value. A single acoustic guitar player can, via advertising, draw people in to an indoor expo or gear-swap event. For only $100 to $200 you can change the dynamic of an event, and with minimal management requirements. The return on investment can be very good with this format. Similarly, DJs can bring good value to an event by providing not only music but a professional voice to MC. It is important to provide a script and lay out a timeline that the DJ (or other MC) can use throughout the event. By giving sponsors opportunities to write a few sentences to promote themselves, you earn goodwill that might pay off in the future.

The difference between scrambling behind the scenes and everything running like a well-oiled machine is in the foresight and time spent on each detail. For example, if a band is booked three months prior to the event, and their commitment is confirmed two weeks before the event, and then again two days before the event, the administrator must feel she has communicated well. But when the band shows up without a sound system, she realizes a vital detail has slipped. The band assumed the sound system was provided. Perhaps the administrator can find a rental in just the nick of time, but how much stress did this oversight put on event staff, who were supposed to be handling other duties?

## Speakers, Classes, and Clinics

A simple speech, class, or clinic becomes a special event when multiple options are offered over the course of a day or weekend. Speakers, classes, and clinics provide opportunities to market an outdoor program and educate the community on a topic, skill, or experience (The Five Rivers MetroParks and Wright State University, 2011). Speakers come in many packages, ranging from local outdoor enthusiasts with a slide show to share, to the Everest climber who charges a small fee, to a nationally known outdoor adventurer or professional athlete. Costs may range from free to several thousand dollars, or way more if you want Lance Armstrong.

Any time an outdoor program has something to market it is an opportunity to get word out about the program. Bringing in local adventurers and enthusiasts to present a slide show or a how-to clinic is an easy way to enthuse others about the possibilities available through outdoor recreation. This event costs the program very little and can do so much to create enthusiasm for experienced and novice adventurers alike. The public also learns that outdoor adventures are accessible to everyday people. By offering a series of these programs, the outdoor program administrator can build community. Staff might also become inspired and be more likely to check out skill-building programs offered by the organization in order to go out and have their own adventure (Wright State University, 2008). Local presenters can often be found in large numbers through contacting local outdoor and sport-specific clubs and retailers (Junction Trail Festival, 2009).

By moving up a level to a local outdoor celebrity, a program administrator can increase marketing power and pull in a bigger audience. The audience will be willing to travel from a greater distance, which broadens the program's reach. Also, the local celebrity becomes familiar with the event or program, which creates a connection that might be used in the future.

If a nationally known speaker is brought in, the presentation must fit the expectations and goals of the program and event. Many speakers at the national level have a stump speech, which may or may not be to the organization's liking. However, many speakers are willing to customize a speech for a higher fee. An organization might save money by working directly with a speaker rather than using a Speakers Bureau (The Five Rivers MetroParks and Wright State University, 2011).

Before investing in bringing in a big-name presenter, make sure the budget allows for properly marketing the event to make the investment of the presenter worthwhile. There is no point in breaking the bank for the presenter if you cannot afford to get the word out to the audience. If funds are available, it might be worthwhile to build a larger event around the big-name speaker, such as an expo or a festival. This allows accommodating different interest and user groups and brings a larger community of enthusiasts to the venue, exposing them to outdoor programs.

## Food

Once an audience arrives at a special event it is imperative to hold them there until the event ends. Regardless of how cool an event is, if basic necessities such as restrooms and food are not provided the average length of stay will be short. For festivals and expositions, food choices should be diverse and amounts abundant. For competitions, basics such as fruit, bread, juice, coffee, and energy drinks and bars should be available for competitors and spectators.

Try to prepare the food service provider for success by matching the expected attendance with enough food service to accommodate. Missing the mark greatly in either direction can cause disappointment in the food provider or a sense of being overwhelmed and unprepared. Either way, the provider might not want to be involved the following year. Also, if the food vendor is overwhelmed, this will cause delays in meals being served to customers, who might respond by leaving, or not returning (Junction Trail Festival, 2009).

The following are three good choices to make when providing food at an event:

1. Have the event staff handle it. When food is purchased, prepared, and sold by festival event staff, an opportunity exists to generate significant revenue; however, along with the opportunity for revenue comes legal responsibilities and logistical burdens. A significant deterrent to managing food distribution with internal staff is the demand that it places on the available human resources of the event. Additionally, the sale of food is regulated by most states to ensure that proper food handling, hygiene, and sanitation practices are maintained by employees.

2. Arrange for a nonprofit club or local organization to provide and serve food. Many nonprofit or local organizations use food preparation and sale at festivals as a means of generating revenue. Many of these groups own and maintain portable equipment that allows them to produce and sell food onsite. Outsourcing the responsibility of food to these vendors allows you to have food available for participants without the burden of managing logistics. Ensure that vendors comply with local regulations for food handling, hygiene, and sanitation practices. Vendors should demonstrate that they are registered with the local tax commission as a legitimate food vendor.

3. Arrange for commercial food vendors. Outsourcing food services to a commercial food vendor is often the most efficient way to provide food because food vendors just want an opportunity to reach customers, with no cost to the event organizer. Contracting professional food service vendors limits the logistics required to provide food to participants, and often is a means of passive revenue generation because the event organizer can charge the vendor a commission on food sales.

## Contests

Contests are an exciting part of any event, and the buzz they create can be a valuable marketing tool for the outdoor program administrator. Contests are different from competitions in that contests are designed to create excitement for the event as a promotional technique, whereas competitions provide opportunities for athletes to vie against others in a specific challenge, such as bouldering or cycling. Contests, such as raffles, social media challenges, gear giveaways, and so on, can help build momentum leading up to an event and provide a venue for manufacturers or retailers to speak to their targeted audience. Often, if you are already working with mainstream media (e.g., a radio station), you can get increased coverage by teaming with them to add a contest to the advertising package (The Five Rivers MetroParks and Wright State University, 2011).

Be wary of creating contests that can be overwhelming to manage; consider the logistics of running a raffle, awarding prizes, and so on. Make sure you fully understand how the contest will affect timing, and assess the return on investment. Contests can range from low level to high level in the amount of time that must be committed to them. A low-level commitment may require the organizer to solicit prizes that will be given away randomly to competitors, or staffing a booth where prizes will immediately be distributed to winners. A medium-level contest commitment may require coordinating with media to have prizes distributed live to competitors and spectators. A high level of time investment may be required for a contest that is raffle based, offers a high dollar prize, and stretches over multiple months or locations. Regardless of the type of contest, you must know the state laws and institutional rules for items donated and items given away, where the prizes will be coming from, who is and is not eligible to win, and the amount of fiscal resources that will need to be devoted to hosting the contest.

## Components of a Competition

Competitions can build excitement for an activity or program because they generate an incentive for participants to pursue ongoing self-improvement. Hosting a competition brings attention to an outdoor program's facilities. Participants might be inspired to take a class or clinic leading up to the competition. A competition is also an opportunity to showcase other aspects of outdoor programming to a core group of people who may already

A bouldering competition can build excitement for a program and inspire participants to take a class prior to the competition.

Courtesy of Wright State University.

have an interest in the programs being promoted (Five Rivers MetroParks, 2011a). At a university program, it is often the students who benefit most from a competition by being exposed to athletes performing at a higher level than they typically see in their program. A really strong and fluid climber performing above the norm at a university wall, for example, may inspire students to join a climbing program. Competition also promotes a sense of community in which all are welcome and encouraged to participate regardless of personal barriers (Loue, pers. comm.).

Most outdoor programming is not set up to be competitive, but people by nature are drawn to competitions. Thus holding a competition is a way for outdoor programs to tap in to people's predisposition to compete. It is also a way for outdoor administrators to generate public enthusiasm and awareness for adventure sports. Almost any combination of activities can be turned into a competition. The Maumee Valley Tri-Adventure Race combines portaging a canoe or kayak a quarter-mile, 6 miles (9.6 km) of paddling, 9 miles (14.4 km) of backpacking with 20 percent of bodyweight, and a 36-mile (58 km) road cycling route (The Naturalist Scouts, 2011). The following are some of the components of a competition:

- Competitors
- Sponsors and prizes
- Equipment
- Staff and volunteers
- Host, announcer
- Plan for spectators and seating
- Restrooms
- Food and aid stations
- Rules and regulations
- Risk management and response plan
- Risk waivers
- Marketing
- Parking
- Registration
- Security and course management

## Who Will Participate?

When designing a competition, the outdoor program administrator identifies target competitors and how they can be reached. Programs must often be proactive when it comes to recruiting participants for a competition. Simply posting a competition on a website and putting up a few fliers is generally not enough marketing to fill a competition.

Targeting a desired audience for a competition is different from targeting for other events. For example, if a program is interested in hosting a bouldering competition, a good start is to involve the local climbing community. Does your university have a climbing club? If so, recruit the club to get involved. Their involvement will help spread the word at local climbing hubs. If there is no climbing club in your community, consider starting one. Sometimes it is necessary to build a community to support an event. A foundation of support makes a big difference when trying to pull off a special event (Wright State University, 2008).

## Involve the Community

Once your local club or community is involved, have them contact other climbing organizations, both local and regional. Contact local climbing gyms and coalitions. The National Intramural-Recreation Sports Association is a great resource; their annual directory lists all universities with outdoor programs and specifies which have climbing clubs. Depending on the scope of the competition, it might be best to invite only clubs within a three-hour radius, or to invite all clubs regardless of location. It must be decided who the competitors should be, and then they should be invited to the competition.

If your event staff is promoting a triathlon, consider going to other running, swimming, cycling, and triathlon events in your region, or calling race coordinators and finding ways to cross-promote together. Think e-mails, letters, phone calls, announcements, and social media including resources like Facebook and Twitter. Competitions require a heavier dose of grassroots marketing than an outdoor festival does.

Because competitions attract a niche audience that lends itself to grassroots marketing, the cost to advertise the event may be limited. This allows event staff to invest financial resources in other areas beyond advertising. Sponsors will often provide prizes in exchange for brand awareness at the event.

## Exceed Standards

When hosting a competition, it is important to meet or exceed competitor and industry standards on equipment with regard to competitor expectations and safety. Staff and volunteer needs are event or competition specific. Needs are generally based on the number of participants and the number of volunteer or staff stations at the event. A static event, held in a controlled and contained area, will have different needs than that of a dynamic event that occurs in a less-controlled and moving venue. Think bouldering competition vs. adventure race (Five Rivers MetroParks, 2011a).

For an indoor bouldering competition most needs are static. The registration area is close to the competition area and the awards area; restrooms are also probably near the competition location. Signs can cover most of the event's directional needs. Volunteers who help with registration may also act as competition spotters or judges, and may be able to tally the scores at the end of the competition. For an outdoor adventure race, volunteers may need to help with parking and directing participants to the registration area. Depending on the length of the race, multiple aid stations may be needed (e.g., on-site first responders, safety boaters, volunteers to set up rappel stations) (Wright State University, 2008).

It is important to have a dependable person to coordinate volunteers to ensure all event areas are covered. Volunteers should feel valued and be able to enjoy the competition. Be aware of how many hours volunteers have been working. Direct the coordinator to schedule adequate breaks and to try not to leave any volunteer in an undesirable location for too long. Free food and event T-shirts are always appreciated by volunteers, but get creative with what you offer them and they are even more likely to come back to help again in the future (Five Rivers MetroParks, 2011a).

## Build a Strong Team

To be the *coordinator* of a competition does not automatically put a person in the spotlight and make it necessary to play the outward role of host, announcer, and commentator, but every competition does require a coordinator. The coordinator should be the "go to" person for all participants and also be available to support the program host. The person who acts as *master of ceremonies* must have a full working knowledge of all competition rules and regulations, not only for the specific competition but for the facility and grounds and the agency or program hosting the event. The *program host* might need to answer competitor and spectator questions (or be able to quickly find the answer for them), anticipate challenges in the competition going smoothly and communicate that to the coordinator, and generally be aware of the overall operation of the competition to serve as the liaison to the coordinator.

At every competition, regardless of size, competitors should be welcomed, introduced to the competition site, have the rules explained to them, and be given the opportunity to clarify rules by asking questions. If at any time during the competition announcements or updates need to be made, they should be made by the program host or a *commentator*. Think about customer service at each step of the process. Be welcoming and appreciative of

A rail jam competition. Riders create excitement by performing tricks on rails, boxes, and so on.

Courtesy of Joni Williamson.

participants' choices to come to your competition. Customer service is all about managing expectations, so figure out a way to exceed expectations of your participants. Often the key to exceeding participant expectations is being thorough in the details (Wright State University, 2008).

Depending on the competition venue, there may be spectators unfamiliar with the competition's intricacies, so providing commentary may add to the spectator's enjoyment and understanding of the sport. A spectator watching a Snowboard Rail Jam competition might not understand the various levels of difficulty associated with each trick; a novice kayaker watching a Flat Water Freestyle competition might enjoy learning the names of the various tricks the boaters are demonstrating (The Five Rivers MetroParks and Wright State University, 2011).

Most competitions end with an awards ceremony of some sort; many are casual, and some are formal.

The advantage of having only a few key point people is professionalism. The competition will run more smoothly and come across as more professional if there are not half a dozen people walking around giving directions or talking over one another over the public address system.

## Consider Spectator Accommodations

Whether your competition is at a level at which spectators will flock to cheer on their favorite athlete or is a first-time climbing competition at a new facility, you should be prepared for spectators. Even the smallest competition will need to accommodate the friends and family of its competitors. Consider the length of the competition and what spectators will need to be comfortable.

A minimum requirement for comfort is restroom facilities. If restrooms are not located onsite, arrange to bring temporary facilities to the site. If this is not feasible, are there restroom facilities nearby that can be made available for spectators? For example, if hosting an ultramarathon, it might be worthwhile to check in with local businesses near the route to find out where public restrooms are located and which businesses are willing to accommodate spectators. Spectators will also need to know if food and drink are available on location. If not, encourage them to bring their own. Consider also advertising food vendors if you plan on having them be part of the event. Finally, there will need to be a comfortable place to watch the competition. Consider temperature, shelter from sun and rain, and seating. Let people know in advance if they need to bring their own chairs.

Participants need food and water to compete at top performance levels. If there will not be food and water made available to competitors during the competition, advance notice should be given so they know to eat before they arrive and to bring snacks and water bottles.

## Registrations

Taking registrations prior to the day of the competition is critical so you know, roughly, how many people are coming. A discount for early registration is an incentive for participants to register early, which allows you to get an early idea of how many total participants to expect and how much additional marketing will be necessary to fill the event. You need to know how many participants to expect when ordering T-shirts, food, medals, and so on, and when signing contracts with outside vendors. Once the critical components of the event have been arranged and ordered, you might choose to offer additional registration at the regular price, as long as you have purchased extra supplies to prepare for this. By offering a pricing structure that includes an early bird discount and then a regular rate up until the event, you manage expectations better than offering a "late" registration price. The event organizer should avoid managing late registrations, which are perceived as an opportunity to raise the price. This comes into clarity when you realize you do not have enough competitors for the event and must begin a marketing campaign to solicit more participants, and thus must resort to getting people to sign up "late." Preevent registration is important also because competitors like to train, and they will only train and travel to a competition if they know they will be able to compete. The simplest way is to allow online registration with credit card payment. If you do not have the ability to take payments online, you can accept registrations online or via e-mail, phone, or mail without payment and then allow competitors to make payment on the day of the competition when competitors check in. There might be a small percentage of no-shows but you get a good idea of interest prior to the competition, which is important for planning purposes (Wright State University, 2008).

## Clear Communication

Imagine this scenario. Your organization is hosting an adventure race. As the outdoor program administrator, you are concerned that many teams might not have their own canoe. This concern is laid to rest as teams begin to register and the event is sold out two weeks before the race. But on race day, as teams arrive, many have no canoe! Though you did not advertise that canoes *would be* supplied, neither did you say they would. The promo and application material did not address the issue one way or the other. Many competitors assumed that because they were not specifically told to bring their own canoe that it would be supplied by the event host. You are able find canoes at the last minute through a desperate phone call to a local canoe livery, but imagine how much smoother your morning would have been if those canoes had been secured and in place leading up to the event. Or imagine your embarrassment, and participants' frustration, if there were no canoes to be found.

This scenario could be easily avoided by stating on the registration form that competitors must bring their own canoe, or by charging a higher registration fee and providing canoes. That said, the most thorough outdoor program administrator will plan to have a small selection of backup canoes on hand regardless of how clearly instructions were written for the competitors.

# RISK MANAGEMENT FOR SPECIAL EVENTS AND COMPETITIONS

Whether you are running a stand-alone film festival or a 24-hour ultramarathon, risk must be considered. Many institutions have appropriate liability coverage, but each event may present different intricacies, especially when the event is hosted away from your facility. If using a pool facility in which the general public is invited to try kayaking, all participants should be required to sign a risk-release form, and this process will have to be managed along with general safe site management techniques. For some events it may be appropriate to invite the local EMS to be onsite or to hire a private ambulance company. Even if EMS is only a minute away from the event site, the safety and public relations benefits of having them onsite if a competitor has an injury is priceless (Five Rivers MetroParks, 2011a). Many times it is a competitor's ego that poses the biggest risk-management concern during a competition. For example, in a bouldering competition a climber may try a route well above his ability, try a route without a pad because he is too impatient to wait for one, not down climb because it's more dramatic to jump, and simply not listen to his body when it has maxed out (Loue, pers. comm.). Your primary action to avoid such situations is to be proactive and set clear expectations in writing as part of a competitor code of conduct. Then remind everyone verbally in a precompetition briefing. This preparation combined with closely monitoring participants and taking action when needed will help provide a safe event.

## Incident Prevention

Incident prevention is critical to all event planning but presents unique challenges when holding a competition at a dynamic site. As in any program that travels over the land or water, the outdoor program administrator must be aware of the potential hazards along the route and design the event to minimize this risk and handle the crowd and competitive mindset. In a competition ordinary hazards can often be taken to the next level. Imagine competitors running on a single track trail through the woods. They try to pass each other on a narrow section. Spectators might be squeezing the trail corridor, limiting sight lines on a steep rocky section. What might happen? Also, in the heat of competition, it is not at all unusual for athletes to push themselves beyond their physical and mental limits, perhaps miles from the nearest aid station.

These factors make the potential for injury or accident skyrocket when compared to a casual noncompetitive trail run on the same course. Proper site selection processes should be followed, with an emphasis on how the event and competitors' mindsets will change the dynamic of the safety of that site. Be aware of the weather forecast; be prepared to implement plan B, which may involve canceling or postponing the event. Work out your communication process long before the week of the event.

## Incident Response

Plan out different scenarios with appropriate responses, and train your staff on what those responses are. Orient local first responders to the event, and invite them to participate in a mock scenario at the event site. Do this early so there is time for staff to adjust to the findings of the mock run-through. All staff and volunteers should carry the incident-response plan with them after being briefed and trained on how to use it (Five Rivers MetroParks, 2011a).

# ASSESSING AND PLANNING FOR YOUR EVENT

An outdoor program administrator has been dreaming of hosting a bouldering competition, or a film festival, or maybe a complex regional outdoor exposition. That dream should first be planned on paper, and then filtered through the following assessment to determine if it is a realistic event to try to tackle. The assessment might show the event to be a good fit for the program, or that it might be best to start small this year and try this event in the future (The Five Rivers MetroParks and Wright State University, 2011).

Before putting a timeline or planning team in place to organize and plan an event, determine if the initial thoughts on dates, scale, scope, and so on will really work. Though the same components make up every event, the size and complexity of the event will determine the degree of planning and preparation required to successfully execute the event. Before publicizing the event, assess the landscape of the project. Starting down one road only to backtrack can cause a planning team and initial timeline to implode. Prior to organizing a planning team, think through the factors that might influence the success of the event. Taking the following steps will help you assess whether your idea for a special event will end in success. These assessments do not have to be done in a specific order, but they should all be completed before fully committing to and publicizing an event (see figure 21.2).

## Scope Assessment and Market Analysis

What will an event look like? As the outdoor program administrator, you must take time to consider who might come and where they will likely come from. When might the event get the best turnout? How many people can your facility safely handle? Are there a variety of facilities that could accommodate the event, or will the facility requirements limit your potential attendance? What other community members might want to get involved, and what might they bring to the table? Should manufacturers or retailers exhibit? Can anyone from the community be involved, or will the event be an internal production? Is there a need for this event in the community, or should it be tied to something similar that is already established? All of these questions need answers before you move ahead with planning an event (Five Rivers MetroParks, 2011a) (Wright State University, 2008).

An outdoor program administrator completes a market analysis to determine if the market can indeed support the event or product. You should be developing a product that can "sell" in the marketplace. This analysis helps set the event up for success before energy and resources are committed

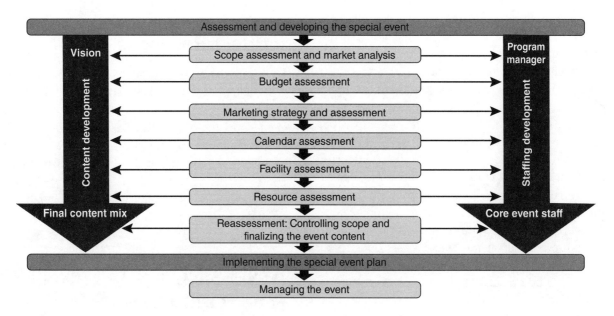

**Figure 21.2** Steps in the event-planning process.

to, perhaps, duplicating a product in the market or developing a product that nobody wants. Say your goal is to have a fund-raiser. Your initial thought is to hold a 5K run. But after you complete the preliminary market research, you find that four runs are already established in your community, and that the newest race struggles most in registering the desired quantity of runners. Thus it might be prudent to scrap the 5K idea and try instead to develop your area's first-ever film festival, which, from running your market analysis, you have learned your community is more than ready for.

By developing a unique product (event), you are more likely to get free media placement and an increased interest from sponsors. After all, sponsors are assessing your event to determine their return on investment (ROI) in terms of exposure and increased brand awareness by the demographic the event is able to deliver. If you had developed the fifth 5K run in the community, your local running shop might not have been interested in participating because they already reach the running community by sponsoring the other races. Look for ways to differentiate your event in the market, or to develop a new niche, but always keep your organization's institution mission and your program strategy foremost in mind when going through the decision-making process. Consider the following questions to determine the programmatic bottom line:

- Are there enough time and resources to plan the special event as envisioned?
- Can the event stay on budget?
- Is there time to promote the event?
- Does the event work for the targeted audience?
- Does the event work with the targeted content (exhibitors, competitors, speakers)?
- Are there adequate facilities to host the event?
- Does the event fit the underlying mission of your organization?
- Does event staff have the time to plan the event?

## Budget Assessment

It is important to consider budget framework and understand institutional policies and process from the beginning because this will have a dramatic effect on your choices later. Will the organization pay for the entire event out of the department budget? If so, will you need to wait another year until the cost of the event can be planned for in the next budget cycle? Will there be fund-raising, participant fees, or other outside funding to supplement the internal budget in part or in full? Does the host agency or institution have a marketing department to cover some marketing costs or to help determine the cost of the marketing strategy? Are there agency or institutional policies regarding fund-raising, accepting sponsorship monies, or contractual conflicts? Some organizations might not allow revenue that the event generates to be directly applied to expenses that have not been allocated in that year's budget. Accurate creation of revenue targets will keep you from overcommitting to bills and charges from the facility, rentals, and other expenses.

Hidden costs often sting the outdoor program administrator who is new to special event planning. Does your organization have a contingency budget or other funds to cover unknown costs? As the design of an event develops, new items to rent, unanticipated signage needs, more staff hours, last-minute printing and marketing materials, and an unfathomable amount of small costs add up to stress the budget.

Unless your organization has a lot of resources (i.e., cash), event sponsors might be needed to offset costs of holding the event. Sponsors can supply cash, prizes, event resources, and SWAG (stuff we all get).

Your event might require various sponsorship levels, depending on the size of the event, and it might be necessary to create a "sponsorship package," which highlights the benefits potential sponsors will receive for their involvement at various levels.

The more a sponsor gives, the more they should receive in return. For example, a sponsor who donates a large sum of money or event resources will expect to receive more from the event host (e.g., having their name mentioned on all radio and television advertising; placing their logo on all print materials, the event website [logo links to sponsors homepage], and event T-shirts). A lower level sponsor (e.g., donating small product samples to registered competitors) might receive logo placement only on the website and selected print materials (The Five Rivers MetroParks and Wright State University, 2011).

Before going after sponsors, define your event's needs. Market your sponsorship opportunities to potential sponsors that are a good fit with the event mission and are able to assist with the resources needed for the event. Larger sponsors will need time to plan the event into their annual budget. Solicit larger sponsors two years to six months in advance, and smaller sponsors nine months to three months in advance. All sponsors will want to know what the event will look like, the audience and competitor demographics, and numbers of competitors and attendees. It is often worthwhile to have as much of this detail in place before making your pitch (Five Rivers MetroParks, 2011b).

Be creative and flexible with potential sponsors. At a bouldering competition, sponsors may be able to donate products like climbing rope and hangboards, which make great prizes in lieu of cash. But perhaps your local climbing gym is willing to set routes in exchange for marketing associated with the event. Or a local running shop might be willing to set the course and provide volunteers for an adventure race. For example, the Brady's Leap Adventure Race presented by Kent State University includes Standing Rock Cemetery and the Kent Historical Society on their list of sponsors in exchange for being able to use Standing Rock Cemetery as a checkpoint (Herpy, pers. comm.).

Finally, if you want their help again in the future, be entirely honest with potential sponsors about the scope of your event. Building relationships is part of the reason to host an event. If you build your event on honesty and mutual gain, your workload will decrease the next time you are seeking program support.

## Marketing Strategy and Assessment

The prudent outdoor program administrator develops a preliminary strategy to deliver the desired audience to the event in terms of quantity and demographic. Will your budget preclude you from reaching your audience or force you into less expensive grassroots marketing strategies that may have less known outcomes? Or will the budget need to be adjusted to incorporate more fund-raising and sponsorships to deliver on the proposed marketing strategy? How many people can you realistically expect to attend this event? Can the event budget afford traditional print, radio, or television advertisements, or is the strategy to get editorial coverage and on-air interviews instead of (or in addition to) paying for time? Are editorial coverage and interviews realistic? Some stations will grant interviews only to those paying for advertising time; if free placement is your strategy, are you confident it will work? If grass roots and viral marketing approaches are planned, does event staff have enough time to deliver on that strategy? Grassroots and viral efforts are low cost but can be time intensive (Five Rivers MetroParks, 2011b).

Sketch out a timeline of milestones for marketing the event. Without proper advertising or a grassroots effort, you might be disappointed by the turnout for the special event. There is nothing more disappointing than investing your heart and soul in an event, and then no one shows up.

The meticulous outdoor program administrator strives to fully understand the event's target audience and what it will take to reach them. In some cases, cheaper and more labor intensive methods bring greater results. Grassroots, viral, and guerilla marketing have been woven into the fabric of marketing campaigns, and these techniques are becoming more important every year in their ability to reach niche audiences through technology and other methods.

In the old days, when there was one newspaper and a couple of radio and television channels, it was not difficult to reach the masses. Today, with the increasing dissemination of media into hundreds of outlets, it has become increasingly difficult to reach everyone in one or two ways. Fortunately, however, technology advances also make it possible to target audiences in new and diverse ways. You can now advertise or reach web-based audiences based on their interest or geography, target a specialized television channel that aligns with your event, or do one of a hundred things through e-mail, online radio, social networks, or text messaging. For example, you can run a text campaign where someone can text a predetermined word to an account you have previously set up, and then you can begin creating a target list based off of the text responses. If done right, these techniques can provide more impact than the old avenues of reaching an audience (The Five Rivers MetroParks and Wright State University, 2011).

Traditional methods of marketing (radio, print, TV campaigns) can be effective for many events and should not be disregarded based solely on cost. These methods can help reach the mass public audience, if that is the target, such as with a large exposition. A bouldering competition, however, might be served best through more niche and grassroots marketing to climbing gyms within a three-hour radius, social-networking strategies, and e-mail blasts (Wright State University, 2008). Make sure to plan in the time it will take to create a website, logos, and posters, allowing plenty of time to get these marketing materials on the street in time to make an impact.

As outdoor program administrator, be true to your organization's mission and strategy. If the hosting program of the special event has no opportunities open to the general public, and has a strict mission to serve a university community, then your program does not directly benefit by targeting the general public with marketing resources set aside for the event. Targeting the public would not be within the mission of the special event.

A website devoted to the special event is a key tool for the public, potential sponsors, and content providers, such as exhibitors and speakers, for finding information. Devote sections of the website to providing information to competitors who are already signed up, and to exhibitors to find information on setup time, scheduling, and more. Your website is often the first impression people have when considering whether to attend the event. Thus a clean, informative site is important. Get a professional's help, if necessary. If you are putting all your time and energy into planning a first-class event, you do not want your brother's buddy creating your website for you. A website is a great help when done right, but if done poorly the site will do more harm than good (The Five Rivers MetroParks and Wright State University, 2011).

## Calendar Assessment

An early question to answer is "When is the best time to hold the event?" When assessing your calen-

dar, refer to the local and regional outdoor program and event schedule, the outdoor industry association calendar, and any marketing milestones. Don't overlook your own organization's event calendar because you will likely need to share resources such as tables, tents, and audiovisual equipment, not to mention likely marketing to the same audience, such as students (Five Rivers MetroParks, 2011a).

The event should not be planned on the same weekend as a local blues festival or sporting event if the same audience is being targeted. Be aware of how a local event can be positioned to either help or hinder your special event. If a large snowboard competition is being held in your region, it might be smart to partner with them to be onsite and promote your film festival, which you have strategically scheduled two weeks later. You can leverage their audience, which is also your target market, and encourage them to come to your event. Placing your film festival on the same date as an established snowboard competition would likely work against you.

Keep in mind when retailers and manufacturers in the outdoor industry may be available to support the event. It is often tough to get a canoe livery to loan you canoes for an outdoor triathlon on a Saturday in July during their peak season. Industry representatives and retailers often want to be involved and will support events if they are not in their heavy sales season or at a trade show.

Finally, don't try to set a date for the event if it sacrifices the event staff's ability to hit marketing milestones, such as getting the website live or sending out invitations to exhibit at the event. Once again, if there are no exhibitors at your event because they heard about it too late, and if they were planned to be a big part of the event, then what are you left with?

## Facility Assessment

The future-thinking outdoor program administrator considers the needs and availability of facility resources required for the event. Think through the projected space, be it a mountain bike trail or an auditorium. Will the restrooms onsite be enough for the projected crowd? Will you need to rent additional tent space? Is parking available? Will the parking lot handle all the vehicles? If the facility is not available on your optimal weekend, can you get it for your second choice? If you can't, you might need to assess which is preferable (or possible)—rescheduling your event for another time or finding a different facility.

After a suitable venue has been identified, it is time to work with the facility to reserve that space, fill out event applications, and begin coordinating with the facility's operations manager. It might be beneficial to look two to three years down the road and book the second annual event so you can promote it during the first event.

Be aware of the impact the event can place on the facility's operations staff, and work with them to offer assistance. The event staff can often assist in manual labor tasks such as moving furniture or stacking tables to alleviate stress on the facility staff. By providing labor, costs can often be cut down on rental fees.

## Resource Assessment

Perform a resource inventory, listing all potential resources available to event staff—volunteers, equipment, sponsors, local web-development companies willing to help in return for exposure, and so on. This is your chance to truly evaluate if you have what it takes to turn your dreams into reality.

Fine-tune your event budget with all intended resources in mind. Event budgets can get complicated if you must target sponsors to assist in funding the event. Sponsorships can come in the form of cash, product, or in-kind agreements. The trick comes in getting the cash sponsorships prior to your need to commit to expenditures. Product and in-kind sponsorships are valuable but not as helpful when paying the bills at the end of the event (Junction Trail Festival, 2009).

A model that can work is to book your "anchor" content for the event, such as your keynote speaker, in order to sell a sponsorship. For example, if you book a big name athlete, such as a top tier climber, you will be able to sell sponsorships to climbing manufacturers and local climbing gyms much more effectively. This will create momentum for other sponsorships outside of the climbing realm. Leave yourself plenty of time to sell those big sponsorships before your contracts leave you with no outs (Junction Trail Festival, 2009).

To avoid unforeseen hurdles, outdoor program administrators should work with their parent organization's finance department to assist in contracts and sponsorship agreements. Otherwise you might be in for an unpleasant surprise when you learn that your primary sponsor for your event is in competition with a chief sponsor for your organization. For instance, you might have your eye on Soft Drink X to sponsor your triathlon, only to discover that your parent institution has a noncompete contract with Soft Drink Y.

Sponsors are a big part of legitimizing any special event and providing financial support to actually run the event. Be realistic in how much cash, product, or in-kind resources event staff will be able to raise, especially in the first year of an event that has no track record.

Think through all costs, from printing fliers to buying advertising. Budget for extra operations staff, security, or other labor in a reserve in case they are needed at the last minute. This will help cover unexpected costs.

When considering equipment and facility needs, take the blinders off—tunnel vision can ruin an event. For a bouldering competition, crash pads, climbing shoes, rocks, and scorecards are needed, but what about audiovisual equipment, event fencing, signage, and extension cords? How are the restroom facilities? Will there be food and water? Wifi? Communication tools? Shade? From parking to spectators, and from competitor gear storage to registration, what is needed for the event to run smoothly from when the first volunteer arrives to when the last staff member leaves (Wright State University, 2008)?

We highly recommend creating a list and keeping it accessible so event staff can continue to add to it as new concerns arise and equipment needs are revealed. Many programs have a general event needs list with amendments for specific events. If your program does not have an equipment checklist then ask a similar program to share their list. Make sure to revisit the list postprogram to make updates for future events. Use all available resources. Most institutions have professional event and volunteer coordinators. Their professional experience can help make or break an event. A marketing department should also have experience with event planning and someone to help assist with special events.

If event staff does not know how something is going to work, figure it out, or it might not work on event day. Leave nothing to chance—because what can go wrong *will* go wrong. Having the right equipment, and having it work when you want it to work, makes the event and host organization look professional. We all have enjoyed a rainy day holed up in our tents, as long as the equipment manager remembered to pack the footprint, guy lines, and playing cards.

If sales are not going as intended, or if it wasn't as easy as you thought to get Climbing Company X to write a check for your bouldering competition event, then you might find yourself without the funds to deliver the event. In this case, try to negotiate a date to opt out of other financial commitments, such as payment for the facility or marketing materials. Otherwise you will not stay within budget. When your revenue targets are not being hit, you might need to rescale the event to achieve lower costs.

## Reassessment: Controlling Scope and Finalizing the Event

Now that you have assessed the major components of the event, developed a plan, and made the commitment to announce that the special event will occur, take a step back to ensure that event planning stays on track and fits the mission of the overarching organization.

Take care not to say yes to every opportunity that comes along because that might increase the scope of the event beyond what was established and derail you from operating within the program mission and event budget. Focus on doing the event that was envisioned during the planning stages; this will keep the event team aligned and on target. Redesigning the event on the fly can inadvertently spread out resources and threaten the success of the event. It is likely that during the weeks leading up to the event that event staff will lose their attention to detail because they are spread too thin trying to make all aspects of the event successful. When dealing with outdoor-oriented events, inattention to detail can lead to unwanted risk-management issues.

If an unexpected opportunity to add an exciting component to the event arises, scrutinize its effect on the existing scope of the event. For instance, a sponsor might offer to contribute a certain amount of product but would like to see a large contest created to tie the event to a local retailer. Consider carefully whether it is worth the extra time and effort to organize the contest and manage that partnership in exchange for what that would bring to the event in terms of excitement, energy, exposure, and legitimacy. What is the return on investment (ROI), and what resources might the contest pull away from existing scope? Will the opportunity dilute the event and stretch the ability of staff to manage the event with the quality you desire?

As sponsorships come in, focus on developing the event based on budget and revenue targets; don't overcommit hoping for sponsorships that might only be pipe dreams. Observe with a critical eye as the event develops to maintain a reasonable scope of practice. Consider the following questions:

- Are there time and resources enough to plan the special event as originally envisioned?
- Can the event stay on budget?
- Is there still enough time to adequately promote the event?
- Does the event work for the targeted audience?
- Does the event work with the targeted content (exhibitors, competitors, speakers)?
- Are the planned facilities still adequate to host the event?
- Does the event still fit the underlying mission of the organization?
- Is the projected event staff still adequate to manage the event?

## STAFFING

The special event staff and planning team are crucial to the success of a special event, but do not pull your team together too early, when the event idea remains vague. The risk is having too many voices trying to sketch out the look of the event. Attention to detail and program vision might be lost along the way. Pull the bulk of the team together after the vision and mission of the event have been clearly defined, when you are ready to assign roles and responsibilities (Junction Trail Festival, 2009).

Going through the assessment process detailed in this chapter should help you define your vision prior to presenting it to your event team. Once the team is together, you might want to revisit the assessments to gather more input from the team, create ownership, and assess the team's interests and strengths. Try to create systems and processes that make it (relatively) easy for others to understand their vision and for them to take action to help make it happen. Don't unleash staff to chaos. They must be given a logical framework. (Comeskey, pers. comm.).

If your organization is an institution, such as a university, it might be helpful to consider how this special event could be coordinated with other departments, such as marketing and finance. The event, regardless of size, is likely to include a few contractual agreements. Make sure they are in writing and follow procedures that are likely already established by your organization. Pull in at least one other professional staff member to work on items such as contracts, budgets, and marketing, and be sure to work closely with your event service staff (The Five Rivers MetroParks and Wright State University, 2011).

If the event team is made up solely of volunteer community members (rather than coworkers) a different dynamic is created. Community members can bring a lot of passion and dedication to the project, but sometimes they lack the focus to work toward common goals. There are also limits to what can be expected of volunteers because there may be no real consequences if they do not follow through on an assigned task (see chapter 13 on managing volunteers). On the other hand, a well-chosen and well-led committee made up from the community can be the best way to leverage event growth by tapping into other resources and local experts. Of course, inviting others in to the event-planning process involves some loss of control, and perhaps anxiety about the final product. Figure 21.3 illustrates a common process to promote, recruit, train, and task a volunteer to an assignment.

## MANAGING THE EVENT

Prior to the event, identify major components that need to be managed on the day of the event and establish a lead coordinator for each area. Regardless of the complexity of the event, areas of responsibility should be split for detailed management and accountability. A common error of new administrators is to try to handle single-handedly the massive influx of decisions and details that need to be managed during the event. A recipe for success is to identify these areas of necessary oversight and assign your team members to head them—food coordinator, exhibition coordinator, music coordinator, and so on. As outdoor program administrator, you must delegate as much as possible. You cannot do it all yourself, and trying to do so only demotivates and isolates your staff. People need to be productive and want to be productive.

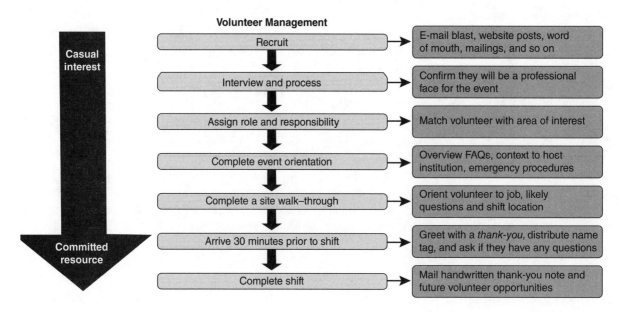

**Figure 21.3** Volunteer management.

Give them tools, give them direction, and get out of their way (Comeskey, pers. comm.).

Even for a small event, it is wise to train key volunteers or staff members to act in supervisory roles during the event. This is a good idea even if these individuals have never coordinated that particular area before. For example, you might assign an exhibition coordinator to lead a team of volunteers to assist in the check-in, setup, and management of the exhibitions. Much of the management of the event happens in a short window of time during setup. As the event administrator, you should be free of any assigned responsibilities in order to be able to respond to questions and "put out fires." Depending on the complexity of the event, it would be prudent to have several people in this "firefighter" role acting as part of an interchangeable management team (Five Rivers MetroParks, 2011b). To maintain consistency, area coordinators should remain the point of contact for their areas throughout the event.

## DEVELOPING TIMELINES FOR SUCCESSFUL EVENTS

It is critical to be able to accurately assess whether deadlines are being met during the development and implementation of a special event. For example, knowing whether marketing materials have been distributed, entertainment is under contract, and port-a-potties have been ordered is necessary for a smoothly run event. Important details will likely be missed if realistic timelines are not developed. When developing your overall event plan, create a calendar with as much detail as possible related to tasks. Many of these tasks can be completed well in advance of the event, which leaves time closer to the event to deal with the unexpected (which is to be expected). Table 21.1 details the three common phases of event planning. The timing of each phase depends on the structure of the event.

## PUTTING THE PLANNING INTO MOTION

Once the plan is made, projects completed, timelines met, and participants begin to arrive, you have arrived at the point of no return. For an event to run smoothly, the event staff must have resources in hand to understand the details for the entire event. Even if responsibilities are split up it is important to see how all the parts of the event fit together. All staff should receive training on key components

**Table 21.1** Phases of Event Development

| Phase I (6-18 months before event) | Phase II (3-9 months before event) | Phase III (1-6 months before event) |
|---|---|---|
| • Book anchor content that can be used to sell sponsorships.<br>• Book facility.<br>• Create sponsorship materials.<br>• Create marketing plan.<br>• Develop marketing materials.<br>• Implement early phases of marketing plan.<br>• Book high-demand rentals such as party tents, etc.<br>• Decide on event content.<br>• Create a potential sponsor and donor list.<br>• Create a potential partner list.<br>• Develop event staff.<br>• Create roles and responsibilities of target team.<br>• Recruit national involvement. | • Book supporting program content.<br>• Book ancillary pieces such as Port o' Johns and event security.<br>• Recruit sponsors.<br>• Begin fund-raising.<br>• Seek event partnerships.<br>• Send out contracts.<br>• Check inventory of local resources (clubs, retailers, individuals). | • Implement final phase of marketing plan.<br>• Design and order any event-specific or branded merchandise.<br>• Collect all contracts.<br>• Recruit sponsors.<br>• Continue fund-raising.<br>• Collect and inventory prizes.<br>• Get the local community involved.<br>• Send out media kits and press release. |

of the event and then have pertinent information included in a resource packet that can be used as a resource for the duration of the event. Resource packets should include basic information on logistics, a schedule of events, and critical information, such as the following:

- Risk-management plan and emergency response plan
- Emergency response and staff phone
- Equipment (rentals—tent, cords, generators, table, chairs, bouldering pads, and so on)
- Food (permit, institutional policy, electricity)
- Electrical needs, security, and parking
- Facility reservations (permits, pool space, conference rooms, and so on)
- Event layout and setup timeline
- Written agreements with all of your event providers

## SUMMARY

A special event makes for special relationships as it develops, often starting with a vision and a plan and ending with a mass celebration of weary but euphoric workers. The road between the start and the end is very dynamic, forcing the need for ongoing decisions and adjustments. The outdoor program administrator's job when preparing for and managing special events is a never-ending tangle of deadlines, details, and change. It is imperative to stay disciplined in developing and managing the scope of the event, tracking the status of each entangled project, and working within the budget and other limiting factors. However, it is the astute outdoor program administrator who can balance the dynamic development of an event by saying *no* to the lure of some opportunities as they arise to open the possibility of finding a way to say *yes* to others.

Encompassing considerations of risk management, site selection, marketing, managing volunteers, community involvement, fund-raising, budget concerns, and public speaking (just to name a few), special events are complex and complicated projects that involve every aspect of an outdoor program coming together at once. The visionary and well-organized outdoor recreation administrator can make it through the test of producing a special event to create a lasting legacy woven deep into the fabric of their program and the community.

# References and Resources

## CHAPTER 1

Cordell, H.K. (2008). The latest on trends in nature-based outdoor recreation. *Forest History Today.* Retrieved July 2011 at www.foresthistory.org/publications/FHT/FHTSpring2008/Cordell.pdf.

Nicolazzo, P. (2007). *Effective outdoor program design and management.* Winthrop, WA: Wilderness Medicine Training Center.

Raiola, E. (1990). Outdoor leadership curricula. In J.C. Miles & S. Priest (Eds.), *Adventure Education* (pp. 233-240). State College, PA: Venture Publishing.

## CHAPTER 2

American Camp Association. (2009). American Camp Association 20/20 initiatives. Retrieved May 2011 at www.acacamps.org/sites/default/files/images/2020/documents/2020MembershipInitiative.pdf.

American Camp Association. (2010). Camp trends fact sheet. Retrieved July 2011 at www.acacamps.org/media-center/camp-trends/fact.

American Camp Association. (2011). About ACA. Retrieved July 2011 at www.acacamps.org/about/who-we-are.

American Canoe Association. (2008). Frequently asked questions about ACA instructor certification. Retrieved July 2011 at www.americancanoe.org.

American Canoe Association. (2010). ACA 2009 annual report. Retrieved July 2011 at www.americancanoe.org.

American Mountain Guide Association. (n.d.) *About us + programs.* Retrieved July 2011 at http://amga.com.

Anderson, L.M. (2006). The playground of today is the republic of tomorrow: Social reform and organized recreation in the USA, 1890-1930's. *The Encyclopaedia of Informal Education.* Retrieved July 2011 at www.infed.org/playwork/organized_recreation_and_playwork_1890-1930s.htm.

Aron, C.S. (1999). *Working at play: A history of vacations in the United States.* New York: Oxford University Press.

Association for Challenge Course Technology. (2010). *About ACCT + practitioner certification.* Retrieved July 2011 at www.acctinfo.org.

Association of Outdoor Recreation and Education (AORE). (2006). A brief history of the conference of the Association of Outdoor Recreation and Education. In J. Turner (Ed.), *Proceedings and Research Symposium Abstracts of the 19th Annual Association of the Outdoor Recreation and Education (AORE) Conference* (pp. 1-5). Boise, ID: Association of Outdoor Recreation and Education.

Attarian, A. (2001). Trends in outdoor adventure education. *Journal of Experiential Education, 24*(3): 141-149.

Bachert, D.W. (1999). The National Outdoor Leadership School: 40,000 wilderness experiences and counting. In J.C. Miles & S. Priest (Eds.), *Adventure Programming* (pp. 85-91). State College, PA: Venture Publishing.

Ball, A. & Ball, B. (2000). *Basic camp management.* Martinsville, IN: American Camping Association.

Barry, J., & Erb, B. (n.d.). WMS footprints: Past, present, and future. (Wilderness Medical Society website.) Retrieved July 2011 at www.wms.org/about/history.asp.

Bialeschki, M.D. (1992). We said, "Why not?"—A historical perspective on women's outdoor pursuits. *JOPERD, 55*(2): 52-56.

Blair, K.J. (1991). Women's voluntary associations. In J.A. Garraty & E. Fonner, *Reader's Companion to American History.* Retrieved July 2011 at www.answers.com/topic/women-s-voluntary-associations.

Boys and Girls Clubs of South Puget Sound. (n.d.). History of Boys & Girls Clubs of America. Retrieved July 2011 at www.bgcsps.org.

Brehony, K.J. (2001). A "socially civilizing influence"? Play and the urban degenerate. Paper given at the International Standing Conference for the History of Education XXIII, University of Birmingham, UK. Retrieved February 15, 2010 from www.inrp.fr/she/ische/abstracts2001/BrehonyP.rtf.

Brinkley, D. (2009). *The wilderness warrior—Theodore Roosevelt and the crusade for America.* New York: HarperCollins.

Brower, D. (Ed.). (1960). *The Sierra Club—A handbook.* San Francisco, CA: Sierra Club.

Brown, D.E., & Carmony, N.B. (Eds.). (1990). *Aldo Leopold's wilderness—Selected early writings by the author of* A Sand County Almanac. Harrisburg, PA: Stackpole.

Cain, K. (1985). Wilderness Education Association certification. In J.C. Miles & R. Watters (Eds.), *Proceedings of the 1984 Conference on Outdoor Recreation—A Landmark Conference in the Outdoor Recreation Field* (pp. 53-61). Pocatello, ID: Idaho State University Press/1984 Conference on Outdoor Recreation Steering Committee.

Canberg, A.S., & Daniels, M.J. (2004). The diffusion of outdoor adventure leadership degree programs in the United States. *World Leisure Journal, 46*(4): 22-34.

Carlson, J. (2009). *Never finished . . . just begun.* Edina, MN: Beaver's Pond Press.

Climbing Wall Association (CWA). (2011). CWA website. Retrieved September 2011 at www.climbingwallindustry.org/index.php.

Cockrell, D. (1987). The professionalization of outdoor leadership. In J.F. Meier, W.W. Morash, & G.E. Welton (Eds.), *High-adventure outdoor pursuits* (2nd ed.) (pp. 510-521). Columbus, OH: Publishing Horizons, Inc.

Cole, C.C. (1980). Instructional implications of the Outward Bound program. In J.F. Meier, W.W. Morash, G.E. Welton (Eds.), *High Adventure Outdoor Pursuits* (pp. 127-136). Salt Lake City, UT: Brighton Publishing. (Originally published in 1976.)

Cordell, H.K. (2002). The way is was, the way it is—ORRRC at 40! *Parks and Recreation, 37*(10): 62-64.

Cousineau, C. (1977). *A Delphi consensus on a set of principles for the development of a certification system for education in the outdoor adventure programs.* Unpublished doctoral dissertation. Greeley, CO: University of Northern Colorado.

Crandall, D. (1994). *Outdoor recreation policy development—1960 to the 104th Congress.* Retrieved May 2004 at www.wildwilderness.org/docs/nfra94.htm.

Dewey, J. (1897). My pedagogic creed. *School Journal, 54*(January): 77-80. Retrieved July 2011 at http://dewey.pragmatism.org/creed.htm.

Dewey, J. (1916). *Democracy and education—An introduction to the philosophy of education.* New York: MacMillan.

Dewey, J. (1943). *The school and society* (Rev. ed.). Chicago, IL: University of Chicago Press. (Originally published in 1900.)

Dulles, F.R. (1965). *A history of recreation—America learns to play* (2nd ed.). New York: Meredith. (Originally published in 1940.)

Elverum, K.A. & Smalley, T. (2008). *The drowning machine.* St. Paul, MN: Minnesota Department of Natural Resources. Retrieved July 2011 at http://files.dnr.state.mn.us/education_safety/safety/boatwater/drowningmachine.pdf.

Garvey, D. (1999). A history of the Association for Experiential Education. In J. C. Miles & S. Priest (Eds.), *Adventure Programming* (pp. 71-76). State College, PA: Venture Publishing.

Gibson, H.W. (1968a). The history of organized camping, Chapter 1. In D.R. Hammerman & W.M. Hammerman (Eds.), *Outdoor Education—A Book of Readings* (pp. 89-96). Minneapolis, MN: Burgess Publishing. (Originally published in 1936.)

Gibson, H.W. (1968b). The history of organized camping, Chapter 3. In D.R. Hammerman & W.M. Hammerman (Eds.), *Outdoor Education—A Book of Readings* (pp. 96-103). Minneapolis, MN: Burgess Publishing. (Originally published in 1936.)

Gillis, H.L., & Ringer, T.M. (1999). Adventure as therapy. In J.C. Miles & S. Priest (Eds.), *Adventure Programming* (pp. 29-42). State College, PA: Venture Publishing.

Glazer, S. (2005). Gender and learning: Background. *CQ Researcher, 25*(19): 458-460, 462.

Grimm, G.O & Hilbert, H.H. (1973). An operational definition and description of college outdoor programs. Unpublished paper presented at the conference of the Association of College Unions–International, March 17-21, 1973, San Diego, CA.

Guthrie, S.P. (1992). Minutes of first open forum of International Conference of Outdoor Recreation. Calgary, CN. (Available from Steven Guthrie, Lock Haven University of Pennsylvania, Lock Haven, PA 17745.)

Guthrie, S.P. (1993). Minutes of the first AORE Board meeting, held at the International Conference on Outdoor Recreation, Corvallis, OR. (Available from Steven Guthrie, Lock Haven University of Pennsylvania, Lock Haven, PA 17745.)

Guthrie, S.P. (2001). A brief history of the AORE. *AORE Newsletter* (June). (Available from Steven Guthrie, Lock Haven University of Pennsylvania, Lock Haven, PA 17745.)

Guthrie, S.P. & Yerkes, R. (2007). Adventure education programming and career paths. In D. Prouty, J. Panicuci, and R. Collinson (Eds.), *Adventure Education—Theory and Applications.* Champaign, IL: Human Kinetics.

Hammerman, D.R., Hammerman, W.M., & Hammerman, E.L. (2001). *Teaching in the outdoors* (5th ed.). Danville, IL: Interstate Publishers.

Heeg, P. (1996). Why is outdoor recreation worth $30 million to the air force? In P. Joyce & R. Watters (Eds.), *Proceedings of the 1992-1993 Conference on Outdoor Recreation* (pp. 121-128). Pocatello, ID: Idaho State University Press/Idaho State Outdoor Program.

Howat, J.K. (1972, June/July). *The Metropolitan Museum of Art Bulletin.* New York: Metropolitan Museum of Art. Retrieved January 2010 at www.metmuseum.org/publications/bulletins/1/pdf/3258969.pdf.bannered.pdf.

Ibrahim, H., & Cordes, K.A. (2002). *Outdoor recreation—Enrichment for a lifetime* (2nd ed.). Champaign, IL: Sagamore.

Jensen, C.R. & Guthrie, S.P. (2006). *Outdoor recreation in America* (6th ed.). Champaign, IL: Human Kinetics.

Jones, C. (1976). *Climbing in North America.* Berkeley, CA: University of California Press.

Jones, C.D., Lowe, L.A., & Risler, E.A. (2004). The effectiveness of wilderness adventure therapy programs for young people involved in the juvenile justice system. *Residential Treatment for Children & Youth, 22*(2): 53-67.

Kaufman, P.W. (2006). *National parks and the woman's voice—A history* (Updated edition). Albuquerque, NM: University of New Mexico.

Kohlstedt, S.G. (2005). Nature, not books—Scientists and the origin of the Nature-Study Movement in the 1890s. *Isis, 96*(3): 324-352.

Leave No Trace Center for Outdoor Ethics. (2008). *Leave No Trace history.* Retrieved July 2011 at www.lnt.org/aboutUs/history.php.

Leopold, A. (1990a). The wilderness and its place in forest recreation policy. In D.E. Brown & N.B. Carmony (Eds.), *Aldo Leopold's Wilderness—Selected Early Writings by the Author of* A Sand County Almanac (pp. 146-151). Harrisburg, PA: Stackpole. (Originally published in 1921.)

Leopold, A. (1990b). Ten new developments in game management. In D.E. Brown & N.B. Carmony (Eds.), *Aldo Leopold's Wilderness—Selected Early Writings by the Author of* A Sand County Almanac (pp. 113-121). Harrisburg, PA: Stackpole. (Originally published in 1925.)

Lewis, J.G. (2005). *Forest service and the greatest good: A centennial history.* Durham, NC: Forest History Society.

March, B. (1985a). Wilderness leadership certification—catch 22—assessing the outdoor leader—an insoluble problem?

In J.C. Miles & R. Watters (Eds.), *Proceedings of the 1984 Conference on Outdoor Recreation—A Landmark Conference in the Outdoor Recreation Field* (pp. 37-42). Pocatello, ID: Idaho State University Press/1984 Conference on Outdoor Recreation Steering Committee.

March, B. (1985b). A reply to Wilkinson's comments. In J.C. Miles & R. Watters (Eds.), *Proceedings of the 1984 Conference on Outdoor Recreation—A Landmark Conference in the Outdoor Recreation Field* (pp. 47-51). Pocatello, ID: Idaho State University Press/1984 Conference on Outdoor Recreation Steering Committee.

Meier, J.F., Morash, T.W., & Welton, G.E. (1980). The Outward Bound concept. *High adventure outdoor pursuits—Organization and leadership* (Chap. 4). Salt Lake City, UT: Brighton Publishing.

Miles, J.C. (1987). The problem of judgment in outdoor leadership. In J.F. Meier, W.W. Morash, & G.E. Welton (Eds.) *High-adventure Outdoor Pursuits* (2nd ed.) (pp. 502-509). Columbus, OH: Publishing Horizons, Inc.

Miles, J.C., & Watters, R. (1985). *Proceedings of the 1984 conference on outdoor recreation—A landmark conference in the outdoor recreation field*. Pocatello, ID: Idaho State University Press/1984 Conference on Outdoor Recreation Steering Committee.

Military Homefront (n.d.). History of MWR. Department of Defense Military Homefront web page. Retrieved July 2011 at www.militaryhomefront.dod.mil/sp/mwr/moreinformation.

Miner, J.L. (1999). The creation of Outward Bound. In J.C. Miles & S. Priest (Eds.), *Adventure Programming* (pp. 56-63). State College, PA: Venture Publishing.

Mitchell, E.D. (1968). The interests of education in camping. In D.R. Hammerman & W.M. Hammerman (Eds.), *Outdoor Education—A Book of Readings* (pp. 107-111). Minneapolis: Burgess Publishing. (Originally published in 1938.)

Moore, R.L., & Driver, B.L. (2005). *Introduction to outdoor recreation—Providing and managing natural resource based opportunities*. State College, PA: Venture.

Mountain Rescue Association (n.d.). MRA website. Retrieved July 2011 at www.mra.org/.

Nash, R. (2001). *Wilderness and the American mind* (4th ed.). New Haven, CT: Yale University Press. (Originally published in 1967.)

National Association for Search and Rescue. (n.d.). ". . . that others may live"—NASAR history brochure. From the About Us section of the NASAR website. Retrieved December 2010 at www.nasar.org/nasar/downloads/NASAR_Book.pdf.

National Ski Patrol. (2011). NSP website. Retrieved July 2011 at www.nsp.org.

Olson, B.A. (2010). Paper trails: The Outdoor Recreation Resource Review Commission and the rationalization of recreational resources. *Geoforum*. In press. Retrieved September 2011 at http://brentaolson.com/wp-content/uploads/2011/07/Olson-2010-01-01-Geoforum.pdf.

Outward Bound. (2010). About outward bound. Retrieved July 2011 at www.outwardbound.org/index.cfm/do/ind.about.

Paris, L. (2008). *Children's nature: The rise of the American summer camp*. New York: New York University Press.

Poff, R., & Webb, D.J (2007). *Outdoor recreation program directory & data resource guide* (4th ed.). Bowling Green, KY: Raymond A. Poff.

Price, J. (1999). *Flight maps—Adventures with nature in modern America*. New York: Basic Books.

Priest, S., & Gass, M.A. (1997). *Effective leadership in adventure programming*. Champaign, IL: Human Kinetics.

Professional Climbing Instructors Association. (2011). PCIA website. Retrieved July 2011 at http://pcia.us/newpro.

Professional Ropes Course Association. (2011). PRCA website. Retrieved July 2011 at www.prcainfo.org.

Professional Ski Instructors of America–American Association of Snowboard Instructors (PSIA-AASI). (n.d.). The PSIA-AASI website. Retrieved July 2011 at www.thesnowpros.org/index.php/PSIA-AASI/info-center/about.

Prouty, D. (1999). Project adventure: A brief history. In J.C. Miles & S. Priest (Eds.), *Adventure Programming* (pp. 93–101). State College, PA: Venture Publishing.

Punke, M. (2007). *Last stand—George Bird Grinnell, the battle to save the buffalo, and the birth of the new West*. Smithsonian Books. New York: HarperCollins.

Ringholz, R.C. (1997). *On belay!—The life of legendary mountaineer Paul Petzoldt*. Seattle, WA: Mountaineers.

Russell, H.R. (1982). 75 years of nature study. *The Outdoor Communicator, 13*(2): 32-36.

Russell, K.C., & Hendee, J.C. (2000). *Outdoor behavioral healthcare: Definitions, common practice, expected outcomes, and a nationwide survey of programs*. Technical Report #26. Moscow, ID: Idaho Forest, Wildlife and Range Experiment Station.

Scott, D. (2004). *The enduring wilderness—Protecting our natural heritage through the wilderness act*. Golden, CO: Fulcrum Publishing.

Sellars, R.W. (1997). *Preserving nature in the national parks*. New Haven, CT: Yale University Press. From the National Park Service History website. Retrieved July 2011 at www.nps.gov/history/history/online_books/sellars/index.htm.

Senosk, E.M. (1977). *An examination of outdoor pursuit leader certification and licensing within the United States in 1976*. Unpublished Master's thesis. Eugene, OR: University of Oregon.

The Sierra Club. (1989). *The Sierra Club: A guide*. San Francisco, CA: Sierra Club.

Simmons, G.A. (1985). The role of academic departments in outdoor recreation programs. In J.C. Miles & R. Watters (Eds.), *Proceedings of the 1984 Conference on Outdoor Recreation—A Landmark Conference in the Outdoor Recreation Field* (pp. 63-69). Pocatello, ID: Idaho State University Press/1984 Conference on Outdoor Recreation Steering Committee.

Smith, J. (1968). Fitness through outdoor education. In D.R. Hammerman, & W.M. Hammerman (Eds.), *Outdoor Education—A Book of Readings* (pp. 65-67). Minneapolis, MN: Burgess Publishing. (Originally published in 1957.)

SOLO. (n.d.). *SOLO history*. Retrieved July 2011 at http://soloadventures.wordpress.com/solo-an-in-depth-look.

Stiehl, J., & Ramsey, T.B. (2005). *Climbing walls*. Champaign, IL: Human Kinetics.

Surgenor, P. (2009). Camping in America: Proud tradition, lasting impact. *Perspective*. Retrieved July 2011 at www.acacamps.org.

Taft, S.L. (2001). *The river chasers—A history of American whitewater paddling*. Mulkiteo, WA: Flowing Water Press & Alpen Books.

Teeters, C.E., & Lupton, F. (1999). The Wilderness Education Association: History and change. In J.C. Miles & S. Priest (Eds.), *Adventure Programming* (pp. 77-83). State College, PA: Venture Publishing.

Turner, F.J. (1893). The frontier in American history. *Report of the American Historical Association* for 1893. From the American Studies at the University of Virginia website. Retrieved July 2011 at http://xroads.virginia.edu/~HYPER/TURNER/home.html.

Unrau, H.D., & Williss, G.F. (1983). *Administrative history: Expansion of the NPS in the 1930s*. Denver, CO: National Park Service Denver Center. From the National Park Service website. Retrieved July 2011 at www.cr.nps.gov/history/online_books/unrau-williss/adhi.htm.

U.S. Army MWR. (2010). *MWR History*. From the U.S. Army MWR website. Retrieved July 2011 at www.armymwr.com/commander/aboutfmwrc.aspx.

U.S. Bureau of the Census. (1975). *Historical statistics of the United States, Colonial times to 1970, Bicentennial edition, Part 2* (Series J 3-7). Washington, DC: U.S. Government Printing Office.

U.S. Navy MWR Headquarters. (2010). Armed forces MWR internships and career opportunities? PowerPoint presentation. Retrieved July 2011 at www.indiana.edu/~r231/MWRinternshipinfo.ppt.

Wagstaff, M. (2003). *A history of challenge courses*. From the Association for Challenge Course Technology website. Retrieved July 2011 at http://acct.affiniscape.com/associations/5266/files/HistoryOfCCourses.pdf.

Waterman, L., & Waterman, G. (1993). *Yankee rock and ice: A history of climbing in the northeastern United States*. Mechanicsburg, PA: Stackpole Books.

Watters, R. (1985). Historical perspectives of outdoor and wilderness recreation programming in the United States. In J.C. Miles & R. Watters (Eds.), *Proceedings of the 1984 Conference on Outdoor Recreation—A Landmark Conference in the Outdoor Recreation Field* (pp. 103-114). Pocatello, ID: Idaho State University Press/1984 Conference on Outdoor Recreation Steering Committee.

Weaver, R.B. (1939). *Amusements and sports in American life*. Chicago: University of Chicago.

Webb, D.J (1991). *Outdoor recreation program directory & data resource guide*. Boulder, CO: Outdoor Network Communications.

Webb, D.J (2000). *Outdoor recreation program directory & data resource guide* (3rd ed.). Bowling Green, KY: Raymond A. Poff.

Wilderness Medicine Associates. (2010). *Our history*. From the WMA website. Retrieved July 2011 at www.wildmed.com.

Wilkinson, K. (1985). Another look at outdoor leadership certification. In J.C. Miles & R. Watters (Eds.), *Proceedings of the 1984 Conference on Outdoor Recreation—A Landmark Conference in the Outdoor Recreation Field* (pp. 43-45). Pocatello, ID: Idaho State University Press/1984 Conference on Outdoor Recreation Steering Committee.

Wood, W. (1913). *The playground movement in the U.S. and its relation to public education*. Board of Education Educational Pamphlets, #27. London: Byrb & Spottiswoodk. Retrieved February 2010 at www.archive.org/stream/playgroundmoveme00wood/playgroundmoveme00wood_djvu.txt.

Yerkes, R. (1985). Certification: An introduction behind the growing controversy. *Camping Magazine, 57*(6): 12-13.

# CHAPTER 3

Dudley, C.M. (1935). *60 centuries of skiing*. Brattleboro, VT: Stephen Daye Press.

Goldenberg, M., McAvoy, L., & Klenosky, D.B. (2005). Outcomes from the components of an outward bound experience. *Journal of Experiential Education 28*(2): 123-146.

Grimm, G.O., & Hilbert, H.H. (1973). *An operational definition and description of college outdoor programs*. Pocatello: Idaho State University Outdoor Program.

Guthrie, S.P. (1999). Outdoor program models: Placing cooperative adventure and adventure education models on the continuum. In R. Harwell & K. Emmons (Eds.), *Proceedings of the 13th Annual International Conference on Outdoor Recreation and Education* (pp. 227-234). Boulder, CO: Association of Outdoor Recreation and Education.

Hooke, D. (1987). *History of the DOC*. From the Dartmouth Outing Club website. Retrieved July 2011 at www.dartmouth.edu/~doc/about/history.

Intercollegiate Outing Club Association. (2011). Directory of IOCA clubs. Retrieved July 2011 at www.ioca.org.

Miles, J.C., & Priest, S. (1999). *Adventure programming*. State College, PA: Venture Publishing.

National Park Service. (2010). Noncommercial river trip regulations. Retrieved July 2011 at www.nps.gov/grca/planyourvisit/upload/Noncommercial_River_Trip_Regulations.pdf.

Sacks, B. (2002). *History*. From the Williams Outing Club website. Retrieved July 2011 at http://woc.williams.edu/index.php/about-woc/history.

The Sierra Club. (2011). Website. Retrieved July 2011 at www.sierraclub.org.

Waterman, L., & Waterman, G. (1993). *Yankee rock and ice: A history of climbing in the northeastern United States*. Mechanicsburg, PA: Stackpole Books.

Watters, R. (1999a). The common adventure model of outdoor programming: Philosophical foundations, definition and the effect of filtering. In R. Harwell & K. Emmons (Eds.), *Proceedings of the 13th Annual International Conference on*

*Outdoor Recreation and Education* (pp. 95-113). Boulder, CO: Association of Outdoor Recreation and Education.

Watters, R. (1999b). Revisiting the common adventure concept: An annotated review of the literature, misconceptions and contemporary perspectives. In R. Harwell & K. Emmons (Eds.), *Proceedings of the 13th Annual International Conference on Outdoor Recreation and Education* (pp. 82-94). Boulder, CO: Association of Outdoor Recreation and Education.

Webb, D.J (2001). The emergence and evolution of outdoor adventure programs, 1863-2000: A history of student initiated outing programs. In P. Joyce & R. Poff (Eds.), *Proceedings of the 15th Annual International Conference on Outdoor Recreation and Education* (pp. 40-52). Bloomington, IL: Association of Outdoor Recreation and Education.

Wyman, R.A. (1972). A memorandum regarding the tort liability of self-directing university outdoor wilderness programs. Eugene, OR: University of Oregon Outdoor Program.

# CHAPTER 4

*An inconvenient truth.* (2006). (Video.) Hollywood, CA: Paramount Classics. L. Bender & L. David (producers).

Burmeister, M. (2008). The 7 most effective ways to recruit, retain and motivate your youngest generation. Retrieved July 2011 at http://ezinearticles.com/?The-7-Most-Effective-Ways-to-Recruit,-Retain-and-Motivate-Your-Youngest-Generation&id=786583.

California State Parks. (2008). California outdoor recreation plan 2008. Retrieved August 2011, at www.parks.ca.gov/pages/795/files/2009-2014%20corp.pdf.

Carlton, M. (2009). The challenge of the Millennials. Retrieved July 2011 at www.carltonassociatesinc.com/wp1.cfm?id=64.

Centers for Disease Control and Prevention. (2010). U.S. obesity trends: Trends by state 1985–2009. Retrieved July 2011 at www.cdc.gov/obesity/data/trends.html#State.

Chesapeake Bay Foundation. (2010). No child left inside. Retrieved July 2011 at www.cbf.org/Page.aspx?pid=687.

Collins, J. (2001). *Good to great.* New York: HarperCollins.

Cordell, H.K. (2004). *Outdoor recreation for 21st century America.* State College, PA: Venture Publishing.

Cross-Bystrom, A. (2010). What you need to know about Generation Z. Retrieved July 2011 at www.imediaconnection.com/content/27425.asp.

Easterlin, R.A., Schaeffer, C.M., & Macunovich, D.J. (1993). Will the baby boomers be less well off than their parents? Income, wealth, and family circumstances over the life cycle in the United States. *Population and Development Review, 19*(3): 497-522.

Federal Interagency Forum on Aging-related Statistics. (2008). *Older Americans 2008: Key indicators to well-being.* Washington DC: U.S. Government Printing Office.

Ford, P., Blanchard, J., & Blanchard, A. (1993). *Leadership and administration of outdoor pursuits.* State College, PA: Venture Publishing.

Harmon, L.K., & Gleason, M. (2009). Underwater explorers: Using underwater remotely operated vehicles (ROVs) to engage youth with underwater environments. *Children, Youth and Environments, 19*(1): 125-143.

Heimlich, J.E. (2007). Research trends in the United States: EE to ESD. *Journal of Education for Sustainable Development, 1*(2): 219-227.

Howe, N., & Strauss, W. (2000). *Millennials rising: The next great generation.* New York: Vintage Books.

Louv, R. (2008). *Last child in the woods: Saving our children from nature-deficit disorder.* Chapel Hill, NC: Algonquin Books.

National Center for Health Statistics. (2011). Health, United States, 2010: With special feature on death and dying. Hyattsville, MD. Retrieved August 2011 at www.cdc.gov/nchs/data/hus/hus10.pdf#specialfeature.

National Park Service. (2011). Glacier Bay's glaciers: Then and now. Retrieved July 2011 at www.nps.gov/glba/nature-science/glaciers.htm.

Outdoor Industry Association. (2006). *State of the industry report 2006.* Boulder, CO: Outdoor Industry Association.

Outward Bound. (2008). Outward Bound awarded $3.5M grant to serve military veterans from Iraq and Afghanistan. Retrieved August 2011 at www.outwardbound.org/docs/Grant_to_Serve_Military_Veterans.pdf.

Rideout, V.J., Foehr, U.G., & Roberts, D.F. (2010). Generation M$^2$: Media in the lives of 8- to 18-year-olds. Research report. Retrieved July 2011 at www.kff.org/entmedia/mh012010pkg.cfm.

Roberts, D.F., Foehr, U.G., & Rideout, V.J. (2005). Generation M: Media in the lives of 8-18 year-olds. Research report. Retrieved July 2011 at www.kff.org/entmedia/entmedia030905pkg.cfm.

Schuman, H., & Scott, J. (1989). Generations and collective memories. *American Psychological Review, 54:* 359-381.

Trunk, P. (2009). What Generation Z will be like at work. Retrieved July 2011 at http://blog.penelopetrunk.com/2009/07/27.

United States Census Bureau. (2004). U.S. interim projects by age, sex, race, and Hispanic origin. Retrieved August 2011 at www.census.gov/population/www/projections/usinterimproj/.

United States Department of Health and Human Services, Centers for Disease Control and Prevention, National Center for Health Statistics. (2008). Life expectancy at birth, 65 and 85 years of age, United States, selected years 1900–2004. Trends in health and aging. Retrieved August 2011 at www.cdc.gov/nchs/data/hus/hus06.pdf.

Virginia Department of Conservation and Recreation. (2007). Virginia outdoors plan: Charting the course for Virginia's outdoors. Retrieved July 2011 at www.dcr.virginia.gov/recreational_planning/vop.shtml.

# CHAPTER 5


Arenas, A., Tabernero, C., & Briones, E. (2006). Effects of goal orientation, error orientation and self-efficacy on performance in an uncertain situation. *Social Behavior and Personality, 34*(5): 17.

Cline, P. (2004). *The merging of risk analysis and adventure education.* Paper presented at the Wilderness Risk Management Conference, Banff, Canada.

Committee, E.R.M. (2003). *Overview of enterprise risk management.* (Self-published.)

Gregg, R. (1999). *Issues in outdoor recreation liability.* Paper presented at the Wilderness Risk Managers Conference, Sierra Vista, Arizona.

Hansen-Stamp, C. (1999). *Thoughts on risk management in the recreation industry: A different perspective.* Paper presented at the Wilderness Risk Management Conference, Sierra Vista, Arizona.

Meyer, D. (1979). Management of risk. *Journal of Experiential Education, 2*(2): 5.

Priest, S., & Gass, M. (2005). *Effective leadership in adventure programming* (2nd ed.). Champaign, IL: Human Kinetics.

Van der Smissen, B. (1990). *Legal liability and risk management for public and private entities.* Cincinnati, OH: Anderson Publishing Company.


# CHAPTER 6


Aguilar, F. (2006). *Scanning the business environment.* New York: Macmillan.

Carver, J. (1997). *Creating a mission that makes a difference.* San Francisco: Jossey-Bass.

Collins, J. (2005). *Good to great and the social sectors.* Boulder, CO: Jim Collins.

Cooperrider, D.L., Whitney, D., Stravos, J.M., & Fry, R. (2008). *Appreciative Inquiry handbook: For leaders of change.* San Francisco: Berrett-Koehler.

Cornell Outdoor Education. (2008). *Cornell Outdoor Education Strategic Plan: 2008-2013.* Ithaca, NY: Cornell Outdoor Education (unpublished document).

Drucker, P.F. (1990). *Managing the nonprofit organization.* New York: HarperCollins.

Drucker, P.F. (1999). *The Drucker Foundation Self-Assessment Tool: Process guide.* San Francisco: Jossey-Bass.

Fields, J. (2003). *Social capital.* London: Routledge.

Miner, T. (1993). Building internal support for experiential education programs. *Journal of Experiential Education, 16*(2): 21-25.

Miner, T. (2003, November). "Cash, Clout, and Counsel: Building Program Excellence Through Advisory Boards," Association for Experiential Education 2003 International Conference, Vancouver, BC, Canada.

Peters, T. (1988). *Thriving on chaos.* New York: Harper.


# RESOURCES

Many valuable resources related to grant or proposal writing can be found on the web. Also don't forget internal resources to one's institution.

## Grant Writing

www.cpb.org/grants/grantwriting.html—Aimed at those seeking funds for public broadcasting, the general principles are appropriate for any proposal.

www.mcf.org/mcf/grant/writing.htm—From Minnesota, a brief and general overview of grant writing.

www.npguides.org/index.html—Good solid generic information and suggestions on grant and proposal writing.

http://theideabank.com/onlinecourse/samplegrant.html—Mainly focused on public safety (fire, emergency response, paramedic, etc.), this site offers many examples of successfully funded grants.

## Grant and Proposal Sources

www07.grants.gov/applicants/find_grant_opportunities.jsp—A good place to get started on looking for U.S. Government grants and funding.

http://school.discoveryeducation.com/schrockguide/business/grants.html—A source for K-12 educators to find funding.

www.necedlinks.org/grants.htm—A list of major grant sources including government, corporate, and foundations.

# CHAPTER 7


Black, H. (1990). *Black's law dictionary.* St. Paul, MN: West.

Crego, S. (1997). Liability insurance: A primer for college and university counsel. *Journal of College and University Law, 23:* 609.

Cloutier, R., Garvey, D., Will, L., Moss, J., & Vadade, G. (Eds.) (2000). *Tort law, legal liability and risk management in adventure tourism.* Kamloops, BC: Bhudak Consultants.

Cotten, D., & Wolohan, J. (2003). *Elements of negligence. Law for recreation and sports managers* (3rd ed.). Dubuque, IA: Kendall/Hunt.

Cotten, D., & Wolohan, J. (2003). *Negligence law. Law for recreation and sports managers* (3rd ed.). Dubuque, IA: Kendall/Hunt.

Diamond, J.L. (1991). Assumption of risk after comparative negligence: Integrating contract theory into tort doctrine, *Ohio State Law Journal, 52:* 717.

Dobbs, D. (2001). *The law of torts.* Saint Paul, MN: West.

Dobbs, D., & Hayden, P. (1997). *Torts and compensation.* St. Paul, MN: West.

Fried, G. (1999). *Applicable legal terms and principles. Safe at first, a guide to help sports administrators reduce their liability.* Durham, NC: Carolina Academic Press.

Gregg, C. (2005). Managing the risks of a lawsuit. In D. Ajango (Ed.), *Lessons Learned II: Using Case Studies and History to Improve Safety Education* (pp. 181-207). Palm Springs, CA: Watchmaker Publishing.

Hansen, C., & Duerr, S. (1993). Recreational injures & inherent risk: Wyoming's recreation safety act. *Land & Water Law Review, 28:* 149.

Hansen-Stamp, C., & Gregg, C. (2001). The elusive reasonable person. *The Outdoor Education and Recreation Law Quarterly, 1*(1): 3-15.

Hicks, E. (2000). A defense lawyer's perspective on risk management and crisis response. In D. Ajango (Ed.), *Lessons Learned: A Guide to Accident Prevention and Crisis Response.* Anchorage: University of Alaska Press.

Hronek, B., & Spengler, J. (Eds.) (2002). The negligence cause of action. *Legal Liability in Recreation and Sports* (2nd ed.). Champaign, IL: Sagamore.

Knutson, T., & Collins, D. (Producers). (2005). State of risk—Risk management in the outdoor industry [DVD]. Available at www.traceyknutson.com.

Knutson, T., & Larson, K. (2009). Legal considerations during expedition planning. *Expedition and Wilderness Medicine.* New York: Cambridge University Press.

Prosser, W.L., & Keeton, W. (1984). *Prosser & Keeton on torts.* St. Paul, MN: West.

Sugarman, S. (1997). Assumption of risk. *Valparaiso University Law Review, 31:* 833.

Wilson, B. (2005). Lee v. Sun Valley Company: Public duty or abdication of free will and personal responsibility. *Idaho Law Review, 41:* 429.

# CHAPTER 8

Blanchard, L.A. (2006). *Performance budgeting: How NASA and the SBA link costs to performance.* Washington, DC: IBM Center for the Business of Government.

FASAB. (1995). Federal Accounting Standards Advisory Board (FASAB) managerial cost accounting concepts and standards for the federal government. Statement #4. Retrieved July 2011 at www.fasab.gov/pdffiles/handbook_sffas_4.pdf.

FASAB. (1996). Federal Accounting Standards Advisory Board (FASAB) overview of federal accounting concepts and standards. Report #1. Retrieved July 2011 at www.fasab.gov/pdffiles/con_stan.pdf.

Rubin, I.S. (2000). *The politics of public budgeting—Getting and spending, borrowing and balancing* (4th ed.). New York: Seven Bridges Press.

Schick, A. (1966). The road to PPB: The stages of budget reform. *Public Administration Review, 26*(December): 245-256.

# CHAPTER 9

American Marketing Association. (2004). Definition of marketing. Retrieved July 2011 at www.marketingpower.com/AboutAMA/Pages/DefinitionofMarketing.aspx.

Andreasen, A. (2002). *Marketing research "that won't break the bank."* San Francisco: Jossey-Bass.

Jacobs, H. (2008). *Emory's beloved online community.* Emory Quadrangle, 10-13. Retrieved August 2011 from http://college.emory.edu/home/assets/documents/quadrangle/Q08S.pdf.

Johnson, W. (2004). *Powerhouse marketing plans.* New York: American Management Association.

Kaden, R.J. (2006). *Guerrilla marketing research.* Philadelphia: Kogan Page Limited.

M. Booth & Associates. (1995). *Promoting issues & ideas: A guide to public relations for nonprofit organizations.* New York: Foundation Center.

Mullin, B.J., Hardy, S., & Sutton, W.A. (2000). *Sport marketing* (2nd ed.). Champaign, IL: Human Kinetics.

NetMBA. (2009). The product life cycle. Retrieved July 2011 at www.netmba.com/marketing/product/lifecycle/.

Straugh, T.B., Converse, P., & White, K. (2004). *2003 deer hunter survey summary statistics.* Juneau, AK: Alaska Dept of Fish and Game. Division of Wildlife Conservation.

Strong, E.K. (1925). Theories of selling. *Journal of Applied Psychology, 9:* 75-86.

# CHAPTER 10

*DOI Quick Facts.* (2009). Retrieved August 2011 at www.doi.gov/facts.html.

Marion, J., & Reid, S. (2001). Development of the United States Leave No Trace programme: A historical perspective. In M.B. Usher (Ed.), *Enjoyment and Understanding of the Natural Heritage* (pp. 81-92). Scottish Natural Heritage, Edinburgh: The Stationery Office Ltd., Scotland.

New Jersey Department of Environmental Protection. (2006). *Open Space and recreation plan guidelines.* Green Acres Program.

Outdoor Industry Association. (2008). OIA homepage. Retrieved July 2011 at www.outdoorindustry.org/careercenter.html.

USDA Forest Service. (1997). *Outfitter-guide administration guidebook.* Northern Region, USDA Forest Service.

USDA Forest Service. (2006). Fiscal year 2006 president's budget overview. Retrieved July 2011 at www.fs.fed.us/publications/budget-2006/fy2006-forest-service-budget-overview.pdf.

USDI Bureau of Indian Affairs. (2007). *Performance & accountability.* Washington, DC. Retrieved November 2011 at www.doi.gov/pfm/bur_annual_rpt/bia_2007_par.pdf.

USDI Bureau of Land Management. (2003). *Recreation permit administration handbook.* Washington, DC. Retrieved August 2011 from www.blm.gov/pgdata/etc/medialib/blm/wo/Planning_and_Renewable_Resources/recreation_images/trip_planning.Par.30501.File.dat/h2930-1.pdf.

USDI Bureau of Reclamation. (2003). *Resource management plan guidebook: Planning for the future.* Washington, DC. Retrieved August 2011 at www.usbr.gov/pmts/planning/RMPG/RMPG.pdf.

USDI National Park Service. (1989). *Colorado river management plan.* Grand Canyon, AZ: Grand Canyon National Park.

USDI National Park Service. (2006a). *Commercial use authorizations: Interim guidelines.* Washington, DC: Department of the Interior.

USDI National Park Service. (2006b). *Management policies.* Washington, DC: United States Government Printing Office.

Vincent, C.H., Baldwin, P., Calvert, K., Corn, M.L., Gorte, R.W., Johnson, S.L., Whiteman, D., & Zinn, J. (2004). *CRS Report for Congress.* Congressional Research Service, Library of Congress.

# CHAPTER 11

Anderson, H.W., Hoover, M.D., & Reinhart, K.G. (1976). *Forests and water: Effects of forest management on floods, sedimentation, and water supply.* USDA Forest Service, General Technical Report PSW18.

Buckley, R.C. (2002). Managing tourism in parks: Research priorities of industry associations and protected area agencies in Australia. *Journal of Ecotourism, 1*: 162-172.

Business Wire. (2007). REI introduces eco-sensitive icon to identify outdoor products with reduced environmental impact. Retrieved July 2011 at www.businesswire.com/portal/site/google/index.jsp?ndmViewId=news_view&newsId=20070816005178&newsLang=en.

Clawson, M., & Knetsch, J. (1966). *Economics of outdoor recreation.* Baltimore, MD: John Hopkins.

Cohen, M.P. (1988). *The history of the Sierra Club: 1892-1970.* San Francisco: Sierra Club Books.

Cole, D. (1996). Wilderness recreation: Trends in use, users and impacts. *International Journal of Wilderness, 2*(3): 14-18.

Cole, D. (2004). Environmental impacts of outdoor recreation in wildlands. In M. Manfredo, J. Vaske, B. Bruyere, D. Field, & P. Brown (Eds.), *Society and Natural Resources: A Summary of Knowledge* (pp. 107-116). Jefferson, MO: Modern Litho.

Cole, D., & Monz, C. (2003). Impacts of camping on vegetation: response and recovery following acute and chronic disturbance. *Environmental Management, 32*(6): 693-705.

Corbett, J.D. (2006). *Communicating nature: How we create and understand environmental messages.* Washington, DC: Island Press.

Dickman, M., & Dorais, M. (1977). The impact of human trampling on phosphorous loading to a small lake in Gatineau Park, Quebec, Canada. *Journal of Environmental Management, 5*: 335-344.

Environmental Protection Agency Environmental Stewardship Staff Committee. (2005). *Everyday choices: Opportunities for environmental stewardship.* Retrieved November 2011 at www.epa.gov/environmentalinnovation/pdf/techrpt.pdf.

Ewert, A., Place, G., & Sibthorp, J. (2005). Early-life outdoor experiences and an individual's environmental attitudes. *Leisure Sciences, 27*: 225-239.

GreenYour. (n.d.). 10 ways to green your camping gear. Retrieved July 2011 at www.greenyour.com/lifestyle/leisure-recreation/camping-gear/tips/rent-outdoor-gear.

Gutzwiller, K., Riffell, S., & Anderson, S. (2002). Repeated human intrusion and the potential for nest predation by gray jays. *Journal of Wildlife Management, 66*(2): 372-380.

Hammitt, W.E., & Cole, D.N. (1998). *Wildlands recreation: Ecology and management* (2nd ed.). New York: John Wiley & Sons.

Hendee, J., & Dawson, C. (2001). *Wilderness management* (3rd ed.). Golden, CO: Fulcrum.

Ibrahim, H., & Cordes, K.A. (2002). *Outdoor recreation: Enrichment for a lifetime* (2nd ed.). Champaign, IL: Sagamore.

Jensen, C., & Guthrie, S. (2006). *Outdoor recreation in America* (6th ed.). Champaign, IL: Human Kinetics.

Klyza, C.M., & Trombulak, S.C. (1999). *The story of Vermont: A natural and cultural history.* Hanover, NH: University Press of New England.

Knight, R., & Cole, D. (1995). Factors that influence wildlife responses to recreationists In R. Knight & K. Gutzwiller (Eds.), *Wildlife and Recreationists—Coexistence Through Management and Research.* Washington, DC: Island Press.

LaPage, W.F. (1967). *Some observations on campground trampling and groundcover response.* USDA Forest Service Research Paper NE-68.

Leopold, A. (1968). *A sand county almanac.* London: Oxford University Press.

Leung, Y., & Marion, J. (2000). *Recreation impacts and management in wilderness: A state-of-knowledge review.* USDA Forest Service Proceedings, RMRS-P-15, Vol. 5. Retrieved August 2011 from www.wilderness.net/library/documents/science1999/Volume5/Leung_5-4.pdf.

Liddle, M.J. (1997). *Recreation ecology: The ecological impact of outdoor recreation and ecotourism.* London: Chapman and Hall.

L.L. Bean. (n.d.). Social responsibility. Retrieved July 2011 at www.llbean.com/outdoorsOnline/conservationAndEnvironment/index.html?nav=ln.

Louv, R. (2005). *Last child in the woods: Saving our children from nature deficit disorder.* Chapel Hill, NC: Algonquin Books.

Manning, R.E. (1979). Impacts of recreation on riparian soils and vegetation. *Water Resources Bulletin, 15*(1): 30-43.

Marion, J.L., & Reid, S.E. (2001). *Development of the U.S. Leave No Trace program: An historical perspective.* Boulder, CO: Leave No Trace.

Moore, R.L., & Driver, B.L. (2005). *Introduction to outdoor recreation: Providing and managing natural resource based opportunities.* State College, PA: Venture.

National Park Service. (April 14, 2009). Noncommercial river trip regulations. Retrieved July 2011 at www.nps.gov/grca/planyourvisit/upload/Noncommercial_River_Trip_Regulations.pdf.

Outdoor Industry Association. (2008). La Sportivia refines environmental and social responsibility platform.

Retrieved July 2011 at www.outdoorindustry.org/media. outdoor.php?news_id=3753.

Outdoor Industry Foundation. (2007). The next generation of outdoor participants: For the years 2005/2006. Retrieved July 2011 at www.outdoorfoundation.org/research. nextgeneration.html.

Queensland Outdoor Recreation Federation. (n.d.). Outdoor recreation in Queensland: The big issues. Retrieved July 2011 at www.qorf.org.au/01_cms/details.asp?ID=135.

Ward, W. (2005). Minimizing mountaineering impacts in Denali National Park. *International Journal of Wilderness, 11*(2): 37-40.

# CHAPTER 12

Ajango, D. (2000). *Lessons learned: A guide to accident prevention and crisis response.* Anchorage: Alaska Outdoor and Experiential Education, University of Alaska.

Arenas, A., Tabernero, C., & Briones, E. (2006). Effects of goal orientation, error orientation and self-efficacy on performance in an uncertain situation. *Social Behavior and Personality, 34*(5): 17.

Bandura, A. (1997). *Self-efficacy: The exercise of control.* New York: Freeman.

Cline, P. (2004). *The merging of risk analysis and adventure education.* Paper presented at the Wilderness Risk Management Conference, Banff, Canada.

Committee, E.R.M. (2003). *Overview of Enterprise Risk Management.*

Curtis, R. (1995). *Outdoor action guide to outdoor safety management.* Princeton, NJ: Outdoor Action Program. Retrieved September 30, 2009, from www.princeton.edu/~oa/safety/safeman.shtml.

Curtis, R. (2002). The risk assessment & safety management system. Retrieved December 2011 at www.outdoored.com/articles/article.aspx?ArticleID=151.

Drury, J., Bonney, B., Berman, D., & Wagstaff, M. (2005). *The backcountry classroom* (2nd ed.). Guilford, CT: Globe Pequot Press.

Elliot, E.S., & Dweck, C.S. (1988). Goal: An approach to motivation and achievement. *Journal of Personality and Social Psychology, 54*: 5-12.

Gookin, J., & Leach, S. (2004). *The NOLS leadership educator notebook: A toolbox for leadership educators.* Lander, WY: The National Outdoor Leadership School.

Gregg, R. (1997). *Issues in outdoor recreation liability.* Paper presented at the Wilderness Risk Managers Conference, Sierra Vista, Arizona.

Hansen-Stamp, C. (1999). *Thoughts on risk management in the recreation industry: A different perspective.* Paper presented at the Wilderness Risk Management Conference, Sierra Vista, Arizona.

Howell, C. (2009). *OPC staff handbook.* Lubbock, TX: Texas Tech University Outdoor Pursuits Center.

Meyer, D. (1979). Management of risk. *Journal of Experiential Education, 2*(2): 5.

Narciss, S. (2004). The impact of informative tutoring feedback and self-efficacy on motivation and achievement in concept learning. *Experimental Psychology, 51*(3): 214-228.

Nicolazzo, P. (2007). *Effective outdoor program design and management.* Winthrop, WA: Wilderness Medicine Training Center.

Paulcke, W., & Dumler, H. (1973). *Hazards in mountaineering.* New York: Oxford University Press.

Petzoldt, P. (1974). *The wilderness handbook.* New York: Norton.

Priest, S., & Gass, M. (2005). *Effective leadership in adventure programming* (2nd ed.). Champaign, IL: Human Kinetics.

Priest, S., & Naismith, M. (1993). A model for debriefing experiences. *Journal of Adventure Education and Outdoor Leadership, 10*(2): 16-18.

Propst, D., & Koesler, R. (1998). Bandura goes outdoors: Role of self-efficacy in the outdoor leadership development process. *Leisure Sciences, 20*: 319-344.

Rosenshine, B., & Stevens, R. (1986). Teaching functions. In M.C. Wittrock (Ed.), *Handbook of Research on Teaching* (3rd ed.) (pp. 376-391). New York: Macmillan.

Schunk, D. (1983). Ability versus effort attributional feedback: Differential effects on self-efficacy and achievement. *Journal of Educational Psychology, 75*(6): 848-856.

Schunk, D.H. (2008). *Learning theories: An educational perspective* (5th ed.). Upper Saddle River, NJ: Pearson Education.

Van der Smissen, B. (1990). *Legal liability and risk management for public and private entities.* Cincinnati: Anderson.

Weiner, B. (1986). *An attributional theory of motivation and emotion.* New York: Springer-Verlag.

Zimmerman, B.J., & Kitsantas, A. (1997). Developmental phases in self-regulation: Shifting from process goals to outcome goals. *Journal of Educational Psychology, 89*: 29-36.

# ADDITIONAL RESOURCES

Climbing Wall Association. (2007). *Industry practices: A sourcebook for the operation of manufactured climbing walls* (3rd ed.). (Self-published).

Hirsch, J., & Sugerman, D. (2007). *Administrative practices of AEE accredited programs* (2nd ed.). Boulder, CO: Association for Experiential Education.

# CHAPTER 13

Anderson, L.W., & Krathwohl, D.R. (2001). *A taxonomy for learning, teaching, and assessing—A revision of Bloom's taxonomy of educational objectives.* New York: Addison Wesley Longman.

Bannon, J. (1999). *911 management: A comprehensive guide for leisure service managers.* Champaign, IL: Sagamore.

Bloom, B.S. (Ed.) (1956). *Taxonomy of educational objectives: The classification of educational goals (handbook 1: cognitive domain).* New York: David McKay.

Chelladurai, P. (2006). *Human resource management in sport and recreation* (2nd ed.). Champaign, IL: Human Kinetics.

Dessler, G. (2005). *Human resource management* (10th ed.). Upper Saddle River, NJ: Pearson Education.

Silsbee, D.K. (2004). *The mindful coach: Seven roles for helping people grow.* Upper Marshall, NC: Ivy River Press.

United States Department of Labor. (n.d.). Fact sheet #18: Section 13(a)(3). Retrieved July 2011 at www.dol.gov/elaws/flsa.htm.

# CHAPTER 14

Campbell, D.E., & Campbell, T.A. (2000). The mentoring relationship: Differing perceptions of benefits. *College Student Journal, 34*(4): 516-524.

Neyer, L., & Yelinek, K. (2007). Mentoring the new millennium. *Pennsylvania Library Bulletin,* June/July: 10-17.

Nicolazzo, P. (2007). *Effective outdoor program design and management.* Winthrop, WA: Wilderness Medical Training Center.

Stuessy, T. (2010). *Outdoor leadership practicum course guide.* Unpublished manuscript, Green Mountain College.

# CHAPTER 15

Andrade, H.G. (2005). Teaching with rubrics: The good, the bad, and the ugly. *College Teaching, 53*(1): 27-31.

Boston, C. (Eds.) (2002). *Understanding scoring rubrics.* University of Maryland: ERIC Clearinghouse on Assessment and Evaluation.

Cawley, B.D, Keeping, L.M, and Levy, P.E. (1998). Participation in the performance appraisal process and employee reactions: A meta-analytic review of field investigations. *Journal of Applied Psychology, 83*(4): 615-633.

Craig, S., & Hannum, K. (2006). Research update: 360-degree performance assessments. *Consulting Psychology Journal: Practice & Research, 58*(2): 117-124.

DelPo, A. (2005). *The performance appraisal handbook: Legal and practical rules for managers.* Berkeley, CA: Nolo.

Eichinger, R.W., & Lombardo, M.M. (2003). Knowledge summary series: 360-degree assessment. *Human Resource Planning, 26*(4): 34-44.

Goodrich, H. (1997). Understanding rubrics. *Educational Leadership, 54*(4): 14-17.

Hill, C.W., & Jones, G.R. (2004). *Strategic management theory: An integrated approach* (p. 16). Boston: Houghton Mifflin Company.

Jawahar, I.M. (2006). An investigation of potential consequences of satisfaction with appraisal feedback. *Journal of Leadership and Organizational Studies, 13*(2): 14-27.

Longenecker, C.O., & Nykodym, N. (1996). Public sector performance appraisal effectiveness: A case study. *Public Personnel Management, 25*(2): 151-164.

Lund, L.L. (1999). Creating rubrics for physical education. In D. Tannehill (Ed.), *Assessment Series: K-12 Physical Education.* Publication of the National Association for Sport and Physical Education.

Maylett, T., & Riboldi, J. (2007). Using 360-degree feedback to predict performance. *Training and Development, 61*(9): 48-52.

Mondy, R.W., & Mondy, J.B. (2010). *Human resource management.* Upper Saddle River, NJ: Prentice Hall.

Moskal, B.H. (2000). Scoring rubrics: What, when and how? *Practical Assessment, Research & Evaluation, 7*(3). Retrieved July 2011 at http://PAREonline.net/getvn.asp?v=7&n=3.

Pelchat, C., & Kinziger, M. (2009). Whitewater rafting. In M. Wagstaff & A. Attarian (Eds.) *Outdoor Adventure Technical Skills: A Curriculum Guide* (pp. 567-621). Champaign, IL: Human Kinetics.

Roberts, G.E. (2003). Employee performance appraisal system participation: A technique that works. *Public Personnel Management 22*(1): 89-98.

Sachs, R.T. (1992). *Productive performance appraisals.* New York: American Management Association.

Simmons, A. (2003). When performance reviews fail. *T&D,* September 2003, pp. 47-51.

Wagstaff, M., & Quinn, W.J. (2007). The challenge course facilitator technical skills assessment tool. *Australian Journal of Outdoor Education, 11*(1): 29-40.

# CHAPTER 17

Climbing Wall Association. (2007). *Industry practices: A sourcebook for the operation of manufactured climbing walls* (3rd ed.). Boulder, CO: Climbing Wall Association.

Climbing Wall Industry Group. (1993). *Specifications for artificial climbing walls.* Boulder, CO: Climbing Wall Industry Group.

deBrun, G., & Turner, D. (2008, October). *What's happening on the wall? A survey of climbing wall incidents.* Presented at the Association of Outdoor Recreation and Education Conference, San Diego, CA.

European Committee for Standardization. (1998). *CEN EN 12572: Artificial climbing structures. Protection points, stability requirements and test methods.* Self-published.

Hansen-Stamp, C. (1999). *Thoughts on risk management in the recreation industry: A different perspective.* Paper presented at the Wilderness Risk Management Conference, Sierra Vista, Arizona.

Long, J. (1994). *Gym climb.* Evergreen, CO: Chockstone Press.

Outdoor Foundation. (2010). *Outdoor recreation participation report.* Retrieved September 2011 at www.outdoorfoundation.org/pdf/ResearchParticipation2010.pdf. Washington, D.C.: Outdoor Foundation.

Outdoor Foundation (2011). *Outdoor recreation participation topline report.* Washington, D.C.: Outdoor Foundation.

Rockwerx Natural Rock—Aesthetic and Functional Design (n.d.). Retrieved July 2011 at www.rockwerxclimbing.com/3488.xml.

Smutek, R. (1974). Spire rock grows. *Off Belay, 17*(October): 39-41.

Spear, B. (2003). *Climbing gym instructor program technical manual.* Canmore, Canada: Association of Canadian Mountain Guides.

Stiehl, J., & Ramsey, T.B. (2005). *Climbing walls: A complete guide.* Champaign, IL: Human Kinetics.

Thomas, R. (1988). Building your own climbing wall. *Rock and Ice, 28*(November/December): 35-37.

## CHAPTER 18

Association for Challenge Course Technology. (2008). *Challenge course and zip line/tour standards.* (7th ed.). Deerfield, IL: Association for Challenge Course Technology.

Association of Experiential Education. (n.d.). *What is experiential education?* Retrieved at http://www.aee.org/about/whatIsEE.

Attarian, A. (2001). Trends in outdoor adventure education. *Journal of Experiential Education 24*(3): 141.

Dewey, J. (1938/1997). *Experience and education.* New York: Macmillan.

Martin, B., Cashel, C., Wagstaff, M., & Bruening, M. (2006). *Outdoor leadership: Theory and practice.* Champaign, IL: Human Kinetics.

Porouty, D. (1999). Project adventure: A brief history. In J.C. Miles and S. Priest (Eds.), *Adventure Programming,* pp. 93-101. State College, PA: Venture.

Professional Ropes Course Association. (2011). PRCA website. Retrieved July 2011 at www.prcainfo.org.

Rohnke, K., & Butler, S. (1995). *Quicksilver: Adventure games, initiatives problems, trust activities and a guide to effective leadership.* Dubuque, IA: Kendal/Hunt.

Rohnke, K., Wall, J., Tait, C., & Rogers, D. (2003). *The complete ropes course manual* (3rd ed.). Dubuque, IA: Kendall/Hunt.

Sanford, N. (1966). *Self and society: Social change and individual development.* New York: Atherton Press.

Siedentop, D. (2008). *Introduction to physical education, fitness, and sport* (7th ed.). Boston: McGraw-Hill.

Wilson, S.J. (2000). Wilderness challenge programs for delinquent youth: A meta-analysis of outcome evaluations. *Evaluation and Program Planning, 23*(1): 1.

## CHAPTER 19

Ajango, D. (2000). *Lessons learned: A guide to accident prevention and crisis response.* Alaska: Alaska Outdoor and Experiential Education. University of Alaska Anchorage.

American Mountain Guides Association (AMGA). (1999). *Technical handbook for professional mountain guides.* Boulder, CO: American Mountain Guides Association.

Bandura, A. (1997). *Self-efficacy: The exercise of control.* New York: Freeman.

Cervone, D. (1989). Effects of envisioning future activities on self-efficacy judgments and motivation: An availability heuristic interpretation. *Cognitive Therapy and Research,* (13): 247-261.

Council for Higher Education Accreditation (CHEA). (2003). Statement of mutual responsibilities for student learning outcomes: Accreditation, institutions, and programs. Washington, DC: Council for Higher Education Accreditation. Retrieved July 2011 at www.chea.org/pdf/StmntStudentLearningOutcomes9-03.pdf.

Curtis, R. (1995). Outdoor action guide to outdoor safety management. New Jersey: Outdoor Action Program. Retrieved July 2011 at http://www.princeton.edu/~oa/safety/safeman.shtml.

Drury, J., & Bonney, B. (Eds.). (2005). *The backcountry classroom* (2nd ed.). Connecticut: The Globe Pequot Press.

Ellis, S., & Davidi, I. (2005). After event reviews: Drawing lessons from successful and failed experience. *Journal of Applied Psychology, 90*(5): 857-871.

Ewell, P.T. (2001). Accreditation and student learning outcomes: A proposed point of departure. Washington, DC: Council for Higher Education Accreditation. Retrieved July 2011 at http://www.chea.org/award/StudentLearningOutcomes2001.pdf.

Fredston, J.A., & Fesler, D. (2001). *Snow sense: A guide to evaluating snow avalanche hazard* (4th ed.). Anchorage, AK: Alaska Mountain Safety Center.

Gass, M. (Ed.). (1998). *Administrative practices of accredited adventure programs.* Needham Heights, MA: Simon & Schuster Custom Publishing.

Gookin, J., & Leach, S. (2004). *The NOLS leadership educator notebook: A tool box for leadership educators.* Lander: The National Outdoor Leadership School.

Howell, C. (2009). *OPC staff handbook.* Lubbock: Texas Tech University Outdoor Pursuits Center.

League of American Bicyclists. (2010). American community survey: Bicycle commuting trends, 2000 to 2008. Retrieved July 2011 at www.bikeleague.org/resources/reports/pdfs/acs_commuting_trends.pdf.

Leemon, D., & Schimelpfenig, T. (2005). *Risk management for outdoor leaders: A practical guide for managing risk through leadership.* Lander: The National Outdoor Leadership School.

Long, J. (2004). *How to rock climb!* (4th ed.). Guilford, CT: Morris Book Publishing.

Merrill, D., Reiser, B., Merrill, S., & Landes, S. (1995). Tutoring: Guided learning by doing. *Cognition and Instruction, 13*(3): 315-372.

The Mountaineers. (2010). *Mountaineering: The freedom of the hills* (8th ed.). Seattle, WA: The Mountaineers Books.

Narciss, S. (2004). The impact of informative tutoring feedback and self-efficacy on motivation and achievement in concept learning. *Experimental Psychology, 51*(3): 214-228.

Nicolazzo, P. (2007). *Effective outdoor program design and management.* Winthrop: Wilderness Medicine Training Center.

National Outdoor Leadership School. (2000). *NOLS climbing instructor notebook.* Lander, WY: National Outdoor Leadership School.

Petzoldt, P. (1974). *The wilderness handbook.* New York: W.W. Norton and Company, Inc.

Priest, S. & Naismith, M. (1993). A model for debriefing experiences. *Journal of Adventure Education and Outdoor Leadership, 10*(2): 16-18.

Propst, D. & Koesler, R. (1998). Bandura goes outdoors: Role of self-efficacy in the outdoor leadership development process. *Leisure Sciences,* (20): 319-344.

Schunk, D.H. (2008). *Learning theories: an educational perspective.* New Jersey: Pearson Education, Inc.

Sullivan, B.F., & Thomas, S.L. (2007). Documenting student learning outcomes through a research-intensive senior capstone experience: Bringing the data together to demonstrate progress. *North American Journal of Psychology, 9*(2): 321-330.

## CHAPTER 20

American Canoe Association. (1996). *Introduction to paddling: Canoeing basics for lakes and rivers.* Birmingham, AL: Menasha Ridge Press.

American Canoe Association. (2004). *Essentials of river kayaking.* Birmingham, AL: Menasha Ridge Press.

American Canoe Association. (2005). *Essentials of kayak touring.* Birmingham, AL: Menasha Ridge Press.

Dillon, P., & Oyen, J. (2008). *Canoeing.* Champaign, IL: Human Kinetics.

Dillon, P., & Oyen, J. (2009). *Kayaking.* Champaign, IL: Human Kinetics.

FEMA. (2010). Thunderstorms and lightning. Retrieved September 2011 at www.fema.gov/hazard/thunderstorm/index.shtm.

Gona, D. (2004). *A guide to multiple use waterway management.* Mentor, OH: National Water Safety Congress & National Association of State Boating Law Administrators.

United States Coast Guard (USCG). (2010). Personal flotation devices & lights. Retrieved September 2011 at http://uscg.mil/hq/cg5/cg5214/pfd-lights.asp.

US Sailing: *Community sailing handbook.* Retrieved September 2011 at http://training.ussailing.org/ProgramMgmt/Community_Sailing_Handbook.htm.

US Sailing: *Modular program planner.* Retrieved September 2011 at http://home.ussailing.org/Page5062.aspx?SourceId=0&ArticleId=5111.

Zeller, J. (2009). *Canoeing and kayaking for people with disabilities.* Champaign, IL: Human Kinetics.

## CHAPTER 21

Backpacker Magazine. (2011). *Get Out More!* www.getoutmoretour.com.

The Banff Centre. (2011). Banff Mountain Film Festival. Banff, Alberta, Canada. Retrieved July 2011 at www.banffcentre.ca/mountainfestival.

Bluegrass Wildwater Association. (2011). National Paddling Film Festival. Frankfort, KY: Retrieved July 2011 at www.bluegrasswildwater.org/NPFF/.

Boise State University. (2010). Sawtooth Mountain Film Festival. Boise, ID. Retrieved July 2011 at http://rec.boisestate.edu/sawtoothmountainfilmfest.

Brumitt, G. (2005). *The culture factor: Culture and economic vitality in Dayton, Ohio.* University of Cincinnati.

Five Rivers MetroParks. (2011a). Five Rivers Outdoors. Dayton, OH. Retrieved September 2011 at www.metroparks.org/GetOutside/outdoorrecreation.aspx.

Five Rivers MetroParks. (2011b). GearFest. Dayton, OH. Retrieved July 2011 at www.metroparks.org/gearfest.

Five Rivers MetroParks & Wright State University. (2011). The Adventure Summit. Dayton, OH. Retrieved July 2011 at www.theadventuresummit.com.

Junction Trail Festival. (2009). Junction Trail Festival. Milford, OH. Retrieved September 2011 at www.thejunctiontrailfest.org/.

The Naturalist Scouts. (2011). Maumee Valley Tri-Adventure Race. Defiance, OH. Retrieved July 2011 at http://maumeetriadventurerace.net/.

Wright State University. (2008). Outdoor Resource Center. The Adventure Summit. Dayton, OH. Retrieved June 2008 at www.theadventuresummit.com.

# Index

*Note:* The italicized *f* and *t* following page numbers refer to figures and tables, respectively.

**A**

accreditation 44-45, 230-231. *See also* certification courses and programs
activity-specific training 228-232
actual risk 55
Adirondack Mountain Club 19*t*
administration. *See also* future of program administration
    about 3
    beginnings of 16-20, 19*f*, 22
    defined 4
    professionalization 44-45
    structures and models for 35-38
administrators
    administrative competence 8, 8*f*
    certification courses 11-12
    challenges for 12-13
    conferences 11
    coursework and trainings 9, 11-12
    defined 4
    educational skills 6, 6*f*
    human skills 5-6, 6*f*
    management skills 6-7, 6*f*, 7*f*
    outdoor skills 5, 5*f*
    personal experiences 9
    policy and procedure development 187
    professional affiliations 11
    professional development 8-9, 9*f*, 10-12, 11*t*
    scouting trips 12
    skill acquisition 8-9, 9*f*
    skill sets for 4-7, 5*f*, 6*f*, 7*f*
    staff training 12
    supervision roles of 211-212
    vocational experience 9-10
    work week and hours 203
Adventure Cycling Association 330
adventure education programs 34
adventure programming
    current status of 24-29, 26*t*
    emergence of 22-24
adventure therapy 24

adventure therapy programs 34
adventuring 9
advertising 141
advisory boards 77-78
age and outdoor programs 42-43
American Alliance for Health, Physical Education, Recreation and Dance 9
American Camp Association 18, 27
American Canoe Association 9, 12, 27, 29, 33-34, 183
American Canyoneering Association 12
American Institute for Avalanche Research and Education 183
American Mountain Guides Association 12, 27, 183, 280
American Red Cross 19*t*
Anchorage City Park and Recreation Department 224
Appalachian Mountain Club 19*t*
assessment, outcome 50-51
assessment, staff
    about 214-215, 235-236, 256-257
    appraisal meetings 254-256
    challenge courses 306-307
    checklist assessments 241-243, 242*t*, 244*f*
    criteria 240-241
    environment for 236-239, 238*t*, 239*f*
    rubric assessments 243-250, 245*f*, 246*f*, 250*t*
    system for 250-256, 253*f*, 255*f*
    tools for 241-250, 242*t*, 244*f*, 245*f*, 246*f*, 250*t*
    water-based programming 338-341
Association for Challenge Course Technology 9, 28, 294, 311
Association for Experiential Education 9, 25, 231, 294, 311
Association of Canadian Mountain Guides 280
Association of College Unions International 9
Association of Outdoor Recreation and Education 9, 26-27, 311
Audubon movement 17, 19*t*

**B**

baby boomers 41
backpacking 318-320, 319*t*

Balach, Ernest 18
Bikes Belong 330
bodyboarding 354
bouldering 284-285, 285f, 320, 322
Boys Club of America 19t
branding 76-77, 140-141
budgets or budgeting
    about 109-110, 126-127
    activity-based costing 116t, 118-120, 119t
    budget management 125-126, 126t
    challenge courses 303
    components of 110-114, 110t
    development strategies 114-120, 115t-116t, 117t, 118t
    forecasting 120-122, 120t
    incremental line item 115t, 116-117
    for land-based programming 315-317, 315t, 316t
    performance-based 115t, 117-118
    revenue management 122-125, 122f, 123f
    for special events 369-370
    water-based programming 335
    zero-based 116t, 118
Bureau of Indian Affairs 148, 154
Bureau of Land Management 21, 148, 152-154, 152f, 153t
Bureau of Reclamation 148, 154

**C**
Camp Directors' Association of America 18, 19t
canoeing 343-344, 348-350
canopy tours 301
cash management, daily 122-123, 122f, 123f
causative risk 188-189
caving 323-325, 324t
cell phones 192
Center for Outdoor Ethics 9, 183
certification courses and programs 26t
    about 9, 11-12
    and policies 183
    professionalization 44-45
challenge course programs
    about 293
    administrator concerns 304-311, 305f, 308f, 309f
    belay systems 299-301, 299f, 300f
    bidding process 304, 305f
    building process 304
    choosing and designing a course 301-304, 301f, 302f

    design and outcomes 294-295
    equipment 310
    and experiential education 295
    facilities 35, 296-301, 297f, 298f, 299f, 300f
    high-element courses 298-301, 299f, 300f, 301f
    history 24, 294
    influences on 295-296, 296f
    low-element courses 298, 299f
    organizational support and resources 311
    portable courses 296-298
    staff training 309-310
    terms 293-294, 297f
    zip lines 301
Charleston County Park and Recreation Commission 73, 79
Children and Nature Network 46t
climbing 320-323, 321t
climbing gyms or walls. See indoor climbing walls
Climbing Wall Association 280
Climbing Wall Industry Group 280
collaborations 50
college outing clubs 36
Colorado Mountain Club 19t
commercial activity, USFS 155
commercial programs 32
Commercial Use Authorizations 150-151
common adventure model 37
competency-based trainings 9
competency creep 10
competitions, components of 363-367
conferences, professional 11
conservation organizations, history 19-20
contests, at events 362-363
Cornell Outdoor Education 68, 73
county parks and recreation departments 158
credit cards 124
curriculum development 7f
cycling 328-330, 329t

**D**
Dartmouth Outing Club 19t, 36
decision-making protocols 188f
demographics, population 40-43, 40t
deposits, managing 123-124
Dewey, John 17, 18, 295
discipline-specific skill certifications 12
discipline-specific training 221
Drucker's model 71-73

**E**
Echo Park dam  21
educational skills  6, 6f
*Effective Outdoor Program Design and Management* (Nicolazzo)  5
emergencies, response to. *See* incident-response policies
emergency contacts  192-194
employees. *See* staff or staffing
Endangered Species Act  21
environmental education programs  34, 45
environmentalism  16-21
environmental stewardship
    about  163, 174
    applied  168-172, 169f
    by associations  171
    by government  172
    history of  163-164, 164f
    by individuals  169-170
    by providers  170-171
    recreation impacts  166-168, 166t
    recreation integration with  172-174, 173f
equipment
    backpacking  319
    budgets  111-112
    caving  324
    challenge courses  310
    climbing  321
    cycling  328-329
    indoor climbing walls  290
    mountaineering  325
    policies, procedures, and guidelines  179-180, 181f
    skiing  327
    water-based programming  336-338, 337f
equipment rental centers  35
Erickson, John  48
ethics, outdoor  49
ethnicity and outdoor programs  43
evacuation routes  192
experiential education  17, 295
expositions  359-360

**F**
facilities and resources
    about  34-35
    budgeting  113
    for special events  371-373
facility management  7f
Fair Labor Standards Act  203

federal lands map  149f
festivals, components of  358-363, 360f
field policies and procedures  187-195, 189f, 191f, 193f, 194f, 195f. *See also* incident-prevention policies; incident-response policies
film festivals  359
finances and funding
    fiscal management  7f
    grant and proposal writing  79-82
    sustainability  78-79
fiscal management  7f
focus groups  132
food, at events  362
forecasting, budget  120-122, 120t
Forest Reserves Act  18
future of program administration
    about  39
    age and participation  43
    collaborations and partnerships  50
    demographics  40t
    generational cohorts  40-42
    outcome assessment  50-51
    participant characteristics  40-44, 40t
    professionalization  44-45
    race and ethnicity  43
    sustainability  47-50
    technology  46-47
    youth  45-46, 46t

**G**
Gateway Academy  34
gear swaps  360-361
generational cohorts  40-42
Generation X  41
Generation Z  42
Get Outdoors USA  46t
*Good to Great and the Social Sectors* (Collins)  76-77
government programs  32-33
grant and proposal writing  79-82
guides and guide services
    guided adventures  38
    guide services  32
    USFS guiding  155

**H**
Hahn, Kurt  294
higher education associations  11t
history of outdoor recreation
    about  15-16, 22-24, 29-30

history of outdoor recreation (*continued*)
    adventure programming current status 24-29, 26*t*
    adventure programming emergence 22-24
    challenge courses 294
    conservation organizations 19-20
    environmentalism 16, 20-21
    experiential education 17
    indoor climbing walls 279-280
    natural resource protection 18
    program administration field 16-20, 19*f*, 22
    rise of sports 17
    women and outdoors 20
    women's clubs 17
    youth organizations 18-19
Hubble, Frank 28
Hudson River School 16
human skills 5-6, 6*f*
human waste 168-169

**I**
ice climbing 320, 322-323
incidental business permits 150
incident-prevention policies
    backpacking 320
    caving 324
    climbing 323
    cycling 330
    developing 188-191, 189*f*, 191*f*
    flat-water venues 345-346
    indoor climbing walls 288-292
    for land-based programming 314
    mountaineering 326
    moving-water venues 350-351
    open-water venues 354-355
    risk management and 56
    skiing 327, 328
    at special events 367
incident-response policies
    backpacking 320
    caving 324-325
    climbing 323
    cycling 330
    developing 191-195, 193*f*, 194*f*, 195*f*
    indoor climbing walls 292
    for land-based programming 314-315
    mountaineering 326
    risk management and 56
    skiing 327, 328
    at special events 367

indoor climbing walls
    about 28, 35, 279
    accident rates 286-287
    activities 284-287, 285*f*, 286*f*, 287*f*
    anchor types 283-284, 284*f*
    angles and features 283
    bouldering 284-285, 285*f*
    construction types 281-282, 281*f*
    flooring 284
    history of 279-280
    hold types 283
    lead climbing 286
    operations 288-292
    programming 287-288
    risk management 288-292, 291*t*, 292*t*
    surface types 282-283, 282*f*
    top rope climbing 285-286, 285*f*
institutionally directed program model 37-38
institutional outfitting 155-156
instruction program model 38
insurance and liability 104-107. *See also* negligence
International Mountain Bike Association 330
internships 204
interviews 132
Izaak Walton League of America 19*t*

**K**
kayaking 343-344, 348-350

**L**
land-based programming
    about 313-314
    backpacking 318-320, 319*t*
    caving 323-325, 324*t*
    climbing 320-323, 321*t*
    cost analyses 315-317, 315*t*, 316*t*
    cycling 328-330, 329*t*
    incident prevention 314
    incident response 314-315
    learning outcomes 317-318
    mountaineering 325-326, 326*t*
    risk management 318
    ski programs 326-328
lands use, public. *See* public lands use
*Last Child in the Woods: Saving our Children from Nature Deficit Disorder* (Louv) 45, 46-47
lead climbing 286, 322
League of American Bicyclists 330
learning theory 295
Leave No Trace 27, 49, 170, 172-174, 183

legal considerations. *See* negligence
Leopold, Aldo  21
liability and insurance  104-107. *See also* negligence
libraries, resource  35
location assessments
     backpacking  319-320
     challenge courses  302-303
     and policy development  179, 180*f*
Lupton, Frank  26

**M**
management skills  6-7, 6*f*, 7*f*
Manifest Destiny  164
marketing
     about  7*f*, 129-130, 144
     advertising  141
     branding  140-141
     market identification  130-132
     marketing mix  132-136, 134*t*
     marketing plan development  138-140
     market segmentation  132, 133*f*
     methods  141-144
     personal selling  143
     print materials  141
     product life cycle  136-138, 136*f*
     promotions  143
     publicity  141-143, 142*f*
     research  130-131
     social media  143-144
     for special events  370-371
Marshall, Bob  21
Massachusetts Audubon Society  19*t*
Mather, Stephen P.  20
media communication  196
mentoring  222-223, 222*f*, 224
Military Family Outdoor Initiative Project  50
Millenials  41-42
Mills, Enos  20
Minerals Management Service  148
mission statements  68-71
Moore, Tim  27
morale, welfare, and recreation programs  33, 71-72
mountaineering  325-326, 326*t*
Mountaineers Club  36
Mountain Rescue Association  29
multipitch climbing  322
municipal governments  158-159
municipal park and recreation programs  32
music, live  361

**N**
National Association for Search and Rescue  29
National Association of Girls' Private Camps  18, 19*t*
National Association of Underwater Instructors  352
National Diffusion Network  294
National Intramural-Recreational Sports Association  9, 364
National Outdoor Leadership School  22, 294
national parks  18
National Park Service  18, 20, 46*t*, 148-152, 151*t*
National Parks Omnibus Management Act  150
National Public Lands Day  50
National Recreation and Park Association  45, 231
National Ski Association  19*t*
National Ski Patrol  28
National Trails System  21
National Wildlife Refuge System  21
Nature Study movement  17, 20
negligence
     assumption of risk  95-103
     breach of standard of care  87
     causation  87
     comparative negligence  94-95
     coparticipant liability  90
     damages  87-88
     defenses against  94-103
     defined  85-86
     duty of care  86-87
     express assumption of risk  98-102
     failure to warn  92
     implied assumption of risk  96-98
     industry standards  92-94
     inherent risk  95
     insurance and liability  104-107
     negligent hiring  92
     negligent medical care or rescue  90-91
     negligent supervision or instruction  91-92
     postaccident procedures  103-104
     premises liability  89-90
     products liability  89
     release and waiver agreements  100-102
     vicarious liability  88-89
No Child Left Inside  45
nonprofit programs  31-32
North American Association for Environmental Education  45
Northbay Adventure Camp  48-49
North Carolina Museum of Natural Sciences  46*t*

**O**

Office of Surface Mining 148
Open Space and Recreation Plans 159
operational expenses 112
organizational justice 213-214
outcome assessment 50-51
outdoor adventure pursuits programs 33
outdoor clubs 36
Outdoor Recreation Coalition 46t, 280
Outdoor Recreation Resources Review Commission 21
outdoor skill instruction programs 33-34
outdoor skills 5, 5f
outfitting, USFS 155
Outward Bound 22, 34, 50, 294

**P**

participants
    assessment and policies 180-181, 182f, 319t, 321t, 324t, 326t, 329t, 338
    for challenge courses 302, 306
    characteristics of 40-44, 40t
    for competitions 364
    indoor climbing walls 288-290
    population demographics 40-43, 40t
partnerships, collaborative 50, 75-76, 147, 159, 359, 361, 364, 369-370, 373
perceived risk 55
performance assessment. *See* assessment, staff
permitting process, land use 147-148, 159-162, 160t, 161t
personal selling 143
personnel 111
personnel policies 214, 215f
petty cash 124-125
Petzoldt, Paul 22, 26
Pieh, Jerry 294
Playground Association of America 19t
Playground Movement 17
policies, procedures, and guidelines. *See also* risk management, administrative
    about 175-176
    adaptations and improvements 186-187
    administrative 187
    characteristics of 176-178, 177t
    equipment assessments and use 179-180, 181f
    feedback 183-184, 185f
    field policies and procedures 187-195, 189f, 191f, 193f, 194f, 195f
    incident prevention 188-191, 189f, 191f
    incident response 191-195, 193f, 194f, 195f
    for land-based programming 313
    location assessments 179, 180f
    participant assessment 180-181, 182f
    program progressions 184-185
    staff training 182-183, 183f
Portland (OR) Mazamas 19t
press releases 142f
pricing 133-135, 134t
print materials 141
private lands use 159
product life cycle 136-138, 136f
professional affiliations 11
Professional Association of Diving Instructors 352
professional associations, history of 25-29
Professional Climbing Instructors Association 9, 12, 27-28, 280
professional development
    about 8-9, 9f, 10-12, 11t
    coursework and trainings 9, 11-12
    future of 44-45
professionalization 44-45
Professional Ropes Course Association 28, 294, 311
Professional Ski Instructors of America-American Association of Snowboard Instructors 28
profit loss 126t
program design
    about 7f, 67
    advisory boards 77-78
    branding 76-77
    change management 82
    Drucker's model 71-73
    financial sustainability 78-79
    grant and proposal writing 79-82
    mission statements 68-71
    process of plan writing 73-74
    program progression policies 184-185
    sustainability 75-76
    vision 67-68
programmatic types
    about 33
    adventure education 34
    adventure therapy 34
    environmental education 34
    outdoor adventure pursuits 33
    outdoor skill instruction 33-34
Project Adventure 24, 294
promotion 135-136

promotions 143
publicity 141-143, 142*f*
public lands use
    about 145, 162
    Bureau of Indian Affairs 154
    Bureau of Land Management 152-154, 152*f*,
      153*t*
    Bureau of Reclamation 154
    county parks and recreation 158
    Department of Agriculture 155-157, 156*t*
    Department of the Interior 148
    federal lands map 149*f*
    municipal governments 158-159
    National Park Service 148-152, 151*t*
    outdoor programs and 145-147, 147*f*
    permit avoidance 148
    permitting process 147-148, 159-162, 160*t*,
      161*t*
    state management agencies 157-158
    United States Army Corps of Engineers 154
    U.S. Forest Service 155-157, 156*t*, 157*t*

**Q**
questionnaires 131

**R**
race and outdoor programs 43
rafting 343-344, 348-350
recreation associations 11*t*
rental operations
    about 261
    budgeting 263
    depreciation values 264-265, 265*f*
    equipment 274-276
    inventory management 270-272, 271*f*, 271*t*
    needs assessment 262
    operations 268-278
    operations plans 262-263
    planning 261-265
    pricing 263-264, 264*t*
    purchasing 265-268, 266*t*, 267*t*
    rental agreements and policies 272-274
    sales tax 265
    special concerns 276-278
    staffing 268-270
    staff planning 263
    technology use 272
retreats, staff 221
revenue 113-114

risk management, administrative. *See also* policies,
    procedures, and guidelines
    about 7*f*, 55
    causative risk 188-189
    challenge courses 305, 308-309, 309*f*
    comprehensive plan creation 56-57, 56*f*
    defined 56
    field risks 57*f*, 61-63, 62*f*
    financial risks 57*f*, 58-59, 59*t*
    indoor climbing walls 288-292, 291*t*, 292*t*
    land-based programming 318
    monitoring and updating 64-65
    operational risks 57*f*, 59-61, 60*f*, 61*f*
    and policy 176
    rental operations 277-278
    risk elimination strategy 64
    risk factor identification 57-63, 57*f*, 58*t*, 59*f*,
      60*t*, 61*f*
    risk reduction strategy 64
    risk retention strategy 64
    risk transfer strategy 64
    special events programming 367
    staff and site assessment 63
    strategic risks 57-58, 57*f*
    strategies for 64
    terms and definitions 55-56
river classification scale 347*t*
Rohnke, Karl 294

**S**
sailing 344-345, 353
Saint Michaels College wilderness program 231-232
school-camp idea 17, 18
scouting trips, location 12
scuba diving 352
Scuba Schools International 352
Seattle Mountaineers 19*t*, 28
service sectors of programs
    about 31
    commercial programs 32
    government programs 32-33
    nonprofit programs 31-32
shared responsibility model 37
Sharp, L.B. 17, 18
Sierra Club 21, 32, 50
ski programs 326-328
Smith, Julian 19
snorkeling 352
SOAP note 192, 193*f*

social media 143-144
soil, impacts on 167
special events programming
    about 357-358
    assessing and planning 367-373, 368*f*
    components of competitions 363-367
    components of festivals 358-363, 360*f*
    event management 374-375, 375*f*
    risk management 367
    staffing 373-374, 374*f*
    timelines for 375, 375*f*
special-use permits 150
spectators, at competitions 366
sponsorships. *See* partnerships, collaborative
sport climbing 320
sports 17
staff or staffing
    assessment 214-215, 235-257, 306-307, 338-341
    for challenge courses 302
    disciplining 215-216
    hiring 210-211
    human resource planning 199-206, 205*f*
    interviewing 207-210, 209*f*
    job analysis 200-203
    organizational justice 213-214
    organizational structure 204-205, 205*f*
    productivity *vs.* satisfaction 212-213
    recognition of 215
    recruitment 206-207
    rental operations 268-270
    selection of 206-211, 207*f*, 209*f*, 210*f*
    special events programming 373-374, 374*f*
    staff exit 216-217
    supervision of 211-217, 215*f*
    training of 7*f*, 12, 182-183, 183*f*, 219-233
    volunteers 204
state management agencies 157-158
strategic plans
    challenge courses 303-304
    customer identification 71-72
    customer values 72-73
    Drucker's model 71-73
    end results 73
    format 74
    implementation 74-75
    and mission 71
    organizational analysis tools 74
    processes and tasks 73-74
    writing process 73-74

Student Affairs Professionals in Higher Education 9
surfing 354
SWOT analysis 237, 238*t*

**T**
technical training associations 11*t*
technology and outdoor programs 7*f*, 46-47, 272
Tempe City Park and Recreation Department 224
theory of challenge and support 296
360-degree feedback 237-238
top rope climbing 285-286, 285*f*, 320, 321
training, staff
    about 219
    and accreditation 230-232
    activity-specific training 228-232
    assessment and evaluation 223-226, 225*f*
    certification courses 11-12, 230
    challenge courses 309-310
    cycling 329-330
    discipline-specific training 221
    educational skills 227-228
    human skills 226-227
    indoor climbing walls 290, 291*t*
    integrated model for 226-228
    mentoring 222-223, 222*f*, 224
    needs assessment 219-220
    outdoor skills 227
    policies 182-183, 183*f*
    progression 220-221, 220*f*
    in rental operations 269-270
    retreats 221
    skills in 7*f*
transportation and travel expenses 112

**U**
university programs 32-33
U.S. Army Corps of Engineers 154
U.S. Department of Agriculture 155-157, 156*t*
U.S. Department of the Interior 46*t*, 148
U.S. Fish and Wildlife 148
U.S. Forest Service 21, 46*t*, 155-157, 156*t*, 157*t*
U.S. Geological Survey 148

**V**
vegetation, impacts on 166-167
vision 67-68
volunteers or volunteerism 32, 204, 374*f*

**W**

water, environmental impacts on  167

water-based programming

about  333

bodyboarding  354

canoeing  343-344, 348-350

cost assessments  335

equipment  336-338, 337*f*

equipment progression  343

flat-water programming  343-346

incident prevention and response  333-334, 345-346, 350-351, 354-355

kayaking  343-344, 348-350

leader qualities  341-342

moving-water programming  346-351, 347*t*

needs assessments  334-335

open-water programming  351-355

participant assessments  338

rafting  343-344, 348-350

sailing  344-345, 353

scuba diving  352

snorkeling  352

staff assessments  338-341

surfing  354

venue progression  343

venue selection assessments  336

whitewater programming  346-351, 347*t*

Wild and Scenic River System  21

Wilderness Act  21

Wilderness Education Association  9, 12, 25-26, 231-232

wilderness emergency medical training  12

Wilderness First Aid  183

Wilderness First Responder certification  183

Wilderness Medical Society  28-29

Wilderness Society  21

wildlife, impacts on  168

women and outdoors  17, 20

**Y**

Young Men's Christian Association  352

Young Women's Christian Association  17

youth and outdoor programs

future of  45-46, 46*t*

youth organizations  18-19

**Z**

zip lines  301

# About the Editors

**Geoff Harrison, MS,** has been working in the field of health and recreation for over 20 years and has been fostering student and staff development at Boise State University since 1998. Geoff serves as the associate director of education and recreation at Boise State University, where he oversees multiple programs and service areas, department partnerships, and initiatives. He also serves as an adjunct faculty member for the department of kinesiology. Prior to his work at Boise State, Geoff worked in the fields of publishing, event promotion, and domestic and international adventure travel.

Geoff has served the Association of Outdoor Recreation and Education as a committee chair, board member, conference host, and interim national director. In 2010, Geoff was the recipient of the Association of Outdoor Recreation and Education's Jim Rennie Leadership Award.

**Mat Erpelding, MA,** has been working in the field of physical education and outdoor leadership for over 15 years. Currently, he teaches at the College of Western Idaho in the physical education department and at Boise State University in the leadership studies minor. Additionally, Mat guides mountain climbers and teaches courses for the American Alpine Institute and teaches wilderness medicine courses for the Wilderness Medicine Training Center. Before making the transition to outdoor education, Mat worked as a developmental therapist and in the mental health industry.

Mat is a past president of the Association of Outdoor Recreation and Education and served on committees and the board of directors and as a conference host. In 2006, Mat was the recipient of the Association of Outdoor Recreation and Education's Jim Rennie Leadership Award, and in 2010 he received the Instructor of the Year Award from the Wilderness Education Association.

Mat and Geoff co-own Experiential Adventures LLC. They provide training and consulting services to organizations that foster leadership development, help organizations manage change, develop positive organizational cultures that promote success, and build professionalism in outdoor programs through trainings and certifications.

# About the Contributors

**Amy A. Anslinger** is the assistant director of outdoor recreation at Wright State University in Dayton, Ohio. She has a degree in outdoor education from Northland College in Ashland, Wisconsin. Amy has worked for numerous environmental and adventure-focused organizations around the country and gained significant experience with event organization during the two years she worked with *Backpacker* magazine as part of the Get Out More! road team. Amy is a founder of the Adventure Summit, one of the largest expositions of outdoor recreation in the region, in conjunction with Five Rivers MetroParks. The Adventure Summit draws over 6,000 outdoor enthusiasts to Wright State University. Amy has backpacked and paddled extensively throughout the United States. She completed hikes of both the 2,650-mile Pacific Crest Trail and Ohio's 1,400-mile Buckeye Trail.

**Brent D. Anslinger** is the program operations manager for Five Rivers MetroParks in Dayton, Ohio, a conservation agency that manages 16,000 acres and 25 facilities using programming, facilities, and events to connect people to nature and transform Dayton into the outdoor adventure capital of the Midwest. Beyond facility development and policy, Brent's role is to manage several of the largest outdoor events in the Midwest, including GearFest. He is a cofounder of the Adventure Summit. He received his bachelor of science degree from Otterbein University, during which time he hiked the Appalachian Trail from Georgia to Maine before he worked around the country in the field of outdoor recreation and education from the National Park Service in Glacier National Park to a variety of outdoor school settings in New Mexico, California, and New England. Brent, along with his wife, Amy, hiked the 2,650-mile Pacific Crest Trail from Mexico to Canada for his honeymoon before working with Amy as the *Backpacker* magazine Get Out More! road team and hiking the 1,400-mile Buckeye Trail. Brent cofounded the Junction Trail Festival in Milford, Ohio, and enjoys introducing his two young daughters to the outdoors.

**Todd M. Bauch** is the associate director of operations and student development of campus recreation at Portland State University. Prior to this he was an outdoor program coordinator at the university. He received his bachelor's degree in commercial recreation at Illinois State University and his master's degree in recreation resource administration at Southern Illinois University. Todd has nearly 20 years of experience in leading outdoor recreation activities and managing outdoor programs across the country. He also served as the vice president of AORE from 1997 to 2000. For his master's thesis, Todd wrote "Risk Management Practices of University Based Adventure Programs," which was the first attempt to gather information on the diverse perspectives held and techniques used by outdoor programs to mitigate the risks associated with their activities.

**John Bicknell** is an American Mountain Guide Association (AMGA) certified rock and alpine guide and owner of the Boulder Rock Club and Colorado Mountain School Guide Service. He has spent the last 20 years as a mountain guide and climbing instructor. He helped develop the climbing wall program for the AMGA and is a member of the AMGA instructor pool training climbing instructors. He has a master's degree from the University of California at Santa Barbara and a bachelor's degree from Harvard. He is also a past president of the AMGA.

**Adam Bondeson** is the president of Lodestone Adventures, Inc., a corporate development and team-building organization. Through this challenge course company, Adam continues to design and implement programs for corporations throughout America. He attended Prescott College, a private accredited four-year school in Prescott, Arizona. During that time he designed an undergraduate program and graduated with a bachelor's degree in therapeutic use of the wilderness experience. He was the teaching assistant for several Prescott classes and designed independent study courses. As part of his graduating process, he designed a three-month internship in which he developed and implemented outdoor and ropes course programming. For several years he facilitated and managed outdoor programs for various ropes course companies assisting many corporations in the area of change. Adam has over 22 years of experience in the field of outdoor and experiential education. He has a background working with many companies and organizations, assisting them in the development of effective teamwork and leadership. He has facilitated programs throughout the country as well as in Europe and Israel. Adam's expertise is in the designing of programs to meet the needs of each client, whether in the classroom or in the wilderness.

**Christina Carter Thompson** serves as a family teacher with her husband and son at Father Flanagan's Boys Town. Prior to that, Christina served as the director of the Experiential Learning and Adventure Center for the University of San Diego, where she also was an adjunct faculty member for the School of Education. She has been on the board of directors for the AORE for two terms, serving as president and hosting the annual conference. She earned her bachelor's and master's degrees in educational psychology and exercise physiology and the University of Nebraska at Lincoln. Christina works as both a consultant for and director of various challenge courses.

**Bryan J. Cavins** is the owner and principal consultant for Cavins Custom Solutions and a longtime adjunct faculty member of recreation and tourism at Bowling Green State University (BGSU). Dr. Cavins has taught courses in recreation leadership, recreation programming, outdoor recreation, tourism and event planning, and environmental studies. He earned his doctorate in leadership studies at BGSU as well as his master's and undergraduate degrees in recreation and tourism. Dr. Cavins is the founder of the BGSU outdoor program, where he served as the director for 10 years. During his tenure with the outdoor program, he developed all areas of the operation, including the trip and workshop policies and procedures, climbing wall management system, team development program, and staff development curriculum. He has studied outdoor recreation for two decades and is a past board member of AORE.

**Guy deBrun** is the assistant director for adventure programs at James Madison University. He received a master's degree from James Madison University and a bachelor's degree from Messiah College. Guy has been managing indoor climbing facilities at private and public institutions of higher learning

since 2001. He has been an active member of the AORE's climbing wall committee, where he served as cochair for two years.

**Heidi Erpelding-Welch** is the former land and special programs coordinator in the outdoor education department at Cornell University. She earned a master's degree in recreation, parks, and tourism administration from Western Illinois University. Before working at Cornell University, Heidi was the coordinator of outdoor adventures at the University of Nevada at Las Vegas and the recreation supervisor for outdoor excursions at the University of California at Riverside. She served on the board of directors of AORE from 2007 to 2009. Heidi lives, works, and plays in Big Bend National Park with her spouse and daughter.

**Jerome Gabriel** is the assistant director of recreation and wellness at Bowling Green State University, where he manages the outdoor program. Jerome received his master's degree in recreation and tourism from Bowling Green State University and his bachelor's degrees from Bluffton University and Columbia Bible College. Jerome's work with the outdoor program focuses on bringing the outdoor recreation experience, including rock climbing, rappelling, and caving, to the students of the Midwest. In 2009 the BGSU outdoor program was awarded the David J Webb Program Excellence Award by AORE. Jerome is a member of AORE, the Leave No Trace Center for Outdoor Ethics (LNT COE), and the National Speleological Society (NSS).

**Steven P. Guthrie** is an assistant professor of outdoor recreation in the recreation management department at Lock Haven University of Pennsylvania. Prior to that, he taught at Unity College in Maine and also was previously the program coordinator of the Outdoor Venture Center at the University of Nebraska at Omaha. He worked his way through graduate school leading and teaching outdoor pursuits for the University of Oregon and for local park and recreation districts. He received his bachelor's degree in philosophy from the College of Wooster in Ohio. His master's degree is from the University of Oregon in physical education with emphasis in adaptive physical education, sociology of sport, and outdoor recreation. For his doctorate at Oregon, he combined his love of philosophy with physical education, doing his doctoral work in the philosophy of sport, focusing on philosophy of art, philosophy of the body, knowledge as social construction, and social science aspects of sport and physical education. In 1986, he began attending the various outdoor recreation conferences, which led to the formation of AORE in 1993. He was on the founding committees and was a board member of AORE every year (but one) until 2005, serving as secretary, many years as treasurer, and one year as president of AORE. He received AORE's Jim Rennie Leadership Award. He coauthored the sixth edition of *Outdoor Recreation in America* (Human Kinetics, 2006).

**Laurlyn K. Harmon** is an assistant professor of parks, recreation, and leisure studies at George Mason University and a registered landscape architect. She received her doctorate in leisure studies from Pennsylvania State University and her bachelor's and master's degrees from Michigan State University. Her research focuses on the relationship of person and place and its effect on stewardship actions and behaviors, and the effect of technology on understanding natural environments. Her work with youth and underwater remotely operated vehicles (ROVs) has been an important part of enhancing outdoor experiential learning opportunities for young people.

**Will Hobbs** is an assistant professor of outdoor education and coordinator of applied learning in the department of outdoor education at Georgia College, one of four academic programs in the United States accredited by the Association for Experiential Education. He taught in the adventure education program at Green Mountain College before arriving at Georgia College in 2008. Will earned his doctorate from Indiana University and his bachelor's and master's degrees from Western Kentucky University. He is also a certified outdoor leader and level II instructor with the Wilderness Education Association.

**Curt Howell** is an assistant director of recreational sports at Texas Tech University, where he directs the Outdoor Pursuits Center. He received his bachelor of arts degree from Hardin-Simmons University and holds a master's degree in educational psychology from Texas Tech University. Since 2001 he has worked with students of all ages in the fields of outdoor recreation and education, primarily as a rock-

climbing instructor. Curt works with college staff members at the Outdoor Pursuits Center in developing a relational leadership model that emphasizes the value of genuine dialogue in effective leadership. He also teaches leadership and education courses for the university's environment and humanities degree program through the TTU Honors College. He is a certified single pitch instructor and climbing wall instructor program provider for the American Mountain Guides Association (AMGA). In 2010, Curt began a term serving on the board of directors for AORE.

**Steve Hutton** serves as the director of recreation for Charleston County Park and Recreation Commission, which protects over 10,000 acres of parklands and services 2 million visitors annually. Steve holds a master of arts degree in recreation management and administration from the University of Nebraska at Omaha and a bachelor of arts degree in music from Dana College. His work experiences include university outdoor programming as well as private-sector commercial recreation. Steve was on the AORE board of directors from 1997 to 2003, serving as president from 2001 to 2002. He received AORE's Jim Rennie Leadership Award in 2005. Steve is also active with the American Canoe Association, is an instructor trainer educator in multiple disciplines, and is the vice chair of the Safety, Education and Instruction Council.

**Leigh Jackson-Magennis** manages the REI Outdoor School New England market. She received her master's degree in outdoor education administration. She has served in leadership positions in colleges and universities in the Southeast. Before working at REI, she led the Georgia Institute of Technology program known as Outdoor Recreation Georgia Tech (ORGT). During her six-year tenure, Leigh hired, trained, and supervised 140 employees and volunteers. She has two decades of field experience. Leigh is a wilderness first responder and a certified sea kayak instructor with the American Canoe Association. She has led extensive expeditions around the world and has a passion for introducing beginners to the outdoors.

**Susan L. Johnson** is the director of the EDGE-Mason Center for Team and Organizational Learning. The EDGE is a provider of experiential learning, team building, and organizational development training in the Northern Virginia and DC metro area. Susan also serves as an adjunct faculty member of Mason's School of Health, Recreation and Tourism and New Century College. She specializes in experiential education, outdoor recreation, program design and administration, interpretation, and landscape design. She worked for the National Wildlife Federation before moving to Mason and is a contract instructor for the U.S. Fish and Wildlife Service. She is also a graduate of Leadership Prince William.

**Robert (Rob) E. Jones** is the manager of the outdoor recreation program at the University of Utah. He received his master's degree in parks, recreation, and tourism from the University of Utah in 2002 and his bachelor's degree from the University of California at Berkeley in 1985. In 1999 he was awarded the Jim Rennie Leadership Award from the AORE, and in 2006 the University of Utah's outdoor program was honored with the David J Webb Program Excellence Award from AORE.

**Jennifer Kafsky** is an associate professor and coordinator of wilderness leadership and experiential education. She earned her undergraduate degree in elementary education, a master's degree in physical education focusing on adventure recreation management, and doctorate of philosophy in parks, recreation, and tourism management. She has been working in administration and teaching of outdoor recreation since 1991. She managed a university outdoor program for four years, managed a university campus recreation aquatic program for seven years, and coordinated a college academic outdoor program for eight years. Her dissertation, *The Effect of a Freshman Adventure Orientation Program on the Development of Social Interest*, was published in 2001. She has received the AORE Jim Rennie Leadership award and the Exemplary Teaching Award from the General Board of Higher Education and Ministry of the United Methodist Church, and was recognized as the Outstanding Faculty Member of the Year in her academic division.

**Tracey L. Knutson** is a lawyer in Anchorage, Alaska. Her primary practice involves working with recreation and adventure sport commercial operators, public land administrators, and recreation-oriented educational groups. An experienced trial lawyer, Tracey defends recreation companies and sport groups from liability claims, often negotiating pretrial conclusions that minimize time and expense. In addition, she provides risk management and training services.

**John C. McIntosh** is an associate professor of entrepreneurship and strategic management at Boise State University. He received his doctorate in strategic management from the University of Illinois at Urbana-Champaign, a master's degree in public policy from the Gerald R. Ford School of Public Policy at the University of Michigan, and a bachelor's degree in business administration from Cornell University. Dr. McIntosh's research and commercial activities focus on creation of new ventures in service industries, commercialization of technology, and industrial design.

**Todd Miner** is the executive director of Cornell outdoor education, one of the largest and most comprehensive collegiate outdoor education programs in the country. At Cornell, Miner is responsible for a nearly $1.5 million budget, 90 percent of which is self-support. He started the Cornell Wilderness Medicine program, a unique collaboration between Cornell's medical school and Cornell outdoor education. Before working at Cornell, Miner served as a tenure-track faculty member, a chief administrator of an outdoor education program, and a wilderness guide in Alaska for nearly 20 years. He earned his bachelor's degree in anthropology from the University of Alaska and his doctorate from Boston University. Miner enjoys a variety of outdoor adventures with his family, on his own, and as an outdoor leader.

**Timothy J. Moore** is the director of recreational sports at Massachusetts Institute of Technology (MIT). He has been working in collegiate recreation since 1988; 15 of those years were spent in outdoor recreation and education. He earned his bachelor's degree in leisure studies and a master's degree in education. Timothy has opened two new recreational sport centers at major universities and developed business plans for four new recreational sport facilities. He has been responsible for significant growth of programs in outdoor recreation at three major universities. Timothy also wrote *A Survey of Selected Climbing Walls in North America*, published by the Outdoor Recreation Coalition of America. This started a national dialogue about elements and standards of design for climbing walls. He followed this survey with another unpublished but widely distributed study that continued to look at the evolution of design in climbing walls in North America in the mid-'90s. Timothy has received the Jim Rennie Leadership Award from the AORE for leadership and contributions to the association and the field of outdoor recreation and education. He has also received the David J Webb Program of Excellence Award from the AORE for excellence in outdoor programming and student development.

**Rachel M. Peters** is the director of field operations for Prescott College in Arizona. Rachel received her bachelor's degree from the University of Northern Iowa in leisure services and her master's degree from Prescott College in environmental studies focusing on education, policy, and public lands. Since 1998, Rachel has been committed to bridging academic institutions and nonprofit organizations with federal, state, and local land management agencies. She has also dedicated much of her time and energy to the River Management Society, where she has served on the executive committee, as well as AORE, where she has served as access committee chair.

**Bruce Saxman** is the director of adventure programs at Green Mountain College. He has a bachelor's degree from Clemson University and a master's degree from the University of Nebraska at Omaha. He is a swiftwater rescue, canoe, whitewater, and coastal kayak instructor with the American Canoe Association and a telemark instructor with the Professional Ski Instructors of America. As the adventures coordinator at the University of Wisconsin at Stout, he won the Staff Outstanding Service Award for service to the university, community, and students.

**Brien Sheedy** has been the director of the Whitman college outdoor program since 2001. He holds a bachelor's degree in environmental studies from SUNY ESF at Syracuse and a master's degree in geography from the University of Texas at Austin, where he studied Nepali for two years and conducted his thesis research on ecotourism in Nepal. In addition to running the program at Whitman, Brien works internationally as a high-altitude mountain guide for Alpine Ascents International and has climbed the highest peak on every continent. He also serves as a senior instructor for the

National Outdoor Leadership School, where he has worked for over a decade, accumulating over 200 field weeks.

**Christopher Stec** is the chief operating officer for the American Canoe Association (ACA). Before that position, Chris worked as a program director at a prominent summer camp, a raft guide for the Nantahala Outdoor Center, and in the ACA's safety education and instruction department. Chris has served on various committees for the National Safe Boating Council, the National Association of State Boating Law Administrators, and the PFD Manufacturers Association. He is also a lifetime member of American Whitewater. Chris holds the following paddlesport certifications: instructor trainer educator for advanced whitewater canoeing, instructor trainer for stand-up paddleboarding, advanced swiftwater rescue instructor, and adaptive paddling endorsement. In addition to publishing articles and poetry in several magazines, Chris has contributed to two books and was one of the writers of the revised Boy Scouts of America canoeing and whitewater merit badge pamphlets. Chris lives in Fredericksburg, Virginia, with his wife and two children. A love for competition has allowed him and his wife to place at regional and national downriver races in tandem canoe. When not in the office, he can probably be found either paddling or fishing with his son and daughter on a section of the Rappahannock River.

**Tom Stuessy** is an associate professor at Green Mountain College in Vermont, where he serves as the program director of adventure education. He earned his doctorate from Indiana University, his master's degree from Aurora University, and his bachelor's degree from Western State College of Colorado. Over the years Tom has served the Wilderness Education Association and AORE in various capacities and is a founding board member of the *Journal of Outdoor Recreation Education and Learning*.

**Jeff Turner** is an associate professor of outdoor education at Georgia College and State University. He coordinates the outdoor education academic programs and teaches graduate and undergraduate theory and technical skills courses. His scholarly interests include outdoor leadership development and the role of the social and environmental setting in the adventure learning process. He received his